State College
at
Framingham

5M-6-65-940607

*English Poetry
in the Later
Nineteenth Century*

English Poetry
in the Later
Nineteenth Century

Benjamin IFOR EVANS

Provost of University College London
Sometime Professor of English Language and Literature
in the University of London

METHUEN & CO LTD
11 NEW FETTER LANE LONDON EC4

First published 1933
Second edition, revised, 1966
Printed in Great Britain
by W. & J. Mackay & Co Ltd, Chatham
© *Ifor Evans, 1966*

TO THE MEMORY OF
OLIVER ELTON

CONTENTS

PREFACE		*page* ix
INTRODUCTION		1
1	Dante Gabriel Rossetti	17
2	Algernon Charles Swinburne	45
3	Christina Georgina Rossetti	87
4	William Morris	104
5	Minor Pre-Raphaelite Poets: William Bell Scott, William Allingham, Thomas Woolner, Arthur O'Shaughnessy, John Payne, Philip Bourke Marston, William Sharp (Fiona MacLeod)	128
6	Coventry Patmore and Allied Poets: Coventry Patmore, Francis Thompson, Mrs Alice Meynell	154
7	George Meredith	188
8	Thomas Hardy	205
9	James Thomson	226
10	Robert Bridges and his Associates: Canon Dixon, Mary Coleridge; Digby Mackworth Dolben; Robert Bridges	236
11	Gerard Manley Hopkins	268
12	Lighter Verse: Austin Dobson, Edmund Gosse, Andrew Lang; Comic and Nonsense Verse: Edward Lear, 'Lewis Carroll', William Schwenck Gilbert, Charles Stuart Calverley, James Kenneth Stephen	286

CONTENTS

13 *Minor Poets: I: George MacDonald; Robert Buchanan; David Gray, Gerald Massey, Alexander Anderson, Joseph Skipsey*   307

14 *Minor Poets: II*   326

15 *William Ernest Henley and Robert Louis Stevenson*   357

16 *John Davidson*   372

17 *Oscar Wilde, Ernest Dowson, Lionel Johnson and the Poetry of the Eighteen-Nineties*   390

18 *Rudyard Kipling*   421

19 *Alfred Edward Housman*   429

NOTES   442

INDEX   468

PREFACE

This volume was first published in 1933: it has long been out of print, and there have been frequent requests that it should be reissued. Its purpose is a simple one, the same that guided Professor Oliver Elton in preparing his *Survey of English Literature*. An attempt is made to discuss the whole of the verse in the period under consideration. Work once popular, but now ignored, is assessed, as is the production of minor writers. It may be thought that too much space is given to these less important poets, but their work is now difficult to obtain, and so the reader who may wish to know the part they once played becomes dependent on this chronicle as a sole source.

This volume is a chronicle and criticism of English poetry from 1860 to the end of the century. In most instances I have limited the study to writers whose main work appears after 1860. I have omitted the later work of Tennyson, Browning, Matthew Arnold, and others who begin in the earlier part of the century.

In 1933, when the volume was first published, I thought there would be a reawakening interest in later nineteenth-century poetry. The variety of work in these decades is notable, and the contrast with the first half of the century is profound. The facile generalization is sometimes made that there is little in English poetry between the Pre-Raphaelites and the poets of the nineties. Nothing could be more false: Patmore, Meredith, Hardy, Bridges, Hopkins, and many others, had all begun earlier, nor do the nineties present one compact movement, but a thrusting forth of conflicting talents. This reawakening of interest in Victorian romanticism has not come about. Meredith remains a great neglected writer, and Professor Lang recently in editing Swinburne's *Letters* describes how utterly even Swinburne's best work has been ignored.

I am convinced that a change of taste will ultimately come, and that English romanticism from Shelley onwards will regain a more conspicuous place in the English literary scene. The notes to this volume will show that if the general reading public has followed other ways many students of literature have remained faithful. The notes to this volume will show new studies of the writers here surveyed by scholars, and particularly by American scholars. To them all I am deeply indebted. I recognize my more detailed debts in the notes to the various chapters.

The end of the nineteenth century was more than the end of an era in time: it was the close of a spiritual epoch. We still turn back to that Victorian age with a complicated mixture of contempt, envy, misunderstanding, and sometimes half-conscious affection. The contempt has been overdone; the envy is futile; and so out of affection for the age I have attempted to portray one aspect of its endeavour. Poetry was no mean part of its achievement, and if ultimately we would trace our relationship with tradition, we must come to a closer understanding of these last decades of the nineteenth century.

Tennyson and Browning so dominated their age that Victorian poetry has frequently been considered as an activity confined to the values of their work. This study has attempted to adjust that perspective. The reaction against Tennyson and Browning was so sweeping that most Victorian poetry was carried along with it. Some reaction against Tennyson had to come, and in its time was salutary enough, for his imitators were alarmingly numerous and dangerously prolific, as this volume shows. Browning's eclipse was for a time even more complete, and must surely soon come to an end. Indeed, younger poets, even when they disliked his thought, have found something instructive in the verbal asperities of his verse.

PREFACE

Apart from Tennyson and Browning, the later nineteenth century has movements in poetry whose significance cannot well be ignored. A new Victorian romanticism develops in the Pre-Raphaelites and is seen to exhaust itself in the nineties. It was but the last phase of that larger movement which found its origins in the Gothic revival of the eighteenth century, and its earlier poets in Coleridge and Keats. Increasingly, under the stress of industrialism and its devastating ugliness, romanticism had become the poetic quest for an idealized past, clean, courteous, and richly emblazoned. Before the century was out the poets knew that their romanticism was only an anodyne and that its sedative powers were becoming rapidly ineffective. Arthur, Gawain, the symbols of chivalry, even courtesy itself, were vanishing like wraiths into the mists. For more reasons than can be enumerated here we have shut out romanticism from our poetry: the trappings are packed into the robing cupboard, too threadbare to be used. But the time will come.

One element detached itself from romanticism and was awarded a distinguished expression. The religious side of medievalism, which is Catholicism, had gained but little recognition in the Romantic Revival, but after the Oxford Movement, in the work of Patmore, Hopkins, Francis Thompson, and others it came to maturity. I have tried, as one who watches this movement only as an observer, to do justice to this impressive influence. It affects not only the religious writers but enters variously into the work of Rossetti, Wilde, Lionel Johnson, and Dowson. This religious poetry, so frequently neglected as a phenomenon in the later nineteenth century, extends beyond Catholicism into the devotions of Christina Rossetti and the philosophy of Robert Bridges. Further, this aspect of romanticism alone survived into twentieth-century poetry.

Outside this religious poetry, a number of writers gather up the problems of faith in their age and attempt individual solutions. It was thus in the sixties, and not in the nineties, that the revolt against Victorian complacency began, and it was found with varying emphasis throughout this half-century in Meredith,

Swinburne, Hardy, and James Thomson. Compact philistinism remained unmoved by these new voices, but that has been its habit in most ages. The poetry of John Davidson, so strangely neglected, showed a later Victorian struggling and even writhing in an attempt to reveal the problems and the attitudes for which the twentieth century has still failed to find an adequate poetic expression.

Despite all the contacts between our own time and the nineteenth century, one returns to the conception that with the close of the Victorian age we have reached 'the end of a chapter'. Poetry had exploited so many overworked traditions, Elizabethan and romantic, that some change seemed imperative. Above all, the nineteenth century had lost contact with the classical conception that a great work must be an organized unity and in attempting long works had grown content to produce amorphous pieces, well decorated with incidental beauties but lacking cohesion. The twentieth century has not yet found the way to recover this sense of classicism which the nineteenth century mislaid. It is not only that we have lost the old mythologies, but that the architectonics of poetry, which despite troublesome accretions was the lesson of classical criticism, have become a dim conception, misunderstood and misprized. Unfortunately this decay in proportion has coincided with a decline in classical education in the audience of poetry. The gods who came down from Olympus in the sixteenth century and offered themselves for three centuries as material for poetic symbol and imagery have disappeared, like the troops of chivalry. All the legends from which poetry was once constructed have grown strange to the newer audiences of poetry, and the poet himself is left denuded of the shapes with which once his mind had been clothed.

In continuity and in contrast the poetry of the later nineteenth century lies in intimate contact with our own age. Even the prosodic experiments of our contemporary verse find their beginnings tentatively, but surely, within these decades, while the wilder extravagances of our modern irregular verse can be

PREFACE

understood in part as protest against the sweetness of Tennyson and his multitude of followers. It is in this belief that our spiritual origins must be found in the nineteenth century, in what we have rejected from that age and in what we have accepted, that I have attempted to trace the history of poetry in that period.

I.E.

1933 and 1964

INTRODUCTION

In the living organism the moment of birth and death can never be precisely traced, and so with poetry no absolute periods emerge; but the death of old ideas and the birth of new forms continue in a perpetual motion. Yet in certain decades the contrast between ascendant and disintegrating schools gains a keener emphasis, and it is then that the values of the new developments can be most easily perceived. Such an instructive juxtaposition of old and new occurs in English poetry during 1850-1860. The present volume isolates the fresh activities which began in that decade, and with them as a point of departure outlines the chronicle of English poetry from 1860 to the close of the century. This introductory note gives, in general perspective, the relation of the poetry of the early nineteenth century to the new forms which emerged in and around 1860.[1]

The years 1821-1834 mark one of the most melancholy interludes of mortality in the history of English poetry. The first manifestation of English romanticism comes to an abrupt end, not through any exhaustion of purposes but by the removal of its poets with calamitous swiftness: Keats, born in the same year as Carlyle, had died of consumption at Rome in 1821; in 1822 Shelley was drowned off Leghorn, and in 1824 Byron succumbed to marsh-fever at Missolonghi; Scott, wearied by the struggle to meet his creditors, died at Abbotsford in 1832; two years later Coleridge, despite the care of the Gillmans, gave up his long and unequal struggle with ill health. Most of these lives had come to an untimely end; accident, disease, frustrated effort accompany their memory, with the suggestion of high talents still maturing, or of genius struck off at its height. It is true that a few figures of the previous age remained with their earlier impulses numbed: Wordsworth, who passed through the horrors in France in 1792 without losing faith in humanity, lived on, petrified, a reactionary and a pensioner from whom 'the breath and finer spirit' of poetry had departed. Sincere and consistent in his new doctrines, he was conscious of loneliness; the best he had known had departed, and the troubled days from which great verse had been made. Southey continued in pedestrian worthiness with a pension from Peel, until 1843; Leigh Hunt, another pensioner, survived his imprisonments and skirmishings in radical journalism, to produce essays and editions of poems, until his long life ended in 1859. By 1830 all that was effective in the movement of English romanticism that began with Wordsworth and Coleridge had come to an end.

Nor were the romantic poets fortunate in the reputation that pursued them after death, for during the period 1830-1860 they all endured diverse misrepresentations. The legend of 'cockneyism' clung to Keats even after the publication of his *Life and Letters* by Lord Houghton in 1848. Matthew Arnold, writing in 1880, was expressing an estimate far more appreciative than that of the earlier half of the century when he commented: 'His *Endymion*, as he himself well saw, is a failure, and his *Hyperion*, fine things as it contains, is not a success. But in shorter things, where the matured power of moral interpretation, and the high architectonics which go with complete poetic development, are not required, he is perfect.'[2] Tennyson had shown by 1830 how the early nineteenth century could gather up the technical ingenuity of the 'shorter things', but Keats's aesthetic philosophy and his profound if incomplete interpretation of experience were left for later decades to rediscover. Shelley was scarcely more fortunate. His lyrical skill was recognized, but his wide-ranging power of converting an upstart philosophy into a noble poetic reality was denied him, and once again Matthew Arnold, writing in 1888, crystallized into a single phrase a generous estimate of the stunted impressions of Shelley's work held in the early nineteenth century. 'The man Shelley, in very truth, is not entirely sane, and Shelley's poetry is not entirely sane either. The Shelley of actual life is a vision of beauty and radiance indeed, but availing nothing, effecting nothing. And in poetry, no less than in life, he is a "beautiful *and ineffectual* angel, beating in the void his luminous wings in vain".'[3] Browning, for a moment in *Pauline*, seemed prepared to see Shelley plain ('Sun-treader, life and light be thine for ever!'), but he withdrew from this early admiration into his own philosophical preoccupations. In this nineteenth-century depreciation of the early romantic poetry Byron suffered most of all. It was not that he was forgotten. There was extracted from his poetry and his life all that was least memorable, and having idolized these selected features, readers grew tired at length of the image that they had created.[4] From the great Byron of *Beppo*, *The Vision of Judgement*, and *Don Juan* the mid-nineteenth century turned with disdain. Matthew Arnold favoured Byron, for had not Byron also in his own day fought the compact majority of British Philistinism? But Arnold contrived to write his long essay on Byron without mentioning *Don Juan*.[5] Nor, as it will appear later, did the later nineteenth century ever rediscover in poetry the intense satiric power of Byron. The Chaucerian frankness, the cascading laughter, the subtle union of pathos and comedy, the roguery and irony of *Don Juan* were lost from one end of the century to the other. This failure to reintroduce into poetry the mature qualities of the Byronic genius is the clearest perspective into the taste of the century,[6] and Byron had already drawn his own conclusion on the contrast between himself and the age which was to follow: 'The truth is, that in these days the grand *primum mobile* of England is *cant*; cant political, cant poetical, cant religious, cant moral.'[7]

Equally serious was the nineteenth-century misconception of Coleridge. Over him lay heavily the double condemnation of incoherent speculation and of a life wrecked by opium. He had a group of loyal followers, but in the popular imagination he remained as the poet of a few magnificent but harmless verses, a moment of brightness in a clouded life. His poetical skill entered richly into the form and diction of early nineteenth-century poetry, and can be seen as a strong formative influence on Tennyson. Yet these isolated poetic excellencies disguised the thinker, more learned than any man of his age, who had attempted to bring together the broken fragments of thought into a single image of truth. 'My system, if I may venture to give it so fine a name, is the only attempt I know, ever made to reduce all knowledges into harmony. . . . I wish, in short, to connect by a moral *copula* natural history with political history; or, in other words, to make history scientific, and science historical – to take from history its accidentality, and from science its fatalism.'[8] Coleridge in this passage was already defining the central problem of Victorian thought, but only a few alert minds realized his profundity. John Stuart Mill as early as 1838 coupled him and Bentham as 'the two great seminal minds of England in their age',[9] but it has been left for the twentieth century to shatter completely the legend of Coleridge's indolence, and to establish all that he might have contributed to the Victorian dilemma.[10] Yet even in the period (1830-1850) when he was most misprized his 'seminal' quality was working. His influence on religious thought has been well summarized in the phrase, 'Coleridge was, in fact, the father of the broad-church movement: and he was the godfather of the high-church'.[11] His influence on Newman and on the Oxford Movement has yet to be fully recognized.

The year 1830 is thus a real date in the history of English poetry: the early movement of romanticism had been submerged or diverted; the old poets were dead, or ineffective; apart from minor writers, such as Beddoes, Darley, Elliott, Wade, and Clare, the field was empty. There was a more distinct break here than at any other period in the century; indeed, the poetry of the later nineteenth century in many of its aspects was the rediscovery in a new form of the romantic tradition which had been driven underground between 1824 and 1830. The early nineteenth century from 1830 constructed a new poetry, with

INTRODUCTION

Tennyson and Browning emerging as dominant figures. They began their effective work in the same years, Tennyson with *Poems* (1832) and Browning with *Pauline* (1832); they achieved recognition and gained the major expression of their genius in the same period, Tennyson with *Poems* (1842) and *In Memoriam* (1850), and Browning with *Men and Women* (1855). In their later work, despite *The Idylls* (1859) and *The Ring and the Book* (1868), they may have changed technically, but they showed no important development either poetically or spiritually. At first it is difficult to realize how clearly Tennyson came to separate his poetic purposes from the romantic movement. His apprenticeship was romantic; frequently even in his later work the décor was medieval and up to 1842 he frequently went questing after the poetic methods and effects of Wordsworth, Keats, and Coleridge. But already in 1842, and more persistently after that date, he narrowed his underlying poetic motives to the elucidation of contemporary problems. His purposes were strangely akin to those of Pope in *An Essay on Man* and *The Moral Satires*, with the satiric element eliminated. He was exploiting poetic resources for contemporary controversies and moral discussion, and in a language intelligible to the layman. Unlike Pope, he had behind him the whole tradition of romantic poetry to colour his work with melody and suggestive phrasing, while a personal urgency of spiritual exploration transfigured his endeavour:

> I stretch lame hands of faith, and grope,
> And gather dust and chaff.

Browning was more obviously removed both in motive and technique from the poets who preceded him. Despite his references to Keats and Shelley and his Gothic extravagances, he was only incidentally affected by the romantic tradition. If his early blank verse owed something to Shelley, his later verse and his couplets seem all his own, vocabulary, syntax, and rhythm all flung from his own mind. He had obvious Elizabethan contacts, and one is frequently reminded in his work of the metaphysical poets and of the prose of Carlyle, but once his tutelage passed it would be difficult to attach him in any way to the poetry that immediately preceded him.

Tennyson and Browning devoted themselves to the debate of the century – the attempt to construct a faith that would incorporate personal immortality in a liberal, even personal, interpretation of Christianity. It was here that they approached more closely to Coleridge than to any of the romantic poets; only Coleridge in his mature period realized that poetry was not the right medium for effecting this discussion. They went further and attempted to consider institutional morality in verse; they portrayed morbid and abnormal types who were infected with moral indiscipline, and the dilemma of those who remain within a faith and are yet uncertain of its relation to truth. With such themes they explored that compact and insular controversy which dominated the early nineteenth century and penetrated all forms of imaginative literature. Carlyle was the central figure in the discussion which developed later into the debate between the scientists and the representatives of organized religion. As has already been suggested, much of the work of Tennyson and Browning, particularly in their earlier periods, was free from these preoccupations; to adapt Arnold on Keats, 'the shorter pieces' were frequently absolved, but the larger effort of their mature endeavour was directed to these purposes. They employed verse to register their passage from spiritual uncertainty to individual spiritual security. Browning from the first had a consistent optimism which Tennyson did not always possess, for though he masqueraded under different dramatic disguises, it is possible to detect his underlying emphasis on a faith jubilantly held despite difficulties, with personal immortality as a sure but unproven result of a life where evil is the necessary accompaniment of moral growth. He defined his position most clearly in *Christmas-Eve and Easter-Day* (1850), *Saul* (1855), and in the Pope's monologue in *The Ring and the Book*. His security was asserted rather than proven, and it remained unshaken by the hordes of grotesque figures – Sludge, Guido and the rest – which haunted his imagination. After his marriage with Elizabeth Barrett in 1845 his attitude began to harden into dogma.

The virtues and limitations of the period 1830-1860 were more absolutely defined in Browning's work than in that of Tennyson. It is true that Tennyson, in the verse of his central period, represented the success and belief in prosperity that lay in all early Victorian thought. He shared particularly the faith in a happy future for England with a somewhat complacent security within well-defined frontiers. He appealed successfully to the traditional virtues of the English people, and he honoured some of their traditional heroes, yet he attempted honestly to face the perplexities which scientific conceptions and changing institutions were developing, nor did he cloister himself in any illusory palace of art, insusceptible to the gradual disintegration around him. With *In Memoriam* (1850) he restated his faith as he had reviewed it since Arthur Hallam's death in 1833. This poem, published nine years before Darwin's *The Origin of Species*, had within it a summary of evolutionary thought, derived possibly from Chambers's *The Vestiges of Creation* (1844), and attempted to relate this to the Victorian conception of the possibilities of human life. Tennyson stated clearly the philosophical scepticism which arose from a material conception of history based on science. He saw Nature, not as a mellowing influence, disciplined by order and harmony, as it had appeared in Wordsworth's poetry, but as a ruthless struggle of type with type in which human history might be a passing incident. This scarified vision of life might have converted Tennyson into a poet of tragic stress, and there were moments in *In Memoriam* when this seemed possible. Instead he withdrew, before the poem closed, a frightened, huddled figure sheltering behind a faith which he could not justify. He came, as Browning had done, to the haven of spiritual security, with a belief in a beneficent Providence and in personal immortality as essential credentials of entry.

Tennyson and Browning continued their work late into the century, but by 1860 their effective purposes had been revealed in their personal solutions of the Victorian controversy. In prose the controversy continued, in Huxley, and in Spencer, but in poetry, with some minor exceptions, it exhausted itself by 1860. This indeed was one of the most impressive contrasts between the earlier and later nineteenth century. After 1860 controversy and discussion in poetry ceased: some poets removed from argument into an aesthetic world of their own creation; others adhered to a tradition of Catholic Christianity which rendered argument unnecessary and released poetry for the exploration of mysticism; a few attempted out of their recognition of new knowledge to construct a new synthesis of belief. Between Tennyson and Browning and the later nineteenth century there remained, however, a number of notable figures whose work helped to determine the perspective of later nineteenth-century verse. Foremost stood Matthew Arnold, the pivotal figure who related the earlier with the later tradition. For the more the poetry of the nineteenth century is explored, the more does it appear that Arnold gathered into his own perplexity the most varied features of the poetic image of the whole century. Arnold in his long weary years as an inspector of schools saw the ordinary life of England more clearly than any other poet: he knew the harsh, cruel values of those decades, and he saw how industrialism was destroying not only the face of England, but man's very power of perceiving beauty. As a critic he set himself against this national Philistinism; and while Tennyson and Browning were occupied with more abstract problems, he made his audience aware of a society that was closing its ugly doors on the arts. Through him we learn something of that bleak isolation of the artist in a world otherwise occupied, a situation which appeared and reappeared in later nineteenth-century poetry. In his own verse he presented three distinct motives which struggled for supremacy in his mind, and they are all instructive. First, like Tennyson and Browning, he attempted out of spiritual distress to create a satisfying faith. In prose, he succeeded, but the synthesis contented his intellect only; his poetry from *Resignation* (1849) is the record of one tortured by the disintegration of all that he would wish to hold secure. Among its many expressions the most poignant is in *Dover Beach*:

INTRODUCTION

> The Sea of Faith
> Was once, too, at the full, and round earth's shore
> Lay like the folds of a bright girdle furl'd.
> But now I only hear
> Its melancholy, long, withdrawing roar,
> Retreating, to the breath
> Of the night-wind, down the vast edges drear
> And naked shingles of the world.

Arnold, like Tennyson and Browning, entered 'the valley of intellectual doubt but unlike them he never comes through'.[12] Much of his most memorable verse was thus occupied in exploring a spiritual dilemma which he was impotent to resolve. This first element in Arnold was paralleled in his friend Arthur Hugh Clough (1819-1861),[13] who dwelt amid the same perplexities; but a comparison of their poetry shows how clearly in Arnold this first motive was modified by other susceptibilities. For, opposed to this poetry of spiritual distress, there lay his own critical doctrine reasserted in his essays and given its most formal expression in his preface to *Poems* (1853). Here, more consciously than any other poet of his age, he rejected romanticism, and attempted to restore to poetry the cool, sane qualities of classical narrative, the portrayal of 'excellent actions', such as 'most powerfully appeal to the great primary human affections'.[14] He would detach himself from the decorative excess of the Gothic and equally from the analytical poetry of his own age. Yet the strange anomaly soon appeared that Arnold's critical precepts failed to satisfy him emotionally, just as his erection of a religious belief in his prose essays had failed to satisfy him spiritually. It is true that he attempted to evolve a poetry based on his criticism, and *Merope, Sohrab and Rustum, Balder Dead* are the cold idols of a literary faith to which his whole nature could not respond. More definitely his rejection of *Empedocles on Etna* showed the gap between his critical precepts and his creative impulses. For there remained in his poetry, and there intruded shyly into his criticism, an element opposed to all that he had asserted, a suppressed romanticism, which joined him intimately, not to his own age, but to the later nineteenth century. It can be seen most clearly in *The Forsaken Merman*, where the Merman describes his lost bride:

> Once she sate with you and me,
> On a red gold throne in the heart of the sea,
> And the youngest sate on her knee.
> She comb'd its bright hair, and she tended it well,
> When down swung the sound of a far-off bell.
> She sigh'd, she look'd up through the clear green sea;
> She said: 'I must go, for my kinsfolk pray
> In the little grey church on the shore to-day.'

So Arnold repressed the 'red gold thrones' of romanticism for the 'grey' duties of his own age, but memories remained: they dominated *The Strayed Reveller*; Callicles represented them in *Empedocles on Etna*; they intruded even into *The Scholar-Gipsy*. This tentative romanticism, with its desertion of contemporary problems, was the element in Arnold which many in the later decades were to follow. Nor was it in thought only that he led into strange places where he did not intend to lead, for prosodically in the tepid irregularities of *The Strayed Reveller*, and of other poems, he set an early example for later prosodic adventure.

To isolate Tennyson, Browning, and Arnold, and to study them alone in relation to the later nineteenth century would be to simplify unduly, for many minor movements flourished between 1830 and 1860; some of these are considered later in contact with the poetry which they influenced, but others had almost exhausted themselves before 1860. In the large perspective of the whole century such writers as Sir Henry Taylor[15] (1800-1886), the mild Wordsworthian of *Philip van Artevelde*, will have no distinct place, although he joins in that retreat from romanticism of the earlier half of the century. The 'Spasmodic' poets, undigested as is much of their work, have a more formative influence. Under the influence of Goethe's *Faust* and of cosmic dramas such as *Manfred* and *Prometheus Unbound*, which have elements derived from it, a number of poets between 1830

INTRODUCTION

and 1850 had evolved a vague, grandiose, sometimes incoherent but frequently spectacular poetry. Philip James Bailey (1816-1902) had inaugurated it with *Festus* (1839); Richard Hengist Horne (1803-1884) had continued with *Orion* (1843); while Alexander Smith (1830-1867) in *A Life Drama* (1853) and Sydney Dobell (1824-1874) in *Balder* (1855) pursued the tradition. The wide popularity of their verse, ebullient with its own enthusiasms, may account in part for the sluggish reception which the Pre-Raphaelites gained in the fifties. The influence of the school marked the early work of Bell Scott, while Meredith, James Thomson, and Tennyson himself, were not untouched by its influence. Bell Scott showed a minor poet emerging from Spasmodic training into contact with the new poetry of Rossetti. In the fifties the reputation of the school suffered a sudden decline with the publication of Aytoun's review in *Blackwood's* for May 1854 of a supposed Spasmodic drama *Firmilian*, and of the full hoax tragedy a few months later.[16]

Other minor poets influenced the later nineteenth century in unexpected ways. Richard Monckton Milnes, Lord Houghton (1809-1885), is remembered less for his poetry than for reviving an interest in Keats (1848); he opened the doors of his library to Swinburne and he was the patron of David Gray. Ebenezer Jones (1820-1860), a poet of Spasmodic affinities, had an incidental influence on Meredith, while Rossetti proclaimed his virtues along with those of other neglected writers. More impressive is the influence of Emily Brontë, achieved in the few deathless lyrics in which she gave expression to a rebellious rejection of creeds, and an adherence to some vague but strenuously defined pantheism:

> Vain are the thousand creeds
>   That move men's hearts: unutterably vain;
> Worthless as withered weeds,
>   Or idlest froth amid the boundless main.

Such lines impressed Swinburne, who was generous in his recognition of Emily Brontë's talent, and they enter more precisely into his conception of *Hertha*. In a firmer manner, Edward Fitzgerald (1809-1883) pervades the later period, and had he possessed greater energy his rare aptitudes might have been organized into a major influence. He retained an independence in taste, and, despite a friendship with Tennyson, he refused to carry his admiration for Tennyson's verse much beyond *Poems* (1842), apart from his enthusiasm for the songs in the Arthurian *Idylls*. The same independence pursued him in his small but precious output of creative work. *The Rubáiyát* (1859), in which Omar Khayyám's verses are 'tessellated into a sort of Epicurean Eclogue in a Persian Garden',[17] entered into the poetry of the Pre-Raphaelites and continued as an influence into the closing decades of the century. Rossetti bought a remainder copy for a penny at Quaritch's and introduced the poem to Swinburne; the stanza is embedded in *Laus Veneris* and the philosophy penetrates widely into Swinburne's work.

The conditions already described make the decade 1850-1860 a period of profound transition in nineteenth-century poetry. Tennyson and Browning, still at the height of their reputation, are seen by some discerning minds to have reached their climacteric. Arnold's position was already defined, though his most memorable work was to appear a little later in *New Poems* (1867). Rossetti had been working as early as 1847; in 1850 *The Germ* appeared and in 1858 Morris's *The Defence of Guenevere*. Swinburne had published *The Queen Mother* and *Rosamond* in 1860, and Patmore *The Angel in the House* in 1854. Here in the fifties the old met the new, and the function of this volume is to trace the history of English poetry from this period of transition to the end of the century.

The changed quality of the new schools of poetry can be discovered most easily by contrasting their governing motives with those of early nineteenth-century verse. The simplest single perspective can be gained by the generalization that the old controversy of faith and unfaith receded from its dominant position as a poetic theme. It is as if the Oxford Movement, culminating in Newman's retreat to Rome (1845), had acted as a catharsis for that conflict as far as poetry is concerned, though the debate is a submerged motive until the end of the century. There arose, as one fresh element, a new religious poetry, Catholic and mystical in motive, removed entirely from the earlier disputes, and owing a spiritual allegiance to the religious poetry of the seventeenth century. Coventry Patmore achieves an additional importance when it is remembered that he was the first poet in this group to gain wide recognition. Gerard Manley Hopkins, its greatest poet, had to wait for the second decade of the twentieth century before the major part of his work was published. Christina Rossetti, as an early figure, united this work to the poetry of the Pre-Raphaelites. Nor can the later verse of Robert Bridges be seen faithfully unless his indebtedness to this poetic tradition be allowed.

Such poets accept a faith and explore its symbolism and experience. With the Pre-Raphaelites there developed a school that withdrew from all such discussion. They solved the Victorian debate by excluding it from their poetry, and yet they were conscious of its existence. Morris, rejecting the High Church movement, which as an undergraduate had attracted him, protected his verse from his own age by a retreat to medievalism. Rossetti remained content to employ the ritual and legend of Catholicism without stating any obligation to the faith. Swinburne, despite his temporary allegiance to a pantheism not unlike Shelley's, his frequent vituperations of the Deity, and his excursions into politics, erected in his most formative period a world of artistic experience independent of current discussion. These writers, despite their widely varying methods, form the most compact movement in the earlier decades under discussion (1860-1880). With them romanticism returned, but it had suffered changes. It had lost its liberal contacts with philosophy and politics. No French Revolution aroused it into new hope or creative despair; neither Swinburne's enthusiasm for Italy nor Morris's socialism was an adequate substitute for that earlier stimulus. Further, it would appear that romanticism while dormant in England had visited France, and now on its return the sea-change is apparent. The broader contacts of earlier

English romanticism have been narrowed by a passage through the minds of Théophile Gautier and of Baudelaire; the taint of mortality was upon it with an increased emphasis on its detachment from morals, while its technical methods have gained a certain preciousness through contact with the theory of *l'art pour l'art*. This was emphasized, even where there is no direct French influence, by the conscious withdrawal from life which characterizes the whole group. Not that this is without English precedent, as appears in the influence of Keats on Swinburne, and even Tennyson in his early poems had suggested an artistic detachment of which he would not have personally approved. The Pre-Raphaelites gathered from early romanticism what they could best assimilate; Keats as an influence was dominant; Shelley appeared intermittently; Byron, whom they appreciated, they failed, unfortunately, to imitate; Blake they rediscovered and he entered frequently into their work. Yet beyond all this general conditions separated them widely from earlier romanticism, for if the French Revolution was a stimulus to poetry at the close of the eighteenth century, the society resulting from the industrial revolution was the plague from which Victorian romanticism tried to escape. Coleridge in the earlier days of romanticism had suggested the independence of the imagination; now from the dread of the unloveliness around them later poets were led to advocate its isolation. This gave a sense of pathos to the revival of medievalism in nineteenth-century poetry. Tennyson had used it, but apart from his early poetry which the Pre-Raphaelites admired, his motive was to display his own age. Now it was employed definitely as an escape. Sometimes one feels that Victorian romanticism is a ghostly masquerade; only when all is quiet in the night do these poets come out and, donning their antique costumes, revive their dreams of long-faded beauty. When day has come they are gone, and the waking world knows them not. While thus they have narrowed the motives of romanticism and elevated love into a supreme position, they enriched the technical resources of their poetry; Rossetti restored a more intimate contact with Italy than had existed since Eliza-

INTRODUCTION

bethan times; Swinburne brought Greece and France equally to his service; and Morris exploited Icelandic resources which, despite Gray's experiments, had remained strangely neglected. Through all their achievement, the sense of resignation implicit in their work gave the suggestion that there romanticism was entering on its last phase, and that impression was strengthened when one approached the work of their adherents in the nineties.

While religious verse and the poetry of the Pre-Raphaelites dominated the period under survey, much else remains within these last four decades of the nineteenth century. Hardy and Meredith, for instance, respond in a fresh way to the main Victorian controversy by attempting to construct in verse a new synthesis of their belief and of their knowledge, incorporating evolutionary conceptions into their formula. Their conclusions and their prosodic methods lay widely apart, but their endeavour added a keen, newly quickened motive to poetry. Meredith remains with Swinburne the most neglected poet of the whole period.

This is not the place to consider the intricate problem of later Victorian taste, though one can record the impression that in these decades while literacy was increasing the audience of poetry was changing. The tradition of humane education which had served England from the sixteenth century was breaking down, and there is a decreasing familiarity with the mythology which had served poets for over two centuries. The new public found contentment in fiction rather than in poetry, and though fiction can equal the achievements of any art form it had obviously a larger tolerance of pedestrian talents. Meredith and Hardy were driven from poetry to fiction, and increasingly poetry ceased to be a profession and became a subsidiary activity of men whose main employment lay elsewhere. Hardy returned to poetry when he was economically secure, dissatisfied by the compromises that he had to make in fiction to meet the taste of the time. Both the creation and the reading of poetry became esoteric rather than popular, and the period lacked any figure such as Shakespeare, or Pope, or Byron, who could dominate the general audience without sacrificing any element of artistic identity. Kipling is the major exception, yet Kipling seems an inexplicable phenomenon, not to be judged by any ordinary standards. There was, in addition, poetry for larger audiences, but it was a poetry infected by the taste of the audience and ephemeral. It is not what was once popular but what has sufficient integrity to remain that matters, and in these decades there emerges a varied body of poetry, traditional and experimental, which survives that ultimate test.

Dante Gabriel Rossetti

At times a writer appears whose significance extends beyond his work or its intrinsic merit. He establishes himself, by a strength of personality, in a symbolic relation to his time, and his influence permeates his contemporaries and successors. This power, which Coleridge once possessed, is the commanding characteristic of Dante Gabriel Rossetti[1] (1828-1882). Through him the changing values in Victorian poetry become apparent, and around him are the men who divert poetry from the purposes and motives employed by Tennyson and Browning and Matthew Arnold. Not that Rossetti occupied himself in any sterile attack on Tennyson and Browning, for he admired Tennyson's early work, and he imitated Browning, but when his mind and creative power came to their maturity he found that he was working in a different way. Whatever may be true of painting, the Pre-Raphaelite movement in poetry is little more than the emergence of Rossetti, a fiery, disruptive mind, sometimes disordered, but always stimulating young writers to new poetic methods.

His whole tradition was fresh. The grandfather was an Italian blacksmith of Vasto. His father, Gabriele Rossetti,[2] driven out of Naples by the despotism of Ferdinand, spent his exile in England teaching Italian and indicating an anti-papal significance to the *Divina Commedia*. Thus Dante Gabriel had grown up outside the traditions of English life. His mother was a sister of that erratic physician, John William Polidori, a member of one of those human menageries that accompanied Byron on his continental travels. English life and even the traditional approach to English literature were to Rossetti of strangeness all compact. The one unity to which he gave passionate loyalty was that of his own family. Born in 1828, and christened Gabriel Charles Dante, he was one of four children; Maria, the eldest (b. 1827), became a nun in an Anglican order; William Michael (b. 1829) was the dull but exhaustive chronicler of the family; in December 1830 Christina was born, the last of the children, whose births all date within three years and ten months.

While the background of his life was Italian, it was a background he never saw. He visited France and Belgium, but never set foot in Italy. Catholicism lay in his past and rose at times with its symbolism to colour his poetry. He assimilated the aesthetic possibilities of Catholic ritual and legend without being affected by the faith. His mother's devout Protestantism dominated the home, but left him untouched. His father's life had been sacrificed to political conviction, and the Charlotte Street house was once illuminated with the presence of Mazzini, but to the problems of politics and social institutions Rossetti remained indifferent. He discovered his own world in poetry and pictorial art and there he found complete occupation. Had he been captured before adolescence by the traditional machinery of education he might have evolved into a foreign-looking Englishman, not too indistinguishable from the pattern, and possessing the right opinions and the right prejudices. He escaped. He had irregular tuition, first at a day school of indifferent merits, and later (1837-1843) at King's College School and at King's College, where his father was a Professor of Italian. This education, combined with his father's instruction and the services of a German tutor, left him ignorant of many things, but preserved a mind passionately free for its own devotions. Freedom was his privilege, but an absence of discipline was the penalty: it left a telling mark on his painting; it smudged and blurred a number of his poems. Millais, who had the discipline without the genius, comments on one of his drawings: 'A very clever and original design, beautifully executed . . . chairs out of perspective', and his brother, William Michael, adds the laconic comment that Gabriel never mastered perspective nor paid much attention to it.

After certain preliminary instruction in painting, Rossetti entered himself in 1846 as a student in the antique schools of the Royal Academy, but the restlessness which dominated his life soon became apparent, and in March 1848 he wrote to Ford Madox Brown for permission to become his pupil. Brown, a young man of 27, accepted the young stranger and set him to work on still-life themes ('pickle-jars and bottles'), a sobering discipline, which Rossetti considered as little better than the Academy Schools. Chafing for a freer atmosphere where accomplishment could be achieved without restrictions, he was attracted by the work of Holman Hunt, who was then only 21. With the impetuousness which marks his every action at this period, Rossetti called on Hunt and asked him plaintively if pickle-jars were an essential preliminary to painting. Hunt decided that they were not, and Rossetti was allowed to struggle with original compositions in oils, early among which was *The Girlhood of the Virgin Mary*. Of all his painter associates Hunt was the most generous and suffered later more than any member of the group in his struggle for recognition. He introduced Rossetti to Millais, the brilliant boy of mid-Victorian painting, who had exhibited in the Academy at 17 and who now at the mature age of 19 years was settling down to a career of artistic prosperity.

Such were the three young men who set before themselves the task of founding a new movement to reform English painting. It is probable that all they wished at first was to associate with one another, to strengthen their common belief in the high purposes of their art. Millais, the most facile and the most shallow, pampered and successful, had more technical skill than the others with less imaginative insight. Hunt, sincere and slow, firm in his convictions, and with a keen religious faith, clung to his conception of Pre-Raphaelitism long after the others had lost touch with the movement. Rossetti knew little of painting and less of the history of art, but with his great forehead, his delicate tapering fingers, his deep voice and large sensuous eyes, he was a figure that easily commanded leadership. A vague association was not enough for him; his Italian tradition suggested closer alliances, and so he combined the knowledge of his associates with his own purposes and enthusiasms to form a sort of secret society, a Pre-Raphaelite Brotherhood, with definite principles and methods of work.

The Pre-Raphaelite Brotherhood, formed in 1848, was by 1851 largely disbanded. Men of such varied temperaments could not long agree, nor was Rossetti an easy or even a fair associate. The fact that the movement ended in discord has led to confusing accounts of its purposes. In most general terms it was a revolt against contemporary English art as represented by the Academy. The simplest and clearest statements are those of William Michael Rossetti, who acted as major-domo to the group, and of Ruskin, who championed it, partly because he thought that its principles were rather like his own.[3] W. M. Rossetti enumerates[4] the objects of the Brotherhood: (1) To have genuine ideas to express; (2) to study Nature attentively, so as to know how to express them; (3) to sympathize with what is direct and serious and heartfelt in previous art to the exclusion of what is conventional and self-parading and learned by rote; (4) to produce thoroughly good pictures and statues. Ruskin in his famous *Times* letter of 13 May 1850, explained more critically what he believed Pre-Raphaelite aims to be. 'The Pre-Raphaelites (I cannot congratulate them on common-sense in the choice of a *nom de guerre*) do not desire or pretend in any way to imitate antique painting as such. They know very little of antique paintings who suppose the works of these young artists to resemble them. As far as I can judge of their aim – for as I said, I do not know the men themselves – the Pre-Raphaelites intend to surrender no advantage which the knowledge or the invention of the present time can afford to their art. They intend to return to early days in this one particular only – that, as far as in them lies, they will draw either what they see or what they suppose might have been the actual facts of the scene they desire to represent, irrespective of any conventional rules of picture-making; and they have chosen their unfortunate, though not inaccurate, name, because all artists did this before Raphael's time, and after Raphael's time *did* not this, but sought to paint fair pictures rather than represent stern facts; of which the consequence has been that from Raphael's time to this day historical art has been in acknowledged decadence.' It is for the students of English art to determine the importance of the movement in the history of English painting. Even if its principles were wrong, or even if the pictures produced failed to conform to the principles, it served at least to awaken in English minds a recognition that painting was an art of importance, not an appendage to household decoration, or a substitute for fiction.

The term Pre-Raphaelite Brotherhood would not enter into the history of English poetry except for two accidents: first, Rossetti was a poet, and had been engaged in writing verse from his earliest days as a painter, and secondly, he was fortunate in influencing forward minds in poetry as well as in painting. Yet little of his own work, or of that of his associates, conforms to the principles set out by the Pre-Raphaelite Brotherhood. As has been already suggested, the Pre-Raphaelite movement in poetry is little more than an inconvenient synonym for Rossetti's personal influence. The Brotherhood itself had a brief literary venture in a periodical named *The Germ*; it first appeared in January 1850, and after two numbers it was renamed *Art and Poetry*; it ceased with the fourth issue in April 1850. Its policy was never clearly defined, but it served as a means for the publication of Rossetti's *The Blessed Damozel* and of ten other poems, and of his prose narrative *Hand and Soul*. Christina Rossetti also contributed verse, and here appeared, too, an early draft of Thomas Woolner's *My Beautiful Lady*, and work by Coventry Patmore.

It was one of Rossetti's most barren projects that brought him seven years later (1857) into contact with two younger men whom he was to influence, and with the woman Jane Burden, later Morris's wife, who so profoundly affected his life. He had undertaken to adorn the Debating Hall (now the Library) of the Union at Oxford with frescoes painted by himself and his friends. Among his pupils was a young Oxford man, Edward Burne-Jones, whom he had persuaded to abandon regular undergraduate studies for painting. Burne-Jones brought to his notice one of his own set, a stocky, thick-set, bearded fellow, William Morris, who had already written poems. As they worked on these Arthurian frescoes, which damp and the fumes of naked gas-jets were soon to obliterate, there came to Rossetti an undergraduate from Balliol with Birkbeck Hill to introduce him as Algernon Charles Swinburne. So Rossetti met two men to whose creative powers he was to give keen impetus. They both developed to produce work that is widely different from his, and neither of them is Pre-Raphaelite as the term was understood in 1848, but, like Rossetti himself, they brought fresh elements into the poetry of the century.

Rossetti's published work is contained in three volumes – *The Early Italian Poets* (1861) (republished as *Dante and his Circle*, 1874); *Poems* (1870) (republished 1881); *Ballads and Sonnets* (1881). In 1886 W. M. Rossetti published *The Works* (reissued in an enlarged edition in 1911), with a number of additional pieces not previously published. In 1930 *The Ballad of Jan Van Hunks*, an early piece revised later, was published. The information which chronology presents is frequently misleading: it does not necessarily bear a close relationship to that secret time sequence formed by the ordering in the mind of imaginative experience. With Rossetti the dates of volume publication bear often little relation to the period of actual composition, and in pursuing this difference one comes into contact with the intimate side of his life. In 1850 one of Rossetti's friends, Walter Deverell, had seen in a London milliner's shop a young woman assistant of exceptional beauty, named Elizabeth Siddal,[1] whose features have become known as one of the types which Rossetti repainted with unwearying tenacity. Miss Siddal was beautiful, but not robust; probably even when Rossetti first knew her she was consumptive. No one was generally less well designed to express considerate affection than Rossetti; what he wanted he seized and used it tempestuously for his own purposes. Friends, patrons, acquaintances, all suffered from an egoism so natural that it was almost unconscious. The only exception was to come later in his solicitous care of Jane Morris. Miss Siddal was to suffer. She had sufficient talent in drawing to attract Ruskin's approval, but her cultural background and physical strength were ill adapted to struggle with Rossetti's fiery and irresponsible spirit. Nor was the situation simplified by Rossetti's encounter in 1857 with Jane Burden, later Mrs William Morris, who exercised a deep influence upon him. The view may be reasonably held that he married Elizabeth Siddal from a sense of obligation at a time when he was already in love with Jane. His treatment of her may well have been affected by this complication in his emotional life. His marriage to Elizabeth was delayed until 1860, and in 1861 she gave birth to a stillborn child. In 1862, suffering equally from phthisis and from Rossetti's neglect, she took an excessive dose of laudanum and died. The balance of evidence must lead to the conclusion that she committed suicide, that Rossetti knew this and that he was deeply remorseful, though remorse, like other emotions, could not hold him with any consistency. Overcome by his immediate grief, he placed the manuscript of his poems, as a gesture of expiation, in her coffin. It is difficult to stand in judgement over such actions, which viewed dispassionately may seem emotional quixotism. But, as Meredith could have told Rossetti, the price of sentiment is a high one. Rossetti discovered it to be excessive. Urged by numerous friends, he was led in 1869 to gain Home Office permission to disinter the poems, which he used in preparing the 1870 volume. Part of the price to be paid for Rossetti's excursion into sentiment lies in the difficulty of chronology in his poetry. His first volume, apart from the Italian translations, was published in 1870, but the poems it contained belong mainly to the periods 1847-1853 and 1868-1870.

While these spectacular moments in his life are associated with Elizabeth Siddal, Janey Morris had a much deeper influence. Like Elizabeth, she was of humble origins, the daughter of an Oxford groom. Rossetti met her, in October 1857, when she was still Jane Burden in an Oxford theatre. She was then a girl of 17, and two years later she married William Morris. Some have said that Rossetti urged Morris to marry her in order to keep 'Janey' in the circle. Morris is so reticent, so honourable, that no open comment on this complex relationship is to be found among his records, but it is clear that his estrangement from Rossetti derived largely from this source. As a model for Rossetti's painting, as an influence on his poetry, as a companion and a lover, she had a dominance for some of the most important years of his life. The complete story of their relationship is still unrevealed, but it is clear now that many of his letters to her are available,[1] that, unlike most of those who met her, he discovered in her not only a most beautiful woman of the Pre-Raphaelite character, but an intelligent companion with whom he could discuss his pictures and his problems. He seems to have married Elizabeth Siddal, as has been suggested, because he felt committed to her; his obsessive love for 'Janey' came from the fact that he was more happy in her company than with any other human person. He was continuously concerned for her health, and her well-being, and, galling though it must have been to Morris, when the firm of Morris, Marshall, Faulkner & Co., broke up, Rossetti handed his share to 'Janey'. So far did his possessiveness go that he extracted from Ford Madox Brown's son the only painting of 'Janey' done by Morris. A third woman entered Rossetti's life and stayed there longer than either Elizabeth or Janey. This was the large-framed, vulgar, exuberant, but apparently very lovable Frances Cornforth. She was present in his days with Lizzie and with Janey Morris, and somehow she survived them both in certain levels of his affections. She was variously married to Timothy Hughes, by all accounts an undesirable character, and later in 1879 she married John Bernard Schott, with whom she kept a public house in Jermyn Street, the Rose Tavern, at No 96.

Later they cashed in on the Rossetti vogue and Schott had 'The Rossetti Gallery' in Bond Street. But Fanny had some quality, though Rossetti's family could not be expected to recognize it. Probably many of his most relaxed hours, particularly in his more tormented years, were spent with her, and their association presents the problem of his personality and his life.

He was a natural Catholic who had fallen on a Puritan world. It was not a Puritan world he could ignore, for he had a great respect for his mother and for his sister, Christina, yet all they represented was remote, even hostile to his life as an artist. His studio they did not visit, and Fanny they never met. What his ultimate relation to his mother must have been has not been explored, but Christina was very close to him and yet shut away in an inhibited and religious life, away from all the practical joking, the bawdiness, and the mistresses. The simplest explanation would be that much in his private life frightened her, though other interpretations are open if one accepts some of the theories of her relation with Bell Scott. His art has an element of the unreal because it falls between these two worlds. He had not the courage or the stamina to be a Victorian Byron. He might have been if his life had been devoted solely to poetry, but he was a painter as well as a poet, and painting was ultimately his main concern. Further, it allowed him to idealize the subject without thinking out the main problems of his life and times.

In 1862 he moved to Cheyne Walk, Chelsea, where for a period he had Swinburne and Meredith as co-tenants. The years that followed were his fullest and most prosperous. He had freedom for his own habits of life, as much work as he desired, and as many friends as he wished. In 1868 Jane Morris reappeared as a sitter for his paintings, and under the influence of her personality he laid the foundation, in 1868-1871, to his sonnet sequence *The House of Life*. In 1868 and 1869 he visited Penkill Castle, in Ayrshire, where William Bell Scott was staying under the patronage of Miss Alice Boyd. The 1869 visit, while it did little to improve his health, led him to write a number of poems, *Troy Town*, *Eden Bower*, *The Stream's Secret*. In 1869 he began to take chloral to induce sleep, and from that year to the end he was consistently struggling with various degrees of ill health. 'I am hardly my own ghost', he wrote to Allingham in 1870. The *Poems*, which appeared in 1870, some of them composed in the late forties, were warmly received, and this encouraged Rossetti to reissue his Italian translations in an enlarged form as *Dante and his Circle* in 1874. Amidst the praise there came the insidious attack of Robert Buchanan, who, under the pseudonym of 'Thomas Maitland', wrote an article in *The Contemporary Review* for October 1871, entitled *The Fleshly School of Poetry – Mr D. G. Rossetti*. The article was elaborated in 1872 into a volume, *The Fleshly School of Poetry, and other Phenomena of the Day*, and Swinburne was included in the diatribe. Rossetti was deeply affected by the virulence of this criticism; the phrase which particularly hurt him was the suggestion that he was binding himself by solemn league and covenant 'to extol fleshliness as the distinct and supreme end of poetic and pictorial art'. Buchanan, later, withdrew this vulgar misappraisement, but at the time it wounded Rossetti deeply. He prepared an effective reply, which was published in *The Athenaeum* in 1871, but the incident helped to develop in him a feeling, which later grew into a mania, that he was being persecuted. Between 1872 and 1874 he recovered sufficiently, in the company of Jane Morris at Kelmscott, to paint *La Ghirlandata* and other oils for which she was the model, but little poetry was produced. In the closing years of that decade, while ill health was continually dominant, he continued to paint, and his work remained popular with buyers. Between 1879 and 1881 there came a return to poetry with *Rose Mary*, *The White Ship*, *The King's Tragedy*, and some additional poems to *The House of Life*. The early volume of 1870 had been a continued success, and in 1881 he republished it with revisions, and with the addition of *The Bride's Prelude*. *The House of Life*, in an expanded form, and the new poems and ballads were published in the same year as *Ballads and Sonnets*. In April 1882, at the age of 54, he died.

This biographical account has served to show that the dates of volume publication (1870 and 1881) are a misleading guide to the chronology of Rossetti's work. His poetry is concentrated in certain groups of years, and even then it is written in the scanty leisure of a professional painter. The first period contains the tentative work before 1847, in which year *The Blessed Damozel* was written. He was already engaged on the Italian translations which belong mainly to 1845-1849. The major part of the early verse is produced between 1847 and 1854 in the period before he had established himself as a professional painter. There follows a lull in poetic production until 1868-1870, when he writes vigorously, mainly upon the expansion of *The House of Life*, and finally, in the period of his last ill health, there emerges a short period of intensive revision and composition between 1879 and 1881. In the following survey the poems are discussed chronologically with reference to these years of poetic activity.

Rossetti approached poetical composition with a background of reading very different from that of his contemporaries. Italian was to him a second language, and to this had been added instruction in German and in French. His own reading had lain mainly in stories of romance, in Terror Tales and in supernatural themes: Scott had mingled with 'Monk' Lewis's *Tales of Terror* and *Tales of Wonder* and with Meinhold's *Sidonia the Sorceress* and *The Amber Witch*. Ballads had early attracted him, and he found in his German reading a close union of ballad form with weird and supernatural themes. One of his earliest pieces was a ballad attempt, *Sir Hugh the Heron*, and his first successful plunge into poetry is a translation of Bürger's *Lenore* in 1844, a remarkable piece of work for a boy of 16 despite its prosodic inadequacies. The influence of German poetry was strong at this early period; he read parts of *Faust*, mainly, one may imagine, for the sake of Mephistopheles, and in 1846 he rendered Hartmann von Aue's *Der Arme Heinrich* as *Henry the Leper*. Further, he was already attempting translations from the Italian. He chose his own reading in English poetry: he early recognized his affinities with Keats; he admired and imitated Browning, and he was frequently making his own discoveries among less well-known poets. The record of these years shows that Rossetti's reading and learning were much wider than they often appeared to be.

A number of the poems in the years 1847-1854 are experimental. *A Last Confession* (begun in 1849) is in style an exercise in Browning's dramatic monologue form. The theme of jealousy and murder with an Italian setting Rossetti may have contrived by combining suggestions from Byron's *The Giaour* with recollections of some refugee at his father's house. He has given his narrative, particularly at the close, the vibrant urgency of Browning's style, but he appears restless amidst the continued realism which the tale demands. In two memorable passages he leaves the dramatic situation and its necessities to describe more pleasing scenes where sensuous and mystical elements unite; one is a description of a woman's face, a recognizable verse account of the Rossetti type, and the other a dream:

> I know last night
> I dreamed I saw into the garden of God,
> Where women walked whose painted images
> I have seen with candles round them in the church.
> They bent this way and that, one to another,
> Playing: and over the long golden hair
> Of each there floated like a ring of fire
> Which when she stooped stooped with her, and when she rose
> Rose with her. Then a breeze flew in among them,
> As if a window had been opened in heaven
> For God to give His blessing from, before
> This world of ours should set; (for in my dream
> I thought our world was setting, and the sun
> Flared, a spent taper;) and beneath that gust
> The rings of light quivered like forest-leaves.

In *Jenny* (1848 and 1858-1869) he attempted a more lyrical expression in the dramatic monologue form. Rossetti thought well of this poem and wrote to William Allingham in 1860: 'Jenny . . . I reckon the most serious thing I have written.' He explores in the four-beat couplets the thoughts of a man who sits with a tired prostitute asleep beside him. Very diverse judgements have been expressed on the poem, whose language, despite its psychological insight, seems frequently sentimental and overstrained. *Jenny* was an experiment, with Browning again as the model, in portraying the mind of a character as revealed in a dramatic situation. Rossetti discovered that while he could treat such themes of human experience they were not the material in which his poetic power could best be revealed.

From the poems of 1847-1854 there emerge dominant motives, which show how Rossetti is separating his own individual quality both from imitation and from preconceived poetic theories. In the early poem, *My Sister's Sleep* (1847-1849), he had attempted to obey the major Pre-Raphaelite principles of accuracy in detail and truth to nature:

> Our mother rose from where she sat:
> Her needles, as she laid them down,
> Met lightly, and her silken gown
> Settled: no other noise than that.

Here it is apparent that he has attempted to restrain himself into a mosaic of accurate detail disciplined to attain an effect of poetic realism. But as in painting so in poetry this self-prescribed emphasis on minuteness came into conflict with a mystical element in his mind, elusive, fugitive, fashioning its dream thought into dim and intangible images. This conflict of material detail with Dantesque vision yields his most original poetry in this period. It appears clearly in his best-known poem, *The Blessed Damozel*, written by 1847 and frequently revised. The scene is that of a woman in heaven watching her lover on earth. Rossetti gained suggestions from Poe, and possibly he knew Herrick's *Comfort to a Youth that had Lost his Love*;[5] a number of the details arise from direct memories of *The Divine Comedy*.[6] The treatment, however, is fresh, and illustrates these two contrasting elements in Rossetti's mind. The theme is of mystical suggestion, a moment in the *Paradiso*, but its purpose is to praise the human love of man and woman. This contrast of mystical and material is not incongruous but pleasurable and surprising. It is emphasized by the description of heaven as 'the rampart of God's House', and by the earthly imagery through which the figure in heaven is portrayed:

> The blessed damozel leaned out
> From the gold bar of Heaven.

We see the universe from heaven, but it is with the simple imagery of our own world: the earth, 'a midge'; the curled moon, 'a little feather'; and the souls mounting to God 'like thin flames'. The submersion of these two elements in Rossetti's imagination and their consequent union in a poem can be paralleled in a number of pieces of this period, notably in *The Card Dealer* (1849). The poem opens as a precise excerpt of realistic description. Rossetti, with a picture by Theodore von Holst in mind, portrays a woman dealing cards. The following stanza illustrates the luxurious wealth of coloured detail in the opening movement of the poem:

> Her fingers let them softly through,
> Smooth polished silent things;
> And each one as it falls reflects
> In swift light-shadowings,
> Blood-red and purple, green and blue,
> The great eyes of her rings.

Later this world of realism is dissolved into dream, symbolical in its purpose and medieval in suggestion, and it is with this mood that the poem closes:

> Thou seest the card that falls, – she knows
> The card that followeth:
> Her game in thy tongue is called Life,
> As ebbs thy daily breath:
> When she shall speak, thou'lt learn her tongue
> And know she calls it Death.

Love's Nocturn (1854), a poem which rests in a twilit obscurity, shows the triumph of fantasy over the world of fact. Rossetti, describing the house of a magician who sends dreams into sleeping minds, imagines that he might himself penetrate this 'vaporous unaccountable' storehouse to send his dream to his lady. This theme is evolved subtly, from a background of elaborate dream detail. The stanza, as the following example illustrates, was one of the most intricate, both in rhyme and numbers, that Rossetti evolved:

> Poets' fancies all are there:
> There the elf-girls flood with wings
> Valleys full of plaintive air;
> There breathe perfumes: there in rings
> Whirl the foam-bewildered springs;
> Siren there
> Winds her dizzy hair and sings.

Further, Rossetti contrives a dim, intangible imagery to sustain the mood, as in this description of the approach to this dreamworld:

> Groping in the windy stair,
> (Darkness and the breath of space
> Like loud waters everywhere.)

It is as if all the solid details which decorate his Pre-Raphaelite exercises in verse had disappeared in a night of storm, whence all that can be seen and touched is banished, so that one gropes, terrified and yet fascinated, in a world where sound and wind and water are all that remain of the scenes of common day. Such are the two elements which struggle for supremacy in Rossetti's mind, and part of the history of his poetical development is the increasing mastery of the Dantesque visions over the world of reality.

This conflict, while it rests at the centre of the problem of Rossetti as a poet, will not alone serve as an interpretation of his poetic purposes. In the period 1847-1854 he disentangled his poetry from its prescribed Victorian duties of expounding the ideas of the time; he released it from its obligations to investigate the conditions of moral or spiritual consciousness. This he achieved naturally, almost secretly, as if he were unaware of his own purposes. He never had to revolt against his century, because he was never in it; spiritually he existed not in an age of scientific discovery with an emphasis on 'the condition of the people', but in a world of his own which had the décor of Dante's Italy. Seldom does he choose a contemporary theme: in 1849 he wrote a series of discursive poems describing his journey to Paris and Belgium, but these were, with one exception, not published with his permission. In 1852 he was led for some unexplained reason to write an ode on *Wellington's Funeral*. But his characteristic poetry is marked by a withdrawal from contemporary problem and circumstance. It can be seen in *The Burden of Nineveh* (1850 and later), where he shows how distasteful and unreal was the modern world in which by an unkind accident of time he found his physical existence:

> In our Museum galleries
> To-day I lingered o'er the prize
> Dead Greece vouchsafes to living eyes, –
> Her Art for ever in fresh wise
>   From hour to hour rejoicing me.
> Sighing I turned at last to win
> Once more the London dirt and din;
> And as I made the swing-door spin
> And issued, they were hoisting in
>   A wingèd beast from Nineveh.

And the same approach is continued later in the poem:

> Now, thou poor god, within this hall
> Where the blank windows blind the wall
> From pedestal to pedestal,
> The kind of light shall on thee fall
>   Which London takes the day to be:
> While school-foundations in the act
> Of holiday, three files compact,
> Shall learn to view thee as a fact
> Connected with that zealous tract:
>   'Rome – Babylon and Nineveh'.

In withdrawing to his own world, he felt no antagonism to religious belief, as Shelley and Swinburne had done. One may trace an autobiographical sentiment in the lines in *The Bride's Prelude*:

> But though I loved not holy things,
>   To hear them scorned brought pain, –
> They were my childhood.

His mind delighted in the rich symbolism of Catholic ritual, and he employs it without believing in the faith which it represents. He used it as he would have used any other material whose form and suggestion attracted him. This explains the presence of *Ave* (1847 and later) among the poems of this period. Written in four-beat couplets derived from his study of Blake, the poem is a moving account of the life of the Virgin Mother, ending in what seems almost a confession of faith. The note attached to the poem in 1869, however, reveals his purpose: 'This hymn was written as a prologue to a series of designs. Art still identifies herself with all faiths for her own purposes.' Similarly, the other poems on religious themes are closely connected with painting, and with the possibilities of Christian story for allied pictorial and literary purposes: it is this motive that governs both *The Portrait* and the sonnets on *Mary's Girlhood*. The latter are closely connected with his early picture of *The Annunciation*:

> This is that blessed Mary, pre-elect
>   God's Virgin. Gone is a great while, and she
>   Dwelt young in Nazareth of Galilee.
> Unto God's will she brought devout respect,
> Profound simplicity of intellect,
>   And supreme patience. From her mother's knee
>   Faithful and hopeful; wise in charity;
> Strong in grave peace; in pity circumspect.

Swinburne summarized Rossetti's approach to Christianity when he wrote: 'Rossetti has felt and given the mere physical charm of Christianity with no admixture of doctrine or of doubt.'

In examining the main features of Rossetti's poetic consciousness it has been necessary to concentrate on poems which suggest more emphatically his personal qualities; others remain, and among them some of his most popular pieces. He had, through his early reading of Scott and of Percy's *Reliques*, supplemented by Bürger and Goethe, attained a strong interest in the ballad form. He realized both the intention and method of the ballad, the allusive presentation of a theme swiftly developed, and the depth of feeling simply and unerringly conveyed. This he understood, but the complexity and conflict of his creative impulses led him frequently to modify the direct simplicity of the ballad form to meet his sophisticated purposes. He frequently introduces subtleties of verbal suggestion, inherited from Keats and Tennyson, and intricacies of mood derived from his other poems. His earliest verse experiments were in this form. *The Ballad of Jan van Hunks*, made when he was 18, was much refashioned in his last years. It is an unusual piece for Rossetti, an exercise in comic grotesque, based on memories of a story which he had read in childhood of the devil's wager with a Dutchman for a smoking match. Slighter than the other poems, it confirms the generalization that the Pre-Raphaelites had little talent for humour in poetry. *David Shand*, another early poem, is a close approximation to ballad form, while it is only half serious in theme. With *The Staff and Scrip* (1851-1852), he entered successfully into possession of the ballad form. The story, adapted from the *Gesta Romanorum*, is of a pilgrim who, having fought for a lady, leaves her at his death his staff and scrip. In the medieval legend, when rich suitors approached her, she grew ashamed of this humble legacy, but Rossetti makes her faithful to her champion and gives the poem a mystical conclusion:

> The lists are set in Heaven to-day,
>   The bright pavilions shine;
> Fair hangs thy shield, and none gainsay;
>   The trumpets sound in sign
>   That she is thine.

The stanza is complex and leads Rossetti into a riot of imperfect rhymes, yet the story is conveyed in the ballad way, while his own values and colouring have been added without incongruity. *Sister Helen*, the other ballad poem of this early period, was frequently revised. First drafted in 1851, it was published in 1854 in *The Düsseldorf Album*,[7] with only thirty stanzas, and this early version gains in conclusiveness over the forty-two stanza version of 1881. The poem has original quality and has been variously appraised. Medieval in setting, it tells of a woman who, witch-like, burns a waxen image of her unfaithful lover so that she may damn him, body and soul. It arises from Rossetti's early interest in witchcraft, and its long, trailing refrains capture the appropriate atmosphere of magic. Yet the length of the poem, particularly in the later version, detracts from its effect, and what should have been weird is in danger of being monotonous. Apart from ballads Rossetti achieved in the period 1847-1854 two narrative pieces. *The Bride's Prelude* (1848 and 1859), an unfinished poem, though medieval in setting, is a study of human feeling in the story of a woman forced to marry the man who had once seduced her. The movements of the poem are powerfully conveyed and a rich imagery sustains them. Rossetti left a prose memorandum indicating a conclusion to the theme, but he never discovered the mood in which to complete it. In *Dante at Verona* (1848-1850 and 1869-1870) he extended his interest in Dante into an imaginative narrative which is the longest portrayal of normal circumstance in his work.

The poetry of this period, while it suggests the dominant moods in Rossetti's poetry, shows at the same time a variety of sympathy and of experiment. Later, the major and individual motives conquer the whole of his poetic consciousness. Nothing served more to direct and concentrate these purposes than his translations of Dante and his contemporaries, first published as *The Early Italian Poets* (1861), and enlarged as *Dante and his Circle* in 1874. Not only had the work a profound effect on Rossetti himself, it served to influence the development of Victorian romanticism; here more than anywhere else Swinburne found himself indebted to Rossetti; Patmore seems aware of it; the approach to sentiment, the very colour and diction of these translations occur and re-occur in the poetry of the later nineteenth century. Much of Rossetti's most secure work occurs in this volume. He knew both languages, and he had a mastery of phrase which transferred delicate poetic sentiment from one language to another, uninjured and almost undisturbed. His approach to Dante shows how he recognized his own poetic sympathies; for he is aware that it is the Dante of the *Vita Nuova* and the sonnets, not the Dante of the *Commedia* that attracts him. He shuts out from his work disturbing metaphysical conceptions. It was not that he did not admire the *Commedia*, but that its 'mighty voice' dealt with problems outside the self-imposed structures of his limited world. While retaining the features of the Italian, Rossetti achieved pieces that have the strength and integrity of original poems. This can be seen from his translation in the following sonnet from the *Vita Nuova*:

> My lady looks so gentle and so pure
>   When yielding salutation by the way,
>   That the tongue trembles and has nought to say,
> And the eyes, which fain would see, may not endure.
> And still, amid the praise she hears secure,
>   She walks with humbleness for her array;
>   Seeming a creature sent from Heaven to stay
> On earth, and show a miracle made sure.
>
> She is so pleasant in the eyes of men
> That through the sight the inmost heart doth gain
>   A sweetness which needs proof to know it by:
> And from between her lips there seems to move
> A soothing essence that is full of love,
>   Saying for ever to the spirit, 'Sigh!'

Rossetti rightly asserted that an important element in his work lay in his rendering of lesser-known poets who were of Dante's age. He introduced to English readers a range of writers who had been previously little known, and at the same time revealed new suggestions of theme and idiom to English poetry. The result is more varied than has often been allowed, and whatever minor distortion of phrase Rossetti permitted himself, he seldom failed to render the Italian original adequately into an English poem. His success is noticeable in his renderings of Guido Cavalcanti, who, despite the 'stiffness and cold conceits', which Rossetti suggests as an occasional disfigurement, has a vigour and freshness which yield themselves to the English version. The following version of one of Cavalcanti's sonnets shows Rossetti adapting himself to a style very different from that required for his renderings of Dante:

> Beauty in woman; the high will's decree;
>   Fair knighthood armed for manly exercise;
>   The pleasant song of birds; love's soft replies;
> The strength of rapid ships upon the sea;
> The serene air when light begins to be;
>   The white snow, without wind that falls and lies;
>   Fields of all flower; the place where waters rise;
> Silver and gold; azure in jewellery: –
> Weighed against these, the sweet and quiet worth
>   Which my dear lady cherishes at heart
> Might seem a little matter to be shown;
>   Being truly, over these, as much apart
> As the whole heaven is greater than this earth.
> All good to kindred natures cleaveth soon.

The work of translation, apart from its effect on his approach to sentiment in his own poems, had a marked influence on his style. The translation of *Lenore* shows that he had an early tendency towards the use of imperfect rhymes, and to rhyming a stressed syllable with an unstressed ending in the following line. He felt, possibly from his Italian reading, that English was weak in rhyming words, and that the concession of imperfect rhymes would alone compensate for this deficiency. He certainly found in his Italian translations that the complex verse patterns could not be maintained unless imperfect rhymes were used. He retains the practice in his own work and frequently employs it with dangerous licence. It has been suggested that a contributory explanation can be found in his early reading of ballads, though Rossetti by no means confines its use to his ballad imitations. In the

Italian poems he discovered also the use of a symbolical description of Love and Death as abstract qualities which he retained in his own work.

The influence of his Italian studies is seen most impressively in his sonnet sequence, *The House of Life*;[8] some of the poems in this work belong to the period 1847-1853, the largest group to 1869-1871, and others to 1879-1881. Rossetti was diffident in admitting an autobiographical element in the poems. William Rossetti summarized the situation by saying that *The House of Life* 'embodies salient incidents and emotions in his own life. There are very few of the sonnets which are not strictly personal, and not one through which his individual feelings and views do not transpire.' At the centre of this was his love for Janey Morris, though the sources were heavily literary as well as personal, deriving from the Italian sonnet tradition which he knew so well. To estimate the quality of this work is to approach the penetralia of Rossetti's poetic life, for here, apart from a few detached sonnets, he exposes his approach to love and art, and his philosophy of experience. The influence of Dante is marked both on style and conception, and Walter Pater devotes his essay on Rossetti largely to elucidating this relationship. 'Like Dante,' Pater suggests, 'he knows no region of spirit which shall not be sensuous also, or material.' By Rossetti this union is applied to Love alone, for the other regions of spirit have been banished to the outer edges of his mind. Apart from this difference, more than the gulf of time separates Rossetti from Dante, for the conflict of motives, apparent in his other poetry, enters here to a marked degree. First, he possessed towards Love an element of worship, rarefied and complex, that 'ideal intensity of love – of love based upon a perfect yet peculiar type of physical or material beauty – which is enthroned in the midst of those mysterious powers; Youth and Death, Destiny and Fortune, Fame, Poetic Fame, Memory, Oblivion and the like'. Strangely contrary to this, there existed in his life a disordered restlessness of passion, a vigorous sensuality, at times a broad coarseness. Both these elements were in his life; the first alone was allowed to escape into his poetry, always admitting that his relation to Jane Morris remains unexplained and was in marked contradiction to much else in his life and in the manifestations of his personality. There are men in certain periods who resolve into their imaginative creations all that is within their consciousness; Rossetti exercises a certain intellectual censorship upon his conceptions, and one of the masters of that censorship is Dante.

It is not that sensuality is excluded – the 'Nuptial Sleep' sonnet which led to the 'Fleshly School' attack is evidence of that – but that its portrayal has the sombre sobriety of ritual. The effect is as if a chastity of mind had combined with a corruptness in experience, and a gracious idealism of sentiment existed without innocence. In his analysis of emotion and passion he knows nothing of joy or that geniality towards love which allowed Chaucer to describe it as the 'olde daunce'. He lacks, as do all the romantic poets except Byron, the intrusion of broad human laughter. This solemn apotheosis of Eros penetrates the whole texture of *The House of Life*. 'As a god self-slain on his own strange altar' he performs this oblation of his personality to Love, and presiding dimly over the sacrifice is the ever-present figure of Death.

The sequence is divided into two parts: Part I, Youth and Change, has, as its main argument, Rossetti's approach to Love. Part II, Change and Fate, portraying later moods, expresses a more general approach to life, with a confession of remorse and a realization of mistaken purposes. At the same time many of the poems are incidental. Each sonnet embodies a single mood:

> A Sonnet is a moment's monument, –
> Memorial from the Soul's eternity
> To one dead deathless hour.

The moment is explored with an intricacy of imagery, whose landscape belongs to intangible, twilight things, waters, and silence, moonlight, and still, half-shadowed shapes. The realistic detail of the earlier Pre-Raphaelite experiments has been exorcized so that these sombre dream shapes may exist unchallenged. In such phrases as 'the dim shoal and weary water of the place of sighs', 'Wild images of Death, Shadows and shoals that edge eternity', he maintains consistently the sombre landscape in which the thought of the poems may dwell. In Part I he portrays Love enthroned above Truth and Hope and Fame, and Youth, and he explores its development, using both a Christian symbolism and a deeply sensual detail to indicate the union of spirit and matter. From the earlier sonnets it would appear that the conception of Love arises from his attachment to one woman, but in Sonnet XXXIV it becomes apparent that the loved one is only an instrument through which some mystical abstract quality, Love, becomes momentarily apparent:

> Lo! what am I to Love, the lord of all?
>   One murmuring shell he gathers from the sand, –
>   One little heart-flame sheltered in his hand.
> Yet through thine eyes he grants me clearest call
> And veriest touch of powers primordial
>   That any hour-girt life may understand.

So in Sonnet XXXVI, after the death of the first love, he finds the mystical quality of Love revealed through a new woman, and in Sonnet XXXVII, when Love charges him with inconstancy, he replies that only by this new attachment can Love's own worship be fulfilled. The new love, unlike the old, is secret, difficult, with the suggestion of the forbidden hanging over it. Yet the longings caused by this new love lead to some of the most poignant poems in the sequence:

> What of her glass without her? The blank grey
>   There where the pool is blind to the moon's face.
>   Her dress without her? The tossed empty space
> Of cloud-rack whence the moon has passed away.
> Her paths without her? Day's appointed sway
>   Usurped by desolate night. Her pillowed place
>   Without her? Tears, ah me! for love's good grace,
> And cold forgetfulness of night or day.
>
> What of the heart without her? Nay, poor heart,
>   Of thee what word remains ere speech be still?
>   A wayfarer by barren ways and chill,

> Steep ways and weary, without her thou art,
> Where the long cloud, the long wood's counterpart,
> Sheds doubled darkness up the labouring hill.

In Part II he surveys life, and particularly his own life, and reveals a sense of lost purposes, of futile and delayed endeavour:

> So it happeneth
> When Work and Will awake too late, to gaze
> After their life sailed by, and hold their breath.
> Ah! who shall dare to search through what sad maze
> Thenceforth their incommunicable ways
> Follow the desultory feet of Death?

The only hope that underlies life, and that is dimly conceived, a fancy rather than a faith, rests in Beauty and the possibility of reunion with the one that is loved. Despite this centre of despair, the second part contains sonnets of considerable variety and power: 'The Monochord', intelligible only as music is intelligible; 'The Sun's Shame', a powerful adaptation of Elizabethan mannerism; the poignant and personal sonnets, 'Newborn Death' and 'The Hill Summit' with their richer background of natural landscape than is usual in Rossetti. All that he could reveal of his mind poetically he placed in this sequence, and in a few related lyrics such as 'Cloud Confines' and 'The Stream's Secret'. In 'Cloud Confines', he explored the meaning of life only to leave the matter a question unanswered.[9] 'The Stream's Secret' (1869), a poem written in Ayrshire from a title derived from Bell Scott, was once thought to be his reflections on his wife's death, but appears to be an expression of his unhappiness in the absence of Janey Morris. The poem recalls the moods of *The House of Life*, the penetration into those half-lit recesses of his mind, where Love dwells, and Death with her:

> Nay, why
> Name the dead hours? I mind them well:
> Their ghosts in many darkened doorways dwell
>   With desolate eyes to know them by.
>   The hour that must be born ere it can die, –
> Of that I'd have thee tell.

The House of Life bridges his early and later poetry. In 1869 he returned to ballad poetry and attempted to adjust two of the great world stories, *Paradise Lost* and the *Iliad*, to the necessities of this form. In *Eden Bower*, Lilith, the snake woman, the first wife of Adam ('Not a drop of her blood was human'), conspires with the snake to undo Adam and Eve. Much of the poem is her account of the Fall, and of her revenge. Rossetti had been attracted by the Lilith legend in Goethe,[10] and had employed it in *The House of Life*. Here he uses Lilith's figure to portray the whole fate of Adam and Eve from a fresh standpoint. Lilith's imagery serves to give unity to her narrative:

> O and Lilith was queen of Adam!
> (*Sing Eden Bower!*)
> All the day and the night together
> My breath could shake his soul like a feather.

Rossetti seldom wrote more simply and effectively; he reduced a large theme to the brief allusive phrases of Lilith's speech and yet retained in her an intensity of passion. In *Troy Town* (1869), the most subtle of the ballads, he contracts the whole of the epic theme to a prayer of Helen's made in dedicating to Venus a cup fashioned in the shape of her breast. One cannot deny the laden sensuality, but this should not obscure its technical perfection. Rossetti considered it among the best of his poems. Its swift movement, its prophetic refrain full of foreboding, and an imagery as exotic as that of the *Song of Songs*, serve to unite a number of Rossetti's dominant qualities conveyed with mature craftsmanship. In *Stratton Water* (1854, revised 1869), he sets aside these individual purposes in order to achieve ballad imitation in theme and form. The effects are broader, and the theme lucidly conveyed, but the story of Lord Sands and of Janet, who believed him unfaithful, and of their marriage in the kirk with its flooded kirkyard, lacks the complete seriousness and sincerity of Rossetti's more individual poems. The adherence to traditional form and vocabulary, while it increased clarity, eliminated the tortuous and yet powerful quality of his mind. In his last years he returned in *The White Ship* (1878-1880) and *The King's Tragedy*

(1881) to this simpler ballad method. In these poems, the product of the lucid intervals of a man ridden with ill health and mental distress, he seems to disengage himself from the motives of his earlier poetry and find freedom in clear narration. The story of the death of Henry I's son, which he retells in *The White Ship*, had long been known to him, while his interest in the theme of *The King's Tragedy*, the death of James I of Scotland, arose from Bell Scott's affection for *The King's Quair*. Neither poem is disturbed by the ballad mimicry which frets the poetic sincerity of *Stratton Water*, yet they both possess a simplicity like that found in William Morris. Ballad poetry has affected English romanticism in many ways, and Rossetti makes an individual contribution: he begins his poetry in the ballad, later he impregnates it with his own purposes, and then at last, when with the increase of physical disability he loses contact with his earlier poetic motives, he reveals himself in the ballad as a narrative writer, with action and pathos and tragedy equally under his control.

Closely related to his ballads is *Rose Mary* (1869), the most complex of Rossetti's narratives, told in five-line stanzas with strophic choruses, dividing the three parts. The theme is ballad material united to Rossetti's own interest in spiritualism. He had heard of the 'dreaming stone' of Dr Dee, the sixteenth-century astrologer,[11] and so in ballad setting he imagines a girl gazing at a beryl stone of her mother's to see if any danger faces her lover. None but the pure can glimpse the message of the stone, and the girl, no longer a maid, fails to see the danger that faces her knight. In the second part, after a strophic interlude by the spirits of the stone, the knight is brought in dead, and on his person the girl's mother discovers letters written by another woman. In the third part Rose Mary breaks the beryl stone with her father's sword, releases its evil spirits, and so brings destruction upon herself. She dies feeling that she is returning to her knight. This poem, so compact and moving, loses only in the inadequacy of its final crisis and in its technical overelaboration. Rossetti's addition of the strophic beryl songs serves to make intricate a narrative which is already overstrained with circumstance.

Yet in its mixture of magic and human motive it possesses an unusual power, not unlike that of *The Ancient Mariner*, but with a suggestion that the poetic purpose was never fully envisioned, or at least never completely revealed.

The limitations of Rossetti's poetry have frequently been defined: his imperfect rhymes, prosodic licences, tortured vocabulary, the absence of natural landscape or normal human interest, the rejection of faith, and of all ethical or social preoccupations. He seems to stand in between the poetic philosophy of Keats and that of the eighteen-nineties; he has lost many of the generous impulses which strengthened Keats's conception of Beauty, while his contacts are wider than those of some of the lyrists who follow him at the close of the century. Many of his limitations can be recognized and admitted, and yet it cannot be denied that his influence gave poetry a new direction in the later nineteenth century. If his vocabulary is difficult, he cannot at least be accused of carelessness: his letters are filled with minute discussion of alternative phrasings, and he revised his work continuously. The integrity of his art lies in the fact that there arises from his most individual poems a single image: Love dimly shrined; Life wreathing flowers for Death to wear and 'darkness and the breath of space, Like loud waters everywhere'. Victorian romanticism is marked by its narrowing content, and Rossetti contributes to that close resifting of the material thought suitable for poetry. Even if his art was esoteric he served by his whole life to emphasize the importance of art in a society that was alien to such a faith. Much of his active life was occupied with painting, and that art enters frequently into his poetry; he writes of pictures and further allows his vivid visual powers to colour his poetic imagery. His life was confused, untidy, in the later years under the influence of chloral morbid and irresponsible. But the fifties and sixties of the nineteenth century were an unsympathetic atmosphere for any artist. Whatever the biographers may say of the more sordid details of his life, he valued poetry for its own sake and strove to bring perfection to its form and phrasing.

Algernon Charles Swinburne

Around the personality of Algernon Charles Swinburne[1] (1837-1909) literary critics were once as restless and tormenting as a pack of midges. Vaguely sensing a legend in his life, they failed to determine what that legend should be. He could not, like Shelley, be converted into a hero; his very appearance was too incongruous, and Sir Edmund Gosse enforced this impression very clearly: 'In the case of Swinburne the physical strangeness exceeded, perhaps, that of any other entirely sane man of imaginative genius whose characteristics have been preserved for us.'

Sir Edmund Gosse's life of Swinburne, published in 1917, had been discreet. Where abnormal features of Swinburne's personality had been indicated the suggestions had been vague and general. Yet along with his published biography Gosse had written in 1917 a manuscript essay now, at last, published by Cecil Y. Lang in his masterly edition of Swinburne's letters.[2] Prior to publication this essay acquired a major degree of notoriety, including questions in the House of Commons. Now, as Lang suggests, the 'force is spent'. All that Gosse writes has long been known and the evidence could be derived from the letters and other sources. For a decade and a half Swinburne was a chronic alcoholic. He was also a masochist. Whether he was also a homosexual remains undefined, for Gosse's essay, as Lang states, is 'as remarkable for what it omits as for what it includes'.

All that can be said is that there was a persistent oral rumour. That he had no inclination or success in heterosexual love is shown in his failure with Miss Menken, the circus performer, to whom he had been introduced by Rossetti. In the midst of all his ineffectuality he boasted of her to George Powell, his scabrous Welsh friend: 'I must send you in a day or two a photograph of my present possessor – known to Britannia as Miss Menken, to me as Dolores (her real Christian name) – and myself taken together. We both come out very well. Of course it's private.'[3] His real addiction, which seems to date from his Eton days, was for flagellation. Gosse describes the establishment in St John's Wood which he visited for the services of two 'scourging ladies' and quotes G. R. Sims as an authority for the story of how Swinburne would pause on a particular bench in Regent's Park and write one or other of his *Songs Before Sunrise*, of all his poems the most idealistic, before he proceeded to be 'whipped at a bawdy house'.

Of all English poets Swinburne represents the clearest example of one whose experience at its most degraded is separated from his poetry. Gosse suggested that 'extravagant, even vicious, as might be many sides of Swinburne's conduct, they were not essential, but accidental'. His private conduct until he was nursed by Watts-Dunton was, to a degree, excessive, and often seemed to have concealed within it an element of fantastic bravado. Such was his letter to that strange Welsh squire, George Powell, where he reminds him that the day is the anniversary of the death 'or shall I say the translation – of that great and good man the Marquis de Sade'.

Of all personalities in English literature he seems the most unreal. The life he led was far from that of ordinary men. Yet the degree to which his poetical personality impressed his contemporaries can be witnessed by many instances. When the social reformer, J. M. Ludlow, wished to lead a prosecution against Swinburne for the publication of *Poems and Ballads* he received from Ruskin a rebuke that must have surprised him: 'Swinburne is infinitely above me in all knowledge and power, and I should no more think of advising him and criticizing him than of venturing to do it to Turner if he were alive again.'

It was through this figure that the public first gained cognizance of the changed values in the poetry of this century. Today this is difficult to realize, for, as Cecil Lang writes, 'Swinburne has long been out of fashion. Of the great English poets he remains the most unappreciated.' One can compare this with the enthusiasm of George Saintsbury, who, as a young man, could recall the scandal and success of *Poems and Ballads* on its first appearance. Rossetti, Meredith, and Morris had published work before Swinburne, but they had been quietly ignored. Christina Rossetti was awarded a genial reception in 1862, but around her no stormy controversies arose. Swinburne by the brilliance and violence of his *Poems and Ballads* made 1866 a turning-point in poetical history. Nothing was quite the same after that. Then with the changing fashions after the First World War neglect crept in, so that the massive twenty-volume *Bonchurch Edition* prepared by Gosse and Wise in 1926-1927 seemed more like a tomb than a living memorial.

He was of a pure English tradition and of noble family; his father was Admiral Charles Henry Swinburne and his mother was a daughter of the Earl of Ashburnham. Hampshire, Northumberland, and a little of London, where by an accident of residence he was born, were the background of his childhood. He enjoyed Nature, the life of the country and the sea. Both father and mother contributed to the education of this child, born all but dead, and certainly not expected to live an hour. His father, who remained throughout life attached to the 'afflictive phenomenon' of a son, swam with him in the sea and awakened in him a lasting passion for that least restrictive of elements. From his mother he gained early a knowledge of French and Italian, and her tact prevented any permanent breach between him and his family. He entered Eton in 1849 when he was 12; he left, a little precipitately, in 1853. His temperament kept him outside the normal life of a public school, and his courage prevented him from being tormented. Those who knew realized that there was 'something a little formidable about him', and those less sympathetic thought him 'a horrid little boy, with a big red head and pasty complexion, who looked as though a course of physical exercise would have done him good'.[4] Some of his leisure was well occupied. He was to become one of the best-read poets of his age, and already he was consuming the work of the romantics and eighteenth-century poets, some of the Elizabethans, with Greek poetry and a few of the Latins, including Ovid and Catullus. Byron he had promised his mother not to read. In 1851, when Queen Victoria visited Eton, he wrote a poem in the manner of Pope, *The Triumph of Gloriana*: the satirist could embroider the incident, but it shall pass.

In 1856 he entered Balliol College, Oxford, and though he paid but limited attention to prescribed studies he read widely; he continued with the poets he had known at Eton, and Byron was no longer excluded. He went farther afield in verse and prose, studying *Wuthering Heights*, *Aurora Leigh*, and less-known works which were to influence him, Charles Wells's *Joseph and His Brethren* and Beddoes's *Death's Jest Book*. During the late autumn of 1857 he met the group of Pre-Raphaelites who were invading Oxford to cover with frescoes the walls of the Union Debating Hall, and later Rossetti, Morris, and Burne-Jones were all to become his friends. Morris's early poetry was the most immediate influence, but the verse and personality of Rossetti were destined to leave a more permanent impression. Some of his best letters were written to Rossetti, until a breach, never fully explained, terminated their relationship.[5] He had friends of his own generation in a group of brilliant undergraduates led by a young Scot, John Nichol. They called themselves the 'Old Mortality' and met to discuss literature and philosophy and to engender conviviality. Nichol introduced him to republican enthusiasms, a hatred of Napoleon III and a love of Mazzini, both to appear as motives in his poetry. During the later years at Oxford he came under the influence of Benjamin Jowett, then Professor of Greek; it was strange how some mutual regard and even respect grew up between dignity and what must have appeared to dignity as impudence. A love of Greek literature was a common bond, and through Jowett's assistance Swinburne continued his Greek studies with an enthusiasm that had its creative effect in *Atalanta in Calydon* and *Erechtheus*. Oxford had given him much, but he showed little gratitude, and his conduct was sufficiently unsatisfactory for him to be sent away in 1859 to study with William Stubbs at Navestock, and later, in 1860, he was 'rusticated and all but expelled'. He left hating Oxford, but not the friends whom he had found there. Ten years later he was welcoming the Master of Balliol as a guest in his father's house.

The record of Swinburne's life from 1860 to his death is different from that of other men. He formed no ties beyond those of friendship; he had no responsibilities beyond that of looking after himself, and in this he failed conspicuously. It is usual to note in that life two periods; both of them lack normality. In the first he is like some gaudy bird flaunting its plumage in the drab, foggy air of London, and then he is a bird caged, content to be caged and fed. The first period extends from 1860 to 1879. His main centre is London, though he has to flee at times to recuperate in the country. It is a period meagre in outward event, but crowded with his own perverted experience and also with intellectual excitement. In the first edition of this book I accepted Gosse's account that 'The Triumph of Time' arose from Swinburne's 'solitary romance' with Jane Faulkner, the niece and adopted daughter of Sir John Simon. I am now completely convinced that I was wrong by Professor Lang's analysis of all the available evidence.[1] Jane Faulkner was only 10 in 1862 when Swinburne wrote his poem. Gosse wrote under circumstances of great difficulty and Professor Lang lets him down lightly. The only lady who will fit the picture is his cousin Mary Gordon (to whose mother Swinburne dedicated 'The Sisters'), and this despite her explicit denial that 'there was in all our years of friendship, an ounce of sentiment between us'. That their relationship was close is known and one day Mary Gordon told him that she was to be married. This, she adds, 'caused something of a gap in our constant correspondence and intercourse, though he was always the same when we did meet. I have been unable to trace the letter he wrote when I announced to him my engagement.' If Swinburne was deeply in love with Mary Gordon everything in the poem will fit in:

> I will say no word that a man might say
> Whose whole life's love goes down in a day.

Mary Gordon married in 1865, a man twenty-one years her senior. Swinburne's love for her, as the poem states, was undeclared and unguessed at. Lang also discovers autobiographical elements that will fit into this general picture in his epistolary novel, *A Year's Letters* reprinted in 1905 as *Love's Cross Currents*, and in the fragmentary novel published after his death, in 1952, as *Lesbia Brandon*.

Swinburne formed new friendships of deep influence. Monckton Milnes (afterwards Lord Houghton), a man of 50, a traveller, who had known the world of diplomacy and politics and savoured the fashionable life of a dozen capitals, welcomed Swinburne to his estate at Fryston.[6] Monckton Milnes, the discreet editor of Keats, possessed a library with a collection of erotica 'unparalleled perhaps in Europe'. After Gosse's biographical essay it is easy to see how Swinburne appreciated access to these treasures, particularly to the comprehensive collection of sadistic literature. It would be false to suggest that Monckton Milnes initiated Swinburne into these studies or even forced them on his attention. Rather Swinburne discovered that he had at Fryston something that would be crucial to the development of his creative work. While, on the one hand, all this encouraged him as a poet, it also led to a febrile excitement and G. Lafourcade has enumerated the acquaintances who could have encouraged him to an unbalanced life, from Burton, the orientalist and explorer, to others such as George Powell, equally Rabelaisian, but of more dubious literary worth. He retained contact with Rossetti and met George Meredith, but an attempt of the three to form a joint *ménage* should have shown Swinburne and

Meredith[7] that their temperaments were too diverse for companionship.

Apart from friendships, Swinburne formed literary adorations, which persisted throughout his life, giving a wan stimulus to his later poetry. Among the objects of this hero-worship were Victor Hugo, Baudelaire, Walter Savage Landor, Mazzini and Walt Whitman, whom later he dethroned amid a storm of vituperation. This period (1860-1879) is crucial in Swinburne's poetic creation. The poetical volumes published in those years are: *The Queen Mother* and *Rosamond* (1860); *Atalanta in Calydon* (1865, April); *Chastelard* (1865); *Poems and Ballads* (1866); *A Song of Italy* (1867); *Songs before Sunrise* (1871); *Bothwell* (1874); *Songs of Two Nations* (1875); *Erechtheus* (1876); *Poems and Ballads (Second Series)* (1878). Apart from poetical work, Swinburne commenced, in this period, critical work in prose. He was a contributor to *The Spectator* from 1862, and to *The Fortnightly* from 1867; in 1868 appeared his study of *William Blake*, important as a revelation of his own early aesthetic position. In 1875 he published *George Chapman*, one of his early studies of Elizabethan drama. He produced also a large amount of unpublished work, including the prose romance *Lesbia Brandon*. This was published in 1952 with an elaborate historical and critical commentary by Randolph Hughes, which makes major claims for Swinburne as a novelist.

The second period of Swinburne's life (1879-1909) has been the subject of much controversy. There emerges the figure of Theodore Watts, known later as Theodore Watts-Dunton, a lawyer of St Ives, who had helped a number of the Pre-Raphaelites in their legal difficulties. Business relationships ripened into friendship, so that when in 1878-1879 Swinburne's health was lacerated by the life he was leading and no appeal of friends or family could move him, Watts-Dunton took him first to his own rooms, and then in September 1879 to 'The Pines', in Putney, a house he had taken for their joint tenancy. The bird was caged, but he would have died had it been otherwise. This joint *ménage* at 'The Pines' has been often described; the late rising; the

Framingham State College
Framingham, Massachusetts

regular morning walk; lunch at 1.30 p.m.; a siesta from 2.30 to 4.30; work until dinner, and after dinner a reading from Dickens's novels with Theodore, and then work and reading until midnight. There were visits abroad and at home, and there were friends, but Watts-Dunton supervised all with an anxious eye. Gosse expressed soberly what has been often expressed satirically when he described Swinburne's life at 'The Pines' as 'an existence of the greatest calm, passivity and resignation, without a struggle and apparently without a wish for liberty of action'. To affirm that Swinburne's work is less spirited during these last decades is merely to record a fact, but to suggest that Watts-Dunton stifled the fire of Swinburne's spirit is to suggest something less than a half-truth. The crisis in Swinburne's emotional and creative life had passed before he entered 'The Pines', and had not Watts-Dunton nursed him back to health in 1879 probably he would have died in 1880 and not in 1909. These last thirty years of Swinburne's life were a period of great industry and the record of volumes is impressive evidence. In poetry, *Songs of the Springtides* (1880); *Studies in Song* (1880); *The Heptalogia* (a volume of parodies published anonymously) (1880); *Mary Stuart* (1881); *Tristram of Lyonesse* (1882); *A Century of Roundels* (1883); *A Midsummer Holiday* (1884); *Marino Faliero* (1885); *Locrine* (1887); *Poems and Ballads (Third Series)* (1889); *The Sisters* (1892); *Astrophel* (1894); *The Tale of Balen* (1896); *Rosamund, Queen of the Lombards* (1899); *A Channel Passage and other Poems* (1904); *The Duke of Gandia* (1908). Apart from poetry the period is rich in critical work, including studies of Shakespeare (1880), Victor Hugo (1886), Ben Jonson (1889), and Charles Dickens (published in part in the *Quarterly Review* in 1902 and the rest posthumously in 1913), and shorter studies of many Elizabethan dramatists and of nineteenth-century writers.

The history of Swinburne's mind must be separated from the biography of his daily life. His mental development shows a consistency, a positive, virile quality which finds no counterpart in the timid negations and wild excesses of his practical existence.

From his boyhood days at Eton to the closing years at Putney he pursued literature with enthusiasm and scholarly methods of precise, effective reading. His creative mind impinges at different periods with varying effect upon these accumulated resources, yet even when creation is sluggish or dormant the passion for literature, the sanest and most prolonged passion of Swinburne's mind, is ever awake. The study of Swinburne must begin with Swinburne's studies. It reveals him as one of the best-read poets of his age, a writer whose letters are full of references to books and problems arising from them, whose friendships were, as the years went on, increasingly literary friendships. In the middle period political figures intrude, but even here the men from the world of activity are chosen, in part at least, as illustrations of general precepts of liberty, which he has found in his Greek reading.

Swinburne's creative work reached its imaginative definition in the crisis which preceded *Atalanta in Calydon* in 1865. The growth of his poetic mind lies in the long years of experiment which anticipate that crisis. This can be more clearly realized now that his early, previously unpublished work has been printed.[8] The early period, whatever the intrinsic merits of the work, has therefore an importance in his poetic development. He remained to the end an admirer of work very different from his own; he began in experiments which diverged widely from the work he later produced. At Eton there was his attempt to write for Queen Victoria's visit a poem in the couplets of Pope, *The Triumph of Gloriana* (1851):

> Here humble shepherds purer pleasures know
> Than what your gay resplendent courts bestow.

At Oxford the most important influence was that of the Pre-Raphaelites. His admiration for William Morris's early verse led him during the period 1857-1860 to write a number of closely imitative poems. The unfinished *Queen Yseult* is the most considerable, the theme showing an early interest in the medieval legend which occupied him so considerably in later life; the stanza and rhythm are an exact memory of Morris's *'Twas in Church on Palm Sunday*. It is difficult to compare *Queen Yseult*, which has the direct simplicity of a ballad, with the massy and grandiose form of the later *Tristram of Lyonesse*: the earlier poem is more successful within its range; the narrative breathes naturally from the verse; the values of the legend are delicately perceived, and the imagery has a keen visual clarity:

> Sidelong to him crept she close,
> Pale as any winter rose
> When the air is grey with snows.

Prosodically the firmness and economy of the verse are sustained throughout. The rhythmical movement, which Morris discovered, has been matched and perhaps surpassed, but it is the same movement not only in its general form but in the devices of rhyme and pause:

> Then he thought him, lying there,
> Of Queen Yseult's golden hair
> And the brows of Guinevere.

A number of other pieces[9] show similar affinities, with a predominant interest in Arthurian scenes.

While a Pre-Raphaelite influence is supreme in the Oxford period, it does not stand alone. In 1860 Swinburne wrote an unsuccessful prize poem on *The Death of Sir John Franklin*, where the Pre-Raphaelite accent is modified by memories of Elizabethan dramatic verse. As the piece is an occasioned one, it is not strange that the two predominant influences on Swinburne's mind should enter equally. Alongside such obviously Pre-Raphaelite lines as:

> Is this the end? is praise so light a thing
> As rumour unto rumour tendereth.

Elizabethan effects occur:

> There is no nobler word
> In the large writing and scored marge of time.

Nor is the Elizabethan influence confined to prosody, for Swinburne has contrived to express a sombre pleasure in the tragic endurance of brave men:

> Like those dead seamen of Elizabeth
> And those who wrought with Nelson or with Blake.

From his childhood days a further powerful and permanent influence worked upon him. He had heard Northumbrian ballads in and around his father's home, and these he had supplemented with early reading in Scott and other collections. Contact with Rossetti and Morris had shown him how two of his contemporaries were manipulating ballad poetry for their own purposes, and so from 1859 to 1861 his interest in the form was reawakened. He studied ballad collections assiduously, with the intention of publishing a collection. He formed his own versions from variants and developed an unusual skill in adding stanzas and phrases, so conformable to the originals that they did not obviously betray a modern hand. From this background he proceeded to construct original ballads, borrowing the suggestion of theme or phrase.[10] Some of these he reprinted in *Poems and Ballads* (1866, 1878, 1889). Lafourcade has noted that the ballad themes which attract him are all of love, frequently of love that ends in tragedy and in crimes which arise from passion. After 1861 ballad imitation becomes submerged, but the vocabulary and prosodic effects of ballad poetry remain a permanent influence.

An additional creative stimulus he derived from Keats. It is to be seen most clearly in an unfinished piece on the *Hyperion* theme, and the numerous verbal resemblances show that at this period Swinburne studied closely a poet whom, later, under Arnold's influence, he was to misprize. Keats had always been a favourite of the Pre-Raphaelites; they and their associates had helped to establish his growing reputation in the nineteenth century, while he had affinities with Swinburne's own mind both in aesthetic theory and in a common enthusiasm for Elizabethan poetry. These matters are developed in George Ford's *Keats and the Victorians*, 1944. Further, Swinburne was already extracting from Emily Brontë's poems that fierce yet melancholy defiance of fate which later developed into his personal approach to life. Amid all this poetic experiment Pre-Raphaelite and Elizabethan elements were combating for supremacy, and the Elizabethans conquered. In 1860 he produced two dramas, published together, *The Queen Mother* and *Rosamond*.

Rosamond is an experiment in dramatic blank verse. Swinburne fought for success in this piece, revising his work with persistence. The resulting verse is competent, but without definitely marked characteristics, except for a few memories of Browning and Rossetti. In later years[11] Swinburne spoke contemptuously of *Rosamond*, particularly of its defects of dramatic construction. As a drama it has obvious deficiencies, but his own criticisms have told against it too heavily. The story of Rosamond, the mistress of Henry II, and her death at the jealous hand of Eleanor is known in ballad literature, and had been retold by Samuel Daniel in *The Complaint of Rosamond* and by Drayton in *Heroical Epistles*. It was a favourite theme with the Pre-Raphaelites: both Rossetti and Burne-Jones had chosen Rosamond as themes for paintings. Whatever Swinburne's defects in *Rosamond*, he has portrayed a beautiful, pathetic woman, in whom love is inevitable, and for whom pain is bound close to love. Swinburne has further achieved success in the concluding conflict of Rosamond and Eleanor, culminating in Rosamond's death and the King's intervention. As a play *Rosamond* may be unactable, but as a poem it has incidents and lines of marked distinction.

The Queen Mother, a blank-verse drama, composed during 1859-1860, is the work in which Swinburne closes his period of tutelage. More elaborate than *Rosamond*, it attempts to interlock two themes in a single dramatic action. The massacre of St Bartholomew's Eve planned by Catherine de Medici is the culmination of the public political action, while the private intrigue centres in the love of Catherine's son, Charles IX, for Denise de Maulévrier. The union of the actions is gained in the tragic story of Denise, a maiden of a dissolute Court, trained to the intricacies of refined sensuality, and yet so revolted by the whisper of the slaughter of St Bartholomew's Eve that life and the pleasure of love, and the person of the King, her lover, are bitterness to her. She is an intricate personality, incompletely realized, and yet rising to strength in the closing scenes. As sources for this play Swinburne studied not only Brantôme but Merimée's *Chronique du règne de Charles IX* and Dumas' *La Reine Margot*.[12] In style *The Queen Mother* is full of gestures adapted from Elizabethan drama; the phrases seem imitated at times, rather than imaginatively reconceived. Swinburne retains the movement of Elizabethan imagery, but the splendour occasionally gives way to the confusion in such lines as:

> I will not do it;
> Lest all that regiment of muffled years
> Now huddled in the rear and skirts of time
> I must walk through, take whips into their hands
> To bruise my shame withal.

Swinburne did not gain much critical encouragement with these two dramas. *The Athenæum* wrote:

> We should have conceived it hardly possible to make the crimes of Catherine de Medici dull, howsoever they are presented. Mr. Swinburne, however, has done so. There is more of real drama in Mr. Browning's short poem of the French poisoner in the laboratory than in the entire hundred and fifty pages here wearily spun off. Having had such ill-luck with one wicked Queen, we were unable to cope with a second one; and thus the Tragedy of Woodstock, once again told, though shorter as a play, is gladly handed over to others who are disposed to venture into the labyrinth.

For five years Swinburne published nothing of importance, and yet that period (1860-1865) was the emotional crisis of his life. Publication when it came was plentiful and varied: *Atalanta in Calydon* (1865, April), a Greek lyrical drama, to be followed later by *Erechtheus* in 1876; *Chastelard* (1865), the first of his trilogy of plays on the life of Mary Stuart; finally *Poems and*

Ballads (1866, August), the first volume of his lyrical poetry. Instead of examining Swinburne's poetry in strictly chronological order, it has been found preferable to discuss separately each of the three genres – drama, lyric drama, and lyric. Such a method, whatever it may lack, serves to show the mental persistence of Swinburne, his power of grappling with large themes in poetry, and it emphasizes that his work as a writer of poetic drama cannot be ignored in the brilliant fanfare of his lyrical verse.

Chastelard was published in November 1865, seven months after *Atalanta in Calydon*, but the piece was begun at Oxford in 1860 and completed before *Atalanta* was commenced. Swinburne's dramas have so often been condemned unread that it has been thought advisable to give a narrative as well as a critical account of their content. *Chastelard* opens with the return of Mary Stuart from France to Scotland. She is in marriage negotiations with Lord Darnley, leader of the Scottish Catholics and a claimant after Mary to Elizabeth's throne. In her retinue is Chastelard, a French poet who loves her and is loved by her. Chastelard persuades Mary Beaton, one of the Queen's ladies whom he has once loved, to bring him to the Queen secretly. Instead Mary Beaton impersonates the Queen; the two are discovered and the news of Chastelard's treachery is borne to the Queen. In impulsive anger and grief she announces her betrothal to Darnley. Mary Beaton, held thrall to Chastelard's influence, introduces him to a hidden place in the Queen's chamber. The Queen yields to his love in a mood that is compounded of pain and overwrought passion. She and Chastelard are thus discovered by Darnley, and Chastelard made prisoner. The climax is reached in the intrigue, and from now to the end the play resolves itself into a study of the Queen's character. In the fourth act she dangles with the life of Chastelard, now in an ecstasy of perverse cruelty wishing him dead, and now turning her thoughts towards pardon. Finally after an interview with Darnley she signs his release. Chastelard in the fifth act refuses to accept the pardon. He has a painful talk with Mary Beaton, who loves him with a passion that frets and sickens her. The Queen visits him; she and Chastelard enter once again into a mood of passion. In the last scenes, which have a Greek economy of control, the waiting maids, with Mary Beaton among them, watch the execution of Chastelard from a balcony window.

Swinburne's achievement in this drama has been frequently underestimated. Drawing the main narrative from Brantôme, he handled the historical material freely and yet honestly. He created the character of Mary Beaton, deriving suggestions possibly from Hugo's *Marie Tudor*, and elaborated and remodelled Chastelard to meet his dramatic purpose. The modifications of historical incident, the antedating of the Darnley marriage, and the reprieve of Chastelard are done with full knowledge and for clearly defined dramatic purposes. The setting has a cunning dramatic skill. The play opens in the upper chamber in Holyrood with Mary Beaton singing a French lyric and with the other maidens around her; the conclusion is the same scene, but Chastelard's death is watched through the casement. Similarly the verse, apart from beauties that are detached and lyrical, has frequent dramatic gesture, gained from Swinburne's study of the Elizabethan verse. Such is the description of John Knox:

> That is Master Knox.
> He carries all these folk within his skin,
> Bound up as 'twere between the brows of him
> Like a bad thought.

The tragedy of Chastelard is so manipulated that it is Fate's prelude to the greater tragedy of the Queen. The dramatic irony of *Chastelard* is only apparent when the whole trilogy has been read. Thus Chastelard says to the Queen:

> I made this yesterday;
> For its love's sake I pray you let it live.
> 'Après tant de jours, après tant de pleurs,
> Soyez secourable à mon âme en peine.'

It is this very song that Mary Beaton sings shortly before the Queen's execution, and after the song the Queen speaks:

> Nay, I should once have known that song, thou say'st,
> And him that sang it and should now be dead:
> Was it – but his rang sweeter – was it not
> Remy Belleau?

Incidents could be multiplied to show Swinburne's skill. The main difficulty of the play, as its earliest critics detected, lies in the person of the Queen herself. She has passion alternating with cruel, calculating coldness; she knows neither gentleness nor affection. At times the sadistic conceptions of love, found so clearly in *Poems and Ballads*, seem to govern her actions, and she appears fickle and ambitious, possessed of a flame, illuminating, destructive, and soon dead. Chastelard understands her well when he says:

> I know her ways of loving, all of them;
> A sweet soft way the first is; afterward
> It burns and bites like fire; the end of that,
> Charred dust, and eyelids bitten through with smoke;

and later he tells the Queen:

> I know not: men must love you in life's spite;
> For you will always kill them; man by man
> Your lips will bite them dead.

The passion revealed is a perverted one, and she is its victim. Judged morally she is heartless and it is thus that she has been most frequently judged, and the unnaturalness of her conduct has led to an underestimate of the positive qualities of the play.

Chastelard is a manageable romantic tragedy; *Bothwell* (1871-1874) is gargantuan in comparison. An early reviewer, attempting to describe its length, wrote that it 'had about as many lines as *Hamlet* supplemented by *Paradise Lost*'. It is simpler to consider each act as a separate play, as Swinburne by giving each a different title would seem to suggest. The length of *Bothwell* arises in part from Swinburne's modifications of his conception of historical drama, for he attempts to incorporate something of both epical and chronicle methods. Still more is it due to his methods of manipulating his sources. It has been shown by E. F. James[12] that Swinburne was mainly dependent in his Mary Stuart plays on Froude's *The History of England from the Fall of Wolsey*. Froude began publishing his history in 1856 and the last volume appeared in 1870. Swinburne's method as he progressed was increasingly to versify Froude. He saw in Froude his Plutarch, but instead of using him as Shakespeare had used his source, Swinburne came to turn morsels of Froude into verse, and frequently lost all conception of the relationship of these isolated fragments to any organic and dramatic unity. As he progressed in his work between 1871 and 1881 he studied the large Mary Stuart literature more widely and increased knowledge of historical detail seems only to have added to his difficulties.

Bothwell thus lacks the clearly etched outline of intrigue of *Chastelard*. No longer is Swinburne content with the loves of the Queen: he enters into the worlds of politics and history to show the form and pressure of Mary's mind. The only unity of structure that is easily discoverable lies in his determination that each act must culminate in a dramatically effective crisis. Act i, Rizzio (9 March 1566), portrays the uneasy passage of Mary's married life with Darnley. Darnley, morbidly jealous of his Queen, ambitious and yet cowardly, has grown 'doubtful and evil-eyed against himself', while Mary's position towards the nobles is weakened by the fact that her husband is a Catholic. She has already recalled Lord Bothwell to strengthen her position, and she is driven back for counsel upon her Italian secretary, Rizzio. Swinburne develops no intrigue between the Queen and her adviser: they are friends in affection and in policy, but no more. Darnley, with some associated nobles, conceives a plot against Rizzio, who is, further, unpopular with the people, led by John Knox, and the culminating scene of this act is the murder of the secretary in the presence of the Queen. The act is clogged with historical detail, and possesses no human conflict until its movement is clarified in the last scene. Here Mary shows her queenliness as the nobles surround her and Rizzio lies dead at her feet. The turgid blank verse in the earlier scenes is replaced by the lucid simplicity of Mary's plea against the injustice that has been done to her:

> What have I done?
> What thing am I that ye should use me thus?
> O miserable and desertless that I am,
> Unkingdomed of mine honour!

The clue to the second act, Bothwell (10 March 1566 to 9 February 1567), is to be found at the close of Act i, where the Queen says:

> I am content.
> Now must I study how to be revenged.

The second act, surely the longest in dramatic literature, shows within its twenty-one scenes how that revenge is accomplished. The earlier scenes are again slow, heavy-moving masses of political incident and intrigue re-expressed in blank verse. The verse is never incompetent; lines of rare excellence shine through even the dullest passages, but all this emphasizes the undramatic qualities of the scenes and the absence of action. All this changes with the concluding scenes. Scene 17, where Darnley is shown completely unmanned by the death which he believes awaits him, is one of the finest in the trilogy. Mary adds to his terror by entering his chamber on the night before his murder and singing the song that Rizzio was singing before his death. The culminating scene of this act displays a dramatic economy which Swinburne, at his best, possesses. Darnley's murder is not shown, but the mental torture of the hours before death are revealed with as much emphasis on the horror of a captured and terrified soul as is found in Browning's study of Guido in *The Ring and the Book*.

From Act iii to the end more continuity is apparent. Swinburne named the acts: Act iii, Jane Gordon (10 February to 11 June 1567); Act iv, John Knox (15 and 16 June 1567); Act v, The Queen (20 July 1567 to 16 May 1568). The time divisions are more useful than the names, for Jane Gordon appears only incidentally in Act iii, while the Queen is not more obviously the centre of the play in Act v than elsewhere. The theme throughout is the presentation of Mary's harassed life after Darnley's death, the opposition of the nobles, the trial of Bothwell, the divorce of Bothwell from Jane Gordon, his marriage to the Queen, and the multitudinous troubles that pursued her and her reckless lord. The play closes with Mary bidding Scotland farewell:

> . . . seven years since
> Did I take leave of my fair land of France,
> My joyous mother, mother of my joy,
> Weeping; and now with many a woe between
> And space of seven years' darkness, I depart
> From this distempered and unnatural earth
> That casts me out unmothered, and go forth
> On this grey sterile bitter gleaming sea
> With neither tears nor laughter, but a heart
> That from the softest temper of its blood
> Is turned to fire and iron.

These last acts possess a much more clearly defined human conflict. Mary and Bothwell are pitted against the nobles and against the people led by John Knox. In continual danger, she bears herself as one who finds a sad fascination in distress. Bothwell is ambitious, quick-tongued, an egoist and lawless, yet she finds moments of joy in his love. In the dangerous delight of their love Swinburne finds the clearest portrayal of his heroine. Nowhere does he reduce to so clear a symbol Mary's motive for action as in her soliloquy in Act iv:

> I would not lose for many fortunate years
> And empire ringed with smooth security
> The sharp and dangerous draught of this delight
> That out of chance and peril and keen fear
> Springs as the wine out of the trampled grape
> To make this hour sweet to my lips.

Swinburne retains in these gigantesque acts an even level of excellence in the verse, with more subtlety in the portrayal of character than he has previously shown. Not only in his studies of Mary and Bothwell, but even with the minor characters, the psychological evaluation of motive is cunningly contrived, though great dramatic action is lacking. There are approaches to it, but no commanding and developing movement. As in the early acts, there are incidents and speeches of much power: an outstanding instance is the very long speech of John Knox in Act iv, which forms a poetical recapitulation of the whole action. The speech is perhaps Swinburne's greatest achievement apart from his lyrical poetry. The poetry of the acts seems at times to have all the 'air and fire' of the Elizabethans. Such is the speech of the Queen, who has been confined to Lochleven Castle, to Lady Lochleven in Act v:

> I am not tired of that I see not here,
> The sun, and the large air, and the sweet earth
> And the hours that hum like fire-flies on the hills.

Excellencies there are within *Bothwell*, but nothing can quite compensate for its length; it is like some pathological thing, some diseased monster, blown up and unnatural.

Mary Stuart (1881) is the play with which Swinburne brought his trilogy to a close. The time duration, as given by Swinburne, is 14 August 1586 to 18 February 1587. The scene has changed from Scotland to England. We are shown Mary in captivity; the plots made for her release, and the final decision of Elizabeth to sign her death-warrant. The movement is brisker than in *Bothwell*; Swinburne has grown content with a method of narration closer to chronicle than to epic. Again he is defeated by the absence of adequate dramatic conflict in the earlier scenes, but this he discovers later in the relationship of Mary and Elizabeth. His brief portrait of the English Queen is effective and sympathetic: at first she is warm-hearted and wishes, if possible, to avoid an execution. Mary's letters to her are penned with pathetic pleas for pardon:

> Howe'er she have sinned, what heart were mine, if this
> Drew no tears from me: not the meanest soul

> That lives most miserable but with such words
> Must needs draw down men's pity.

Swinburne, to draw the play to a climax, allows Elizabeth to see the letter that Mary is credited with having written, in which she details all the gross calumnies that the Duchess of Shrewsbury had spoken to her against the Queen. He rises to dramatic as well as poetic effectiveness in Act iv, Scene 3, where he portrays the change from compassion to anger in Elizabeth when she hears this news. In the final scene Mary Beaton and one other lady watch from a balcony window the death of the Queen, and memories of all the previous crises of the plays come back, the death of Chastelard more particularly, that minor tragedy which had foreshadowed this great doom.

Swinburne's other verse plays are *Marino Faliero* (1885) and *Locrine* (1887), *The Sisters* (1892), *Rosamund, Queen of the Lombards* (1899), *The Duke of Gandia* (1908).

In *Marino*, Swinburne used for a blank verse drama, political in theme, a figure whom Byron had employed in *The Doge of Venice*. The play is written possibly as a pendant to Swinburne's attack on Byron's dramatic competence. In *Marino* Swinburne re-fashions the *Songs before Sunrise* into a dramatic mould. The result lacks dramatic effectiveness; all has been subordinated to the thought conveyed in such speeches as Faliero's final prophecy that liberty will one day arise. Swinburne seems to have realized the dramatic limitation of the play and claims Chapman as a model: 'The fifth act of *Marino Faliero* hopelessly impossible as it is from the point of view of modern stagecraft could hardly have been found too untheatrical, too utterly given over to talk without action by the audiences which endured and applauded the magnificent monotony of Chapman's eloquence.'[11] To this tradition of poetical rhetoric all is subdued and the play emerges as a sombre yet powerful prophecy of Mazzini's principles. In *Locrine*, working on the memory of a play now attributed to Peele, he reverts to legendary Britain for his theme. Here he exercised a barren, technical virtuosity in constructing a dramatic work in varying lyrical stanzas: Petrarchan sonnets, octaves, and even *terza rima* contribute to the prosodic texture of this strange experiment. If *Locrine* is an experiment in form, *The Sisters* is an innovation in theme, and one of even more dubious success. So far Swinburne's drama has obeyed the Shakespearian tradition in basing its fable on some noble, historical theme. Here, in blank-verse drama, he invents a plot of contemporary life, but mingles with it the trappings of Elizabethan revenge tragedy. The setting is Northumberland and, despite its meagre dramatic value, the play serves to reveal Swinburne's enthusiasm for Nature and for his country of the North. *Rosamund* and *The Duke of Gandia* appear as the attempt of his later years to discipline his lyricism to dramatic intrigue. Action recovers its importance, and the characters become distinct figures. The plays remain, however, study pieces, in which competent craftsmanship is uninspired by any urgency of expression or depth of passion.

Swinburne exploited a number of romantic traditions to the exhaustion of their possibilities. Among them was the construction of a verse play unrelated to the stage and relying for its main suggestion upon Elizabethan blank-verse drama. At best it was an artificial practice, though it had produced notable work by Shelley, Byron, and Browning. In the Mary Stuart plays he contrived to add qualities that were his own, and in those plays the best of his dramatic work rests. These later experiments, cold, varied, ineffectual, suggest that here, as in many other ways, he was at the end of a tradition. Throughout his dramatic work Swinburne's deficiency had been his willingness to exult in brilliant isolated passages, without attending adequately to dramatic conflict and to unifying motives. His methods of versifying Froude, sometimes in a piecemeal manner, emphasized this amorphous quality in the Mary Stuart plays, but it characterizes his work elsewhere. The decline in formal criticism had drawn attention away from the essential organizing singleness of design which any long work demands. In non-dramatic literature such works as Wordsworth's *Excursion* had given models for lengthy products whose merits lie rather in detail than in the central conception. Swinburne himself, with his passion for Lamb's *Selections,* had a keen understanding of Elizabethan blank verse, but it may be questioned whether he ever mastered the dramatic principles of Shakespearian drama. One may speculate what Swinburne's success as a poet might have been, and indeed how his whole life might have been different if the Victorian age had possessed any theatre of distinction. If he had moved in a company of players as Shakespeare did, living within the theatre and daily made aware of its problems, he might have developed a flourishing dramatic talent. Shakespeare, had he worked in isolation, might well have succumbed to the temptations of rhetoric.

The plays already mentioned are those which arise directly or indirectly from Swinburne's study of Elizabethan drama. Two lyrical dramas of an entirely different order owe their main outline of form to Swinburne's study of Greek drama. *Atalanta in Calydon* (1865, April), written between 1863 and 1865, was the work which first announced Swinburne as a new force in English poetry. To estimate *Atalanta in Calydon* merely as an imitation of Greek tragedy is to lose most of its virtues and Swinburne realized how far he had deviated from his models. 'It was perhaps', he writes, 'too exuberant and effusive in its dialogue as it certainly was too irregular in the occasional license of its choral verse.' The play assumes 'the likeness of Greek tragedy', but combines with it a romantic profusion of lyrical verse, and from that combination creates a new form. As he expanded the scheme of the Elizabethan drama into the immense Mary Stuart plays, so his tendency here is to expand: *Atalanta* possesses six episodes and five main choruses, while a Greek play was more restricted in both movements. This inflation allows him room for the lyrical commentary which is the poem's main excellence.

Swinburne had studied the classical sources of his theme;[13] he knew the allusions to the story in Aeschylus and Euripides; he knew Ovid and Apollodorus; while the references to the Jason and Medea story were drawn from Apollonius of Rhodes. The fable is one of the most clearly managed themes that Swinburne manipulated. Althæa, Queen of Calydon, had two brothers,

Toxeus and Plexippus, and a son, Meleager, whose life she could control by a brand which, when thrown into the fire, would cause his death. The goddess Artemis, angered at neglect of her sacrifices, allows a wild boar to enter Calydon, but for her love of the maiden Atalanta she allows it to be slain. Meleager, who loves Atalanta, gives her the spoils, and so angers his uncles that they would attack Atalanta. Meleager slays them. Althæa on hearing of their death throws the brand into the fire and so Meleager dies, nor does she herself long survive him. The first impression made by Swinburne's rendering is of the lyrical power and variety, the intricate ecstasies of the choruses, the cadenced words awakening a music that is new to the language. Arising from this sensuous delight comes the second impression that Swinburne is expressing certain ideas on religion and of the duty of man to the gods. Finally one becomes conscious of the characters and their story, more particularly of Althæa, who is baffled by the harshness of the immortals. Such is the order of impressions, but the logical order seems the reverse of this, demanding that one should begin with the treatment of the legend and its characters. Althæa is the most carefully wrought character. Her early speeches prelude the tragedy which the later scenes confirm; distrustful of the gods, and of Atalanta, above all distrustful of love, her one aim centres in her maternal love and her desire to protect her son from passion and from divine vengeance:

> Child, if a man serve law through all his life
> And with his whole heart worship, him all gods
> Praise.

The clarity of Althæa's prevision adds to the tragedy that follows: the gods deceive her, for Artemis's maiden Atalanta entraps Meleager in love, and leads him to murder:

> Love is one thing, an evil thing, and turns
> Choice words and wisdom into fire and air.

Swinburne concentrates all the passionate fervour of his language in the study of the sad, unwrathful vengeance of Althæa. She undergoes a fierce and fevered mental agony which culminates when she throws the brand into the flames:

> I know not if I live:
> Save that I feel the fire upon my face
> And on my cheek the burning of a brand.
> Yea the smoke bites me, yea I drink the steam
> With nostril and with eyelid and with lip
> Insatiate and intolerant.

Atalanta is more slightly drawn, but Swinburne has allowed this splendid intruder one moving speech, in which she pleads the loneliness of a maiden of Artemis, 'one who shall have no man's love forever, and no face of children born'. Her modesty, physical grace and lightness make a symbol of the play's swift lyrical movement. The men are types, yet recognizable; Toxeus and Plexippus, uncouth and jealous; Meleager, impetuous but honourable; Œneus, the King, baffled yet sane in action and advice. A study of the characterization reveals that the play is not a series of magnificent choruses, but a drama with some unity of structure.

From the study of characterization it appears that Swinburne is emphasizing two ideas; first he attacks the gods who make pain such an essential aftermath of pleasure, and secondly he recognizes in love the fiercest example in human life of this union of agony and joy. Both ideas bear some relationship to the dramatic action, but Swinburne expresses them with a disproportionate emphasis. It is here that he departs widely from Greek tragedy. The attack on the gods is most clearly elaborated in the chorus which opens:

> Who hath given man speech? or who hath set therein
> A thorn for peril and a snare for sin?

The thought behind this passage has been expressed in gentler form in the 'creation' chorus, 'Before the beginning of years'. The portrayal of love girt around with pain emerges in the magnificent verses, 'We have seen thee, O Love, thou art fair; thou art goodly, O Love'. Both characters and ideas are affected by the lyrical quality of the drama, for they are submerged in its enchantment. From the first chorus, the famous 'When the hounds of spring are on winter's traces', to the last fevered speeches of Althæa, the drama exults in words that sway into perfect rhythms, and rhythms that become symbols of such buoyancy and strength that they seem to mock at the intellectual ideas of the poem, the hate of God, and the fearfulness of love. Here, beyond intellectual discussion, is a reality in melodious words, imaging eternal youthfulness and grace which emerge and re-emerge from life.

Swinburne had discovered himself prosodically; in the lyrical measures by an apotheosis of the anapaest, served and strengthened by iambs, he had invented new harmonies which were sustained by a daring employment of alliteration and of double rhymes.[14]

In *Erechtheus* (1876), Swinburne's second drama modelled on Greek tragedy, the pattern and restraint of the original are more closely retained. The pedantic pleasure gained in appreciating this imitative skill is not adequate compensation for a loss of spontaneity. Gosse praised the poem justly when he wrote: 'It is the most Greek of all the compositions of Swinburne because it follows with the greatest success, closely and yet vividly, the exact classical models.' The scale of the drama and the romantic variety of the choruses have been reduced; it is Swinburne's attempt, under Jowett's discipline, to represent Greek tragedy as perfectly as possible in English. Yet the fable itself is less compact than that employed in *Atalanta*. Erechtheus is a descendant of an earth god whose shrine is among the holy places of Athens. Athens is attacked by the Thracians, and Erechtheus and his wife, Praxithea, fear the disaster of their sacred city. The oracle says that the city will be saved if their daughter Chthonia is sacrificed. The second movement of the play is largely a study of the mind of Praxithea and Chthonia once faced with this tragedy which culminates in Chthonia's death and an announcement by the herald of Athens's triumph. But the play does not end there; Erechtheus is made to die, and yet despite the double tragedy

Praxithea is left at the close praising the gods who have saved Athens ('I praise the Gods for Athens'). Intellectual criticism can find little to comment on adversely in the play. It might ask that the tragedy of Chthonia should have no sequel in the death of Erechtheus, or that the sense of suffering should not be divided between Praxithea and Athens. In all else it can but admire the close interlocking of choruses and episodes, the cunning episodical narration in one of the choruses of the rape of Oreithyia, elder sister of Chthonia, by Boreas, and above all the calm, deeply moving portrayal of the Queen. Poetical judgements, however, comprise much that escapes intellectual criticism, and *Erechtheus* fails to achieve the same poetical reality as the less soberly ordered *Atalanta*. Both dramas suggest that the final duty of mortals is the pursuit of honour; so Althæa instructs Meleager, and so Praxithea, Chthonia. The charm of *Atalanta* lies in the exultant passages which praise beauty, and challenge the gods who have prescribed such narrow and unpleasant ways for men. In *Erechtheus* all is calm acquiescence. The difference between the two moods is in part the result of an attempt to follow classical models more closely, but it arises, too, from changes, which are examined below, in Swinburne's own mind between 1865 and 1876.

The study of Swinburne's dramatic work may impress with the massiveness of his talent, though for decades now there is no indication that it is doing so: the return to his lyrical poetry reveals his genius. In August 1866 he published *Poems and Ballads*. The volume is the most momentous in the whole period under survey. It marks the intrusion of those new influences which separate the romantic poetry of the early and later nineteenth century. While its immediate reception was marked with a vituperative storm, most memorably portrayed in John Morley's condemnation of Swinburne in *The Saturday Review* as 'the libidinous laureate of a pack of satyrs', the following decades show how deeply its influence had penetrated into the values of English poetry. Romanticism was entering upon that last phase, decadent yet beautiful, which found its culmination in the poetry of the nineties. Further, the volume was the crisis of Swinburne's own poetical achievement, and even now its intensity, the variety and pungency of its stanzas, the words that assault with almost a physical impact, and the daring of its themes, leave the impression not merely of a volume that is read but of a haunting and powerful experience lingering within the mind. It is with this volume under consideration that it becomes harder to realize the truth of Lang's comment as already quoted that 'of all the great English poets he remains the most unappreciated'. Underlying its varied contents is a philosophy of aestheticism, flamboyantly amoral, which is the central theme of the opening poems *A Ballad of Life* and *A Ballad of Death.* In the first, Lucrezia Borgia is figured as some Unblessed Damozel who transfigures Fear, Shame, and Lust into Pity, Sorrow, Love. The poem is Pre-Raphaelite in its allegorical setting. The stanza form is imitative of the Italian *canzone,* for which Swinburne had models close at hand in Rossetti's *Early Italian Poets. A Ballad of Death,* another Lucrezia poem, expresses the same doctrine in a more extreme form. Beauty can transfigure all hideousness, all sin:

> O Sin, thou knowest that all thy shame in her,
> Was made a goodly thing;
> Yea, she caught Shame and shamed him with her kiss,
> With her fair kiss, and lips much lovelier
> Than lips of amorous roses in late spring.

This philosophy of beauty was derived ultimately from Théophile Gautier and Baudelaire,[15] but it grew naturally from Swinburne's Pre-Raphaelite affinities and his admiration during this period for the poetry of Keats. It had found fullest expression in his study of William Blake. From Gautier he had derived further a hatred of the bourgeois, and of conventional restraints, and from Baudelaire the preoccupation with death and the substitution of the painfully beautiful for good and evil as a value within his poetry. These theories combine naturally with Swinburne's Greek enthusiasms to substitute for a Christianity which is a repellent faith of pity and self-denial an idealized paganism where the gods demand suffering, but reveal beauty as its partner. In

Hymn to Proserpine Swinburne enlarges this element in his thought, and suggests that behind the tumult of life, in which Beauty is quickened by the pangs of anguish, there lies Proserpine, the goddess of sleep who will continue after all other gods, new and old. *The Garden of Proserpine* concentrates upon certain aspects of the *Hymn*, and images the desire of eternal rest in the sad melody of its stanzas.

It was not the novelty of the philosophy, however, which gave *Poems and Ballads* its peculiar power, but the brilliance and variety with which its moods were recorded. The volume contains poems written between 1857-1865.[16] The poems composed before 1862 are, with few exceptions, the less distinctive pieces, such as *Before Parting*, *A Song in Time of Order*, *A Song in Time of Revolution*. But Swinburne has gathered from these years some of his ballad pieces, *The Leper*, *May Janet*, *The Sea-Swallows*, keen, poignant poems, which commemorate his study of the ballad form. Apart from these, *At Eleusis* stands out as an early achievement in a blank-verse manipulation of a classical theme for which Landor may have been the model. In 1862 Swinburne completed *The Masque of Queen Bersabe*, a piece in the manner of the miracle-plays which attaches itself to the influence of William Morris.

The poems, for which *Poems and Ballads* are mainly remembered, belong to the crucial years 1862-1865. Such is their variety both in mood and in prosody that it is difficult to suggest any satisfactory grouping. The dominating theme is obviously that of love, but love approached through devious ways. Two poems stand apart, *The Triumph of Time* and *A Leave-Taking*. In *The Triumph of Time* Swinburne commemorates in the same magnificent stanza as he used in the first chorus of *Atalanta* a love unannounced and unfulfilled. The unhurrying onslaught of its verses elevates the personal mood into a universal reality, while in *A Leave-Taking*, with quieter tone but rare lyrical success, he bids farewell to this subject:

> Let us go hence, my songs; she will not hear.
> Let us go hence together without fear.

The other love poems are portrayals of the intricate and abnormal in passion. They centre in the great sequence of dramatic poems, *Laus Veneris, Dolores, Faustine*, and Swinburne has brought dominating ingenuity in verse to their expression. In *Laus Veneris*, with a stanza reminiscent of Fitzgerald's *Rubáiyát* he fashions the Tannhäuser legend which Wagner and Heine had treated. Morris was considering the same theme during this period for the story of *The Hill of Venus* in *The Earthly Paradise*; 'Owen Meredith' and Julian Fane issued their version in 1861, while later in the century John Davidson retold it in ballad form. Swinburne found within the legend the very values with which his mind was agitated: love was not pleasure but a fever of desire and pain and an unending satiety:

> Ah yet would God this flesh of mine might be
> Where air might wash and long leaves cover me,
> Where tides of grass break into foam of flowers,
> Or where the wind's feet shine along the sea.

In *Dolores*, Swinburne uses with great skill an eight-line stanza, basically trisyllabic; he employs double rhymes freely and balances its singing music with a short final line. The poem reveals a picture, symbolic, and yet dramatic, of Dolores, who afflicts men with a passion cruel but irresistible. The sadistic element ('on thy mouth though the kisses are bloody') intrudes more openly here, and the picture of dread satiety is outlined with stark emphasis. *Faustine* is a more dramatic expression of the cruelty and sadness that dwell with love. Swinburne in his notes has described the origin of his conception. 'The chance which suggested to me this poem was one which may happen any day to any man – the sudden sight of a living face which recalled the well-known likeness of another, dead for centuries, the noble and faultless type of the elder Faustina as seen in coin and bust.' Within his poem Swinburne imagines a gladiator who has been Faustine's lover, standing up in the arena at the moment before he dies and denouncing her pitiless cruelty:

> You have the face that suits a woman
> For her soul's screen –

> The sort of beauty that's called human
> In hell, Faustine.

Throughout 'Faustine' occurs as the last word in each stanza, and a corresponding rhyming word is found in the second line; the effect of this deliberate repetition is to emphasize the sickened lust of the dying man.

A similar theme in varied form intrudes into a number of poems of classical suggestion. *Atalanta* had immediately preceded *Poems and Ballads*, and it is not strange that Swinburne should employ classical themes again in this volume. The Proserpine poems are one reflection of this interest. *Phædra* uses suggestions from Euripides, while *Anactoria*, in which Swinburne presents 'that violence of affection between one and another which hardens into rage and deepens into despair', is based on the fragments of Sappho. The poem most completely associated with classical legend, yet modified for Swinburne's own purposes, is *Itylus*. Here he achieves a calmer mood, a rare beauty, undisturbed by the perfervid, forced atmosphere which affects even some of his most finished poems. The degree to which he has transfigured a crude legend can only be realized to the full when his poem is compared with the story in its primitive form. Tereus had violated his sister-in-law, Philomela, and in revenge Procne, his wife, served up Itys, her son, as a dish before him. Itys was turned into a pheasant, Tereus into an owl, Procne into a swallow, and Philomela into a nightingale. Swinburne, relying on a number of classical suggestions and aware of Ovid's version, seizes upon a single incident in the legend and treats it in an allusive way. He pictures Philomela mourning that her sister, the swallow, has forgotten the death of Itys:

> O sister, sister, thy first-begotten!
> The hands that cling and the feet that follow,
> The voice of the child's blood crying yet
> *Who hath remembered me? who hath forgotten?*
> Thou hast forgotten, O summer swallow,
> But the world shall end when I forget.

The legend is transfigured into a fresh poetic reality, and prosodic skill reveals the ensanguined poignancy of the mood. It evokes memories different from those of the other poems, and one is tempted to wish that Swinburne's poetic intensity had been nourished thus, more often, with wider sources of suggestion.

Such were some of the poems which make *Poems and Ballads* a critical volume of English poetry. Its intrinsic merits do not comprise the sum of its importance in poetic history. Underlying its lyrical moods, and implicit in its themes, there lay a protest, almost satiric in purpose, against the placid measures of Tennyson and the more guarded moods of early Victorian poetry. The faith of liberty, to which Swinburne dedicated his next volume, had already here found expression of provoking daring. The volume marked the culmination of the romantic movement in its technical aspects. The prosodic variety which Coleridge, Shelley, and Keats had given to English poetry, applied by Tennyson for his own purposes, was carried to the limits of verbal music and stanzaic ingenuity. All that would follow would either be imitative or hollow unless poetry could discover new ways, and much of the poetic history of the later nineteenth century is an attempt, only partially successful, to break from this tradition and discover new forms. Some of the later hostility to Swinburne is that, within his own tradition, he had done his work so well. Some of the later neglect is the realization that down this road one could not travel farther.

The stimuli which had aroused *Poems and Ballads* had been strange, specialized, and unnatural. They were never replaced by others of equal strength. *Songs before Sunrise* ('My other books are books, *Songs before Sunrise* is myself') is Swinburne's partially effective attempt to gain fresh sources of suggestion for his poetical creation. Late in 1866 he had already conceived the possibility of modifying his principle of art for its own sake, and he set himself the task of constructing poetry political in theme and philosophical in its ultimate purpose. The first results were two elaborate pieces published separately in 1867, *Ode on the Insurrection in Candia* and *A Song of Italy*. This enthusiasm for Italian liberty was strengthened by a meeting in 1867 with

Guiseppe Mazzini. Jowett and other friends, who felt that this change of interest would have a healthy influence, had engineered the encounter, and Swinburne was charmed by the idealistic Italian refugee who instructed him to 'dedicate his writing power to do good'. The result was *Songs before Sunrise* (1871), though how much it affected his personal conduct can be questioned now that Gosse's manuscript monograph has been published. His sudden adoption of the Italian cause gives the volume an artificial atmosphere, which was noted by Gosse, who commented on the 'apparent causelessness of the emotion, and the vain violence as of a whirlwind in a vacuum'. Yet it must be allowed that Swinburne's ultimate enthusiasm is a philosophic conception of liberty, and that Italy is adopted merely as a central example of this theme. The poems can thus be grouped into two categories, those definitely Italian in theme, and those in which the more comprehensive political philosophy is outlined,[17] and while the localized Italian poems have a vapidity of mood, the philosophical pieces possess a contrasting solidity and strength.

The topical poems commemorate incidents in Garibaldi's revolt in the autumn of 1867. *Blessed among Women* is an Ode to Signora Cairoli, whose sons, with a small band of Garibaldians, were repulsed in attempting to approach Rome. *Mentana* reflects upon Garibaldi's encounter with French and Papal troops in which his band was finally routed. *The Halt before Rome* relates the 1867 campaign to that general struggle for Liberty which Swinburne conceived as the one worthy aim of political endeavour. Despite their strenuous rhetoric these pieces seem lost in the ephemeral, while a perfervid mood agitates throughout them. Transition to elegies which express more general sympathy for Italy is gained in such poems as *Super Flumina Babylonis*, where Swinburne contrives an effective contrast of long and short lines, to give the mood of contemplation in which the poem dwells. Emerging from these Italian poems there appear a number of poems, such as *The Eve of Revolution*, *The Litany of Nations*, and *Quia multum amavit*, in which Swinburne pleads for a revolution to remove from Europe the type of tyranny with which Italy had been oppressed. Throughout, these poems have an air of unreality, an absence of contact with the movement of events in 1871, while the references to Italy contained within them approach a mood which is ecstatic:

> We are but men, are we,
> And thou art Italy;
> What shall we do for thee with our desire?
> What gift shall we deserve to give?
> How shall we die to do thee service, or how live?[18]

As a pendant to these pieces are poems, such as *To Walt Whitman in America*, in which Swinburne complains of the inadequate role which England appears to him to be playing. Further, he dedicates individual poems to personalities such as Shelley and Mazzini, who have advanced the cause of Liberty. All these political poems retain the prosodic virtuosity which had distinguished *Poems and Ballads*, though they miss something in verbal cunning. The sexual imagery of the earlier poems intrudes frequently, even when the theme is narrowly political; so in his appeal to France in *Quia multum amavit* he writes:

> Thou hast mixed thy limbs with the son of a harlot, a stranger,
> Mouth to mouth, limb to limb,

and anti-Christian elements are also allowed to intrude into the imagery of many of the poems. In these and other pieces, Italian and political, he constructs the groundwork of the philosophical poems. Their mood is anticipated in *Prelude*, an expression of personal faith which reveals his adoption of the Italian cause as part of a conscious effort to modify his poetic purposes:

> Then he stood up, and trod to dust
> Fear and desire, mistrust and trust,
>   And dreams of bitter sleep and sweet,
>   And bound for sandals on his feet
> Knowledge and patience of what must
>   And what things may be, in the heat
> And cold of years that rot and rust
>   And alter; and his spirit's meat

> Was freedom, and his staff was wrought
> Of strength and his cloak woven of thought.

In a later stanza he pleads, in a vocabulary derived from Shelley, for the quest of an ideal freedom which is liberated from the tyrannies of earth and heaven.

Prelude serves to introduce the poems in which Swinburne's philosophy is conveyed, *Hertha, Genesis, Hymn of Man*, and, less directly, *Mater Dolorosa* and *Mater Triumphalis*. The summary of his thought can be gained from a study of this poetic sequence. The world, he suggests, was first a chaos; it has developed by the contraries of life, death, and change, 'the rhythmic anguish of growth'. The creator and the created are one, and the spirit in them should live in liberty. Man has made for his own torment a shadow, which he calls god, and to overthrow that god is the most powerful step towards man's spiritual regeneration. Liberty is the spiritual in man, and through that life of liberty man gains contact with the eternal. This thought is clothed with magnificence of expression. In *Hertha* the unity of life is outlined, and Swinburne himself spoke justly when he wrote of this poem, 'Of all I have done, I rate *Hertha* highest as a single piece, finding in it the most of lyric force and music combined with the most of condensed and clarified thought.' In *Hymn of Man* his attack upon the God of established religion flames forth with malevolent power. Certain poems are allied to these philosophical pieces; they are more incidental in application and more dramatic in form. In *Tiresias*, Swinburne exploits classical incident and adapts the dramatic monologue form to show his faith in Liberty. The poem is brought into such close alliance with his Italian enthusiasms that its classical movement is warped. Indeed, its full purport is made clear only by Swinburne's note: 'Tiresias, at the grave of Antigone, i.e. (understand) Dante at the grave of Italia.'[19] A more memorable poem in this group is *Before a Crucifix*, in which Swinburne possesses himself of a keener dramatic method for his attack on Christianity than he shows elsewhere in the volume.

Songs before Sunrise is the critical volume in Swinburne's development. He had formulated in *Poems and Ballads* certain aesthetic theories, and had discovered a sufficient strength of imagination to render them a poetic reality. He had travelled down that road as far as it was possible to go. In *Songs before Sunrise* he had fallen from the earlier theories, and attempted to replace them with others which would lead his poetry back closer to the common ways of life. He succeeded only in part. The imagination had not kindled to response with spontaneity, but the work achieved had solid and sober qualities. And now what of the future?

The years between 1871 and Swinburne's retirement to 'The Pines' in 1879 were rich in publication. Of dramatic work, the enormous *Bothwell* was completed by 1874, and *Erechtheus* by 1876. In lyrical work the yield is less. *Songs of Two Nations* (1874) is merely a reprint of earlier work. Swinburne gathers into the volume *The Song of Italy* (1867), *Ode on the French Republic* (1870), and the series of sonnets *Diræ*, directed against Napoleon III, written in the years 1868-1869. The single volume which remains is *Poems and Ballads (Second Series)* (1878). Here he achieved the most calm expression of his lyrical genius, detached from those pulsating qualities which had agitated the earlier work. The themes of *Songs before Sunrise* are retained incidentally; in *The Last Oracle* he continues the anti-Christian mood of *Hymn of Man*, while his political enthusiasms are variously expressed in *To Kossuth* and *Rizpah* and *The White Czar*. None of these pieces can parallel the quality of the greater poems in *Songs before Sunrise*, and they appear as only a minor contribution to the poetical emphasis of this volume. Many of the poems suggest preoccupation with literature, not with life. It is as if the sources of creative suggestion arising from his own experience had been exhausted, so that he turned his rare technical powers to secondary purposes. So he writes a number of poems in which the metrical interest exceeds the poetical, verses in Latin and French, experiments with choriambics and the sestina. He translates a number of Villon's ballades, excluding wisely the pieces rendered by D. G. Rossetti, and he contrives to endow them with the fresh energy of original poems. He writes poems on Théophile Gautier, Victor Hugo, Barry Cornwall, and a *Ballad of François Villon*. He begins the versification of his critical enthusiasms: a sonnet capturing pictorially the mood of Cyril Tourneur's plays, and *In the Bay*, where he recalls the career and the poetical significance of Christopher Marlowe. Allied to the literary interest is the elegiac mood: the outstanding piece *Ave atque Vale* (1867) appears here only by an accident of publication, but *Inferiae*, a poem to Swinburne's own father, and *Epicede* on James Lorimer Graham are examples of this genre.

One group of poems, of which the most distinguished representatives are, *A Forsaken Garden*, *At a Month's End*, *The Year of the Rose*, *A Ballad of Dreamland*, *A Vision of Spring in Winter*, lies apart from these literary preoccupations. Here he has captured a series of moods, sombre, passionate, and beautiful, and conveyed them on a background of natural suggestion, bringing to their expression the mature powers of his poetical skill. They possess certain common elements, and a more varied sympathy of nature with human mood is shown than elsewhere. In *A Forsaken Garden* the desolate scene portrayed symbolizes with a powerful melancholy, reminiscent of Anglo-Saxon poetry, the desolation of love and of life, while in *At a Month's End* the storm on the sea and the passionate movement of a human mind are brought into symbolic contact. Throughout all the poems there is a sense of loss, memories of 'the heaven of dear times dead to me', of the old love 'dead and buried'. This emphasis appears even in the softer magical mood of *The Year of the Rose* and *A Vision of Spring in Winter*; it recurs at the close of *A Ballad of Dreamland*:

> In the world of dreams I have chosen my part,
>   To sleep for a season and hear no word
> Of true love's truth or of light love's art,
>   Only the song of a secret bird.

The achievement within this volume, calm and mature though it is, does not fulfil the promise of either *Poems and Ballads* or

Songs before Sunrise. Swinburne has abandoned many of his earlier theories, aesthetic and philosophical. He has dissolved his feverish urgency into calmer melodies, but the resulting quiet of this volume suggests sequestration. It is as if the future may hold mirrored before him but fading shapes of past experience.

Swinburne published over twenty volumes after his retirement to 'The Pines' with Theodore Watts-Dunton in 1879. Among these are eight volumes of lyrical verse. The *Heptalogia* (1880) lies apart as a collection of clever verse parodies in which the mannerisms of Coventry Patmore and Elizabeth Barrett Browning and others are successfully entrapped. The same year (1880) saw the publication of both *Songs of the Springtides* and of *Studies in Song*. With these it is impossible not to feel disappointment. He is preoccupied with the poetical treatment of literary themes: in *Birthday Ode* he celebrates Hugo in a mosaic of intricate reference, while *Song for Landor* has such elaborate allusions to Landor's works that Swinburne's notes are necessary to make the poem intelligible. Poetry seems smothered in the massed verbiage. Not more successful were Swinburne's attempts at nature description and the portrayal of landscape effects. Gosse has suggested that Swinburne was led to this type of work by Watts-Dunton's influence. The results were either the resurrection of old matter in new form, as in *By the North Sea*, or the ineffectual attempt to portray localized natural effects, as in *The Garden of Cymodoce*, a poem on the Island of Sark, and in *Evening on the Broads*.

One poem stands out from the verse of these two volumes, *Thalassius* in *Songs of the Springtides*. This is a spiritual self-confession, idealized out of autobiography and rendered allegorically. Thalassius, a foundling, a child of Apollo and the sea, is educated by an idealized figure who taught him of Liberty, of the power of song, of love that turned 'God's heart toward man and man's to God', and of hatred towards all that imprisoned either body or soul. So educated he passed into life and met the god of love, and later when the god had gone he dedicated himself to dangerous delights; he

> Sat panther-throned beside Erigone,
> Riding the red ways of the revel through
> Midmost of pale-mouthed passion's crownless crew.

After this episode he returned to his mother, the Sea, 'communed with his own heart, and had rest', and once again the power of song grew within him. His father, too, consoled him with the promise that he should sing

> The song of all the winds that sing of me,
> And in thy soul the sense of all the sea.

The mythological movement cannot disguise the personal interpretation. Swinburne was reasserting his belief in Liberty, in the life that is completely unshackled, but he was suggesting further that the fevered years of *Poems and Ballads* were but an episode in his spiritual life, and that his richer service to poetry lay in his later nature poetry. So he may have believed and so he reasserted in his prose, yet *Thalassius* itself is a denial of this faith, for its most spectacular passage is the long simile describing Nero's throne, used to illustrate the fevered years. The glamour of this passage renders it an unintentional confession that all that is quickened into poetry in his later work owes its origin to the recollection of the spiritual crisis which centres in *Poems and Ballads*. Creative development was arrested there, and much of what is vital in his later work rests in memories, shadows, and a few flashes of sudden recollection.

The remaining volumes show clearly the damp that fell about Swinburne's path in the later years. *A Century of Roundels* (1883) displayed a continuance of technical ingenuity in the mastery of a difficult form, without a corresponding strength in content. Nature has been supplemented by an interest in baby life; the 'libidinous laureate' of *Faustine* has become the laureate of babyhood. His admiration for Blake led him to believe that he, too, could capture innocence with power, and it is pathetic to watch his failure. The daintiness of the roundel volume is lost in *A Midsummer Holiday* (1884), where he returns to landscape poetry, to literary themes, to Hugo, and to an attack, due to

Tennyson's peerage, on the House of Lords. *Poems and Ballads (Third Series)* (1889) was mainly memorable for the publication of a number of ballads which he had written before 1865; the contrast between these and the other poems shows what had disappeared with the years. In *Astrophel* (1894) he turned to write of personal associations, of Morris, Richard Burton, and Bell Scott; but the other pieces in this volume, the nature studies and the boastful patriotism, were hollow-sounding work. *A Channel Passage and other Poems* (1904), the last published volume of lyrical work, is the strangest medley. Landscape pieces are mixed with baby verses, attacks on the Boers and Irish with a plea for a strong navy, and there are the usual number of verse obituaries. The one attractive element lies in Swinburne's prologues to a number of Elizabethan plays. Apart from these, he wrote not only less well than in his earlier verse but to meaner purposes. He fell, like Wordsworth, too soon into the sere, the yellow leaf, and, like Wordsworth, he failed to realize his own falling off. Quantities of unpublished work testified to his unswerving diligence.

Swinburne's most successful poetry in the years at 'The Pines' was not in lyric but in two longer pieces, *Tristram of Lyonesse* (1882) and *The Tale of Balen* (1896). *Tristram*, his longest poem, has suffered from the first from superficial criticism; each critic seems to have done little more than to copy the impressionistic judgements of his predecessors. Swinburne's own statement summarizes the values behind the poem: 'My aim was simply to present that story, not diluted and debased as it had been in our own time by other hands, but undefaced by improvement and undeformed by transformation as it was known to the age of Dante wherever the chronicles of romance found hearing, from Ercildoune to Florence; and not in the epic or romantic form of sustained or continuous narrative, but mainly through a succession of dramatic scenes or pictures with descriptive settings or backgrounds.' In Tennyson he found the Tristram story compressed into an inadequate episode. Arnold had forced it equally into subservience upon didacticism. Redeeming it from such purposes, he wished to render it not simply as a story as Morris would have done, but exploiting all its 'finer shades' as in the best tradition of the chronicles of romance. The heavy-laden verse of this later period threatens at times to frustrate him. It has an elaborate imagery without sustaining power, which disintegrates and diffuses the narrative; this is most emphasized in the early books, particularly in the description of Iseult in Book I: 'Iseult, more fair than foam or dawn was white.' As the poem develops one realizes that its strength is neither narrative nor lyrical but dramatic; it lies in such scenes as that of Iseult's prayer in Book V, or in the address to love in Book VI, or in the strength of the scene of Tristram's death in Book IX. Swinburne has applied the most courtly of medieval narrative traditions for his own purposes, and has achieved a modified success.

The interest in the Tristram legend had been with Swinburne since his earliest years as a poet, and the magnificent invocation to love which preludes the poem had been written as early as 1871. It is not strange therefore that this piece so intimately connected with his early years should possess, more than any of his later poetry, the strength of his great poetic years. He investigated the sources for this poem with thoroughness. His main authority was Sir Walter Scott's edition of *Sir Tristrem*, but he knew Malory and he was aware of the earlier treatments of the legend. The poem fails in the fullness of its effect. Romanticism had overworked the Arthurian legend in the nineteenth century, and Swinburne comes late into the field. The crises he managed with success and the moods of passion, but the poem lacks a unifying narrative texture to give it a continued interest and a consistency of purpose.

In *The Tale of Balen* he retold, with close, sometimes verbal, adherence to Malory's narratives, a story which Tennyson roughly mishandled in *Balin and Balan*. Less ambitious than *Tristram*, this lyrical poem is more secure, and in a tail-rhyming stanza not unlike that of *The Lady of Shalott* he gave without his customary grandiloquence a fresh rendering of a medieval theme.

He was doing here at the end of his career what in his early years in *Queen Yseult* he had achieved for the Tristram story.

Swinburne, in writing of Byron's poetry, suggested that his greatest work as a poet was the mass of his poetry taken altogether. This certainly is not true of Swinburne's work. Viewed as a whole, it cannot escape a suggestion of waste in the exploitation of the overworked blank-verse tradition of unactable drama, and in the diffuseness apparent in so much of the later work. He comes through at his greatest in individual lyrics, and in single passages in the dramatic and narrative pieces. The motives from which his poetry arose were so unusual that they tend to emphasize the withdrawal of poetry from life and ordinary human action, which has already been noticed in Rossetti's work. Unlike Rossetti, he had strong sentiments on matters of faith and politics, but here, too, he was in revolt against contemporary values; in religion he was mainly destructive and rebellious, and in politics without cognizance of realities. His mind gained its keenest poetic expression in the years 1862-1866, when, guided by his study of Keats and Blake and Gautier and Baudelaire, he was led to believe in art for its own sake. Rossetti, too, had come to that position, but he had reached it naturally, out of his own poetical purposes; he lacked Swinburne's aggressive insistence on its validity. Swinburne's later work is an ineffectual attempt to modify that early position. His main contribution to the poetry of the later nineteenth century lies in those early moods. He emblazoned them with such verbal and rhythmical designs that, whatever poetry might achieve, nothing more seemed possible of accomplishment within this narrow exotic conception of romanticism which he had marked out as his own territory. A conviction may be expressed that the best of his lyrics are still widely read. Some of them, such as *Itylus*, are incomparable. One day the battle of the conflicting schools will end and English romanticism gain its proper place among the audiences of poetry. When that day comes Swinburne will not be neglected.

Christina Georgina Rossetti

Numerous lives of Christina Rossetti (1830-1894) have been written,[1] and her brother, William Michael, that pedestrian Boswell of the Pre-Raphaelites, issued a memoir and some letters. All the later lives were dependent on William Michael, until Lona Mosk Packer issued her study in 1963. She had access to a great deal of unpublished material, including letters, and notebooks with manuscript versions of the poems. She maintains with great self-confidence a theory that Christina's emotional life was concentrated on William Bell Scott. With much ingenuity she contrives to show how passages in the poems can be interpreted with reference to this theory.

Lona Packer has, it may be admitted, shown that Bell Scott's influence was far greater than has been previously realized. According to William Michael she had two suitors, both of whom, if he knew the truth and told it, she rejected on religious grounds. Neither was of outstanding attraction. First there was James Collinson, a minor Pre-Raphaelite, whose work attempts to combine contemporary themes with Pre-Raphaelite device, and then came Charles Bagot Cayley, whom William Michael describes as scholar, author, linguist, translator of the *Divina Commedia*.[2] Collinson became a Catholic and Cayley was but indifferently orthodox, and so Christina, according to William Michael, remained unwedded. Lona Packer indicates that the Collinson affair ended in 1850 and that Cayley's courtship did not begin until 1862. 'Yet', she adds, 'the major part of her love poetry falls within that period of her young womanhood, in the twelve years between the ages of twenty and thirty two.'

When Christina first met Bell Scott she did not know that a Mrs Scott existed. The lady, never conspicuous in Scott's life, was a Letitia Norquoy and, according to Lona Packer, during her engagement she 'contracted an illness which resulted in her incapacity for marriage'. She offered him his release, but Scott went through a form of marriage, and certainly she gave him in the years that followed all the freedom that his strong and roving nature required. His central friendship was with Alice Boyd, the owner of Penkill Castle. Scott spent long periods in the castle, which was situated near Girvan on the Firth of Clyde. He enjoyed all the comforts, sometimes alone with Alice and sometimes accompanied by Mrs Scott. In 1866 Christina herself visited Penkill, and obviously enjoyed the visit. It is conceivable that Bell Scott brought into her life for a time a liveliness of emotion that no one else created, though Lona Packer pursues the theme, one might think, too absolutely and does not set it in the background of Christina's life as a whole.

She was the youngest child in a family of four and overshadowed by both her brothers. William by his domestic righteousness had an importance in practical affairs which she could not emulate. Gabriel was a genius: 'You must not expect me to possess a tithe of your capacities,' she wrote to him, 'though I humbly – or proudly – lay claim to family likeness.'[3] To her mother she was deeply attached: the four volumes of poems published in her mother's lifetime are all dedicated to her. This love for her mother was strengthened by their long association, their attempts to start private schools, and their trips, under William's guidance, to the Continent. Further, she shared with her mother a deep piety and an attachment to High Anglicanism which appears as the most consistent motive in her life. Her whole adult life was threatened by ill health, culminating in Graves's disease in 1871. On her partial recovery in 1873 she became a novice, and later a sister, of an Anglican Order in

London. Her mother died in 1886, and the last years of her own life were scourged by disease: cancer was discovered in 1892; in 1894 she died, and was buried in Highgate Cemetery. Such is the meagre biographical record, and very little illumination can we find within it for the experience that discovered *Goblin Market* or *The Prince's Progress*, unless with Lona Packer one is to rely solely on Bell Scott.

Her poetical work is contained in a number of volumes published in her lifetime and in posthumous collections. The volumes she herself published were *Verses* (privately printed by her maternal grandfather) in 1847; *Goblin Market and other Poems* (1862); *The Prince's Progress and other Poems* (1866); *Sing-Song* (1872); *Goblin Market, Prince's Progress*, etc. (1875); *A Pageant* (1881); *Verses* (1893). W. M. Rossetti collected her unpublished work, and with uncritical enthusiasm issued this, along with pieces already published, in *New Poems* (1896), and in *The Poetical Works* (1904). Her contributions to periodicals were numerous, including poems written under the pseudonym 'Ellen Alleyn' to *The Germ* (1850).[4] She published in 1870 a volume of short stories, *Commonplace*, which reveals an irony and humour that does not intrude frequently into her poetry. She also wrote a number of prose devotional pamphlets for the Society for Promoting Christian Knowledge.

Certain persistent motives govern her creative work, varying in their outward form, in the shape and fashion of the symbol, but recognizably the same in origin. However she may have appeared in daily life, that portion of herself which she converted into poetry is possessed of a singular consistency, a definable continuity of desire. Even in her juvenile pieces there arises the same poetic argument that one finds in her mature work. A warm desire kindles within her for joy and love, the pleasurable and sensuous acceptance of life. Before she can gain this breath of warm experience, fear chills her: life is insecure, refusing to yield what it has promised, its joys but brief preludes to enduring sin. Her early poetry dwells in a latent conflict between these two motives. They resolve themselves, a little sadly, in a faith in

Christianity which is at once passionate and sombre. This devout otherworldliness leaves Christina Rossetti with a deep, somewhat baffled antagonism to life. It is here that she endures a world-weariness, similar in expression to Swinburne's in *Poems and Ballads*, though reached by a very different sequence of experience. So she is led to write to Dante Gabriel during his last illness: 'I want to assure you that, however harassed by memory or by anxiety you may be, I have (more or less) heretofore gone through the same ordeal. I have borne myself till I became unbearable by myself, and then I have found help in confessions and absolution, and spiritual counsel and relief inexpressible.' In poetry her treatment of this desire that life should end is frequent. So in *Dream Land*:

> Rest, rest, a perfect rest
> Shed over brow and breast;
> Her face is toward the west,
>   The purple land.
> She cannot see the grain
> Ripening on hill and plain,
> She cannot feel the rain
>   Upon her hand.

This central conflict gains frequent expression and colours moods and incidents which seem at first sight unrelated. The ubiquity of a single theme has often been suggested as the most limiting factor in Christina Rossetti's poetical work. Dante Gabriel recognized it and told her ironically that she was ever '"sulking" beside the grave of twice-buried hope!' Christina admitted that the impulses behind her work were closely confined. She writes to Dante Gabriel: 'It is impossible to go on singing out-loud to one's one-stringed lyre. It is not in me, and therefore it will never come out of me, to turn to politics or philanthropy with Mrs Browning: such many-sidedness I leave to a greater than I, and, having said my say, may well sit silent.'[5] Yet these circumscribed motives give her work a consistency and integrity, as if its many parts, *Goblin Market*, her nature poetry, and *The Convent Threshold*, were but contributory to one symbolic intention.

Her irony and humour, which disappear after Dante Gabriel's death, allow her to detach herself sometimes from her usual preoccupations. In the *Goblin Market* volume she has a poem, *Winter, My Secret*, which would seem to forewarn the critic from attempting any psychological evaluation of her lyrical work:

> I tell my secret? No indeed, not I:
> Perhaps some day, who knows?
> But not to-day; it froze, and blows, and snows,
> And you're too curious: fie!
> You want to hear it? well:
> Only, my secret's mine, and I won't tell.
>
> Or, after all, perhaps there's none:
> Suppose there is no secret after all,
> But only just my fun.

In a preface to the 1847 volume her grandfather pleads that he may be excused 'for desiring to retain these early spontaneous efforts in a permanent form and for having silenced the objections urged by her modest diffidence'. The volume contains little of poetical distinction. Most of the verses are juvenile pieces completed before she was 16, and are little more than intelligent exercises with no distinct promise of her later accomplishment. The volume has interest in showing her early preoccupation with death, and with the motive of unfulfilled love which precedes in her poetry the appearance in her life of either of her suitors or of Bell Scott. The opening poem, *The Dead City*, preludes certain elements found in *Goblin Market*, while a number of the poems show her interest in Italian. In brief, some of the motives of her later poetry are already apparent, but the poetry itself has not yet appeared.

Goblin Market and other Poems (1862) was the first volume issued by the Pre-Raphaelites and their associates to gain wide public recognition. After *The Germ* (1850) their zeal for publication seems to have been frustrated. Rossetti's first volume of original verse was not to appear until 1870; Morris's *Defence of Guenevere*, published in 1858, had attracted little attention; Swinburne's *The Queen Mother* and *Rosamond*, 1860, had been uniformly neglected. It remained for Christina Rossetti, 'the Jael who led our host to victory', as Swinburne called her, to make the reading public aware that a new poetry was developing. In *Goblin Market* itself she evolved a completely Pre-Raphaelite poem, and yet one whose elements could be easily assimilated and accepted without hostility. Exact detail, a Pre-Raphaelite dictum, not only exists in the poem but is fashioned into one of its main ornaments; 'bloom-down cheeked peaches', 'swart-headed mulberries', such are the fruit, and the goblin men are minutely described:

> One like a wombat prowled obtuse and furry,
> One like a ratel tumbled hurry skurry.

Yet the poem cannot be adequately described in the terms of Pre-Raphaelitism, and its contact with the movement seems more accidental than deliberate. *Goblin Market* is one of the mysterious poems of the period, raising the same problems as *The Ancient Mariner*, though a solution cannot be gained as completely as with Coleridge's poem. In both a moral is suggested, as an incongruous anticlimax to a poetic narrative full of glamour and magic. In both the metre has novel elements and an unusual importance in producing the poetic effect. In both the coherent witchery of the poem seems to have developed from wide associations of reading and memory. Of the moral conclusion to *Goblin Market* little can be said. It is much more logical than that of *The Ancient Mariner*. Two sisters Laura and Lizzie were tempted with dangerous fruits by goblin men; Lizzie succumbed, and Laura saved her; and so if there is to be any moral, 'For there is no friend like a sister' is not an unnatural one. The moral has no importance for the appreciation of the poem, though it has its place in the analysis of Christina Rossetti's mind. It is very like the moral she had seen so frequently in her childhood's books, such as *Peter Parley's Annual*,[6] and which she introduced later into the child verses in *Sing-Song*. Her motive in placing it here was to suggest that this was another child poem, a fantasy to which no profound meaning was to be attached. Prosodically the poem is cunningly contrived, and yet the form seems a mass of irregularities which by design or instinct she has succeeded in manipulating to serve her poetic purposes. Lines vary in length from ten syllables to four syllables; trochaic mingles with iambic and dactylic movement. No counting of syllables or numbering of accents can torture this prosody into a single pattern. Licence is equally used in rhyme; assonance and imperfect rhymes appear, and one rhyme is frequently carried through a number of lines. Yet throughout there is the sense of control, even, at times, of restraint. It is gained by repeating lines of the same rhythm as if a motive were repeated, by adjusting the rhythm, particularly in its speed, to the meaning, and by asserting regular decasyllabics or octosyllabics after passages in which all regular movement seems in danger of being lost. Nor is the poem so irregular as it appears on the printed page; many of the short lines unite in couplets to give single lines of some five-foot variety. In much of her work Christina Rossetti was careless prosodically, flat, and occasionally incompetent. Here she achieved that rare prosodic success of giving a poem the only form in which, one feels, it could ever have been held.

The main problem of discovering the background of association behind this poem remains. Much of its colour and details derive from early reading in *The Arabian Nights*. Her volume of 1847 has a poem, *The Dead City*, a version of an Arabian Nights theme of a city of marble men, a story used also by Meredith and James Thomson. Already before her eyes there lies the image of rich, bright-coloured fruit, that leads to temptation:

> In green emerald baskets were
> Sun-red apples, streaked and fair;
> Here the nectarine and peach
> And ripe plum lay, and on each
> The bloom rested everywhere.

> Grapes were hanging overhead
> Purple, pale, and ruby-red;
> And in panniers all around
> Yellow melons shone, fresh found,
> With dew upon them spread.

The temptation with the fruits is a recollection gained from Keightley's *Fairy Mythology*.[7] Further, there lay a more homely source, Hone's *Every Day Book*, which is known to have been one of her favourite childhood volumes.[8] From that delightful miscellany she could have found many cries like that of the goblin men:

> Come buy our orchard fruits,
> Come buy, come buy,

from the call of Autolycus to those of the London street criers. Her knowledge of the ballads – and, like Dante Gabriel, she was a ballad reader – gave her a number of suggestions in detail; while the 'wombats' of which she drew a competent pencil drawing were derived from personal observation in the Zoological Gardens.[9] Much else must have been gathered out of her memories and caught by her capacity of poetic creation into the unity of this poem. Without further data one cannot trace the working of that forming process of the imagination. Yet it is not without significance that the two central motives, the temptation of a sister and the attraction and danger of all that delights the senses, are important throughout her secular poetry. The sister theme, found frequently in her ballad poetry, recurs with the accompaniment of irony and humour in *Commonplace*.

The other poems in *Goblin Market* are lyrics, many possessing an originality of atmosphere unequalled by any woman poet of the century. In a number of pieces, *Cousin Kate*, *Noble Sisters*, and particularly in *Maude Clare* and *Sister Maude*, she uses the ballad form with poignant and tragic themes and a consciousness that the ballad demands quick and allusive presentation. A love motive dominates a number of the most memorable poems. It is unnecessary to assume that the prosaic figure of Charles Bagot Cayley inspired these haunting pieces or that they resulted from some undefined relation with Bell Scott: enough that somehow Christina Rossetti possessed herself of the experience which lies in them. In *A Birthday* ('My heart is like a singing bird') she uses imagery exotic and oriental, caught from The Song of Songs and *The Arabian Nights*, to express a moment of exultant acceptance of love. All the other pieces dwell in the memory or the denial of that moment. So in *Echo*, one of the keenest lyrics in this volume:

> Yet come to me in dreams, that I may live
> My very life again though cold in death:
> Come back to me in dreams, that I may give
> Pulse for pulse, breath for breath:
> Speak low, lean low,
> As long ago, my love, how long ago.

This sense of a love grown dead leads to world-weariness and a desire for death, and so are produced two of the best-known pieces in the volume, *Up-hill* and *Song* ('When I am dead, my dearest').

Closely allied to this theme are the nature poems *The First Spring Day*, *Bitter for Sweet*, *Spring*, and *Winter Rain*. Throughout the motive is that out of winter comes spring, and out of spring, winter, with the symbol suggested that in the human heart the spring that turns to winter remains winter, always. Christina Rossetti was a town child, and despite the visits to Somerset she never possessed a wide interest in natural scenery. On occasion she describes detail happily, as she describes the fruit in *Goblin Market* and flowers in *Another Spring*:

> I'd have my crocuses at once,
> My leafless pink mezereons,
> My chill-veined snow-drops, choicer yet
> My white or azure violet,
> Leaf-nested primrose; anything
> To blow at once, not late.

But usually nature is for her not a theme for description but a symbol, an image of warmth and cold, of sun and frost, of hope followed by despair. In thus avoiding the complex emotions which the romantics had found in nature she gives to her poems the poignant simplicity of a medieval 'seasons' poem. True, she has added more symbol, but such a poem as *Bitter for Sweet* seems to retain a medieval simplicity in the central theme, however dim and far-reaching are the ultimate symbolic implications:

> Summer is gone with all its roses,
> Its sun and perfumes and sweet flowers,
> Its warm air and refreshing showers:
> And even Autumn closes.
>
> Yea, Autumn's chilly self is going,
> And Winter comes which is yet colder;
> Each day the hoar-frost waxes bolder,
> And the last buds cease blowing.

Already in 1862 one section of her volume is set apart for *Devotional Pieces*; later this interest will exclude entirely the secular, bright-coloured, poignant images which figure in *Goblin Market*. As a prelude to this section stands *The Convent Threshold*, which would seem to be the answer of Christina Rossetti's piety to *The Blessed Damozel*. In this keen dramatic monologue love is no compensation for the loss of heaven:

> You sinned with me a pleasant sin:
> Repent with me, for I repent.

The devotional poems conquer the difficult problem of conveying mystical experience in poetical form, which can only be achieved by arresting the mind of the reader with an adequate imagery, and by resolving devoutness and mysticism into the terms of normal activity. This she achieves in such poems as *A Better Resurrection*, which possesses a greater simplicity than the work of the seventeenth-century religious poets, but does not lack their urgency. Two poems stand out for their originality of conception, *The Three Enemies* and *Sleep at Sea*. In the first she converts the temptation theme which she frequently uses into dramatic conversations of the soul with the Flesh, the World, and the Devil. So the Flesh asks, 'Sweet, thou art pale', and the soul replies:

> More pale to see,
> Christ hung upon the cruel tree
> And bore His Father's wrath for me.

Sleep at Sea is as if the most eerie elements of Coleridge's ship of dead men had been isolated from *The Ancient Mariner* and applied to the purposes of religious allegory. It has the same compactness as Cowper's *The Castaway*, the same unfailing strength in the narrative.

Disappointment must attend a reading of her second volume, *The Prince's Progress*, which, with Dante Gabriel's promptings, she published in 1866. The same motives predominate as in *Goblin Market* – the sister theme, the lost-love theme, temptation poems, love-ballad poems, nature 'seasons' poems, devotional poems, and the narrowness of interest, already a marked feature of her poetry, gains emphasis. The most sustained piece is the title poem *The Prince's Progress*. Its theme is of a bridegroom prince who sets out to meet his bride, but delays so long by the way that when he arrives it is but to find that she is dead, and her maidens sing to him the lyric which is the most moving feature of the poem:

> Too late for love, too late for joy,
> Too late, too late!
> You loitered on the road too long,
> You trifled at the gate.

This lyric was in 1863 a separate poem and was published independently in *Macmillan's Magazine*.[10] Later, at Dante Gabriel's suggestion, it was attached to the narrative of the Prince's journey which is described with a Pre-Raphaelite, even dilatory, emphasis on detail. In the same volume is the lyric *Songs in a Cornfield*, a poem admired by Swinburne, which repeats the motive of *The Prince's Progress* in rustic setting.

Despite similarities with *Goblin Market*, this volume has an increased emphasis on personal weariness and distress which now appears more persistently and penetrates deeper. In *Life and Death* she demands an annihilation of all that is life in a desire for rest:

> Life is not sweet. One day it will be sweet
>   To shut our eyes and die;
> Nor feel the wild flowers blow, nor birds dart by
>   With flitting butterfly,
> Nor grass grown long above our heads and feet,
> Nor hear the happy lark that soars sky-high,
> Nor sigh that spring is fleet and summer fleet,
>   Nor mark the waxing wheat,
> Nor know who sits in our accustomed seat.

Elsewhere, in *What would I Give?* and *Autumn*, a more distinctly personal element is added to this pessimism. *Memory* is the only poem in the volume where this sickness of the spirit emerges into original poetic expression. The theme attaches itself to that motive of lost love and broken betrothal which pursues all her love poetry, but it is maintained with such strong and consistent imagery that the poem has the lucid clarity of a single symbol. The imagery is one which she has used before, and so is the motive, but it is represented with freshness and urgency:

> I have a room whereinto no one enters
>   Save I myself alone:
>   There sits a blessed memory on a throne,
> There my life centres.
>
> While winter comes and goes – oh tedious comer! –
>   And while its nip-wind blows;
>   While bloom the bloodless lily and warm rose
> Of lavish summer.
>
> If any should force entrance he might see there
>   One buried yet not dead,
>   Before whose face I no more bow my head
> Or bend my knee there;
>
> But often in my worn life's autumn weather
>   I watch there with clear eyes,
>   And think how it will be in Paradise
> When we're together.

As *Goblin Market* had already shown, one of Christina Rossetti's most delightful powers was to play with the images that delight children and use them for the purposes of the imagination. In *Sing-Song* (1872) she uses this same fancy, but for childish purposes. The poems vary from nursery rhymes to poems of innocence comparable with those of Blake if indeed not definitely influenced by him. A moral element is often allowed to intrude, but in compensation there are nonsense pieces such as 'If a pig wore a wig', and brief studies such as 'Who has seen the wind?' Christina Rossetti published this volume when childhood verse and nonsense verse were beginning to gain popularity; it shows, too, that the Goblin Market element in her mind is not dead, but that unfortunately it is separated from her main imaginative purposes.

In 1875 *Goblin Market* and *The Prince's Progress* were reprinted as one volume, with a few omissions and with a number of new poems added. *A Pageant and other Poems*, the last volume before Dante Gabriel's death, appeared in 1881. The volume confirms this impression of ever-increasing seriousness not unmingled with morbidity. Its outstanding expression can be found in the poetic allegory, *A Ballad of Boding*, where in a dream the poet sees three ships – one of Love, filled with revel and feasting; one, the ship of the Worm, of wealth and strife; and a third, a ship of Suffering without brightness or display:

> Their sails were patched and rent,
> Their masts were bent,
> In peril of their lives they worked and went.
> For them no feast was spread,
> No soft luxurious bed
> Scented and white,
> No crown or sceptre hung in sight.

The allegory is a simple one: the Love ship and the Worm ship go down, but the third survives the storms. The poetic manipulation of this theme lifts it out of the commonplace. As has already been seen in *Sleep at Sea*, Christina Rossetti's mind dwelt on some dream seascape, aroused by memories of *The Ancient*

Mariner, from whose eeriness arose symbols and images which she mingled with memories of her childhood reading in *Perils of Flood and Field* and fashioned into her poems.

This volume marks her increased interest in the sonnet form; she issued two sequences, *Monna Innominata* and *Later Life*, along with a number of miscellaneous sonnets. It was a natural development; the family letters reveal that the Rossetti children used the sonnet as a literary exercise, while Italian reading and Dante Gabriel's notable example, coupled with that of Mrs Browning, would all lend encouragement. Like Dante Gabriel, Christina Rossetti keeps to the rhyme of the Petrarchan sonnet form, though she pays little attention to the balance of octave and sextet and other niceties of structure. She explains the theme of *Monna Innominata* in an introductory note. She imagines a lady, of the Provençal Renaissance period, loved by a poet as Beatrice and Laura were later loved, and herself sharing her lover's poetic aptitude, 'while the barrier between them might be one held sacred by both, yet not such as to render mutual love incompatible with mutual honour'. She suggests that the theme would have suited Mrs Browning had she been 'unhappy instead of happy'. Despite this dramatic setting, little pretence at historical detail intrudes into the poems, and the revelation of Christina Rossetti's own moods soon becomes their dominating purpose. In Lona Packer's volume all this is worked out in the terms of Christina's relationship with Bell Scott, and as part of the evidence she quotes William Michael's note that the sonnets were 'a personal utterance – an intensely personal one'. From the early sonnet,

> I wish I could remember that first day,
> First hour, first moment of your meeting me,

to the last beautiful sonnet,

> Youth gone, and beauty gone if ever there
> Dwelt beauty in so poor a face as this,

she reveals in simple, poignant verses the moods of a love that is persistent but unfulfilled. She is removed from the Elizabethan tradition by infrequency of conceit, and by an increased earnestness. Yet, despite her simplicity, imagery enters freely, and at times she allows a Shakespearian gesture in vocabulary, a play and antithesis in words. This occurs in the sextet to the sonnet in which she invites her lover to take another love if it will add to his happiness:

> For if I did not love you, it might be
>   That I should grudge you some one dear delight;
>   But since the heart is yours that was mine own,
>   Your pleasure is my pleasure, right my right,
> Your honourable freedom makes me free,
>   And you companioned I am not alone.

She never revealed her poetical autobiography more fully than in this sequence, where she explores the moods of one who desires love, who knows of its awakening, but who has known not of its fulfilment, but only of memories and imaginings.

It is difficult to make any ultimate assessment of Christina's emotional life. Possibly she struggled against heterosexual love as fiercely as John Addington Symonds struggled in his father's lifetime against homosexuality. Her religious faith, her health, and indeed the very circumstances of her life would make any liaison with Scott, or indeed with anyone else, impossible. But it need not have precluded her from a consciousness of what she was missing, and an accompanying sense of guilt that she should feel that she was missing anything. Her time, her personality, her associates, especially Gabriel and Bell Scott, may thus have united to contribute something very rare to her emotional life and to her poetry.

Later Life is less a sequence than a miscellaneous collection of sonnets, though a certain unity is gained by the prevalence of religious themes. It is the aftermath of *Monna Innominata*, the renunciation of earthly love for spiritual salvation. The Elizabethan intrusions in the earlier sequence have disappeared; one seems to sense an increased severity and distress:

> So tired am I, so weary of to-day,
> So unrefreshed from foregone weariness.

Occasionally a more genial imagination lingers to give a keen and successful interpretation to the religious theme. Usually this occurs in poems where the personal element and the emphasis on weariness have been obviated, as in *Sonnet* 10 ('Tread softly! all the earth is holy ground').

A Pageant (1881) shows a fuller preoccupation with religious themes, and the last volume, *Verses* (1893), published in the year before her death and under the direction of 'the Tract Committee' of the Society for Promoting Christian Knowledge, is entirely religious and devotional in character. Nowhere in this later religious verse does she show the imaginative power which sustained *Sleep at Sea*, *The Three Enemies*, and *A Ballad of Boding*. Her distinctive achievement had been to reveal in poetical terms the conflict of the world and the spirit in the religious soul. In this later verse the spirit has conquered: the Church, its feasts and fasts, are celebrated, and the relation of the worshipper to God. Yet neither imagery nor emotion converts these poems into great religious verse such as that of Donne or Herbert. Even when she records experience she lacks the reality of the earlier pieces and approaches at times the luxury of spiritual self-flagellation. Influences are difficult to detect, and it would be well to assume that most of these poems arose more from genuine and deeply felt experience, even if the poetic representation is incomplete. Sometimes she uses an antithesis not unlike that found in some of Donne's religious verse, as in *Ash Wednesday*:

> My God, my God, have mercy on my sin,
>   For it is great; and if I should begin
> To tell it all, the day would be too small
>   To tell it in.

> My God, Thou wilt have mercy on my sin
>   For Thy Love's sake: yea, if I should begin
> To tell This all, the day would be too small
>   To tell it in.

She also has in some of her poems a movement imitated from medieval verse:

> The twig teacheth,
> The moth preacheth.

In the main the imagery and the numbers do not differ widely from those which she had previously employed.

Such was the verse that Christina Rossetti published; but two years after her death William Michael, in *New Poems* (1896), contrived to make a large volume out of previously unpublished pieces, without issuing anything which adds substantially to Christina's reputation. Even the faithful *Athenæum* administered a rebuke when the volume appeared, and William Michael's only defence was that he had left some pieces in manuscript still unpublished. In 1904 he issued a complete edition of Christina Rossetti's poems, with a further selection from her unpublished work. Brotherly piety can seldom have rendered a greater disservice than did William Michael Rossetti in this collected edition. The rearrangement of the poems, the addition of so many poems which Christina Rossetti had not herself published, the absence of a complete title index, and the solemn, trite memoir all help to obscure the poetry that lies concealed. To turn from this collected volume to the original volumes of 1862 and 1866, adorned with Dante Gabriel's illustrations, is to gain a new perspective on Christina Rossetti's work. She had made her individual contribution to later nineteenth-century poetry. Few writers united so fully the two main and usually distinct movements of the period – the poetry with Pre-Raphaelite décor and the poetry of religious sensibility. In however narrow a range, there exist in her work both the enthusiasms which began with Rossetti and those which find their ultimate source in the Oxford Movement.

4

William Morris

Rossetti never influenced a man more unlike himself than William Morris (1834-1896).[1] His family was of Welsh descent, although it retained nothing of Welsh tradition. His father, a successful bill-broker, who had unexpected luck in a copper-share deal, represented that upper middle-class tradition which can educate a son at Marlborough and Exeter College, Oxford, and leave him with a competence. Morris was born at Walthamstow, then a pleasant village on the edge of Epping Forest, but which he described in 1883 as 'now terribly cocknified and choked up by the jerry-builder'. He went to school at Marlborough, which he later said was in his day 'new and very rough'. But it was situated in beautiful country which he much enjoyed, and he later recalled how his enthusiasm was aroused for the historical monuments which were 'thickly scattered' over the district. The domestic atmosphere of Morris's home was one of narrow evangelicalism, but his school brought him into contact with men affected by the Anglo-Catholicism of the Oxford Movement, and he entered Oxford with the determination to become a priest.

Oxford was the determining period of his life, and it is in these years that we meet for the first time the baffling difficulty present in all discussion of Morris's mental development. The outward facts of his life are known, but the inner, spiritual values remain a secret. He is as noisy and active as the wind, but once he has passed we cannot trace his passage. We know that Oxford deepened his medieval romanticism, through a study of Malory and Tennyson. It aroused in him a hatred of the classics, and still more of the way in which they were taught. It gave him a lifelong friend and associate, a young Birmingham man, Edward Burne-Jones, the painter. Something, too, happened in these years to his faith; but Morris was not in the Victorian tradition which regarded the discussion of belief as one of the main purposes of poetry. At Oxford he had been for a time under the influence of the 'High Church or Puseyite school'. He himself suggested that this phase was 'corrected' by the revelation of reading Ruskin's work. He lost interest in religion, but he kept quiet about it, and turned his attention to other things. He had already written poems, but he did not treat the accomplishment very seriously. 'Well, if this is poetry,' he said once during this period, 'it is very easy to write.'

It was in this unsettled period (1855-1856), the end of his Oxford career, that Morris first came under Rossetti's influence. He and Burne-Jones had talked things out during a long holiday in France in the summer of 1855; Burne-Jones was to be a painter, Morris an architect. A 'Brotherhood' was to be formed on the model of the Pre-Raphaelite Movement, and, in imitation of *The Germ*, a journal, *The Oxford and Cambridge Magazine*, was to be published. Rossetti himself was gained as a contributor, and his *Burden of Nineveh*, *The Blessed Damozel*, and *The Staff and Scrip* appeared in *The Magazine*. In the period 1855-1857 Rossetti was the dominating influence in Morris's life. When Burne-Jones challenged him with too much subordination to Rossetti he replied, 'I have got beyond that. I want to imitate Gabriel as much as I can.' Rossetti told him that every art and every occupation was inferior to painting, and within a year Morris had left architecture to devote himself to painting. It was at the end of this youthful, impulsive period that he published in 1858, at the age of 24, his volume of poems, *The Defence of Guenevere*.

Nine years separate *The Defence of Guenevere* from Morris's second work in poetry, and within that decade he found the practical activities which were to fill the greater part of his very energetic life. The occupation of rooms with Burne-Jones in London, and later his own marriage in 1859 to Jane Burden, who appears in so many of Rossetti's paintings, led him to think of the beauty and utility of all household decoration. He concentrated his energy on reorganizing the Brotherhood into Morris, Marshall, Faulkner & Co., which commenced business, on a very inadequate capital, in 1861. He abandoned painting just as previously he had abandoned architecture and became a craftsman. Mural decoration, carving, stained glass, furniture, wall-papers, carpets, chintzes, all were within the final activities of the firm. It is outside the present purpose to discuss the effect that the work of Morris and his associates had upon middle-class Victorian taste; enough that for a number of years it exhausted even his amazing capacity for work. His return to poetry is marked by the publication of *The Life and Death of Jason* in 1867 and of *The Earthly Paradise* (1868-1870).

By 1870 Morris was a successful man of business; his inherited income had decreased, but his losses had been compensated by the success of his enterprise. This removal of financial stress shows itself by Morris's entry into a number of fresh activities. In 1871 he purchased Kelmscott Manor House, a residence on the upper Thames, intimately associated with the work of his middle years. He commenced, too, in the autumn of 1868, the study of Icelandic literature under the guidance of Eiríkr Magnússon. Morris was immediately attracted by the qualities of Icelandic literature, and with Magnússon he executed a number of translations, including a prose version of the *Volsunga Saga* in 1870, and *Three Northern Love Stories* in 1875. A journey to Iceland in 1871, followed by a second journey in 1873, aroused in him still more deeply the conception of the imaginative possibilities of the Northern myths. His journals of these two journeys are the most intimate documents of Morris's yet published.[2] He first realized the possibilities of the Northern stories for his own poetry in *The Lovers of Gudrun*, a rendering of the *Laxdaela Saga*, which he had included as one of *The Earthly*

Paradise stories. Further, with a verse refashioning of the *Volsunga Saga*, issued as *Sigurd the Volsung* in 1876, he produced his most considerable poetic work. Icelandic influences, although they dominate this period, were not all-absorbing; in 1872 he published *Love is Enough*, a dramatic poem fashioned on the pattern of the medieval morality play.

Within the decade 1870-1880, which marks these new poetic interests, may be traced a number of new developments in Morris's life and outlook. He had long exhausted the influence of Rossetti in his poetry, and he was now forced to an open breach with him. Rossetti had been a joint tenant at Kelmscott in 1871; it was an arrangement which resulted in subdued mutual irritation. Further, Rossetti had been a very inactive partner in Morris & Co., and, with Madox Brown and Marshall, insisted on a financial compensation which Morris regarded as excessive. The friendship of 1855, frustrated in Rossetti's complex relationship with Janey Morris to which reference is made in chapter one, was finally lost in lengthy and unpleasant legal negotiation in 1875. In the same period Morris, who had been a poet and a craftsman, developed into a man of affairs. The change is an almost imperceptible one. He was led first by his anger at the 'restoration' of ancient buildings into public controversy and into the treasurership of the Society for the Protection of Ancient Buildings. This seemed only a natural extension of his earlier interests, but the Eastern Question of 1876 drew him away from his crafts to the world of politics. The Eastern crisis led him into personal contact with Radical leaders, and in 1879 he was Treasurer of the National Liberal League. Radicalism held him for a time, but soon he found himself searching for some more fundamental solution of social difficulties. The biographical information is again perplexing; the facts are in our possession, but the mental adjustments, the conflict, if there was a conflict, remain unknown. He was at the height of his professional prosperity: he was to decorate with damasks the walls of the Reception Rooms at St James's Palace and to adorn the hangings of the Throne; his college was to make him a Fellow; he had new, ambitious poetic themes ready to be attempted. But something urged him to leave this spectacular triumph and, in January 1883, register himself as a member of the Social Democratic Federation. It may have needed a struggle; but it would be like the man to do it light-heartedly, almost carelessly, because it seemed to him the obvious thing to do.

It was the natural political consummation of his other activities. His whole life had been a protest against the production of goods for profit without consideration of the craftsman or of the beauty and utility of the thing produced. 'Time was when everyone that made anything, made it a work of art besides a useful piece of goods; *and it gave them pleasure to do it.* Whatever I doubt, I have no doubt of that.' For twenty years he had attempted to persuade the rich and the middle classes to retain in their houses only the beautiful and the useful; in that task he had done all that it was within him to do. At the same time he had watched the ugly cities where the purposeless labour of men who were not craftsmen produced work that was shoddy or pretentious. His socialism was an emotional protest against this world, a logical outcome of Ruskin's influence on his mental activity. He summarizes his sentiments and Ruskin's place within them in a May Day article in *Justice* in 1896, the year of his death:

> I cannot help saying, by the way, how deadly dull the world would have been twenty years ago but for Ruskin! It was through him that I learned to give form to my discontent. . . . Apart from the desire to produce beautiful things, the leading passion of my life has been and is hatred of modern civilization. . . . The struggles of mankind for many ages had produced nothing but this sordid, aimless, ugly confusion. Was it all to end in a counting-house on the top of a cinder-heap, with Podsnap's drawing-room in the offing, and a Whig Committee dealing out champagne to the rich and margarine to the poor in such convenient proportions as would make all men contented together, though the pleasure of the eye was gone from the world and the place of Homer was to be taken by Huxley?

The whole Pre-Raphaelite group was in protest against the Victorian age; Morris alone attempted in the world of politics to effect structural changes in society. He had to learn, in a severe school, the difficulties of practical political action, and he soon became aware of the wilder associates who surround a leader in a revolutionary party. The crisis of his socialist career came in 1884, when he quarrelled with H. M. Hyndman and left the Social Democratic Federation, to inaugurate the Socialist League with *The Commonweal* as its journal. Hyndman, writing years later, was able to give a just estimate of the effect of Morris's entry into English socialism:

> For Morris was ever too eager to take his full share in the unpleasant part of our public work, and speedily showed that he meant to work in grim earnest on the same level as the rank and file of our party. That was Morris's way from the first. He was never satisfied unless he was doing things which, to say the truth, he was little fitted for, and others of coarser fibre could do much better than he.[3]

Morris was surrounded with strange companions in the Socialist League, and he was committed to a policy of extreme socialism. Friction with the police was not infrequent, and in 1885 he found himself in the dock of a Thames police court, though it was his temper rather than his politics that had brought him there. 'What are you?' asked the magistrate. Rage overcame habitual modesty: 'I am an artist and a literary man, pretty well known, I think, throughout Europe.' Despite this spirited reply, Morris realized during these years that scuffling and street-corner oratory would not initiate that England of Utility and Beauty which dwelt in his mind. He witnessed 'Bloody Sunday' in November 1887, and saw from the scenes in Trafalgar Square how dangerous the indiscriminate use of force might become. He came to feel that education must precede any adequate revolutionary movement, and that the way to the ideal State could not come up suddenly with the dawn as he had once imagined. He grew more tolerant of other political methods, of the Fabians and the Independent Labour Party. G. B. Shaw furnished me with an impression of Morris's mood in these years:

Morris's attitude towards Fabianism was at first one of very strong distaste for its official and administrative detail and its adaptation to the sort of average public character with which he had no patience. But after experimenting pretty exhaustively with the Socialists who sympathized with him in this, and finding that they were hopeless Impossibilists, his great practical sense came into play. He dropped the Socialist League, which immediately perished, and declared that he had now no doubt that Socialism would come about in Sidney Webb's way, but that, as that way did not offer him a job at which he could be as useful as he could be at his own artistic activities, he would return to them, and content himself with keeping the cause of ultimate Communism alive in the little Hammersmith Socialist Society which had grown up round his house. And in that attitude he remained until his death.

This last period adds little to the record of his achievement in poetry, and yet it is full of varied literary productivity, much of which is in prose. His lectures on the position of the craftsman and the relation of literature to art were collected in a number of volumes: *Hopes and Fears for Art* (1882); *The Aims of Art* (1887); *Signs of Change* (1888), with a posthumous volume, *Lectures on Socialism* (1915). His most original work in prose is a series of prose romances: *The House of the Wolfings* (1889); *The Story of the Glittering Plain* (1891); *The Wood Beyond the World* (1894); *Child Christopher* (1895); *The Well at the World's End* (1896); and the romances published posthumously, *The Water of the Wondrous Isles* (1897), *The Story of the Sundering Flood* (1898). With these are two prose romances with a definitely political bias, *A Dream of John Ball* (1888) and the *News from Nowhere* (1891), a volume which for political rather than from literary reasons has gained a European currency. He added in these years to the crafts which he had mastered. After his withdrawal from active socialism in 1890 he founded at Hammersmith the Kelmscott Press for the production of finely printed books. The Press produced over fifty volumes between 1891 and 1898, when it was wound up by Morris's executors. The poetical work in these years is less significant. In 1875 he translated Virgil into English verse as *The Aeneids*; in 1887 *The Odyssey*, and in 1895 *Beowulf* with the assistance of A. J. Wyatt. He gathered together a number of old pieces and added some new ones to his last volume of original verse, *Poems by the Way*, issued from his own Kelmscott Press in 1891. In 1896 he died. The study which follows, confined as it is to Morris's poetry, cannot do justice to his whole life and personality, one of the most active and varied in the later nineteenth century.

Morris broke into English poetry, in 1858, at the age of 24, with *The Defence of Guenevere*, a volume which was a fresh contribution to Victorian romanticism. No volume by Rossetti had yet appeared; it was four years before Christina Rossetti was to publish *Goblin Market*, and seven years before Swinburne entered effectively into English poetry. The volume in which every poem is of medieval suggestion shows Rossetti's influence, but Morris has developed in his own way under this stimulus. Rossetti had kept his own age out of poetry, but Morris contrived to keep himself out as well. Every poem, except the charming aubade, *Summer Dawn*, is impersonal. 'I abominate introspective poetry', he once wrote, and here at an age when most poets are undertaking self-scrutinies, and in a decade when introspection was the dominant motive of poetry, Morris brusquely shows the door to all subjective discussion of mind and soul. Sentiment, action, and passion are substituted as motives, and these are revealed on a medieval background, arising from suggestions of Malory and Froissart, and presented in lyric, narrative, and dramatic forms.

The lyrics arise mainly from moods of magic, embroidered with Pre-Raphaelite device, memories of that beautiful, unreal world of dream medievalism which exists in Keats's *La Belle Dame sans Merci*. *The Blue Closet, Near Avalon, The Gilliflower of Gold, The Tune of Seven Towers, Rapunzel* and others were airy, gossamer designs which Morris was never again to attempt. Occasionally as with *The Blue Closet* he is writing with one of Rossetti's pictures as a starting-place for his imagination. At times his lyrics seem mere tunes, pattern without rational content, and yet in Morris the insubstantial is never the meaningless.

He was once challenged on the refrain in the lyric *Two Red Roses Across the Moon*:

> There was a lady lived in a hall,
> Large in the eyes, and slim and tall;
> And ever she sung from noon to noon,
> *Two red roses across the moon.*

It seemed that the refrain was a melodious but meaningless intrusion. Morris at once replied that the roses and the moon comprised the emblem on the shield of the Knight: what might appear to the reader as a mere collection of pretty words was all as solid to his mind as a row of bricks.

The dramatic and narrative pieces which are distinct in mood from the lyrics are of two types: in the one, the memory of Malory prevails and with it the romantic glamour of chivalry; in the other, the influence of Froissart, known to Morris in Lord Berners' translation, introduces into the poems the grim, ugly reality of war. These two contrasting moods remained with him throughout his life. He looked on the medieval world as bright and clean, but he knew that it could be brutal and cruel. The whole of this poetry, whether the original suggestion is from Malory or Froissart, has a tense and piteous quality, full of a penetrating compassion for the tragedy and affliction of those who have suffered deeply. Swinburne, commenting on one of these poems, has written a passage which gives the tone of all of them: 'It has not been constructed at all; the parts hardly hold together; it has need of joists and screws, props and rafters . . . But where among other and older poets of his time and country is one comparable for perception and expression of tragic truth of subtle and noble, terrible and piteous things? Where a touch of passion at once so broad and so sure?'[4]

His method, influenced by Browning's practice in the dramatic monologue, is to seize a single episode and manipulate it freely so that the full human poignancy of the situation can be revealed. Unlike Tennyson and Browning, he is not embarrassed by moral perceptions, but is free to develop character and scene for their own sentiment and value. So in the Arthurian pieces, *The Defence of Guenevere* reveals the Queen fevered and distraught in a long ordeal of inquisition by Gawain and other Knights; *King Arthur's Tomb* is a reconstruction of the last encounter of Guenevere and Launcelot, a portrayal of passionate memories and the maddening onslaughts of repentance; *Sir Galahad*, the third Arthurian poem of importance, is a study of the knight who chose the sacredness of the San Greal quest and doubted temporarily whether he had not lost too much in forsaking the human pleasures which the other knights enjoyed. The poetic quality of the Arthurian poems can be seen from the opening of *The Defence of Guenevere*:

> But, knowing now that they would have her speak,
> She threw her wet hair backward from her brow,
> Her hand close to her mouth touching her cheek,
>
> As though she had had there a shameful blow,
> And feeling it shameful to feel ought but shame
> All through her heart, yet felt her cheek burned so.

The utter impatience with all introductory matter and the sudden ruthless emphasis on the central poignant situation is characteristic of Morris throughout these poems.

The poems whose suggestion arises directly or indirectly from Froissart have a greater economy of effect; they rely less on character, more on the very efficacy of their dramatic setting. Of these *Sir Peter Harpdon's End*, the most considerable piece in the whole volume, is a blank-verse play set out in three scenes. The structure is a little too mechanical for successful dramatic unity, but the three main figures, Peter, Lambert, and Alice, show the courage, cunning, and suffering of the medieval world. Here lies the freshness of the poem: the medieval world had for over a century yielded suggestions for romantic sentiment, the dim glamour of far-away things, but Morris now shows a medieval life, fresh in its own setting, full of its own humanity. The same values yield themselves to more concentrated expression in the narrative poem, *The Haystack in the Floods*. The incident is of Morris's invention, but the background is suggested by Froissart. Robert and his Jehane are overtaken by the tyrant Godmar from whom they are fleeing. The man is taken and killed, and the woman, who has watched her lover die, led back to ignominy. Morris insists with an emphasis derived from Browning's *Porphyria's Lover* upon the cruelty of this medieval world. He thus describes Robert's death:

> With a start
> Up Godmar rose, thrust them apart;
> From Robert's throat he loosed the bands
> Of silk and mail; with empty hands
> Held out, she stood and gazed, and saw
> The long bright blade without a flaw
> Glide out from Godmar's sheath, his hand
> In Robert's hair; she saw him bend
> Back Robert's head; she saw him send
> The thin steel down; the blow told well,
> Right backward the knight Robert fell,
> And moan'd as dogs do, being half dead,
> Unwitting, as I deem: so then
> Godmar turn'd grinning to his men,
> Who ran, some five or six, and beat
> His head to pieces at their feet.

The impression gained here by direct emphasis is enhanced by the ironic undertone of the conclusion:

> This was the parting that they had
> Beside the haystack in the floods.

Similarly in *Concerning Geffray Teste Noire*, a poem which has a closer relationship to Froissart, he reveals suddenly and grotesquely the pain and horror which inevitably accompany war, even war with the superficial trappings of chivalry.

The Defence of Guenevere was a first volume of unbounded promise; the freshness of outlook, the prosodic and technical variety, and the keen, impassioned humanity all suggested the advent of a new poet of magnitude. The prosody was unusually varied and adventurous; *terza rima* in *The Defence of Guenevere*, iambic quatrains in *King Arthur's Tomb* and *Sir Galahad*, dramatic blank verse in *Sir Peter Harpdon's End*, the octosyllabic managed without its fatal facility in *The Haystack in the Floods*, and varied lyrical measures, including the *In Memoriam* stanza in *Golden Wings*. Morris never fulfilled that promise; he achieved much both in poetry and in other activities, but he never attained all that *The Defence of Guenevere* suggests that he had within him. His whole poetical fibre slackened;[5] the fevered passion and bitter wisdom of this youthful work pass into the more placid story-telling of *The Earthly Paradise* period. Swinburne, in a picturesque passage in one of his letters,[6] has described this sweet, untroubled manner which had lost all the splendid poignancy of the early poems:

> His Muse is like Homer's Trojan women; she drags her robes as she walks. I really think any Muse (when she is neither resting nor flying) ought to tighten her girdle, tuck up her skirts, and step out. It is better than Tennyson's short-winded and artificial concision – but there is such a thing as a swift and spontaneous style. Top's[7] is spontaneous and slow; and especially my ear hungers for more force and variety of sound in the verse. It looks as if he purposely avoided all strenuous emotion or strength of music in thought and word; and so when set by other work as good his seems hardly done in thorough earnest.

One can register the change, but one cannot explain it, for it is easier to weave explanations around an introspective soul who for ever tells you why he does things than around an active personality who is too busy doing things ever to explain why they are done. He lost the stimulus of Rossetti, and from this loss the emotional temper of his poetry suffered as the art of Millais had done. It may be that his craft activities occupied so much of his mind that poetry became a pastime; he could weave patterns of beautiful words with the same skill as he could design the pattern of a carpet, and with the same degree of emotional stress. Whatever the cause, the middle period in his poetry suggests a conscious removal of his mind not only from his own century but from all the strenuous moments of human passion and suffering.

Morris's relations with his wife, Jane, must have been one of the main motives for this change. Hall Caine had a story that she had been in love with Rossetti before she married Morris. This need not be accepted, but it is clear that it was under Rossetti's influence that he married her. She had met Rossetti in a theatre in Oxford in October 1857 and she married Morris at St Michael's at the Northgate in Oxford on 29 April 1859. Despite her beauty, she had little to offer Morris either in affection or intellectual companionship. In the earlier years their relationship, though disappointing to Morris, seems to have been tolerable and Jenny was born in 1861 and May in 1862.

In the late sixties Jane Morris and Rossetti were drawn more strongly together. Not only was she the model that dominated Rossetti's pictorial imagination, but she inspired many of the poems in *The House of Life* and other of his poems of that period. She appeared frequently with Rossetti at receptions in London, and it is suggested that, accepting the situation, Morris took Kelmscott Manor as a joint residence. Much of this matter has not yet been disclosed. Morris's closest friend during this period was Lady ('Georgie') Burne-Jones, but it is clear that Mackail was permitted to quote only a few of the passages in the letters which they interchanged. There are letters in the British Museum from Rossetti to Jane Morris and these have been made available to readers in 1964.[1] The mystery remains in the command that 'Janey' had over Rossetti: 'far deeper', he wrote to her, '(though I know you never believe me) than I have entertained towards any other living creature at any time of my life'. This is confirmed by his entry in his notebook:

> My world, my work, my woman, all my own –
> What face but thine has taught me all that art
> Can be and still be nature's counterpart?

In all this Morris did not, as far as is known, deal either in self-pity or in recrimination. He gained a renewed internal happiness once his activities in socialism and public affairs had developed. 'Janey' disliked his socialist friends and even Bernard Shaw could make no impression on her, but this did not modify Morris's own enthusiasm in socialism.

As has been suggested, the major change came in his verse, and it was in this rarefied atmosphere that he constructed *The Earthly Paradise* (1868-1870). In the Prologue he removes himself to a medieval world, a world that is not Rossetti's nor Dante's, but rather Chaucer's, sane, clean, full of the light of common day:

> Forget six counties overhung with smoke,
> Forget the snorting steam and piston stroke,
> Forget the spreading of the hideous town;
> Think rather of the pack-horse on the down,
> And dream of London, small, and white, and clean,
> The clear Thames bordered by its gardens green.

His own function in this world is to relate a story such as a medieval tale-teller at a high table or a minstrel at an inn might have recited, free from the desire to give didactic bias or the emphasis of intricate phrasing. The verses which preface *The Earthly Paradise* seem to show that Morris realized the purpose and the limitation of the design:

> The heavy trouble, the bewildering care
> That weighs us down who live and earn our bread,
> These idle verses have no power to bear;
> So let me sing of names rememberèd,
> Because they, living not, can ne'er be dead,
> Or long time take their memory quite away
> From us poor singers of an empty day.
>
> Dreamer of dreams, born out of my due time,
> Why should I strive to set the crooked straight?
> Let it suffice me that my murmuring rhyme
> Beats with light wing against the ivory gate,
> Telling a tale not too importunate
> To those who in the sleepy region stay,
> Lulled by the singer of an empty day.

The whole of *The Earthly Paradise* is held within the closely prescribed frontiers of this world of beauty removed from life. In the Prologue Morris describes how medieval travellers from Norway set out for a land rumoured to possess the enchantment of eternal life. Their journey leads through many distresses to ultimate disillusionment, and as old, weary men they come to an island inhabited by descendants of ancient Greeks. With this background of mellowed sadness rest steals upon them, and they and the medieval Greeks, as old men, wearied of toil, tell each other tales to while the months away. The tales themselves form the central element in *The Earthly Paradise*; half of them are from classical sources, half from medieval, but they are all told in a medieval manner. Morris, while he interested himself in classical stories, preserved his distaste for classical methods of narration. In writing these stories Morris first chose one with a Greek theme, and *Cupid and Psyche*, one of the most successful tales, was probably the first to be written. He continued with *The Tale of Orpheus and Eurydice*, which he rejected as too weighty. He then attempted to render the quest of the golden fleece, which grew so elaborate in its detail that it found separate publication as *The Life and Death of Jason*. He continued with *Atalanta's Race*, the story of how Milanion outran Atalanta and thus gained her in marriage; *The Doom of King Acrisius*, a re-rendering of the Perseus story; *The Love of Alcestis*, which tells how Alcestis gave her life for Admetus, the theme used later by Browning in *Balaustion's Adventure*. *The Son of Croesus*, one of the shortest of the classical tales, recounted the death of Atys, and *Pygmalion and the Image* retold the story of the statue which with Venus's aid became a living figure. In *The Death of Paris* he described Paris's visit to Ida to see Œnone. *The Story of Acontius and Cydippe* told of the strange wooing of Cydippe by Acontius, a youth of obscure birth. *The Story of Rhodope* recounted how Rhodope became the wife of an Egyptian king. *The Golden Apples* was a brief rendering of the eleventh labour of Hercules. *Bellerophon at Argos* described Bellerophon's adventures at the court of Proteus, and *Bellerophon in Lycia* gave Bellerophon's adventures after he had offended Proteus's Queen. Morris's method was first to read the account of a legend in Lemprière's

Classical Dictionary and to amplify this with such sources as were easily available. Once he had the incidents in his mind he closed his source-books and retold the story, changing its proportion, motive, and incident to meet his own mood and the design of *The Earthly Paradise* as a whole.

The medieval stories were drawn from varied originals. Morris knew the *Gesta Romanorum*, and from this he drew themes for *The Proud King* and *The Man Born to be King*. From Mandeville's *Voyage and Travel* he extracted *The Lady of the Land* and *The Watching of the Falcon*. William of Malmesbury's *De Gestis Regum Anglorum* gave him *The Writing on the Image* and *The Ring Given to Venus*. Northern stories he gathered first from English books: *The Fostering of Aslaug* from Thorpe's *Northern Mythology*, and part of *The Land East of the Sun and West of the Moon* from *Yule Tide Stories* by the same author. *The Lovers of Gudrun* showed the beginnings of his own Icelandic reading in the *Laxdaela Saga*. The *Arabian Nights* yielded *The Man Who Never Laughed Again*. *Ogier the Dane* he found in a fourteenth-century French romance, *Ogier le Danois*, and *The Hill of Venus*, a rendering of the Tannhäuser legend, had an immediate source in Tieck's *Romances*.

The structure of *The Earthly Paradise* is reminiscent of Chaucer's framework for his *Canterbury Tales*. But Chaucer has variety of mood, humour, pathos, ribaldry, and grace; Morris, though the range of the stories is considerable, is held within a single mood dimly revealed, 'Like an old dream, dreamed in another dream'. Among the shorter stories *The Lady of the Land* shows Morris's power of adorning a simple tale with picturesque detail; of the more ambitious pieces *Cupid and Psyche*, drawn from Apuleius, is the most evenly successful. His method throughout is separated from the main nineteenth-century tradition in poetry. Shelley, Keats, Tennyson, and Browning had all used narrative, but with some ulterior motive; symbol or allegory or didacticism was mingled into the simple story elements, and mood and sentiment made more complicated and modern. For Morris the tale was simply a tale; he peddled these beautiful wares, unfettered by allegory, without concentration on mood or character. Nor is the story supported by rich coruscations of imagery: the language is easy like the narrative method. He substitutes for passion and sentiment the thronged pictures which arose easily to his pictorial mind, so that we forget human action in a dim pageantry of inanimate scenes. Yet it must be remembered that the tales are not merely narratives but the monologues of ageing, disillusioned men, told one to the other when glamour and romance, and the aching unrest of high feelings had faded. Morris could advance Chaucer's plea:

> Whoso shall telle a tale after a man,
> He moote reherse, as ny as evere he kan.

This slackened pace, consistent with the dramatic purpose, leaves the poem in some distant dreamland where the air is rarefied, the footfall silent, the wind noiseless, and where the reader, isolated from his own life, its philosophy and humour, is left contemplating the dimly mirrored forms of a dream enchantment. Morris has suffered for this apparent placidity, this pronounced reaction from analytical and introspective methods. It was in other ways that poetry was to develop in the closing decades of the century.

One poem in *The Earthly Paradise* stands apart. It is *The Lovers of Gudrun*, Morris's version of the *Laxdaela Saga*, the one poem in *The Earthly Paradise* based directly on Icelandic sources. Morris achieved little in verse that can compare with this poem. He combated the difficulties of a legend whose outline is tortuous and obscure, and elevated the central theme into a tragic conflict; and he tightens the whole fabric of his poetry to give it adequate presentation. Within this story we feel some return of the keener human interests present in his early verse; the dim multicoloured veil of *The Earthly Paradise* breaks apart, and we see Kiartan, Bodli, and Gudrun, mighty opposites, capable of tragic suffering and the tragic strength of endurance. For Morris found in the Northern literature, beyond a mere collection of stories and a new literary influence, a view of life, heroic, fatalistic, where action dominated thought, and suffering was endured with a dogged, unmurmuring acquiescence. He has expressed in a number of lines written in the manuscript of his translation of the *Eyrbyggia Saga* the effect of this northern *Weltanschauung* on his mind:

> Tale-teller, who 'twixt fire and snow
> Had heart to turn about and show
> With faint half-smile things great and small
> That in thy fearful land did fall,
> Thou and thy brethren sure did gain
> That thing for which I long in vain,
> That spell, whereby the mist of fear
> Was melted, and your ears might hear
> Earth's voices as they are indeed.
> Well ye have helped me at my need!

The interest in the Northern literature preludes a still wider human interest which gained its expression in politics rather than in poetry. With this intrusion he comes out of the craftroom where in the middle years his beautiful wares have been prepared and joins with the thought and endeavour of his own century once again. A passage in one of the Lectures[8] recounts an incident which seems a symbol of the changing sympathies of his life:

Look you, as I sit at my work at home, which is at Hammersmith, close to the river, I often hear go past the window some of that ruffianism of which a good deal has been said in the papers of late, and has been said before at recurring periods. As I hear the yells and shrieks and all the degradation cast on the glorious tongue of Shakespeare and Milton, as I see the brutal reckless faces and figures go past me, it rouses the recklessness and brutality in me also, and fierce wrath takes possession of me, till I remember, as I hope I mostly do, that it was my good luck only of being born respectable and rich that has put me on this side of the window among delightful books and lovely works of art, and not on the other side, in the empty street, the drink-steeped liquor shops, and the foul degraded lodgings.

He broke the window; he stepped out into the world; he came to strange places – the hustings, the police court, and the dock. It is fortunate that before politics became the dominant expression of this changed mental consciousness he had leisure to give it poetic expression in *Sigurd the Volsung* (1876). He experimented in both rhythm and vocabulary in this poem. Technically the verse may be described as a rhyming couplet of six feet, frequently anapaestic in movement with a hypermetrical syllable before a pause in the middle of the line. It resembles closely in effect the metre of the *Nibelungenlied*, except that Morris has used the anapaest generously in developing the movement of his line. The monotony of the fourteen-syllable line is missing, and for the rhymelessness of blank verse has been substituted a form capable of lyrical strength, strong, adaptable, varied; its invention and use constitute one of Morris's most considerable prosodic achievements. The vocabulary has strong Anglo-Saxon elements and is coloured by the insertion of words and phrases, such as 'bath of the swan' for the sea, which look as if they had been paraphrased out of Old English poetry. This contact with Old English verse is strengthened by the frequent use of alliteration. The story is told in four books, of which the first recounts the life of Sigmund, Sigurd's father. The theme here dwells with scenes of horror and incest, grim and inhuman in outline, yet essential to the main narrative as indicating the Volsung tradition from which Sigurd springs. In the second book Morris recounts Sigurd's education by Regin, who knows the secret of the gold of Andvari, and in the moving scenes at its close Sigurd gains supernatural insight into Regin's treachery, kills him, and seizes the treasure. He rides away until he reaches Hindfell, where he awakens Brynhild from an enchanted sleep and pledges love to her. The third book has an intricate movement, and includes Sigurd's fatal marriage to Gudrun, and Brynhild's marriage to Gunnar the 'Niblung', both achieved by the crooked ways of magic, and it culminates in the death of Sigurd and Brynhild and the passing of Andvari's gold to the 'Niblungs'. The fourth book is Gudrun's revenge. This she achieves, but not before the 'Niblungs' have buried the gold in the Rhine, so that with the death of Gunnar, the last of their race, its secret is lost. The narrative closes as Gudrun plunges into the sea to be carried away to fresh adventures:

> Then Gudrun girded her raiment, on the edge of the steep
>   she stood,
> She looked o'er the shoreless water, and cried out o'er
>   the measureless flood:
> 'O Sea, I stand before thee; and I who was Sigurd's wife,
> By his brightness unforgotten I bid thee deliver my life
> From the deeds and the longing of days and the lack I
>   have won on earth,
> And the wrong amended by wrong, and the bitter wrong of
>   my birth.'

Morris found in *Sigurd* much that Keats found in *Hyperion*: the equation of being, set out in terms of myth. The Northern heroes believed in no Earthly Paradise, but in a quiet, strenuous enduring of the worst that life might bring. Morris never allowed this symbolic attraction of the myth to enter into his presentation of the legend, but it remains within his mind, a residuum left after the telling.

Icelandic stories have not entered easily into the imaginative memory which lies behind English poetry. There had been an Icelandic tradition since Gray, but it had not been a popular tradition. The Greek world has had centuries of mental companionship with our national tradition. Prometheus and Hercules, Helen and Ulysses have become names rich in association; Loki and Odin and Gudrun and Brynhild are comparative strangers. Morris, undaunted by these difficulties, attempts to retell the most titanic of all the Icelandic stories, an epic massive and at times inhuman. The importance which Morris attached to the Sigurd story can be seen from a prefatory passage in his prose translation of the *Volsunga Saga* in 1870: 'This is the Great Story of the North which would be to all our race what the Tale of Troy was to the Greeks – to all our race first, and afterwards, when the change of the world has made our race nothing more than a name of what has been – a story too – then should it be to those who came after us no less than the Tale of Troy has been to us.'

Morris's very honesty of purpose entangles him in the poem. As a piece of creative reconstruction the story might be simply that of Sigurd, but as a refashioning of a national myth the whole fate of the Volsung house must be displayed. The first book, *Sigmund*, becomes a poetic overture to the main theme, but its incidents, magical, incestuous, and grotesque, may perturb an imagination accustomed to the more placid outline of the Arthurian tales. The second and third books are relatively compact, but despite unity of theme some unity of emotional interest has been lost. Morris's method may have been right, but its diffuseness robs the poem of that supreme simplicity of outline which allows one in the *Iliad* and the *Odyssey* to summarize the central action in a single phrase. It remains a great but not a companionable poem; the reader is spectator and not protagonist; he must leave behind his own life before he comes to witness this strange conflict of the 'fell incensèd pass of mighty opposites'. *Paradise Lost* imposes a similar limitation on the reader: one may watch the scene, but it is too strange for one to act a part as one may do in *Hamlet*. But Milton, while he shuts the reader out of the narrative, welcomes him into the imagery, where human scenes and incidents caress the imagination with memories of experience. This Morris could not achieve. Further, despite the towering magnificence of the theme, he is still the Earthly Paradise story-teller, content to narrate without assaulting the imagination with phrases that conquer the mind and hold it in bewildered wonder.

In following Morris's Icelandic interests to their culmination one has to leave by the way the dramatic poem, *Love is Enough*, of 1872. It is strange that the possibilities of imitating the medieval morality play have not appealed more widely to modern writers. Morris adapts the form here, employing a somewhat overconscious artistry that impairs the fresh *naïveté* of the original. He uses five different verse measures to bring out the various sections of the poem; one can gain some intricate intellectual pleasure from the result, as one gains pleasure from the intricate pattern of a carpet, but the unerring and commanding effects which make great poetry are absent. Based on a theme in *The Mabinogion*, the central story in *Love is Enough* has a suggestion of *Alastor*, caught into a medieval setting. It recounts the journeyings of Pharamond, a king, who has left his kingdom and his victories for a dream country where he finds Love. He returns at length to his own people, only to find that he has been forgotten, and that his place is occupied by another. Yet he gains satisfaction from the fact that he has loved. Behind this simple outline of human action, Morris has inserted the symbolical figure of Love, and to his teaching the action of the poem seems dedicated. In his early speeches Love seems romantic and sensuous:

> Yea, in the heaven from whence my dreams go forth
> Are stored the signs that make the world of worth:
> There is the wavering wall of mighty Troy
> About my Helen's hope and Paris' joy:
> There lying 'neath the fresh dyed mulberry-tree
> The sword and cloth of Pyramus I see:
> There is the number of the joyless days
> Wherein Medea won no love nor praise:
> There is the sand my Ariadne pressed;
> The footprints of the feet that knew no rest
> While o'er the sea forth went the fatal sign:
> The asp of Egypt, the Numidian wine,
> My Sigurd's sword, my Brynhild's fiery bed,
> The tale of years of Gudrun's drearihead,
> And Tristram's glaive, and Iseult's shriek are here,
> And cloister-gown of joyless Guenevere.

Later in the poem these trappings of romance are laid aside and in their place Love decks himself in the sober garments of social duty and virtuous action:

> Have faith, and crave and suffer, and all ye
> The many mansions of my house shall see
> In all content: cast shame and pride away,
> Let honour gild the world's eventless day,
> Shrink not from change, and shudder not at crime,
> Leave lies to rattle in the sieve of Time!
> Then, whatsoe'er your workday gear shall stain,
> Of me a wedding-garment shall ye gain.

Morris within the poem seems searching for a philosophy of action. He found it on a grander scale in the Icelandic poems, and he applied it as seemed best to him in the socialism which occupied the later years of his life.

The life of action is difficult to combine with consistent creative work. Morris had always been a man of many activities, and yet he found time for poetry. When harassing political propaganda was added to the rest the poetry began to suffer. The translations of this last period have already been enumerated; they do not add to one's conception of Morris as a poet. Very different is the last volume, *Poems by the Way* (published 1891). Though it may do nothing to increase the sum of his achievement, it illustrates every aspect of his poetic activity. Early lyrics of *The Earthly Paradise* mood are there, including *A Garden by the Sea*, one of the most charming, gentle lyrics in all Morris's work, and one which he had already used in the fourth book of *The Life and Death of Jason*:

> I know a little garden-close,
> Set thick with lily and red rose,
> Where I would wander if I might
> From dewy morn to dewy night
> And have one with me wandering.

Icelandic lyrics represent the middle period, including the illuminating personal poem, *Iceland First Seen*, while the later enthusiasms are represented by socialist songs; further, certain lyrics, such as *Error and Loss*, suggest the essential moods of his poetical character, the melancholy and the pathos of 'lost delights' which enter even into the most brightly coloured of his poems.

The whole of Morris is not in his poetry. His interpretation of life lies largely in his workshops, his reform of domestic decoration, his revival of fine printing, his keen sense of political and social injustice. One might see his importance more fully if one could gather up his various activities into a single conception of his personality. He himself stands between us and that. 'I abominate introspective poetry', he himself wrote, and apparently his letters were few. Miss May Morris has written to me on this:

> I don't think he wrote at great length on all the subjects he had at heart – considering the amount of work he got through in his life, there would not have been time for it. Of course there are interesting letters, but, I think, no sustained correspondence with friends on literary subjects.

He is the bluff, open-hearted, active man, whose states of mind remain unanalysed; the only way to trace him is to see the mark of his activity on the history of the century.

Minor Pre-Raphaelite Poets:

William Bell Scott, William Allingham, Thomas Woolner, Arthur O'Shaughnessy, John Payne, Philip Bourke Marston, William Sharp (Fiona Macleod)

'Pre-Raphaelite' is but a lightly fitting formula even when applied to Rossetti, Morris, and Swinburne; still less does it have any close significance when used to discriminate between the work of the minor writers of the period. In this chapter those poets have been gathered together who had some personal or technical allegiance to one of the three major poets, but they have not been cramped to do service to a theory, and their work is described even when it departs from Pre-Raphaelite purposes. Rossetti's personal influence upon his contemporaries emerges: he could fire a sluggish mind to produce better work even though that work may not be a close imitation of his own poetic methods. Yet it must be admitted that the Pre-Raphaelites produced no great successor. The movement was itself in many ways a last phase, romanticism working itself out technically and spiritually, and the minor writers instead of finding new themes and forms are driven to imitation and repetition on patterns already tried. Much of their work, however, is outside the central formulas and in lyric they possess more variety and spontaneity than has generally been allowed.

William Bell Scott[1] (1811-1890) is worth remembering mainly because he was one of Rossetti's close personal associates. Further, if one is to accept the views and evidence advanced in Lona Mosk Packer's biography of Christina Rossetti, he was the main emotional influence in Christina's life. He was the son of Robert Scott, an Edinburgh engraver. Trained as an artist, he assisted his father for a number of years. He was writing poetry as early as 1834 and he continued to write till the late eighties. In 1837 he moved to London, buoyed by optimistic hopes of supporting himself by engraving and painting, but the prospect of matrimony and the attraction of a secure income drove him back to the provinces in 1843 as a design master at Newcastle upon Tyne. Here he remained for over twenty years and he led a busy life, for apart from professional duties he executed drawings and paintings, acted as a critic of painting and literature, and wrote poetry. His marriage, as described in the chapter on Christina Rossetti, seems to have been a nominal affair, and his wife seems to have consented to the numerous outlets that his amorous nature required. In 1859 he formed the most important intimate attachment of his life, a friendship with Miss Alice Boyd of Penkill Castle, Ayrshire: he visited her frequently and, on his introduction, Dante Gabriel Rossetti was also her guest, as was Christina. In 1870 he settled in London once again, at Chelsea, and gathered around him a considerable literary acquaintance. In his last years he wrote his *Autobiographical Notes*, posthumously published in 1892, valuable not only as a personal record but for the numerous portraits he gives of the Pre-Raphaelite group, though it is marred by his unkindly portrait of Gabriel and his general mood of disparagement of his friends. His last years, marred by *angina pectoris*, were spent under the care of Alice Boyd at Penkill.

Bell Scott's published works are numerous: he edited Shakespeare, Coleridge, Scott, Keats, and others; he wrote numerous lives of painters, and histories of art – useful work, but of little permanent value. His poetry may one day attract the bibliographer; it was published now in London, now at a provincial press, and the earlier volumes are difficult to procure. In 1838 appeared *Hades or The Transit*, to which is added an ode on *The Progress of Mind*; then followed *The Year of the World* (1846), a philosophical poem; *Poems* (Newcastle and London, 1854); *Poems* (London, 1875); *A Poet's Harvest Home* (1882); and an enlarged edition of the same volume in 1893. The difference in format in these volumes is of interest. *Hades* is a poverty-stricken little volume in grey-brown cloth, and so are some of the earlier volumes; but *Poems* (1875) is a rich decorative volume, with etchings by Alma-Tadema and by Bell Scott himself.[2]

The poetry of Bell Scott divides itself into clearly defined periods. The early work derived from the Spasmodic School has a kinship in ambition with the great things in poetry; unfortunately it has not an equal kinship in accomplishment. To write on religious and philosophical themes, to make Blake and Shelley one's masters, is also to demand of the gods the gift of genius. *Hades*, a poem in irregular verse reminiscent of Shelley's early poetry, deals with the refashioning of the soul in the underworld. It attempts much more than it achieves: the thought is vaporous, and technically it is equally deficient. The same criticism applies to the accompanying *The Progress of Mind*, an irregular ode, the suggestion of which Scott ascribes to Shelley. The verse exploits irregularity for the development of poetical rhetoric. *The Year of the World* (1846), an even more ambitious piece, gained the praise of Emerson and Rossetti, and apparently of nobody else. Scott has described the purport of the poem in his *Autobiographical Notes*. A dull 'cosmic poem', its scheme and opening books result from the study of Blake, while the last book is due to Scott's absorption of Shelley's combined belief in radicalism and science. Both influences are modified by Scott's own religious beliefs, which were more conventional than those of either of his masters. The poem has little to commend it philosophically, and less poetically. Blank verse is the main medium, and as Bell Scott could have learnt from Shelley, blank verse leaves no room for mediocrity. The poem is a tomb of its own dead verse; the verse of *Orion*, to which it bears some similarity, is immeasurably superior.

After 1846 the religious and philosophical poems ended; the influence of Rossetti came into Bell Scott's poetical work. As a young aspirant, Rossetti had written to Bell Scott an extravagant eulogy of his early poetry; he found such excellence in Bell Scott that he sent the manuscript of *The Blessed Damozel* to be revised by the author of *The Year of the World*. Their acquaintance developed into friendship, and the disciple remained as the master. The influence is seen less clearly in *Poems* (1854) than in *Poems* (1875). The earlier volume is a collection of miscellaneous lyrics, some on philosophical themes, but many showing an interest in ballad, in medievalism, and in mystery, all a direct outcome of Pre-Raphaelite contacts. In *Poems* (1875) Scott collected a number of early pieces and added many new poems. His preface suggested that the volume contained all of his poetry that he would most wish to preserve. How clearly Rossetti caused a momentary glow in Scott's sluggish poetic spirit can be seen in the ballad *Lady Janet, May Jean*, with which *Poems* (1875) opened:

'Tween sleeping and waking, 'tween fever and fear,
The lady Janet, May Jean,
Felt her mothering hour draw near;
So wearily dreaming 'tween fever and fear;
The shards have cut the shoeless feet.

It is true that the poem retained a certain obscurity which Rossetti was the first to observe, but the poetical accomplishment had advanced a long way from the bleak verse of *The Year of the World*. It was in such verses and in a few ballads, such as *Kriemhild's Tryst*, that Scott quickened for a while into poetry, but only a little while. The last volume, *A Poet's Harvest Home*, had the virtue of being simple; it is a collection of short lyrics which Scott wrote in the early eighties as an old man.

Very little of Scott's verse has the magic and glamour of his Pre-Raphaelite models. His large poetic purposes never gained fruition, and his prose prefaces, with their solemn air of mock modesty, have an atmosphere of the unreal bred from pretension. He set out his position in poetry in the preface to the 1875 volume: 'No external or adventitious merits, nor even purely intellectual qualities, can altogether determine the value of poetry. It must affect us like music or wine, but it must certainly have wisdom, like an instinct, directing it from within. Every excellent poetic work has a physiognomy of its own, an organic character of its own, the possession or non-possession of which the world will sooner or later sympathetically determine.' By this high tribunal not much of Scott's poetry stands exempt from condemnation. In a few of his lyrics only did he approach excellence, and most of what is good derives from the fructifying contact with Rossetti and the other Pre-Raphaelites.

William Allingham[3] (1824-1889) was mainly independent of Pre-Raphaelite traditions, but he was a friend of the Pre-Raphaelites. He admired Rossetti; some of Rossetti's best letters were written to him, and it was Rossetti's personality, if not his poetry, that emboldened him into the achievement of creative work. An able minor poet, he is free to a considerable extent from English contemporary influences, though he has his contacts with nineteenth-century Irish literature. He knew the great poetic names of his time: Leigh Hunt encouraged him as a young poet; Rossetti, Tennyson, and Browning listened to his opinions with respect; he was allowed to argue with Carlyle and to be the friend of Coventry Patmore. Born at Ballyshannon, Donegal, in 1824, Allingham, after a meagre education, followed his father's occupation of bank official, but later gained a post in the Customs, which he occupied from 1846 to 1870. He paid frequent visits to London, where he was fortunate in his contacts with men of letters. He became a contributor to periodical literature, and in 1870 he retired from the Customs to become sub-editor of *Fraser's Magazine*. In 1874 he succeeded Froude as editor, and continued in this post until 1879. The last decade of his life was spent first at Witley in Surrey and later at Hampstead. He died in 1889.

His poems were printed in many different forms, and finally gathered with a fresh arrangement into a collected edition (1889-

1893). His first volume was *Poems* (1850), and selections from this, with some new poems, appeared as *Day and Night Songs* (1854). In 1855 a new selection, *The Music Master*, was issued, and a further rearrangement in 1860 appeared as *Day and Night Songs and the Music Master*. In 1860, under the pseudonym 'Giraldus', he issued *Nightingale Valley*, 'a great number of the choicest lyrics and short poems in the English language'; he included six of his own pieces among these 'choicest lyrics'. *Laurence Bloomfield in Ireland*, Allingham's main work, and his only long poem, appeared in 1864 and was frequently reissued. In 1877, in *Songs, Ballads and Stories*, he reprinted many of his poems and added some new ones, so that all his most representative lyrical verse can be found in this volume. In 1883 he published *Evil May-Day*, which W. B. Yeats has described as 'a heavy argumentative experiment in philosophic poetry', and a drama, *Ashby Manor*, partly in blank verse, dealing with the Civil War period. In 1884 appeared *Blackberries*, a volume of poetical aphorisms; and in 1887 *Irish Songs and Poems*; illustrations, made by Rossetti and Millais for earlier volumes, were re-used in this edition. His wife, Helen Allingham, a watercolour painter of distinction, collected a number of his miscellaneous poems and fragments under the title *By the Way* (1912). Apart from these volumes of verse, Allingham issued a volume of selections, a collection of English ballads (1864), a series of travel sketches, and a collection of miscellaneous essays, *Varieties in Prose* (1893). A number of his fairy poems were also issued separately from time to time.

Of his early pieces, *The Music Master* is a simple story of love and untimely death, told in the manner of Wordsworth's early ballads, but with some eighteenth-century mannerisms. Similarly, *The Pilot's Song* and *Lady Alice* are simple ballad narratives, well turned, but adapted to the unsophisticated taste of the *Household Words* audience; it was his approach to broadside literature and the popular Irish song. He wrote also a few poems for children, fairy pieces of delightful movement and fancy, and here he attained to more individual and imaginative work. Of these lyrics, *The Fairies*, a nursery song, which has been frequently reprinted, is rightly the best known:

> Up the airy mountain,
>   Down the rushy glen,
> We daren't go a-hunting
>   For fear of little men;
> Wee folk, good folk,
>   Trooping all together;
> Green jacket, red cap,
>   And white owl's feather!

This mood of fancy, as airy as Mercutio's Queen Mab speech, he repeated less successfully in lyrics and ballads of Irish suggestion and frequently with themes of magic, as in *The Witch-Bride*. He possessed, further, the power of setting down occasionally an impression in its uttermost simplicity and risking the possibilities of the banal. An extreme example is found in a short poem in *Evil May-Day* (1883):

> Four ducks on a pond,
> A grass-bank beyond,
> A blue sky of spring,
> White clouds on the wing;
> What a little thing
> To remember for years –
> To remember with tears!

If the words seem too simple they are given power, as are the words of many of Allingham's lyrics, when once they are put to music. He attempted the same method in nature lyrics such as *An Evening*, where mere statement set by statement reconstructs the image of a mood:

> A sunset's mounded cloud;
>   A diamond evening-star;
> Sad blue hills afar;
>   Love in his shroud.
>
> Scarcely a tear to shed;
>   Hardly a word to say;
> The end of a summer day;
>   Sweet Love dead.

The emphasis is upon mournfulness, that grey, autumnal sadness which may be a product of his Irish studies. In certain lyrics he exploited this romantic melancholy for its own sake, and constructed in *Æolian Harp*, *Would I Knew*, and *Therania* poems reminiscent of Rossetti and Tennyson. Here the sombre melody and twilit atmosphere are Allingham's closest approach to the Pre-Raphaelite manner.

Much in Allingham does not live up to the quality of his best work. Yet there is ample evidence that he strove to fashion his experience into adequate poetical form. Referring to *Laurence Bloomfield in Ireland*, he wrote in his *Diary*: 'It's not properly compacted as to plan, and never will be now. But with indefinite time at command I should most probably, as so often before, have tried a dozen different shapes and ended by throwing the thing aside.' The hundreds of bright, keen lines collected in *By the Way*, the glittering waste from the workshop of an honest craftsman, show how he revised and rejected in his work.

Laurence Bloomfield in Ireland by its length and its accomplishment will remain his most memorable poem. The form is the heroic couplet, showing study of Pope, Goldsmith, and Crabbe, a sudden and refreshing example of cool eighteenth-century verse amid the more perfervid styles of the late nineteenth century. The theme is a study of contemporary Ireland, seen in the return to his Irish estates of Bloomfield, English-educated, idealistic. The dinner of the wealthy landlords, the portrait of the agent, Pigot, the Ribbon Lodge plotters, the evictions, the poor farms and homes of the peasants, are all so clearly conveyed that one can credit Turgeniev's comment that he had not understood Ireland until he read this volume.[4] The poem was first written for periodical publication in *Fraser's Magazine*, and it lacks a consistent unity of form. In compensation it possesses freshness, and alert couplets give a neat satiric flavour to the description:

> Grown sick of London's huge and flimsy maze,
> Polite, luxurious, ineffectual days.

So Allingham begins a description of Bloomfield's mood on his return to Ireland, and he is equally compact in his comment on the landlord, Sir Ulick Harvey:

> His judgment feeble and his self-will strong,
> He had his way, and that was mostly wrong.

Allingham comments in his preface on the difficulty of making poetry out of contemporary circumstance. It is a difficulty not to be minimized, yet he contrived to restore to poetry some of those purposes which it possessed in Dryden, of illuminating a modern theme.

Pre-Raphaelite interest, though it entered into some of his lyrics, does not explain him fully as a poet. His sources of suggestion lay somewhat apart from those of other Irish poets. He caught some of the landscape of Ireland, her dim grey background out of which fairies and magic shapes appear, and most compactly he described her contemporary life. When the best has been isolated from his work he appears as a writer of individuality, who can use poetic methods with economy to attain effects clearly identifiable as his own.

Thomas Woolner[5] (1825-1892) was among the original members of the Pre-Raphaelite Brotherhood, and his verses, *My Beautiful Lady* and *Of My Lady in Death*, stand as the first contribution in the original number of *The Germ*. Apart from a few short verses in the later numbers of *The Germ*, they are the sum of his poetic work at this period. His chief artistic endeavour was to express himself through sculpture, and Bell Scott reports that he once said, 'But poetry is not my proper work in this world; I must sculpture it, not write it.' He had been trained from an early age as a painter and sculptor, and only after meeting Rossetti and his associates in 1847 did he turn his attention to literature. In sculpture he was ambitious but not successful at first, and in 1852 he decided to go out to Australia to try his luck in the gold diggings. The mines proved less remunerative than the studio, and in 1854 he was back again in England. From that time his success as a sculptor was continuous; he made medallions of most of his distinguished contemporaries, and this led in time to more ambitious commissions. He gained the friendship of Tennyson and Mrs Tennyson, and executed a popular bust of Tennyson in 1857. Further, according to Dr Richard Garnett,[6] it was Woolner who gave to Tennyson the narrative basis for *Enoch Arden* and for *Aylmer's Field*. Poetry came fitfully amid his preoccupations as a sculptor. *My Beautiful Lady*, expanded from *The Germ*, appeared in 1863; *Pygmalion* in 1881; *Silenus* in 1884; *Tiresias* in 1886; *Poems* (*Nelly Dale* and *Children*) in 1887. The example of Woolner's work most generally known is neither a sculpture nor a poem, but the delicate vignette which was reprinted as a prefatory illustration to early editions of Palgrave's *The Golden Treasury*.

In poetry his vein is a thin one, with almost as little gold as he himself found in the Australian diggings. 'Poetry is not my proper work'; the words were a gesture imitative of Rossetti, but they were the truth. The only poems by Woolner that have a compelling quality are the two lyrics in *The Germ*. Coventry Patmore admired these pieces and they have something of the clear honesty of motive which distinguishes Patmore's *The Angel in the House*. When Woolner published a whole volume entitled *My Beautiful Lady*, the original fragments had been inflated by the addition of blank verse and couplet passages, and heaviness had intruded where lightness was before. Even the fragments themselves have been modified, not without mutilation. If *The Angel in the House* was the model for these expansions, it was a model that led Woolner astray. The only moment when fresh poetic quality wakened in Woolner was during the years in the late forties when he first met Rossetti and the other Pre-Raphaelites. It was then that he wrote the fragmentary lyrics on 'My Lady' which hold within them the sum of his poetic individuality:

> I love my lady; she is very fair;
> Her brow is white, and bound by simple hair;
>   Her spirit sits aloof, and high,
>   Altho' it looks thro' her soft eye
>   Sweetly and tenderly.

Through this and other stanzas of *My Beautiful Lady* music may be tenuous, but it has a note which is Woolner's own.

The rest of Woolner's work belongs to a later period and has very different characteristics. The friendship of Tennyson allured him into classical blank-verse themes: *Pygmalion*, *Silenus*, and *Tiresias* are mainly in blank verse, but choric interludes are allowed to intrude. *Silenus* is more successful than the others, but Woolner is in a tradition and has little of his own to add. When all has been said of Woolner he is a very minor poet. Yet a comparison of *My Beautiful Lady* in the first number of *The Germ* with Woolner's other poems serves to show how Rossetti's personality quickened the imagination of those around him.

Mystery surrounds the life of Arthur William Edgar O'Shaughnessy[7] (1844-1881). He was credited with being a natural son of Lord Lytton, and it was said that he took the maiden name of the Irishwoman who was his mother. His education was private, and at the age of 17 he was already earning his living as a junior assistant in the library of the British Museum. In 1863 he was appointed to an assistantship in the zoological department. As he knew nothing of natural history, the appointment caused much offence to zoologists, but he worked strenuously and became an authority on certain sections of his subject. His environment, as it is described in Mrs Moulton's life, does not seem to have been the likeliest for a poet: 'A queer little subterranean cell, strongly scented with spirits of wine, and with grim creatures pickled all round him in rows on rows of gallipots.'

He had friends, principally John Payne, the poet and translator, and J. T. Nettleship, the painter who did the designs for his first volume of poetry, *An Epic of Women*. He found an entry into the literary society, and at Ford Madox Brown's house he met the Rossettis, and Morris, Bell Scott, Swinburne, and Theodore Watts-Dunton. As early as 1869 O'Shaughnessy and Payne contracted a friendship, which influenced their poetical work, with a Mrs Helen Snee. There was a close attachment between Helen Snee and O'Shaughnessy which seems to have ended in 1873, when he married Eleanor, the daughter of Westland Marston and sister of Philip Bourke Marston. O'Shaughnessy's poetry is found in four volumes: *An Epic of Women* (1870); *Lays of France* (1872); *Music and Moonlight* (1874); and *Songs of a Worker* (1881), a posthumous publication. He also published, with his wife, a volume of prose stories for children, *Toyland* (1875). The bulk of his poetical work is found between 1870 and 1874, the period which marks his friendship with Helen Snee.

An Epic of Women, his first volume, which was favourably received, contains two contrasted groups of poems. One is miscellaneous, with an emphasis on sentiment and the ideality of love; the thought in these poems is thin and desultory, and their movement vaporous. Their quality can be seen in *The Lover*:

> But more and more he seemed to seek
>   My heart: till, dreaming of all this,
>   I thought one day to hear him speak,
>   Or feel, indeed, his sudden kiss
>   Bind me to some great unknown bliss:
> Then there would stay upon my cheek
>   Full many a light and honied stain,
>   That told indeed how I had lain
> Deep in the flowery banks all day;
>   And round me too there would remain
> Some strange wood-blossom's scent alway.

The other group gives the volume its strange title. Here the poems are precise and mordant, without any of the vague and intangible qualities of the miscellaneous pieces. The governing mood is one in which passion is portrayed with a cynical emphasis on the faithlessness of woman who awakens it. The opening piece, *Creation*, adapting a motto from Boccaccio, shows woman created from all the most radiant of unearthly elements:

> So the beginning of her was this way:
>   Full of sea savours, beautiful and good,
>   Made of sun, sky, and sea – more fair than they –
> On the green margin of the sea she stood.

> The coral colour lasted in her veins,
>   Made her lips rosy like a sea-shell's rims;
> The purple stained her cheeks with splendid stains,
>   And the pearl's colour clung upon her limbs.

God, according to the legend, having made woman, loved her, and only when He had grown weary did He give her to man, splendid but incomplete:

> He feasted her with ease and idle food
>   Of gods, and taught her lusts to fill the whole
> Of life; withal He gave her nothing good,
>   And left her as He made her – without soul.
>
> And lo, when He had held her for a season
>   In His own pleasure-palaces above,
> He gave her unto man; this is the reason
>   She is so fair to see, so false to love.

The poems which follow exploit the mood of this introductory poem and portray crucial incidents in the lives of famous women, *The Wife of Hephæstus*, *Cleopatra*, and *The Daughter of Herodias*. Decorative, sensuous, and cynical, these studies are the most compact and effective work that O'Shaughnessy achieved. Their quality can be estimated from the opening stanza of the first of the Cleopatra poems:

> She made a feast for great Marc Antony:
>   Her galley was arrayed in gold and light;
> That evening, in the purple sea and sky,
>   It shone green-golden like a chrysolite.

A French influence is obvious in O'Shaughnessy's first volume. He spoke French fluently, and he knew the poetry of nineteenth-century France – Hugo, Leconte de Lisle, Baudelaire, and Gautier. One poem, *Bisclavaret*, which is prefaced with a motto from Marie de France, showed an interest in medieval French poetry. In Marie de France the lay tells of the lady whose husband was turned into a werwolf; O'Shaughnessy constructs in a dramatic monologue the thoughts of the man-beast. Though an effective poem once the situation has been understood, he has made no effort to reveal the situation by those allusive details which distinguish Browning's monologues.

His second volume, *Lays of France*, is a series of five poems based on five of the *Lais* of Marie de France: *Laustic*, or *The Lay of the Nightingale*; *The Lay of the Two Lovers*; *Chaitivel*, or *The Lay of Love's Unfortunate*; *The Lay of Eliduc* and *The Lay of Yvenec*. These O'Shaughnessy has rendered in the manner of a medieval romance writer. He has abandoned the octosyllabic couplets of Marie de France and used an irregular rhyming stanza with an octosyllabic line, suggestive of the stanzas of the medieval romances. He has inflated the *Lais* to three or four times their original size; Marie de France's *Laustic*, for instance, has one hundred and sixty lines, while the corresponding poem in O'Shaughnessy has over seven hundred and fifty. In the original, brevity and succinctness are the two main charms, and one can find no adequate motive to compensate for O'Shaughnessy's expansion.

In 1874 O'Shaughnessy published a further volume of original lyrics, *Music and Moonlight*. Here an indefiniteness of purpose seemed to suggest that a halt has been called in his poetical progress. Its vocabulary and stanza, the very gesture of its speech, are more derivative than in the earlier work. Swinburne is followed on occasions with servility and throughout with excess, as in *The Disease of the Soul*:

> My red mouth fashioned for joy,
>   Rich bloom of the world's fairest hour,
> Is pale with faint kisses that cloy
>   And sadden and wither and sting;
> My form, like a blue-veined flower,
> Has learned to droop and to cower;
> And my loves are griefs that destroy
>   The lovers to whom I cling.

All the love poems, even those which are not Swinburnian, have lost the positive and satiric quality found in *An Epic of Women*.

The classical background which O'Shaughnessy used so freely

has been replaced in such poems as *Song of Palms* and *Azure Islands* by a vaguely oriental atmosphere, adapted, perhaps, in deference to the oriental enthusiasms of John Payne. As the first poem in this volume O'Shaughnessy placed the *Ode*, which anthologies were to make the best known of his poems:

> We are the music makers,
>   And we are the dreamers of dreams,
> Wandering by lone sea-breakers,
>   And sitting by desolate streams; –
> World-losers and world-forsakers,
>   On whom the pale moon gleams:
> Yet we are the movers and shakers
>   Of the world for ever, it seems.

With facile Swinburnian diction, and with a vague complacency of thought, the poem is saved by its pleasing melody. O'Shaughnessy has done better work, but for once he found a theme which he could express definitely and with emphasis. The title poem, *Music and Moonlight*, the longest of O'Shaughnessy's original pieces, attempted, among other things, to present in verse some of the effects of Chopin's music. The defects of O'Shaughnessy's poetry are more marked in this second volume and the positive qualities have declined. He was incapable of loading each rift with ore, and lazy, unmusical, meaningless lines come in. He had an excessive desire for decoration and for detail, qualities which led him away from precision to a vagueness that is occasionally unintelligible.

O'Shaughnessy's last volume, *Songs of a Worker* (1881), though a posthumous volume, was in the main prepared by him for publication before his death.[8] In part it is occupied with his translations from the French: François Coppée, Paul Verlaine, Ernest D'Hervilly, Sully Prudhomme, Henri Cazalis, Catulle Mendès. The original poems are of unequal strength. Some few of them in the series *Thoughts in Marble* possess the limited excellencies which his poetry can display: they return to the mood of *An Epic of Women* and possess an unusual combination of sensuousness with ironical commentary. The other poems attempt more idealistic themes, though with dubious success. Of these *Christ will Return* was the most substantial; it possessed a moral strenuousness absent in much of O'Shaughnessy's verse, though its poetical quality did not transcend that of effective rhetoric. The poem *Colibri*, with its flamboyant South American setting, showed how decorative elements baffle and betray a narrative theme in O'Shaughnessy's later work.

His weaknesses are palpable: they include an inability to maintain an even quality of verse in a single lyric, a vagueness in thought, an excess in decoration. The later work suffers in being blatantly derivative, and in adapting the pessimism of the greater Pre-Raphaelites and diluting it to a persistent languorousness. In some few poems a more independent mood emerges, and it is that mood which gives O'Shaughnessy his place as a minor poet at the close of the century.

John Payne[9] (1842-1916), O'Shaughnessy's companion in poetry, was the son of a prosperous family fallen on less happy days, and in early life he pursued a variety of occupations. He showed early an aptitude for languages, and he acquired, mainly by private study, an acquaintance not only with a number of European tongues but also with Turkish, Persian, and Arabic. In London, as a solicitor's clerk, in 1861, he was encouraged by reading Emerson to attempt original work, and a friendship with O'Shaughnessy and an acquaintance with the Pre-Raphaelite poets led him into literary circles. His first volume, *The Masque of Shadows*, was published in 1870; it was followed by a volume of sonnets, *Intaglios* (1871),[10] and in 1872 by *Songs of Life and Death*. These volumes mark the close of Payne's first period as a poet. In the following years he devoted himself to translation, both in verse and prose. His range was remarkable, and the authors and works which he rendered include Villon, *The Arabian Nights*, Boccaccio, Bandello, Omar Khayyám, Hafiz, and Heine. Amid these preoccupations he produced a new poem, *Lautrec*, in 1878, and *New Poems* in 1880. Later he returned again from translated to original work and issued a series of volumes:

Collected Poems (1902), *Vigil and Vision* (1903), *Songs of Consolation* (1904), *Carol and Cadence* (1908), *Flower o' the Thorn* (1909), *The Way of the Winepress* (posthumous publication, 1920). He died in 1916.

Payne suffered from extravagant contemporary praise, and subsequent complete neglect, apart from the overzealous partisanship of a few adherents. He would appear to have been a crotchety person, a mixture of considerable talents, little whims, and some venom, who flourished in the atmosphere of a coterie. Unfortunately, he believed that his age was against him, and the mood of his later poetry is sometimes marred by embittered disillusionment.

His original poetry seems puny when compared with his translated work. He was attracted by the same themes as O'Shaughnessy and has the same unevenness in accomplishment. He is susceptible to Pre-Raphaelite influences, but their significance diminishes in his verses. One can distinguish a number of prevailing themes: medieval stories and ballads of which *The Rhyme of Redemption, Sir Floris, Sir Winfrith* are the main examples; sonnets of sentiment and of philosophy with a prevailing emphasis on death; and dream poems or fantasies, such as *The Masque of the Shadows*. His most successful work is his simplest, his ballad and verse narratives. Here his work was a direct continuation of the Pre-Raphaelite interest, though his ballads are more frankly medieval than the novel and sophisticated poems evolved out of the form by Rossetti. *Sir Floris*, a Graal story, is the most successful example of his achievement in this form. Told in the manner of a medieval romance, without any further motive than the imitation of a medieval form, its success within its limited range is adequate. The romance stanza transmutes metrical deficiencies into quaintness, though the result is that the poet makes things too easy for himself. In *The Rhyme of Redemption* he attempted the ballad stanza, only to find that it was more strenuous and exacting than the long rhyming stanza of the romances, and he added to his difficulties by enslaving himself with internal rhymes. Of the shorter poems in this group *The Ballad of Shameful Death* is the most memorable, and is one of the outstanding poems in Payne's work. The thought of the piece is summarized in the lines from Baudelaire which form a motto to the poem:

> Le regard calme et haut,
> Qui damne tout un peuple autour d'un échafaud.

The motive is elaborated by the narrative in the poem:

> I go in the felons' cart, with my hands bound fast with the cord,
> And nothing of brave or bright in the death I ride toward:
> The people clamour and jeer with a fierce and an evil glee,
> And the mothers and maids that pass do shudder to look on me.

All this work shows a marked influence of William Morris, found less in theme, though Payne does retell the Rapunzel story in *Sir Winfrith*, than in the general method and conception. On more than one occasion he re-echoes the sentiment of the introductory verses to *The Earthly Paradise*, in which Morris refers to himself as 'An idle singer of an empty day':

> Ah! who shall cure the sickness of the time?
> Who shall bring healing to the wounded age?

Ballad and romance, though the most successful element in his poetry, form but a small portion of the whole. With the volume of sonnets *Intaglios* (1871) Payne began a career as a sonnet writer which he maintained to the end. The dominating element was sentiment, but criticism and the praise of poets and friends were also among his purposes. He was a talented versifier in his sonnets, clear in his detail, competent in diction, but without much to express. The following sonnet from *Intaglios* gives a conception of his skill, and shows equally the decorative elements which both he and O'Shaughnessy derived from Rossetti:

> A place of woven flowers and singing winds,
> Jewell'd with moss and plumed with nodding ferns;
> A hall of silver silence, wherein burns
> A soft star-glamour. Through the moss that binds
> Fern-roots with gold, a slow clear water winds,

And slackens into tiny pools of light,
Pale topaz, amethyst and chrysolite,
Set in the gilded tracery of the grass:
And there the charmed hours do lingering pass
Unwilling to forsake so fair a place.
In such a haunt I picture thee by day,
Stirring the air to rapture with the grace
Of thy sweet songs, and wonder of thy face
Until the slow West gloom to purple-grey.

The sonnets as a whole miss all urgency of expression; their detail and decoration arise and flourish, but their imaginative purpose is only dimly conceived.

The life of Philip Bourke Marston[11] (1850-1887) is a keen legend of misfortune. The fates had seemed favourable. He was the son of John Westland Marston (1819-1890), the writer of historical and poetic drama, who, if he could not offer his son a competence, could give him the companionship of the main literary figures of the day. But disaster after disaster followed in his life. At the age of 3, through a series of accidents, he lost his sight: partially at first, and then completely. Despite this calamity he contrived, largely through the help of his mother, to educate himself to literature. In 1870 his mother died. As a young man he became betrothed to Mary Nesbit; she died in 1871. In 1874 Oliver Madox Brown, his best friend, died suddenly. His sister Cicely died in 1878, and in 1879 his remaining sister, Eleanor, the wife of O'Shaughnessy the poet. With this melancholy roll-call of death recurring with such persistence in his life, we are prepared for the sadness of his poetry. His published work is found in three volumes: *Song-Tide* (1871) *All in All* (1875); *Wind-Voices* (1883).[12] In 1891 a posthumous volume, *A Last Harvest*, was issued by Louise Chandler Moulton, an American lady of letters who was a friend of many English poets of the period, and in 1892 she also issued his *Collected Poems*, including some additional material. Bourke Marston had a far wider recognition in America than in England

and during his later years he was dependent for an income largely upon American editors and publishers.

His poetry raises problems that are psychological as well as literary. What images from the world of experience can penetrate to a mind that saw dimly for a few years and then not at all? For Marston, sounds and depths and odours are more impressive than shapes and colours; the images of the sea and tides, and clouds, and, in kindlier moments, the qualities of flowers are the resources of his poetry. Above all, the varied qualities of sound suggest to his mind the imagery which normal men gain from visual sensation. *Song-Tide* contains a sonnet, *Speechless, Upon the Marriage of two Deaf and Dumb Persons*, which might be passed over as an exercise in the grotesque did it not suggest Marston's unusual consciousness of how each of the senses contributes to life. His infirmities led him here to a pathological study, but a kindlier mood dwells in most of his poems.

His main medium was the sonnet, with love as its theme, and intricate patterns of mood and phrase as its texture. Rossetti is the main influence, though Marston does not attempt any imitation of the colour and sensuous glamour of *The House of Life*, nor has he Rossetti's skill in intangible images, clearly seen but in dim light. Yet the general attitude to love, the emphasis on its supreme importance, and much of the poetical vocabulary, are directly inherited from Rossetti. The influence of Swinburne, who knew Marston and admired his verse, is present though less obviously and persistently. Further, he derived, partly from the Pre-Raphaelites and partly from the circumstances of his own life, that mood of spiritual nostalgia which finds no rest on earth nor hope in the life beyond the earth. In *Song-Tide* he attempted to track 'through its dark and devious windings a heart which, loving passionately and with reason, had, for all, no hope of ever meeting with the response for which it yearned'. In *All in All* he attempted to continue this analysis of love, now showing 'how the love, so longed for and despaired of, is at last vouchsafed with all attendant peace and blessedness, until the beloved one is withdrawn, and the mourner is left but a memory'. This second series, which possesses a most consistent mournfulness, is written with the memory of Mary Nesbit in his mind. The love theme expressed in sonnet form is less conspicuous in the final volume, *Wind-Voices*, and such poems as deal with it seem to suggest a happier mood, made buoyant by the thought of some final spiritual reunion. Marston wrote the sonnet in a variety of forms: he had mastered the medium though he allowed himself, as did Rossetti, considerable licence in rhyme. His verse had a certain inevitable monotony; images of troubled black waters pursue us and mock at us through his poems. The strange thing remained that, shut off from visual sensation, he could express so much. The crisis of the following poem, one in which Pre-Raphaelite imitation is most marked, is made dependent on an act of sight, 'lifting up my eyes, I looked'; and yet the poem is maintained with an almost complete independence of visual imagery:

> In places that have known my lady's grace,
>   Seeing how all my soul and life lay there,
>   I sat; when lo, so sitting, I was 'ware
> Of breath that fell in sighs upon my face,
> While like a harp, where through the night-wind plays
>   A sorrowful, delicious, nameless air,
>   A voice wherein I felt my soul had share
> Made music in the consecrated place.
>
> Then, lifting up my eyes, I looked, and lo!
>   A fair sad woman sitting all alone
>   Where Love brief while ago had made his throne:
> Against her pale still breast I leant my brow,
>   'Thy name,' I said, 'is Grief; take then my vow
>   That I and thou henceforward be as one.'

It is in the final volume, *Wind-Voices*, and in the posthumous *A Last Harvest*, that Marston seems to have experimented most freely outside the sonnet form, and as a welcome accompaniment there is more variety of mood than in the earlier volumes: *The Old Churchyard of Bonchurch*, a poem with Swinburnian reminiscence; *The Ballad of Monk Julius*, one of a number of simple narrative pieces; and the whole of *New Garden Secrets*, a continuation of earlier nature moods, suggest that Marston was maturing as a poet when he died in 1887 at the age of 37.

William Sharp (Fiona Macleod)[13] (1855-1905) was born at Paisley. Despite his desires to go to sea or to escape to the gipsies, his parents contrived to give him a regular education, including a period at Glasgow University. After a sailing voyage to Australia, taken to ward off consumptive tendencies, he obtained a clerkship in London and began to devote himself to literature. In 1881 he had the good fortune to meet Rossetti, who introduced him to men of letters. The rest of the life is marked by prolific production both in verse and prose. Immediately on Rossetti's death he wrote his biography (1882). This he followed with many other studies, including *Heine* (1888) and *Browning* (1890); he edited *The Canterbury Poets* and produced numerous essays, critical works, novels, and short stories. In addition to this varied activity he also wrote verse. His early work written under his own name included *The Human Inheritance* (1882), *Earth's Voices* (1884), and *Romantic Ballads and Poems of Phantasy* (1888), and some rhymeless verses, *Sospiri di Roma* (1891). Meanwhile Sharp had met in Rome a lady who seemed to carry within her memories of the heroic past of Greece and of the North. She stimulated him to convert these memories, particularly in their Gaelic features, into literary forms. Sharp seems to have alleged that when he wrote under the influence of this friend he was a second personality, and this other self he named Fiona Macleod. From 1890 he maintained a dual personality. Though writing still as William Sharp, he also produced under the name of Fiona Macleod works both in verse and prose, beginning in 1894 with a prose romance, *Pharais*. In verse the earliest volume was *From the Hills of Dream* (1897); two dramas, *The House of Usna* (mainly in prose) (1900), and *The Immortal Hour* (1900); other poems and prose rhythms were issued, and a posthumous collection appeared finally (1909-1910).

Sharp's early verse in *The Human Inheritance* shows poetic

ambition combined with unequal powers, and so it remained throughout his work. The title poem is a dim, visionary account of man's development, reminiscent of the early work of Bell Scott. Sharp created an atmosphere of diffused dreaminess which allowed a loose poetical texture:

> Below, the wide waste of the ocean lay.
> League upon league of moonled waters, spray
> And foam and salt sea-send: a world of sea
> By strong winds buffeted.

Much more concrete and effective is *Motherhood*, the first part of which, describing the birth-throes of a tigress, is Sharp's most decisive poetical composition. He used a Pre-Raphaelite detail for purposes of which the Pre-Raphaelites would not have approved. The detail, reminiscent at times of O'Shaughnessy, has gained from Sharp's own voyagings, and the grimness of the motive makes vivid contrast with his usual themes:

> Deep 'mid the rice-field's green-hued gloom
>   A tigress lay with birth-throes ta'en;
> Her swaying tail swept o'er her womb
>   As if to sweep away the pain
> That clutched her by the gold-barred thighs
> And shook her throat with snarling cries.
>
> Her white teeth tore the wild-rice stems;
>   And as she moaned her green eyes grew
> Lurid like shining baleful gems
>   With fires volcanic lighten'd through,
> While froth fell from her churning jaws
> Upon her skin-drawn gleaming claws.

Much of *Earth's Voices* he devoted to pastel studies of Nature, where the effect is usually marred by the diffuseness of the verse. In *Sospitra*, the outstanding poem in this volume, he returned to the metre of *Motherhood*, and to a narrative borrowed from Ouida. The poem has clarity, but it is infected with luxuriant and unnecessary epithets. As in the earlier volume he introduced a fresh, Australian background into a number of the poems. The

Romantic Ballads (1888) were Sharp's attempt to free the ballad from the 'literary' qualities which Rossetti had fastened to it. His performance is unequal. In *The Son of Allan* he remains Rossetti's disciple in movement and refrain, while *The Weird of Michael Scott* gains simplicity only by a thinness in thought matched to a glib facility of movement. In 1891 *Sospiri di Roma* shows how Sharp's tendencies towards tenuity of thought were encouraged by irregular and rhymeless verse. Such patterns leave all the responsibility for control with the poet, and Sharp is unable to restrain the dreamy rhetoric which rose so easily within his mind.

Despite all discussions on dual personality and psychic memory, the 'Fiona' poems are, both in theme and vocabulary, merely Sharp's fuller exploitation of romantic inclinations apparent in his earlier work. These, it has been suggested, were strengthened by memories of stories told by his old Highland nurse, and they certainly gained further definition by the reading he had done in preparing his edition of Ossian (1896). Nor was 'Fiona' as a poet, particularly as a dramatic poet, without the help and encouragement of W. B. Yeats. The resulting verse suffered from diffuseness, but its dim, twilight colouring resuscitated the interest of earlier romanticism in ruins, legends, and far-off forgotten things, seen through a mist of vague but not unpleasant Ossianic rhetoric. The following, which is the opening passage from *The Immortal Hour*, shows how mechanical is Sharp's use of the adjective which suggests atmosphere, and how loose is the texture of the verse:

> By dim moon-glimmering coasts and dim grey wastes
> Of thistle-gathered shingle, and sea-murmuring woods
> Trod once but now untrod . . . under grey skies
> That had the grey wave sighing in their sails
> And in their drooping sails the grey sea-ebb,
> And with the grey wind wailing evermore
> Blowing the dun leaf from the blackening trees,
> I have travelled from one darkness to another.

He seems like a gleaner going through all the places where romantic poetry has been harvested and gathering what is left into his verses. *The Immortal Hour* had the good fortune to attract Rutland Boughton as a possible libretto for his music, and as a result it has had a successful stage history. There is nothing in this play or in *The House of Usna* to suggest that they would have sufficient strength in themselves to survive as dramas.

The legend of Fiona Macleod gave the poetry of William Sharp a temporary popularity disproportionate to its merit. He never realized the distinction, essential in art, between the reception of experiences or emotions and their successful portrayal in an adequate medium. He is frequently content, as in *Dreams within Dreams*, to make a rhetorical statement and feel that his duty as a poet is at an end:

> I have gone out and seen the lands of Faery,
>   And have found sorrow and peace and beauty there,
>   And have not known one from the other, but found each
>   Lovely and gracious alike, delicate and fair.

If this be poetry, then anyone who has stated that some experience has moved him deeply is a poet. Similarly, he relies on a small cohort of romantically coloured adjectives and nouns which he sends into his poems: 'dim' and 'grey' occur profusely, while the 'flittermice' that steal in and out of the poems both of William Sharp and Fiona Macleod serve as liaison officers between the dual personality. He had a poetic quality which appeared most clearly when his verbal fluency could be restrained. It can be found in his early poems, and recurs, less consistently, in some of the short-line lyrics of the Fiona Macleod period, as in *The Vision*:

> In a fair place
>   Of whin and grass,
>   I heard feet pass
> Where no one was.
>
> I saw a face
>   Bloom like a flower –
>   Nay, as the rain-bow shower
> Of a tempestuous hour.

> It was not man, nor woman:
> It was not human:
> But beautiful and wild
> Terribly undefiled,
> I knew an unborn child.

Encouraged at one period by Rossetti and at another by Yeats, he had little of that passionate attachment to the craftsmanship of verse which marked their work, but he possessed a facile habit for refashioning the material from which romantic poetry is made.

6

Coventry Patmore and Allied Poets:
Coventry Patmore, Francis Thompson, Alice Meynell

The Pre-Raphaelites developed and exploited a fresh element in the later phases of English romanticism, but the boundaries of their poetical world excluded many themes. In the main, their aestheticism had no place for mystical or religious experience; Rossetti's contacts with Catholic ritual were wayward and unconvincing; Swinburne's efforts towards philosophical poetry and political poetry as in *Songs before Sunrise* were highly subjective and awkwardly self-conscious. William Morris had kept all such themes away from his verse; his politics were left to his prose, and religion was excluded both from prose and verse. Contemporary with the Pre-Raphaelites there existed more than one group, influenced largely by the Oxford Movement, who gave poetical expression to their religious beliefs and who had a formal contact with some section of the Christian Church. Christina Rossetti is the only Pre-Raphaelite who shared such interests. These religious poets do not all belong to one group; Coventry Patmore forms one centre and he had close personal contacts with Francis Thompson and Alice Meynell. The others are more heterogeneous. At one, imprecise, centre is Robert Bridges, though his own religious position is obscure; he begins as an Anglican, is obviously disturbed when his closest friend, Gerard Manley Hopkins becomes a Jesuit, and ultimately ends with a highly personal philosophy. But Bridges, by an accident of friendship, was a centre, however uncertain. He had felt that the Pre-Raphaelites, particularly Morris, had mutilated their medievalism by the exclusion of religion. He was led, therefore, to champion Canon Dixon, an associate of the Morris group, who remained faithful to his earlier beliefs, and similarly he praised Mary Coleridge. Above all, though later criticism has given him little credit for it, he was the first interpreter and editor of Gerard Manley Hopkins, the most original religious poet of the century, whose verse had such a marked influence on Bridges's own work. These divisions of the religious poets and mystical poets into groups are not close or exclusive: Hopkins, for instance, in his earlier verse had poetical contacts with Patmore, and was affected by Walter Pater, the philosopher of aestheticism. In the main, however, the associations of Patmore and of Bridges serve to group the important development of religious and philosophical verse in the later nineteenth century.

Coventry Kersey Dighton Patmore[1] (1823-1896) was the son of Peter Patmore, a journalist of the romantic period and an associate of Hazlitt and Lamb. The father seems, especially when compared with his son, an irresponsible character; he was reputed to have played a dishonourable part in a literary duel; he had absconded from his creditors, and he had published in 1854, the year before he died, three volumes entitled *My Friends and Acquaintances*, lively but indiscreet volumes of reminiscences which led to much controversy. His kindliest feature was his affection for his son, and the son was loyal to the father. His father encouraged Coventry Patmore's reading in such a way that at 15 he 'cared little for any but the classics of English literature'. His father also led Patmore to put together the early volume of his poems in 1844 and a publisher was ready at hand. Patmore's early life up to 1845 is one of freedom for education and the exercise of literature without financial embarrassment. He had no formal instruction apart from a few months in the Collège de France in 1839.

In 1845 his father fled from his creditors, and Patmore was

left to his own resources. A period of hackwork and penury followed, which was relieved when Monckton Milnes (Lord Houghton) nominated him to an appointment in the Printed Books Department of the British Museum (1846): 1846-1862 was the period of his graduation as a poet, and it synchronizes with his friendship with Tennyson, who had a strong influence over him. In 1847 he married Emily Andrews, and in 1854 he began publication of *The Angel in the House*, a poem intimately associated with her personality and his love of her. Patmore and his wife diverged widely in religious belief; it was not an open conflict, for Patmore seems to have restrained his High Church proclivities in deference to her merciless Puritanism. In 1862 Emily Patmore died. It was a crisis in Patmore's development. *The Angel in the House*, though continued, was developed in a new way, and never rightly completed. In 1864 Patmore adopted the Roman Catholic faith, and married a Catholic, Caroline Byles, who had been an intimate friend of Cardinal Manning. Miss Byles had a considerable fortune, and in 1865 Patmore gave up his position in the Museum and retired to Heron's Ghyll in Sussex. Here he developed the estate with practical efficiency, as he has described in *How I managed and improved my Estate*. Later he sold his property at a sound profit and settled in Hastings. His literary product during this new period is represented mainly by the Odes which centre in the various editions of *The Unknown Eros*. He engaged also in prose literary criticism and in journalism. Among his prose works were literary essays and a number of religious meditations, including *Principle in Art* (1889); *Religio Poetae* (1893); *The Rod, the Root and the Flower* (1895). Frederick Page collected in 1921 a number of the essays as *Courage in Politics and Other Essays, 1885-1896*, and to this last volume Page added a bibliography of Patmore's prose writings. In 1880 his second wife died, and in 1881 he married Miss Harriet Robson. When he was nearly 70 he met Alice Meynell and a deep friendship developed between them. After his death she burnt all his letters and there is little substantial evidence to support Derek Patmore's view 'that the ageing poet experienced a grand physical passion which Mrs Meynell rejected'.[1] He died at Lymington in 1896.

Patmore's revisions to his published work led to so many reissues that a number of bibliographical difficulties arise. The main editions have been listed in an appendix.[2] *Poems* (1844) was the earliest production, to be followed by *Tamerton Church-Tower and Other Poems* (1853). These two volumes form his early work. The middle period is filled by *The Angel in the House* and its associated poems. The first portion was issued in 1854 and the poem approached its final form in 1863. In 1878 *Amelia* appeared, with a number of early poems, and a long prefatory study of English metrical law; 1877 saw the first edition of *The Unknown Eros*, which was enlarged until it reached its final form in 1890.

Poems (1844) consists of four narratives told in lyrical measures. *The River* is a story of bride and bridegroom and of the lover who kills himself in failing to gain a love he has not expressed. *The Woodman's Daughter* is a ballad theme of love of high degree for the lowly maiden and its tragic consequence in child murder and madness, recalling Tennyson's *Dora* and *The Gardener's Daughter*, and less obviously Wordsworth's *Ruth*. *Lilian* is the monologue of a worthy lover rejected for a rival of lighter charm and less substantial worth. *Sir Hubert* is the story of the Falcon from Boccaccio's *Decamerone* (fifth day, novel nine). The interest lies not so much with the stories as with the tentative approach of a young writer to his medium. Widely differing influences have been suggested, and yet the main poetical inheritance seems openly revealed. Most definitely impressed is the bewitching melody of Coleridge. In *The River* Patmore uses a stanza reminiscent of Tennyson's *Sir Galahad*, and mingles into it memories derived from *The Ancient Mariner*:

> The guests are gay; the minstrels play;
>   The hall is liker noon than night;
> From side to side they toast the Bride,
>   Who blusheth ruby light;
> For youth and age, for clown and sage,
>   It is a cheerful sight!

The influence of Wordsworth is less frequent, but not less distinct. The Wordsworth of *Lyrical Ballads* modified by memories of Tennyson's English idylls intrudes clearly into such stanzas as the following from the opening of *The Woodman's Daughter*:

> In 'Gerald's Cottage', on the hill,
> Old Gerald, and his child –
> His daughter, Maud – dwelt happily –
> He worked, and she beguiled
> The long day at her spinning-wheel,
> In the garden, now grown wild.

Allied to these precise influences on diction, all the poems, except *Lilian*, have varieties of ballad form and a suggestion of medieval setting. *Lilian* stands apart, and it is from this poem that the mood of *The Angel in the House* derives. The subject is contemporary, and both form and theme have been strongly influenced by Tennyson's *Locksley Hall*. It is with rejection of romantic influence and the substitution of contemporary for medieval themes that Patmore's poetry is to find its development. Throughout this volume the verse is tentative, with some weak, flat lines, 'hammered up out of old nail-ends', as Tennyson said. Further, an unconscious bathos sometimes intrudes, as if one were in the presence of a humourless mind: so in *Lilian* the rival lover is described, with 'lips, still most expressive, though deform'd with quoting French'. Shining through the deficiencies are moments of observation and feeling keenly expressed, suggesting that a new poet is working his way through. For such an early volume there was much favourable comment and criticism. Browning admired the volume, so did Leigh Hunt, and *The Examiner* was kindly in a review, supposedly by Sir John Forster, and Bulwer Lytton wrote an appreciative letter. On the other hand *Blackwood's* were still scenting out any suggestion of romanticism in English poetry, and their comment on Patmore shows what virulence review criticism could still employ in 1844: 'Indeed we question whether the strains of any poetaster can be considered vile when brought into comparison with this gentleman's verses ... This is the life into which the slime of the Keatses and Shelleys of former times has fecundated.'

If the first volume suffered from contact with romanticism, the second, *Tamerton Church-Tower*, had to endure confusion with the work of Peter Patmore, the father, whose recollections appeared in 1854. Even in places where the work of father and son was not confused, the father's reputation told against the son. The volume consisted of a republication of the earlier pieces in revised form and of new poems. These show that Patmore had released himself from the romantics, except for memories of Wordsworth, and that he retained independence from the new influences of Browning, Arnold, and Rossetti. To Tennyson alone he owed kinship, particularly to the Tennyson of the English idylls. The title-poem had an original theme developed in simple ballad form. Three separate incidents are recorded: first, the poet and his friend ride out from Tamerton and discuss the ladies whom they are to wed; secondly, the friends, now wedded, are in a boat off the Cornish coast, and Blanche, the poet's wife, is drowned in a storm; thirdly, the poet himself rides by Tamerton and thinks of life and of his personal experience. The reconciliation to life with which the poem closes reaffirms the influence of Wordsworth, particularly in the scene when the poet is overtaken by a girl, an alms-taught scholar, who sings:

> 'Saint Stephen, stoned, nor griev'd nor groan'd
> 'Twas all for his good gain;
> For Christ him blest, till he confess'd
> A sweet content in pain.
>
> Then Christ His cross is no way loss,
> But even a present boon:
> Of His dear blood fair shines a flood
> On heaven's eternal noon.'

While the interpretation of human emotion through the memory of natural scenery recalls Wordsworth, the contemporary scene and the simple, unadorned verse is a continuance of the poetic purposes initiated in *Lilian*. Still, the final effect is inconclusive.[3]

Two of the new poems in this volume, *Ladies' Praise* and *Love's Apology*, suggest the road down which Patmore is to travel. These were adapted later as parts of *The Angel in the House*, and in them Patmore finds, for the first time, the content and mood of the poetry of his middle period. Love is the theme, a love not dominated by the sensual or enclosed by morality. For Patmore's conception of love arises in the sacramental and finds its expression in a mystical adoration:

> She is
> 'Our most effectual means of grace
> And casket of our worldly bliss'.

This newly discovered and individual approach to poetry and experience, Patmore developed in *The Angel in the House*. He was conscious of an original and difficult purpose. He pursued his task with courage, integrity, and success. The poem was to prove one of the most popular in the whole period and before his death a quarter of a million copies had been sold. Other poets had emphasized the erotic, the sensual, and the lewd aspects of love, and all these had some element of excitement possessing immediate if superficial attraction. For him the love in marriage of man and woman, nuptial love, should be the theme, and he would show its transcendency, for here was the root

> Of all our love to man and God.

His view of love was highly individual. Philosophically he had derived much from Swedenborg. In a manuscript note in the Princeton Collection he wrote that 'bodily conjunction without mutual passion' is something that 'horribly outrages' the 'personal sanctity' and 'though it would not do to preach the doctrine – it is absolutely true that adultery with such love is far less essentially immoral than the most exemplary marriage without it'.

The scene in *The Angel* was to be contemporary and the setting realistic. Patmore knew the dangers of the too-familiar setting, but he regarded its successful presentation as part of his task: the spirit of Dante was to be expressed in the setting of the Trollope novels. Similarly, he made simplicity the main feature of his verse form, the octosyllabic quatrain with alternate rhymes, and to those who found it 'easy reading' he replied that it was 'often damned hard writing'. Both versification and diction were influenced by Tennyson and derived from *The Day Dream*, *The Miller's Daughter*, and other poems of that order. It had no 'fatal facility', but it tends to dullness, and this Patmore triumphantly overcomes. His success is due to a very close study of Tennyson and possibly to his knowledge of Crabbe's use of the stanza.

The setting and theme must be recounted if Patmore's achievement is to be estimated. To elude the dangerous suggestion that the poem is autobiographical, he imagines a poet, Vaughan, writing to his wife on the eighth anniversary of their wedding a poem in which he recounts his love and wooing of her. This device Patmore employs in Books I and II, and his manipulation of it is more elaborate than is frequently allowed. Each book, apart from introductory and concluding poems, is divided into cantos, containing a number of separate but related poems. The earlier pieces are reflective, mainly abstract in vocabulary and philosophical in approach. These are followed by neat, realistic narratives, portraying incidents describing the development of love. Against these quiet recitals of apparently ordinary circumstance the main critical attack was directed. But this placid background was essential to Patmore's philosophy. He recounts how Dean Churchill had three daughters. When Felix Vaughan returned from abroad he discovered that of these he loved Honoria, and he was pleased to find that in his absence she had not been captured by his naval cousin Frederick Graham. The incidents which follow are trivial to the rational onlooker, but momentous to the lover: an invitation to dine; a gift of violets from Honoria; a formal talk with the Dean; a visit to church; a dance; and so to the engagement with which the first book closes:

> Her soul, which late I loved to invest
> With pity for my poor desert,
> Buried its face within my breast,
> Like a pet fawn by hunters hurt.

The actual incidents in *The Espousals* are still more difficult to control. The prattle of relations, and the good nights of the lovers,

> 'These "Good-nights", Felix, break my heart,
> I'm only gay till you are gone':

the county ball, Felix's attempts to become a politician by studying 'ethics, politics, and laws', and more successfully to escort the Dean's girls to the Cowes Regatta; and so home to his own house, which is soon to be hers. Even the most trivial of the incidents are often keenly contrived. For instance, on one occasion, Honoria sits playing the piano; Vaughan enters and Honoria reacts Aunt Maude's comment on the engagement:

> 'You, with your looks and catching air
> To think of Vaughan! You fool! You know,
> You might with ordinary care,
> Ev'n yet be Lady Clitheroe.'

And Honoria makes Vaughan take this very aunt in, on his arm, to dinner. So a mosaic of commonplace detail is pieced together into the story of the wedding, the honeymoon, and the meeting with Frederick Graham, the unsuccessful lover.

The texture of this poetry and its material are in revolt against all that nineteenth-century poetry had inherited from the romantic movement. It goes back in its acceptance of the commonplace scene to Crabbe and in its faith in the ordinary life to Wordsworth's ballads of 1798. Its strength can best be judged by comparison with either of those earlier exploitations of the same type of material. Frederick Page suggests that Patmore like Wordsworth carried his artistic theory too far and so offended against the decorum of verse, and this and not his characters and theme constitute any weakness he possessed. The main aspect of the romantic tradition accepted by the nineteenth-century poets was that of Coleridge and Keats, the marvellous, the weird, the magically adorned. Victorian poetry had achieved much upon that background, but the danger was a narrowing of interest, a belief that poetry had to be of one type. Patmore was reasserting that poetry could do other things, and from his close study of Tennyson he had developed a vocabulary and method of his own to achieve them. It was easy to parody the manner and theme, and Swinburne was amongst those who fell into the temptation. But Wordsworth cannot be revealed in the terms of Anti-Jacobin criticism, and Patmore cannot be judged by the parody of his weakest lines. Weak lines exist, such as Honoria's farewell to her family:

> 'Mary, you'll make Papa his tea
> At eight exactly.'

Such flat lines only reveal the incredible risk involved in conveying this contemporary and commonplace theme in a poetic medium, and their infrequency is a measure of Patmore's poetic success.

The criticism so far has been confined to the narrative sections of Books I and II; but swathing these around are the Preludes and Epigrams which reveal Patmore's philosophy of nuptial love. They are the sections that Patmore remodelled most severely in successive editions. The general trend of that revision was to separate more distinctly prelude and narrative in style and diction. Patmore seems increasingly to suggest that the narrative of lovers' lives seems commonplace, but that their elucidation reveals a meaning as profound as life itself. He continued to expand the Preludes as fresh elaborations occurred to him, without modifying the original conception.

This philosophy of love and marriage loses much once it is wrenched away from Patmore's words. The purpose of the whole poem, he confesses, is a moral one: 'You shall be sweetly help'd and warn'd.' The Primal Love is God, the power that grants wings and voices to the singing birds, and through Love man may come to the Godly. Woman 'less marr'd than man by mortal fall' is the only way to this Love, and so she is the Angel, the representative of God:

> And round her happy footsteps blow
> The authentic airs of Paradise.

Woman's presence is a check to evil and the uncouth; to her, the arts and the sense of the decorative owe the source of their inspiration. Man will do anything for woman, and woman should not disregard her degree or cheapen her qualities. Man can only develop by honouring woman, and if she insists on that honour man will cast off his 'gross regality of strength' and the true, mystical, nuptial love will arise. For woman is Love and Man is Truth; Love is the substance, man the form:

> So, dancing round the Tree of Life,
> They make an Eden in her breast.

Some do not see the strength of nuptial love: they seek the airy insubstantiality of Plato or the earthiness of Anacreon. For Patmore nuptial love is permanent in life and is more spiritual than virginity:

> Virgins are they, before the Lord,
> Whose hearts are pure: the vestal fire
> Is not, as some misread the word,
> By marriage quench'd but burns the higher.

With marriage wooing does not cease, for the 'undrest, familiar' style is not for the friend that we respect. The philosophy found in Books I and II is later set out more consecutively in *The Wedding Sermon*, the concluding poem of *The Victories of Love*. Here Patmore shows that all love is of desire or benevolence, but all desire we owe to God, and through nuptial love desire transmutes itself to Divine benevolence.

Justice has seldom been done to the subtlety of Patmore's thought nor to the poetic strength with which it is expressed. Ruskin represents the popular view when he quotes a passage from *The Angel in the House* in *Sesame and Lilies*, and wishes that the lines 'were learned by all youthful ladies of England'. The following is the powerful and closely packed extract which Ruskin selected:

> Ah, wasteful woman, she that may
> On her sweet self set her own price,
> Knowing he cannot choose but pay,
> How has she cheapen'd paradise;

> How given for naught her priceless gift,
> How spoil'd the bread and spill'd the wine,
> Which, spent with due, respective thrift,
> Had made brutes men, and men divine.

Let the youthful ladies of England learn them if they wish, but such lines, with their cunning recall of Satan's speech to Eve in *Paradise Lost*[4] ('I of brutes, human, ye of human Gods'), need not be confined to them or to their moral edification.

Patmore wrote two other parts to *The Angel*, and then left the poem incomplete. Already in Book II he had written a pathetic poem of the lover who has premonition of the death of the beloved, and at the close of the year 1862, when his wife died, he wrote: 'I no longer have at every step, the needful encouragement of an approval which was all that my heart valued of fame'; and he adds that the poem, as first conceived in his mind, was to have concluded with 'the subject of the hope which remains for individual love in death'.

Faithful for Ever and *The Victories of Love* differ in form and mood from the first two books. They are set out as letters between the main characters, and their metrical form is the octosyllabic couplet. We see Frederick Graham, the unsuccessful suitor of Honoria, a naval officer with deeds in India to his credit, married to Jane, the chaplain's daughter. The opinions on Jane of friends and relations are contrived with a satiric finish not unworthy of an Austen novel. Conscious of the grandeur of her husband's world, Jane writes a pathetic little note to her mother. Once she has children of her own she opens out a little in her correspondence and displays a deal of good-heartedness mingled with a little vulgarity. She so improves her manners that Lady Clitheroe, who had once said of her

> H is her Shibboleth. 'Tis said
> Her mother was a Kitchen-Maid

revises her judgement and discovers her '*outrée* and natural'. Jane and Frederick visit the Vaughans and Frederick discovers a modified attitude in Honoria:

> I confess
> I love her rather more than less!
> But she alone was loved of old;
> Now love is twain, nay, manifold;
> For, somehow, he whose daily life
> Adjusts itself to one true wife,
> Grows to a nuptial, near degree
> With all that's fair and womanly.

Jane loses two of her children and finally feels the touch of death on herself. In her letter she discusses the immortality of love, and tells Frederick that love without immortality is mockery. Her letters are the simplest and most poignant expression of Patmore's teaching. Jane by her love has developed love in Frederick, and so these third and fourth parts develop the argument of Books I and II.

It has been frequently suggested that these later sections fall far beneath the level of Books I and II. Such criticism mistakes the scheme of the poem. Books I and II elaborate the philosophy related only to the happily-wedded Vaughans. The picture of the Grahams shows the growth of nuptial love from less hopeful circumstances. In these later books there is a richer view of humour and satire, a more generous basis of evidence for Patmore's theories. He has contrived to present in verse the content of a domestic novel, attempting even more than in the earlier books to bring back into poetry the breath of common life. We are reminded frequently of Crabbe's matter-of-fact methods and brazen disregard of possible bathos: so Jane to Mrs Graham,

> Also to thank you for the frocks
> And shoes for Baby. I, (D.V.),
> Shall wean him soon. Fred goes to sea
> No more.

Yet in the later sections Patmore creates securely a group of characters – Frederick, Jane, Mrs Graham, Lady Clitheroe, and others – who possess distinct features. So clearly fashioned are they that the Vaughans appear sometimes a little colourless by their side. *The Angel in the House*, as a whole, constitutes such an original and daring element in the poetry of the century that it may be suggested that Patmore should stand with Tennyson, Browning, and Arnold as one of the major poets of his age.

It is difficult to tell when Patmore first began to write odes. The earlier ones are so filled with memory of Emily Patmore that it is natural to feel that they were written soon after her death in 1863.[5] The nine odes printed in 1868 were all republished in *The Unknown Eros* collection of 1877.[6] There were elaborate revisions of individual odes from one edition to another. Patmore early hoped through the odes to give poetic expression to varied aspects of one idea. In 1868 he already states this ambition: 'I meant to have extended and developed this series of odes until they formed an integral work expressing an idea which I have long had at heart.' He adds, rather incongruously, that his despair at the 'disenfranchisement of the upper and middle classes in 1867 by the false English nobles and their Jew' discouraged him from his attempt. Only in 1890 did he present *The Unknown Eros* as a sequence in two books possessive of a unity of purpose, and it is from this volume that the poems have been examined. Much of the background came from his reading in mystical literature: to his early reading in Swedenborg he had added a deep study of Aquinas. More specifically for *The Unknown Eros* the influence is St John of the Cross. Frederick Page quotes from one of Patmore's notebooks: 'This poem is to consist of a series of poems on texts from the Canticles, and to contain all the essential matter of St John of the Cross.'

In form and diction these poems differ widely from the octosyllabics of *The Angel in the House*. The lines may vary from two syllables to sixteen syllables and there are no stanzas. One would imagine that such poems were irregular Pindaric (*numeris lege solutis*), but Patmore had very different ideas on the form. The odes, he asserted, depended upon pause, and on its true interpretation all the lines were of the same length from the 'long-drawn sigh of two syllables to the passionate cataract of sixteen'. He described the measure[7] as 'iambic tetrameter with unlimited catalexis, which is commonly called "irregular" ode, though it is really as "regular" as any other English metre', and even much more so, if its subtle laws are truly considered and obeyed. With something approaching complacency Patmore added: 'Owing, again, to the peculiarly and essentially *fluent* character of this metre, it can hardly be used with full success by any poet who has not acquired by long practice in simpler rhythms, that *sense* of metre which is rare even in very good poets.'[8] In 1878 Patmore published as a preface to *Amelia* an essay on *English Metrical Law*, in which he defines these principles at greater length, but with less clarity. Patmore's theory gained little support, but in the odes he wrote poems of irregular line lengths which have been acknowledged to possess at their best some inner principle of harmony, though at their worst they fall into the arid flatness of the irregular Pindaric. He seems to have realized the esoteric nature of these poems, for in the ode *Dead Language* he suggests that his language will not be understood, while in *Prophets who Cannot Sing* he comments on the rarity of verse that shows 'views of the unveil'd heavens'.

The First Book of *The Unknown Eros* contains the pieces most usually quoted; the selection of themes is more varied, more human than in the closely argued mysticism of the Second Book. Of these odes in Book I, *Toys* is the best known, and the simplest in its analogy from human to religious experience. This and a group of other powerful poems deal with Patmore's moods after his wife's death. The most poignant is *Departure*, in which he tells his wife,

> It was not like your great and gracious ways!
> Do you, that have nought other to lament,
> Never, my Love, repent
> Of how, that July afternoon,
> You went,
> With sudden, unintelligible phrase,
> And frighten'd eye,
> Upon your journey of so many days,
> Without a single kiss, or a good-bye?

Closely allied with these is *Tired Memory*, in which Patmore describes himself as releasing his wife's memory from earth to heaven, and since love on earth was still necessary for him, he asks God for bliss in which his wife has no part. He admits some treachery in this reunion of himself with love on earth, but pleads that he is 'dead of devotion and tired memory':

> When a strange grace of thee
> In a fair stranger, as I take it, bred
> To her some tender heed,
> Most innocent
> Of purpose therewith blent,
> And pure of faith, I think to thee.

With such subtle poignancy does Patmore pass from his first marriage to his second.

Combined with these poems of Love in Book I are Patmore's political poems. He is opposed to democracy, to the franchise, to Gladstone, to 'the Jew', and from the midst of this network of reaction he sees England's irretrievable decline. England still possessed 'the ghostly grace of her transfigured past', but that was all. Fortunately Patmore's poetry usually dealt with the things he loved, but the barrenness of the vain, protesting voice is heard more clearly in this First Book than elsewhere.

Book II of *The Unknown Eros* is Patmore's final expression of his philosophy of Love. If in *The Angel* he considered how human love can lead to heaven, he here contemplates how all earthly love is but the symbol of the Soul's love for God. The central poem is *Sponsa Dei*, where this philosophy is most clearly expounded:

> Who is this Fair
> Whom each hath seen,
>
> . . . . .
>
> Who is this only happy She,
> Whom, by a frantic flight of courtesy,
> Born of despair
> Of better lodging for his Spirit fair,
> He adores as Margaret, Maude, or Cecily?

The conception found in *Sponsa Dei* permeates the other odes. The opening poem suggests that this esoteric love of God and the Soul will demand an unusual expression:

> In what veil'd hymn
> Or mystic dance
> Would he that were thy Priest advance;

and in the odes which follow he isolates different aspects of this mystical union. In *The Contract* he describes the nuptials of Adam and Eve, who seek some voluntary discipline to the 'mutual free contract' of their 'virgin spousals'. In *To the Body*, the ode which comes closest to a seventeenth-century manner, he speaks in an impassioned way of the glory of the body:

> Little, sequester'd pleasure-house
> For God and for His Spouse.

So in *Deliciæ Sapientiæ de Amore* he associates the love of the Virgin Mother, and that of the brides of Christ in their cells, with the love of all to whom 'generous Love, by any name, is dear'. There follows a series of odes in which the figures of Eros and Psyche are substituted for those of God and the Virgin, or of God and the Soul. Though described in the terms of human love, the full intent of these poems lies in their symbolical interpretation. Patmore endeavours to explore the relationship of the soul to God, and, of this, human love at its purest is only an image. The poems reveal at the same time the motions and moods of human love with detailed subtlety. The culmination of this purpose can be seen in *The Child's Purchase*, the most elaborate poem, both in form and thought, in the whole sequence. Here he attempts to transcend all other praise he has made of woman in a direct hymn of praise to the Virgin-Mother herself. The poem is varied at irregular intervals by the prayer 'Ora pro me', which gives a strophic effect not found in the other pieces.

In 1890 *Amelia* and other poems in the ode form were published in the same volume as *The Unknown Eros*. *Amelia*, an irregular ode with a narrative theme, portrays the poet's love for his second wife, though the memory of his first dead love is still quick within him. The solemnity of movement cannot extinguish a latent sentimentality, and certainly the poem has nothing of the rare sensitiveness of approach which marked the treatment of the same subject in *Tired Memory*. Of the other poems in the 1890 volume *Regina Cœli*, a simple address to the Virgin, 'mild, silent little Maid', is a pendant to *The Unknown Eros*, and there are poems on miscellaneous themes.

The irregular ode in Patmore's hands became an intricate form. His themes were unusual, and even when his vocabulary was simple the words were often fashioned into such strange symbols and thoughts that his meaning was difficult to unravel. So in Psyche's words to Eros in *Eros and Psyche*:

> And this thy kiss
> A separate secret by none other scann'd;
> Though well I wis
> The whole of life is womanhood to thee,
> Momently wedded with enormous bliss.

Though no word is strange the content cannot be revealed without some knowledge of Patmore's whole philosophy. In a few of the poems Patmore uses unusual words ('shaw', 'photosphere', 'prepense-occulted', 'draff'), but although the vocabulary is more involved than in *The Angel*, difficulties arising directly out of vocabulary are infrequent. In his early poetry Patmore had avoided imagery, and had even suggested that the highest poetry existed without it. Into the odes imagery intrudes, an imagery like that of the metaphysical poets, original, difficult, intellectual. So, in *Saint Valentine's Day*, Love is told to go to all-amorous May:

> Go to her summons gay,
> Thy heart with dead, wing'd Innocencies fill'd,
> Ev'n as a nest with birds
> After the old ones by the hawk are kill'd.

Further, the irregular line in the odes leads to difficulties of syntax which serve to obscure a meaning already complex. Yet when all is allowed it is the theme, the combination of sensuous and mystical elements, that gives the odes their esoteric quality. Further, by some unusual combination of abstract and concrete words, he has developed an individualized vocabulary, which, strangely enough, seems to have gained suggestions from his reading of Ford.[9] To the generality the First Book of *The Unknown Eros*, with its recognizable human themes, will probably yield more than the passionate symbolism which Patmore valued so much in the poems of the Second Book, yet it is in these later pieces that his most individual contribution is to be found.

Those who read the life of Patmore by Richard Garnett[10] may be startled by the summary of his personality: 'Instead of an insipid amiability, his dominant characteristic was a rugged angularity, steeped in Rembrandt-like contrasts of light and gloom. Haughty, imperious, combative, sardonic, he was at the same time sensitive, susceptible, and capable of deep tenderness.' Patmore does not reveal his whole personality in his poetry: sometimes one feels that his poetic personality existed apart from his ordinary individuality. It is true that his gloomy, reactionary preoccupations intrude sometimes, and his aggressive Catholicism. He is led even to make the Pythoness say to Psyche:

> Child, anyone, to hear you speak,
> Would take you for a Protestant.

But from his poetry we could not have pictured that arrogance before friends, that desire to lecture fellow poets, which occur frequently in the life. Nor does the poet of *The Angel* always figure well in his comments on women: 'Mrs. Tennyson has had a son born dead; I am very sorry for this, as I think, that the sooner Tennyson has a few children about him the better it will be for his mental health and comfort.'[11] The standpoint is selfish and masculine for the creator of Vaughan; Mrs Tennyson and the children are regarded as sops to Tennyson's mental comfort. Within his poetical work, however, a distinct personality is found, and it is not essential that it should coincide with the words and manners of the Coventry Patmore of ordinary life. The content and method of that work are one of the original enterprises in the poetry of the later part of the nineteenth century, and it has important parallels and developments.

Among those who owed allegiance to Coventry Patmore none was more openly a disciple than Francis Thompson, and though their work comes to differ widely in content and poetic skill, Patmore consistently welcomed the association of his name with that of Thompson. ('I feel a personal and sort of proprietary interest in the metrical qualities of much of Mr. Thompson's work.')

Francis Thompson's[12] life (1859-1907) has all the qualities of legend. He was born in Preston, where his father was a doctor. Both his parents were converts to the Roman Catholic Church, and in 1870 he was sent to Ushaw College, near Durham, to be trained for the priesthood. Here he studied until his father received, in 1877, a letter from the President regretting that 'a natural indolence' made Thompson unsuited for the Church. In the same year he was entered as a student of medicine at Owens College, Manchester. His father seems to have persuaded him to this course, and although Thompson had a physical repulsion for the sight of blood, or of dead bodies in the dissecting-room, he appears silently to have acquiesced. He was in Manchester for six years, although little of his time was spent in medical studies. A serious illness in 1879 and the presentation by his mother of a copy of De Quincey's *The Confessions of an English Opium Eater* led him to take opium. His father made a further attempt to give him a career, by entering him as a student at Glasgow University, but failure was inevitable. After a number of shifts he found himself back in Manchester in 1885. He failed to declare to his family his poetical ambitions ('If the lad had but told me') and, to his long-suffering father, he appeared as merely an idle fellow who liked to 'lead a dawdling, sauntering sort of life'.

In November 1885, almost destitute, and without hope, he came to London. Everard Meynell[12] has told the story of the years that follow: the doss-houses; the odd jobbing; the free library when a few shillings had been sent from home; opium; the writing of prose and verse in old account-books and sometimes at night the shelter of a railway arch or of an Embankment seat; then the manuscript sent to *Merry England*; the delay; the publication of a poem; the encounter with Wilfrid Meynell, the editor, and the discovery that the wife of the editor was a poetess, Alice Meynell, who could give encouragement that was more valuable than charity.

The turning-point in Thompson's career, both physically and as a poet, dates from his friendship with the Meynells. It was they who persuaded him to enter a hospital and to fight his drug habit, and they who sent him to Storrington Priory to recuperate. At Storrington he wrote most of the pieces which appear in his first volume, *Poems* (1893). *Sister Songs* followed in 1895. From 1893 to 1897 Thompson spent most of his time at Pantasaph, in North Wales, in a Franciscan monastery, and here he composed most of the *New Poems* (1897), along with a number of prose pieces. The last years, despite all the ministrations of friends, were darkened by his ill health and the gnawing desire for drugs and for alcohol. In the summer of 1907 he entered the Hospital of St Elizabeth and St John in London and there in November of the same year he died. Much of his prose, including the Shelley essay (1909), was published posthumously, and in 1913 Wilfrid Meynell issued his collected *Works* in verse and prose in three volumes.

Francis Thompson has never been judged dispassionately: he fell among friends, who nurtured his talent, shared his faith and found joy in his poetic expression of mystical experience. It was only natural that critics outside the group should approach this favoured poet with a mood of potential disparagement. This conflict of opinion sets in with the first volume of 1893. Coventry Patmore[13] concurred in the opinion that he was a 'greater Crashaw', and looked to him to explore 'the inexhaustible and hitherto almost unworked mine of Catholic philosophy'. Andrew Lang,[14] a month later, wrote in an article on *The Young Men* that the general effect of Thompson's poetry was 'not of originality but of a conscientious and strenuous *bizarrerie*'. Adverse criticism was more general after the publication of *New Poems* in 1897, and Patmore was no longer alive to praise the poet.

Poems (1893) contained three groups of poems: *Love in Dian's Lap*; *Miscellaneous Poems*, including *The Hound of Heaven*; and *Poems on Children*. *Love in Dian's Lap* comprises a series of odes, describing a love at times Platonic and at times mystical, into which influences from Shelley's *Epipsychidion* and Patmore's *The Unknown Eros* have intruded. The poems arose from Thompson's reverence for Alice Meynell. Throughout these pieces he has undoubtedly fresh thought to express, but it is a thought which never gains adequate poetic embodiment. Frequently he allows himself to be deceived by a fine-sounding, meaningless rhetorical phrase:

> Within your spirit's arms I stay me fast
>   Against the fell
> Immitigate ravening of the gates of hell![15]

He tortures sentences out of their grammatical word order without introducing compensating effects of euphony:

> Too wearily had we and song
> Been left to look and left to long,
> Yea, song and we to long and look,
> Since thine acquainted feet forsook
> The mountain where the Muses hymn
> For Sinai and the Seraphim.[16]

With the pattern of the metaphysical poets before him, particularly of Donne and Crashaw, he is led, as Alice Meynell detected, to elevate imagery to the supreme place in poetry. Unfortunately he lacked the mental alertness, the intellectual strenuousness which, as Donne had shown, can alone sustain such a method. His images are frequently trailing draperies of fustian rhetoric. His vocabulary, with its far-sought words, confirms this impression. Patmore had given his authority for the employment of an esoteric language in poetry, and the crabbed, hard terms of the metaphysicals presented a further model. Thompson in employing these devices is seldom free from poetical dependence upon one or other of his predecessors. Nor is it the type of derivation which enriches the poetry of Milton and Gray, where the borrowed phrase is so aptly introduced that its beauty is increased by the memory of its previous employment. Frequently Thompson, like Wilde, has the dependence of one who has not sufficient native strength to move without support.[17] *The Athenæum* detected this element in Thompson when the volume of 1893 first appeared: 'He has been impressed by certain styles, in themselves incompatible, indeed implying the negation of one another – that of Crashaw, for instance, and that of Mr. Patmore – and he has deliberately mixed them, against the nature of things. Thus his work, with all its splendours, has the impress of no individuality; it is a splendour of rays and patches, a very masque of anarchy.'[18]

The Hound of Heaven, which is the central poem in the *Miscellaneous* section, is not without some of the disfiguring qualities of the love odes, but in strength of conception and in achievement it is of a different category. One has to exempt it, as Johnson was led to exempt the *Elegy* from his general strictures on Gray's poetry, and for some of the same reasons. It has a universality which gives it an appeal to many who are not interested in poetry as a whole, nor studious of the niceties of form and vocabulary. Its central theme, familiar to mystical writers, was derived by Thompson from the *Confessions* of St Augustine. Thompson's strength lay in his power to illustrate poetically the pursuit of the soul by God, and seldom has spiritual experience been wrought with such certainty into the symbols drawn from the images of possible human experience. Here he controlled his decorative virtuosity to the central poetic purpose. He was not equally successful in *A Corymbus for Autumn*; the poem dazzles the reader with its imagery, but it is imagery in riot:

> Gipsy of Seasons, ere thou go winging;
> Ere Winter throws
> His flaking snows

> In thy feasting-flagon's impurpurate glows!
> The sopped sun – toper as ever drank hard –
> Stares foolish, hazed,
> Rubicund, dazed,
> Totty with thine October tankard.

He exercises more restraint in his ode on Cardinal Manning, *To the Dead Cardinal of Westminster*:

> I will not perturbate
> Thy Paradisal state
> With praise
> Of thy dead days.

With this simpler movement, which he uses again in *Any Saint*, he attains his effect with that same economy employed by George Herbert in *Discipline*.

The *Poems on Children*, with which the volume concludes, form Thompson's least ambitious but possibly most effective poetic achievement in this volume. Poetic borrowing is again marked. *To Monica Thought Dying* is consciously imitative of Patmore's *Odes*, and a gentle and gracious poem, *The Making of Viola*, develops a more distinct Pre-Raphaelite influence than is frequent in Thompson's work. Above all these is *Daisy*, which has a lyrical quality that transcends in poetical value the rhetorical effects of Thompson's more elaborate poems. In its closing epigrammatic stanza he captures the movement of Gray's conclusion to his *Eton College* ode, yet for once he has given a fresh reality to the borrowed element.

Sister Songs, as Thompson states in the first edition of the poem, 'though new in the sense of being now for the first time printed, was written some four years ago, about the same date as the "Hound of Heaven" in my former volume'. In contrast, this long poetic rhapsody is Thompson's *Prelude*; a record of his spiritual experience mingled with praise of nature and of the two sisters (Monica and Sylvia) who helped him to attain possession of himself and of his own powers. Unfortunately, the poetic medium is not disciplined blank verse as in Wordsworth's

Prelude, but an irregular form with occasional reminiscence of the *Ode* on *Intimations of Immortality*. In this, his longest poem, the imperfections of his craftsmanship are apparent, despite the strong interest of his central theme. He is dominated by the conception that poetry lives in imagery, and his mind evolves tortuous comparisons which obscure his meaning. The nature images have been frequently praised, and the following example shows their peculiar quality:

> I know in the lane, by the hedgerow track,
>> The long, broad grasses underneath
> Are warted with rain like a toad's knobbed back;
>> But here May weareth a rainless wreath.

Spontaneity has been deliberately avoided, and any pleasure derived must arise from the triumph of the reader's intellect over perplexing material. Thompson's inadequacy can be more clearly seen in passages where the phrasing or the sense seems to derive from one of frequent memories of earlier poets. For example, in *The Ancient Mariner* Coleridge uses the image of music to describe the sounds of a troop of angelic spirits:

> And now 'twas like all instruments,
> Now like a lonely flute.

Coleridge's simple sufficiency of phrasing has been distraught by the hordes of prismatic words in Thompson's description:

> 'Twas like no earthly instrument,
> Yet had something of them all
> In its rise, and in its fall;
> As if in one sweet consort there were blent
>> Those archetypes celestial
> Which our endeavouring instruments recall.
> So heavenly flutes made murmurous plain
> To heavenly viols, that again
> – Aching with music – wailed back pain.

Nor is this more than a small portion of his elaboration. An ornate style can possess many virtues, complicated, sophisticated beauties which a direct style has to sacrifice, but such effects can only be gained if there lies a centre of clarity in the writer's own mind. Thompson confuses intricacy with poetic success; he evolves a poetic baroque, and loses himself in the *bravura* of detail, until words infect his poetry like a multicoloured plague. To employ the terms of romantic criticism, the poem sacrifices imagination to fancy, the revelation of the significant experience to incidental device. In one passage of *Sister Songs* Thompson describes the most moving incident of his destitute days: he was penniless and starving, and a prostitute sheltered him, fed him, and asked nothing in exchange. In prose Thompson has described this with complete adequacy, but in the verse he has decked and bejewelled it beyond all recognition. The prostitute has become 'a flower fallen from the budded coronal of Spring', and all else has suffered from decorative periphrasis.

On his last volume, *New Poems* (1897), Thompson left an explanatory note in manuscript: 'This book represents the work of the three years which have elapsed since my first volume was prepared for the press, my second volume having been a poem of comparatively early date. The first section exhibits mysticism in a limited and varying degree. I feel my instrument yet too imperfect to profane by it the higher ranges. Much is transcendental rather than truly mystic. The opening poem, *The Mistress of Vision*, is a fantasy with no more than an illusive tinge of psychic significance.'[19] The poem to which Thompson refers is the most original in the volume. It opens with a description of Paradise:

> Secret was the garden;
> Set i' the pathless awe.

Within dwells the Mistress of Vision, and the poet wishes that he could capture into verse her sweet, wise, sorrowful song. While distrusting his own powers, he ventures to recall a few moments of her vision, but the attempt leads him back to recognize his deficiencies:

> O dismay!
> I, a wingless mortal, sporting
> With the tresses of the sun?

> I, that dare my hand to lay
> On the thunder in its snorting?
> Ere begun,
> Falls my singed song down the sky,
>   even the old Icarian way.

The conclusion is a dialogue between the poet and the lady, in which she attempts to initiate him into the ways of wisdom. The poem has a vocabulary which is not self-conscious and rhetorical; the theme transcends the words, and the style is subservient to the creative intention. More than in any other of his poems one senses the poet breaking through and taking possession. Yet certain elements mar its perfection, and seem a product of that 'natural indolence' against which the President of Ushaw College complained. It is strange, for instance, to find in a poem which dwells in memories of Crashaw a line which has suddenly slipped in from Kipling:

> So fearfully the sun doth sound
> Clanging up beyond Cathay;
> For the great earthquaking sunrise rolling up beyond Cathay.

Apart from such incidental grotesque features the poem has a lack of unity, as the brief summary has shown. Possibly the memory of Coleridge's 'damsel with a dulcimer' from *Kubla Khan* is responsible for the sudden divergences of theme. Thompson confesses, however, that the poem was fantasy, and to demand a close sequence in the argument is to exact more than has been promised. The other poems in this volume share with *The Mistress of Vision* a developing discipline in poetic method; it appears in the mystical poems, *The Dread of Height* ('Though sweet be great, and though my heart be small'), and *To Any Saint*; it gives cohesion to the series of love poems, *A Narrow Vessel*, and it reveals itself in the form of simple verses, on the model of R. L. Stevenson, *Ex Ore Infantium*:

> Little Jesus, wast Thou shy
> Once, and just so small as I?

Thompson, however, has not deserted his profuse and irregular splendours; they are emblazoned on such poems as *Ode to the Setting Sun*, *An Anthem of Earth*, and *Orient Ode*. They can be studied more precisely in his translations from Hugo's *Feuilles d'Automne*.

The Collected Works (1913) added a number of miscellaneous pieces, but little of importance. He had written journalistic poems, without deserting his intricate vocabulary or his irregular ode form: Queen Victoria had thus been commemorated on her Diamond Jubilee, and so was Cecil Rhodes celebrated on his death in 1902. A series of sonnets displayed openly a debt to Mrs Alice Meynell, whose influence on his poetry appears to have been of a pervasive and salutary nature.

Thompson's reputation will probably change more than that of most of his contemporaries. Seldom, one imagines, will he be again compared to Shakespeare as he was in his lifetime. Some few of his verses will enter into that small collection of poems generally known, the anthology common to persons of good taste: *Daisy* will be there, and *The Hound of Heaven*, perhaps some others. Those who share his faith will find in many of his poems the expression of a Catholic mysticism, and their enthusiasm for the subject-matter cannot fail to excuse the possible inadequacies of the verse. In judging Thompson one is driven to judge him by the standard of the great writers, Donne, Crashaw, Coleridge, Shelley. Such were his models, and lines from them dart in and out of his poems like lightning flashes, and sometimes, though rarely, he has an original quality, not unlike that of the masters he imitated.

His prose is more secure than his verse; *Shelley*, *Paganism Old and New*, the essay on poets and prose writers have a consistent strength and clarity of purpose. In the essay on *Shelley* he speaks in general terms of the poetry of his time: 'Contemporary poetry in general, as compared with the poetry of the early nineteenth century, is mildewed. That defect is the predominance of art over inspiration, of body over soul. We do not say the *defect* of inspiration. The warrior is there, but he is hampered by his armour. Theoretically, of course, one ought always to try for the best word. But practically, the habit of excessive care in word-selection frequently results in loss of spontaneity; and, still worse, the habit of always taking the best word too easily becomes the habit of always taking the most ornate word, the word most removed from ordinary speech. In consequence of this, poetic diction has become latterly a kaleidoscope, and one's chief curiosity is as to the precise combinations into which the pieces will be shifted. There is, in fact, a certain band of words, the Praetorian cohorts of poetry, whose prescriptive aid is invoked by every aspirant to the poetical purple – against these it is time some banner should be raised.' Thompson's strictures on contemporary verse can be applied in every particular to his own poetry, though it would not be right to suggest that he made any such application himself. Yet signs are not wanting that by 1897 he was realizing, partly through the influence of Alice Meynell, that his trust in the cohorts of poetic words had been misplaced. 'I who can scarcely speak my fellows' speech', he writes in *Sister Songs*, and so one feels that he is struggling in some of his poems to the expression of an experience which is strange in a medium which he has not fully comprehended. He has, however, like Coleridge, a poetic transfiguration in some few poems; his defects are transcended and he sees with heightened clarity, uniting vision to expression.

A unity of faith and personal contacts brings Alice Meynell[20] (1847-1922) into intimate association with Patmore and Thompson. Her life seems to the outward observer a fortunate one: she was born into a family of artistic tastes and accomplishments. Her mother, Christina Weller, was a musician of professional competence, and her father, Thomas James Thompson, who lived on an income inherited 'from property in the West Indies and in Lancashire', occupied himself, after an unsuccessful interlude in Liberal politics, with travel and the arts. The two daughters of the Thompson family had the education of leisured and cultured nomads: Elizabeth (Lady Butler) soon showed an aptitude for drawing and she has presented her life vividly in *An Auto-*

biography. Alice was interested in words, and strict paternal supervision of studies gave her a wide background in at least three literatures.

In 1877 she married Wilfrid Meynell. Her literary interest, which had already found expression in *Preludes* (1875), now extended into journalism. Wilfrid Meynell started the short-lived *Pen*; he had a strong and continued connexion with *The Dublin Review*, and, in 1883, he started a new monthly, *Merry England*, which not only had the distinction of discovering Francis Thompson but had among its contributors most Catholic writers of merit. Alice Meynell shared in all phases of this journalistic work. She wrote frequently, and her prose became a distinct institution in the literature of the period. Editors, unconnected with Wilfrid Meynell, called for her work – Henley in *The National Observer*, *The Pall Mall Gazette* (for the series found in *Ceres Runaway*), *The Spectator*, and *The Saturday Review*. Apart from journalism, her family life developed. Critics have spoken sometimes of the small poetic output of Alice Meynell; it is easy to forget that, unlike the Brontës, George Eliot, and Christina Rossetti, she was the mother of eight children, among whom were Everard, who wrote the life of Francis Thompson, and Viola, a novelist of distinction and Alice Meynell's biographer.

Her literary activity, as a bibliography of her work shows, was mainly in prose essays and in editing anthologies, and selections. Her poetic output is small, though it is spread over a large number of individual volumes. *Preludes* (1875) was written when she was still Alice Thompson, and had 'illustrations and ornaments' by Elizabeth. There followed at considerable intervals slim volumes: *Poems* (1893); *Other Poems* (1896) (a private issue); *Later Poems* (1901); *The Shepherdess and Other Verses* (1914); two privately issued volumes, *Poems on the War* (1915) and *Ten Poems* (1915); *A Father of Women* (1917); *The Last Poems* (a posthumous publication) (1923). Apart from these, a collected edition entitled *Poems* had been issued in 1913, and this was published with additions in 1921 and 1923. The whole of this work can be effectively gathered in one small volume of lyrical poetry.

Her life must have been crowded with activity and experience, but the image of her that dwells in the poems is of silence and withdrawal. 'Her wish', writes her sister, 'was to keep her personality always retired.' This she achieves within her poems, although the mood is often lyrical and personal. In close keeping with this restraint lay her poetic sense of verbal economy. Among her prose criticisms can be found estimates of the two foremost women poets of the century. Of Mrs Browning she wrote: 'Her poetry has genius. It is abundant and exuberant, precipitate and immoderate; but these are faults of style and not deficiencies of faculties. When she is gentle she is classic and all but perfect.'[21] On Christina Rossetti she comments: 'Much of her work, indeed, would be greatly the better for the friction of what D. G. Rossetti called "fundamental brain-work". Ease is good, but – if the paradox may be permitted – it must be ease won at a certain cost.'[22] Ease and exuberance she exorcized from her verse, aiming at a classic severity of effect, simple and compact. It accounts, along with other reasons, for the smallness of her output.

Her art becomes thus hedged in with inhibitions, both from her discipline of style and the delicacy of her personal reticence. The cloistral perfection of her verse has been gained by rejecting the temptations of much that has added powerful, stormy, immoderate qualities to the verse of other poets. In her best pieces there dwells a quiet security imaged with unerring clarity, as in *Renouncement*, a sonnet which has been frequently isolated as her best single poem:

> I must not think of thee; and, tired yet strong,
>   I shun the thought that lurks in all delight –
>   The thought of thee – and in the blue Heaven's height,
> And in the sweetest passage of a song.

Such is the first quatrain; the movement of the poem gathers additional strength in the changed mood of the sestet:

> But when sleep comes to close each difficult day,
>   When night gives pause to the long watch I keep,
>   And all my bonds I needs must loose apart,

>Must doff my will as raiment laid away, –
>With the first dream that comes with the first sleep,
>I run, I run, I am gathered to thy heart.

She knew the sonnet from her early reading of Dante and Petrarch, and it is the Italian form that she employs. In such poems, as *We Never Meet, My Heart shall be Thy Garden, I Touched the Heart that loved Me*, she showed how well adapted was the precision of the sonnet to her studied art. She used a number of other lyrical forms, and, though it is difficult to assign definite influence, her deep admiration of Tennyson and Rossetti, of Mrs Browning and of Christina Rossetti enters fitfully into her work. Her metrical command gives all her work an identity of quality, the impress of her gentle yet austere personality; this can be seen at its simplest in *The Shepherdess*:

>She walks – the lady of my delight –
>A shepherdess of sheep.
>Her flocks are thoughts. She keeps them white;
>She guards them from the steep;
>She feeds them on the fragrant height,
>And folds them in for sleep.

The same severe control can be seen in the more elaborate cadences of the poem which opens:

>Oh, not more subtly silence strays
>Amongst the winds, between the voices,
>Mingling alike with pensive lays,
>And with the music that rejoices,
>Than thou art present in my days.

In her later collections she rejected a number of pieces from *Preludes* (1875), including the long blank-verse dramatic monologue *A Study*. She was right in detecting in them the sadness of adolescent *malaise*, yet this first volume had a larger and more generous movement than the narrower perfection of her later verse. Three main themes penetrate into the quietude of her mature poetry: love, nature, and religion. Her love poetry has a keenly individual vocabulary, as can be seen in the sonnet

Renouncement. The nature poetry is a rare capturing of mood, a presentation of verbal miniatures: *A Dead Harvest, In Kensington Gardens* is an example which does justice to her achievement:

> Along the graceless grass of town
> They rake the rows of red and brown –
> Dead leaves, unlike the rows of hay
> Delicate, touched with gold and grey,
> Raked long ago and far away.
>   .   .   .   .   .
> A futile crop! – for it the fire
> Smoulders, and, for a stack, a pyre.
> So go the town's lives on the breeze
> Even as the sheddings of the trees;
> Bosom nor barn is filled with these.

The religious poetry grows into a dominating interest. She does not attempt the mystical themes of Patmore and Thompson; her mind was unattracted by theology and the philosophy of religion. Her power lies in presenting the adoration of the individual worshipper. She explained her attitude in one of her letters: 'You have never realized how incapable I am of philosophy. I really cannot answer your questions. I can only say that when I find a thought worthy of poetry I immediately give thanks for it, and also for such expression as I may have achieved.'[23] Within this range, which she realized so surely to be her own, she developed her religious experience into poems, clear and intelligible. So in the first stanza of *Meditation*:

> No sudden thing of glory and fear
> Was the Lord's coming; but the dear
>   Slow Nature's days followed each other
>   To form the Saviour from his Mother
> – One of the children of the year.

In her latest work she made an excursion into war poetry, speaking more passionately, even more stridently, than was her custom. Some of these poems may suffer the taint of ephemerality, but *Summer in England* (1914) has a humanity that transcends the conditions under which it was written.

In each of the women poets within this period there has been a sense of withdrawal from life, which affects their poetry. Alice Meynell had a richer human experience than any of them, and yet in a subtle way she holds herself apart. 'With her children,' her daughter writes, 'she had always preserved the privacy and formality of a stranger in her personal things so that even in all the crowded life of their childhood they had never once seen her unfinished or unprepared.' So in her poetry, all has been examined and set in place before it appears in the publicity of print, but one feels that in process of rejection much that was valuable in that 'crowded life' was expunged.

George Meredith

George Meredith (1828-1909), like Hardy, was known to his own age mainly as a novelist, yet poetry came first and remained with him to the last years of his long life. His biography has been frequently delineated,[1] and here only its main features will be recalled. He emerged from a family of naval outfitters in Portsmouth. About these origins he was always a little mysterious, but he has given the background and a portrait of his grandfather, the memorable Melchizedek Meredith, in *Evan Harrington*. His father, a dim, genial figure, continued the family business without success. Meredith was an only child, and his mother died when he was 5. His childhood recollections were coloured with unhappiness, the result probably of his own sensitiveness, rather than of any positive action of his father's. He missed the regular methods of education, and this emphasized both the originality and the waywardness of his nature. It kept him clear of the Victorian background, and detached him from a too close preoccupation with his own age. He was educated at private schools in England, and later, when he was 14, he was sent to the Moravian School at Neuwied. This contact with Germany proved the most formative influence of his younger years, and German literature, particularly the works of Heine, Goethe, and Schiller, remained a permanent influence on his mind.[2] Before 1846 he had appeared in London, a handsome youth of brilliant conversational powers. He was articled to a solicitor and had the good fortune to work under Richard Stephen Charnock, whose literary contacts encouraged his interest in letters. It was in Charnock's manuscript magazine *The Monthly Observer* that Meredith's first published poem *Chillianwallah* appeared in 1849. In the same year he published five translations from Heine in *The Monthly Observer*.[3] His poems also gained an entry into *Household Words* and *Chambers's Journal*, and through Charnock he developed an acquaintance with a number of men of letters. Chief among these was Thomas Love Peacock, whose prose style influenced his novels, and in 1849, without resources or a profession, he married Peacock's daughter, a widow nine years his senior. He also gained the friendship of R. H. Horne, whose dimly mystical *Orion* had early attracted him. In 1851 he published *Poems*, a selection of his verse, mainly the product of the years 1849-1851. Prose was already occupying him; in 1855 appeared his first prose volume *The Shaving of Shagpat*, and from that year his main literary occupation was novel-writing. His marriage proved a disaster of maladjustment which culminated when his wife deserted him in 1858. A son, Arthur Gryffydh, had been born in 1853, and one of the personal tragedies of Meredith's life was the later alienation and death of this only child. The memory of this marriage coloured the title-poem of his second volume of verse, *Modern Love and other Poems* (1862).

From 1862 Meredith's literary occupations were distractingly diverse. Novel-writing was his main work, but there were periods of journalism, and an episode as correspondent in the Italian-Austrian War of 1866 which gave him the background for his novel *Vittoria*. Further, from 1860 to 1894 he had to combine his own writing with the routine duties of publisher's reader for Chapman and Hall. His second marriage, contracted in 1864, was as happy as the first had been unfortunate, and Meredith's deep sense of loss in his wife's death in 1885 is recorded in his poem *A Faith on Trial*. Poetry remained an active interest in these crowded middle years, though there was limited leisure for actual accomplishment. In the last decades he returned to the medium which he had always held in the highest regard, and a number of his most memorable volumes were published: *Poems and Lyrics of the Joy of Earth* (1883); *Ballads and Poems of Tragic Life* (1887); *A Reading of Earth* (1888); *Poems, The Empty Purse, with Odes, etc.* (1892); *Odes in Contribution to the Song of French History* (1898); *A Reading of Life* (1901); *Last Poems*, posthumously published in 1909. In 1868 he had moved to Flint Cottage, Box Hill, and Surrey scenes colour the nature references in these volumes. In 1909, at the age of 81, he died. Meredith's poetry aroused most contrary critical judgements; all are agreed that it was difficult and that it was new, but varying estimates have been made of its poetical worth. In the mid-twentieth century his verse and his prose have been completely neglected. While many minor writers have been revived, he has remained with a negligible number of supporters.

A chronological study shows that much of his early verse was simple enough, in theme and diction, but that in later years he attempted to reveal poetically a profound philosophical conception. His outlook was so fresh that it demanded for its expression a new style, and a new vocabulary, and symbolism, and here he was faced with the most difficult task that can confront a poet. He succeeded in defining his philosophy, but he had to banish the easy melodies of his early verse and call frequently upon the service of a language that was harsh and obscure. In some of his later verse this difficult vocabulary, initiated in the philosophical poems, became a habit, and so extended its dominion into lyrical and narrative poems where its presence has no rational justification.

Meredith's *Poems* (1851), issued when he was only 23, passed unnoticed apart from friendly reviews by W. M. Rossetti and Charles Kingsley. In later life he spoke abusively of this 'worthless, immature stuff', and he destroyed three hundred 'unwanted copies'. Yet he had already found himself as a poet and achieved some effects which he was never to find again. The best known of all his lyrics, *Love in the Valley*, now appeared in its earliest form. In 1851 it was a poem of only eleven stanzas: in 1878 he issued a longer version completely remodelled. Both poems share the same exquisite stanza, which, with its cunning quadrisyllabic movement, has given *Love in the Valley* an individual voice amid the lyrics of the century:

> When her mother tends her before the laughing mirror,
> Tying up her laces, looping up her hair,
> Often she thinks, were this wild thing wedded,
> More love should I have, and much less care.

Meredith found suggestions for the stanza in George Darley's *Serenade of a Loyal Martyr*:

> Sweet in her green cell the Flower of Beauty slumbers,
> Lulled by the faint breezes sighing thro' her hair;
> Sleeps she, and hears not the melancholy numbers,
> Breathed to my sad lute amid the lonely air?

In treatment the two versions are widely diverse: the 1851 poem is a simple lyric of love-longing with a suggestion of the *Locksley Hall* motive, 'Would she were older and could read my worth'; in 1878 Meredith depicts a more quiescent and secure lover, who contemplates youth and age and death as he sings of his love. In both versions the love description has a rare quality of innocence, marred only by a few touches of Keats in his Leigh Hunt manner, and in them both the keenest poetic element lies in the relation of nature to the love theme; the second poem has more to give here, although it misses the earlier simplicity.

Love in the Valley was but one of the nature poems in the 1851 volume. *Pastorals, The Two Blackbirds, The Wild Rose and the Snowdrop, The Flower of the Ruins*, and *South-West Wind in the Woodland* all arose from the same interest. Much in these poems is descriptive, and Meredith, the chief nature poet after Wordsworth, has a much closer eye for colour and detail than Wordsworth possessed. From nature he was to draw largely the experience which shaped his philosophy: in these early poems the contemplative elements are frequently Wordsworthian in both content and vocabulary. So in *Pastorals*:

> A valley sweeping to the West,
> With all its wealth of loveliness,
> Is more than recompense for days
> That taught us to endure.

In *The Flower of the Ruins* he uses nature openly for moral purposes, and, re-echoing the thought of Wordsworth's *Ode to Duty*, insists on the necessity for discipline and a consciousness of duty in the Universe. Up to 1851 he has no original thought to add, and the merit of the poems lies rather in their keen description than in their contemplative elements. His developing originality of approach comes through in *South-West Wind in the Woodland*. Of all nature poets Meredith, next to Shelley, was conscious of wind and sky and of their close union with earth: he feels the wind not as Shelley did as a chastener, but as an invigorating experience. His poetic method is widely removed from that of the romantic poets. The poem has a strange, formal effect, as if the poet were returning quite naturally to the classical tradition of Gray. Nature throughout is described in the terms of art:

> Æolian silence charms the woods;
> Each tree a harp, whose foliaged strings
> Are waiting for the master's touch.

The wind loosens 'all his roaring robes'; the boughs have 'their prophet harmony of leaves'; the oak has an 'organ harmony' which amid its upper foliage 'sounds, a symphony of distant seas'. The growth of the wind is like the growth of a crescendo in music. This imagery is one of Meredith's chief poetic achievements in the volume; its appeal is intellectual rather than sensuous, but the intellect is made a gateway to the imagination. The conclusion is contemplative, the suggestion that the mystery of the wind gives a deeper insight into life than 'hours of musing' in the lore of men. It is possible that this thought derives from Wordsworthian memories, and yet Meredith must have revalued the experience, for, in 1862, in *Ode to the Spirit of Earth in Autumn*, he returned to this scene, of 'the wind-swept world' and added elements of his own philosophical thought.

Within these nature poems can be found the awakening of the more individual elements found later in his poetry, but the 1851 volume has many other types of verse. He began here the construction of narrative poems and dramatic monologues on classical themes, a type of verse which Tennyson had made popular in *Œnone* and *Ulysses*. Meredith seems to have thought well of his classical pieces, which included *The Shipwreck of Idomeneus* in blank verse, *Antigone* an irregular rhyming scheme on the basis of the decasyllabic line, and *Daphne* in the *Locksley Hall* metre. He continued this refurbishing of classical legend throughout his poetical career. Frequently he adds little to the myth, and even reveals that in poetry his quick-glancing mind could not easily be controlled to regular narrative developments. He was approaching most closely here to one of the traditions of Victorian poetry, but seldom, except in *Phoebus with Admetus*, did he make it peculiarly his own.

The other poems in this volume, apart from a series of epigrams on the poetry of writers from Chaucer to Keats, may be considered as an overflow from Meredith's periodical writing: generically it is his *Household Words* poetry. These simple ballads and incidents, such as *London by Lamplight* and *The Sleeping City*, show how intelligible his verse can be when he is not under the stress of conveying his more intimate and original thought. One poem in this unambitious tradition contains suggestions of his later thought; in *The Olive Branch* he outlines the possibility of social and material prosperity derived from scientific knowledge, which Tennyson had voiced with such confidence in *Locksley Hall*. Later he detached himself from this enthusiasm for material progress, and saw that the prime necessity of man lies in moral and spiritual development. English taste in poetry, dominated by the mature work of Tennyson and Browning, passed the volume by, just as it had passed a year before the first poetry of the Pre-Raphaelites in *The Germ*. Yet here was the first volume of the poet whose work contributed fresh elements to the poetry of the century.

Meredith waited over a decade before he published his second volume, and then, when the tragedy of his first marriage had been finally played out, he issued, in 1862, *Modern Love and Other Poems*. A cold reception greeted his second volume, with apathy accompanied in some quarters by attack. *The Spectator* even defined him as 'a clever man, without literary genius, taste or judgment', a criticism which called out Swinburne's genial championship of him as 'one of the masters of English literature'. It is not strange that Meredith waited more than twenty years before he issued another volume of verse. The main feature of this second volume was the sequence *Modern Love*, in poems of sixteen lines which have a sonnet effect. The range of Meredith as a poet can perhaps best be gauged when it is remembered that he never wrote again in the manner which here he affects with such mastery, and that there is no poem in the century which attempts this same psychological analysis of sentiment in imaginative form. Nowhere is Meredith's detachment from the work of the Pre-Raphaelites more clearly seen. For them the pursuit of Eros had elevated itself into mystical passion, to be pursued in the dim and lovely intricacy of *The House of Life*. Meredith's setting for the analysis of love is realistic and modern, and his purpose is to discover every mood in the lover from pettiness and jealousy to passion. Equally he removes himself from Tennyson and the moral background of the *Idylls*. In the early sixties he has stepped outside Victorianism into the modern world.

It is inevitable that the crisis of his own first marriage should form the background, though it cannot be asserted to what extent the portraits are biographical. The sequence unfolds a story which is as vivid as anything in Meredith's novels. The narrative movement is not obvious, so its main development may be summarized. A wife hushes her weeping at night as she realizes that the husband who lies beside her is awake and listening. No word is spoken, but distrust arises. The man, estranged from her, notes her added beauty as she meets her lover, and is disgusted that he is aroused by these fresh charms. His moods are intricate; anger is exchanged for compassion when he realizes that she, too, is suffering. Philosophy brings no consolation, nor the memory of what he hoped love might be, and in a weaker mood he seeks consolation in a 'golden-haired' lady, a relic of his past. Such is the intricacy of love that the wife, though conscious of her own unfaithfulness, is aroused to jealousy. Life demands that, despite this discord, the show of married love shall continue, and an attempt to maintain these appearances leads to situations of tragic irony. The husband discovers but little consolation in his old love; the wife is tortured in her new passion, and they are drawn together in their unhappiness and in a mood of self-consolation seek to be reconciled. But what can pity fulfil when it is a substitute for love? The old complications return, a tangle of jealousy and bitter memories that only resolves itself in tragedy. And so the wife seeks death as a solution, and the husband stands over her body, the tortured image of their disaster.

Each poem is made an emotional crisis in these two lives. An incident is first realistically presented, and then its implications are explored in an imagery of rich and involved associations. It is in this mixture of commonplace externals with a resultant, far-reaching, passionate intricacy of mood that the individual quality of the poems lies. So, for instance, as guests at a Christmas country-house party, husband and wife are shown to 'an attic crib'; in their estrangement the situation is ironic, and the poem has a simple description of their solution:

> I enter, and lie couched upon the floor.
> Passing, I caught the coverlet's quick beat.

But the emotional residuum of the situation is far from simple, and very different is the poetry in which it is imaged:

> Come, Shame, burn to my soul! and Pride and Pain –
> Foul demons that have tortured me, enchain!
> Out in the freezing darkness the lambs bleat.
> The small bird stiffens in the low starlight.

Elaborate quotation could alone reveal the wealth of circumstantial detail which gives these poems their basis in actuality, or the keen, resourceful imagery by which their moods are explored. Imagery mingles frequently with statuesque symbolism, as in the first poem, when the wife has ceased her sobbing once she knows that her husband lies awake and listening. Each situation is first stated in its simplicity, but a majestic symbolism follows, so that the fact already advanced looms reflected upon a gigantesque shadow background which emphasizes the tragedy of the human scene and imbues it with unearthly grandeur:

> Then, as midnight makes
> Her giant heart of Memory and Tears
> Drink the pale drug of silence, and so beat
> Sleep's heavy measure, they from head to feet
> Were moveless, looking through their dead black years,
> By vain regret scrawled over the blank wall.

Meredith's achievement as a poet can be most easily remembered for this sequence. Later his work becomes more esoteric, and the technical involutions already apparent grow more complex. In *Modern Love* he established a poetic portrayal of a phase of modern consciousness: the invention is admirable; its contriving is masterly.

A number of the shorter poems published in the 1862 volume had already seen periodical publication. They include some simple dramatic poems, such as *Juggling Jerry, The Beggar's Soliloquy, The Old Chartist, Grandfather Bridgeman*. These sketches in humour and pathos, developed through clearly imagined characters, seem the poems of a novelist who is awakening to dramatic sympathy. Technically the most marked intrusion is a close imitation of Browning's manner, allusive and abrupt. This influence, though it is a temporary one, may have led in Meredith to his philosophical preoccupations, to that peculiar and personal obscurity which almost disintegrates his later poetry.

One poem in this volume, *Ode to the Spirit of Earth in Autumn*, initiates the philosophical nature poetry which is the most individual element of his later work. He re-works in the *Ode*, the mood of *South-West Wind in the Woodland,* as if he had only now become aware of its full philosophical implication. The thought which gains first adequate expression here is elaborated in *The Lark Ascending* (1881), *The Woods of Westermain* (1883), *Earth and Man* (1883), *A Faith on Trial* (1888), *Hymn to Colour* (1888), *Ode to the Comic Spirit* (1892), *The Empty Purse* (1892), and *The Test of Manhood* (1901). He developed within these and other poems an attitude to experience which has almost the consistency of a formal philosophy. He set out to rediscover a personal faith, and a faith for humanity, postulating the truth of the evolutionary origins of life. As thought, apart from all considerations of a poetical expression of thought, the poems have importance in the mental history of the century, and it has therefore been thought best to summarize Meredith's position as found in these later poems, and then to consider the technical problems which the poetic expression of philosophy has created.

Meredith pictures Earth first as a primeval mass 'of mud'[4] with the power of giving birth to living organisms. The life of animals and the life of man derive equally from the Mother that is Earth, and consequently man has no right to claim a title to a special creation. Man's weakness lies in the shame he feels in this kinship with Earth and his quest of a God in the Heavens away from Earth: 'Now to the Invisible he raves.'[5] To ignore Earth is to deny the meaning of life; to follow Earth is to develop in fullness. Earth has prescribed the method by which all life shall progress, a method of struggle between types, and a survival of the fittest. This is Earth's 'cherishing of her best endow'd'. To recognize this purpose of selection and development in Earth is to achieve fullness in life:

> She winnows, winnows roughly; sifts,
> To dip her chosen in her source:
> Contention is the vital force,
> Whence pluck they brain, her prize of gifts.[6]

The sentimentalist and the 'totter-knee'd' fail to distinguish this purpose and seek kindliness and indulgence.[7] Further, man, unable to concentrate upon development in contact with Earth, seeks to know the meaning of the whole of life, the Whence and Whither.[8] Such a craving for personal contact with all-knowledge is philosophical sensuality.[9] Behind Earth there lies some Lord of Earth, but man, a cross of brute and spirit nourished by Earth, can only gain contact with this reality by the disciplined life that Earth exacts.[10] All knowledge comes from Earth: 'Earth that gives the milk, the spirit gives.'[11] The other faiths which man constructs are symbols disguising his fear of life and death. Earth gives man no final answer to the problem of immortality; her purposes extend beyond the individual life. The degree to which man extends Earth's purposes to a future generation is in itself one immortal fulfilment,[12] though Earth, while demanding Faith and gathering and re-gathering so much back into herself, suggests that there are elements which endure.

Meredith then proceeds to outline the conduct that Earth demands of man. Man's delusion has been to regard himself as a creation different from the rest of life, but human life begins with its 'pasture amid the beasts'. Man beginning with an animal origin has by Earth's selection, and by his contact with her, developed a larger, more complex nature, which is a trinity of 'Blood', and 'Heart', and 'Brain'.[13] Man's danger is to allow any one of these elements to dominate and so prevent the purposes of his development in Earth. Blood alone is sensuality, the memory of the beast. Frequently Blood exhorts Heart or Sentiment to give a decorative cloak to animal lust. In such a combination Egoism, the degenerating atavism of man, flourishes, frustrating Earth's purposes. Sentimentalism is its expression, and it is to this aspect of humanity's frailty that Meredith directs his main attention in the novels. Brain alone is arid, but brain in contact with Heart and Blood can discipline man to a state of the Earthly normality, which Meredith names Common-Sense.[14] Earth uses two weapons in urging man's development; by Change, 'the strongest son of life', she fights egoism, and by the Spirit of Comedy she displays man's foibles, mirroring his deviations from her standard of Common-Sense: 'With laughter she pierces the brute.' This progress in man is not a mechanical or inevitable development. History is full of the 'slip in relapse'.

Meredith proceeds to describe in greater detail the nature of this State of Reality or Common-Sense at which man should aim. Love under the discipline of Common-Sense is neither a habit nor a lust, but an element in which Beauty and Brain and Reason enter and from which Pain and Fear depart. Nature demands generation, but she yields to man her richest experience in the accomplishment of her necessity. This theme of Love's relationship to Earth Meredith elaborates in *With the Persuader* (1901) and in *The Test of Manhood* (1901). Similarly, in *The Empty Purse* (1892) he outlines the social and economic application of the doctrine of Common-Sense. Meredith, in the poems to which reference has been given, elaborates a more logical system of thought than any poet of the period. This system permeates into other poems not primarily philosophical, and it is found suggestively in some of the later classical pieces, such as *Phoebus with Admetus* (1880) and *The Teaching of the Nude* (1892). Meredith's faith as outlined in his poems is incomplete. He would seem to admit that teleological conceptions are beyond human intelligence. Even the fate of the individual after death, that search for eternal tenancies, which had preoccupied so much of early Victorian poetry, he sets aside. Occasionally, as in *A Faith on Trial*, he seems to suggest the possibility of personal immortality, yet for him the real problem lies elsewhere. He seeks only such elements of faith as are necessary for the construction of a moral life. He recognizes the history of biological development, and the motives that govern the struggle for life which nineteenth-century scientific thought was expounding; on this basis he constructs a principle of living, strenuous and yet optimistic. The main conception is original, and worked out from his own experience, though at times one can detect Carlyle's influence in his thoughts and in his epithets.

Meredith's poetry grew intricate in his endeavour to express these new elements of thought. He developed a vocabulary, individual, unexplained, and often uncouth. 'Yaffles on a chuckle skim'[15] is his method of describing the laughing cry of the green woodpecker. 'The Temple of the Toes'[16] is a dancing-hall. 'Heaven a place of winging tons'[17] is his description of the primeval cosmos. Such examples are not difficult in themselves: they suggest merely an individual approach to vocabulary, simple in its elements, but fanciful and involved in its effects. Such phrases are more difficult when Meredith is applying to them an unusual value arising from his own thought. Thus the two lines in *The Woods of Westermain*:

> Straightway venom winecups shout
> Toasts to One whose eyes are out.

Not immediately may the uninitiated reader perceive that the second line constitutes an image of Death. It is true that Meredith explained many of these more difficult images to G. M. Trevelyan, and these definitions are incorporated in the notes to the poems.[18] But poetry should be self-explanatory; an 'edification by the margent' is not part of the game. Combined with these difficulties of phrase are found almost every possible grammatical inversion. Beyond all these complexities lie Meredith's specialized philosophical vocabulary and his use of allegory. 'Heart', 'Brain', 'Blood', 'Common-Sense', 'Comedy', all represent newly devised concepts, and their full meaning is only revealed when they are studied in relationship to his whole thought. His allegory is almost medieval in its arbitrary abruptness: *The Woods of Westermain* appears to have elements of a medieval Bestiary imaginatively applied to the necessities of nineteenth-century thought. So in the passage descriptive of one of the dread animals in the Wood:

> Heed that snare.
> Muffled by his cavern-cowl
> Squats the scaly Dragon-fowl,
> Who was lord ere light you drank,
> And lest blood of knightly rank
> Stream, let not your fair princess
> Stray: he holds the leagues in stress,
> Watches keenly there.

Without G. M. Trevelyan's kindly note that ' "The Dragon", or "Dragon-fowl" is self, egoism' the allegorical sense of the passage could not easily be gauged.

The value of Meredith's poetical method is difficult to estimate. Occasionally it seems to be a mere wantonness in words. As in the novels, he sometimes creates deliberately difficult passages, signposts to the dull-witted to proceed no farther, so in his poetry he appears to delight in verbal convolutions. Such an exercise in dexterity is intellectual revelry, a harlequinade of the mind. These metaphysical fancies account, however, for but a small part of Meredith's vocabulary: the real source of difficulty is more deep-rooted. He has related his spiritual affirmations to all that knowledge and experience have shown him of life, and demanded not unnaturally a fresh vocabulary for their poetic expression. Consequently the perplexing elements, once they have been unravelled, render a rich yield of thought which could not have been otherwise fashioned. They serve to colour the philosophical poetry with an atmosphere not inappropriate to its content, a suggestion of quick energy, violent at times and explosive, but never inert. It is the poetical counterpart of the torrential eloquence of Carlyle. The melody of Tennyson's verse and Swinburne's poetic sensuousness do not enter here: sometimes Meredith seems, as does Hardy, to be in conscious revolt against them, as was Donne against the Petrarchans. His crabbed, hard effects have at their best a vigour that seems suggestive of a new poetic vitality.

The intricacy of the 'Earth' poems is carried with declamatory emphasis into his *Odes in Contribution to the Song of French History* (1898). As a result these poems are the most difficult and least satisfying portion of his poetical achievement. Meredith's strong intellectual attachment to Germany had been emphasized by education, by Carlyle's influence, and by his philosophical attachments. In the decades after the Revolution of 1848 he had noted with approval Germany's development of civic virtues. Bismarck's policy of unifying Germany under Prussian leadership had aroused suspicions, but they had been quelled by his faith in the solidarity of the German people. To France he had always paid homage, as the home of the 1789 Revolution and as the patroness of Reason, but she had sinned for him by her worship of the disruptive genius of Napoleon I and her submission to Napoleon III.

Meredith first approached this theme poetically in *France, An Ode* (1870). Sedan had been fought, the Germans were victorious: a republic had been established in Paris. Meredith resented such opinion in England as was uncompromisingly hostile to France and within the ode he pities a chastened and defeated nation, which yet he regards as the treasury of much that is valuable in the spiritual life of Europe. She was misled by Napoleon I and tricked by Napoleon III, but yet she is the inheritress of Reason, a people that speaks the language of Voltaire:

> Inveterate of brain, well knows she why
> Strength failed her, faithful to himself the first:
> Her dream is done, and she can read the sky,
> And she can take into her heart the worst
> Calamity to drug the shameful thought
> Of days that made her as the man she served
> A name of terror, but a thing unnerved:
> Buying the trickster, by the trickster bought,
> She for dominion, he to patch a throne.

This early poem on France is much simpler than those which followed some twenty years later. It exploits somewhat generously an irregularity in verse form, and employs a brusque semi-abstract vocabulary; yet if the verse is sometimes clamorous, the general movement of argument is not concealed. Of the three new poems added in 1898 two precede *France* in theme. *The Revolution* outlines France's contribution in 1789 to the development of the human spirit, while *Napoléon* depicts her captured by the false glamour of one whose mind was 'cannon's cave':

> Cannon his name,
> Cannon his voice, he came.
> Who heard of him heard shaken hills,
> An earth at quake, to quiet stamped.

The final poem, *Alsace-Lorraine*, gives Meredith's impression of France's recovery by 1898 from the calamity of 1870. He suggests that her saint should be Joan of Arc, 'She had no self but France', and not Napoleon I, who had 'no France but self'. He is confident that France will make her own contribution to Europe, and that instead of seeking to recapture the lost provinces, she will aid the development of a warless Europe:

> On France is laid the proud initiative
> Of sacrifices in one self-mastering hour.

Meredith's politics, despite their concluding optimism, have a sense of realism to which Swinburne's seldom attained. In the later odes, however, poetic expression is enmeshed in verbal intricacies. It is as if Meredith had stolen the hurricane rhetoric of Carlyle and, robbing it of explanatory detail, had substituted an allusive and symbolic vocabulary borrowed largely from his own theory of Earth. It is true that he explained to G. M. Trevelyan what the verses meant, but one suspects that he must have known how they would confuse the general reader. The most effective of the poems is *Napoléon*, a character by whom Meredith, despite his antagonism, is fascinated. Yet even in the simpler passages in this poem, where the subject-matter is simply the description of Napoleon, the style struggles to conceal the meaning:

> Incarnate Victory, Power manifest,
> Infernal or God-given to mankind,
> On the quenched volcano's cusp did he take stand,
> A conquering army's height above the land,
> Which calls that army offspring of its breast,
> And sees it mid the starry camps enshrined;
> His eye the cannon's flame,
> The cannon's cave his mind.

The difficulty of this later poetry need not disguise Meredith's important contribution to the poetry of the century. In *Love in the Valley* he had written a lyric which yields its meaning as easily as a tune its melody; in *Modern Love* he had applied verse to nervous, tangled modern moods; and in the 'Earth' poems he had won expression for his own attitude to life, an individual philosophy arising out of the Victorian problems of knowledge and faith. The 'Earth' poems which led him to exploit a new vocabulary beguiled him finally into mannerism; it was as if he were uttering a secret language in the belief that it was a universal speech. At its best, even if it is a secret language, it contains a body of thought and intuitions that are worth unravelling. Its neglect is one of the mysteries of nineteenth-century literary history.

Thomas Hardy

The changed purposes in later nineteenth-century poetry reveal themselves in the work of Thomas Hardy (1840-1928).[1] Born at Higher Bockhampton in the parish of Stinsford, Dorset, he came of a family which had been associated with the West counties since Elizabethan times. His father was a small farm-holder and builder, and the boy grew up in a county into which industry had not penetrated, and where mass education had not affected the varied, old-fashioned manner of life. Local traditions were still strong, including Napoleonic reminiscences, and village merry-makings, with fiddlers and song; a background remote from the later part of the century, and colouring Hardy's work in an individual way. His early years were lived in the period of the sudden violent change to industrialism. The railway came to Dorchester only seven years after his birth. As a child he was delicate, but so interested in books that even as a village school-boy he discovered Dryden and Johnson and enjoyed them: Dryden's *Virgil*, Johnson's *Rasselas*, and *Paul and Virginia* had been an early gift from his mother. Also he unearthed an old periodical which portrayed the Napoleonic Wars: his grandfather had contributed to the serial parts and had himself been a volunteer when Napoleon threatened invasion. So were made his first contacts with the theme which he was to use in *The Trumpet Major* and *The Dynasts*. When later he was sent to a Dorchester day school he showed an interest in Latin and had the good luck to find a master who was anxious to teach him. Largely through the encouragement of his mother, he added lessons in French and German to his ordinary studies. At 16 he was apprenticed to an architect in Dorchester, but he found time to study Greek, and to continue, with quiet persistence, his reading in other languages. He remained in Dorchester for six years, the most formative period of his life. The experiences he gathered were unusual, and the background unlike that of any other contemporary man of letters. Without a university education he had found the humanities, and their form, without pedantry, entered later into his creative work. He saw the new England of railways and mechanized life beginning to affect the country town of Dorchester, but he saw also the old life, the fairs, and dances where with a fiddle under his arm he was a welcome figure.

In 1862 Hardy came to London to continue his architectural studies, and from 1863 he began to write with some consistency. Most of his early work was in verse, though his first published piece was a prose essay in *Chambers's Journal* (1865), *How I Built Myself a House*. His life in London was desultory, and without literary companionship he pursued his reading and formed plans for writing which were never fulfilled. Some of the earliest pieces printed in his later volumes date from this period. It was in 1867, when a request for a church-restorer recalled him to Dorchester, that the impulse to write first found generous relief. He wrote a prose fiction, *The Poor Man and the Lady*; John Morley and Meredith both read it in their capacity as publishers' readers and advised Hardy on its inadequacies. Attempting to adjust himself to contemporary needs, he completed by 1870 a second novel, *Desperate Remedies* (1871). So, at the age of 30, literature began to supersede architecture as a profession. It was not an easy road, but the man, dark, thick-bearded, with alert and kindly eyes, as he appears in the portraits of those years, had adequate resources to meet the game that was on foot. For twenty-seven years his main occupation was prose fiction, and in that period he completed seventeen volumes, short stories and novels, which gave him a notable and permanent position in the history of the English novel. Yet if we are to credit his statements, and there is no good reason for not doing so, his main interest, from the beginning, lay in verse: he told Sir Sydney Cockerell that he would never have written in prose had not money considerations forced him to do so. He allowed even the best of his work to be modified for serial publication: his verse he kept inviolate.

After 1897, the year in which *The Well-Beloved* was published, and a year after the publication of *Jude the Obscure* in volume form had aroused a storm of criticism, he resolved to publish nothing but poetry. Throughout the period of prose he had not been inattentive to verse, and one finds a remarkable unity of tradition between his early poems in the mid-sixties and the last verses written in the third decade of the twentieth century. Hardy's short poems were issued in a number of volumes: *Wessex Poems and other Verses* (1898); *Poems of the Past and the Present* (1902); *Time's Laughingstocks and other Verses* (1909); *Satires of Circumstance, Lyrics and Reveries* (1914); *Moments of Vision* (1917); *Late Lyrics and Earlier with many other Verses* (1922); *Human Shows, Far Phantasies, Songs and Trifles* (1925); *Winter Words in Various Moods and Metres* (1928). Apart from these he issued his epic-drama *The Dynasts* in three parts (1903, 1906, 1908), and in 1923, *The Famous Tragedy of the Queen of Cornwall*, a play arranged for mummers. The volume publication frequently bears little relationship to the chronological order of composition, though Hardy often clarifies matters by adding the date of composition at the end of a poem.

The earliest of his published lyrics were written in the days of *Enoch Arden*, *Atalanta in Calydon*, and *The Princess's Progress*; the last verses appeared amid the experimental work of postwar lyrists. It is difficult to find the mark of any contemporary influence, though he would have willingly admitted that he had been influenced in his metrical experiments and ballad pieces by William Barnes (1801-1886), the Dorset dialect poet, a selection of whose verse he edited. Yet, basically, he and Barnes have little in common. In his obituary notice on Barnes he seems to define a poet whose temperament is very far from his own; 'one', he wrote, 'who entirely leaves alone ambition, pride, despair, defiance and other of the grander passions which move mankind great and small. His rustics are, as a rule, happy people, and very seldom feel the sting of the rest of modern mankind – the disproportion between the desire for serenity and the power of obtaining it.'

No marked change of poetical purpose can be discovered throughout the whole range of Hardy's work; skill increases as the poet grows older, but there is consistency of vision. He is so seldom subjective that it is unusually difficult to trace his personal development, though this must be modified in view of what is written below of poems of two women he had once loved. A few of the very early poems, such as *Amabel* ('Can there indwell, My Amabel?'), have the movement of Tennyson's early lyrics, while in later work he imitated French forms. The Boer War enters into a number of dramatic and contemplative poems in *Poems of the Past and Present*, while in the same volume *Poems of Pilgrimage* arise out of his Italian journey of 1887. In *Late Lyrics and Earlier*, he remembers the European War (1914-1918) and the troubled days that followed it. All these instances are exceptional, for while aware of his age, his poetical experience arises not from topical incident but from timeless moments of human passion and conflict.

Hardy's departure from the poetical traditions of the century is apparent both in subject and form. Form affects his treatment of subject, and it is in form that his achievement is most difficult to assess. His obstinate originality has led to a number of adverse judgements. Samuel Hynes[2] calls attention to some of the unfavourable criticisms made of Hardy's verse when the poems first appeared, including Lytton Strachey's on *Satires of Circumstance*: 'It is full of poetry and yet it is also full of ugly and cumbrous expressions, clumsy metres, and flat, prosaic turns of speech', and Hynes adds, 'Any reader of Hardy's verse will agree that some of these judgments, at least, are just. Hardy's poems do seem awkward, halting and often ungrammatical. The language ranges from the dialectal to the technical, and is full of strange, tongue-twisting coinages. The sentences move crabwise across the page, or back toward the subject of the verb: "They know Earth's secrets that know not I", a characteristic poem ends.' To this may be added Leavis's comment on how small a proportion of his verse has any great quality; he would reduce it to a dozen poems, adding that 'these are lost among a vast bulk of verse interesting only by its oddity and idiosyncracy'. All this is to miss the originality of Hardy's poetry in relation to the period in which it was composed, and its merit by any standard however severe.

Many nineteenth-century poets, Tennyson and the Pre-Raphaelites, and equally lyrists of the nineties, had emphasized the importance not only of form, but of form that yielded rich melodious effects. Hardy seeks in poetry severity rather than delight. Without any open assault on the schools of romantic verse, and while preserving traditional verse patterns, he implies a distrust of rich verbal melodies. Frequently the significance in his poetry is transferred to matter in the prose sense of the word, and he appears deliberately to break up a stanza so that its musical effect may be afflicted. The following verse from *Old Furniture* is an example of what is a frequent practice in Hardy's work:

> On this old viol, too, fingers are dancing –
>   As whilom – just over the strings by the nut,
> The tip of a bow receding, advancing
>   In airy quivers, as if it would cut
>   The plaintive gut.

The same retention of the outward pattern of forms, accompanied by the apparently deliberate dissolution of rhythm and melody, can be seen in the following stanza from *The Woman I Met*:

> 'Why do you trouble me, dead woman,
>   Trouble me;
> You whom I knew when warm and human?
>   – How it be
> That you quitted earth and are yet upon it
> Is, to any who ponder on it,
>   Past being read!'
> 'Still, it is so,' she said.

In well-marked contrast to such stanzas are the poems in which Hardy imitates the well-defined melody of the ballads.

Apart from his conscious withdrawal from harmony, there appear not infrequently passages when movement differs but little from that of prose. This effect can be seen in this first stanza *At Madame Tussaud's in Victorian Years*:

> That same first fiddler who leads the orchèstra to-night
> Here fiddled four decades of years ago;
> He bears the same babe-like smile of self-centred delight,
> Same trinket on watch-chain, same ring on the hand with the bow.

It is not merely that the lines, despite rhyme and a certain regularity of accentuation, have a prose movement, but that the poem as a whole has a diffused prose effect, lacking the resolution of scattered prosaic materials into a united poetic image. Hardy's life was spent mainly as a prose writer, and the prose writer at times intrudes into his poetry. Yet the seeming direct prose-like statements have their own imaginative cunning, defined by their distinctiveness, and their remoteness from anything achieved by his contemporaries. He can also use other methods where the prose element has been entirely sublimated: in *Moments of Vision*, for instance, there occurs the lyric 'Near Lanivet, 1872', which is the most uniformally poetic of all his short poems. A tired woman leans for a moment against a 'stunted handpost', and her outstretched arms make her look 'in this dim-lit cease of day' like a woman crucified. As an incident robbed of its poetical expression the poem might seem trivial, but the poetical transcription elevates it into a symbol of human suffering, a moment in experience whose associations are indefinitely various.

In vocabulary, too, Hardy is individual: he has revalued words for himself, but his selection adds no sudden revelation of verbal beauty. Strange words intrude significantly, but frequently with harshness, as Hynes suggested in his comments which have already been quoted. Hardy has in store a considerable heap of words learned in his profession as architect and builder, and they are emptied, sometimes a little indiscriminately, into his poetry. His finest effects are often obtained through specialized knowledge, his intimacy with the Wessex country, its contours, and the habits of its men and women. But this specialized knowledge rests on a generous humanity, while the architectural vocabulary has the same incongruity as Browning's casual allusions to unfamiliar names and events. Words such as 'adze', 'cusp', 'ogee', though most of them have been used in poetry before, are employed by Hardy in a way that holds up the mind and disturbs appreciation. Apart from this architectural vocabulary one finds other groups of hard, unusual words, such as 'lewth', 'leazes', 'dumble-dores', 'spuds', 'cit', 'wanzing'. Some of these arise from an attempt based on his interest in William Barnes to introduce a dialect word into a poem whose basis is standard English; they reaffirm his belief that common words can settle into a poem without incongruity. Like Coleridge, he does not object to 'bucket' as a unit in his poetical vocabulary, but he is less careful than Coleridge in finding for such words their appropriate setting. Despite the occasional use of strange, unexpected words, the basis of Hardy's poems is a simple vocabulary; poetic diction, in its more rhetorical and decorative phases, he consciously avoids. The total effect is expressiveness and dignity without sensuous beauty. His vocabulary is, in one instance, impelled by the requirements of an experience that is new to poetry. He sees man frequently as a determinist, the helpless plaything of forces outside himself. To express this view poetically Hardy is forced to use words such as 'automaton', 'foresightlessness', 'mechanize', 'fantocine', 'artistries in Circumstance', 'junctive law'. These words are not new in themselves, but their application to human life suggests new angles of vision. In thus separating himself in form, vocabulary, and thought from his contemporaries he gained contact with the metaphysical poets whose work, particularly that of Donne, he so much admired.[3] As Evelyn Hardy writes:[4] 'Both were in conscious revolt against the mellifluousness of their predecessors: each had a liking for the Gothic and strange . . . Both are permeated with the philosophical and *scientific* thought of their day which they use allusively.'

In estimating the contents of Hardy's poetry it is difficult, as has already been suggested, to forget his achievement in prose: he forces the recollection by giving lyrical expression to isolated incidents from the novels. His prose method relies upon the slow and architectonic manipulation of detail, until each fresh incident is seen with a richly associated background. This elevates even the sordid scenes in the novels, endowing them with the large vision associated with epic narration. Poetically it is only in *The Dynasts* that Hardy achieved a similar effect. The short poems suggest the absence of these large qualities; with them the mean incident often remains, despite vivid portrayal, a mean incident and nothing more. This effect is emphasized in that the poems are often stark transcripts of human experience in moments when passion, or jealousy, or the irony of circumstance reflects, unrelieved, the grimness of life. So frequent are these poems that there arises from Hardy's poetry a permanent image of human frustration: a man and a woman are thrown together by the irony of circumstance, and from their union arises a moment of passion which they call love, only to discover that its aftermath is a dreary record of semblance and deceit.[5] The record of his life with his first wife Emma, as recounted below, and the poetry which miraculously came from it forty years after her death, suggest that more of his poems than was once thought are autobiographical.

The mood varies, but the theme is the same; in *In the Days of the Crinoline* the deception resolves itself into comedy, while in *The Duel* it results in tragic consequences; yet both are illustrations of the same theme. Hardy has justified this concentration on the drab motives of men and women in two ways. He asserts, in the preface to *Poems of the Past and the Present*, 'Unadjusted impressions have their value, and the road to a true philosophy of life seems to be in humbly recording diverse readings of its phenomena as they are forced upon us by chance and change.' This is an assertion that the poet must accept isolated appearances as they come into his consciousness, resting content that the aspects of life which he perceives are part of some unperceived unity. In the *Apology* prefaced to *Late Lyrics and Earlier* he states a second justification, more didactic in its intention: 'Let me repeat what I printed in this relation more than twenty years ago, and wrote much earlier, in a poem entitled "In Tenebris":

> If way to the Better there be, it exacts a full look at the Worst –

that is to say, by the exploration of reality and its frank recognition, stage by stage, along the survey, with an eye to the best consummation possible: briefly, evolutionary meliorism.' The explanation is intellectually permissible, while it does not serve to lift the cloud that overhangs this large section of his poetical work. Yet the true position of Hardy in these lyrics of human inadequacy can only be estimated historically. They are in part a protest against the idealization of love in the poetry surrounding him, from Browning's conception that love is the centre of successful human activity to Rossetti's apotheosis of the earthly Eros. Read with these poems as a background, Hardy's short lyrics, economical in phrase, and pungent in the expression of their dark realism, recall the poetry of the century to moods in life which it had forgotten.

As thus stated, the poems are dramatic explorations, with little relation to his own personal experience, and that obviously is the impression that Hardy himself would wish to give. More recent comment has, however, revealed a different picture. He, himself, was diffident about the publication of biographical material. Superficially this inhibition seems to have been overcome by the publication of two volumes by his second wife, Florence Hardy,[1] but these are mainly items and extracts carefully prepared and edited by Hardy himself and eliminating all the intimacies. They give the outward events in a way that leaves no image of the man. There has more recently come to light some evidence[6] to suggest that as a very young man he was betrothed for some years to Tryphena Sparks, who, when the engagement was broken off, became a Mrs Gale and died in 1890. In the preface to the first edition of *Jude the Obscure* Hardy refers to having been influenced by the death of a woman in 1890. He would seem to refer to her in a poem 'Thoughts of Ph—a on news of her death', which is dated March 1890:

> Not a line of her writing have I
> Not a thread of her hair.

Among other poems closely related to her memory it is suggested are, 'In Eweleaze near Weatherbury', 'Her Immortality', 'To an Orphan Child', and 'The Little Old Table'; this last is said to refer to the desk at which Hardy worked and a gift from Tryphena.

Later Hardy met Emma Lavinia Gifford, sister-in-law of the Rector of St Juliot in Cornwall, where he had been doing some architectural work, and in 1874 they married. At first they seemed romantically happy and, in her *Recollections*, Emma described the day of the wedding: 'a perfect September day – the 17th, 1874 – not brilliant sunshine, but wearing a soft sunny luminousness; just as it should be'. Later the marriage suffered a number of stresses, and Emma became increasingly conscious of the fact that however distinguished her husband might be she was of a superior social class. Further she tried to modify Hardy's atheism with her piety, as she wrote: 'I have had various experiences, interesting some, sad others, since that lovely day, but all showing that an Unseen Power of great benevolence directs my ways.' In the early years she shared his life, and followed closely his creative work, but the growing rift between them found its open expression in her antagonism to *Jude the Obscure*. She became depressed and introspective, and as if to compete with Hardy she wrote verses, some of which found publication. Finally, in 1912, after their stubborn antagonism and isolation had broken into open and acrimonious conflict, she died. Hardy was in his seventy-second year: two years later he married Florence Dugdale, who brought a quiescent happiness and devotion to his later years.

If there were nothing more to tell than this, it would not be worth recording. But Emma's death led in Hardy to a period of profound contrition. Among her papers he found her manuscript headed *Recollections*. Some sections of these were printed in the official life: they were edited and represent only a fifth of the total manuscript, and it was not until 1961 that Evelyn Hardy and Robert Gittings published the complete text.[7] Emma's narrative is in a natural and lively prose, and it recalled to Hardy the early happy years of his married life, and he regretted that he and Emma had not revisited the scenes and places that had given them so much pleasure. So deeply affected was he that these recollections of forty years earlier led him, an ageing man of over 70, to the composition of some of his most moving lyrics. It is calculated that fifty poems concerning Emma were written in the year immediately after her death and that the total number associated with her is over one hundred. The poems most intimately associated with Emma he published in *Poems of 1912-13 (Veteris vestigia flammæ)*. Evelyn Hardy and Robert Gittings print fourteen poems, especially influenced, where 'words, phrases, incidents, emotions, and even rhythms, are echoed or repeated'[7] from Emma's narrative. These are 'Rain on a Grave', where Hardy employs the passage in *Some Recollections*, in which Emma describes how she was as a child taken to see the daisies as some children are taken to see the sea; 'During Wind and Rain', one of Hardy's best-known lyrics, but a poem whose detail has been difficult to interpret. It is now clear from *Some Recollections* that the scene is Plymouth and refers to two houses occupied by Emma's family. 'The Marble-Streeted Town' and 'The West-of-Wessex Girl' are again reminiscent of Emma's narrative, and it is Emma who charmingly mistook the limestone paving-stones of Plymouth for marble. 'Places', a poem of Emma's childhood, catches up phrases from *Some Recollections*. 'Lonely Days' is of their life at Max Gate:

> In the house where the gate was
> Past finding at night.

Some similar recollections can be found in 'The Five Students', 'She Opened the Door', 'The Interloper', 'I found her out there', 'Beeny Cliff', 'A Man was drawing near to me', 'After a Journey', 'Under the Waterfall'.

Thus memories of forty years ago came to illumine a number of his lyrics, and influence many others, and leave one with a changed awareness of his poetry as a whole, and for the first time some intimacy with the man himself.

In the dramatic lyrics Hardy's poetry is not confined to the depiction of the mere baseness of humanity. The perception of cruelty is strangely mingled with compassion, and from this union of pity and severity he derives his strongest poetic intuitions. It is as if he were some traveller to earth, who had explored human life and, finding it 'flat and unprofitable', had at the same time discovered that the fault lay in the necessity of outward events rather than with the human creatures themselves. So he turns from condemning the system to caress the human children in their weariness and to comfort them. His philosophy absolves his pity from sentimentality and his pity absolves his philosophy from cynical indifference. This mood of compassion colours and modifies many of his poems, more particularly those which approach ballad form; it lightens the gloom of *A Trampwoman's Tragedy*; it mingles with irony in *The Rival*.

Many of these poems reveal Hardy using poetic form for psychological exploration. They are, despite the limitations already suggested, the most notable element in his verse. His patience in the analysis of human motive and his revelation of intricate moods of passion sustain interest, even when that interest is not poetic. Next in importance to this psychological group are the poems which display a metaphysical bias. Hardy suggests that we should not extract from his portrayal of varying moods a metaphysical system, and label it as his own. He reaffirms this warning in uncompromising form in the preface to his last volume, *Winter Words*: 'I also repeat what I have often stated on such occasions, that no harmonious philosophy is attempted in these pages – or in any bygone pages of mine, for that matter.' Yet however cautiously we proceed it is impossible not to detect within a large number of verses a similarity of attitude, a permanent angle of vision, colouring experience ever with the same shades of belief. The most persistent mood is a consciousness of the purposelessness of life, the irremediable disorder of the cosmos. Its keenest expression can be found in *Nature's Questioning*:

> Has some Vast Imbecility,
> >Mighty to build and blend,
> >But impotent to tend,
> Framed us in jest, and left us now to hazardry?
>
> Or come we of an Automaton
> >Unconscious of our pains? . . .
> >Or are we live remains
> Of Godhead dying downwards, brain and eye now gone?

Such a mood is important not less for the thought it contains than in the degree to which the thought has been transferred into poetic reality. Lascelles Abercrombie has commented judiciously on this poem, and on its contact with a conception of Hardy's metaphysic: 'The notion . . . is one of those inventions in artistic metaphysic which can do without, and even go against, the approval of reason, because they excite in us the sense of vague, notorious feeling finally reduced to vivid and unique form.'[8]

Despite the general uniformity of these metaphysical poems they possess a variety of mood. *A Meeting with Despair* suggests a fleeting renunciation of his despair:

> >Then bitter self-reproaches as I stood
> >>I dealt me silently
> >As one perverse, misrepresenting Good
> >>In graceless mutiny.

Yet the whole intent is to emphasize that this self-reproach was momentary and unjustified. Rarely there intrudes a mood of joy:

> >>Let me enjoy the earth no less
> >>Because the all-enacting Might

> That fashioned forth its loveliness
> Had other aims than my delight.

Even here we are made to feel the impermanence of this forced elation. In *The Mother Mourns*, the Earth condemns the development of assertive, conscious thought in man. She prefers the days when he saw the sun as a 'Sanct shape' and the 'moon as the Night-Queen'; resignation rather than bitterness is the governing mood. Very different is *New Year's Eve*, a poem expressive of God's confessed purposelessness in relationship to his creation; here Hardy voices the bitter resentment of some trapped creature watching its tormentor. Examples could be multiplied to show that the mood and even the thought changes, but something deeper than these remains. It is as if creatures with different shapes came out of a fog and proclaimed separate identity for their varying forms, and we who watched confessed that the fog itself was far more important and impressive.

In certain poems, mainly later ones, Hardy gives infrequent expression to a more positive philosophy. A tentative persuasion, that 'evolutionary meliorism' may possibly effect progress, possesses him. It may be that this, too, is nothing more than a mood. If so, it is a mood which returns frequently into his consciousness, and gives him intuitions of a positive faith based on evolutionary conceptions. Possibly this was as far as he could be moved in concession to Emma's piety. One of the keenest expressions of this attitude is in the poem *In a Museum*:

> I
> Here's the mould of a musical bird long passed from light,
> Which over the earth before man came was winging;
> There's a contralto voice I heard last night,
> That lodges in me still with its sweet singing.
>
> II
> Such a dream is Time that the coo of this ancient bird
> Has perished not, but is blent, or will be blending
> Mid visionless wilds of space with the voice that I heard,
> In the full-fugued song of the universe unending.

When all Hardy's metaphysical poems have been gathered

together the group is still less impressive than the simple, terse lyrics and ballads of human experience; yet in these philosophical poems he approaches that central debate of the century, the adjustment of the individual's life to that of the universe in the terms of faith. He has abandoned Christian cosmology: he sees the world as the scientists see it; he has embraced scepticism without that spiritual nostalgia for earlier faiths which saddens some of the Great Victorians. It is unnecessary to seek in Schopenhauer or elsewhere for the origins of his conceptions, for they possess neither finality nor close philosophic discipline. They are intuitions such as sensitive minds of this and other periods must frequently have possessed. The sole difference is that Hardy found in these intuitions sources of suggestion for which he contrived to discover poetic language.

Hardy's poems on war form a convenient link between his short poems and *The Dynasts*. Three main groups of poems appear: verses on the Boer War, and the European War (1914–1918), and ballads and poems on the Napoleonic War. The governing mood behind the two groups is different. Hardy sees clearly the pain and waste of modern warfare, which he reviews in terms of realism. The Napoleonic struggle, despite all recognition of distressing aspects, has a residuum of romance. *Poems of the Past and the Present* opens with an interesting collection of Boer War poems, and the sense of glory and glamour has disappeared. He summarizes the mood in a concluding lyric, *The Sick Battle-God*, in which he describes the gradual dethroning of Mars, the warlike spirit:

> In days when men found joy in war,
> A God of Battles sped each mortal jar;
>   The peoples pledged him heart and hand,
>   From Israel's land to isles afar.
>
>   . . .
>
> Yet wars arise, though zest grows cold;
> Wherefore, at times, as if in ancient mould
>   He looms, bepatched with paint and lath;
>   But never hath he seemed the old!

> Let men rejoice, let men deplore,
> The lurid Deity of heretofore
> Succumbs to one of saner nod;
> The Battle-god is god no more.

For the European War of 1914-1918 he speaks with greater emphasis. In the *Poems of War and Patriotism* he confesses a belief in the justice of England's cause (*England to Germany in 1914*), and appeals to America for Belgium (1914); but later he commemorates the personal and human aspects of war, the tragedy of the common man that lies deeper than the policies of the nations. He remembers in *The Pity of It* the common lineage of the English and German peoples and sets his curse on those who have put them asunder. His song in honour of the soldier was sung early (September 1914) and memorably:

> What of the faith and fire within us
> Men who march away
> Ere the barn-cocks say
> Night is growing gray,
> Leaving all that here can win us;
> What of the faith and fire within us
> Men who march away?

Such is his tribute to humanity that goes bravely to war, but the ugliness and waste of the conflict remain longest in his mind. In *Then and Now* he considers the different forms of warfare, from the time of chivalry to the present day, and he sees honour and cleanliness dying out, to be replaced by unillumined cruelty.

The Napoleonic struggle aroused him in a very different way. We have already seen how that story penetrated deeply into his mind and had been a part of his family tradition: it was his boyhood reading; out of it grew in prose *The Trumpet Major* and in verse *The Dynasts*. It is not strange that he should reflect on it frequently in his lyrical verse. In *The Alarm* he reminds us in the sub-title (*In memory of one of the writer's family who was a volunteer during the War with Napoleon*) that he had close, personal contacts with the struggle. The ballad form dominates his treatment of the Napoleonic theme: typical of his method are

Valenciennes, Leipzig, The Peasant's Confession, The Dance at the Phœnix, The Bridge of Lodi, and *One We Knew*. It is not that he is blind to the cruelty of the Napoleonic Wars, but that the incidents he records glow in his mind as they might in the reminiscences of some old soldier. Most of these poems are earlier than *The Dynasts*, and they serve to show his many associations with Napoleonic legend before his imagination realized fully the implications of Napoleon's career.

The Dynasts, which Hardy completed in September 1907, is one of the ambitious poetical achievements of the period. He transfers into it all that impressive accumulation of detail which is the distinguishing characteristic of his prose work. The imagination is conquered by a sense of mass, co-ordinated to make one coherent impression. The work conforms to no recognized literary form. Hardy himself describes it as 'an epic-drama of the war with Napoleon, in three parts, nineteen acts, and one hundred and thirty scenes'. This vast material is organized into several types of action. The main movement consists of human scenes expressed in dramatic blank verse, depicting crucial moments in the ten years that precede Waterloo. These are connected by prose scenes, mainly descriptive of large movements that cannot be dramatically portrayed. Further, colloquies of phantom spirits in the Overworld, expressed in strophic stanzas, occur at intervals in the drama. It is small wonder that Hardy felt that the piece was intended 'simply for mental performance'. The human scenes are those most closely parallel to the work of earlier writers. If they stood alone, they would have the appearance of a pre-Elizabethan chronicle play; they have the same wealth of character and diffusion of scene as in the English Shakespearian chronicles, where the action seems too great for full emphasis on any individual character. Man is seen only in relationship to incident, and unity is sought in some abstract conception that summarizes the purport of the variegated movement of men and events. Yet from the complexity of action and character Hardy contrives to give a detailed presentation of Napoleon. The lyricism and the powerful gesture of the single line, from which Shakespearian blank verse derives its individuality, are absent. Examined passage by passage, the blank verse has a frequent flatness, and a severity that is almost drab, but the appropriateness of each speech and the dramatic rightness of the scenes give the whole a noble strength.

Hardy was not content to write a chronicle play. He sought devices to contrive a more coherent structure and a philosophical bias. The prose 'Dumb-Shows' which frequently divide the human dramatic scenes have a more important influence here than has been usually allowed. They serve, obviously, to unite the human action, but, more than this, they give the physical standpoint from which the spectator is to view the whole. The following is a typical passage of the prose in the 'Dumb-Shows': 'A view of the country from mid-air, at a point south of the River Inn, which is seen as a silver thread, winding northward between its junction with the Salza and the Danube, and forming the boundaries of the two countries. The Danube shows itself as a crinkled satin riband, stretching from left to right in the far background of the picture, the Inn discharging its waters into the larger river. A vast Austrian army creeps dully along the mid-distance, in the form of detached masses and columns of a whitish cast. The columns insensibly draw nearer to each other, and are seen to be converging from the east upon the banks of the Inn aforesaid.' The scene is viewed from above, at a distance from the human participants, and the spectator is made thus to feel that the individuals are but the minute puppets in some cosmic movement. In this way the Dumb-Show prepares the reader for the spiritual values of the epic-drama and for the scenes in the Overworld.

The figures in the Overworld are described by Hardy in his preface as 'supernatural spectators of the terrestrial action, certain impersonated abstractions or Intelligences, called Spirits'. They are divided into two main groups. The Spirit of Pities 'approximates to the Universal Sympathy of human nature – the spectator idealized', and the cognate spirits, Ironic, Sinister, emphasize moods in which human experience may be viewed. The Spirit of the Years, in Hardy's own phrase, 'approximates to the passionless Insight of the Ages'. Not only do these spirits comment on the action, but they are allowed at times to assume human form and mingle with the human scene. The Spirit of Rumour enters the House of a Lady of Quality in London and disturbs the company by his whispers; Pities whispers admonitions into the ear of Napoleon as he is crowned King of Italy, while Pities and the Spirit of the Years, in the form of sea-birds, influence Villeneuve in the crucial hours of his life. It is in the Overworld discussions, however, that the Spirits make their main effect. Hardy suggests that they are a modern counterpart for epic machinery and that 'their doctrines are but tentative, and are advanced with little eye to a systematized philosophy warranted to lift "the burthen of the mystery" of this unintelligible world'. Whatever may have been his initial purpose the Overworld does impose a closely defined interpretation upon the human action.

Such is the form of the work; its strength lies in the variety of the human scenes, and the close grasp on dramatic appropriateness that Hardy retains throughout. We see passengers in a Wessex coach quarrelling over England's war policy; Sheridan speaking in the Old House of Commons; George III receiving Pitt amid the leisure of his Weymouth distractions; Napoleon and Josephine; the death of Sir John Moore; the wooing of Maria Louisa; and the little boy who can prove that 'Mr Pitt killed Uncle John's parrot'; and so to the climax of Waterloo. Retaining closely the outline of historical fact, Hardy has wrought from the Napoleonic story its rich human and dramatic possibilities. Only once does he turn from the press of men in events to dwell caressingly with an individual. The death of Nelson so delays him, and in consequence produces the drama's most lyrical passage of blank verse. Nelson, as he dies, has asked Hardy, the Wessex captain, what he is thinking of, and Hardy replies:

> Thoughts all confused, my lord: – their needs on deck,
> Your own sad state, and your unrivalled past;

> Mixed up with flashes of old things afar –
> Old childish things at home, down Wessex way,
> In the snug village under Blackdon Hill
>
> Where I was born. The tumbling stream, the garden,
> The placid look of the grey dial there
> Marking unconsciously this bloody hour,
> And the red apples on my father's trees,
> Just now full ripe.

It would seem that Hardy revenged upon himself this moment of excessive concern at Nelson's death, for later he makes Nelson's body the cause of one of the few grotesque scenes in the drama. An old boatman is made to recount how Nelson was brought home 'in a cask of sperrits . . . But what happened was this. They were a long time coming, owing to contrary winds, and the Victory being little more than a wreck. And grog ran short, because they'd used near all they had to peckle his body in. So – they broached the Adm'l . . . the plain calendar of it is, that when he came to be unhooped, it was found that the crew had drunk him dry.' The scene is one of the strange, gothic elements in *The Dynasts*, an incident that only the Spirit Ironic can interpret.

When all comment on detail has been made the vast impression of the whole work returns to capture the mind. The scientists have envisioned a larger cosmos since Milton wrote *Paradise Lost* and Hardy is alone among the modern poets in attempting to capture these illimitable elements into imaginative form. This panoramic show, 'a spectacle in the likeness of a drama', intended only for mental performance, rises in its unity to give an impression of strength which is absent from the single scenes considered in isolation. This quality gives to the work, apart from its novelty of form, a classical structure, an economy in the parts arising from their due subordination to a unity in design. The same architectonic control as gives to the novels their sombre strength pervades this epic-drama, though the canvas is here more extended. The underlying values are the same as those found in the novels, and in many of the short poems. They accumulate into a view of life, emotional and intuitive, without the logical clarity or argued consistency of a philosophy. Over human life hangs a malignant destiny which leads all human endeavour to frustration and cruelty. In the midst of this calamity there remains a spectator piteous and deeply affected but impotent to assist. The intellect suggests that gradually this tragedy may be alleviated, but the suggestion is only momentary and finds no confirmation in events. It is with such a momentary relaxation into optimism that *The Dynasts* closes:

> But – a stirring thrills the air
> Like to sounds of joyance there
>   That the rages
>   Of the ages
> Shall be cancelled, and deliverance offered from the darts that were,
> Consciousness the Will informing, till It fashion all things fair!

Hardy's one other adventure into poetic drama is of a much more modest type. *The Famous Tragedy of the Queen of Cornwall* (1924) is his version of the Tristram and Iseult story 'arranged as a play for mummers'. His intention in this drama[9] was to preserve, as in classical drama, the unities and a Chorus, named The Chanters. He demands at the same time a licence to modify the legend. The resulting play is slight and unsatisfactory. He has completely perverted the values of the traditional Tristram and Iseult story and has had nothing to substitute for the loss of its grace and loveliness. His play ends by the King stabbing Tristram and Queen Iseult stabbing the King. The Queen rushes out and promises to commit suicide. Hardy, in reducing the legend, has made it a meaner thing, nor does his model of a mummer's play, despite his citation of classical parallels, allow for any adequate development of character or dramatic conflict. Having made the cosmos his stage in *The Dynasts*, he chose here to work with puppets, and the effect is not equally satisfying. The interest in the play can only remain an interest in experiment: it is elsewhere that one must look for his individual contribution to nineteenth-century poetry.

James Thomson

James Thomson (1834-1882),[1] popularly known as the poet of one poem, *The City of Dreadful Night,* presents a record of half-frustrated poetic expression, with moments of dark splendour, arising from a life dominated by misfortune. He was born at Port Glasgow in 1834. His mother died when he was 6, and from her close evangelicalism he was later to revolt. His father was a sailor stricken with paralysis, and some of Thomson's unstable characteristics have been traced to his influence. Thomson found sufficient schooling in London in the Royal Caledonian Asylum, later the Royal Caledonian Schools, at Ballincollig, near Cork, and at the Royal Military Asylum, Chelsea, to qualify him for an army-schoolmastership, and from 1854 to 1862 he served in army schools in Ireland and England. Like Leopardi, who influenced his poetry, he loved unsuccessfully; the one to whom he was deeply attached was Matilda Weller and she died in 1853, and in the most ambitious of his prose essays, *A Lady of Sorrow,* he has commemorated the attachment in language influenced by De Quincey. His years as a schoolmaster were the most untroubled in his life, though there are many signs that he found the work uncongenial and questioned his own abilities. He had worked to gain a knowledge of Italian, French, and German, and had read widely in English literature: he translated Heine, who had an influence on his poetry, and Novalis. It was then that poetry began, and as yet the poverty and self-inflicted distress of the later years had not mastered him. He was dismissed from his post in 1862 for a breach of discipline which appears to have been of a venial character. In his early days at Ballincollig he had met, at Cork, Charles Bradlaugh, the rationalist politician who carried his atheism so aggressively into English public life. His influence on Thomson was profound, and it was to Bradlaugh that he turned after his dismissal, whose home was the first family background he ever knew. Bradlaugh found him work on his paper, the *National Reformer*, and from 1862 to 1874 Thomson wrote regularly for the rationalist Press. His satiric prose in such pieces as *The Story of a Famous Old Jewish Firm*[2] has an assaulting power: the work that Swift might have produced had he been an atheist and not a Christian. Unfortunately his rationalist associations and his poverty barred him from the society and the literary journals where his poetical work might have found acceptance. His interests remained wide: the initials 'B. V.' ('Bysshe Vanolis'), under which he wrote, showed his admiration for Shelley and Novalis, while his prose essays mark his retention of wide literary enthusiasm and discrimination.[3] Yet rationalist thought was definitely penetrating his outlook and exercising a developing influence on his creative work. Apart from one visit to Colorado and another to Spain, a garret in London was the centre of the rest of his life, and the dim gas-lit streets of London appear frequently in his poetry, though relieved in the expression of a Londoner's pleasure as in *Sunday at Hampstead* and *Sunday up the River*. Yet after he left the Bradlaugh home melancholy possessed him with the strength of physical disease, and he grew into a habit of drinking which his will was powerless to control. It was towards the close of this period that *The City of the Dreadful Night* appeared in the *National Reformer*, March–May 1874.

In 1875 Thomson quarrelled with Bradlaugh, and his association with the *National Reformer* ceased. He struggled to gain other journalism, and some of his work appeared in that most curious Victorian periodical *Cope's Tobacco Plant*, in which a Liverpool firm advertised its tobacco by printing reputable literature. These were temporary exploits, and Thomson's condition was frequently not far from destitution. He had the good fortune to gain the friendship of Bertram Dobell, bookseller and publisher, who arranged for the appearance of his first volume of verse, *The City of Dreadful Night and other Poems*, in 1880. The title-poem had already gained the attention of George Eliot, Meredith, and Philip Bourke Marston, and the volume was in every way successful. Later in the same year (1880) appeared a second volume, *Vane's Story, Weddah and Om-el-Bonain and other Poems*. Recognition had come at last, and had Thomson a settled health or temperate habits he could have developed the opening offered him in periodicals such as the *Fortnightly* and the *Cornhill*. But dipsomania possessed him, until even his friends found difficulty in associating with him. He died in 1882 in University College Hospital, where he had been taken by Philip Bourke Marston and other friends. After his death a third volume of verse, *A Voice from the Nile and other Poems* (1884), was published with a memoir by Bertram Dobell, and in 1895 the collected *Poetical Works* were issued, to be followed by a selection of the prose.

Thomson's poetry was issued in volume form only in the last years of his life, though some of it had been composed more than twenty years before. The order of composition can be generally determined by the dates of periodical publication and by biographical information, and the development of Thomson's mind and creative power can be more clearly perceived once the poems are so arranged. The first period in his work dates from the middle fifties until his dismissal from the army-schoolmastership in 1862. He had not yet absorbed atheism as a creed: he stands as Arnold did in the 'valley of the shadow of hesitation'. An expression of this spiritual self-probing lies in *Suggested by Matthew Arnold's 'Stanzas from the Grande Chartreuse'* (1855); poetically the piece is flat, but it shows Thomson torn between the faith of his childhood and a belief that Christianity is

> a mighty Creed outworn –
> Its spirit fading from the earth.

If *Suggested* is an attempt to express his early position intellectually, *A Recusant* (1858) forms, again under Arnold's influence, an emotional approach to the same dilemma:

> The Church stands there beyond the orchard-blooms:
> How yearningly I gaze upon its spire!
> Lifted mysterious through the twilight glooms,
> Dissolving in the sunset's golden fire,
> Or dim as slender incense morn by morn
> Ascending to the blue and open sky.
> For ever when my heart feels most forlorn
> It murmurs to me with a weary sigh,
> How sweet to enter in, to kneel and pray
> With all the others whom we love so well!
> All disbelief and doubt might pass away,
> All peace float to us with its Sabbath bell.
> Conscience replies, There is but one good rest,
> Whose head is pillowed upon Truth's pure breast.

Apart from the poems which express this central approach to faith, he wrote within this period a number of lyrics, varied in mood, and frequently of distinct accomplishment. Among them is *Withered Leaves* (1857), an epitaph, possessing more technical virtuosity than he usually displays:

> Let the roses lie, dear,
> Let them lie;
> They are all thrown by, dear,
> All thrown by:
> What should they do now but quickly die?

One poem in this first period, *The Doom of a City* (1857), preshadows much in his later work. The poem opens with a voyage in a boat, which has suggestions of *Alastor*, to a city of stone people, a notion derived directly from *The Arabian Nights*.[4] These elements are harnessed, somewhat incongruously, to a Judgement scene followed finally by an account of the return voyage. Thomson was conscious that he had not succeeded in inducing unity upon his diverse thought and material; in a manuscript note he wrote, 'I call it a Fantasia, because (lacking the knowledge and power to deal with the theme in its epical integrity) I made it but an episode in a human life.'[5] This self-criticism must be accepted and it needs emphasis. His theme belongs distinctly to his earlier period; the recognition of a Providence has not been rejected and even a faith in human amelioration is expressed. Looseness of poetic form and unevenness of thought both detract from the merit of the piece, yet certain characteristics of his poetical work appear here for the first time. Despite his failure in the work as a whole, he has scattered through its diverse parts brilliant single lines and short passages of descriptive strength. Such is the picture of a city of stone, and such is the following simile around which clings an element of personal pathos:

> As one who in the morning-shine
>   Reels homeward, shameful, wan, adust,
> From orgies wild with fiery wine
>   And reckless sin and brutish lust:
> And sees a doorway open wide,
>   And then the grand Cathedral space;
> And hurries in to crouch and hide
>   His trembling frame, his branded face.

Yet he is capable of destroying his strongest passage by some gesture of crudity that would have led the reviewers of the romantic period to dub him a 'cockney-atheist'. Apart from developing characteristics of style, the poem possesses the peculiar image which moves in and out of his later poetry and dwells in *The City of Dreadful Night*: a single man, alone in a city at night, where darkness is broken only by the gas-lights and silence is not broken at all:

> I paced through desert streets, beneath the gleam
> Of lamps that lit my trembling life alone.

So emerges the symbol in which Thomson endeavours to express imaginatively his spiritual loneliness and melancholy.

The second poetic period (1860-1874) is roughly contemporaneous with his employment by Bradlaugh on the *National*

Reformer (1862-1874); this culminates with *The City of Dreadful Night*, though much of the work is of a different character. *Sunday at Hampstead* (1863) and *Sunday up the River* (1865) are poems of the cockney worker at rest. The earlier piece has memories of Heine, a number of whose poems Thomson translated and whose influence on his work is marked. The holiday mood of the later piece is interrupted with historical discourses. Both poems have an individual atmosphere, the country near the gas-lit streets, the love-making of the worker at rest. The occasional cockneyisms merely help to define the frolic mood. The detachment of these poems from atheistical discourse is retained in *The Naked Goddess* (1866) and *Weddah and Om-el Bonain* (1868), two of his most secure poems, which suggest that he possessed elements of suppressed romanticism. *The Naked Goddess* is an allegory of pagan beauty transcending the sombre, furtive ways of priest and philosopher. In couplets, of a mainly trochaic movement, he has maintained his theme with even power; he has consolidated the elements of fable, satire, and description into one impressive whole. A larger work, no less adequately contrived is *Weddah and Om-el Bonain*, a story expanded, in *ottava rima*, from a brief prose incident in Stendhal's *De l'Amour*, and showing an unusual control of narrative. It has the same range of ambition as Keats's *Isabella*; decorative elements enter without corrupting the development, and the memory left from the poem lies not merely in incident but in a piteous image of beauty's unfair struggle with power. Meredith's comment is memorable: '[The poem] stands to witness what great things he would have done in the exhibition of nobility at war with evil traditions.' These poems show clearly that Thomson had wider potentialities than his actual achievement might suggest, but the dark melancholy that dwelt within him gradually reduced all promise of colour and variety to its own sombre mood.

Two poems emerge in these years, personal in character and anticipatory of *The City of Dreadful Night*: *To Our Ladies of Death* (1861) and *Vane's Story* (1864). The earlier poem derives from De Quincey's *Suspiria de Profundis*, and resolves itself into verbal statuary, figuring Our Lady of Beatitudes, Our Lady of Annihilation, and Our Lady of Oblivion. In a stanza derived from Browning's *The Guardian Angel* he attains a classical restraint and dignity of expression. This breaks down at the close as a mood of personal suffering enters in; for with Thomson as emotion increases poetic effectiveness declines. The poem marks his first full declaration of pessimism, the consciousness of *l'ultimo inganno della vita* which had led him to kinship with Leopardi:

> Weary of living isolated life,
>   Weary of hoping hopes for ever vain,
> Weary of struggling in all-sterile strife,
>   Weary of thought which maketh nothing plain,
> I close my eyes and hush my panting breath,
> And yearn for Thee, divinely tranquil Death,
>   To come and soothe away my bitter pain.

Vane's Story (1864), a more uneven work, has definitely autobiographical elements. After a brief prologue in Skeltonics, the speaker narrates how he encounters the vision of his dead beloved. They speak together, he of his atheism and she of her simple, self-consoling faith. Abruptly the poem changes with the recital of Heine's *Ich bin die Prinzessin Ilse*. The lady ceases to be a vision, gains definite human qualities, and goes off with the speaker to a working-men's ball. Here they meet Brown and Jones with their rough, enthusiastic pleasure-making, and so Vane's dream ends. The poem has marked defects, including this ill-contrived transition from fantasy to realism. Thomson, who knew Browning's work, had a model in *Christmas Eve and Easter Day* for the union of satire and discourse which he wished to convey. He failed to make use of it, and his poem is marred with grossness and with sly, ogling lines; he admits their presence, but excuses them with Heine's example:

> Grossness here indeed is regnant,
> But it is the grossness pregnant;

Heine growled it, ending thus
His wild *Book of Lazarus*.

Again the anti-Christian satire lacks dramatic appropriateness; the journalist belabouring his opponents has intruded, as in the lines on the creation:

> He cursed
> The work He thought so good at first;
> And surely Earth and Heaven evince
> That He has done but little since.

Despite these inequalities, the poem possesses autobiographical interest, and isolated images and passages have the excellence frequently found as a partially compensating element in Thomson's uneven, introspective poems. The terror with which he recognizes the necessity of accepting this misshapen life is expressed in lines reminiscent of Blake:

> As well a thorn might pray to be
> Transformed into an olive-tree;
> As well a weevil might determine
> To grow a farmer hating vermin.

He portrays how in his own life the earlier happiness has been overshadowed; melancholia and mental isolation are poisoning him:

> The stream fell stagnant, and was soon
> A bloated marsh, a pest-lagoon;
> The sweet flowers died, the noble trees
> Turned black and gaunt anatomies;
> The birds all left the saddened air
> To seek some other home as fair.

From 1870 to 1874 Thomson was engaged on *The City of Dreadful Night*. In other poems he is more secure, but here more creative, and a strange, distinctive world emerges, a symbol of Despair fashioned only for those who know its 'dolorous mysteries'. Thomson seems fascinated by London, as a city of loneliness and gloom, a mood which appears in his autobiographical poem *In the Room*, 1867-1868. He confesses that life is a tortured

Death-in-Life (the phrase itself he derived from Heine's *Confessions*) and poetry may give

> some sense of power and passion
> In helpless impotence to try to fashion
> Our woe in living words howe'er uncouth.

Though much in the poem is similar to Leopardi's pessimism, it is clear from *The Doom of a City* (1857) that Thomson had his own intuitions of despair before he found confirmation of them in the Italian's work. The poem opens with a geographical description of the City, curiously detailed, as if a metaphysical poet had written it, but impressive with glimpses of waste marshes that shine and glisten in the moon. A succession of pictures follows, not closely connected, but all displaying scenes in the dread life of the City. These are expressed in varying verse forms, and set alternately with them are passages in a seven-line stanza showing the progress of the speaker. Thomson evokes images of sombre power to present the grim pageantry: a weary figure shows life void of meaning as a watch without hands or marks on the dial-face; another appears tortured by his loss of the woman who could have given him hope; some of the inhabitants of the dread City attempt to escape to Hell and find that the citizens of the Dreadful City are 'shut alike from Heaven and Earth and Hell'. He emphasizes this mood of despair by his portrayal of the Mansion of love that is frustrated, the voice of a preacher, the River of the Suicides, the sphinx amid shattered statuary, and, as a culminating episode, a verbal rendering of Albrecht Dürer's 'Melencolia'. Behind these scenes are the recurrent impressions of the speaker, stifled and lonely, moving in silence through the gloom of the gas-lit streets:

> Although lamps burn along the silent streets;
> Even when moonlight silvers silent squares
> The dark holds countless lanes and close retreats;
> But when the night its sphereless mantle wears
> The open spaces yawn with gloom abysmal,
> The sombre mansions loom immense and dismal,
> The lanes are black as subterranean lairs.

The mood of despair penetrates deeper than the spiritual nostalgia of the romantics or the prayer for life's cessation of Swinburne's *The Garden of Proserpine*. Life is here an aching and inescapable futility like the maddening wakefulness of insomnia. The strength of the poem lies in the imaginative quality that has sustained these dark phantoms without monotony; and it increases in the later sections, so that the fallen statuary and the transcript of Dürer's 'Melencolia' and the description of the sphinx are among the most marked and individual passages in the whole of Thomson's work. Despite unevenness he has poetic integrity, and not infrequently poetic power. His contacts lay closely with the earlier nineteenth-century discussion of faith and disbelief. He carries on that theme where Arnold left it, in self-frustrating doubt. He penetrates farther than Arnold and arouses from his scepticism an image of despair.

10

Robert Bridges and his Associates:
Canon Dixon, Mary Coleridge, Digby Mackworth Dolben, Robert Bridges

A number of poets in the later nineteenth century are closely associated with Robert Bridges: he knew them personally and championed them, though some of their ways in verse, and their motives, including the poetical expression of religious experience, lay removed from his own achievement. The earliest, Canon Dixon, had been, as a young man, a member with William Morris of a group intimately connected with the Pre-Raphaelites. Later he removed himself from that allegiance, and his poetry, like that of Bridges and of the other writers in this chapter, is marked frequently with a conscious reaction from Pre-Raphaelite methods and motives. More notable than Bridges's praise of Dixon is his support of D. M. Dolben and, above all, his friendship with Gerard Manley Hopkins, which is discussed in the next chapter.

Digby Mackworth Dolben (1848-1868) showed an early, almost precocious, talent in verse. Bridges, who knew him at Eton and was related to him, published his poems and portrayed his brief life in a memoir (1911). He presents him as a keenly emotional nature, one who could be aroused to passionate attachments, whether for friends, or religion, or verse. His life from his adolescence onwards was dominated by religious enthusiasms. Though he did not actually enter the Roman Church, his thought from his Eton days onwards was continually turned towards that direction. In his poetry he seems conscious not only of religion and the cloister but of the beauties of a pagan world. So in the dramatic monologue *From the Cloister*, Brother Jerome speaks:

> O sunny Athens, home of life and love,
> Free joyous life that I may never live,
> Warm glowing love that I may never know, –
> Home of Apollo, god of poetry.

This conflicting attraction of Greece and Christian Rome he never completely resolved. Possibly had he lived to more mature years he might have come to produce very different work, but in the record that remains religious poetry stands out as the strongest element. He captured some fragrance of Christian medievalism, and sometimes, as in *Homo Factus Est*, deliberately imitated a medieval hymn:

> Come to me, Belovèd,
> Babe of Bethlehem;
> Lay aside Thy Sceptre
> And Thy Diadem.

Bridges speaks cautiously of Dolben's talent, possibly too cautiously, for despite his championship they belonged to different schools. Bridges had a strong classical rectitude in his work, while Dolben, even in his religious verse, is thrusting out excessively towards romantic effects. This Bridges himself realized: 'Our instinctive attitudes towards poetry were very dissimilar, he regarded it from the emotional, and I from the artistic side.' Yet Bridges makes it clear that he saw in Dolben a potentially rich talent that might, had it developed, have made an important contribution to later nineteenth-century poetry.

Richard Watson Dixon[1] (1833-1900), eldest son of a celebrated Methodist minister, was in the group of undergraduates who were associated with Morris and Burne-Jones in the days of the 'Brotherhood' at Oxford, where he was a member of Pembroke College. Most of those young men were destined for the Church: Dixon alone fulfilled that destiny. He held many offices, though he never gained the preferment which his friends thought he deserved. He wrote an elaborate *History of the Church of England*, the main literary accomplishment of his life. Poetry was a fitful occupation. His verse was issued as, *Christ's Company* (1861); *St John in Patmos* (1863); *Historical Odes* (1864); *Mano* (1883); *Odes and Eclogues* (1884); *Songs and Odes* (1896); *Last Poems* (1905); *Selected Poems* (1909). Canon Dixon's claims for poetical recognition have been ably championed by Robert Bridges and by Mary Coleridge, though unfortunately Bridges attempted to elevate him by special pleading and the unnecessary disparagement of Morris. Such was Dixon's wayward occupation with poetry that he never mastered its technical problems. He assumed those privileges of imperfect rhyming and stress variation which the Pre-Raphaelites employed, merely to override the difficulties that he encountered. Four lines more bleak than those with which his *Story of Eudocia* opens can hardly be imagined:

> Theodosius the Roman Emperor,
> Son of Arcadius, was named Junior,
> Being grandson of Theodosius the Great,
> And in weak nonage raised to his estate.

The same technical difficulties crumble and corrupt the verse of *Mano*, an experiment in a *terza rima* presentation of a tenth-century theme. Dixon cannot, however, be judged from his narrative poetry, though the same deficiencies often intrude to mar his lyrics. In the following poem, which Mary Coleridge praised in high terms, one doubts if the mood is helped by the persistent imperfection of the rhymes:

> The feathers of the willow
> Are half of them grown yellow
> Above the swelling stream;
> And ragged are the bushes,

>   And rusty now the rushes,
>   And wild the clouded gleam.
>
>   The thistle now is older,
>   His stalk begins to moulder,
>   His head is white as snow;
>   The branches all are barer,
>   The linnet's song is rarer,
>   The robin pipeth now.

As Bridges detected, Dixon's poetical work grew better in his later periods. His early verse has an occasional influence derived from Morris in Pre-Raphaelite mood, with an exploitation of a religious melancholia that left life dull and inert. This atmosphere was partly relieved, and there was a greater compensating strength, in the *St John* volume, where the most successful poem, *St Mary Magdalene*, is closely Pre-Raphaelite. The volume entitled *Historical Odes* has more variety: the historical pieces themselves are ponderous and creaking poems, on Wellington (with an abstract but able picture of Waterloo), and on Marlborough. Dixon also wrote dramatically of a number of religious incidents: *Legion*, *St Thomas in India*, and the Pre-Raphaelite *Joseph of Arimathea* and *Nicodemus*. A few lyrics, including *The Feathers of the Willow*, showed more colour than the earlier work possessed.

The later lyrics were issued privately after a gap of more than twenty years. They possess an increased mastery of form, using a classical reserve and formality mingled with some archaism and eccentricity of vocabulary. Religious themes dominate, pervaded by a persistent melancholia, yet in *The Mystery of the Body*, *Ode on Conflicting Claims*, and *I Rode my Horse to the Hostel Gate*, Dixon has explored successfully moods which the technical resources of his earlier poetry would not have sustained. These volumes gained variety by Dixon's use of classical themes – *Ulysses and Calypso*, *Mercury to Prometheus*, and others; in a genre which the nineteenth century flogged threadbare Dixon contrived an individuality by directness and simplicity. The most memorable of these later poems is *The Fall of the Leaf*, a nature study, sustained by a melancholic imagery similar to that in his contemplative poems, although even here a technical casualness mars the perfection of effect:

> Rise in their place the woods: the trees have cast,
> Like earth to earth, their children: now they stand
> Above the graves where lie their very last:
> Each pointing with her empty hand
> And mourning o'er the russet floor,
> Naked and dispossessed:
> The queenly sycamore,
> The linden and the aspen, and the rest.

As a poet Dixon was held captive both by technical waywardness and limitation of mood. When he broke through his depression, to poems of nature and fancy, as in *Fallen Rain*, or in *Ode: The Spirit Wooed*, he had a rare gift of phrase and imagery. It was this element that attracted Bridges, and Dixon is best read in the few passages selected in Bridges's preface.

Mary Elizabeth Coleridge[2] (1861-1907), who had Samuel Taylor Coleridge among her forebears, published in her lifetime but little poetry, and that under the pseudonym of 'Anodos'. In 1896 Robert Bridges persuaded her to issue a private and limited edition of poems, *Fancy's Following*, and a modified form of this collection appeared in 1897 as *Fancy's Guerdon* in one of Elkin Mathews's *Shilling Garland Series*. The main collection of her verses was made in 1907, after her death, by Sir Henry Newbolt.

Poetry occupied but a small part of her life; she wrote prose romances, some of which, like *The King with Two Faces*, brought her a wide popularity, and she had many charitable and social activities. There comes through the scanty biographical records and there reappears in the poems an impression of a vibrant, keenly living personality. Her *Letters and Diaries* show her arising from a religious atmosphere, and poised in deep concern, before the problems of the modern world. Her contrasting interests are symbolized in her diary entry in 1891: '*Ghosts*, and a sermon fifty-six minutes long, all in the course of one week.'

She seemed, in her earlier poems and in the letters, to seek the sensuous pageantry of colour and form in the living world:

> Pour me red wine from out the Venice flask,
>   Pour faster, faster yet!
> The joy of ruby thought I do not ask,
>   Bid me forget!

Gradually an inwardness of thought developed, a hesitancy and distrust of experience, and an increased preoccupation with religion:

> Bid me remember, O my gracious Lord,
> The flattering words of love are merely breath!
> O not in roses wreathe the shining sword,
> Bid me remember, O my gracious Lord,
>   The bitter taste of death!

All her poems were short lyrics, arising frequently from some suggestion of personal experience. It is difficult without biographical material to trace these moods separately to their sources. Her development had some parallel with that of Christina Rossetti, and the resultant verse is at times similar, though Mary Coleridge's range is much more confined. Both sought within the world, for warmth, colour, and love; both withdrew hesitantly towards religion. The progress is less definitely marked in Mary Coleridge, and one feels that William Johnson Cory, who was her friend and tutor, may have helped her towards the final resolution of this conflict.

Technically her work is secure, and here again Cory's influence may be traced. Of direct reminiscence there is little in her work; Robert Bridges compared her poetry to that of Heine, but this was merely to suggest her concentration of a mood into a short poem with an apparently effortless movement. Certain recurring *idées génératrices* can be traced throughout. The most remarkable is the mood which gained dramatic expression in stories of magic, in pieces such as *Master and Guest*, *The Witch*, *Wilderspin*, which have led a critic to speak of her as 'the tail of the comet, S.T.C.' These poems, apart from the Pre-Raphaelite influence in *Wilderspin*, have much originality. Allied to them are a number of lyrics, fashioning out a mood in a more personal manner; they include the powerful sonnet *Imagination* ('I called you, fiery spirits, and ye came'), and *The Other Side of a Mirror*, a poem suggestive of the Metaphysicals, and expressed with considerable verbal cunning. Many of the lyrics have a less definite background, though their movement and expression are often skilfully contrived. Such a piece is *A Moment*:

>   The clouds had made a crimson crown
>   Above the mountains high,
>   The stormy sun was going down
>   In a stormy sky.
>
>   Why did you let your eyes so rest on me,
>   And hold your breath between?
>   In all the ages this can never be
>   As if it had not been.

Along with these poems of mood she wrote on mystical and religious themes, and these become more prevalent in the later years. Frequently the religious thought was given brief poignant expression as a simple experience, as in *Depart from me, I know thee not*, and *Thee have I sought, divine Humility*.

Mary Coleridge was able to reveal only a part of her personality in verse; her letters and her prose work show that there was a quiet ironic laughter in her spirit which never comes through into her poetry. Like many other women of her time, and among them Christina Rossetti, she had narrow opportunities for experience. Such of her life as she could convert into poetry she rendered with precision and beauty. One wonders whether, if she had been more deeply distressed, with wider clashes of happiness and despair, the resultant yield in poetry would have been richer. Contact with Canon Dixon may have helped to develop her melancholia, though she combated it with a variety of mood to which Dixon never attained. There developed in her work poems such as *Mother to a Baby*, simple, like Blake's early verse, and yet powerful. She could, more perhaps than any woman poet of the century, concentrate her meaning with epigrammatic precision. The following poem is a single thrust unerring and yet controlled:

> Forgive? O yes! how lightly, lightly said!
> Forget? No, never, while the ages roll,
> Till God slay o'er again the undying dead,
> And quite unmake my soul!

Robert Seymour Bridges[3] (1844-1930) was a poet of a different range from those discussed earlier in this chapter. He began publishing verse in 1873 and continued until *The Testament of Beauty* in 1929. Last of the Victorians, he gathered much of what that age held dear and revered in this poem, and, publishing it at the age of 85, he found a strangely wide appreciation from a generation that had turned to other values and methods in its art.

Bridges passed his early years at his parents' house at Walmer on the Kentish coast, where he derived much pleasure from the garden and orchard. His father died in 1853, and his mother married Dr Molesworth, Vicar of Rochdale, in 1854. During most of his Eton years Bridges's home was the Vicarage, Rochdale. He was the eighth child in a family of nine. From 1854 to 1863 he was at Eton, where he distinguished himself in study and in games, and showed equally his power of sympathizing with the wayward personality of Digby Mackworth Dolben. From Eton he moved to Oxford and consolidated the interest in classical studies which penetrated so firmly into his creative work, and at Oxford, as is elsewhere recorded, he met Gerard Manley Hopkins. Poetry attracted him early, though his first volume, a thin pamphlet of lyrics, did not appear until 1873. Poetry seemed already his spiritual profession, but he determined to widen his contacts with life; he spent eight months in Germany and travelled in Syria and Egypt, and later in a number of European countries. He applied himself to scientific and medical studies; he was a student at St Bartholomew's and later a physician at the Children's Hospital, Great Ormond Street, and at the Great

Northern Hospital. In 1882 he gave up medicine and settled at Yattendon, and in 1884 he married. The years spent at Yattendon (1882-1905) were productive poetically, for most of the plays and many of the minor poems were then written. After a stay of some months in Switzerland (1905-1906) he returned to England and built Chilswell House on Boar's Hill, near Oxford. There he lived for the last twenty-five years of his life. In 1913 he was made Poet Laureate, and in 1929 he received the Order of Merit. This year was marked, too, by the publication of *The Testament of Beauty*. On 21 April 1930 he died.

Bridges's lyrical poetry is known to most readers from the collected editions, but it was first published in a number of small volumes, issued privately at frequent intervals. *Poems* (1873) was followed by *The Growth of Love* (1876, 1889, 1898) and by pamphlets of verse (1879, 1880, 1884, 1890, 1893, 1894, 1896). Many of these were revised and issued together in 1899 and in 1912. There followed *Now in Wintry Delights* (1903); *October and Other Poems* (1920); *New Verse* (1921). Apart from these volumes of short poems, *Eros and Psyche*, a narrative poem, had been published in 1885, and plays and masques were issued: *Prometheus the Firegiver* (1883); *Nero* (1885 and 1894); *The Feast of Bacchus* (1889); *Palicio* (1890); *The Return of Ulysses* (1890); *Achilles in Scyros* (1890); *The Christian Captives* (1890); *The Humours of the Court* (1893); *Demeter, a masque* (1905). Finally in 1929 there was published *The Testament of Beauty*.

Apart from verse, Bridges had a deep love of music. Of this the Yattendon Hymn Book and the Yattendon Psalter were a few manifestations and in his later years he did much work on the pointing of the Psalms. Further his love of beautiful things was shown by his interest in handwriting and in fine printing. Again, apart from his poetry, the most popular of all his publications was his very imaginative and unusual anthology *The Spirit of Man* (1916). There he expressed cogently what was probably his ultimate view of human life and experience:

As for the sequence chosen, that might no doubt have been other than it is without damage and perhaps with advantage; but, as will readily be perceived, the main implication is essential, namely that spirituality is the basis and foundation of human life – in so far as our life is a worthy subject for ideal philosophy and pure aesthetic – rather than the apex or final attainment of it. It must underlie everything. To put it briefly, man is a spiritual being, and the proper work of his mind is to interpret the world according to his higher nature, and to conquer the material aspects of the world so as to bring them into subjection to the spirit.

Bridges has affirmed his own approach to poetry in contrasting it with that of D. M. Dolben: 'What had led me to poetry was the inexhaustible satisfaction of form, the magic of speech, lying as it seemed to me in the masterly control of the material: it was an art which I hoped to learn. An instinctive rightness was essential, but, given that, I did not suppose that the poet's emotions were in any way better than mine, nor mine than another's: and, though I should not at that time have put it in these words, I think that Dolben imagined poetic form to be the naïve outcome of peculiar personal emotion.'[4] These principles result in that attraction for prosodic experiment, always present in Bridges's work, leading alike to lyrical success, to the Delilah of experiments in classical and quantitative verse, and to the final genial compromise of the 'loose alexandrines' in *The Testament of Beauty*. His emphasis on form had an influence apart from prosody. In finding poetic suggestion in commonly shared experience he escaped from the romantic excess of much nineteenth-century verse, and equally from the search for the odd and grotesque. He returned to a principle that would have pleased Pope and Dr Johnson – 'What oft was thought but ne'er so well expressed' – though he interpreted this elucidation of the commonplace in his own way. The approach explains, as is noted below, many of the more memorable lyrics, such as *London Snow*.

In this precise discipline he matured his poetic individuality, but certain elements were thus consciously excluded. He seemed to have grown distrustful of imagery, though his appreciation of its successful use can be seen from the passage in his essay on Keats, where he described imagery as the highest gift in poetry:

'I mean the power of concentrating all the far-reaching resources of language on one point, so that a single and apparently effortless expression rejoices the aesthetic imagination at the moment when it is most expectant and exacting, and at the same time astonishes the intellect with a new aspect of truth.'[5] This gift was not entirely absent in Bridges: it adorned *The Growth of Love* and *The Testament of Beauty*; but one is conscious that it has been restrained both by his sense of diffidence and in obedience to self-imposed principles. Reticence penetrated from vocabulary into subject. His early reading in the classics was continued throughout his life; many of his lyrics record the pleasure he thus received. The attraction of classical form, obvious in his dramas and in the quantitative pieces, penetrated in a more subtle way into his other poems. He supplemented it with a close study of English poets who were similarly influenced, of Spenser and Milton, and incorporated their adaptation of Italian models, particularly the *canzone*. Of romantic influences he was more suspicious. Shelley, particularly in his Greek affinities, attracted him, and *The Hymn to Intellectual Beauty* had a place in the development of his philosophy. In his essay on Keats he extracted the frequent perfection of phrase from the relapses into technical inadequacy, while Keats's withdrawal from life into the contemplation of Beauty found a parallel in his own experience. But from the glamour of romantic poetry, with the consequent risk of insecurity, he turned with something like disdain. This attitude is emphasized by a strong distaste for the Victorian romanticism of the Pre-Raphaelites. It arose, in part, out of a personal loyalty to Canon Dixon, who, once an undergraduate companion of Morris, retained his religious faith, and found himself isolated in temper and achievement from the associates of Rossetti. This antagonism, presumably, led to his exclusion of Morris and Rossetti from his anthology, *The Spirit of Man* (1917). Along with these excesses of romantic poetry he avoided instinctively both the coarse, animal elements which occur in Chaucer, Shakespeare, and Burns, and that preoccupation with blood and tears which intrudes into the Elizabethans and into Browning. This fastidiousness can most easily be seen in his attitude to Shakespeare. To the language he surrendered his admiration: Shakespeare mastered the supreme gift which Keats had fitfully possessed, and in *The Testament of Beauty* the *Sonnets* are neatly epitomized:

> Those golden sonnets
> that swim like gondolas i' the wake of his drama.

Yet for the broader humour of the plays and their unabashed contact with the grosser elements in life he expressed in his essays a strong, even prim disapproval.[6] His objections to Browning, who was also excluded from *The Spirit of Man*, were probably more deep rooted. The stridency of Browning's verse, the acrobatics of vocabulary combined with grotesque, unusual themes, and heavy trencher-work in didacticism, served to render his poetry an epitome of all that Bridges would avoid.

Apart from classical influences, he had for himself a conception of belief that arose from art or philosophy rather than from a religious faith, as he has suggested himself in his memoir of Dolben. He seemed to have reverenced religion, and sought contact with religious writers, while standing aside in an independence of thought. The closest glimpse of his own mind in this matter can be found in his summary of Henry Bradley's beliefs: 'He respected all well-accredited opinion, though he never allowed its authority to hamper the freedom of his convictions. . . . Religion in such a mind is inseparable from Philosophy: that part of it which is separable, – habits of devotion, the colour of its mysticism, the congeniality of certain symbols, – are intimate and secret matters inexplicable often to oneself.'[7] At times he seemed not a little exultant that his own values differed widely from those usually received. So he asserted that his loyalty to his friend, William Johnson Stone, led him to persist in his experiments in quantitative verse. Individuality led at times dangerously near to singularity, as when he intruded his experiments in simplified spelling into his essays and into *The Testament of Beauty*. Free from economic restraint, continually in contact with the English countryside, and with Oxford and its associations close at hand, he matured his art. From his published work the kinship of his mind would appear to bear some resemblance to that which has been above outlined; it can be pursued more certainly and in further detail in the study of his poetry.

Bridges's volume of 1873 showed his earliest poetic preoccupations. The first impression is of his discipline and enterprise in prosodic form. Earlier than Gosse and Dobson, he had manipulated the rondeau and the triolet, though unlike them he employed these verse patterns for serious themes. In *Elegy* ('Assemble, all ye maidens at the door') he used an eight-line stanza, reminiscent of Spenser, yet of original movement, while each of the lyrics had its own tune and no pattern was repeated. He had separated himself from the interests of his contemporaries; the rhythms of Tennyson, Browning, and the Pre-Raphaelites were rejected, and for them was substituted a severer harmony, Miltonic already in suggestion, though mingled at times with easier movements that might come from a Jacobean anthology. A Swinburnian suggestion intruded momentarily in 'The wood is bare: a river-mist is steeping', but it only emphasized the contrast with other poems. The themes were equally individual; love lyrics and nature fancies occurred, but the main quality was classical, an avoidance of the grotesque and unusual and the keen portrayal of common elements in adequately sustained language. This can be seen in its simplicity in *Clear and Gentle Stream*:

> Where back eddies play
> Shipwreck with the leaves,
> And the proud swans stray,
> Sailing one by one
> Out of stream and sun,
> And the fish lie cool
> In their chosen pool.

Such lines manipulate common experience without apparent emphasis, and yet contrive to render them poetically. Personal poems appeared, and the most memorable among them was the lyric which begins:

> Long are the hours the sun is above
> But when evening comes I go home to my love.

Bridges erected in this poem the image of himself which remains throughout his work; of one who seeks quietude for the contemplation of the best that nature has given to man of art, beauty, and love. Nor was his prosodic control ever more secure than in his strengthening of the treacherous anapaest with trochee and iamb in this poem.

The poems published in 1879 continued the tradition of the earlier volume. Nature themes dominated, but they were approached in measures reminiscent of the Italian *canzone* as used by Spenser and Milton. Such was the tune of *There is a hill beside the silver Thames*, yet within the formal pattern the verse retained simple diction and an unusual visual clarity:

> Sometimes an angler comes, and drops his hook
> Within its hidden depths, and 'gainst a tree
> Leaning his rod, reads in some pleasant book,
> Forgetting soon his pride of fishery.

The outstanding poem of this type was *The Downs* ('O bold, majestic downs, smooth, fair and lonely'), in which the resources of the stanza were united with cunning manipulation of vowels to construct a nature picture. Here again he preferred classical description in general terms for 'Gothic' exuberance in detail, preserving the elements which were of universal appeal. One poem, *Invitation to the Country*, and *Reply* revealed his personal development, and, as in the earlier volume, suggested a quiet certainty of desire. Here he discussed his art, suggesting that while he did not possess the Dionysiac power to 'play with hidden things', he could yet exercise his art in portraying Nature and Beauty,

> And am content, denied
> The best, in choosing right.

The volume of 1880, while arising from the same poetic methods and motives, possessed a richer range of theme. This can be seen in *London Snow*. Previously Bridges had isolated the commonplace elements in an ordinary experience, and united them into a poetic reality, but never had he so successfully converted the usual into the universal. Prosody aided him; the anapaest used sparingly, and inverted feet quietly intruded on a firm iambic background with swift double rhymes, 'flying', 'lying', and solid single rhymes, 'brown', 'down', 'town', to suggest the mingled movement and stillness of the snow. It remained as a lyric achievement, simple in its final effect, but attained by a rare skill and economy. The deeper content of this volume can be perceived elsewhere, notably in *On a Dead Child*:

> Perfect little body, without fault or stain on thee,

which carries memories of the canzone pattern and of Milton's early and artificial treatment of the same theme in *On the Death of a Fair Infant*:

> O fairest flower, no sooner blown but blasted.

In this volume can be found also the first firm expression of that poetic faith which culminated later in *The Testament of Beauty*. Its outline may be found in *Joy sweetest lifeborn joy, where doest thou dwell?* – a poem in rime royal. Seeking joy, which is the breath of God, the poet is bewildered by earth's cruelty:

> The grinding enginry of blood and breath,
> Pain's random darts, the heartless spade of death.

Yet though neither earth nor God's plan seems organized for joy, the sudden moment returns, quickening the blood and mind. The poet's function is to taste that moment, and then to give it poetical expression. Bridges's conception of beauty as 'most blessed truth' has some parallel with that of Keats, whom he studied closely, nor are suggestions of Pater lacking. He interpreted it, however, as a savour of God, a conclusion which they would not have allowed; he was at one here with Ruskin, with whom he had apparently little contact, and with his friend Gerard Manley Hopkins.

The lyrics of 1893 and 1899 do not modify the conclusions gained from the earlier pieces. Nature lyrics dominate, and they are presented in forms varying from the elaborate movement of *The Garden in September*:

> Now thin mists temper the slow-ripening beams
> Of the September sun,

to the almost ballad simplicity of *The north wind came up yesternight*. The poems of 1893 gained a continuity as nature was pursued through the months, and the seasons, and the changing moods captured in happy sequence. He returned to the themes from which his poetry first arose, and emphasized that poetry seizes joy from life, rejecting 'mournful strains':

> But since I have found the beauty of joy
> I have done with proud dismay:
> For howsoe'er man hug his care
> The best of his art is gay.

During this period of lyrical work Bridges had also been occupied with a sonnet sequence, *The Growth of Love*: an early issue of *XXIV Sonnets* appeared in 1876; this had been increased to *LXXIX Sonnets* in 1889; the final issue (1898) was of *LXIX Sonnets*. Bridges found technical satisfaction in the sonnet; he used mainly the Italian form, though varying this with the easier English pattern. Elizabethan memories enter, though more in structure than in verbal echoes. So in *Sonnet 13*,

> And tho' where'er thou goest it is from me,
> I where I go thee in my heart must bear,

he was using the nice balance of the Elizabethan sonnet, and frequently (as in *Sonnet 15*, 'Who builds a ship must first lay down the keel'), he toyed with a comparison until the sonnet became one prolonged conceit. Yet his seriousness excluded dainty devices and Petrarchan gambadoes. His success was frequently greatest when restraint had infused itself through an

Elizabethan pattern, as when, in *Sonnet 30*, he conducted a simple, sincere argument within a closely antithetical structure:

> My lady pleases me and I please her;
> This know we both.

In theme the sequence portrays love from its early moments to the fears of death, and emphasizes the effect of love on art and life. It became Bridges's fullest expression, up to 1898, of his philosophy. Previously he had shown how in seeking joy he had been bewildered by the world's cruelty. Now he suggested (*Sonnet 3*) that love has dissolved 'that old feud 'twixt things and me', and this was allied to a conception of Divine Love in the closing sonnet. Through love he had been able to renew his search for Beauty, for Love had endowed nature with new values. So he reaffirmed that the quest of beauty was the most satisfying human endeavour (*Sonnet 8*):

> For beauty being the best of all we know
> Sums up the unsearchable and secret aims
> Of nature, and on joys whose earthly names
> Were never told can form and sense bestow;
> And man hath sped his instinct to outgo
> The step of science; and against her shames
> Imagination stakes out heavenly claims,
> Building a tower above the head of woe.

Further, in *Sonnet 16* he imagined the world to be a work of art which God has left for man to complete, a task which can be achieved only by seeking 'the face of Beauty'. Although aware (*Sonnet 62*) that the genius of his own generation is scientific, and that his pursuit of 'beauty' and 'rhyme' may be a lonely one, Bridges is determined to persist:

> I will be what God made me, nor protest
> Against the bent of genius in my time.

Throughout the sequence he commented on his own poetry, suggesting at times that he had now mastered his difficult art (*Sonnet 1*), but frequently he was more diffident and conscious of an inadequate reception (*Sonnet 51*).

Despite the power of individual sonnets, and the variety of mood, the sequence has an air of incompleteness when compared with either *Modern Love* or *The House of Life*. Bridges was far more conscious than either Meredith or Rossetti of the Elizabethan tradition, and the sequence of mood was less emphasized. Superficially, the philosophy seemed more loosely defined, though Bridges was already suggesting within *The Growth of Love* the view of life which finally he stated explicitly in *The Testament of Beauty*.

Two collections of miscellaneous lyrics, *New Poems* (1899) and *Later Poems* (1912), reaffirmed some of the themes found in *The Growth of Love*. *New Poems* opened with a number of Victorian eclogues, a form which Bridges had praised in his essay on poetic diction.[8] Among them was his account of the funeral of Giovanni Duprè, who followed Beauty and not ambition, and so deserved burial with the great of the Earth:

> And number'd with the saints, not among them
> Who painted saints.

The volume had a share of nature poems and elegies, including the choric poem, *The South Wind*. *Later Poems* was a collection of pieces written between 1903 and 1911; they were frequently poems on persons, in which the ode was called on to add dignity to an ephemeral incident. Outstanding was the *Ode to Music, Henry Purcell*, and here Bridges returned to the philosophy of Beauty which he had already been formulating:

> All mankind by Love shall be banded
> To combat Evil, the many-handed:
> For the spirit of man on beauty feedeth.

From 1903 to 1909, and later, though with less persistence, Bridges engaged in experiments in classical prosody. They seem a diversion from his main purposes, a triumph of the prosodic over poetic interests, and yet they left an important trace upon the form of his later work. In 1887 Canon Beeching had asked him to write some notes on Milton's prosody for an edition of

Paradise Lost (1893); later, these were published separately and a keen controversy followed (1901).[9] In this study he was led to define the nature of quantitative and accentual verse in English. These critical works already approached the problems of classical prosody, and in 1901 they were supplemented by *Classical Metres in English Verse*, a volume by Bridges's friend William Johnson Stone. On Stone's early death Bridges felt a personal obligation to test and to expound his theories; he wrote a number of critical papers, and experimented, with *Epistles*,[10] in classical prosody. Stone had attempted to 'think in quantities' and to reduce the English language to a quantitative system, based on English sounds, that should be free from false analogies with classical prosody. Bridges found during his experiments that he had to modify the value which Stone gave to some syllables,[11] but he retained Stone's purpose of constructing English quantitative verse from English sound lengths with as little arbitrary adjustment as was possible. Bridges once wrote, though he did not use the words in this context, that, 'when one is considering prosody and principles of rhythm, it is necessary to attend to that only'. The experiments in classical prosody are mainly of interest as prosody: their poetic interest is certainly subordinate, for they did not achieve success in a field where much poetic ingenuity has been spent since the sixteenth century. It would appear from Bridges's verses that where the line's movement depends on length only, its rhythm is too indefinite to impress the ear. Where length combines with stress, the rhythmic movement is overemphasized and mechanical. Nor do the variations gained largely from his study of Miltonic elision serve to free the verse from these embarrassments which arise from the nature of the language. But despite Bridges's preoccupation with technical ingenuity, he made important developments of his thought in these poems. By choosing the epistle as his form, he allowed a freer conversational approach to themes which have only been implied in the lyrical poems. So in *Wintry Delights* he was led to anticipate *The Testament of Beauty* in his discussion of contemporary thought:

> Boldly a new science of MAN, from dreamy scholastic
> Imprisoning set free, and inveterate divination,
> Into the light of truth, to the touch of history and fact.

In the second and more elaborate epistle, *To a Socialist in London*, his expression was more crabbed; he expounded a sort of spiritual *laissez-faire* which was not unsavoured with self-complacency. Yet it was of interest that he employed here the fable of the bees, which was used later in a memorable passage of *The Testament of Beauty*. *Ibant Obscuri* (1909),[12] a later experiment, was an attempt to make a line for line paraphrase from the *Æneid*, Book VI. Here more than in the original pieces the restrictions under which he worked became apparent, and this was confirmed by his rendering into alcaics of Blake's *Evening*. Bridges, it must be remembered, had never suggested that English poetry should be written in classical prosody; he wished merely to show that it could be so written. Further, the results of his experiments are not to be judged in themselves but from the indirect results which they have upon his later verse: 'The experiments which I have made reveal a vast unexplored field of delicate and expressive rhythms hitherto unknown in our poetry.' Some of those rhythms he explored in the unrhymed verse of his later years.

At a long distance from these earlier works there followed two volumes of lyrics. *October* (1920) contained, apart from lyrics written in 1913, a number of war poems, marked by an unhappy stridency of mood. *New Verse* (1921) was a more legitimate successor to the early work. Bridges's own division of the volume was prosodic: in one division he placed a few more quantitative poems, and in another pieces in 'recognizable old styles': a third was occupied with accentual measures which had attracted him from the earliest days of his verse-writing; the most important was filled with poems written in a manner which he described as 'Neo-Miltonic syllables. It pretends to offer their true desideratum to the advocates of Free Verse.' He expressed a similar faith in this development of 'Milton's inventions in syllabic verse' in his essay on *vers libres*, entitled *Humdrum and Harum-Scarum*

(1922). This new form was presented in lyric in *Cheddar Pinks*, and in longer discursive pieces, notably *Kate's Mother*. Its importance lay in the fact that it was this measure, renamed as 'loose alexandrines', that Bridges employed in *The Testament of Beauty*.

It is significant that these experiments coincided with his final edition of *Milton's Prosody* (1921). He had been attracted by Milton's free use of the alexandrine in the lyrical parts of *Samson Agonistes*. He was equally impressed by the methods of inversion and elision with which Milton had varied the blank verse of *Paradise Lost*. Further, his edition of the poems of Gerard Manley Hopkins (1918) had shown his familiarity with Hopkins's system of counterpointed rhythm: the licence by which varied feet could be introduced somewhat freely upon a basic pattern. From a combination of these experiments he evolved a verse freer than Milton would have allowed, and based on a line of five or of six stresses. In speaking of the dactylic variations which Milton had introduced into his line, he wrote, 'Milton was, therefore, not inventing anything new or unheard, but seeking rather to make a good use of natural English stress rhythms, without falling into their singsong, or setting all his verse to dance. And it should now be clear to the reader by what means he did this.'[13] It may not be equally clear how Bridges attained his effects. He used considerable licence in the position of the stress and in the number of syllables; yet his long experience in prosodic experiments, both in stress rhythms and in quantitative verse, had trained his ear to a subtle appreciation of what could be attained with English sounds. In the longer discursive pieces of 1921 he did not seem to have realized the full possibilities of his discovery; for that he had to wait until *The Testament of Beauty*. The invention of these 'loose alexandrines' was the final reward of his long discipleship in prosody; he found a new medium; he employed it worthily, and it was a medium that could be used only by one who had pursued closely the rhythms of the language. Before *The Testament* itself can be approached, Bridges's narrative and dramatic works must be examined.

In 1885 there appeared two versions of Apuleius's rendering of the Cupid and Psyche myth; Walter Pater embedded a prose version as an episode in *Marius the Epicurean*, while Bridges gave a stanzaic rendering in *Eros and Psyche*. Both had felt the strangeness that a story of Greek form and delicacy should exist in the macabre surroundings of *The Golden Ass*, and they contrived to recover some of that Greek quality in their own versions. Pater, writing of the episode's place in the story, had commented: 'Amid its mockeries, its coarse though genuine humanity, its burlesque horrors, came the tale of Cupid and Psyche, full of brilliant, lifelike situations, *speciosa in locis*', and so Bridges, emphasizing still more its Greek spirit, wrote Eros for Cupid,

> Eros, the ever young, who only grew
> In mischief, and was Cupid named anew
> In westering aftertime of latin lore.

Throughout the poem, not only by its values but in frequent reference to other Greek myths, he kept prominent this intention. Nor in choosing this legend could he have been unmindful that this was a story used by Morris in *The Earthly Paradise*: antagonism to Pre-Raphaelite art may have strengthened his intention of giving to his version a precision which Morris with his genially easy story-telling did not cultivate. He chose a measure which Morris had frequently used, the rime royal, though by changing the rhyme scheme and so avoiding the final couplet he modified its effect. Further, it may not be fanciful to remember that, while the setting of *The Earthly Paradise* is arranged for two stories for each month, Bridges divided his theme into months and apportions one stanza for each day of the month. Although he seems to have fixed himself with fetters he moves easily, but when in one stanza he inserts an acrostic on Purcell's name the suggestion arises that dexterity has itself grown wanton.

Bridges brought his own values and emphasis to the poem. Their origin is to be sought in Keats's *Ode to Psyche*, a motto from which was quoted on the title-page. For Keats the legend has transformed itself into a symbol of all that beauty allied to love could convey to the mind. Bridges, already attracted to that theme, pursued it through the legend:

> And if some beauteous things, – whose heavenly worth
> And function overpass our mortal sense, –
> Lie waste and unregarded on the earth
> By reason of our gross intelligence,
> These are not vain, because in nature's scheme
> It lives that we shall grow from dream to dream
> In time to gather an enchantment thence.

This emphasis appears variously in the poem, both in his portrayal of Cupid and in the philosophical implication of the closing stanzas. Frequently it is relaxed so that the legend may be developed in picturesque detail, but it returns, as a recurrent and governing motive. His discipline over incident, and the power of expressing his own imagination while retaining good faith with the myth, leads to a regret that he did not exploit further the narrative power which he so obviously possessed.

Of the dramas, two are closely related to his lyrical work, *Prometheus the Firegiver* (1883) and *Demeter* (1905). *Prometheus*, the earliest of the dramatic pieces, is described by Bridges as 'a mask in the Greek manner'. Keeping to the form of Greek tragedy, he conveys the Prometheus myth with a lyrical emphasis in the commentary. The dramatic speeches are in blank verse, marked with some Miltonic features, while the theme has suggestions of Satan's conflict in *Paradise Lost*: 'Could I but win this world from Zeus for mine.' In the first part Prometheus is the spokesman of Bridges's philosophy. He is made to describe that searching for beauty which distinguishes the 'spirit of man' from the rest of creation:

> That spirit which lives in each and will not die,
> That wooeth beauty, and for all good things
> Urgeth a voice, or in still passion sigheth,
> And where he loveth draweth the heart after him.

Thus in the first part one is led to imagine that Bridges, following Shelley, is about to refashion the myth for his own symbolic purposes. The second part marks, however, a retreat from this intention, and falling back on the mere recountal of the myth, he allows Prometheus, with Aeschylean precedent, to describe the wanderings of Io. Despite this sense of diminution of poetic purpose, Bridges's earliest essay in dramatic form is possibly his most successful. *Demeter* (1905), 'written for the Ladies at Somerville College and acted by them at the inauguration of their new building in 1904', is a slighter exercise in the same manner. Here blank verse is varied with elaborate choral movement, including the memorable chorus of the Oceanides ('Gay and lovely is earth, man's decorate dwelling'). Its sequence of thought is not unlike that found in *Prometheus*; it opens with philosophy, a discussion on the place of wisdom and joy, of love and passion in life. This recedes in Acts II and III to make room for simple, dramatic elements, the description of Demeter's grief, and a recounting of Persephone's lovely legend. Only as the play closes does Bridges return to the contemplation of the symbolic implications of the myth. Again he seems uncertain of his poetic purpose; at times he would appear prepared to make *Comus* his model and subdue considerations of drama and myth to abstract discussion. He has not the courage to do this consistently, and he is content that some movement in the story shall woo him away from his philosophic purposes. Both the pieces seem therefore to be poetic compromises, in which unity of intention has not been fully conceived. Yet, unlike the other dramas, they seem closely related to the lyrical poetry.

In the later nineteenth century blank-verse drama continued to attract a number of poets who had little knowledge or aptitude for the stage. The narrative power which Bridges had shown in *Eros and Psyche* he refrained from developing, while the dramatic gift which he possessed but fitfully he exercised with persistence. Though his pieces are but dubiously successful as dramas, they show an independence in thought and structure. *Nero*, a work in two parts, which covers the death of Agrippina, the conspiracy of Piso, and the death of Seneca, marks Bridges's dramatic discipleship. The work is inconclusive and overelaborated, with a multiplicity of characters and themes and a discursive handling of the speeches. If tragic values prevail, the play must conclude with Nero's death; instead, we see merely the monotonous extinction of his opponents. If the drama is philosophical, Nero's view of life must be presented and confronted with others that conflict with it. Occasionally this appears as Bridges's intention, but more frequently it is lost in the mêlée of characters and intrigue. Nero frequently suggests that his purpose is to extend indefinitely the material resources of human enjoyment; man 'wounds his happiness against a cage of his own making'. In the second part he asserts the doctrine in a more aggressive form:

> I believe,
> That no man in the world worth calling man
> Is what philosophers term pure and good; –
> Nor woman either. All would gratify
> The strong desires of nature, and all shall,
> While I am emperor.

Nero's sensual hedonism is not consistently opposed until the second part, when Seneca and the Christians affirm a spiritual conception of life and after-life. Bridges admitted that he was only experimenting in this play. Its length and diffuseness make it impossible for the stage, but it has excellent moments, such as the death of Seneca and the feast which precedes the death of Britannicus. The characterization is flat. Bridges seemed a little embarrassed by the unsavouriness of Nero, but he succeeded with Petronius, who, knowing wisdom, does not seek it, and he converted him into the most lifelike portrait in the play. In *The Feast of Bacchus* he experimented in Latin comedy, a parents and children theme, in the Terentian manner. Prosodically the play has interest; it is described as 'a line of six stresses, written according to rules of English rhythm'. The characteristic movement of the verses can be seen in the following lines:

> I came upon her hard at work at her tapestry,
> Dressed in a common gown: no gold about her; none
> Of the rouge and powder, that women bedaub their faces with.

This verse, though difficult to adjust to the necessities of drama, was Bridges's skilful attempt to adapt the Latin *senarius* of Plautus to English verse. The line has a particular interest from its similarity to the form of 'loose alexandrines' which Bridges developed in his later work.

Of the remaining plays, three owe their origin to Bridges's study of Calderon. *Achilles in Scyros*, though possessing a prologue, chorus, and other appurtenances of classical drama, is romantic in form, with eavesdropping, hiding, and with Achilles disguised as a maiden. Little emphasis is given to character, but, as in the earlier plays, room is found for some discursive commentary. Its main success lies in the lyrical power and the movement of thought in the choruses. *The Christian Captives* gives fresh treatment to a situation suggested by Calderon's *El Principe Constante*, and portrays the love of Almeh, daughter of the King of Fez, for Ferdinand the Christian Prince of Portugal. In form, the tragedy is, as Bridges himself suggested, 'mixed'; its values of honour and love could consort with those of heroic drama, yet the play ends more strenuously than heroic drama would permit in the death of the main protagonists. A chorus is retained and used generously, but little else belongs to classical tradition. *The Humours of the Court*, in which Bridges uses suggestions from Calderon and Lope de Vega, is, apart from *The Feast of Bacchus*, his only experiment in comedy. Possibly the most actable of the plays, it preserves a certain consistent sophistication of sentiment which befits its artificiality of situation. It is as if one of Shakespeare's romantic comedies had dropped its coarseness and farce and had been crossed with a play of romantic adventure. The result is a brave and graceful incredibility, which has the honesty never to pose as reality. *Palicio*, the third play which shows the influence of Calderon, owes nothing directly to any Spanish play. It has, however, a Spanish theme, and Palicio himself, the Sicilian brigand who marries Margaret, sister of the Chief Justiciary of Sicily, belongs to the romantic tradition of Spanish drama.

The Return of Ulysses separates itself from the other plays in that it recasts some of the chief scenes in Homer's *Odyssey* into dramatic form. The material, as Bridges seems to have suspected, was too diffuse for dramatic action, nor did he contrive to govern its movement with any adequate conflict. It is difficult to see what he has gained by imposing dramatic form on such obviously narrative texture. He employs the chorus from classical tragedy and uses Athene as prologue, but the values of the play and its loose episodical character have little in common with classical drama.

Despite the outstanding quality of individual passages, his dramas remain as poetic exercises. The interests of his mind, philosophical, prosodic, and descriptive, found no outlet, and to replace them he attempted to manufacture an attachment for intrigue, conspiracy, and human passion. His very quality as a poet exists in his aloofness from this blood and stress; he had announced frequently in his lyrical poetry such a retreat, but the desire to write drama pursued him into his quietude and perplexed his poetic purposes for almost a decade. All that is good within the dramas seems related to his philosophical and lyrical interests, such as the comments in *Nero* and the choruses in *Achilles in Scyros*.

In 1929 Bridges published *The Testament of Beauty*.[14] The poem presents two preliminary difficulties to the reader who meets Bridges's poetry here for the first time: its reformed spelling troubles the eye, even if it does not hold up the mind, while the metre is an extended use of the loose alexandrines which Bridges had employed already in 1921,

> 'wherein so many strange verses amalgamate
> on the secure bedrock of Milton's prosody'.[15]

The *Testament* is a confession of faith, expressed with sufficient consistency of argument to elevate it into philosophy, and diversified with numerous illustrations and episodes. Its thought develops naturally from the earlier poems. Bridges, now an old man, experiences a 're-awakening to a fresh initiation of life', and this leads him to express his philosophy in verse. Modifying Plato's image in the *Phaedrus*, he portrays man's two main instincts, Selfhood and Breed, as two steeds, controlled by Reason, the charioteer. Each of these instincts arises from an impulse shared by all living things, the desire to live and the desire to propagate. Neither impulse is evil, yet uncontrolled by Reason they become cruel and wasteful. Reason by itself can achieve little; its power arises only when it comes into contact with these two instincts. So Selfhood, with Reason's control, develops the altruism of motherhood, which even animals possess. Further, it can proceed to the higher aim of life, the fullest development of individual worth:

> our great endeavour
> is spiritual attainment, individual worth
> at all cost to be sought and at all cost pursued.

Bridges is led here, partly by a bias against political socialism, to deprecate Plato's conception of a communal Utopia and to ridicule the mechanized industry of the beehive as an ideal for human society. Full human individuality can be attained when man aided by Reason perceives Beauty. Similarly, Breed which begins as propagation is led by the same qualities into Love. Through Art, man figures out this Beauty which is his highest attribute. Like Selfhood and Breed, Art is present everywhere in some form in the living world, in the song of birds and in flowers and the dance of animals; but in man Art becomes that enlarged perception of Beauty which is an approach to a contact with God:

> Beauty, the eternal Spouse of the Wisdom of God
> and Angel of his Presence thru' all creation.

Reason is, thus, the great servant of man, and from Reason arises Duty. Some would imagine that Duty is externally imposed on life, but to Bridges, as to Wordsworth, Duty is a natural outcome from Nature. The conception of Duty changes with man's knowledge, and so develops his closer interpretation of Beauty. To make Reason master of man is to lose the contact with Nature, and the instincts, from which man's highest achievement arises, go astray. Nor is Reason or Duty opposed to Pleasure, unless Pleasure becomes an end in itself out of contact with Nature and Beauty. Bridges, while he does not ignore the problem of evil, does not attempt to solve it. Man, he suggests, is not equipped to solve the eternal problem of why life is; he can only approach through the instincts controlled by Reason to a deeper conception of what life may be. Error, perversion, and retrogression are for ever the results of false relation to Nature. The true approach to life as he outlines it rests in Faith:

> But heav'nward tho' the chariot be already mounted,
> 'tis Faith alone can keep the charioteer in heart.

Of all the activities that have been named evil, war is one of the most perplexing, for war 'is like unto virtue, but not virtue itself'. War is closely allied to Selfhood, and seems in the child a natural instinct, but it has developed to loathsomeness and leads to a sickness of spirit. Despite the havoc of the European War and the troubled condition of the peoples at its close, Bridges is not led away from his Faith that man has the possibility of expressing in life, through instinct and Reason, the love that is God. Beauty is the perception of that love, and so Beauty therefore becomes the central doctrine of this Testament and in a number of passages its precise interpretation is defined:

> *What is Beauty? saith my sufferings then.* – I answer
> the lover and poet in my loose alexandrines:
> Beauty is the highest of all these occult influences,
> the quality of appearances that thru' the sense
> wakeneth spiritual emotion in the mind of man:
> And Art, as it createth new forms of beauty,
> awakeneth new ideas that advance the spirit
> in the life of Reason to the wisdom of God.

Such in barest outline is Bridges's argument. Its inadequacies are more obvious in a prose summary than when expressed persuasively with a wealth of illustration and modification in the poem itself. Despite the recognition of evil, Bridges may be felt to dismiss the problem too facilely. He had none of Browning's preoccupation with evil, and one feels that his own neglect of

Browning's poetry was his retreat from the nauseating, obscene thing that was there ever dangling before his eyes. Nor was his conception of life as the development of the worth of the individual fully related to spiritual altruism; it approached at times to a refined egoism not uncoloured by his obvious antipathy to political socialism. His faith in the Universe was asserted rather than justified, nor was its Divine origin reconciled to the instinct of cruelty in all living things. This philosophy is open at places to attack, but the greatness of his achievement as a philosophical poet remains. Alone of the poets of the period he incorporated into a single poem, not merely a philosophy, but a system of aesthetic, and he related these to contemporary knowledge of science, of evolution, and of history. He came back to the problems which perplexed Tennyson in *In Memoriam*, Browning in *Christmas-Eve and Easter-Day*, and Arnold in *Rugby Chapel*; he united the poetry of the early and the late nineteenth century. Unlike the earlier poets, he was not perplexed by doubt: his philosophy arose from a certainty of faith which was combined with a serenity of mood. Tennyson in *In Memoriam*, despite his spiritual self-torturing, offers the closest parallel. The two poems arise from a restatement of a faith after the endurance of a personal grief: this motive was not as emphasized in Bridges, yet it occurred clearly at the close:

> 'Twas at sunset that I, fleeing to hide my soul
> in refuge of beauty from a mortal distress,
> walk'd alone with the Muse in her garden of thought.

Bridges was much more comprehensive in his approach than Tennyson, and he absorbed the knowledge which seventy years of investigation in science had made available. He failed to emphasize as ruthlessly as did Tennyson the cruelty of the struggle for existence, but he showed, as Tennyson failed to do, how the new knowledge of the physical world which the nineteenth century had made available could be reconciled to a philosophy of art in which religious conceptions were dominant. Of the poets of the later nineteenth century the two who approach his purposes most closely are Meredith and Hardy. Meredith, developing a tortuous vocabulary of his own, had evolved in poetry a system of conduct which embraced a recognition of man's contact with the animal world. Hardy, like Bridges, had become aware of evolution, but that recognition had moved his creative vision to emphasize the cruelty and ruthlessness of life and to express pity for all living things which suffered and endured it. In the third decade of the twentieth century, when many minds were filled with misgivings that amounted to despair, Bridges reasserted that faith in abstract virtues, in Beauty and Goodness, which underlies so much Victorian poetry. Strange as it may seem, he gained a far wider recognition for this service than for any other work which he had achieved. In an age that was morbidly distrustful of idealism he reasserted the place of Beauty and Love in experience and in philosophy.

A poem cannot live by philosophical argument alone, and Bridges used all his long-gathered resources as a poet to give *The Testament* an imaginative life. The ease with which he employed his 'loose alexandrines' suggested that he was working in a medium as comprehensive as prose and yet possessing that dexterity of phrase, harmony in numbers, and power of gathering diversity into a single compelling impression which belong to poetry. His vocabulary had such a happy combination of the familiar and the remote that he could describe wireless and communal nurseries without intruding any quaintness into the movement of his verses. The theme necessitated that his vocabulary should at times give to abstract concepts a precise value, and sometimes an inevitable discursiveness intruded as if this were not a poem but a poetical lecture. Such slackening of texture is rare and serves only to show how he conquered these difficulties in the major part of the poem. He coloured his diction with a far more generous employment of imagery than he had previously permitted, and keen, well-discovered phrases flash in and out of the argument, lighting it with a warm and romantic quality which in the earlier years of his poetic asceticism he had denied himself.

Much of the imaginative strength of the poem lay in its descriptions and episodical passages. Bridges's problem was not unlike that of Milton in *Paradise Lost*: he had brought wide human interests into a theme which did not seem obviously to allow of them. He may have had Milton's method in mind when he sought in history, the sciences, and the arts for illustrations, and endowed them with a glamour that gave them value quite apart from the argument which they expounded: so the descriptions of nature and of music; the life of St Francis and 'his hymn in honour of God'; the arts of Greece and of the coming of Jesus; the account of the Crusades and of the beginnings of modern poetry; the brilliant anatomy of the pleasures of eating; the summary of the Orient's absorption of Western science; the excavators amid prehistoric tombs in Mesopotamia, where the bones of the King's servants and his mistresses were found heaped around the grave. Some of these have but a slender contact with the argument; so the poetical essay on 'Pleasure in Food' is, on Bridges's own confession, a digression, and is elaborated for its own delight, while the passage on Mesopotamian exploration, perhaps the most brilliant in the whole poem, is but dimly related to the attack on socialism which is its alleged purpose. Yet it was these very passages, and others such as the opening nature scene, and the discussion on asceticism arising from the refusal of a peach by Gerard Manley Hopkins, that gave the poem its ultimately personal quality. Bridges was expounding his own faith in the terms of his own long-gathered studies of the sciences of human life. Though in form and vocabulary the poem stands apart from the poetry of the period, it is intimately associated with the motives from which Victorian poetry arises. It is with *The Testament of Beauty* that nineteenth-century poetry comes to an end.

11

Gerard Manley Hopkins

Gerard Manley Hopkins (1844-1889) was a nineteenth-century poet whose place and influence it has been left for the twentieth century to determine. Apart from a small circle of intimates, which included Coventry Patmore and Robert Bridges, his work was hidden away in manuscript out of the view of most of his contemporaries until long after his death. His poetic remains were entrusted to Robert Bridges, who allowed a few poems to appear in anthologies,[1] but waited until 1918 before he launched the major work in volume form as *Poems of Gerard Manley Hopkins*. To this was added a separate issue of Hopkins's early poem *A Vision of the Mermaids* (1929). Despite critical attention,[2] there cannot have been many purchasers of the volume, for it was not until 1930 that a second edition was called for; additional poems were added and Charles Williams, a great but discriminating admirer of Hopkins, contributed an introduction. In the thirties Hopkins became a major influence on new poets. They were not interested in his religious themes, for many of them, at that time at least, were agnostics, but they were fascinated by the originality of his rhythms and his vocabulary and, above all, in the contrast of his genius against the whole nineteenth-century romantic tradition. The publication later of his letters and notebooks[3] confirmed the range and distinction of his mind; there were massive volumes of his letters to Robert Bridges, Richard Watson Dixon, and Coventry Patmore, and, in addition, Journals, Sermons, devotional and other writings.

Hopkins was the eldest son of a large family and was brought up in a cultivated home in a comfortable middle-class tradition. His father was the Consul-General of the Hawaiian Islands to Great Britain, an office that he combined with that of an average adjuster in the City. His father's work brought him into contact with problems of nautical law and he wrote learnedly on the subject, and some have thought, plausibly though with little evidence, that it was the father's interest that led his son to choose the sea as the theme of one of his most memorable poems, *The Wreck of the Deutschland*, and of *The Loss of the Eurydice*. His parents were devout, but no narrow tradition prevailed, and painting and music, both of which influenced Hopkins, were cultivated in the family. He was born at Stratford, Essex, but later the family moved to Hampstead. Even as a schoolboy at the Grammar School at Highgate Hopkins showed an unusual interest in study, not unmixed at times with an eccentricity of mood. The devoutness of his parents was of a moderate High Church character, but Hopkins soon became less moderate under the influence of Canon Dixon, then a curate at Lambeth and an occasional teacher at Highgate. Poetry already attracted him, and his earliest verse shows that it was Spenser and the romantic poets, with Keats dominant, who were among his early enthusiasms; this is ironic to recall when it is remembered how younger poets used his work to exorcize the romantic tradition. In 1862 he wrote a poem in couplets to which reference has already been made, *A Vision of the Mermaids*, and in the same year he won a scholarship to Balliol. He entered Oxford in the Easter term of 1863, and in the following Michaelmas term Robert Bridges came from Eton to Corpus Christi. They met in 1863 and there was formed between these men of such different loyalties and temperaments a friendship which was certainly the most powerful human relationship in Hopkins's life; they remained friends until Hopkins's death in Dublin in 1889.

Bridges has been criticized for his share in the association, and the matter has been examined by Jean-Georges Ritz,[4] in detail,

though possibly with less than justice to Bridges. One of the main charges against Bridges is that he destroyed his letters to Hopkins when they were returned to him on Hopkins's death. But in this context one has to remember Bridges's general desire that his personal life should not be recorded and his wish that no biography should be published. On the other hand, Bridges kept Hopkins's letters to him and they were made available for publication in 1935; though by then Bridges was dead. Herbert Read goes as far as to suggest that their friendship was not based ultimately on intellectual interests: 'Hopkins', he affirms, 'had known Bridges for fourteen years before he discovered (and then from a review) that his friend wrote poetry. We can assume therefore that the attraction was instinctive, even physical.'[5] All this is most unjust. E. Thompson, who knew Bridges well, has noted that Bridges's motive may well have been modesty, and it was consistent with his desire that his biography should not be written.[6] Bridges has also been attacked for not issuing the volume of Hopkins's poems before 1918, and for being lukewarm in his appraisal of his friend's verse. So, for instance, Bridges is led to speak of *The Wreck of the Deutschland* as 'a great dragon folded in the gate to forbid all entrance'. Against this it can be urged that at any earlier date Hopkins would not readily have found an audience, and it has been indicated how slow was the sale of the volume in 1918. It is often forgotten by these hostile critics that Bridges was himself a poet, though by today a neglected one. He had himself experimented in verse and must, not unreasonably, have felt that Hopkins's far more complex innovations might detract from the acceptance that he had won for his own work only with great difficulty. Of Hopkins's appreciation of Bridges there is a moving passage by Edward Dowden in the *Fortnightly Review* for July 1894. He says that it was Hopkins who left 'at my door two volumes by Mr Bridges'. Dowden knew that Hopkins was a poet, but had not met him, because 'I took it for granted that he belonged to the other camp in Irish politics'; later he learned that Hopkins 'died of distress and depression' at the political dishonesty he saw in Dublin.

The difference in the religious loyalties of Hopkins and Bridges must not be forgotten, as it was by Hopkins's agnostic admirers in the thirties, who were deeply impressed by the form of his work and for the most part ignored the content. Bridges remained an Anglican, though he developed philosophically into an Anglican agnostic. Hopkins was not only a Roman Catholic but a Jesuit, and it is difficult now to realize what an isolation this imposed on him in mid-nineteenth-century England. The degree to which Bridges was disturbed is unknown, but it must have placed a heavy burden on their personal relation, and the surprising thing is that they remained so close to each other to the end.

The Oxford that Hopkins entered as an undergraduate was filled with religious enthusiasms and controversies. Eighteen years earlier Newman had entered the Roman Catholic Church and the repercussions of his conversion were still strongly felt. Pusey remained at Oxford, the leader of the Tractarian Movement and of Anglo-Catholicism, challenging the more rational and intellectual conceptions of Christianity, represented by Benjamin Jowett, then Professor of Greek. Hopkins, already keenly preoccupied with religion, was strongly influenced by all three men, and by other and more intimate religious instructors. His university career in the 'Schools', where he read classics, was brilliant, but all this seemed to be incidental to the fact that Oxford was the arena in which he settled the form of faith that would gain ascendancy and so determine the shape of his whole life. He moved, largely under Newman's influence, from Puseyism to Roman Catholicism. He was received into the Catholic Church in 1867, the same year as he graduated with a 'First' in Classical 'Greats'. His letters record how deeply his conversion affected his whole being; he offended his family, he complicated his relation with Bridges; he isolated himself from many Oxford personalities whom he admired; a deep cicatrice was left upon his spirit which could be healed only by a passionate devotion to his faith. The depth of his distress can be seen from a letter to Newman: 'I have been up at Oxford long enough to have heard from my father and mother in return for my letter announcing my conversion. Their replies are terrible. I cannot read them twice. If you will pray for them and me just now I shall be deeply grateful.' As has been suggested, by taking the extreme step of becoming a Jesuit Hopkins was forced into a tragic isolation from the world he had known, and his only possibility of consolation lay in a strenuous, fervid, and consuming loyalty to the faith that he had found. The experience of a convert is always different from that of those born into a faith and this was particularly true in the sixties of the nineteenth century. It had this importance on his genius as a poet, that his work had to be developed in an almost aggressive condition of loneliness; this is why the friendship of Bridges and of a few others meant so much to him. His originality may have gained from these conditions, but, at the same time, the element in his work which is extreme and eccentric might possibly have developed in other ways had he been at the centre of a wide and welcoming society.

For Hopkins, after his departure from Oxford, religious experience is the one experience that really mattered. He entered the Society of Jesus in 1868 and subordinated himself passionately to its discipline. Poetry, particularly his first romantic exercises, belonged to another world, and he burned much of his early work. On first leaving Balliol he served at the Oratory School at Birmingham, and Newman initiated him into the ways of the Catholic life. His main studies were in philosophy and mathematics, and he wrote at this time to his sceptical friend, A. W. M Baillie: 'The life here though it is hard is God's will for me as I most intimately know, which is more than violets knee-deep. Later he was at Roehampton and Stonyhurst. Poetry which he had set aside when he entered the Society he was fortunately encouraged to recommence. His highly individual verse, which arose from his faith and his deep and mystical attachment to it belongs to these later years (1875–1889). It can be supplemented by his diaries, which reveal the dark and tumultuous movement of his mind in contemplative and mystical moods. He filled a number of appointments as he was directed, both as a lecture and a teacher. His health was seldom good and he was moved frequently, for reasons never fully explained, from one office to another. After 1877 he served at Jesuit Colleges at Manresa House and Stonyhurst. One has the impression that his mind did not adjust itself easily to the more routine tasks of teaching and lecturing. In 1884 he became Professor of Greek in the Catholic University of Ireland. Five years later he died of typhoid fever.

Though absorbed in his religious experience and duties, he had a strong social awareness, derived in part from Ruskin and Arnold, but also from his own observation. His reactions in these matters could be violent. He abhorred the selfishness of modern materialism and the way that industry had befouled the land: 'Is it not dirty, yea filthy, to pollute the air as Blackburn and Widnes and St Helens are polluted?' In 1871 he wrote with considerable boldness to Bridges: 'I must tell you I am always thinking of the communist future. The too intelligent artisan is master of the situation I believe.' One also knows that his last years were saddened by the sight of the poverty of the Dublin slums.

While Hopkins's adult life was spent in absolute devotion to the Jesuit Order, he had reached that position only with difficulty. The potentialities of his talent as a pictorial artist are now known, and his musical gifts and his wide-ranging interest in verse, including that of his contemporaries, Morris and Rossetti, and, of course, Bridges and his associates. His own poetical work is divided abruptly into two divisions: the early poems up to 1868 and the later verse beginning with *The Wreck of the Deutschland* in 1875. First among the early pieces stands the school-prize poem, *The Escorial*, a clever exercise in Byronic Spenserians. He had studied in detail his theme of the building of the Escorial by Philip II, and his introductory phrase from Theocritus, 'and I compete like a frog against the cicadas', shows his own estimate of the poem. There followed a much more nature poem in couplets, *A Vision of the Mermaids*, held by family tradition to be another school-prize poem, though Humphrey House has shown that there is no proof of this. Keats's influence is marked both in the irregularity of the prosody and in the union of classical and faery elements in the theme. There are some excesses as existed in Keats's *Endymion*:

> Plum-purple was the west; but spikes of light
> Spear'd open lustrous gashes, crimson-white.

But already Hopkins shows his power in imaginative epithet, which later grows into one of his main characteristics. Little of his work of this early period, 1862-1868, survives. Bridges suggests that he was attracted by George Herbert, whose influence continues into his later work. The poems which do remain show what he achieved in traditional forms. Amongst them is the remarkable *Winter with the Gulf Stream*,[7] which, though touched with memories of romantic sadness such as linger in Keats's *La Belle Dame sans Merci*, conveys Hopkins's fresh approach to nature; this is his capacity of looking at ordinary objects as if they had never been seen before, and certainly as if no one had built up a conventional vocabulary for their description. Such, at the close of the poem, is his impression of a sunset on a mild winter day:

> And slendering to his burning rim
> Into the flat blue mist the sun
> Drops out and all our day is done.

Hopkins has himself described[8] his attitude to poetry after he entered the Society of Jesus: 'I resolved to write no more, as not belonging to my profession, unless it were the wish of my superiors; so for seven years I wrote nothing but two or three little presentation pieces which occasion called for.' Though he ceased from writing, he could not cease to think about poetry: 'I had long had haunting my ear the echo of a new rhythm.' So that when in the winter of 1875 he was moved by the death of five Franciscan nuns on board the *Deutschland*, and his rector told him that he wished someone would write a poem on the theme, he was encouraged to transfer this rhythm to paper. 'On this hint' he wrote, 'I set to work', and he composed a poem that had but few points of identity with his earlier verse. Yet, as W. H. Gardner has shown,[9] even in the early period of his romantic loyalties as an undergraduate he had foreseen the possibility that to survive in its full imaginative intensity poetry would have to be constantly submitted to revolutions. While he was under the influence of Walter Pater, who was only five years his senior, Hopkins composed an essay on *Health and Decay in Art*, where he comments:

Perfection is dangerous because it is deceptive. Art slips back while bearing, in its own distribution of tone, or harmony, the look of high civilisation towards barbarism. Recovery must be by a breaking up, a violence, such as was the Pre-Raphaelite school.

Gardner adds the comment that 'this proves that the violence of his own later innovations in poetic style had a conscious or at least a sub-conscious rational basis'. 'The violence' that he now introduced into *The Wreck* was far beyond anything that the Pre-Raphaelites had ever conceived. The prosody was fresh, the syntax individual, the vocabulary and epithets unusual to the point of obscurity. All these elements unite with an inwardness of thought to give this poem a place entirely apart from the work of his contemporaries. W. H. Gardner in his elaborate treatment of the poem writes that it 'presents more problems than any other great ode of equal length in the language'.[10] No one in 1875 was familiar with poetry similar to this found in *The Deutschland*:

> I am soft sift
> In an hourglass – at the wall
> Fast, but mined with a motion, a drift,
> And it crowds and it combs to the fall;
> I steady as a water in a well, to a poise, to a pane,
> But roped with, always, all the way down from the tall
> Fells or flanks of the voel, a vein
> Of the gospel proffer, a pressure, a principle, Christ's gift.

Such verses, had they been printed, would have been unintelligible to an audience in the seventies, and it is doubtful whether later readers could have fully explored their thought without some aid from marginal comments. Bridges suggested, and one might think wisely, that the reader should begin with one of the more direct and factual stanzas, such as stanza 16:

> One stirred from the rigging to save
> The wild woman-kind below,
> With a rope's end round the man, handy and brave –
> He was pitched to his death at a blow,
> For all his dreadnought breast and braids of thew:
> They could tell him for hours, dandled the to and fro
>   Through the cobbled foam-fleece, what could he do
> With the burl of the fountains of air, buck and the flood of the wave?

The Wreck of the Deutschland is a great poem and it will stand high in all that the nineteenth century achieved, but one is not helped by the excessive claims, far greater than his own, of some of Hopkins's admirers. W. H. Gardner, to whom this chapter is much indebted, permits himself to say: '*The Wreck of the Deutschland* has a completeness, an intellectual and emotional unity, a subtlety and variety of verbal orchestration which are unique not only in English but also, we believe in the literature of the world.' Let it be admitted that this is a great poem, as indeed it is, and that given its time it is a miraculous poem, but it is yet not all that Gardner and some of Hopkins's other admirers claim. Ultimately one reaches the problem that many of Hopkins's commentators have not faced the question of whether they admire his great technical originality or whether they appraise him as a Christian poet. F. R. Leavis does, as one would expect, come squarely to terms with this dilemma.[11] 'Hopkins', he writes, 'is the devotional poet of a dogmatic Christianity. For the literary critic there are consequent difficulties and delicacies. But there is something that can be seen and said at once: Hopkins's religious interests are bound up with the presence in his poetry of a vigour of mind that puts him in a different world from the other Victorians.' This successfully dismisses Tennyson and the others, though it is a little hard to see *In Memoriam*, the central poem of the Victorian age, disappearing so easily. But Leavis does not fully explain how one can accept Hopkins's 'vigour of mind' if one cannot identify oneself with the religious purposes to which that vigour was directed. The poets of the thirties, as has already been suggested, pursued him for his prosody, not for his religion, and the prosody, which has profound elements of originality, interested Hopkins himself in an almost compulsive way. He wrote a *Preface on Prosody* for the manuscript collection of his poems. Coventry Patmore wrote an essay on *English Metrical Law* in 1878. He knew Hopkins in the later years of his life and the dates preclude any possibility of contact in prosodic discussions, but the two systems possess some parallels. Patmore's essay gained a delayed notoriety from A. E. Housman's praise of it in *The Name and Nature of Poetry*. Hopkins's own system is not unmarked by eccentricity, particularly in the intrusion of an individual vocabulary partly borrowed from music. Yet its central principle is clearly enunciated and is allied, though in a very loose way, to the oldest elements in English poetry, the rhythm of Anglo-Saxon verse and of *Piers Plowman*. Briefly, Hopkins claimed licence to write in Sprung Rhythm, or in feet in which one accented syllable is followed by one or two or three unaccented ones as the poet may consider necessary. A line may thus vary from four single accented syllables to sixteen syllables, in which four are accented and twelve are unaccented. Usually these extremes are not used, but varying feet are united into a rhythmical pattern. Thus, to quote a single example, Hopkins allows in his alexandrine sonnet on Henry Purcell lines such as

> Of the outward sentence low lays him, listed to a heresy, here.

Allied to this adventure in prosody is his elliptical use of grammatical structure. Like Meredith, he finds the relative pronoun a troublesome element, and his solution, which sometimes befogs the reader, is to leave it out altogether. Bridges has commented on this peculiarity[12] and on its probable origin: 'He needed in his scheme all the space for his poetic words, and he wished those to crowd out every merely grammatical, colourless or toneless element; and so when he had got into the habit of doing without these relative pronouns – though he must, I suppose, have supplied them in his thought – he abuses the licence beyond precedent, as when he writes "O Hero savest!" for "O Hero that savest".'

He possessed throughout his mature work a desire to remove from a poem all that was dross, all explanatory matter, the links and transitions which rob words of that unity of impression which a painting or music possesses. In his sonnet *God's Grandeur* he writes:

> The world is charged with the grandeur of God.
> It will flame out, like shining from shook foil.

It is with such sudden glamour that he would endow his poems. The approach is best described in his own words, and it is not without significance that he realizes the mixture of oddity in his originality: 'But as air, melody, is what strikes me most in music and design in painting, so design, pattern, or what I am in the habit of calling *inscape*, is what I above all aim at in poetry. Now it is the virtue of design, pattern or inscape to be distinctive, and it is the vice of distinctiveness to become queer. This vice I have not escaped.'[13] He intended his poetry to be read quickly, in the trust that the whole would reveal any obscurity that the parts might possess. He used alliteration freely to strike this conception of speed and unity, and, as Charles Williams has indicated,[14] it is not the gently luxuriating alliteration of Swinburne but a rush of alliterative words, which, though at first they may seem to have been flung together impulsively, frequently resolved themselves into a keen and imaginative expression. These licences, except to his uncritical admirers, seemed sometimes mere wantonness, but that Hopkins is conscious of the necessity for restraint can be seen in his remark that he hopes to work out towards a 'more balanced and Miltonic style'. On this Charles Williams, the most level of all his critics, writes: 'His poetic tricks, his mannerisms, his explorations in the technique of verse, are not in his earlier poems and they are disappearing from the later . . . Had he lived, those tricks might have seemed to us no more than the incidental excitements of a developing genius. Since he did not live, they will probably always occupy a disproportionate part of the attention given to him.'[15]

The Wreck of the Deutschland must have been for Hopkins a major and most exacting effort, and the fact that it found no acceptance or understanding, even among his intimates, could not but have been a serious reverse. The poem reveals his central position as a poet. In the first part he explores the distress of a spirit recalled by a sudden catastrophe to a realization of God's scourging of humanity: 'Dost thou touch me afresh.' He feels the agony of disunity in the Universe, the soul afflicted by God: 'Thou heardst me truer than tongue confess, Thy terror, O Christ, O God.' For Hopkins the meaning of such suffering and the reconciliation to God lies in the contemplation of Christ's Passion:

> It dates from day
> Of his going in Galilee;
> Warm-laid grave of a womb-life grey.

The second part of the poem opens with a swingeing description of the storm, with the passages to which Bridges suggested that the new reader should first devote his attention. Here is the description of the Nun who cried to the 'black-about air', 'O Christ, Christ, come quickly.' Hopkins, as far as one knows, had little experience of the sea, the most formidable of all the elements. As has been earlier mentioned, his father wrote learnedly on marine law, and it is ironic to contrast these sober pages with the passages that Hopkins himself wrote about the sinking ship:

> She drove in the dark to leeward,
> She struck – not a reef or a rock
> But the combs of a smother of sand: night drew her
> Dead to the Kentish Knock;
> And she beat the bank down with her bows and the ride of
>   her keel:
> The breakers rolled on her beam with ruinous shock;
> And canvas and compass, the whorl and the wheel
> Idle for ever to waft her or wind her with, these she endured.

The second part of the poem concludes with a resolution of that anguish with which the first part opened:

> Dame, at our door
> Drowned, and among our shoals,
> Remember us in the roads, the heaven-haven of the
>   Reward:
> Our King back, oh, upon English souls!
> Let him easter in us, be a dayspring to the dimness of us,
>   be a crimson-cresseted east,
> More brightening her, rare-dear Britain, as his reign rolls,
>   Pride, rose, prince, hero of us, high-priest,
> Our hearts' charity's hearth's fire, our thoughts' chivalry's
>   throng's Lord.

Contemporary with *The Deutschland* are a few strangely ineffectual regular poems, *Penmaen Pool* and *The Silver Jubilee*. It is as if Hopkins, discovering his own methods in poetry, had grown impatient of the more conventional approaches and while continuing to use them employed them with only indifferent skill.

Distress at sea is a theme that has an unusual attraction for religious minds, apart from any additional interest that Hopkins may have gained from his father, the marine lawyer. In 1878 he returned to such a theme in *The Loss of the Eurydice*. The training ship *Eurydice*, as Gardner mentions,[16] had been overturned off Ventnor, by a sudden squall from land, and there had been only two survivors. Hopkins had a double purpose; first, to show the pathos of the disaster, and secondly, to symbolize the shipwreck spiritually of Christendom and above all of England. In a note[17] he mentions that the poem is written in 'sprung rhythm' and that 'each stanza is rather one long line rhymed in passage than four lines with rhymes at the ends'. In range and ambition this cannot compare with *The Wreck of the Deutschland*. Some phrases in the poem recall Cowper's *Loss of The Royal George*, but Hopkins has a more dynamic purpose to fulfil and this leads to certain differences. The diction and the rhythmic movement are simpler than in *The Wreck*:

> The Eurydice – it concerned thee, O Lord:
> Three hundred souls, O alas! on board,
>   Some asleep unawakened, all un-
>   warned, eleven fathoms fallen
>
> Where she foundered! One stroke
> Felled and furled them, the hearts of oak!
>   And flockbells off the aerial
>   Downs' forefalls beat to the burial.

Hopkins himself confessed to a 'kind of raw nakedness and unmitigated violence in this poem'.

Among Hopkins's most original contributions were the variations which at different periods in his career he brought into the conventional sonnet form. He had begun writing sonnets as early as 1865, but the first main group were composed around 1877 and belong to some of his most widely known poems. Such was *God's Grandeur*, which has already been mentioned, and such again was *The Starlight Night*; they reveal a poet who sees nature and every phenomenon of life as a gift and a glorification of God. Such poetry can easily fall into declamation and rhetoric. Hopkins elevates it by his impetuous epithets, each flushed with new colouring and sent speeding into the poem. Amongst these poems is *The Windhover: To Christ our Lord*, which Hopkins himself described as 'the best thing I ever wrote'; from frequent anthology reproduction this is the poem for which he is best known popularly. The description of the kestrel's flight shows the virtues gained from his poetic methods without the licence that puzzles the less-initiated reader in his more unrestrained adventures:

> I caught this morning morning's minion, king-
>   dom of daylight's dauphin, dapple-dawn-drawn Falcon, in
>   his riding
> Of the rolling level underneath him steady air, and striding
> High there, how he rung upon the rein of a wimpling wing
> In his ecstasy! then off, off forth on swing,
>   As a skate's heel sweeps smooth on a bow-bend: the hurl
>   and gliding

> Rebuffed the big wind. My heart in hiding
> Stirred for a bird, – the achieve of, the mastery of the thing!

There were other memorable poems in this group, such as *Pied Beauty* ('Glory be to God for dappled things'); *Hurrahing in Harvest* ('Summer ends now; now, barbarous in beauty, the stooks arise'); *The Caged Skylark* ('As a dare-gale skylark scanted in a dull cage'); and the simplest and, even if not the most poetically brilliant, one of the most moving of them all, *In the Valley of the Elwy*:

> I remember a house where all were good
> To me, God knows, deserving no such thing:
> Comforting smell breathed at very entering,
> Fetched fresh, as I suppose, off some sweet wood.

Sonnets such as these, with their happy themes and their comparatively mild technical innovations, are in profound contrast to those of the final period. These may be said to begin with the sonnet in honour of 'the divine genius' of Henry Purcell, 1879, which is an alexandrine sonnet with six stresses. Its meaning is lucid, though there is a bold prosodic approach:

> Have fair fallen, O fair, fair have fallen, so dear
> To me, so arch-especial a spirit as heaves in Henry Purcell.

There follows a far more original sonnet, bolder in theme and in poetic execution, *Felix Randal* (1880), which describes the death of a farrier, 'big-boned and hardy-handsome':

> Sickness broke him. Impatient he cursed at first, but mended
> Being anointed and all; though a heavenlier heart began some
> Months earlier, since I had our sweet reprieve and ransom
> Tendered to him. Ah well, God rest him all road ever he
>   offended!

George Orwell described this as 'the best short poem in the language' in his *Observer* review of W. H. Gardner's first volume on Hopkins.

The final sonnets belong to the year 1885. Of these *Carrion Comfort* is the most impressive and must be ranked among

Hopkins's greatest poems. It explores some of the same thoughts as *The Deutschland*, but in a darker and more personal manner. The deep passion of a soul contending with God has frequently been a theme in religious experience and confession. Seldom has it gained an expression quickened by such poetic power. Hopkins's gloom is not like that of the later nineteenth-century poets who turn from life in distaste and weariness. It is a positive and impassioned experience, which can only be identified by those who explore it sympathetically and in religious terms. But its reality is made certain by the poetic manner in which it is revealed:

> Not, I'll not, carrion comfort, Despair, not feast on thee;
> Not untwist – slack they may be – these last strands of man
> In me ór, most weary, cry *I can no more*. I can;
> Can something, hope, wish day come, not choose not to be.

In the same mood is *The Bugler's First Communion* (1879), a theme full of treacheries, and even Hopkins's most ardent admirers have had to comment on the poem's eccentricities, as when he rhymes 'boon he on' with 'communion'. This seems very like one of Browning's verbal audacities, and Browning's influence on Hopkins has yet to be fully explored. Hopkins opens in a deceptively easy, almost conversational mood:

> A bugler boy from barrack (it is over the hill
> There) – boy bugler, born, he tells me, of Irish
> Mother to an English sire (he
> Shares their best gifts surely, fall how things will).

The bugler boy seems almost a pious variant on one of A. E. Housman's soldier lads. Whatever its strangeness, the poem has a touching human quality. Ultimately it is a poem of the Christian sacraments and can be appreciated fully and understood only by those who accept these as Hopkins did:

> Here he knelt then in regimental red.
> Forth Christ from cupboard fetched, how fain I of feet
> To his youngster take his treat!
> Low-latched in leaf-light housel his too huge godhead.

How powerfully this religious passion possessed Hopkins in these later years of his life can be seen in other poems of the same period, including 'I wake and feel the fell of dark not day', with its scarifying sestet. Then there was *Harry Ploughman*, among the boldest of the sonnets, composed in 1887. Of this Hopkins himself thought well, for on 28 September 1887 he writes that he has been touching up some old sonnets and he adds, 'within a few days done the whole of one, I hope very good one and most of another: the one finished is a direct picture without afterthought'.

Hopkins had the power of a great poet to see life afresh, and he demanded an individualized vocabulary and rhythm to express what he had seen. His kinship with the metaphysical poets is obvious. Like George Herbert, he could translate religious experience into the tangible and visible imagery of human life. Like Herbert and Vaughan, he delighted in catalogues of similes or of epithets praising the deity, and here he was obviously influenced by the diction of Anglo-Saxon poetry. The passion of his religious experience recalls that of Donne, though he did not come to the religious life with such a rich background of varied human activity as Donne had. He approached most closely to Donne in some of the religious sonnets where he used an acrid physical imagery for the exploration of a religious mood:

> I am gall, I am heartburn. God's most deep decree
> Bitter would have me taste: my taste was me;
> Bones built in me, flesh filled, blood brimmed the curse.
> Selfyeast of spirit a dull dough sours. I see
> The lost are like this, and their scourge to be
> As I am mine, their sweating selves; but worse.

When all these parallels have been explored there is a central element in Hopkins that allies him to Milton rather than to Donne and his followers. He thought of his own work in relation to Milton: 'My poetry errs on the side of oddness. I hope in time to have a more balanced and Miltonic style.' Elsie Phare in discussing[18] this Miltonic parallel suggests that where Milton exaggerated the Latin elements Hopkins exaggerated the Anglo-Saxon ones. Beyond his poetically 'metaphysical' elements he is, like Milton, genuinely metaphysical in revealing in his poetry a philosophical view of the universe; he would reveal the ways of God if not to man at least to himself. This gives to his most memorable verse a consistency of purpose; to suggest at once the grandeur of God and to explore the terror of God as it afflicts the human soul. In that pursuit he was led at times to eccentricity and as a result of his isolation to obscurity, but he gained new values for words, new impacts between mind and experience.

12

Lighter Verse:
Austin Dobson, Edmund Gosse, Andrew Lang
Comic and Nonsense Verse:
Edward Lear, 'Lewis Carroll', William Schwenck Gilbert, Charles Stuart Calverley, James Kenneth Stephen

Throughout English literature there has persisted as a graceful accompaniment to serious poetry a tradition of lighter verse. It varies in motive from comic verse, through epigram and light satire, to poems, brief with gracious conceit, which comment on life wistfully, but without emphasis. At its best, as in Herrick, or some of the Restoration lyrists, or Prior, it has the illimitable quality of greater imaginative work. The main tendency of poetry in the romantic period and in the nineteenth century leads away from any intrusion of the trivial, and yet lighter verse held its place. Isaac Disraeli, writing in 1796, had made a plea for a poetry, not profound in content, but full of the graces, 'refined, melodious and glowing', and he had quoted Pliny's praise of *poésies légères*: 'It is surprising how much the mind is entertained and enlivened by these little poetical compositions as they turn upon subjects of gallantry, satire, tenderness, politeness and every thing, in short, that concerns life, and the affairs of the

LIGHTER, COMIC AND NONSENSE VERSE

world.'[1] If lighter verse may be interpreted through Disraeli's generous formula, the first half of the century has a number of examples from Thomas Hood (1799-1845), and Winthrop Mackworth Praed (1802-1839), to *The Ingoldsby Legends* (1840) of Richard Harris Barham (1788-1845), and the Bon Gaultier *Book of Ballads* (1849), which William Edmonstoune Aytoun (1813-1865) wrote with Theodore Martin, and the miscellaneous light verse of Thackeray.

After 1850 light verse of diverse forms occupied a large place in poetic production, though its existence is frequently forgotten by those who generalize on Victorian taste. It varies in character, and frequently the light-verse writer is capable of more solemn endeavour: Andrew Lang shows, as Thomas Hood did earlier, that humour was but one aspect of his keenly perceptive mind. Many of the major writers allow themselves occasionally to turn to 'these little poetical compositions'; even Tennyson could trifle at times, and Christina Rossetti's *Sing-Song* is a notable example of light verse from a writer whose mind dwelt frequently amid shadows. Other writers, and they are many in the second half of the century, found in lighter verse their main achievement. In this chapter such writers are considered and their serious work is noticed along with the lighter.

It is difficult to define closely the content of all that can be contained under the term 'lighter' verse. If the Aristotelian method of producing the specimens be allowed, the poems in Frederick Locker's *Lyra Elegantiarum* (1867) should be quoted, and with them the poems in Locker's own successful volume of *London Lyrics* (1857). In the preface to his anthology Locker attempted a definition which is possibly as precise as the miscellaneous character of the material will allow: 'Genuine *vers de société* and *vers d'occasion* should be short, elegant, refined, and fanciful, not seldom distinguished by chastened sentiment, and often playful. The tone should not be pitched high; it should be idiomatic, and rather in the conversational key: the rhythm should be crisp and sparkling, and the rhyme frequent and never forced, while the entire poem should be marked by tasteful moderation, high finish and completeness; for, however trivial the subject-matter may be, indeed rather in proportion to its triviality, subordination to the rules of composition and perfection of execution should be strictly enforced.'

Among the great diversity of writers of light verse one group gained unity in attempting to achieve Locker's requirement of 'perfection of execution' by using the more elaborate forms of French verse, *rondel, rondeau, triolet, villanelle, ballade,* and *chant royal.* This movement would appear to owe its origin to a handbook on prosody, *Petit Traité de la Poésie Française,* published in 1872 by Théodore de Banville. His purpose was to deplore that limiting of verse forms which he considered to have had an enervating influence on French poetry for two centuries: 'la poésie française à partir du xviie siècle, a été non seulement réduite en esclavage mais tuée, embaumée, et momifiée.' He invited poets, before inventing new forms or breaking with all tradition, to attempt to convey their sentiments in some of the older and more complex French measures. Théodore de Banville's treatise was read in England by a group of writers and critics, whose interest lay not in his precise thesis, but in the possibility of applying to English poetry the older French forms which he analysed. Early in the field was Edmund Gosse, then a young critic, who wrote in the *Cornhill,* July 1877, an article on *A Plea for certain exotic forms of verse.* Much of this article is a summary of Théodore de Banville's analysis of French forms,[2] but it is accompanied by the plea that these forms should be used in English. Gosse suggested that further imitation of Tennyson and Browning would be unprofitable, while the Pre-Raphaelites had already shown what could be gained by an extension of form: 'The actual movement of the time', he writes, 'appears certainly to be in the direction of increased variety and richness of rhyme, elasticity of verse, and strength of form. The invertebrate rhapsodies of Sydney Dobell, so amazing in their beauty of detail and total absence of style, are now impossible. We may lack his inspiration and his insight, but we understand far better than he the workmanship of the art of verse.' He emphasizes the kinship of poetry with art rather than with philosophy, and quotes as the aim of poetry, the sentiment in Alfred de Musset's lines:

> D'un sourire, d'un mot, d'un soupir, d'un regard
> Faire un travail exquis.

Gosse's article was followed in the next year (1878) by a short essay by Austin Dobson on *Some Foreign Forms of Verse*,[3] in which the types of verse mentioned by Théodore de Banville were again commended. It would seem unprofitable to analyse closely the sequence in which these forms came into English, though this was a problem which some of the poets in this group were frequently considering. It is of interest to note that the ballade had already attracted Swinburne by 1866. He used it both then and later, but for his own purposes, and not in the way in which Austin Dobson and Andrew Lang used it a decade later. Further, the triolet, a favourite with these poets, was used before it was employed by Robert Bridges, who has triolets in *Poems* (1873). Bridges brings the impress of his own high seriousness to this dainty verse pattern, and his work seems to have no contact with the other experiments of the seventies. An anthology, derived from the work of these writers, was issued in 1887, with an introduction by Gleeson White, and there would appear to have been some continued interest in the forms until some of them were used again in the nineties.

One of the earliest and most representative members of the group was Henry Austin Dobson[4] (1840-1921). His grandmother was French, and he was educated in France and Germany, so that his employment of French forms was a natural development. Like Gosse, Lang, and Henley, his main occupation was not poetry. At 16 he accepted a clerkship in the Board of Trade and there he remained until 1901. For a time Edmund Gosse was his colleague. Like some others who devoted their life to biography, he was sufficiently distrustful of the art to wish that his own life should not be written. His main period of poetical production lies in the years 1864-1885, but he continued to write until his death in 1921. His long retirement was occupied mainly with critical and biographical work. Dobson had been writing in periodicals for almost a decade when his first volume of verse, *Vignettes in Rhyme and Vers de Société*, was published in 1873; *Proverbs in Porcelain* followed in 1877, and *Old-World Idylls* in 1883, mainly a selection from the two earlier volumes; *At the Sign of the Lyre* in 1885 and in 1897 *Collected Poems*. Finally, a complete edition was issued in 1923; this, unfortunately, rearranged the poems and the sequence of the earlier volumes was lost.[5]

Austin Dobson worked within a narrow range and a chill fell whenever he attempted to pass on to larger endeavour. The occasional elegiac pieces, such as *Before Sedan*, Spenserian verses on a classical theme, as in *The Prayer of the Swine to Circe* and *Rondeaus of the Great War*, seem all the work of a poet who has lost his way. Within his own domain he contrived a miniature and artificial perfection. There he is master, but one has to examine that world before one can estimate his comparative excellence. Like all successful light-verse writers, he possessed a playfulness in rhythm, with a mastery of complex stanzas, particularly the French forms. With these he constructed a dainty world, into which an element of sentiment was allowed to intrude. If the emotion goes beyond sentiment, the poet is flustered and uncertain, and even in sentiment he is in danger; propriety and sentimentality tempt him away from the game which he is playing. Strangely enough, he is frequently stimulated by an enthusiasm for the eighteenth century, particularly for that courtly eighteenth-century French society, elegant, sophisticated, perfectly mannered, beautiful, cruel, and gracefully immoral. He moves uneasily in this world that he loves, capturing something of its sentiment, but always afraid that he may see or be asked to do something which both he and his Muse would consider improper. It can be seen in *Une Marquise*, where he wins out of the past a delicately contrived portrait, and then ruins it with a blatant moral conclusion disguising itself as satire:

> We shall counsel to our Chloe
> To be rather good than clever;
> For we find it hard to smother
> Just one little thought, Marquise!
> Wittier perhaps than any other, –
> You were neither Wife nor Mother,
> 'Belle Marquise'.

The best of Dobson must be discovered in poems where these alien elements are absent. It can be found in the delightful ballade *On a Fan that Belonged to the Marquise de Pompadour*. Here sentiment and moral comment are reduced to the wistful sense that bright things die, while the ghosts of past elegance move gracefully in the complex stanzas:

> Chicken-skin, delicate, white,
> Painted by Carlo Vanloo,
> Loves in a riot of light,
> Roses and vaporous blue;
> Hark to the dainty frou-frou!
> Picture above, if you can,
> Eyes that could melt as the dew, –
> This was the Pompadour's fan!

and so to the Envoy:

> Where are the secrets it knew?
> Weavings of plot and of plan?
> But where is the Pompadour, too?
> *This* was the Pompadour's *Fan*!

In the same genre are his two 'characters' of *A Gentleman of the Old School* and *A Gentlewoman of the Old School*, and in this verse portraiture he achieved a number of his main successes. The same quality appears in *The Old Sedan Chair*, where the sentiment, obvious but not uninteresting, moves easily in the rhythm of the anapaests. Great poetry can be made out of memories of the past and from the idea of mortality; Dobson approached these themes more lightly, but at times he arouses pathos, even though he never penetrates into the heart of things. The narrative poems show the thinness of his content and the narrowness of his governing motives. These features appear even in such a delightful piece as *The Ballad of 'Beau Brocade'*. Dobson prefaces the poem with a quotation from *The Beggar's Opera*, which seems only to emphasize all that was lost between Polly Peachum and Dobson's Dolly.

In many of his poems he attempted the French forms which he had commended in 1878. Theme, for him as for some other members of this school, was frequently merely the material for technical virtuosity. So in his well-known triolet:

> Rose kissed me to-day.
> Will she kiss me to-morrow?

He was sometimes denied the title of poet and called 'only a most accomplished writer of verse'.[6] But poetry fulfils itself in many ways, and in that age of sanity, the eighteenth century, to which Dobson was himself so attached, many of his verses would have passed the tests. He is neat, 'correct', too decorous perhaps, but some wistful, shy beauty informs the best of his work.

Sir Edmund Gosse[7] (1849-1928) is more happily to be estimated as a prose writer than a poet. His story of his relationship with his father, *Father and Son*, has a strength to which nothing in his verse approaches. Throughout the greater part of his life he had official duties to perform which made literature a secondary interest. After a vague general education he came to London when he was 17 and was appointed to a post in the Cataloguing Room of the British Museum. Later he migrated to the Board of Trade, and finally gravitated to the Librarianship of the House of Lords. He contrived to perform a large amount of literary commentary, and he was among the first in some fields, and fields as wide apart as Restoration comedy and Ibsenite drama. He knew everybody and had an almost unprecedented capacity for gathering acquaintance. It was not strange that poetry, which he had once believed to be his main interest, lingered for the graceful moments of his leisure. As a young man he had sent some of his verses to Swinburne and asked him if he should make poetry a career. Swinburne's answer is one of the best and wisest passages in his whole correspondence. Gosse's verse was contained in the main in four volumes, *On Viol and Flute* (1873); *New Poems* (1879); *Firdausi in Exile* (1885); *In Russet and Silver* (1894). Already in 1911, when he issued a volume of *Collected Poems*, he commented on these volumes: 'They are almost unknown to readers of the present day, and their titles, which had their moment of notoriety, are, I believe, forgotten.' Gosse's judgement on the early verses of Compton Mackenzie can be justly applied to his own work: 'Your verses are highly accomplished and full of delicate grace, but they are lacking in temperament. There I miss a vocation.'[8] Added to this, one may place George Moore's opinion that Gosse was deficient in the use of idiom. His one ambitious piece was a narrative poem in an octave stanza, *Firdausi in Exile*. He omits the more piquant details of the Persian epic poet's exciting career, and so strains the stanza and diffuses the narrative movement that the poem, while retaining the minor virtue of coherence, lacks unity. His poems in French forms hold a place in a minor poetic movement; his themes are more serious than those of Dobson, but their success is hindered by a turgid vocabulary. In a few poems a keener sensibility is quickened by a desire to escape the sophisticated world, of books, and criticism, and towns; this romantic nostalgia for simplicity and nature can be found in *Philomel in London*, and again in *A Winter Night's Dream*,

> Dreary seems the task assigned me,
>   Dull the play;
> I would fain leave both behind me,
>   Steal away
> Where no hopes nor cares could find me
>   Night or day.

Of far greater poetic accomplishment is the work of Andrew Lang[9] (1844-1912). Versatility in the arts, and still more in the world of scholarship, is always suspect, and doubly so when combined with the gentle vice of self-disparagement. Lang worked in a number of fields and belittled his own work in all of them. Educated at St Andrews and Oxford, with a brief interlude at Glasgow, he was elected to a Fellowship at Merton College and could have begun an academic life under those favoured auspices. He chose instead to be a journalist in London. He wrote an incredibly large number of books, and many of them memorable ones; Scottish history, folk-lore and mythology, fairy-tales, novels, primitive religions, all occupied him. He was a Greek scholar, and he had a share in producing a serviceable prose translation of Homer. In such a life there would seem to be little room for poetry, and Lang himself in his later years gave the impression that he had written little, and that not of much consequence. His published work, both in quality and variety, denies such disparagement. His earliest volume was *Ballads and Lyrics of Old France* (1872); *xxii Ballades in Blue China* followed in 1880, and *xxxii Ballades* in 1881; *Helen of Troy* (1882); *Rhymes à la Mode* (1885); *Grass of Parnassus* (1888); *Ballads of Books* (1888); *Ban and Arrière Ban* (1894). Apart from these and other volumes, Lang wrote a large number of periodical pieces. His verse was collected in a four-volume edition in 1923, edited by Mrs Andrew Lang; unfortunately, but perhaps inevitably, she regrouped the poems so that the sequence of the earlier volumes has been lost, and with less excuse she omitted a number of the shorter poems.[10] The omissions include Lang's translation of Gérard de Nerval's sonnet *El Desdichado*, which had first appeared in *Letters on Literature* (1889). Nothing in Lang's work shows his sensibility and skill more keenly than this neglected poem:

> I am that dark, that disinherited,
>   That all dishonoured Prince of Aquitaine,
>   The Star upon my scutcheon long hath fled;
> A black sun on my lute doth yet remain!
> Oh, thou that didst console me not in vain,
>   Within the tomb, among the midnight dead,
>   Show me Italian seas, and blossoms wed,
> The rose, the vine-leaf, and the golden grain.

> Say, am I Love or Phoebus? have I been
> Or Lusignan or Biron? By a Queen
>   Caressed within the Mermaid's haunt I lay
> And twice I crossed the unpermitted stream,
> And touched on Orpheus' lyre as in a dream,
>   Sighs of a Saint and laughter of a Fay!

His first volume, *Ballads and Lyrics of Old France* (1872), contains translations from French poetry, beginning with Charles d'Orléans and continuing to Victor Hugo; he is already gaining contact with some of the French forms which Gosse and Dobson extol later in the same decade. The most ambitious of the original poems is a lyrical sequence, *Hesperothen*. Greek in theme and allegorical in intention, it describes the land of Phæacia, by which is to be understood 'the place of Art and of fair Pleasures'. Lang, a student of the Pre-Raphaelite poets, is influenced here by Swinburne, and Swinburnian domination leaves little room for independence:

> The languid sunset, mother of roses,
>   Lingers, a light on the magic seas;
> The wide fire flames, as a flower uncloses,
>   Heavy with odour, and loose to the breeze.

Such verses are too full of echoes, and yet Lang has conveyed his theme and a mood of 'sweet melancholy' has been brought to dwell in this poem. The volume also contains two poems of places, *Twilight on Tweed* and *A Sunset on Yarrow*, where he writes a little too easily in a genre to which he paid much attention later.

There followed in 1880 and 1881 his collections of *Ballades in Blue China*. He is here in contact with the movement to which Gosse and Dobson gave critical impetus: one of his ballades is a translation from Théodore de Banville, and many of them are exercises in poetical lightness. Lang retains a variety of mood: the *Ballade of Sleep*, which opens,

>   The hours are passing slow,
>   I hear their weary tread,

adapts a serious theme adequately to a ballade of six-syllable lines; in *Ballade of Autumn* he traffics more safely with sentiment than Dobson ever did; while *Ballade to Theocritus, in Winter* recaptures that mood of wistful melancholy which has already appeared in his verse.

Helen of Troy (1882) shows clearly that he is continuing the ambitious endeavour first apparent in *Hesperothen*. *Helen* is a narrative poem in an octave stanza, influenced both prosodically and in its narrative emphasis by William Morris. The verse varies in quality, but the theme is vividly portrayed and the detail contrived with keen dramatic sense. So, for instance, when Helen is portrayed as distressed by the strife she has caused, Lang writes:

> And once she heard a Trojan woman bless
>   The fair-haired Menelaus, her good lord,
> As brave among brave men, not merciless,
>   Not swift to slay the captives of his sword,
>   Nor wont was he to win the gold abhorr'd
> Of them that sell their captives over sea.
>   And Helen sighed, and bless'd her for that word
> 'Yet will he ne'er be merciful to me'.

The critics complained that Lang had chosen a non-Homeric version of the legend. He had made Helen an innocent figure who acted solely as the instrument of Aphrodite, and added a prose appendix on the fortunes of Helen's reputation from Greek times to the nineteenth century. In this controversy on his treatment of the theme the warm, vigorous qualities of Lang's narrative seem to have been ignored.

The unfavourable reception of *Helen* was crucial: he relaxed his promising approaches towards ambitious work; poetry became an incidental activity, the instrument frequently of light and occasional verse. Much that is best in the later collections has, however, more than lightness: Mrs Lang quotes Andrew Lang as saying, 'My mind is gay but my soul is melancholy', and she adds, 'it was the union – or the clashing – of the gaiety and melancholy that gave him his personality'. These elements unite to give some of his light fanciful verse a quality more purely imaginative. So in *The Fairy Minister* the poem opens whimsically with the adventures of the Rev. Mr Kirk of Aberfoyle, who was carried away by the Fairies, but some more witching quality has entered into the closing lines,

> And half I envy him who now,
>   Clothed in her court's enchanted green,
> By moonlit lock or mountain's brow
>   Is chaplain to the Fairy Queen.

For much of this later work no great claim must be made; the rhymes on golf, cricket, and railway novels are verses decked to give ephemeral pleasure. Yet in each of the later volumes he appears at times as the lost romantic attempting to discover

> Of Fairyland, the lost perfume,
> The sweet low light, the magic air.[11]

It can be seen in *Almae Matres*, in which he commemorates his affection for St Andrews and Oxford, and it reappears in *Romance*:

> And through the silver northern night
>   The sunset slowly died away,
> And herds of strange deer, lily-white,
>   Stole forth among the branches gray;
> About the coming of the light,
>   They fled like ghosts before the day!

Lang's place among the minor poets of the period is larger than is sometimes allowed. His versatility has been punished too severely. Engaged in incessant prose work, he had not the disciplined leisure which sustained poetic composition demands. Nor in his life of preoccupied diurnality would those moments of quickened sensation come so easily. He caught poetic images sometimes from his sober prose tasks; two of his most memorable sonnets are on Homer, *In Ithaca* and *The Odyssey*, while one of his best lyrics is *Three Portraits of Prince Charles*. Much of his verse belongs to the trivial, but when the more worthy poems are collected their number is considerable, and a few, such as the translation from Gérard de Nerval already quoted, show that he had a kinship with the creations of pure imagination.

There existed in the later nineteenth century, along with lighter verse, a rich tradition of comic and nonsense verse, some of which has a distinguishing quality of vivacity and metrical ingenuity. This activity is summarized here through some of its main practitioners. No attempt is made to pursue it further, though the comic periodical verses, with their pen-and-ink illustrations, are a revealing feature of the fugitive literature in the Victorian age.

Edward Lear[12] (1812-1888) makes an original contribution to light verse by gaining a comic effect from sheer nonsense. Born in 1812 of Danish descent, he was one of a family of twenty-one children. He had early to earn his own living, and developing a talent for making coloured illustrations of birds and animals he obtained employment at the Zoological Gardens. In 1832 he published a volume of coloured ornithological drawings, *Family of the Psittacidae*. His work gained the notice of the Earl of Derby, and he was invited to draw the animals and birds at Knowsley; these were privately printed in 1846 as *The Knowsley Menagerie*. He was a favourite with the family, and particularly with the Earl's grandchildren, and it was for them that he published *A Book of Nonsense* in 1846. Much of his later life was spent wandering in Europe and the Far East, and he produced a number of volumes illustrated with landscape studies of great distinction. The early nonsense volume was followed by *Nonsense Songs, Stories, Botany and Alphabets* (1871); *More Nonsense Songs, Pictures, etc.* (1872); *Laughable Lyrics* (1877). Lear's first volume was in the form of limericks, a form which owes its modern popularity largely to the wide diffusion of his verses. Historically the limerick may be described as a variation of Poulter's measure worked out in trisyllabic feet. The nature of the stanza is best seen if the limerick is written out not in three lines as is customary but as five short lines, rhyming a a b b a.

It can then be seen that one's natural intuition for rhyme demands that the rhyme of the first two lines shall be answered and the insertion of the third and fourth lines only stimulates this desire. Lear seems to realize that as long as he completes the verse pattern he may say what he likes, and he makes full use of this licence. He chooses to make simple statements, coherent syntactically, but with a delightful detachment from all that is reasonable. So he begins *A Book of Nonsense* with a limerick, which once one has seen his illustration and his portrait, can be described as autobiographical:

> There was an Old Man with a beard, who said, 'It is just as I feared! –
> Two Owls and a Hen, four Larks and a Wren,
> Have all built their nests in my beard!'

And so he continued. In the later volumes he used other, more elaborate, stanza forms, but the method by which the effect is gained is, however, consistently the same. Lear, like Shadwell, but for different motives, 'never deviates into sense'; he is beyond parody and burlesque in a world where things are not what they seem. He retains a well-defined verse pattern which gives to his statements a sense of the inevitable, and so without any grotesque phrasing or imagery he steps straight into another world:

> The Owl and the Pussy-cat went to sea
>   In a beautiful pea-green boat,
> They took some honey, and plenty of money,
>   Wrapped up in a five-pound note.
> The Owl looked up to the stars above,
>   And sang to a small guitar,
> 'O lovely Pussy! O Pussy, my love,
>   What a beautiful Pussy you are,
>   You are,
>   You are!
>   What a beautiful Pussy you are!'

Charles Lutwige Dodgson[13] (1832-1898), known better by his pseudonym, 'Lewis Carroll', followed a brilliant career at Rugby and Oxford with a mathematical lectureship at Christ Church (1855-1881). His career was punctuated with the publication of works on mathematical subjects, the most interesting of which is reported to be his defence of Euclidian geometry, *Euclid and his Modern Rivals* (1879). A shy personality, he seems to have found pleasure in the companionship of young children and in a world of comic fantasy which he and they could enjoy together. He was writing comic verses as early as 1853, and some of them were published by Edmund Yates, who gave him his pseudonym of 'Lewis Carroll'. Among his child friends was Alice (Mrs Reginald Hargreaves), the daughter of Dean Liddell, and for her he wrote the volume *Alice's Adventures in Wonderland* (1865; reissued 1866), which was followed by *Through the Looking-Glass and What Alice found there* (1871). These volumes were mainly in prose, with verses interspersed, and their popularity was so widespread that, in E. V. Lucas's happy phrase, they constituted 'a new nursery mythology'. The next volume was entirely in verse, *The Hunting of the Snark* (1876), as was its successor, *Phantasmagoria* (1876); these were published together with additions as *Rhyme? and Reason?* (1883). After an interval came the stories *Sylvie and Bruno* (1889) and *Sylvie and Bruno Concluded* (1893).

Lewis Carroll was the most ingenious mind that occupied itself with comic and nonsense verse in this period. His pieces are not written as an adult's concession to the child mind. They are a new world created for children and seemingly natural to their values and interests, yet the adult can derive his own subtle and secondary pleasure. His nonsense always appears to have some inner coherence, to be a secret world, mad from our standards, but yet intelligible enough if only one had the clue. His simplest work is in parody, a motive found in many of the 'Alice' verses and in *Phantasmagoria*. Southey, Swinburne, Tennyson, and Longfellow all have comic motives imposed upon their staid stanzas. Dr Watts was perhaps the main sufferer when out of his lines, 'How doth the little busy bee', Carroll extracted:

> How doth the little crocodile
> Improve his shining tail,
> And pour the waters of the Nile
> On every golden scale!

Beyond the parody of individual writers lay the parody of the ballad form which produced Carroll's best fantastic verses, *Jabberwocky* and *The Hunting of the Snark*. *Jabberwocky*,

> 'Twas brillig and the slithy toves

appears a mere mad carnival of words; yet Carroll showed that some of them had meaning, and even gave instructions on their pronunciation. In *The Hunting of the Snark* he reached his most imaginative work. Let it be conceded that the poem is nonsense, a very pleasing mania perhaps, but still not a property of our sensible world. This is no disqualification, for cold common sense might say the same of *The Ancient Mariner*. Nor can one escape the suggestion that this nonsense is not just nonsense. The rhythm, the movement of the story, is in parody of the ballad form, and the theme frequently has a vague and wistful symbolical suggestion. Bishop Blougram once compared life to a ship's cabin, and Carroll's voyage in *The Hunting* is not far from a similar satire on the incongruity of life and of what we pursue in life. It is Swift's satire on the muddled inadequacy of the human mind carried out with a gentle, comic grace which Swift might not have understood:

> The Bellman himself they all praised to the skies –
>   Such a carriage, such ease, and such grace!
> Such solemnity, too! One could see he was wise,
>   The moment one looked in his face!
>
> He had bought a large map representing the sea,
>   Without the least vestige of land:
> And the crew were much pleased when they found it to be
>   A map they could all understand.

It is neither in parody nor satire that the final quality of the poem lies, but in the ingenuity of its world, where pathos and fun mingle in frolicsome unity. He seemed to have lived in two separate personalities, the one which came to a shy, donnish compromise with the rational world and employed itself successfully in mathematical studies; the other that escaped into a child world consistent with itself, but free from the cramping restrictions of the world in which adult humanity has its being.

Sir William Schwenck Gilbert[14] (1836-1911), son of William Gilbert (1804-1890), the novelist, followed an irregular education at Boulogne and London with a commission in the militia and a government clerkship. He has himself told[15] how a minute legacy led him to throw up the restraints of regular employment; he began to read for the Bar, and at the same time found his real profession in literature. Gilbert's work as a writer divides itself into three groups: his comic verse, contributed mainly to *Fun*, and published as *The Bab Ballads* (1869) and *More Bab Ballads* (1874); his dramas and burlesques, beginning with *Dulcamara* (1866) and including the blank-verse fantasy, *The Palace of Truth* (1870), based on Madame de Genlis's story *Le Palais de la Vérité*; finally, with Sir Arthur Seymour Sullivan (1842-1900) as composer he was librettist for a series of comic operas, beginning with *Thespis* (1871) and continuing with a series, produced under the management of Richard D'Oyly Carte: *Trial by Jury* (1875); *The Sorcerer* (1877); *H.M.S. Pinafore* (1878); *The Pirates of Penzance* (1879); *Patience* (1881); *Iolanthe* (1882); *Princess Ida* (1884); *The Mikado* (1885); *Ruddigore* (1887); *The Yeomen of the Guard* (1888); *The Gondoliers* (1889); *Utopia Limited* (1893); *The Grand Duke* (1896).

Gilbert's greatest achievement was in comic opera: he was able to rescue a dull stage from farce and burlesque. With Sullivan's aid he supplied a light humorous satire, nimble in wit and verse, and if too superficial to possess any Aristophanic quality, yet sufficiently barbed to make itself felt amid the foibles of the day. So *Patience*, which attacked the 'vapours' of aestheticism, was mortally effective as satire, despite its accompanying ripple of laughter. The importance of Gilbert in the theatre of the nineteenth century lies outside this study. It can be easily underestimated: he helped to rid the contemporary drama of dullness; through *The Palace of Truth,* and later through the operas, he gave suggestions for G. B. Shaw's conception of dramatic character, and if the theatre at the close of the century presents a criticism of life, Gilbert was one of the first to show how that could be achieved.

Here he is studied only as a poet, and, strangely enough, most of his later work arose out of these early comic poems. *Trial by Jury* had appeared as a verse incident in *Fun* (April 1868), eight years before it was expanded into a 'comic cantata'. Many of the operas were derived from suggestions in *The Bab Ballads*; *H.M.S. Pinafore,* for instance, owes its origin to the situations already found in *Captain Reece.* His most obvious power lay in verbal and prosodic dexterity. Speed, stress, inversion, have all an additional value and emphasis in comic verse. Gilbert had mastered the comic patterns, and with apparent inevitableness he sent the words gambolling through his stanzas. Further, he possessed the power, which Congreve had, of making his world all comic, without the intrusion, except on a few occasions, of moral sentiment. Alone he might have remained merely a writer of comic poems, dexterous and pleasantly satirical. With Sullivan he was able to bring wit and grace back into popular musical entertainment in England.

Charles Stuart Calverley[16] (1831-1884), born at Martley in Worcestershire, was a connexion of the Yorkshire family of Calverley. His parents were named Blayds, but later they took the name of Calverley. In the sixteenth century his ancestor, Walter Calverley, had been associated with a grim tragedy which had passed into Elizabethan drama: now, by strange irony, three hundred years later, one who had adopted the name was to write verse that was a delicate filigree. He had a brilliant career at Harrow as a schoolboy; at Oxford his tutors thought that a sense of high-spirited fun affected his studies. He transferred himself to Cambridge, where he showed his quality by winning distinctions, mainly for classical verse. He married a lady of the Calverley family and became squire of Oulton Hall, near Leeds. He followed no career, and ill health and disability clouded much of his later life. He died in 1884. His verses are to be found in *Verses and Translations* (1862); *Translations into English and Latin* (1866); *Theocritus translated into English verse* (1869); *Fly Leaves* (1872). He worked in two distinct genres. First, he wrote Latin poems and translated English poems into Latin and Latin into English; secondly, he produced light humorous verse and parody, best represented by *Fly Leaves* (1872). The parodist and the translator have common purpose in their desire to appreciate form, and ultimately it is the same technical skill that allows Calverley to make his comic parody of Browning and his translations of religious poems from the Paris Breviary. He spoke himself of 'form-translation' as an ideal, and by this he would imply not only adherence to the original pattern but a capturing of the tempo and the quality of mood. His prose papers on translation[17] demonstrate how keenly he had considered the problems and ethics of translation, and his own versions show how he brought his metrical grace to master the difficulties of the art.

In original verse he shared with Gilbert the skill of playing with words in a gentle, delicate way. It can be seen in such poems as his A B C:

> A is an Angel of blushing eighteen:
> B is the Ball where the Angel was seen.

His last translation was also an A B C poem, but of a very different kind, a rendering of an 'alphabetical hymn by Thomasius', published in Archbishop Trench's *Sacred Latin Poetry*:

> As a thief, who falls at midnight on his unsuspecting prey,
> When we think not shall o'ertake us the Almighty's Judgment Day.
> Brief shall seem to men the pleasures that they prized in times of yore,
> When they know that as a moment Time hath past, and is no more.

These two poems serve to illustrate the variety of theme in Calverley and the technical dexterity which united them.

Many of his verses were parodies of his major contemporaries. Parodies cannot easily survive the originals from which they derive, and for this reason some of Calverley's pieces have lost their freshness. In *The Cock and Bull* story he captured the restlessness of Browning's verse in *The Ring and the Book*:

> You see this pebble-stone? It's a thing I bought
> Of a bit of a chit of a boy i' the mid o' the day –
> I like to dock the smaller parts-o'-speech.
> As we curtail the already curtail'd cur.

Equally apt was his parody of the Pre-Raphaelite poets who wrote ballads with a refrain. Some of their critics had suggested that the refrain was meaningless, and Calverley emphasized this in his ballad of 'The auld wife sat at her ivied door', where the line 'Butter and eggs and a pound of cheese' is used with gay inanity. Sometimes he writes original light verse, as in the *Ode to Tobacco*, where a rime couée stanza is adapted to his comic purposes.

It is difficult not to remember that behind all Calverley's light-heartedness there lurks the tragedy of ill health. Those who knew him as a young man believed that he might have achieved anything that he wished to do. Yet he accomplished nothing that serves as an adequate record of his great talents, but in light verse, as well as in verse translation, he has a distinctive place.

Calverley's talent is paralleled in that of the brilliant son of Sir James Fitzjames Stephen, James Kenneth Stephen (1859-1892), whose career at Eton and Cambridge came to an untimely end as the result of an accident. Stephen had followed his scholastic successes with preparation for a legal career, though much of his time was devoted to literature and to journalism. He produced, on somewhat unpractical lines, a weekly journal, *The Reflector*, which, despite its short life, contained much commendable work by Stephen himself, with contributions by Meredith and others, who delighted in Stephen's methods of editorial freedom. His verse is contained in two slim volumes, *Lapsus Calami* (1891) and *Quo Musa Tendis* (1891). His collected verses were issued with a memoir in 1896. If parody be the extraction of the virtue of one poem and its transference into another mood or environment where all its intention becomes comic, then Stephen is one of the masters of this light but subtle art. His successes have an easy and unexaggerated certainty of effect. Browning was, of course, at hand as one whose poetry cried out to be parodied, and Stephen has welcomed the opportunity in his dexterous verses, *The Last Ride Together* (*From Her point of view*). Byron, Gray, and the ballade writers are gently mocked. He captured the prosody, syntax, and vocabulary of the writers whom he parodied, and combined this with an ingenious inversion of their sentiment. It is the completeness of his effects, combined with their adroitness, that give his work its main charm. This skill can be seen most obviously in his poem to R.K., where he seizes upon Kipling's more rhetorical style:

> When mankind shall be delivered
> From the clash of magazines,
> And the inkstand shall be shivered
> Into countless smithereens:
> When there stands a muzzled stripling,
> Mute, beside a muzzled bore:
> When the Rudyards cease from kipling
> And the Haggards Ride no more.

When he abandoned parody his verses still showed the same features, a light theme, or a seemingly serious theme turned into lightness by prosodic neatness and a finish in phrasing. None of his original verse possesses the final excellence of his parodies, for Stephen is at his best as the disguised and jesting burlesquer

Minor Poets: I

*George Macdonald, Robert Buchanan, David Gray,
Gerald Massey, Alexander Anderson, Joseph Skipsey*

Into this and the next chapter there have been collected estimates of a selected number of minor writers within the period. Their contacts with the major developments in poetry have been noted, though no attempt has been made to force them unwillingly into schools. The nineteenth century presents in an acute manner the problem of how criticism is to face increased production of written matter which must accompany the general spread of literacy. Much work has been sorted and set aside before the writers here selected were chosen as typical minor poets. The chapter which follows is frankly of a miscellaneous character, but one common feature is that the work of those who suffered some defect in education, some unequal start, has been gathered together. Their work has been treated somewhat more fully, as it seems to be a feature characteristic of one aspect of the period. This verse differs from the dialect poetry of such writers as William Barnes (1801-1886), the Dorsetshire poet. Barnes was a man of wide culture who assumed dialect mainly to confirm his own theories on language and because he was attracted by its possibilities as a poetic medium. The writers in this chapter are all in some way unfinished writers, who with other opportunities might have developed differently. Edwin Waugh (1817-1890), the Lancashire poet, is an example of such a poet in the earlier part of the century.

George Macdonald[1] (1824-1905) had a long career as a novelist and poet, and, in his own day, a wide popularity: interest in him was revived with C. S. Lewis's anthology of his prose in 1946. Born in West Aberdeenshire, he was of farming stock of unrelenting piety. He could trace other, and possibly more romantic, allegiances among his forebears. He has described his early years and his struggle for education in a blank-verse poem, *A Hidden Life*. He relates his first enthusiasm for romance:

> The boy knew little; but he read old tales
> Of Scotland's warriors, till his blood ran swift
> As charging knights upon their death-career,

and later he tells of how his father allowed him to go to King's College, Aberdeen:

> To the plough no more,
> All day to school he went; and ere a year,
> He wore the scarlet gown with the closed sleeves.

On leaving the College, Macdonald prepared himself for the ministry, but his mind was restless, leading to trouble with the 'deacons' for heresy: and so in 1853 he determined to break free and devote himself to literature, but only at the expense of poverty which had intervals of starvation. A long record of published work followed; he was mainly occupied with prose fiction, novels of psychic phenomena, or stories of Scottish life. His best-remembered prose work is the fairy romance, *Phantastes* (1858), which also contains some of his more successful lyrics. He began his career as a writer in verse with a drama, *Within and Without* (1855), and verse continues to punctuate the periods of his prose output: *Poems* (1857); *The Disciple* (1867); *The Diary of an Old Soul* (1880); *Collected Poems* (1893).

Macdonald's whole work shows him as a child of Victorian circumstance and opportunity: the emergence from strict religious discipline, with early educational struggles; the religious doubt, solved by rejecting old faiths for an amalgam of Browning, Carlyle, and such German philosophy as is within reach, and the cheerful but unsupported assumption that God approves of the change. He had passed through the whole of this spiritual saga and had an unusual talent for describing it in verse. Indeed, he possesses such metrical fluency that at moments one might suspect the presence of great poetry, but in reality both thought and verse possess a swollen wordiness. In his religious poems there appears rather the voice of exhortation than of experience, with some flavour of the enthusiasms of the 'confessional bench', while the lyrics, though bright with rhetorical phrases, are never illuminated by images that arrest and satisfy. Macdonald's popularity in his own age lay in his subject-matter and general metrical competence. While poetry was withdrawing away from life he was busy contriving readable verses on most of the important problems both of this life and of the future.

Within and Without, his one attempt at dramatic poetry, deals with such problems as the secular and religious life, love and marital fidelity, sin and the consciousness of sin, the possibility of the survival of good and of the reconciliation of divine elements in the future world. Quite naturally he finds that he has overcrowded his drama, and its numerous and disjointed scenes may be better described as a collection of dramatic episodes than as a play. Further, the thought is somewhat incongruously allied to the narrative basis: it is as if one of Byron's heroes had found himself in a Calderon play which had been finished by Browning in one of his more sentimental moods. Despite all inadequacies, the early scenes which describe Count Julian's desertion of the monastery have a sense of power in exploring spiritual dilemmas, and nothing in his later work equals the best passages in this play. *Poems* (1857), apart from the well-contrived verse autobiography, *A Hidden Life*, contains a series of poems on the women of the New Testament. This metrical presentation of Biblical narrative is a device as old as Anglo-Saxon poetry, when its practical value was more obvious. In Macdonald these pieces have the qualities that an uneducated reader of simple piety would appreciate, but they lack any revelation of blood and tears in fresh-found words and melodies. Though this religious verse remains a dominant element in Macdonald's later poetry, it is varied with many other interests. In *The Disciple* (1867) he writes a number of Scots songs and ballads which have heartiness and rollicking movement seldom discoverable in his English verse. Like Stevenson, he seems, in his own tongue, to penetrate to some parts of his nature, humorous, satiric, which he can never release in English. His Jacobite ancestry seems to take possession of him in such a full-blooded ballad as *The Yerl of Waterydeck*, while there is a roguish humour which did not appear in the English verses in *The Waesome Carl*:

> There cam a man to oor toon-en',
> And a waesome carl was he,
> Snipie-nebbit, and crookit-mou'd,
> And gleyt o' a blinterin ee.
> Muckle he spied, and muckle he spak,
> But the owercome o' his sang,
> Whatever it said, was aye the same: —
> There's nane o' ye a' but's wrang!
> Ye're a' wrang, and a' wrang,
> And a'thegither a' wrang;
> There's no a man aboot the toon
> But's a'thegither a' wrang.

His last and most ambitious poem was *A Book of Strife, in the form of The Diary of an Old Soul* (1880), where he attempts in rime royal to trace a spiritual experience, month by month for a year. Rhetorically competent, these verses have a sermonizing quality that infects their value as a record of poignant religious anguish. In 1876 he had published a volume of verse translations, possessing the same interests and sources of suggestion which govern many of his own poems. Schiller, Goethe's lyrical poetry are here, and Novalis, who had contributed to the conception of *Phantastes*, also a translation of Luther's *Hymn Book*, which reads exactly like Macdonald's own religious poems.

In his poetry one always seems to be on the threshold of great things, but his thought is ever giving way to self-caressing complacency. Even in his religious poems, when there is thunder and storm on the stage we feel that he is already in the wings preparing the inevitable and happy conclusion. His lyrical verses rise at times into short passages that have the compelling power of the imagination, but he does not maintain this strenuousness. In *Songs of the Days and Nights* he has the following passage:

> O night, send up the harvest moon
>   To walk about the fields,
> And make of midnight magic noon
>   On lonely tarns and wealds.
>
> In golden ranks, with golden crowns,
>   All in the yellow land,
> Old solemn kings in rustling gowns,
>   The shocks moon-charmed stand.

That is Macdonald very near his best, but whatever the freshness of its suggestion it remains an image half-formed, as if the poet should have dwelt longer with his creation. One wishes that the Jacobite ancestor could have dominated him more often and allowed him, in writing more Scottish ballads, to have grown into a greater poet.

Robert Williams Buchanan (1841-1901) has been remembered mainly for one unfortunate incident in his literary career, the unhappy attack he made on the Pre-Raphaelites in the *Contemporary Review* (October 1871) under the pseudonym 'Thomas Maitland'. Fifteen years later he had so modified his position that he could write of Rossetti: 'When I contrast his gentle life with the strenuous lives of noisier and more prosperous men it seems strange to think that, at any period of his career, any writer could be found blind enough or hard enough to criticize him adversely.'[2] Buchanan might retract, but the memory of his early virulence, and the wounding effect that it had on Rossetti, remained. Hidden behind this single incident there lay a full and interesting life[3] and a voluminous record of poetical production.

Born in 1841, he was the son of a socialistic free-thinking journalist who edited and owned radical newspapers in Glasgow and so was led to bankruptcy. After a period at Glasgow University, he had to come south in 1860 to try his fortune in London. In the same year his school friend, David Gray, made the same journey in the same poverty-stricken conditions; the story of their early hardship has been told poignantly by Buchanan in *David Gray and other Essays* (1868). Gradually he contrived to attract the attention of editors and men of letters; G. H. Lewes gave him useful advice and T. L. Peacock suggested poetic methods. In 1863, *Undertones*, his first volume of verse, was published. From then until his death he published continuously, poems, poetic dramas, popular dramas, criticism, controversy, and novels. The virulence of his critical work alienated him from many of his contemporaries, and led to depreciation of his own verse. In poetry he attempted the type of work which only the greatest can achieve. He wrote too voluminously and with insufficient self-criticism. When every disqualification has been considered it must be admitted that his poetical importance has been minimized.

His early poetical work consists of five volumes of short poems: *Undertones* (1863); *Idyls and Legends of Inverburn* (1865); *London Poems* (1866); *Ballad Stories of the Affections* (1866); *North Coast and other Poems* (1867). This early poetry marks several distinct lines of endeavour. *Undertones* was described by Buchanan himself as pseudo-classical poems written under the influence of T. L. Peacock. They are tentative pieces of pleasing variety and considerable metric ingenuity. In marked contrast, for instance, to the movement of *The Satyr*:

> The trunk of this tree,
>   Dusky-leaved, shaggy-rooted,
>   Is a pillow well suited
>   To a hydrid like me,
>   Goat-bearded, goat-footed,

is the consciously stronger melody of *Antony in Arms*:

> Lo, we are side by side! – One dark arm furls
>   Around me like a serpent warm and bare;
> The other, lifted 'mid a gleam of pearls,
>   Holds a full golden goblet in the air:
> Her face is shining through her cloudy curls
>   With light that makes me drunken unaware,
> And with my chin upon my breast I smile
> Upon her, darkening inward all the while.

Idyls and Legends of Inverburn are in distinct contrast to these refashionings of antiquity. Here he chooses to write dramatic soliloquies on the background of Scottish village life, simple narratives, such as *Willie Baird*, the tragedy of an old Scotch dominie, and *Poet Andrew*, a poem based on the life of his friend David Gray. Buchanan in this volume leans towards blank verse, of whose treacheries he was never fully aware. *London Poems* were a development from the *Idyls*; Buchanan sought amid the figures of mean streets for themes touched with sordidness and crime. He attempted not an emphasis upon the squalid but a portrayal of the innate goodness of man, distorted by circumstance and environment. His verse developed a greater urgency than he had previously displayed, and in such poems as *The Little Milliner, Jane Lewson,* and *Nell* the realistic scene was keenly portrayed. The dangers were vulgarity and, above all, bathos, and he did not always avoid them, but there was sufficient strength and novelty to explain the interest they aroused in the sixties. *The Ballads of the Affections* marked another new departure. Buchanan had gained some knowledge of Danish, which he here used to render a selection of Danish ballads, both ancient and modern. There had been some continuity of interest in popular Danish ballads since the beginning of the nineteenth century. Robert Jamieson had issued his collection in 1806, and Buchanan confessed that this was one of his models. George Borrow had also translated Danish ballads, and in 1860 Alexander Prior had issued an elaborate collection which was possibly used by Buchanan for his own work. The renderings come through into English as fresh spirited poems. *North Coast*, the last of his early volumes, consisted of a series of miscellaneous poems, mainly on Scottish and Danish themes, such as *The Northern Wooing*, a Hallowe'en poem, and the impressive dramatic monologue of *Sigurd, the Saxon*.

Throughout the whole of this first period Buchanan's work, however varied in theme, was confined to lyric and short dramatic soliloquy and narrative. In 1870 he inaugurated with *The Book of Orm* his more grandiose endeavour to achieve poetical expression for philosophical and mystical visionary poetry. This poetry had kinship with work of the 'spasmodic' group, one of whose members, Sydney Dobell, had been friendly with both Buchanan and his friend David Gray.

Buchanan's 'spasmodic' poetry extended over the whole of the remainder of his career. Apart from *The Book of Orm* (1870), he issued *Balder the Beautiful* (1877); *The City of Dream* (1888); *The Outcast* (1891); *The Wandering Jew* (1893); *The Devil's Case* (1896). Amid the myriad visionary scenes of these poems he maintained one thesis, a belief that there was an ultimate regeneration for all life however depraved or ugly it may now seem, and a belief that Christianity, as it was commonly conceived, bred distrust and cruelty. It was expressed most clearly in the last section of *The Book of Orm*, *The Vision of the Man Accurst*, and he returned to it again at the close of *Balder the Beautiful*:

> 'The White Christ answer'd back, and cried,
>   Shining under the sky,
> All that is beautiful shall abide,
>   All that is base shall die.
>
> And if among thy sleeping kin
>   One soul divine there be,
> That soul shall walk the world and win
>   New life, with thee and me.
>
> Death shall not harm one holy hair,
>   Nor blind one face full sweet;
> Death shall not mar what Love made fair;
>   Nay, Death shall kiss their feet!'

Poetically, the firmest of these poems was *The Wandering Jew*, the story of how the poet met a distressed figure in the streets, only to discover that this was the Christ whom the world had rejected. The central element in the poem is the trial of Christ before the Court of Humanity, and his condemnation by all those who have received torture or cruelty in the name of Christianity, and the sentence that is passed upon Him:

> Since thou hast quicken'd what thou canst not kill,
> Awaken'd famine thou canst never still,
> Spoken in madness, prophesied in vain,
> And promised what no thing of clay shall gain,
> Thou shalt abide while all things ebb and flow,
> Wake while the weary sleep, wait while they go.
>
> And lo! while all men come and pass away,
> That Phantom of the Christ, forlorn and grey,
> Haunteth the Earth with desolate footfall –
> God help the Christ, that Christ may help us all!

Buchanan suggested that Christianity had brought torment to humanity, but that in its misinterpretation there was a perpetual re-crucifixion of Christ Himself. He wrote a number of narrative poems which cannot be included within this philosophical group: *Saint Abe and his Seven Wives* (1872); *White Rose and Red* (1873); *The Earthquake* (1885).

Throughout these decades while he is engaged in ambitious poetry he produced a few lyrics, which have a more certain quality of poetical merit than anything else which he produced, notably the two ballads, *The Ballad of Judas Iscariot* and *The Ballad of Mary the Mother*. The simplicity and imaginative integrity of *The Ballad of Judas* reveal by contrast those elements of verbiage and rhetoric which distress his long poems:

> 'Twas the body of Judas Iscariot
>   Lay in the Field of Blood;
> 'Twas the soul of Judas Iscariot
>   Beside the body stood.

> Black was the earth by night,
> And black was the sky;
> Black, black were the broken clouds,
> Tho' the red Moon went by.
>
> 'Twas the body of Judas Iscariot
> Strangled and dead lay there;
> 'Twas the soul of Judas Iscariot
> Look'd on it in despair.

His career as a poet reached its crisis in the years 1870 to 1873. It was in that period that he attacked the Pre-Raphaelites, and it was then that he abandoned lyric and narrative for cosmological and visionary poetry. His work, whatever its limitations, has greater sincerity than that of some of the minor poets who have gained greater consideration, and in his protest against received religious conceptions he must be remembered as one of the figures of revolt in the later nineteenth century.

David Gray[4] (1838-1861), the friend of Robert Buchanan, is an example of a small group of poets in the later nineteenth century who struggled towards poetry from the peasant and proletarian classes. The son of a hand-loom weaver, he was born on the banks of the Luggie, near Glasgow. He contrived with great privation to obtain university tuition; the ministry was the obvious career that suggested itself, but he had already determined to be a poet. From now to the end there existed in his letters an excited assertion that he had the power within him to achieve the greatest things in literature. He obtained by correspondence the interest in his work of both Sydney Dobell and of Monckton Milnes (Lord Houghton). In 1860 he determined to come to London to pursue a career in literature. Monckton Milnes, who had always set counsels of caution before him, tried to persuade him to go home. In London he would stay, however, and there pulmonary trouble undermined his health. He died in 1861. *The Luggie and Other Poems* was first published in 1862, and an enlarged edition appeared in 1874.

MINOR POETS: 1

David Gray's published poetry consists of one long blank-verse poem, *The Luggie*, a collection of sonnets and a few lyrics. He had impressed Monckton Milnes and others with the possibility of greatness, and his poems show that an unusual spirit is attempting to break through. Unfortunately he never fulfilled himself completely in his poetry; one can only hope to detect amidst its inadequacies the promise of what he might have produced. *The Luggie* is a description of nature in the manner of Thomson's *Seasons*, but quickened with phrases that suggest a more romantic approach. The influence of Keats dominates in diction, and Gray shared to some extent Keats's rare gift of revealing a complete picture in a brief, compelling phrase, though Gray's phrases still have diffuseness intermingled. The following passage, despite its rhetorical flatulence, has moments, as in the last line, of quiet command of theme and diction:

> A bank of harebells, flowers unspeakable
> For half-transparent azure, nodding, gleamed
> As a faint zephyr, laden with perfume,
> Kissed them to motion, gently, with no will.

So it is throughout the poem: keen, unusual words and images mingle with what is commonplace or derived.

Some of the passages in *The Luggie* suggest that Gray had already realized that he was soon to die; the sonnets, *In the Shadows*, the product mainly of his last year, are marked heavily with this sense of approaching death. The inequalities noted in *The Luggie* are emphasized, and one misses the fresh natural descriptions of frost and 'feather-silent' snow which had enlivened the earlier poem. The same sudden intrusion of the imaginative phrase remained. The following sonnet is a typical example of this work of the last year:

> Sometimes, when sunshine and blue sky prevail –
> When spent winds sleep, and, from the budding larch,
> Small birds, with incomplete, vague sweetness, hail
> The unconfirmed yet quickening life of March, –
> Then say I to myself, half-eased of care,

Toying with hope as with a maiden's token —
'This glorious, invisible fresh air
Will clear my blood till the disease be broken'.
But slowly, from the wild and infinite west,
Up-sails a cloud, full-charged with bitter sleet.
The omen gives my spirit much unrest;
I fling aside the hope, as indiscreet —
A false enchantment, treacherous and fair —
And sink into my habit of despair.

Any estimate of Gray's verses must make allowance for what Monckton Milnes described as 'the strange and pathetic incidents of their production'. Yet he can be seen in the work which he left, finding his way to a fresh approach to the poetry of natural description which might have become a valued element in the work of the later nineteenth century.

David Gray, despite his early struggles, had the hard-won advantage of regular tuition. Compared with him Gerald Massey[5] (1828-1907) is a poet self-taught. The son of a canal-boatman, and born near Tring, Massey at the age of 8 was working for his livelihood; at 15 he was an errand-boy in the London streets. The hours he had for study were stolen hours. His enthusiasm mastered these difficulties of circumstance, and as early as 1848 he had produced *Poems and Chansons*. Moved by the social upheavals of the time, he was first attracted by the Chartists, but later, under the influence of F. D. Maurice, he associated himself with Christian Socialism. In 1850 appeared his second volume of verse, *Voices of Freedom and Lyrics of Love*. In 1854 he gained wide recognition with *The Ballad of Babe Christabel and other Poems*, and this was followed by *War Waits* (1855); *Craigcrook Castle* (1856); *Robert Burns* (1859); *Havelock's March* (1861); and *A Tale of Eternity* (1870). Massey found that poetry alone would not provide him with a livelihood. As he naïvely remarked in the preface to his collected edition, 'No one lives by poetry in England except the Laureate.' He entered upon a varied career in journalism, lightened by some gracious patronage. His poetry was collected in 1861, with an introduction by Samuel Smiles, and in 1889 a two-volume edition with some additional pieces was issued as *My Lyrical Life*.

Massey's work won high contemporary praise. Landor compared him to Shakespeare and to a 'chastened Hafiz'; George Eliot used him in her portrait of Felix Holt, the Radical; Tennyson gave his approval and employed Massey's *Sir Richard Grenville's Last Fight* as a suggestion for *The Revenge*. Yet his reputation, despite Churton Collins's[6] able essay, seemed by the beginning of the next century to have suffered a complete eclipse. Poetry in the later nineteenth century became increasingly fastidious and esoteric; its content was narrowed and the emphasis upon form increased. Massey's most effective work existed outside these proscriptions. He was popular, blatant, noisy. He wrote in the sixties, though less effectively, the rowdy verses with which Rudyard Kipling troubled the thin perfections of the nineties lyrists. His themes were national and the sentiment boisterously conveyed in a lusty, shouting voice; Chartism, Italy, the Crimean War, the Indian Mutiny, the whole history of England reviewed with the heartiness of the popular ballad. So in his poem, *Down in Australia*, he gives a verbal fanfaronade from which subtlety and uncertainty are banished:

> Quaff a cup, and send a cheer up for the Old Land!
>   We have heard the Reapers shout,
>   For the Harvest going out,
> With the smoke of battle closing round the bold Land.

He was faced with the dangers of facility and of an easy medium; these he fails to avoid, yet in such poems as *The Sea Kings* and *Havelock's March* he has succeeded in re-creating a popular national poetry. Massey himself spoke modestly of these poems in his preface to *My Lyrical Life*: '[they] are more properly historic photographs, rather than Poems in the Esthetic sense. But they are national; and such things whatsoever the matter might be, I have always written for the subject with all my heart.' The same qualities are found, with the inadequacies emphasized, in his early Chartist lyrics. Here, as in the *Song of the Red Republican*, he would seem to have captured a Swinburnian movement before Swinburne had produced the model:

> Fling out the red Banner! the Patriots perish,
>   But where their bones whiten the seed striketh root:
>   Their blood hath run red the great harvest to cherish:
>   Now gather ye, Reapers, and garner the fruit.
>   Victory! victory! Tyrants are quaking!
>   The Titan of Toil from the bloody thrall starts;
>   The Slaves are awaking, the dawn-light is breaking,
>   The foot-fall of Freedom beats quick at our hearts!

Apart from these political and national poems, Massey wrote numerous lyrics, which are frequently distressed by his diffuse style, and poems of domestic life, including the once popular *Babe Christabel*. In this last he attempts, in a poem reminiscent in purpose of Patmore's *The Angel in the House*, to portray the birth and death of a child. Any age which has a generous vein of sentimentality will be able to detect the pathos of its stanzas. In his later poetry he dealt with his psychic experiences, and in *A Tale of Eternity* showed that he could master eerie circumstance into coherent narrative couplets.

He must remain a minor poet, though as such he has been frequently underestimated. Such probably is the penalty of excessive contemporary eulogy. Landor selected the following passage from Massey's poem on Hood and spoke of it in the strongest terms of praise:

> His wit? – a kind smile just to hearten us! –
> Rich foam-wreaths on the waves of lavish life,
> That flashed o'er precious pearls and golden sands.
> But there was that beneath surpassing wit!
> The starry soul, that shines when all is dark! –
> Endurance, that can suffer and grow strong –
> Walk through the world with bleeding feet, and smile!

Viewed more calmly, this may seem merely effective rhetoric, but it has an impression of vigorous thought which gives Massey's work a decisiveness even when technical sensitiveness is missing.

Alexander Anderson[7] (1845-1909) is a notable example of the working man as poet within the period. Born in Kirkconnel, in Dumfriesshire, in 1845, he left school at an early age to work as 'surfaceman' on a railway. His education was the result of his own search, and it led to Dante and to Goethe. He wrote verse with ease, and published in numerous periodicals, including the popular *People's Friend*. Four volumes appeared in his lifetime: *Songs of Labour* (1873); *The Two Angels* (1875); *Songs of the Rail* (1878); *Ballads and Sonnets* (1879); and a posthumous volume, *Later Poems*, in 1912. In his later years he was Assistant Librarian and then Chief Librarian at the University of Edinburgh. As a railway worker he looks from his portraits rather like William Morris, but in Edinburgh days he develops a genteel, frock-coated benevolence. His poetry belongs mainly to his surfaceman period; in the academic atmosphere, away from the railroad scenes, he lost his poetic power.

His early work is markedly derivative in its technical aspects; its freshness lies in his new material, drawn from the worker's life, and in his enthusiasm for those who toil. Tennyson dominated him prosodically, and the mixture of the Laureate's urbanity with Anderson's fresh, crude themes is frequently interesting, but incongruous. In such poems as *The Song of Labour* he used the metre and vocabulary of *Locksley Hall* to express a democratic enthusiasm which he sincerely felt but was unable adequately to re-conceive.

He gradually emerged from this dependence into forms of expression more properly his own, and discovered a poetic method for the description of railroad scenes. Frequently these were but simple incidents, marred sometimes with a melodramatic taint, but at times converting a moment of experience into an adequate poetic image. Such a poem is *The Cuckoo*, in which two men working on the line hear the song of a bird:

> Two simple notes were all he sang,
> And yet my manhood fled away;
> Dear God! The earth is always young,
> And I am young with it to-day.

Anderson developed in individuality, even apart from these poems of working-class life. The most successful of his extended pieces is a sonnet sequence, *In Rome*, written before he had seen the city, and containing, among other poems, a remarkable description of the Laocoön. The most characteristic poems of this later period were Scottish dialect pieces, in the manner of Burns; here he used homely, humorous verse, supported by some compensating strength. The merit of his performance can be seen in *Cuddle Doon*, the best-known poem of his series:

> The bairnies cuddle doon at nicht,
>   Wi' muckle faucht an' din;
> O, try and sleep, ye waukrife rogues,
>   Your faither's comin' in.
> They never heed a word I speak
>   I try to gie a froon,
> But aye I hap them up, an' cry
>   'I! bairnies cuddle doon.'

Within his range he had achieved something definite in simple narrative poetry. Outside the regular schools of verse he had discovered what he had to express and developed a poetic vocabulary by which to fulfil it.

Joseph Skipsey[8] (1832-1903) struggled with even greater disadvantages than Anderson had done. He was born in 1832, the youngest of eight children. His father was shot by a special constable in a mine strike. He had no schooling, but began work at the age of seven in days when work might mean a fourteen-hour day. He had to teach himself to read, and he found books in a haphazard way: Milton, Shakespeare, Pope's *Iliad*, Burns, and translations of Goethe and Heine. His friends attempted several times to rescue him from coalmining; he tried village school-teaching, a sub-librarianship, the porter's post at Armstrong College, and the curatorship of Shakespeare's house; Rossetti admired his verse and formed a personal friendship with him. Either economic difficulties or the sensitiveness of his personality drove him from them back to the mine, until a Civil

List pension, and help from his children, kept him in modest retirement. His published work included a volume of poems (1859); *Poems, Songs and Ballads* (1862); *The Collier Lad* (1864); *Poems* (1871); *A Book of Miscellaneous Lyrics* (1878); *A Book of Lyrics* (1881); *Carols of the Coal-fields* (1886); *Songs and Lyrics* (1892).

Burne-Jones, speaking of Skipsey, said that he felt that one so sensitive in nature 'must carry about with him the pain of knowing that all he did could only be judged after allowance made'. Of much of Skipsey's work this is true; it is remarkable verse for a miner entirely self-educated to have written, but it is not remarkable, absolutely, as poetry. For a number of his poems no such allowance need be made. In such a poem as *Mother Wept*, Skipsey has mastered the contact of form with the experience which initiates the poem; he has a masterly use, reminiscent of Blake, of simple vocabulary and syntax for the suggestion of a deep emotion:

> Mother wept, and father sighed;
> With delight a-glow
> Cried the lad, 'To-morrow,' cried,
> 'To the pit I go.'
>
> Up and down the place he sped, –
> Greeted old and young;
> Far and wide the tidings spread;
> Clapt his hands and sung.
>
> Came his cronies; some to gaze
> Wrapt in wonder; some
> Free with counsel; some with praise;
> Some with envy dumb.
>
> 'May he,' many a gossip cried,
> 'Be from peril kept.'
> Father hid his face and sighed,
> Mother turned and wept.

Not infrequently he transformed the commonplace detail of mining life into poetry with equal power. He has the power to reproduce a single moment of expression with all the finished quality of an epigram:

> 'Get up!' the caller calls, 'Get up!'
>   And in the dead of night,
> To win the bairns their bite and sup,
>   I rise a weary wight.
>
> My flannel dudden donn'd, thrice o'er,
>   My birds are kissed, and then
> I with a whistle shut the door
>   I may not ope again.

He departs from single incidents to a more sustained portrayal of mining life in ballad poems, such as *Bereaved*, which Rossetti considered one of the best poems, and in *The Hartley Calamity* in which he re-tells, rather more rigidly, one of the most terrible mining disasters of his time. Apart from his mining poems, Skipsey has a few poems of fancy, delicate, courtly pieces, such as *The Violet and the Rose*:

> The Violet invited my kiss, –
>   I kiss'd it and called it my bride;
> 'Was ever one slighted like this?'
>   Sighed the Rose as it stood by my side.
>
> My heart ever open to grief,
>   To comfort the fair one I turned;
> 'Of fickle ones thou art the chief!'
>   Frown'd the Violet, and pouted and mourned.
>
> Then, to end all dispute, I entwined
>   The love-stricken blossoms in one;
> But that instant their beauty declined,
>   And I wept for the deed I had done!

Skipsey's poetry has, at its best, a distinct quality. His work illustrates clearly the difficulties in mid-Victorian times of the working man who is possessed of some elements of genius. Once he is removed from his environment he is shut out from the centres of suggestion which made his poetry possible. Unless he is removed from that environment he is unlikely to acquire the technical skill through which his experience may be expressed. Skipsey was not unaware of this sad dilemma; the strange thing is that he should have escaped from it so often to write poetry that needs no 'allowances'.

Minor Poets and Poetry: II

Into this chapter has been gathered a selection – admittedly it is no more – of the minor poetry of the period. Wherever a minor poet has had contact with one of the major movements, or wherever his work has suggested some fresh tendency, it has already been considered. Here has been assembled the unmanageable mass of competent versifiers which increased literacy made such a formidable problem in the later nineteenth century. These are the poetical *vulgariseurs*, the exploiters of the overworked traditions, the multitude who write often with irritating correctness, but who are poetically sterile, and, last of all, and in a different class, the genuine minor writers who have produced a little that is good and have been content to go no farther.

Some of these writers were highly esteemed in their own day. Such were the claims made for Sir William Watson (1858-1925).[1] Apart from the popularity of individual volumes, *The Collected Poems* had reached a third edition by 1899. He seemed to have a natural claim to be Tennyson's successor and his grandiloquent manner was found by his contemporaries most acceptable. The later neglect of such volumes as *Lachrymae Musarum* (1892) has been nearly complete, though there was a selection of his poems in 1922 and another made by himself in 1928 and an edition of the collected poems was published as late as 1936. If one looks at his work again after this absence of time, it is easy to see how derivative it was, how far from all the succeeding traditions, but often informed with intelligence, and sometimes with a genuine if sonorous poetic style.

The later nineteenth century produced a large audience for easy, intelligible verse, whose sentiment and form were made to render no difficulty in vocabulary or movement. The laureate of this audience was Martin Farquhar Tupper[2] (1810-1889), who in *Proverbial Philosophy: a book of thoughts and arguments originally treated* devised a rough doggerel pleasing to a large nineteenth-century audience, more enamoured of moral reflection than of poetry. The volume first published in 1838 had reached its thirty-ninth edition by 1865. There remained an extensive public, which had been attracted by the simpler verses of Tennyson and wished for more in that manner. Among those who were most effective in meeting this demand was Sir Edwin Arnold[3] (1832-1904). His popularity, deriving from *The Light of Asia* (1879), showed that new subject-matter couched in verse which the unobservant might mistake for that of Tennyson would meet the requirements of the multitude. Arnold had a varied career: his six years' service in India he had employed in learning Sanskrit and Persian. He could have become a scholar, had not chance led him into journalism and finally into the editorship of the *Daily Telegraph*. Already in 1852 his Newdigate Prize poem, *The Feast of Belshazzar*, had shown his interest in oriental themes. The reception awarded his early miscellaneous verse did not predict the fantastic success of *The Light of Asia* on its appearance in 1879. The English public of the seventies knew little of the stories of the Buddha and still less of the religions of India, and Arnold's poem, emblazoned with a new vocabulary, extravagant in its use of detail, and employing strange if cacophonous proper names, initiated readers into the life of the Gautama and the philosophy of Nirvana. Even if Arnold's work fails as poetry, he gave, to his own generation, a new mental horizon. This freshness of material must be considered in estimating his poetical reputation. He had something to reveal which could not be found elsewhere, and Sir Denison Ross in 1932 wrote that the poem still remains 'the best description of the life of Gautama Buddha in our language'.[4] Once Arnold leaves the theme of Buddha his poetical strength fails him. His *Poems National and non-Oriental* (1888) are blatant and ineffective, while his attempt in *The Light of the World* (1891) to treat Christ's life as he had once treated Buddha's is a complete failure. Even his other Indian poems, which included translations from the Sanskrit, missed the appeal of *The Light of Asia*. The eclipse of Arnold's reputation has been, however, too complete. He had descriptive powers and an eye for telling detail, both of which are illustrated in such a passage as his account of the city of Buddha's father:

> here a throng
> Gathered to watch some chattering snake-tamer
> Wind round his waist the living jewellery
> Of asp and nâg, or charm the hooded death
> To angry dance with drone of beaded gourd;
> There a long line of drums and horns, which went,
> With steeds gay painted and silk canopies,
> To bring the young bride home; and here a wife
> Stealing with cakes and garlands to the god
> To pray her husband's safe return from trade,
> Or beg a boy next birth.

All his verse is too easily wrought, but at his best, and with Tennyson to help him, he is not without an arresting quality. He added to this the capacity for organizing detail into narrative. *The Light of Asia* has much of the charm of *The Arabian Nights*, with the added dignity of a great world theme, and while it titillates the reader with its bizarre movement it leaves him with the consolation of knowing that he has absorbed a difficult philosophy without apparent inconvenience.

Nine years after *The Light of Asia*, Kipling was to use the East for more subtle and captivating poetic purposes; while a year later than Kipling, Sir Alfred Comyns Lyall[5] (1835-1911) published *Verses Written in India* (1889), which describe Indian scenes in easy, swinging melodies. Lyall was a distinguished administrator who knew the East well, and had he continued to write and had Kipling not been a contemporary, he might have been more esteemed as a poet. He is sometimes too facile, but he has mastery of the simple monologue and narrative, as poems such as *The Old Pindaree*, *The Amir's Message*, and *Theology in Extremis* show.

For Sir Lewis Morris (1833-1907) less claim can be made than for Arnold, yet nowhere can the demand for Tennyson-made-easy be more readily perceived. He always possessed a clear subject in the prose sense of the term, and he infused his work with the blatant moral values of which his audience approved. He chose themes which a great poet might have found strenuous, and while he never has the imagination to dominate them, he seldom descends to bathos and never to grossness. A wide public, not poetically sensitive, and in revolt against the exotic moods and overcurious phrasing of much of later nineteenth-century verse, mistook him for a great writer in the main tradition, and welcomed him accordingly; of his *Works* published in 1890 sixteen thousand had been sold by 1907. His later blank verse obscures the inadequacies obvious in his lyrics, *Songs of Two Worlds* (1871 and 1878), where he shows a strong but ineffectual influence, derived from Herbert and from Vaughan, whom he eulogizes in *To an Unknown Poet*. He has a slackness in verse texture, and one of his freshest lyrics is *The Organ Boy*, where the measure is admittedly made free so that picturesque detail may be introduced:

> Great brown eyes,
> Thick plumes of hair,
> Old corduroys
> The worse for wear.

Much of his credit for producing this poem disappears when Morris's debt to William Brighty Rands's *Polly*, in *Lilliput's Lyrics*, is recollected.

The Epic of Hades (1876-1877), for which Lewis Morris was best known, remains his most vigorous poem. Exploiting the overworked Victorian pastime of refashioning classical legend, he wrote a poem in three books: Tartarus, the place of torment; Hades, of purgatory; and Olympus, the heavenly place. Each book has suitable narrations, and from these he extracts moral motives, as Tennyson had done from the Arthurian tales. Apollo and Helen may seem somewhat wan and cramped when reduced to the service of didacticism, but the Christian atmosphere was welcome to Morris's audience. He concludes in an optimistic mood, savouring of Tennyson's *Locksley Hall*, and yet more vigorous than anything else in the poem. His quality comes through most pleasingly in such a narrative of pathos as Marsyas's account of his defeat by Apollo, yet here the moral and the poetic themes are more than usually discordant. He is frequently close to poetry in imagery and phrasing, as in his description of fate's cruelty:

> binds us fast
> Within the net of Fate; as the fisher takes
> The little quivering sea-things from the sea
> And flings them panting down to die on the shore.
> Then he spreads his net for more.

Yet he dwells in complacency, with verbal nebulae, rather than in the clear light of poetry. In his later *A Vision of Saints* (1892) he attempts to retell the stories of saints and worthies from St Christopher to Elizabeth Fry. He has abandoned Tennyson and substituted a weak Miltonic gesture in vocabulary and syntax. To consider this volume is one way of instructing oneself to think well of *The Epic of Hades*.

In approaching 'Owen Meredith'[6] (1831-1891), first Earl of Lytton, and son of Lord Lytton, the novelist, one discovers a writer imitative to the point of plagiarism, but with keener sensibilities than Edwin Arnold or Lewis Morris. He combined a distinguished career, culminating in his eventful tenure of the office of Viceroy of India, with considerable activity as a poet. He would seem to belong to the Elizabethan tradition, when letters, diplomacy, and arms had not become divorced activities. As early as 1855 he had published *Clytemnestra* and *The Wanderer*; a volume of lyrics followed in 1859. In 1860 *Lucile*, a novel in verse, appeared, a genre to which he returned in *Glenaveril* (1885). His other work includes *Orval* (1869), based on a Polish poem by Count Krasinski; *Chronicles and Characters* (1868), in which on a plan derived from Victor Hugo he recounts memorable moments in great lives, a device used later by Lee-Hamilton in *Imaginary Sonnets*. In 1874 he produced a less ambitious but more successful volume, *Fables in Song*. His elaborate blank-verse fantasy, *King Poppy*, appeared posthumously in 1892, though there is a version with the date 1874. Swinburne in *Last Words to a Seventh-Rate Poet* in *The Heptalogia* parodies the more marked features of Lytton's verse.

The most marked feature of Lytton's work is its strongly derivative quality; this was noticed by his contemporaries, and it continues to trouble any reader of his work. He has a nimble movement of his own, placid at times, but beautiful, too, though with a bias towards mere prettiness. One feels, however, that the impression which Lytton himself is making is apt to be marred by passages closely modelled on Tennyson, Browning, and Swinburne, or by more general memories of Victor Hugo. His own ambitious attempt towards originality was in the verse novel. The genre had gained a general sanction from Mrs Browning's *Aurora Leigh*, while Patmore in a different way had shown how poetry could be evolved out of contemporary circumstance. In *Lucile*, on a plot derived in part from George Sand's *Lavinia*, Lytton attempted to tell an elaborate story of love intrigue in a four-beat line, anapaestic in movement. The verse form never justifies itself as a medium for the narrative. *Glenaveril* is more ambitious, but not more successful: Lytton attempts to hold an elaborate plot with heredity as a main motive and a mass of contemporary detail as décor, within an *ottava rima* stanza. The novel in verse demands the energy of Byron in the mood of *Don Juan*; Lytton lacks the gusto, the right emphasis, and the wit and entertainment which he generously provides do not compensate. His more secure work is to be found in some of the lyrics and fables; they are fanciful and too easily evolved, but they have a daintiness which gives them an identity. To them one may add *King Poppy*; half allegory and half fairy-story, with a mixture of moods from solemnity to fantasy and satire, this has a fresher quality. Even here he returns at times to imitate Browning and Tennyson so closely that one might feel that he had copied passages from their works and inserted them by error into his own poem. His residence in Venice and his knowledge of Wagner led him to collaborate with his friend Julian Fane to compose *Tannhäuser* (1861). Julian Fane (1827-1870), a son of the Earl of Westmorland, was Lytton's companion in the diplomatic service, and Lytton's memoir of him, *Julian Fane*, gives generous recognition to his poetry, which included *Poems* (1852) and translations of Heine (1854).

Traditional verse possessed a much more sensitive practitioner in the work of John Byrne Leicester Warren, Lord De Tabley[7] (1835-1895). A cultured, delicately attuned mind, he wrote an elaborate but dimly coloured verse, never inept but without commanding quality or urgency. He adhered to the tradition founded by Tennyson in his classical poems and English idylls, and to this he added features from Matthew Arnold and a few Swinburnian memories. In reviewing his careful verses one is at first surprised that in his own day he gained so little popularity and that his posthumous fame has not been more notable. This neglect arose from his failure to establish poetic independence. He is content with forms already worked, and with a tenancy in a Palace of Art, whose wan perfections had already been overdisplayed. He seems to be searching, almost indiscriminately, for themes which may be patterned into a delicate fabric. His main endeavour lay in refashioning classical legends, and in dramatic monologue or narrative form he retells the stories of Iphigenia, Anchises, Ariadne, Daedalus, and Niobe; it is Tennyson's work lithographed. His methods are shown in the monologue *Philoctetes*, the theme of which he used later for one of his plays. He gives a firm portrait of an outcast, who waits knowing that the day of revenge is certain to come, but strong memories of Tennyson arise in the form, and in some of his lines he echoes Tennyson's *Ulysses*:

> I hate this island steep, this seam of beech,
> This ample desolation of gray rock.

He is more independent once he has set aside classical themes, and in such a dramatic monologue as *The Cardinal's Lament* he gives an aroused, spirited presentation of the case for Catholic Christianity. But Greek themes seem to haunt him, and he carries their refashioning from narrative to dramatic form in *Philoctetes* (1866) and *Orestes* (1868). The blank-verse closet play of classical form attracted poets in the nineteenth century, as Swinburne's work shows, and yet it seems a poetic cul-de-sac, heavily encumbered with dead verse. It was in this form, however, that De Tabley gained his most individual success. He began with Matthew Arnold's example before him, and always aware of Swinburne's choruses, yet he asserts his own purposes. In *Philoctetes*, while indebted to Sophocles's treatment, he develops the story of the banishing of Philoctetes and his later recall in his own way. The early part of the play is contemplative, Philoctetes considering the unfairness of the gods in a manner reminiscent of *Atalanta in Calydon*. Then Pyrrhus enters with Ulysses, who makes one of the best speeches in De Tabley's work, and Philoctetes is persuaded to rejoin the Greek forces. The early motive of the evil of fate is eluded in this second part, thus leaving the play inconclusive, despite the strength of individual speeches. *Orestes* (1868), though less well known, is far more effective dramatically. The play deals, not with the well-known Orestes, but with the prince of Larissa, whose mother's paramour plans to enjoy the throne once the heir is disposed of. The dramatic movement is complicated and the plot savours of a romantic play. The clear picture of the developing manhood of Orestes and the sickening passion of the Queen for her lover show that could De Tabley have freed himself from nineteenth-century classicism he might have achieved something fresh in poetic drama.

His shorter poems have variety, but seem the miscellanea of one who consciously sought for themes. In *The Sale at the Farm* he reworks Tennyson in the English idylls manner, though he supports the poem with his own close knowledge of country life. *The Garden of Delight* and *A Heathen to his Idol* confirm the evidence of the dramas that he has remembered Swinburne's melodies, while *The Strange Parable* shows him producing a strong poem on Browning's models. Yet it would not do De Tabley justice to suggest that his shorter poems are confined to these derivative pieces. He does not attain easily to lyric; the mildly decorative quality of his verse is nurtured more easily in blank verse, yet in some short-line lyrics, notably in *A Hymn to Astarte*, he works with economy to a well-defined effect:

> Parent of Change and Death,
> We know thee and are sad, –
> The scent of thy pale wreath,
> Thy lip-touch and the glad
> Sweep of thy glistening hair:
> We know thee, bitter-fair.

De Tabley's talent is more considerable than has been usually allowed, and his quiet, sincere verse is lost amid the many challenging voices at the close of the century.

Though De Tabley can be affirmed to have made a definite contribution to verse drama less certainty can be expressed in any judgement of the voluminous work of 'Michael Field'.[8] This pseudonym was used by two ladies, aunt and niece – Katherine Bradley (1846–1914) and Edith Cooper (1862–1913) – who wrote in collaboration and produced their work as that of a single masculine personality. They began their joint career as dramatists with *Callirrhoë* in 1884, where the Greek theme is freely treated to illustrate love and self-sacrifice, in a blank verse that has enthusiasm but sometimes lacks discretion. There followed between 1884 and 1890 a series of ambitious plays on themes from English and Scottish history: *Fair Rosamund* (1884), *The Father's Tragedy* (1885); *William Rufus* (1885); *Canute the Great* (1887); and *The Tragic Mary* (1890). In this last the Mary Stuart history is retold with greater brevity than Swinburne employed. They followed these plays with a lengthy Roman trilogy of the second and third centuries A.D. *The World at Auction* (1898); *The Race of Leaves* (1901); *Julia Domna* (1903). They had attempted to dramatize Gibbon's theme of the decline of the Empire, and this and later material is exploited further in *Stephania* (1892) and *Attila, my Attila* (1896). Finally were produced plays on Cesare Borgia (1905), on Tristram (1911), on Deirdre (posthumously published 1918), on Herod (1911), and on other themes. Their work aims at the most ambitious heights in poetry, both in form and theme. At first there were many to tell them that they had been successful, and Browning's voice joined in the applause. Later, when their work became neglected, they pursued their studies and their prolific production unabashed, and even ill health could not deter them. They form possibly the most absolute example of the Victorian inability to distinguish between a blank-verse play that is dramatic and an amorphous work decorated with occasional passages of high-sounding verse. These collaborators, despite their honesty and their patience in working out historical themes, had no sense of the organic coherence which a dramatic work demands. They gathered from their Elizabethan models a happy aptitude in imagery and for brave, extravagant phrases, and some of their contemporaries mistook these splendours for dramatic poetry.

The work of these two ladies serves to show how far from the theatre most nineteenth-century verse drama dwelt. The main interest in the work of Stephen Phillips[9] (1864-1915) was that he attempted to bring back the blank verse as a medium in acted drama. For a brief period (1898-1906) he had a success of coruscating brilliance; then suddenly the praise ceased, and with equal suddenness the virtues which his early poetry possessed shuffled out of his work. He was educated at a number of places, including Oundle School. He studied to enter the Civil Service, but abandoned this to join Sir Frank Benson's Shakespearian Company. He was already writing verse, and his employment in the theatre led him to think of the possibilities of verse for drama. He had first gained recognition with a volume of non-dramatic poetry – *Poems* (1898) – but the extravagant praise given to this volume was eclipsed by his fantastic success as a dramatic poet acceptable to the commercial theatre. *Herod* (published 1901) was performed by Sir Herbert Beerbohm Tree in 1900; it was followed by a production in 1902 of *Paolo and Francesca* (published 1899). Then came in full flood, *Ulysses* (1902); *The Sin of David* (1904); *Nero* (1906); *Faust* (with J. Comyns Carr, 1908); *Pietro of Siena* (1910); and other pieces, including some one-act plays. He had an instability of temperament and habit which success emphasized. After 1906 there is little in his work that is either attractive or original. During some of his later years he lived in a condition which was sometimes little better than vagrancy. His last years (1912-1915), during which he edited the *Poetry Review*, suggest a more settled life, but poetic activity returned without poetic strength.

His non-dramatic work began as early as 1884 with a privately printed volume, *Orestes*; in 1890 he contributed with Laurence Binyon and others to a volume of verse, *Primavera*; *Eremus* followed in 1894, and *Christ in Hades* (1897), and *Poems* (1898). Then after the production of the poetic dramas came, with a decade's interval, *New Poems* (1908); *The New Inferno* (1911); *Lyrics and Dramas* (1913); *Panama and Other Poems* (1915). Phillips's effective work belongs to *Poems* (1898) and to the volumes that precede it. In *Orestes* he had written a blank-verse dramatic monologue, which showed strong influence from Tennyson's classical idylls; it is a brilliant poetic exercise rather than an original poem. *Eremus*, a long blank-verse poem, not reprinted, describes how Eremus, an archbishop, before his death has himself carried up by two monks to a mountain peak. Here he describes the vision which he has had, and portrays a brooding and pessimistic philosophy of life. The poem lacks both dramatic coherence and intellectual strength, and even the strong Miltonic influence in the verse cannot rescue the vaporous rhapsody of the archbishop from dull morbidity. *Christ in Hades*, much stronger and more distinct, is the poem in which Phillips's merits and defects can be most clearly perceived. Employing Miltonic precedent, he mingles Christian and classical elements in the narration; Christ descends into Hell, but it is Virgil, Prometheus, and Persephone who come to greet him. This choice of a large theme is typical of Phillips's method, and he certainly possesses power in marshalling a processional movement. Unfortunately he seems incapable of exploiting the possibilities of the situations which he has invented. The opening of *Christ in Hades* has the gesture of epic, but once Phillips has summoned the spirits he can think of nothing adequate for them to say, and so they are dispersed with a Miltonic simile. Similarly, the verse has the accent of great poetry, yet the suspicion remains that it has been copied as exactly as the clever student in a picture gallery copies a Titian. The following is his description of the hosts of Hades:

> Toward him in faded purple, pacing came
> Dead emperors, and sad unflattered kings;
> Unlucky captains listless armies led;
> Poets with frozen music on their lips,
> Toward the pale Brilliance sighed.

The poem dwells in rhetoric, with a phrasing frequently derivative and a verse texture that is loosely woven. The whole seems a medley of mighty figures, fine words, the gestures of greatness, all standing incoherently together like discarded pageant robes in the wardrobe cupboard of a theatre.

These impressions are confirmed by *Poems* (1898). *Marpessa* continues the tradition of *Christ in Hades*. A more compact poem in the manner of Tennyson's classical idylls yet has the same disquieting sense that the poem rests in skilful imitation rather than in some fresh poetic impulse. The closing lines describe Idas and Marpessa:

> Then slowly they,
> He looking downward, and she gazing up,
> Into the evening green wandered away.

The poetic worth of the passage collapses when one realizes that it arises from a close recollection of the passing from Paradise of Adam and Eve at the close of *Paradise Lost*.

In the shorter lyrics Phillips was dominated by moods of melancholy, facilely rendered, but missing in the same way as the longer poems the qualities of urgency and freshness. Occasionally the expression is sharpened to the point of epigram, and it is here, as in the early poem of *A Dream*, that he is most effective:

> My dead Love came to me, and said:
> 'God gives me one hour's rest,
> To spend upon the earth with thee:
> How shall we spend it best?'
>
> 'Why as of old,' I said, and so
> We quarrelled as of old.
> But when I turned to make my peace,
> That one short hour was told.

He was less successful when he attempted, as in *The Wife*, to follow John Davidson's example, and in converting grim transcripts of contemporary experience into poetic form. In one of his prose essays Phillips lamented the decay of English verse satire. One is led to wonder if he would not himself have succeeded better with Dryden and Pope as his masters, rather than with Milton and Tennyson.

The main interest in his poetic dramas is that they were not closet plays: they were adapted to the needs of the contemporary theatre, and found favour with the practical men of the stage: Sir George Alexander and Sir Herbert Beerbohm Tree. The problem which he set himself was the very problem which the Elizabethan dramatist tried to solve; how to preserve a fine frenzy of poetical language in a theme which would appeal to general audiences and would exploit the scenic possibilities of the popular stage. This the Elizabethans achieved, but they went farther, and showed skill in depicting character, and high passions, and the tragic conflict of mighty opposites. It is here that Phillips fell short. He went far in reconciling poetry and the theatre, but he failed to convert popular drama into an instrument through which tragic experiences could be conveyed. His qualities can be seen in *Herod*, the earliest of the plays to be performed. The main theme is the murder at Herod's command of Aristobulus, the brother of Herod's wife Mariamne. This Phillips contrives to adapt into vivid theatrical situations, yet retaining a lavish use of poetic language. In the first act, for instance, Herod is allowing the Queen's brother to be put to death while she is recapturing him with her charm. They exchange conversation which is lyrical and yet cunningly dramatic:

>*Mariamne*: O world of wearied passion dimly bright!
>*Herod*: Now the armed man doth lay his armour by,
>And now the husband hasteth to the wife.
>*Mariamne*: The brother to the sister maketh home.
>*Herod*: Now cometh the old lion from the pool.
>*Mariamne*: And the young lion having drunk enough.

And while this conversation is being maintained the audience knows that Aristobulus is being killed and that Herod knows that he is being killed. Similarly, at the close of the second act, Phillips exploits the elaborate setting of a modern stage. The act has been tumultuous, and Herod now makes his exit up an enormous stairway, reciting as he goes the names of the provinces which he is to hold under Caesar:

>Hippo, Samaria, and Gadara,
>And high-walled Joppa, and Anthedon's shore,
>And Gaza unto these, and Straton's towers.

Unfortunately *Herod*, though cleverly arranged as a spectacle, and not inadequate as a melodrama, failed to give either penetration into motive or tragic conflict. The play remains a play of situation decorated with poetry. *Paolo and Francesca*, of the same period as *Herod*, is a more even achievement, and is by far Phillips's strongest work as a poet. Basing his play on a story which Dante told so exquisitely, he builds up a four-act tragedy of considerable coherence. Again the characters are phantoms rather than individuals, but the sense of an inevitable yet tragic love is powerfully conveyed. The later plays confirm the evidence of the non-dramatic poems that Phillips works in a narrow field. *The Sin of David* (1904, revised 1912) develops clearly the

Biblical plot in a Commonwealth setting; the excesses common to the later work are absent, but there are few positive qualities. *Ulysses* and *Nero* out-herod *Herod* in exploiting theatrical manipulation amid a display of verbal pyrotechnics.

There is a sense of unusual pathos in Stephen Phillips's career. He seemed to be so near in *Paolo and Francesca* to bringing poetical drama back to the public stages. He was not working for a coterie theatre, but for some of the largest theatres in London. No wonder that it seemed at the time like a renaissance in drama, and that Phillips was hailed as a leader. His essays in *The Poetry Review*, which he edited from 1913 to 1915, show how he clung to that ideal of a poetical drama. Splendour surrounds much of his work, and it is only after examination that it is seen to be a splendid emptiness. Yet nowhere did the example of Tennyson seem for a time to be leading to such fresh possibilities of poetic achievement.

This notice of some of the more popular and traditional writers of the later nineteenth century may be best concluded by a note on Alfred Austin (1834-1913).[10] It is unfortunate that the Laureateship, one of the few national tributes to the arts, should be so frequently rendered ridiculous. Tennyson had adapted himself so sumptuously to the office that Providence might seem to have designed him for it, but no one, not even Lord Salisbury, who recommended him, could have imagined that Alfred Austin would be more than a dwarf straddling in the trappings of a giant. In prose Austin could command a heavy but not ineffective bludgeon, which was discovered to be useful for party purposes; in poetry he was ambitious, but bleakly uncritical and unrestrainedly productive. Further, in order to swell his work he is for ever reincorporating into new volumes poems already issued in his past works, so that to read a fresh volume of Austin is like coming upon tedious acquaintances in places where one imagined that they could not possibly be present. In verse he produced a number of narratives beginning with *Randolph* (1855), dramatic poems, of which the first is *The Tower of Babel* (1874) and the best *Fortunatus the Pessimist* (1892), and many volumes of lyrics from *Interludes* (1872) to *Sacred and Profane Love* (1908).

Austin incurs displeasure both by his solecism in succeeding Tennyson and by his pretentious and waspish criticism of his contemporaries in *The Poetry of the Period* (1870). Here he attacks Tennyson, Browning, and Swinburne for their general incompetence. He rails against the pettiness of modern verse, proclaiming narrative and drama as the two great poetic forms, with Milton and Shakespeare as their masters. As criticism, despite its lack of generosity, it would have had the interest that attaches to impertinence, but Austin loses all sympathy for himself when he attempts to put his own precepts into practice. He had neither a sense of humour to protect him from bathos nor the self-criticism to restrain his own discursive ineptitude. He is a bleak example of ambition without accompanying powers. His lyrical work is easier to read only because it is shorter, and if he has poetical quality at all it must be found in his placid studies of the quieter aspects of the English countryside, the material which he exploited in his popular prose work *The Garden that I Love*. Even in these he cannot guard himself from the discomfitures of clumsy rhyming, of rhythms that mock the sense, and of banal sentiments that trip complacently through his verses. One example may serve, and it is taken from one of his more successful lyrics; here the stanza which begins in some security is suddenly betrayed by a trochaic and dactylic movement in the last line which reduces the whole to parody:

> The crab, the bullace and the sloe,
>   They burgeon in the Spring;
> And when the west wind melts the snow,
>   The red-starts build and sing.
> And Death's at work in rind and root,
>   And loves the green buds best;
> And when the pairing music's mute,
>   He spares the empty nest.
>   Death! Death!
> Death is master of lord and clown;
>   Close the coffin and hammer it down.

This is Austin at his best; of his worst it is not necessary to write here.

The writers so far considered are either popular versifiers or belong to the school of Tennyson. There remain many whose output is smaller and whose verse can be less precisely described: only a selection of these writers can be considered. One of the most interesting of them was William Johnson, who later called himself William Johnson Cory (1823-1892).[11] He was an Eton master from 1845 to 1872, and those who were his pupils spoke of him in the terms of high admiration as a 'vigorous and commanding' intelligence, and he made the same impression on many of his older associates. In an introduction to Cory's poems A. C. Benson wrote of him as one possessed of 'a mental equipment of the foremost order, great intellectual curiosity, immense vigour and many-sidedness'. In *Ionicus* Reginald, Viscount Esher, confirmed the same impression. Cory appears a schoolmaster of dedication and genius. He had many distinguished men among his pupils, including Oscar Browning. Viscount Esher dedicated his volume to the Earls of Roseberry and Balfour, who had been Cory's pupils, and to Asquith, 'who showed him kindness in his old age'. Another pupil was Henry Paul, who gives a most balanced introduction to Cory in an essay in *Stray Leaves*. The depth of his thought about education is shown by his contribution in 1867 to Frederick Farrar's *Essays on a Liberal Education*, and this was republished in 1964 as *On the Education of the Reasoning Faculties* with a note by John Carter. Yet he had his eccentricities; he described his early experiences in Eton as 'bellowing at 55 book-bearing bipeds', and once when soldiers were passing on their way to Windsor he rushed the boys on to the street, crying, 'Brats, the British Army.' He had favourites and intense and emotional friendships with his pupils. To one of them he wrote of University life: 'It is a less beautiful or poetical form of life than the Eton form.' Suddenly in 1872 he left Eton for some reason unexplained, and his name disappeared from his textbooks which were still widely used. Faith Compton Mackenzie bases her account on H. S. Salt's *Memories of Bygone Eton*. 'A parental protest had been made', she writes, 'in terms which the Headmaster Dr Hornby dared not ignore.' She adds 'it would be absurd to get embroiled with parents who did not understand Platonic friendship' and Cory fled. Salt had written: 'Johnson was great enough in his reputation to dispense with decorous pretences; and those who knew him personally and were aware of his high qualities, and essential goodness, cannot but wonder whether, if Eton had then had a wise and strong Headmaster, so great a loss to the school might have been averted.'

In 1871, in two parts, as William Johnson, he published *Lucretilis, An Introduction to the Art of Writing Latin Lyric Verse*: the first part contained a series of exercises for the comparison of Alcaics and Sapphics, and the second, obtainable only from the publisher, and not available to the boys, was the *Key to Lucretilis*, which contained Cory's own renderings. Though limited inevitably by the occasion, the lyrics have been highly praised. John Sparrow in the sumptuous edition which he published with J. W. Carter in 1952 praises them discreetly, but notes H. A. J. Munro's comment that they are 'the best and most Horatian Sapphics and Alcaics . . . that have been written since Horace ceased to write'. They are, at least, evidence of a devotion to the whole art of teaching and Cory's dedication of all his talents to his pupils. His *Extracts from the Letters and Journals* (privately printed 1897 and edited by F. Warne Cornish) confirm this in a record of his personal relationships and again bear evidence of his distinction of mind.

Isolation from Eton must have been the most important event in his life. He still had the resources to live comfortably; first at Halsdon in North Devon and then later with his young wife of 20, whom he married at 56 in Madeira, and in a final phase at Hampstead. Nor did he lack personal contacts with old Eton friends, and he continued a voluminous correspondence. The poetical output is small. His devotion to Eton had led him, in his days as a master, to write 'The Eton Boat Song', composed in 1862-1863 and published in 1865:

> Harrow may be more clever
> Rugby may make more row
> But we'll row, row for ever
> Steady from stroke to bow,
> And nothing in life shall sever
> The chain that is round us now.

Apart from this, his verse is contained in *Ionica*, published in 1858, and containing only forty-eight poems. When this was supplemented by *Ionica II* in 1877 it could be seen that Cory had expressed all he had to say in the first volume and this was even more apparent when an omnibus *Ionica* appeared in 1891. Yet this does not diminish the distinguished quality of the most moving of his lyrics. Cory himself described *Ionica* as a 'booklet made up in a fortnight spent in solitude at Pangbourne on the Thames in August 1858 and published secretly at the cost of £40, paid in advance'. Of the most beautiful of all the lyrics, 'They told me Heraclitus you were dead', he merely notes: 'Written for the boys, doing Farnaby', which was a school book containing easy Greek pieces. His quality can be seen at its best in 'Mimnermus in Church', which he wrote while waiting to go to his first dinner of the Apostles:

> Forsooth the present we must give
> To that which cannot pass away;
> All beauteous things for which we live
> By laws of time and space decay.
> But oh, the very reason why
> I clasp them, is because they die.

Of the range of his mind and understanding there can be little dispute. The most unresilient element lay in his aggressive imperialism. One of the milder passages reads: 'The conquest of the Nile Valley, if we persevere, will be a signal, a proof of national vitality as the conquest of the Ganges valley and the Punjab. The duty was forced on us and is an antidote to the temptations towards a Dutch stationary state.' Yet apart from a few lyrics little that was present in his mind entered his poetry.

The position of Thomas Gray comes to mind, though as a scholar Cory could not compare with Gray. It is as if only one mood, that of a Platonic agnosticism, to use A. C. Benson's term, quickened him to poetic expression. Technically he is in the school of Tennyson, but unlike the popular disciples he brings a classical sense of restraint, a poetic cautiousness, which sets his poetry apart from that of his contemporaries. He can write verses, on varied themes, of boyhood, school life, and poems with an easy ballad movement. These, despite their competence, remain merely verses. Within him there dwelt a sensitiveness to beauty, a recognition of the pathos of its fleeting passage through life, and an air of resignation, not acrid, but quiet and pensive. That mood prevented him from attaching his gifts in an ambitious way to other poetic themes, but at the same time the existence of that mood allowed him to create an individual lyrical expression.

Little survives from the fluid and once popular verses of the Hon. Roden Noel[12] (1834–1894). He had neither the discipline as poet nor the coherence as thinker adequately to present his pseudo-pantheism in verse: *Behind the Veil* (1863) and *Beatrice* (1868) show a writer, with Shelley sometimes as a model, attempting more than he could attain. Of his numerous later volumes, which continue to *A Modern Faust* (1888), some, such as *The Red Flag* (1872) and *Livingstone in Africa* (1874), develop either lyrical measures or simple narrative themes. His lyric is always perturbed by diffuseness and a general slackness in style; these elements corrupt even the more easily wrought elegies of *A Little Child's Monument* (1881), which many have considered to be his most secure poem. Possibly his talent is better displayed in *The Water-nymph and the Boy*, a poem in *The Red Flag*. Here the quality of sensuous extravagance, which he contrived to combine with his philosophy, is not inappropriate, and a not unpleasant atmosphere of the early Keats dwells over a poem which is original and a little daring.

Roden Noel is an example of ambition without commensurate talent, and the phenomenon is not infrequent in the later nineteenth century. In contrast there can be instanced a number of writers of a definite minor talent whose main activities were not devoted to poetry. Thus John Addington Symonds[13] (1840-1893) will be best remembered as the historian of the Renaissance in Italy, and as a critic, yet his letters and diaries show that he desired above all else to be a creative writer. He possessed technical knowledge beyond many of his contemporaries, but seldom does he breathe poetry into his patterns of dead perfection. His personality is more interesting than his poetry, for he is an introspective, modern type, sceptical, fastidious, questing for some absolute which he hardly believes to exist. His diary speaks of 'brooding self-analysis without creation', and this sense of frustration, arising partly from physical causes, holds him in fretful impotence. Phyllis Grosskurth has recorded his complex homosexual life with much detail and sympathy. He attempted original verse with assiduity from his early success in the Newdigate to *Many Moods* (1878) and *New and Old* (1880). These were followed by *Animi Figura* (1882) and *Vagabunduli Libellus* (1884), which form a spiritual autobiography mainly in the sonnet form. Here, more than elsewhere, a meticulous correctness in form and an overwrought vocabulary combine to destroy poetic quality. His dilemma which arises from the inhibitions of his fastidiousness can be seen from his admiration of Walt Whitman's vibrant strength and disregard for delicate adjustment of phrase. Matthew Arnold contrived to make poetry out of his spiritual distress, but Symonds is baffled in the attempt. Some of his most interesting poems are made from material gained in the course of his studies, lyrics such as *For One of Gian Bellini's Little Angels* and, despite lapses towards Keats in the Leigh Hunt manner, *Le Jeune Homme caressant Sa Chimère*.

As a translator he was much more successful. His *Sonnets of Michael Angelo and Tommaso Campanella* (1878), with Shakespearian memories in their phrasing, are admirably executed. He was continuing Rossetti's work of making Italian verse available in English. More impressive than these Italian renderings is

Wine, Women and Song (1884), a collection of translations of the songs of the wandering medieval scholars, to which Symonds added an essay on Goliardic poetry. In nimble and idiomatic verse he has caught the roguish, carefree, deep-drinking vagabondage of the scholars. Though of recent years the *vagantes* have received more critical attention, no one has so successfully recaptured the spirit of their songs. Further, one sees Symonds discovering in this volume his own creative spirit, unrepressed for a brief while by its contact with these medieval entertainments. Yet in his prose conclusion he returns solemnly to examine himself and ask if he ought to have done it.

An impressive contrast to J. A. Symonds may be found in the verse of Wilfrid Scawen Blunt[14] (1840-1922), a romantic personality, delighting in the colour, intricacy, and even the cruelty of life. He is worthy of better company than that of many of the writers in this chapter. He contrived to crowd much into his eighty-year span, including travel in the Near and Far East, a championing of Egyptian nationalism, and of Irish Home Rule, with a consequent interlude in an Irish jail. He had excursions into politics and diplomacy, and his prose, particularly in the *Diaries*, has an intimate quality, a mixture of adventure and confession. He found time to write many verses which when collected in 1914 made two substantial volumes and included three plays. It is as a lyrical poet that he achieves distinction. His work includes the *Sonnets and Songs by Proteus* (1875, expanded 1881 and 1892), *Esther* (1892), *The Seven Golden Odes* (1903), and other volumes. In 1898 Henley and George Wyndham made a collection of his verses, 'bowdlerizing' some of the franker passages. His main form is the sonnet, which, unlike the Pre-Raphaelites, he uses with a simple even conversational vocabulary, with imagery employed sparingly. This undress in style gives him an air of modernity and an individuality in the verse of his time. He allows himself some licence in the sonnet form, but not unpleasingly; and again he seems to be anticipating the modern impatience with the fetters of traditional verse. Further, Blunt never writes merely because he has learnt how to write;

his work has always a suggestion of urgency, and it invariably possesses a clearly defined theme. The *Esther* sonnet sequence shows his quality. On the background of the Lyons fair, portrayed with a sympathy for shabby but picturesque detail, he narrates the love of a youth for a kindly, sensual, experienced woman. Sensitive moments of passion are detached from the surrounding sordidness and recounted with a pleasing frankness in vocabulary. An element of autobiography clings to *Esther* and is pursued further in *Proteus*, which includes sonnets, lyrics, and irregular verses. These lack the dramatic conciseness of *Esther*, but despite occasional discursiveness they have freshness. Blunt seems at times indebted to Meredith's *Modern Love* for his portrayal of sentiment in a setting of contemporary circumstance. Of his knowledge of the Near East he makes comparatively little use in his poetry, though in *The Golden Odes* he has rendered the 'Mu'allakât', the Pre-Islamic poems, which Sir William Jones had translated in 1782.

Another definite minor talent can be found in the work of Eugene J. Lee-Hamilton (1845-1907). Diplomacy occupied his early adult years, and his poetry is the product of his last twenty years, spent in Italy under the shadow of physical disablement. His work includes *The New Medusa* (1882), *Apollo and Marsyas* (1884), and *The Fountain of Youth* (1891), which are dramatic and narrative poems, and a number of volumes of lyrics, *Poems and Transcripts* (1878), *Gods, Saints and Men* (1880), *Imaginary Sonnets* (1888), and *Sonnets of the Wingless Hours* (1894). His work has an unmistakable emphasis on the grotesque, with a frequent concentration on the stark, uncompromising description of revolting themes. It is as if Browning had been robbed of much of his morality and all of his intricacy and then modified with influences from Poe. The effect can be seen in *Apollo and Marsyas*, where the god and the satyr sing of their competing desires. Lee-Hamilton seems to image his own preoccupation with the cruel, shadowed, half-obscene things of life; Apollo's songs commemorate in clear chants the worthiness of noble deeds, but for the satyr life's attraction lies elsewhere:

> But oh, I love the caves where all is mute
> Save unseen dropping waters, or my flute,
>   Whose tones are made
> So strange by echo, that, transform'd, increased,
> They ape the voice of some wild wounded beast
>   Or eager hounds; or wail in cavernous shade
> Like souls in Hades wailing unreleased.

What may, a little ungenerously, be called the images of Marsyas occur throughout the early volumes, gaining their strongest expression in *The New Medusa*. They are retained in *Imaginary Sonnets*, which are dramatic monologues in sonnet form, each commemorating some moment in a memorable life. Yet the cruel themes and livid colouring of such poems as *Leonardo da Vinci to his Snakes* mingle here with quieter moods. This development of the normal interests is confirmed by *Sonnets of the Wingless Hours*, where he recounts the moods of his long years of ill health. Lee-Hamilton, of whom no memoir exists, and no critical notice apart from contemporary reviews, has received less attention than he deserves. His verse employs licences which the fastidious would condemn, but he is never wanton, nor are his lines encumbered with verbiage. He approaches forbidding themes, but he is led to them not by whim but by some urgency in his personality, and they possess that sense of power which one finds in the strange, unhealthy hues of the paintings of El Greco.

If Lee-Hamilton has suffered from undue neglect, F. W. H. Myers[15] (1843-1901) has possibly received more than his share of attention. Even as a boy he was recognized for his keen literary sensibilities, and his early work showed aptitudes both for poetry and criticism. His later life was largely devoted to psychical problems, and he was a pioneer in their systematic study. His verse is marked throughout with strong, full-throated melodies, which are not always closely adapted to his subject. This unmistakable quality in his rhythms, bold if never very original, gave his verse a superficial attractiveness. It can be found in his early *St Paul* (1867), a dramatic monologue where, despite the noise of the rhetoric, Biblical phrase and nomenclature have been adroitly employed:

> Christ! I am Christ's and let the name suffice you,
> Ay, for me too He greatly hath sufficed:
> Lo with no winning words I would entice you,
> Paul has no honour and no friend but Christ.

The thought is apt to become overlaid by the masses of words, and the whole has that diffused impression so frequently found in Swinburne's lyrics. His later poems, *The Passing of Youth* (written in 1871 and published in 1882) and *The Renewal of Youth* (1882), are more closely wrought. He employs the heroic couplet, and though he never masters the form it serves to give discipline to his expression. He expounds in these two poems his philosophy of the apprehension of the divine in human life and of the intuitions of immortality that may be gained by recognizing its presence. Another poem in couplets, *The Implicit Promise of Immortality*, written in 1870, also anticipates some aspects of this later thought. His approach to experience sometimes recalls Wordsworth, while his melodies are frequently diluted forms of Tennyson and Swinburne. His couplets are refreshing, but his inadequacy in their employment only serves to recall the absence of the cool 'tessellated' verse of the classical schools from later nineteenth-century poetry.

With Aubrey Thomas de Vere[16] (1814-1902), the son of Sir Aubrey de Vere, whose *Mary Tudor* was published in 1847, one approaches, if not poetical greatness, at least poetical independence. He belongs to that notable tradition of Irish poets who have written in English. James Clarence Mangan (1803-1849) is one of its notable representatives in the earlier half of the century, while many of its later adherents, William Allingham and Lionel Johnson, had such intimate contacts with English movements that their work has been considered elsewhere. As the century closes the tradition has a renaissance in the poetry of W. B. Yeats and of 'A.E.' The movement of Irish verse is more continuous than has sometimes been imagined, and even when it fails to produce great poets it is able to retain the services of faithful minor writers or of critics turned poet, such as Edward Dowden. De Vere's true predecessor in Irish poetry was Sir Samuel Ferguson (1810-1886), who saw the possibility of rendering Irish themes in English verse, and de Vere is generous in his acknowledgement of Ferguson's example. Ferguson, whose early work dates from the thirties, had gained recognition with *Lays of the Western Gael* (1865), and this was followed with *Congal* (1872) and *Poems* (1880). De Vere's early work is lyrical: *The Waldenses* (1842) and *The Search after Proserpine* (1843). With *A Year of Sorrow*, still using lyrical forms, he turns definitely to Ireland and describes the winter of 1846-1847. His conversion to Catholicism in 1851 strengthened his attachment to Ireland, and his later poetry deals either with Ireland's heroic past or the early history of the Catholic Church. *Inisfail* (1862) and *The Foray of Queen Meave* (1882), which contains the story of Cuchullain, show his treatment of Irish themes, while *The Legends of St Patrick* (1872), describing the conversion of Ireland, forms a link with poems where the Christian interest is dominant, *St Thomas of Canterbury* (1867) and *Legends and Records of the Church and the Empire* (1887).

De Vere's verse reveals that his early friendship with Wordsworth left its mark on his poetry; in the sonnet he follows Wordsworth and in blank verse he frequently imitates his unhurried serenity. He detached himself from the subjective moods of his contemporaries and made his purposes the ambitious exploration of legend and religion, with an increasing emphasis on mysticism. His poetry retains throughout a sombre dignity; he never descends to the trivial, but his processional movement is too regular and slow paced ever to give sudden and compelling delight. In lyric, particularly in the sonnet, he is more secure than in narrative; an example of his quality can be gathered from his sonnet to Wordsworth *Composed at Rydal*:

> Wisdom sheath'd
> In song love-humble; contemplations high,
> That built like larks their nests upon the ground;
> Insight and vision; sympathies profound

That spann'd the total of humanity.
These were the gifts which God poured forth at large
On men through him: and he was faithful to his charge.

His narrative poems have been praised more often than they have been enjoyed. All their estimable qualities do not protect them from frequent dullness: they have been, too often, the bedfellows of Wordsworth's *Excursion*.

Among the minor poets of the period are some women writers. Their work is difficult to classify, and on its value the most divergent judgements have been passed. The clearest tradition is that maintained by the popular women poets, the writers of lyric, of facile movement, and of simple, sometimes mawkish sentiment. Even the greater women writers – Mrs Browning and Christina Rossetti – descend at times to this level. Adelaide Anne Procter[17] (1825-1864) is an example of this popular tradition in the earlier part of the century. She was a *Household Words* poet and wrote sometimes the verse that Dickens's heroines might have enjoyed. She can do much better, as *A Legend of Provence* issued in *Legends and Lyrics* (1858-1861) shows. Jean Ingelow[18] (1820-1897), a poet and a novelist, suffered from the same defects, yet she possessed a more definite lyrical quality. Her verse, *Poems* (1863), *A Story of Doom* (1867), and *Poems* (1885), gained a wide audience, and encouraged her innate prolixity. She attempted some ambitious things, but she approaches poetry only in simple ballad and lyric, in *The High Tide on the Coast of Lincolnshire, 1571*, and in *Divided*. Even here she has an overflow of words, and unremitting sweetness in melody reminiscent of some of Tennyson's early lyrics.

In contrast to these practitioners of fluid verse may be found a few writers whose output is small and who have obviously exercised self-criticism. The published work of Margaret Veley (1843-1887) is in such a small compass that probably she would have remained unknown had not Leslie Stephen introduced some of her poems into the *Cornhill* and later prepared an edition of her verses, *A Marriage of Shadows* (1888). Even when assembled her verses seem a slender collection of shy pieces content to be forgotten. She possessed a classical quality in verse, precision without a thrusting for unusual effects, and an economy in vocabulary reminiscent of Robert Bridges. Her best-remembered poem, *A Japanese Fan*, a delicate study in irony and sentiment, shows a lover using the legend on a fan to relate how his mistress ill-used him. The poem has something of Dobson's delicacy, though the stanza is borrowed from Browning:

> Here's a lady, small of feature,
>   Narrow-eyed,
> With her hair of ebon straightness
>   Queerly tied.

Into her other verses melancholy occasionally intrudes, and she returns to the 'When I am dead' mood of Christina Rossetti; but her more individual talent lay in description, which she shows in such poems as *Sunset*, *The Land of Shadows*, *A Town Garden*. She can erect a mood out of a mosaic of detail, and there remains from her poetry an image of twilit waters, bridges, and laden ships, and roads 'dim and ashen-gray'. These nocturnes are executed without any lavish expenditure of verbal resources, and this act of self-denial in style separates her from many of the other women writers of her time, and shows that small as her output may be she possessed the intuitions and the methods of a poet.

Some have found equal strength in the work of Amy Levy (1861-1889), a novelist and poet whose talent was undoubtedly developing when she brought her own life to an end in 1889. Her poetry is contained in three volumes, *Xantippe* (1881), *A Minor Poet* (1884), and *A London Plane-Tree* (1889). In lyric she develops a movement of song on whose somewhat facile melodies the influence of Heine can be traced; but in her last volume, *A London Plane-Tree*, she shows a greater restraint and a capacity for converting significant experiences into compact lyrics. Her two most telling poems are, however, in blank verse. *A Minor Poet* is a study of suicide, reminiscent of Browning's methods, but fresh and independent enough, nor does its whole strength derive from the premonition it contains of her own fate. *Xantippe*, a study of Socrates's wife, has an originality derived from its exposition of a woman's point of view, but the verse is modelled too closely on Browning. Amy Levy has a capacity in verse which is at best unfinished, but the absence of lushness and crudity suggest that she might have grown in strength. Some have discovered her most mature talent in an interesting poem on waltzing, *Swing and Sway*.

It is difficult to discover the same authenticity in the more copious work of Mathilde Blind[19] (1841-1896), the daughter of exiles from Germany after the Revolution of 1848. She travelled widely and used her experiences in her poetry. A visit to Scotland led to *The Prophecy of St Oran* (1882) and *The Heath on Fire* (1886). In the first she was captured by the romantic past, and in the second she pleaded against the evictions of the Scottish peasantry. Her danger is to use accurate but undistinguished verse into which memories from other poets enter with irritating abruptness. More ambitious was her disastrous attempt to render poetically the century's debate on evolution in *The Ascent of Man* (1889). Her later verses, mainly lyrics and sonnets – *Dramas in Miniature* (1891), *Songs and Sonnets* (1893), *Birds of Passage* (1895) – frequently owe their suggestion to travel in Egypt and the Near East. Occasionally she approaches towards an angle of vision which is her own, as in *The Songs of Summer*, *The Hunter's Moon*, and *A Fantasy*. Yet, despite the critical attention of Arthur Symons and Dr Richard Garnett, it will be found that Mathilde Blind seldom passed the gap which divides adroit versifying from poetry.

Mrs Augusta Webster (1837-1894) frequently shared Mathilde Blind's pedestrian quality, but with her the pace can quicken and the verse has interest and variety. She published voluminously: *Blanche Lisle* (1860); *Lilian Gray* (1864); a translation of *Prometheus Unbound* (1866) and of *Medea* (1868); *Dramatic Studies* (1866); *A Woman Sold* (1867); *Portraits* (1870); *Yu-Pe-Ya's Lute* (1874); *A Book of Rhyme* (1881); and verse dramas, including *The Auspicious Day* (1872) and *Disguises*

(1879). Mrs Webster developed under Browning's influence, and much of her early work combines moral strenuousness with heavy blank verse. She is not a mere studio-worker: had that been her aim her work would have been easier to accomplish and might have been more lively. She had definitely a woman's attitude to express: it can be found in *A Woman Sold* (1867), and it reoccurs in *The Castaway*, a poem on the theme of a fallen woman, which gained Browning's admiration. Her feminism gives her poetry a strength, sometimes even a corrosive quality, which distinguishes her work from that of imitators and mere versifiers. Further, she can occasionally gain poetic effectiveness in handling other themes. In *The Snow Waste* (1866) she recounts a Dantesque vision of one who has sinned through jealousy, and the dread allegorical landscape around the speaker is well contrived. She showed also a spirit of experiment, as seen in her attempts in *English Stornelli* to adapt the Italian *rispetto*, an eight-line rural love lyric, into English verse. The poems are lightly turned, if occasionally a little vague and inconclusive. The same grace accompanies her 'Chinese' tale, *Yu-Pe-Ya's Lute*, where fantastic story is made pleasantly to combine with description of Chinese manners and etiquette.

Such were some of the minor writers and major versifiers of the nineteenth century. Their names can be added to, almost indefinitely. Some might look for the inclusion of Richard Garnett (1835-1906), who brought his wide scholarship to the services of translation and whose own lyrics have a piquancy that sometimes approaches cynicism. In prose his work is varied and of solid worth. Many of his original verses have neatness and metrical adroitness, and he should at least be remembered for his merry poem *The Fair Circassian*:

> Forty Viziers saw I go
> Up to the Seraglio,
> Burning, each and every man,
> For the fair Circassian.

In the later volumes of the *Dictionary of National Biography* he wrote discriminating notices on many of the minor poets of the period. Other names have an equal claim. Constance Naden (1858-1889), in her philosophical verses, solemn in thought but frequently Swinburnian in movement, has found high praise for her work. She could number Mr Gladstone among her admirers. This chapter does not, however, attempt to record every writer of verse in the period. The main traditions have been indicated, and enough has been recorded to give an impression of the productiveness and prolixity of the minor verse writers.

William Ernest Henley and Robert Louis Stevenson

William Ernest Henley[1] (1849-1903) was born in Gloucester and educated there at the Crypt School, where T. E. Brown, the poet, was a master. His mother was a descendant of the eighteenth-century poet and critic Joseph Warton. His father was a bookseller, though never a very successful one, and his death forced Henley to leave school in 1867. Tubercular disease affected him even as a child and led to the amputation of a foot. Later, at Edinburgh Infirmary, under the care of Joseph Lister (later Lord Lister), he effected a painful recovery. T. E. Brown had encouraged him towards literature and he remained faithful to his memory of this influence and encouragement. On Brown's death he wrote that he 'came upon me like a call from the world outside – the great, quick, living world – and discovered me the beginning, the true materials, of myself'. If Brown was the first influence, Lister was the second, and possibly the most powerful in Henley's whole life. How he got to the Royal Infirmary at Edinburgh and under Lister's care is unknown: it appears as an act of will, where he was guided solely by himself. It was the turning-point of his life. As 'Connell' writes, 'In Edinburgh in the twenties he laid all the foundations of the man he became; in Edinburgh in the forties he did his best work and was happiest'. He was to marry Anna Boyle, the sister of a merchant officer,

Captain Boyle, who had shared his room in the Infirmary; she remained a constant companion throughout his life. It was at Edinburgh in 1875 that Leslie Stephen brought Henley and Stevenson together: they were both in their early twenties and the effect of the meeting on both of them was profound. Its emotional intensity made inevitable their later estrangement, but for a time they influenced and encouraged each other in their work. Ill health was something which Henley and Stevenson shared, though they dealt with it in different ways. Both were courageous, but Henley was impatient and aggressive, and, unless undermined by pain and disability, determined to labour at his editing, his prose essays and his poetry. It is 'Connell' who gives the fullest exposition of this friendship, describing it in the terms of an unfulfilled homosexual relation: 'a strong, bitter, blinding love, passing the love of women'.

Given all the restriction imposed by his health and his disability, the record of his literary achievement is remarkable. As editor of the *Scots Observer* and the *National Observer*, he contrived to gather around him the most brilliant talent of his day; unfortunately he was less successful in making these journals financially prosperous. His own literary work included a series of dramas which he wrote with R. L. Stevenson, essays and criticism, the supervision of the *Tudor Translations*, and the preparation of numerous anthologies of which the *Lyra Heroica* (1891) was the most popular. His whole life was devoted to literature, but little of it to poetry. His first volume, produced after much periodical publication, was *A Book of Verses* (1888); it was followed in 1892 by *The Song of the Sword*, which included *London Voluntaries*, and both volumes were united in *Poems* (1898). *Hawthorn and Lavender* followed in 1899, and *For England's Sake* in 1900, *The Passing of Victoria* (1901), *A Song of Speed* in 1903. *A Collected Edition* of prose and poetry was issued in 1908. His verse has evoked very little critical attention and no one has attempted to reassess him as T. S. Eliot reassessed Kipling.

Henley's most interesting work occurs in his first volume,

Verses (1888). Its contents are divided into three distinct groups: rhymeless pieces, which, with some poems in conventional form, make a series entitled *In Hospital*; lyrics, in simple stanzas, including the popular *Out of the night that covers me*, and *Or ever the knightly years were gone*; finally, a gathering of ballades, rondels, sonnets, quatorzains, and rondeaus, in which he had adapted himself to the Gosse and Dobson bypath of Victorian romanticism without adding much that is his own. His ballade *Of a Toyokuni Colour-Print* recalls that the cultivation of ballades synchronized with the interest in Japanese art, and suggests that possibly the two fashions had something in common. The irregular, rhymeless pieces of *In Hospital* are, in contrast, revolutionary and modern. In theme they are grim impressions, sparing in vocabulary and realistic. *Operation* is a typical example, though it has a greater regularity of form than some of the other pieces:

> You are carried in a basket,
>   Like a carcase from the shambles,
> To the theatre, a cockpit,
> Where they stretch you on a table.
>
> Then they bid you close your eyelids,
>   And they mask you with a napkin,
>   And the anaesthetic reaches
> Hot and subtle through your being.

The origins of Henley's irregular verse are difficult to ascertain. He has no contact with the rhythmical prose of Walt Whitman; even at its freest, Henley's verse is closer to a regular pattern. He had patterns for irregular verse in Matthew Arnold, in *The Strayed Reveller, Philomela*, and *Heine's Grave*. Arnold had found models for his licences in the Greek odes and tragic choruses, in Goethe's reflective and elegiac pieces, and in the borderland of these two influences which arises from Goethe's own imitations of the antique. It is difficult to prove that Henley made direct use of these models, though he parallels their movement in such poems as *Clinical*, where all stanza pattern seems to be abandoned:

> Hist? . . .
> Through the corridor's echoes
> Louder and nearer
> Comes a great shuffling of feet.

A number of Henley's verses retain a regular stanza pattern, without rhyme, as in *Casualty*:

> As with varnish red and glistening
> Dripped his hair: his feet looked rigid;
> Raised, he settled stiffly sideways:
> You could see his hurts were spinal.

This is the verse of the Spanish ballads and folk-songs, with the modification that they are governed by a liberal conception of assonance, in place of Henley's abandonment of rhyme. Heine had imitated the Spanish form in *Romancero*, and Henley, who shows other derivations from Heine, may have adapted it from that source. Heine would thus give a model for a form which would have the appearance of freedom without necessitating a complete break with tradition. Henley adds the novelty of brutal, unlovely themes, which seem to fit with the bare rhymeless verses. Henley's variety can be seen by the appearance in this same volume of dexterously contrived ballades. While he pirouettes here in accordance with contemporary fashion, he introduces themes of pathos and of the endurance of fate which are marked with his own personality. As in the hospital poems, he has an alert faculty for brief revealing epithets; so in *Ballade of Dead Actors* he holds a complete post-mortem on stage life:

> The curtain falls, the play is played;
> The Beggar packs beside the Beau;
> The Monarch troops, and troops the Maid;
> The Thunder huddles with the Snow.
> Where are the revellers high and low?
> The clashing swords? The lover's call?
> The dancers gleaming row on row?
> Into the night go one and all.

> Prince, in one common overthrow
> The Hero tumbles with the Thrall:
> As dust that drives, as straws that blow,
> Into the night go one and all.

In his irregular poems Henley appears to break away from the overused forms of Victorian poetry. In content and method they traverse new ground and gain from their historical position an interest unwarranted by their intrinsic worth. Unfortunately Henley did not develop poetically, for his most effective work is in these early poems: the rhymelessness and irregularity of *In Hospital* have poetic method and purpose, but later these elements seem occasionally a poetic excuse for an easy rhetoric that cannot be troubled with rhyme. In *The Song of the Sword* he writes irregular verses which have the effect of a diffused translation of Anglo-Saxon poetry. Licence and an absence of rhythmical control are still more apparent in *A Song of Speed*, where he attempts to adapt to poetry the then modern theme of the automobile.

London Voluntaries are among the more successful of the later poems. They give large-flowing impressions of London by night and day, employing a combination of six- and ten-syllable lines, such as Spenser and Milton had used. Rhetorical as is the quality of the verse, it has scattered within it phrases of keen imaginative insight, and the theme has freshness and vigour. Henley is using a more deliberately poetic vocabulary to gain orchestrated effects and diversifying the rhetorical passages with keen, silhouetted pictures. The effect can be seen in the following passage from the second 'Voluntary':

> And lo! the Wizard Hour,
> His silent, shining sorcery winged with power!
> Still, still the streets, between their carcanets
> Of linking gold, are avenues of sleep.
> But see how gable ends and parapets
> In gradual beauty and significance
> Emerge! And did you hear
> That little twitter – and – cheep,

> Breaking inordinately loud and clear
> On this still, spectral, exquisite atmosphere?
> 'Tis a first nest at matins! And behold
> A rakehell cat – how furtive and acold!
> A spent witch homing from some infamous dance –
> Obscene, quick-trotting, see her tip and fade
> Through shadowy railings into a pit of shade!

Heine would appear again to have been the model, for Henley's verses in the *Voluntaries* are paralleled by the effects gained by Heine in the *Nord-See* poems in *Das Buch der Lieder*. In *For England's Sake* he rivalled Kipling in patriotic poetry. The vehemence of his nationalism does not frequently achieve poetic expression, but in one lyric, *Pro Rege Nostro* ('What have I done for you, England, my England?'), he expresses a popular sentiment in strong, plangent language.

Henley's poetic output is small, but it is marked with strong originality. He could write good 'shouting' lyrics, embodying moods and themes that even the least sophisticated reader could understand. He had variety and could step from that romantic Babylon to which Christian slaves had been imported, presumably from the sea-coasts of Bohemia, to the stark, clean cruelty of a hospital. He had an important influence on the employment of freer verse forms, and showed the way in which later poetry was to develop. Heine, as it has been suggested, had influenced him in his experiments, and equally he can imitate Heine in lyric verse, with simple ballad structure, and a tempestuous enthusiasm in sentiment. This frequently results in a fresh and vigorous movement in his lyrical stanzas:

> My songs were once of the sunrise:
> They shouted it over the bar;
> First-footing the dawns, they flourished,
> And flamed with the morning star.

While he was content at times to imitate the contemporary 'bric-à-brac' of ballades and rondeaus, he showed also that he could adapt these forms to the expression of more weighty themes.

His knowledge and sympathy with French literature may be paralleled with that of Andrew Lang. It comes out most clearly in the astonishing boldness of his adaptation of Villon into contemporary slang:

> Villon's Straight Tip to all Cross Coves,
>   'Tout aux tavernes et aux filles'.
>
> Suppose you screeve? or go cheap-jack?
>   Or fake the broads? or fig a nag?
> Or thimble-rig? or knap a yack?
>   Or pitch a snide? or smash a rag?

Yet on turning to his work one finds that the impression of his personality is based on very few poems; Henley, in his preface to his *Poems* (1898), seems to have been surprised himself by the paucity of his production. He assigned his own departure from poetry to economic reasons: 'I found myself (about 1877) so utterly unmarketable that I had to addict myself to journalism for the next ten years.'[2] He is not the only writer of the period who is lured by the economic rewards of prose, though with Henley one wonders whether increased leisure would have proved him to be more than a poet in flashes, however brilliant those individual flashes might have been.

The life of Robert Louis Stevenson[3] (1850-1894) falls naturally into legend, and numerous writers have attended to his biography. Unfortunately an attempt was made to cast an atmosphere of false piety and innocent chivalry around him; it occurs in Graham Balfour's *Life* (1901), and it has entered into Colvin's edition of the Letters (1911). The truth is less innocent but more interesting: its record is due largely to the work of G. S. Hellman and J. A. Steuart. Nor can the biographical problem be ignored in estimating Stevenson's poetry; the influences which helped to model the legend also helped to frustrate the artist. Apart from a few pamphlets: *Not I* (1881); *Moral Emblems* (1882); *Familiar Epistle in Verse and Prose* (1896), the poetry that Stevenson published in his lifetime is contained in a book of children's poems, *A Child's Garden of Verses* (1885), and in two other volumes, *Underwoods* (1887) and *Ballads* (1890). To these a posthumous volume was added, *Songs of Travel* (1896). Yet when the *Complete Poems* were published in America in 1923[4] nearly half the volume was made up of previously unprinted work. One is familiar enough with the collected edition that has been swollen with fugitive pieces, but here the new work is as different from the old as the man himself from the legendary Stevenson. The unpublished work modifies previous conceptions and certainly falsifies Mrs Stevenson's dictum, that the writing of poetry was for him merely a matter of entertainment.

He was born in Edinburgh (1850), an only child, proud and fragile, with pious parents and a sternly religious nurse. His schooldays were spent irregularly, hindered by ill health and indifference, though he was already reading the books that pleased him. His father, a distinguished engineer, hoped that he would follow in the family profession, and entered him as a student at Edinburgh University. He showed ability in his studies, but such distaste for the subject that his family allowed him to abandon engineering and to read for the Bar. He prepared himself fitfully and was finally called in 1875. Yet these Edinburgh years (1867-1875) were the most formative in his life. He came into open conflict with his parents on moral and religious issues; he entered the Bohemian circles of Edinburgh, and formed more than one deep attachment. By 1875 he knew Leslie Stephen, who took him, as has been recorded, to visit Henley in the Edinburgh Infirmary, and from then he realized that literature would be his profession. Between 1875 and 1878 he worked feverishly, publishing comparatively little, but testing his capacities in verse and prose. Ill health was still pestering him, but he was restlessly active, moving from Edinburgh to London and from there to Fontainebleau. These were the years of his tempestuous friendship with Henley which was to leave such a deep mark on both their lives and to end in bitterness. In 1878 *An Inland Voyage* was published, and his career as a prose writer began in earnest. In the years of prose writing that follow he published poems. In

1879 he met at Fontainebleau a Mrs Osbourne, an American lady of Swedish-Dutch extraction, and they became deeply attached. They were married in 1880. Mrs Stevenson's devotion helped Stevenson to survive the many crises that his health was to endure. She became, however, the 'censor' of his personality, and aided by her influence the 'official' legend of chivalric piety was constructed; some of his creative impulses were frustrated and many of his poems left unpublished. From 1880 to 1887 he was establishing his reputation as a prose writer. *Treasure Island*, which was elevated from serial publication in *Young Folks* in 1881 to volume form in 1883, was followed later by *The Strange Case of Dr Jekyll and Mr Hyde* (1886) and *Kidnapped* (1886). Two volumes of verse appear within this period, *A Child's Garden of Verses* (1885) and *Underwoods* (1887). The literary activity was maintained despite severe ill health, which drove him to Davos and Hyères in a fruitless quest for strength.

In 1887, after his father's death, he left with his family for America, and after a period in the United States and some voyaging in Pacific waters, he found a home at Vailima, in Samoa (1891). Here he spent the remaining years, industrious as ever, a genial and willing correspondent of men of letters in England, and on the island a definite personage, with an interest in the welfare of the people. The last volume of verse published in his lifetime was *Ballads* (1890). In the following study Stevenson's published poetry has been considered first, and then the verse issued in 1916 and 1921 from the Stevenson manuscripts.

A Child's Garden of Verses (1885), Stevenson's most popular volume, belongs to that child poetry which follows the developing popularity of Blake in the later nineteenth century. Stevenson has nothing of Blake's mysticism, yet, on the other hand, he avoids the mere nursery-rhyme quality which affects so many of the poems in Christina Rossetti's *Sing-Song*. He has closer contacts with that apt practitioner of child verses, W. Brighty Rands, whose *Lilliput Revels* had appeared in 1870-1872. The adult portraying in simple lyrics the content of the child mind is ever in danger of banality and false sentiment; this Stevenson escapes, though his children have a pre-Freudian innocence and gentleness. His skill lies in the imaginative phrasing with which he decorates these pieces:

> I should like to rise and go
> Where the golden apples grow; –
> Where below another sky
> Parrot islands anchored lie,
> And, watched by cockatoos and goats,
> Lonely Crusoes building boats.

It is an easy genre, but more has been inserted than the genre itself demanded. The poems are not without a biographical interest; if the love of adventure is in them ('My bed is like a little boat'), so too is the necessity for prayer; one wonders what strange combination of irony, pathos, and humour led him to write *System*:

> Every night my prayers I say,
> And get my dinner every day;
> And every day that I've been good,
> I get an orange after food.
>
> The child that is not clean and neat,
> With lots of toys and things to eat,
> He is a naughty child, I'm sure –
> Or else his dear papa is poor.

The volume gained a wide popularity, but Stevenson did not attempt to exploit his success. Two years later (1887) he published *Underwoods*. The memory of Ben Jonson and his school extends beyond the title, for many of the lyrics have Herrick's quality of sentiment and a few have Jonson's epigrammatic brevity. The volume contains both English and Scots poetry. The latter has more variety: social and religious themes are conducted with a pawkiness of humour, in stanzas reminiscent of Burns. Stevenson is more outspoken here than in the English poems; it is as if the satiric tradition of Scottish poetry allowed him to speak his mind:

> While thus the lave o' mankind's lost,
> O' Scotland still God maks His boast –
> Puir Scotland, on whase barren coast
>   A score or twa
> Auld wives wi' mutches an' a hoast
>   Still keep His law.

Among the English poems, *Requiem* ('Under the wide and starry sky') is the best remembered. Many of the other poems arise from the same mood: pictures of voyagings, as in *The Canoe Speaks*:

> But I, the egg-shell pinnace, sleep
> On crystal waters ankle-deep,

and poems of journeyings, such as *A Song of the Road*. Simple themes and stanzas dominate, with a number of octosyllabics where overfacility intrudes. In sentiment there is a suggestion of fixation, as if the writer were playing up to his part of romantic vagrant.

In *Ballads* (1890) Stevenson attempts story-telling in verse. Of the three main pieces, the earliest, *Ticonderoga*, a re-rendering of a Highland theme, has grown diffuse through Stevenson's method of employing the ballad form. The verse has a pleasant lilt, but the central theme, the fatal mystery of the name Ticonderoga, fails to develop effectively. The other two poems are Tahitian stories, told in a manner reminiscent of William Morris. *The Feast of Famine* is a love theme of Stevenson's own invention: a poem where the narrative is choked by local colour that is far too local. *The Song of Rahéro* Stevenson based on an old Tahitian tradition, and the poem grows in strength as it proceeds. It opens with a simple revenge motive, but develops to a climax when Rahéro, whose whole tribe has been destroyed, escapes with a woman and sets out with her to found a new race. The poem concludes as Rahéro addresses her:

> 'Before your mother was born, the die of to-day was thrown
> And you selected: – your husband, vainly striving, to fall
> Broken between these hands: – yourself to be severed from all,
> The places, the people, you love – home, kindred, and clan –
> And to dwell in a desert and bear the babes of a kinless man.'

Songs of Travel (1896), the posthumous volume, is in quality and theme a continuation of *Underwoods*. The same gesture of chivalric vagabondage is maintained. It occurs in the opening and best-known poem in the volume:

> Give to me the life I love,
>   Let the lave go by me,
> Give the jolly heaven above
>   And the byway nigh me.

The same mood is found in the love poems, genial, romantic, and a little too facile, which form one of the major themes in this volume, and so it continues to the closing poem:

> Sing me a song of a lad that is gone,
>   Say, could that lad be I?
> Merry of soul he sailed on a day
>   Over the sea to Skye.

This atmosphere of God is in his heaven and all is right on the open road appears as an official optimism. Stevenson seems to have despaired of singing truthfully 'of a lad that is gone', and to have presented instead an unrevealing picture of a perpetually interested and jolly lad that liked the open spaces. Such sentiments had their influence in the development of English poetry. They combined with Henley's thunderings to form a contrast to the pessimism that underlay much later Victorian work, and they influenced younger poets at the beginning of the twentieth century who were reacting against the nineties. Stevenson found a model for some aspects of his open-air romanticism in Heine, and equally for his exaggerated gestures in sentiment, and the contrasting excess of buoyancy. Occasionally, as in the following poem, he parallels closely some of the moods of Heine's lyrics:

> The infinite shining heavens
>   Rose and I saw in the night
> Uncountable angel stars
>   Showering sorrow and light.

> I saw them distant as heaven,
>   Dumb and shining and dead,
> And the idle stars of the night,
>   Were dearer to me than bread.
>
> Night after night in my sorrow
>   The stars stood over the sea,
> Till lo! I looked in the dusk
>   And a star had come down to me.

Among the poems in *Songs of Travel* is the following brief lyric:

> I have trod the upward and the downward slope;
> I have endured and done in days before;
> I have longed for all, and bid farewell to hope;
> And I have lived and loved, and closed the door.

The reader of Stevenson's poetry before 1916 could not have guessed how much had been closed out of view. It cannot be claimed that the poems issued in 1916 and 1921 by George S. Hellman convert Stevenson into a great poet, but they show that he attempted to express many phases of his experience. An important group of poems dates from his Edinburgh days, particularly from 1871 to 1875; many moods arise, and in keen self-revelatory poems he explores them. Love is a dominant motive, but imaged with greater fervency than in the *Songs of Travel*. *After Reading 'Antony and Cleopatra'* illustrates the mood of many of these poems:

> As when the hunt by holt and field
>   Drives on with horn and strife,
> Hunger of hopeless things pursues
>   Our spirits throughout life.
>
> The sea's roar fills us aching full
>   Of objectless desire –
> The sea's roar, and the white moon-shine,
>   And the reddening of the fire.
>
> Who talks to me of reason now?
>   It would be more delight
> To have died in Cleopatra's arms
>   Than be alive to-night.

The approach to sentiment in some of the love poems in this new work varies; there are a few poems of banter and humour; some that retain the geniality of the published pieces, but more often the emphasis lies with passion, and its distress. So in *Love, What is Love?* he uses the epigrammatic form found frequently in the published poems, though here the mood is more grim:

> Love – what is love? A great and aching heart;
> Wrung hands; and silence; and a long despair.
> Life – what is life? Upon a moorland bare
> To see love coming and see love depart.

Among the love poems is a memorable piece of uncertain date on an unborn child, *God gave to me a child in part*. Stevenson probably remembered Burns's approach to the same theme. His own treatment is quiet but poignant; he explores the sentiment safely, revealing the lyrical potentialities which it possessed:

> My voice may reach you, O my dear –
> A father's voice perhaps the child may hear;
> And pitying, you may turn your view
> On that poor father whom you never knew.
>
> Alas! alone he sits, who then,
> Immortal among mortal men,
> Sat hand in hand with love, and all day through
> With your dear mother, wondered over you.

Apart from the love poems, many other moods occur. An early sonnet sequence, written possibly under Wordsworthian influence, shows how he experimented in a form which he used seldom in his later work. Further, he left a group of translations from Martial which he had hoped to expand into a complete volume. The series is incomplete, but it has a few renderings which have ease and mastery of form, though Stevenson usually avoids with whispered periphrases the smack and salacity of Martial's vocabulary. These renderings show how the study of Martial served to discipline Stevenson's quest of the epigram in his own poems.

The unpublished work reveals, then, a poet who treated poetry much more seriously than the published work would suggest. Only a limited number of these pieces exceed in technical accomplishment the 'official' pieces; many of them fall below. Stevenson had to pay the price of every busy prose writer who puts poetry on 'half-pay'. But the image of Stevenson as a poet demands that these pieces should be considered. We need not doubt that the optimistic, open road mood was one which he sincerely felt, but it is elevated in the official poetry into a dominant, almost an all-prevailing, mood. Distress, self-reproach, poignancy, such are the themes which intrude from the unpublished work and present us with a fuller and more human Stevenson. It has been pointed out that Stevenson in *A Child's Garden* has the couplet:

> The world is so full of a number of things
> I'm sure we should all be as happy as kings,

but that his original manuscript version was:

> The world is so great and I am so small
> I do not like it, at all, at all.

The unpublished work has kinship with that manuscript version. In privacy he records the sentiment that underlies the gesture of optimism with which he faced the world:

> I have left all upon the shameful field,
>   Honour and Hope, my God, and all but life;
> Spurless, with sword reversed and dinted shield,
>   Degraded and disgraced, I leave the strife.

That is not the only mood: valour is there, too, irony and humour. The image of Stevenson the poet grows to completion; it is of one who could write of his errings, his sorrows, as well as of his happiness. The poetry may not be technically better, but the themes are more varied and he has succeeded far more closely in disclosing himself in his verse.

John Davidson

John Davidson[1] (1857-1909) wrote in his will that no biography of him should be published, no unpublished work should be issued, and that no work except of his own writing should appear in any of his books. All that is known of him is the obvious record of dates, occupations, and movements, and nothing emerges that can explain the fiery, troubled movement of his work. He has had little attention after his death except that in 1961 J. Benjamin Townsend published a study, and a selection of his poems appeared, with a preface by T. S. Eliot, edited by Maurice Lindsay, and an essay by 'Hugh McDiarmid'. Eliot stated that he was influenced by Davidson's attempt to transfer verse into colloquial London speech. He added that of the poets that had influenced him as a beginner, 'One was Arthur Symons, some of his poems; another was Ernest Dowson, again one or two poems; and the third was Davidson in "Thirty Bob a Week". From these men I got the idea that one could write poetry in an English such as one would speak oneself. A colloquial English.'[2] Davidson, while he disapproved of biography, conceded in his preface to Shakespeare's Sonnets (1908) that all creative work is to some extent autobiographical, and it is from Davidson's work that we must alone hope to discover him. He was born in 1857, in Renfrewshire, a son of Alexander Davidson, a minister of the Evangelical Union. His education was irregular; at 13 he left school and went into a chemical factory, and a year later he was assistant to the Public Analyst at Greenock. From such beginnings may have been formed his lifelong interest in science. At 15 he was at school again as a pupil-teacher, and four years later he spent a session at Edinburgh University which completed his formal education. From 1878 to 1889 he was a teacher, a profession which he so detested that for one year (1884-1885) he tried clerking instead. In the middle of this period as a teacher he married. He was already writing, and his reading must have been varied, for he shows an acquaintance with Elizabethan and ballad literature, and, later, he knows Nietzsche, Ibsen, and the modern philosophical writers. In 1889 he came to London to seek a livelihood in the world of literature. He had previously written a number of poetical plays: one of them, *Bruce*, had been published in Glasgow in 1886. Little is known of the years that followed, except that he published continuously plays, novels, prose sketches, and poems. His main occupation was journalism, and if his poetry is a record of fact, he was as ill at ease amid the journalists as he had been amid the schoolmasters. Certainly it was a troubled period; recognition he received, but he was often ill and more often poor. In 1906 he was awarded a Civil List pension of £100. His most revealing autobiographical statement on these last years occurs in the preface to *Fleet Street* (1909): 'The time has come to make an end. I find my pension is not enough; I have therefore still to turn aside and attempt things for which people will pay. My health counts too. Asthma and other annoyances I have tolerated for years; but I cannot put up with cancer.' In 1908 he left London for Penzance. In March 1909 he was missing from his house. Six months later a fisherman found his body washed up by the sea.

Davidson's first poetic period belongs to his pre-London days; its content is in complete contrast to the work usually associated with him. For here he is untouched by his own time, and produces a series of plays, based upon suggestions from Shakespearian drama. *Bruce* (1886), the earliest published work, reads like a Shakespearian chronicle piece; he has caught the idiom and the method. The play deals with the struggle of Edward I against Bruce, and though the sympathy is with the Scots, there lurks a greater sense of national unity conveyed in a speech by Wallace in Act III:

> We are your equals, not to be enslaved;
> We are your kin, your brothers, to be loved.

In 1889 Davidson published at Greenock a volume of *Plays*. Two of these antedate *Bruce*: *An Unhistorical Pastoral* (Glasgow, 1877); *A Romantic Farce* (Edinburgh, 1878); one is of later date, the brilliant fantasy, partly in prose, *Scaramouch in Naxos* (Crieff, 1888). *An Unhistorical Pastoral* bears the same relation to Shakespearian comedy as *Bruce* does to the chronicle play. The competent study piece of a young apprentice, it demonstrates that Davidson's early work began in a world of romantic kindliness. Experience taught him savagely to deny these dream contours. *A Romantic Farce* is of the same texture: a romance of long-separated lovers and long-lost children, played with a light-hearted conviction that the end will be happiness. *Scaramouch in Naxos*, a witty, original comedy, with glimpses of darker satire, is of much more mature conception, and despite Davidson's later attempts in drama, it remains probably his most adequate play. Scaramouch, a showman in England, seeking a new attraction, attempts to hire old wine-sodden Silenus to impersonate Bacchus in his entertainment. A number of classical figures are introduced, all living in a modern world and insisting on their pedigree in Lemprière as if it were *Debrett's Peerage*. The play closes with the appearance of the real Bacchus, a god of power, who frustrates the sordid designs of Scaramouch and Silenus. The verse has a strength that derives from Elizabethan originals, but it possesses a fragrant beauty of its own. Such is Silenus's speech, which opens:

> I saw Endymion long ago
> Before the stars were tarnished: with his crook
> Sloped in his hand he wandered down a hill;
> The night shone round him.

In this play, for the first time, Davidson opens that attack on his time which was to frustrate the romantic elements in his poetry; the modern world reveals itself as a shallow vulgar affair, whose God is Silenus of the wineskin, not the young Bacchus. Davidson called the piece a pantomime, but he wrote a prose prologue, the most brilliant of all his prose passages, in which he confesses that the play is too complicated for pantomimic values. *Smith* (1888), a tragedy, was the last play of the Scottish period, and here for the first time Davidson portrays contemporary life. Whenever he enters that world in his poetry his mood is tragic. Out of the past only can he bring not only tragedy but gentleness and the gay colours of romance. Frequently in his poetic career he attempted to use old forms for modern circumstance, and here he uses blank verse for modern characters. Throughout, the effect is a combination of power with incongruity, of poetry with flat, hackneyed lines. Here for the first time there appears in Davidson's work the solution of suicide for those who find the world inadequate to their desires.

In 1889 Davidson left Scotland for London, and with this change began his second poetic period. He wrote much prose during the next decade, novels, and charming essays such as are found in *A Random Itinerary* (1894). His poetic production was unbroken; in 1891 appeared *In a Music Hall,* and there followed, almost annually, little volumes, in glossy blue cloth, all but one of them decorated on the cover with a pleasingly elaborate device of gold: *Fleet Street Eclogues* (1893); *Ballads and Songs* (1894); *A Second Series of Fleet Street Eclogues* (1896); *New Ballads* (1897); *The Last Ballad* (1899). *In a Music Hall* contains, first, six short dramatic monologues in which music-hall artists, refreshing themselves at the bar as they wait their turn, give pictures of themselves and of life. These are the children of Silenus, revealing their sordid, half-pathetic lives, in brisk black-and-white sketches. The mood is staccato, and Davidson seems to have been influenced by Kipling's desire to see the thing as it is and to allow it to speak in its own vocabulary. The scene is nominally Glasgow, but one feels that spiritually Davidson came here into his closest contact with the London of the nineties. The rest of the volume is made up of a selection of miscellaneous poems of the period 1872-1889; short lyrics of pre-London days, historical pieces of the same period as *Bruce*, delicate nature studies, and lyrics of happy, gentle moods. He uses the French forms, popular in those decades, rondeau, roundel, and villanelle, but he uses them in a way fiercely different from that of Austin Dobson and Edmund Gosse. It is as if with deliberate irony he employed these decorative measures to reveal grim scenes such as the struggling artist whose wife and children have to suffer for lack of daily bread.

Fleet Street Eclogues was the first volume with which Davidson attracted marked critical attention. He uses the eclogue, the form of Theocritus and Spenser, for the discussions of Fleet Street journalists. The device has a freshness, but the effect is not without incongruity. Two qualities ever latent in Davidson's work emerge: a romanticism, frequently suppressed, combines with an angry, unrestrained outcry against contemporary life. These two elements meet in his poetry in sudden conflict as if a sleeper had been awakened from the pleasant images of dream by a cry of anguished pain. So in the *Saint Swithin's Day* poem the close is a prayer, almost hysterical in its plea for protection from the modern world:

> Help, ere it drive us mad, this devil's din!

But modernity has not yet worn Davidson down; his love of nature and of pleasing old-world fantasies still allows him to recreate a world of gentle devices and ballad theme. One of the pleasantest recollections occurs in *Good Friday*, when he recounts how Adam and Eve went out of Eden:

> Their haggard eyes in vain to God,
>   To all the stars of heaven turned;
> But when they saw where in the sod,
>   The golden-hearted daisies burned,
>
> Sweet thoughts that still within them dwelt
>   Awoke, and tears embalmed their smart;

> On Eden's daisies couched they felt
> They carried Eden in their heart.

In *Ballads and Songs* this same dual mood prevails, and yet the old-world romanticism again triumphs. The volume contains some of Davidson's best-known pieces, notably *A Ballad of a Nun*, where he retells the story usually known in medieval literature as 'the Nun who goes out to see the World'. It is the beautiful fable of a nun who, deserting her convent, mingled in the world, and who, when she returned, wan with passion, found that the Virgin Mother had impersonated her in her absence. The story is famous in the medieval literature of western Europe, but Davidson, who probably knew Adelaide Anne Procter's version in *A Legend of Provence*, narrates it afresh with economy and deeply conveyed feeling. Had he been satisfied with this medium he could have become the most successful modern exploiter of the ballad, but it was not in his nature to be satisfied, and there occurs already in this volume a strain of fretful, subjective poetry. It is to be found in *A Ballad in Blank Verse of the Making of a Poet*, which is as unlike a ballad as possible. All qualities of pleasant phrasing and melody have disappeared, and instead there emerges a mood of satire, and a wilful self-assertion which preludes the later *Testaments*:

> Henceforth I shall be God; for consciousness
> Is God: I suffer; I am God: this Self,
> That all the universe combines to quell,
> Is greater than the universe; and *I*
> Am that I am.

Closely allied to this is the *Ballad of Heaven*, a poem of personal despair arising from poverty and lack of recognition, a theme already emphasized in his first volume of lyrics:

> He wrought at one great work for years;
>   The world passed by with lofty look:
> Sometimes his eyes were dashed with tears;
>   Sometimes his lips with laughter shook.

> His wife and child went clothed in rags,
>   And in a windy garret starved:
> He trod his measures on the flags,
>   And high on heaven his music carved.

The increased attachment to such moods can be seen in the volumes which follow. Into *A Second Series of Fleet Street Eclogues* the harsh enforced vocabulary intrudes, and with it a bitter commentary on contemporary life; as in *Lammas*:

> The blare of personal and party aims
> In parliaments and journals seems indeed
> No substitute for Sinai; but it serves:
> And from the vehement logomachy
> Of interest and cabal, something humane
> At happy intervals proceeds.

An attempt is made to break away to early moods in the *May-Day* poem, but this lacks the spontaneity of some of his earlier pieces. *New Ballads* reiterates the now persistent theme of the struggling artist and his distressed family; it comes through in *A Ballad of an Artist's Wife*, and in a different way in *A Woman and her Son*, which is a fiercer version of the theme found earlier in *A Ballad of the Making of a Poet*. Despite these preoccupations, this volume has some signal examples of Davidson's varied poetic power. In *Piper, Play!* he contrives to fashion a lyric, whose background is the life of the industrial worker:

> Now the furnaces are out,
>   And the aching anvils sleep;
> Down the road the grimy rout
>   Tramples homeward twenty deep.
> Piper, play! Piper, play!
>   Though we be o'erlaboured men,
> Ripe for rest, pipe your best!
>   Let us foot it once again!

In *A New Ballad of Tannhäuser* he uses again his skill in manipulating ballad form for a traditional theme; the poem seems to be an answer to Swinburne's *Laus Veneris*, for in Davidson the monk does not sicken of his love.

The Last Ballad was the volume with which Davidson brought this second period in his poetic work to a close. Early and late moods seem once again in conflict, and yet most of the poems are occupied with fables of romance. It is as if Davidson were lingering with medieval themes before bidding them a long farewell. In the title poem he isolates an incident in the lives of Lancelot and Galahad, and relates it with that mastery of the ballad medium which he now possessed. He accomplished here an important though neglected contribution to the treatment of Arthurian legend in the nineteenth century. With no moral and sophisticated purpose to fulfil, he recaptured the mood of the ballad without ransoming his modernity to any conscious archaism. *The Ordeal*, the other long poem in this volume, is a narrative poem with a medieval theme which in its insistence on stern and strenuous incident is reminiscent of Morris's *Sir Peter Harpdon's End*. With this volume Davidson completed a notable and individual contribution to the lyrical poetry of the period. He exploited romantic themes when it seemed that the century had exhausted all their possibilities, and then he wrote 'finis' to this type of work and resurrected himself anew as a poet in difficult, philosophical pieces which are powerful and ill-disciplined and through whose strength there lurks an isolation of spirit, not unakin at times to the fantasies of the insane.

Without biographical data one must form a subjective judgement on this change. Whatever may be the intrinsic value of the poetry that follows, one cannot detach from one's mind some image of heroism in relationship to Davidson's last endeavour. The century was in need of a new poetry, a poetry such as Meredith and Hardy had attempted, where poetic creation allied itself to the deep-rooted origins of the modern consciousness. His effort is not completely successful, but the image of endeavour remains, and as he himself wrote in *A Random Itinerary* after a poignant reference to Cowper's *Castaway*: 'I would sooner be a castaway than never sail at all.' Lyrical poetry ceased, only to be fitfully reawakened in *Holiday* (1906), *Fleet Street and other Poems* (1909). The more strident elements, already latent in his lyrical work, possessed him. He conceived afresh his poetical function, and determined that it was within him to create a new poetry and from that poetry a new world. He seemed to envision himself as a lonely saviour of a world that was too busy even to crucify him. From 1901 to 1908 he wrote blank-verse poems and tragedies, all governed by this aim. He summarized his purpose in his prose Epilogue to *The Triumph of Mammon*: 'For half a century I have survived in a world entirely unfitted for me, and having known both the Heaven and the Hell thereof, and being without a revenue and an army and navy to compel the nations, I begin definitely in my Testaments and Tragedies to destroy this unfit world and make it over again in my own image: in my own image because that cannot be transcended; all men, crossing-sweepers or Ministers of State, endeavour to their utmost to make the world to their order; and those who identify their minds and imaginations with the Universe have unusual power and authority.'

The Testaments were all blank-verse pieces. The first three were published, in rapid succession, by Grant Richards as paper-covered pamphlets, and the first two were offered at the attractive price of sixpence each: *The Testament of a Vivisector* (1901); *The Testament of a Man Forbid* (1901); *The Testament of an Empire-Builder* (1902). There followed as octavo volumes, *The Testament of a Prime Minister* (1904); *The Testament of John Davidson* (1908). During the same period he attempted to express his ideas through poetic drama, and hoped, though unsuccessfully, to gain recognition through the performance of his plays. In his preface to *The Theatrocrat* (1905) he has explained his relationship with the theatre. Forbes Robertson had read the volumes of *Plays* which Davidson had written in Scotland, and in the mid-nineties he invited him to prepare a poetical version of François Coppée's *Pour la Couronne*. This Davidson achieved successfully and the play was performed at the Lyceum Theatre in 1896, with Forbes Robertson and Mrs Patrick Campbell in the main parts. He continued with further adaptations and hoped through this connexion to have some of his own plays produced. Though this ambition was unfulfilled, he continued until the end to produce poetic dramas: *Godfrida* (1898); *Self's the Man* (1901); *The Knight of the Maypole* (1903, written in 1900); *The Theatrocrat* (1905); *The Triumph of Mammon* (1907); *Mammon and his Message* (1908). These last two plays were part of a trilogy, the conclusion of which was never published. It has been too often assumed that these poems and plays are merely the record of an angry incoherence. This may be true of isolated passages, and Davidson himself has admitted the difficulties of expression which he encountered: 'There is no language for what I have to say: my meaning hides behind my words.'[3] Yet from the 'Testaments' and the plays there emerges a philosophy, consistently maintained. He asserts that the one reality is the Universe, a living material mass, in which all things are included:

> You and the beasts, and everything that is,
> In every organ, function, grain and drop,
> In every quivering ion, Universe,
> This is the thing the world is waiting for.[4]

Men do not live in this Universe but in some false image of it. 'When the minds and imaginations of all men exist in the Universe itself and not in a symbol of the Universe, we shall have a new world. Is there any thinking person who does not wish to see the world made over again? Is it so lovely? Is it so sweet-smelling? Men tinker and patch with policies and economics. They might as well attempt to cure the plague by an exhibition of rose-water.'[5] All the universe is matter; man is conscious matter, and the suggestion that he possesses spirit and is separated from the animal world is erroneous. Fantasies created by political, religious, and moral deceit have obscured this truth, and the poet's function is to destroy the fantasies and reveal that material universe from which the new world will come. So Davidson pleads in *The Testament of a Vivisector*:

> Expunge the o'erscored script
> That blurs the mind with poetry and prose
> Of every age; and yield it gladly up
> For me to carve with knowledge, and to seal
> With Matter's signet.

The work of revealing this Universe can only be achieved by a strong, ruthless personality, a Superman who has rid himself of pity, fear, and the other vices of the commonalty. Throughout the 'Testaments' Davidson identifies himself with this personality, and it is in this self-assertion that the most unbalanced element in his later works is to be found. The same thought is contained in the dramatic work, where Mammon is given the role of Superman, but even here Davidson insists with excessive vehemence upon the necessity for one strong leader:

> Not two men in a century can think;
> Not two men in an age: I mean to do
> The thinking for a thousand years to come![6]

This theory is seen in its extreme form when Davidson suggests in *The Testament of John Davidson* that it may be through him alone that knowledge can be attained:

> It may be that the Universe attains
> Self-knowledge only once; and when I cease
> To see and hear, imagine, think and feel,
> The end may come.

The Heaven of the Universe is reserved for those who identify themselves with the Superman, those who

> challenged fate and staked their lives
> To win or lose the prize they coveted,
> Who took their stand upon the earth and drew
> Deep virtue from the centre, helped themselves,
> Desired the world and willed what Matter would.[7]

In contrast, the hell of the Universe is occupied by those who deny the reality of the Universe and live in some fantasy:

> All kinds of cowards who eluded fact;
> Dwellers in legend, burrowers in myth:

> The merciful, the meek and mild, the poor
> In spirit.[7]

The fullest and most aggressive statement of his position is to be found in the prose preface to *The Theatrocrat*.[8] Here he insists more than elsewhere on the fact that all life has a chemical basis. Children should be made aware of this, and of nothing else. 'Thus a child would know at once that there has been no philosophy, no religion, no art, literature, hitherto; that there is nothing for him to learn; that everyone must make for himself his own philosophy, religion, literature.' . . . 'The insane part of mankind is the incubus: the world is really a virgin world awaking from a bad dream.'

The commonest reaction of criticism has been to consider Davidson as a muddled materialist who has read Nietzsche, and to leave the matter there. It is true that the name of Nietzsche had filtered into literary circles in England in the mid-nineties. Davidson may have encountered it either in the work of G. B. Shaw or through a series of articles by Havelock Ellis in the *Savoy* in the spring of 1896. Davidson himself denied that he was a disciple of Nietzsche, and maintained throughout that his purpose was poetry and not philosophy. It is unnecessary to suppose that Davidson had, at any time, made a close study of Nietzsche's work, yet undoubtedly he found in that will to power which is beyond good and evil a formula for the superman of his own plays and poems. Also his attack on Christianity as the friend of 'all the feeble, the diseased, the low, the loathsome' seems to have derived some of its vehement strength from Nietzsche. It is dangerous to assume that every superficial similarity indicates some direct borrowing by Davidson from Nietzsche's work. Those who wish to carry this process to its logical conclusion should note the many passages in Davidson's work in which he speaks in the vocabulary of psychoanalytic writers. Yet it is extremely improbable that Davidson, living in England in the first decade of the twentieth century, could have become acquainted with their work.

It remains to give some brief account of the individual works of this last period. Of the dramas, three belong to a mood which is free from philosophical preoccupations. He seems to be attempting original work which does not break too completely with the tradition of the successful verse plays which he had been adapting. *Godfrida* (1898), a romantic drama of incident and intrigue, has its scene in a theatrical conception of fourteenth-century Provence. In his introduction Davidson suggests that he is resuscitating the mood in which his early dramas were written: 'Before I sat down to write *Godfrida* I read over my early plays, and the lot was cast for Romance.' 'My object', he adds, 'was to give delight.' The characters are distinct, but not strongly drawn; the intrigue is involved but not confused; the play retains the attention, without awakening the imagination by any outstanding novelty or charm. *The Knight of the Maypole* (published in 1903 and written in 1900) is comedy of Charles II's reign, where he returns most clearly to the mood of his early drama. *Self's the Man* (1901) is the last play of Davidson's which is not rendered subordinate to his philosophical interests. He sets the scene in Lombardy in the eighth century, and the governing incident lies in the struggle of Lucian and Urban, two claimants for the throne and for the hand of Osmunda, the daughter of the powerful Hildebrand. With *The Theatrocrat* (1905) Davidson has broken with romance and with the desire to give delight, and the play is contemporary, although the blank verse is retained.

The Triumph of Mammon and *Mammon and his Message* are Davidson's last published plays. In them he comes most closely to the expression of his mind during the last decade of his life. They are far more intelligible than the blank-verse 'Testaments', and their dramatic form has been disciplined to the purposes of philosophical expression. The medium is still blank verse; the scene is contemporary, but with the setting in the State of Thule, the values are those of fantasy and not of realism. Davidson has never been given due credit for the invention of a form which has many of the dramatic possibilities of the later expressionist drama. The scene, which is contemporary without realism, allows of an action which is fantastic without incongruity, and so his symbolic and discursive purposes are adequately served. The advance which he made in dramatic invention between *The Theatrocrat* and the 'Mammon' plays is one of the most impressive in his career.

The blank-verse 'Testaments', like the tragedies, were intended to serve the same purpose of emancipating the world. Davidson hurled the first volume, *The Testament of a Vivisector*, at the public with a defiant, almost contemptuous preface. The poem opens with an aggressive statement of his philosophy, in which the terms Matter and Universe and Materialist are used with his peculiar values. From this cramped, abstract exposition the reader is jerked to a concrete illustration which assaults the emotions even more strenuously than the philosophy had confounded the intellect. The poet rescues an old neglected horse, 'pitying his case', and takes him to a meadow:

> A rotten hack,
> Compunctious hideful of rheumatic joints
> Larded with dung and clay, gaunt spectacle
> Of ringbone, spavin, canker, shambled about,
> And grazed the faded, sparse, disrelished tufts
> That the sun's tongue of flame had left half-licked.

There he kills him, and gains some ecstasy of delight from the intense pain of the animal 'terrible in martyrdom':

> The whip's-man felt no keener ecstasy
> When a fair harlot at the cart's-tail shrieked
> And rags of flesh with blood-soaked tawdry lace,
> Girdled her shuddering loins.

The whole incident is unexpected, and superficially there emerges merely the delight of a perverted mind in the sight of pain. Davidson's purpose lies deeper, for he wishes to illustrate that the Universe is all one in Matter, and that Matter one in Pain. All pain that leads to self-knowledge is useful, and all action that leads to the attainment of self-knowledge is justifiable. Yet these general conclusions do not render the central incident less repellent. He contrived to make the first of his

'Testaments' the most tortuous and unintelligible; bewildered reviewers suggested that this was a poem on vivisection, but they were not sure on which side in the controversy lay the sympathies of the poet.

The Man Forbid reveals Davidson's dangerous belief that he is a man apart: 'Mankind has cast me out.' This theme gives the poem, however, a dramatic situation possessed of a human and easily intelligible poignancy. Two images seem frequently present in the background of Davidson's mind, the despairing isolation of *The Castaway* and the triumphant isolation of the Christ. Into his conception of his own relationship with the world he has combined elements from both of these:

> Alone I went in darkness and in light,
> Colour and sound attending on my steps,
> And life and death, the ministers of men,
> My constant company. But in my heart
> Of hearts I longed for human neighbourhood,
> And bent my pride to win men back again.
> I came, a penitent; and on my knees
> I climbed their stairs; I thundered at their doors,
> And cried, 'I am your brother; in your wrath
> As brethren should, destroy me; at your hands
> I must have life or death: I cannot bear
> The outcast's fate.'

But the reconciliation is not achieved and the poet wanders out into the loneliest corners of nature possessed of a faith which he may not communicate. The philosophical elements are reduced to a minimum, but Davidson expresses more simply here than elsewhere his belief in the millenium awaiting the age which banishes Other-worldliness and lives in the reality of the World as it is:

> Olympus stands untenanted; the dead
> Have their serene abode in earth itself,
> Our womb, our nurture, and our sepulchre.

The Testament of an Empire-Builder is a longer and more elaborate poem than either of its predecessors. In the first section the animals hold a congress to discover how man has taken precedence over them, but this satiric and somewhat inconclusive discussion is completely overshadowed by the vision of Heaven and Hell, found in the second part of the poem. Heaven, for Davidson, is the home of the realists and Hell of those who have worshipped any form of deception. But the poetic vision transcends the thought, and he masters within his verse a gigantesque dream sculpture, which possesses the effect of awe attained by some of Blake's drawings. The most terrible portrayal is of Hell as seen from Heaven as a vast amphitheatre of human flesh, a pallid wall:

> Tier upon tier of flesh from base to crown,
> This human amphitheatre was Hell
> Itself, constructed of its denizens.

Though the poem suffers from a lack of unity and a sense of wasted strength, it has individual passages in which Davidson seems possessed of impressive powers of imaginative description.

The Testament of a Prime Minister attempts to express dramatically the theme in the previous 'Testaments'. *The Prime Minister*, a disciple of the poet's, has attempted to break through the trivial discussions of Parliament with an exposition of the new philosophy. Driven out, he endures a number of mental and physical adventures, until hopeless of an understanding audience he goes

> despairing down
> To dust and deep oblivion.

The poem adds little to any constructive statement of Davidson's belief, but it possesses two dramatic scenes of marked contrast. In the first, a little cluster of wretched humanity by the River Lea is awakened for a moment to a sense of the reality of the Universe, while in the second Davidson expounds more fully his anti-Christian feeling by a magnificent vision of the Day of Judgement. Unity the poem lacks, and the blank verse crumbles at times beneath the demands of arid exposition. Such a line as

'In carbon, calcium, metals, vapours, earths' is far removed from the melody of his best verse, yet even in this poem nature scenes intrude, though a little shyly, as if they knew that they were neglected:

> Bird after bird
> Forbore its song as darkness crept abroad,
> Till the last lark dropped breathless from the sky.

In 1908 *The Testament of John Davidson*, the last of these blank-verse poems, appeared. Its dedication *To the Peers Temporal* is a headlong intrusion into contemporary politics; the image that lies behind it is that of the angry and unnerved figure of the hustings. It forebodes ill of the poem that is to follow, but the auguries must be disallowed, for the last 'Testament', whatever its inequalities, has moments of beauty and an underlying sense of power. One comes to suspect that the stridency of Davidson's prose prefaces was due to the fact that G. B. Shaw's models lay too close to hand.

The verse is less secure than in the previous poems. The vocabulary of tortuous words ('scaurs', 'manchet', 'lycanthrope', 'nympholept') increases, and flat, dusty stretches of lines in which theory is expounded. But the method of the poem is more original, and the sustaining powers of the poet are not inadequate. He imagines that he is out above the world in the Milky Way, and here he meets Diana, the last of the gods. The symbolic movement is that man must unite with the goddess and produce a new race of god-like men who shall dwell not with the gods but in the Universe. Diana, in the final scene, affirms this belief with great clarity:

> Greater than the gods,
> O man, immortal in mortality,
> For your delight, for your supreme delight
> I kept my maidenhood. Without a doubt –
> I know it in my sex and in my soul! –
> My womb shall teem with daughters fairer far
> Than their most happy mother.

Linked to this symbolic movement in loose, episodical form, enters Davidson's exploitation of classical myth. He recounts in keen narrative lines the stories of Endymion, Actæon, and Orion, and continues in more cramped passages to describe the death of the gods. The poem concludes with a hideous vision of the Hell in which dead gods are confined.

So closed the published poetic work of John Davidson. Two miscellaneous volumes had appeared in these years: *Holiday*, a volume of miscellaneous lyrics, includes the poignant lyric of stag-hunting – *A Runnable Stag*; *Fleet Street* may be considered as a list of addenda to the thought of the 'Testaments'.

No extravagant claim need be made for Davidson's verse to establish its importance in the poetical history of the century. His lyrical work alone gives him a distinct place, for he brings a freshness to forms that have been frequently exploited. The ballad yielded a new magic to him, and nature and industry alike showed him something that no poet had seen before. He was not satisfied. Both dramatic and narrative poetry were to be curbed to the purposes of his mind, and that mind was possessed of the belief that it could make a new faith out of the scientific thought of his time. The record of his partial success has been given. More than this he seemed conscious of immense powers, accompanied by a tragic frustration; he left no biography, but out of his life he created a legend. So at the conclusion of his last 'Testament' he writes a lyric which presages his own fate:

> My feet are heavy now, but on I go,
>   My head erect beneath the tragic years.
> The way is steep, but I would have it so;
>   And dusty, but I lay the dust with tears,
> Though none can see me weep: alone I climb
> The rugged path that leads me out of time.

Oscar Wilde, Ernest Dowson, Lionel Johnson and the Poetry of the Eighteen-Nineties

Oscar Wilde (1856-1900) once said to André Gide, 'I have put all my genius into my life; I have put only my talent into my works.' Time has confirmed his paradox, and the legend of Wilde, building a large literature around his name, has given his work continued vogue throughout Europe and America. He came through at his best and his worst in his life. There are moments, and the speech on friendship delivered when he stood on trial is among them, that have radiance and beauty; and moods of courage, too, which parallel the thought of his sonnet, *On the Sale by Auction of Keats' Love Letters*. But tawdriness and clatter accompany him, distressing even his best work. Wilde, like Byron, offended society grievously and society rough-handled him. Wilde offended more flagrantly than Byron and was punished more crudely, but this has only served to give his legend an even wider circulation. Wilde's personality thus gave his work a far wider influence on the literature and taste of his time than its intrinsic merit might warrant; and his poetry is but a small part of his literary work.

Oscar Fingall O'Flahertie Wills Wilde[1] was born in Dublin in 1856. His father, Sir William Wilde, was a distinguished surgeon, with a streak of undisciplined passion in his temper, and at times in his conduct. His mother, an accomplished lady, a poetess and journalist, and an Irish nationalist of radical sympathies, gave Wilde an early love of the classics, and from her he inherited a happy gift for languages. His educational career was a record of continual success; at Portora Royal School, Enniskillen, he was a brilliant but unsociable schoolboy; at Trinity College, Dublin, he won the Berkeley Medal for Greek; and at Oxford, at Magdalen College, where his exquisite rooms, with their famous blue china, overlooked the river, he found time to take a 'double first'. In 1877 he travelled in Italy and Greece with Professor Mahaffy, a journey which influenced his poetry, and in 1878 he turned all this to immediate profit by winning the Newdigate Prize with a poem, *Ravenna*. He was already contributing poems to periodical journals,[2] and by the time he left Oxford he was known as an 'aesthete', a brilliant, gaudily-decked *poseur*.

In 1881 his *Poems* were published, and five impressions quickly exhausted: his reputation as an aesthete gave them a notoriety, and as a result a popularity which they did not deserve. His name filtered through to America, and in 1882 he crossed the Atlantic for a lecturing tour, where the curiosity of his audiences led him to emphasize his extravagances of dress and speech. The years after his return were filled with hack-work in lecturing and journalism. In 1884 he married Constance Lloyd, and with the help of her income he was able to settle in Tite Street, Chelsea, in greater comfort than he had known for years. The decade 1885 to 1895 is the period of Wilde's main literary success. He wrote essays, short stories, novels, prose romances, fables, a play in French (*Salomé*), and then four brilliant social comedies in English. This production allowed little time for poetry. A number of pieces appeared in periodicals; they are among his best poems, but so few that they seem produced in the rare leisure of a busy man of letters. There is one exception; in 1894 *The Sphinx* was published, a complete poem, issued separately, the last work he was to publish before disaster overcame him. In 1895 Wilde brought an action for criminal libel against the Marquess of Queensberry. He was unsuccessful, and as a result of information revealed in these proceedings he was himself arrested for offences under the Criminal Law Amendment Act. His homosexuality, his complex relation with Lord Alfred Douglas, the son of the Marquess of Queensberry, the long trials and the savage sentence of two years' imprisonment with hard labour, have all been the theme of much discussion. In prison he wrote one of his most moving prose pieces, the autobiographical fragment of *De Profundis* (1905), the full version of which is published in Rupert Hart-Davis's edition of the letters. On his release he lived abroad at Berneval, and in Paris and Naples. At Berneval he wrote a poem which is in marked contrast to his earlier work, *The Ballad of Reading Gaol* (1898). He died at the Hôtel d'Alsace, Paris, in November 1900.

Wilde's first published poem, apart from pieces in periodicals, was *Ravenna*, his Newdigate Prize poem, issued in 1878. In heroic couplets, as the rules of the Newdigate Prize required, it is a good prize poem, touched but rarely with poetry. The piece is full of echoes of poets from Milton to Swinburne. At times there are moments of nature observation, poetically conveyed, which are rare in Wilde's later pieces:

> Some startled bird, with fluttering wings and fleet,
> Made snow of all the blossoms.

He must have felt that these lines were better than most, for he uses them once again in his sonnet on Genoa in the 1881 volume.

In 1881 Wilde's *Poems* appeared, resplendent in white vellum parchment with a cover device of gold prune blossoms, designed by the author. Purchased by the public, and mildly patronized by the critics, it gave Wilde a place among contemporary poets. Two features stand out: the degree to which he imitates earlier poets and the variety of his themes and interests. The subject of Wilde's use of imitation has been fully explored[3] and only representative examples need be given here. Frequently he turns into verse a paragraph or phrase from a prose passage which has attracted him. The introductory sonnet *Helas* ends:

> with a little rod
> I did but touch the honey of romance –
> And must I lose a soul's inheritance?

In one of the moving passages of the conclusion of his essay on *Winckelmann*, Pater has: 'But Christianity, with its uncompromising idealism, discrediting the slightest touch of sense, has lighted up for the artistic life, with its inevitable sensousness, a background of flame. "I did but taste of little honey with the end of the rod that was in mine hand, and lo, I must die."' In numerous other poems Wilde versifies passages from Pater's *Renaissance*. Pater's phrase from the famous *Conclusion*, 'To burn always with this hard gemlike flame', becomes, 'This hot hard flame with which our bodies burn' in *Panthea*, and 'To burn with one clear flame' in *Humanitad*. Further, he adapts phrases and lines from the poets. In *Sonnets*, which are political in theme, he uses adaptations of Milton. For Milton's sonnet, 'Avenge, O Lord, thy slaughtered saints', we have Wilde's sonnet, 'On the Massacre of the Christians in Bulgaria':

> Christ, dost thou live indeed? or are thy bones
> Still straitened in their rock-hewn sepulchre?

Keats is frequently echoed in individual phrases, as in *Ave Imperatrix*, where the 'Chapman Sonnet' is remembered:

> And many an Afghan chief . . .
> Clutches his sword in fierce surmise.

A more elaborate influence of Keats in form and theme is found in *Charmides*. Swinburne is remembered in single phrases, though Wilde has avoided any mechanical repetition of the more characteristic elements of Swinburnian verse. Arnold enters with Oxus stream in *Ave Imperatrix* and with Bagley Wood in *The Garden of Eros*, while phrases from his poetry slip in almost undetected. The Shakesperian echoes are numerous and distinct and were noted at the time in the *Athenæum*.[4] The clearest examples occur in *The Garden of Eros*, a poem riddled with Shakespearian memories.

The Ballade de Marguerite is in form and style a close imitation of Morris and Rossetti and contains verbal memories of both poets. Sufficient examples have been quoted to show Wilde's keenly assimilative quality, and his borrowings cover most of the major poets from the Romantic period onwards, and some, such as Milton and Spenser, from earlier centuries. Though it is simple to perceive that he is an imitator, it is more difficult to estimate the quality of his imitation. Seldom is he a crude plagiarist, decorating his own poems with ready-found phrases. But his retentive memory holds within it much that is beautiful from earlier poetry. Despite all the derivations, his own verse has a consistency as if he touched what he borrowed with his own genius.

The other outstanding feature of the volume is its width of interest. Its contents fall naturally into four divisions: *Eleutheria*, the poems on liberty and political themes; *Rosa Mystica*, the Catholic and Italian poems; the longer narrative and lyrical pieces, *The Burden of Itys*, *The Garden of Eros*, *Charmides*, *Panthea*, and *Humanitad*; finally, short lyrics, including a series of sonnets, *Impressions du Théâtre*. The political poems are marked with a vigour of expression, but with such an inconsistency of thought that one doubts whether any of them represent a sincere conviction. In *To Liberty* he asserts that he has no interest in Liberty herself, but that her reigns of Terror 'mirror his wildest passions', and yet nonchalantly at the close he commends those who die for liberty:

        and yet
  These Christs that die upon the barricades,
  God knows it I am with them, in some ways.

In the concluding sonnet he undermines every position which he has previously advanced, and postulates, as if Baudelaire had overshadowed Milton, an aesthetic individualism, aggressive and anti-social:

    It mars my calm: wherefore in dreams of Art
    And loftiest culture I would stand apart,
    Neither for God, nor for his enemies.

Here one seems to encounter an avowal that the other sonnets were either whims, forced into seeming passion, or exercises in metrical deception. This impression is carried over into *Ave Imperatrix*, in which Wilde with some skill in detail contemplates England's position as an Imperial power.

The second section, *Rosa Mystica*, opens with *Requiescat*, a poem suggested by the death of his sister, Isola, who died in childhood. It has an unaffected simplicity and integrity, gained by the subtle melody of its short lines,

> Tread lightly, she is near
> Under the snow.

Such was the mood; he never recaptured it, but here for once it matures into a poem evenly maintained. The other poems in this section are all governed by religious or contemplative themes. The sonnets, *On Approaching Italy*, *San Miniato*, and *Holy Week at Genoa*, all arise from some Catholic suggestion. One is led to feel that Catholicism, with its ritual, has appealed to Wilde's imagination, and one remembers his comment that had his father allowed him to be a Catholic when he went up to Oxford the catastrophe of his later life would not have occurred. The mood of these sonnets is summarized by a fragment, *Rome Unvisited*, in the stanza of *In Memoriam*:

> O joy to see before I die
> The only God-anointed King,
> And hear the silver trumpets ring
> A triumph as He passes by!

Wilde had used the *In Memoriam* measure in a number of his early pieces, published in periodicals, nor does the imitation seem accidental, for Wilde, like Tennyson, explores his spiritual experience in these early quatrain poems. With the concluding poem, *The New Helen*, he seems to undermine the sincerity of sentiment which his religious poems had appeared to possess:

> Of heaven or hell I have no thought or fear,
> Seeing I know no other god but thee.

In these lines, adapted from William Morris, he flings aside the spiritual experience previously expressed, attaching himself to an aestheticism which knows neither philosophy nor religion. Possibly these sections show his mind freeing itself of earlier interests, and establishing this confined aesthetic approach to experience, gained under the influence of Pater and Baudelaire, and which he found expressed poetically for the first time in Keats and elaborated later by the Pre-Raphaelites.

The longer lyrical and narrative poems form the central element in the volume. *The Garden of Eros* reaffirms his belief that the pursuit of Beauty is the only commendable form of human endeavour. He continues the plea made so frequently by the Pre-Raphaelites that modern civilization militates against this ideal:

> Spirit of Beauty tarry yet a-while!
>   Although the cheating merchants of the mart
> With iron roads profane our lovely isle,
>   And break on whirling wheels the limbs of Art.

He commemorates the poets who have been votaries of beauty in this modern world, Keats, Shelley, Swinburne, Morris, Rossetti. Tennyson is also praised, for his 'gorgeous-coloured vestiture', and for his painting of the Soul with all its 'mighty questionings'. In this longer poem Wilde's technical inadequacies become more apparent. Defects of rhyme are less important than the patched, unmusical lines with which some of the stanzas are completed. He permits such verbal contortions as 'Its new-found creeds so sceptical and so dogmatical'. The diction, too, is conceited, and here, as elsewhere, he makes excessive use of classical allusion. That Wilde had a considerable classical knowledge need not be denied, but unfortunately he could not resist flourishing a classical allusion, as if its very presence in a poem were a guarantee of success.

The Burden of Itys, though allied in motive to *The Garden of Eros*, is a stronger poem. It opens with praise of England, the common poppies in the wheat instead of the crimson Cardinal on the Esquiline. Wilde asks the nightingale to sing in these unfamiliar English haunts of Grecian themes, and so contrives once again to give a catalogue of classical allusions. From these memories of legend there emerges a plea for beauty such as Wilde has also made in other poems:

> Sing on! sing on! let the dull world grow young,
> Let elemental things take form again,
> And the old shapes of Beauty walk among
> The simple garths and open crofts.

Though derivative in theme and mood, this is the most secure of Wilde's longer poems. The philosophy, even to its very phrasing, is that of Keats. The atmosphere is quite admittedly that of Arnold's *Scholar-Gipsy* and *Thyrsis* ('The horn of Atalanta faintly blown, across the Cumner hills'). The verbal rhetoric remains, as in the description of the nightingale as a 'tiny sober-suited advocate'. Despite technical imperfections, the poem has some urgency of suggestion which gives it an individuality.

In *Humanitad* Wilde attempts a philosophical statement of his position, but the poem develops into a thing of shreds and confusions. It serves to show again how literary and derivative were the sources of his verse. Apart from verbal memories, we find direct references to Giotto, Brunelleschi, Milton, and Wordsworth, while the central theme in this discursive medley of a poem is praise of Mazzini. *Panthea*, a shorter piece, possesses more warmth of movement and a clearer plan. If one had not read Pater and Swinburne, it might pass as a poem of original thought. As it is, one feels that Wilde is a verse reporter with a good memory who has interviewed these two writers. The thundered alliterations come through from Swinburne:

> to make atone
> By pain or prayer or priest,

while Pater's philosophy is paraphrased and vulgarized throughout:

> Nay, let us walk from fire unto fire,
> From passionate pain to deadlier delight, –

I am too young to live without desire,
  Too young art thou to waste this summer night
Asking those idle questions which of old
Man ought to seer and oracle, and no reply was told.

Charmides is Wilde's one narrative poem in this volume. He constructs a mythological story from a number of classical sources: to a name taken from Plato he attaches elements of the story of Hylas and of Tiresias, and mingles these with an anecdote of Charicles at the statue of Venus of Praxiteles, adapted from one of Lucian's *Dialogues*. The manner and mood are informed throughout with Keats's methods, though memories of Arnold intrude here as in other unexpected places in Wilde's work. Unfortunately the lavish sensuousness with which the poem is imbued is not always fully under his control. All the five long poems in this volume have the same six-line stanza, decasyllabic with alternate rhyme in the first four lines and concluding with a couplet, the second line of which is of fourteen syllables. Such were the main poems in the volume which leapt to popularity with the book-buying public in the early eighties. It is rather like a 'beautified' room in some overexpensive boarding-house with rococo decorations, classical statuary, and *objets d'art*, mingled in elaborate profusion but with little taste. Despite its poetic inequality, the volume allows us to see certain aspects of Wilde's personality. Throughout a curious combination of a pursuit of beauty mingled with a confession of sin: the *Dorian Gray* motive intruding into the poetry. Combined with this there is a dependence on Pater and Baudelaire. Though the influence of Baudelaire intrudes but fitfully, it is present both in thought and in direct borrowing, while the history of Wilde as a poet between 1881 and 1894 is the revelation of an increasing dependence on Baudelaire, and a consequent improvement in his work.

It would appear that with many poets but a small part of their thought can gain effective poetic expression. They think of many things, but they capture but few of them adequately into verse. Wilde's poetic interest narrowed after 1881, but the narrowing was an increased effectiveness within a hard, limited, grotesque world. He understood the more blatant elements in Baudelaire as he had understood the most obvious elements in Pater. He was captured by the pursuit of bizarre themes, outside nature, from which new sensations could be created, and so he came to write *The Harlot's House* and *The Sphinx*. *The Harlot's House* is the most original and beautiful poem that Wilde achieved. Decoration now achieves a purpose and the baroque rhymes (*grotesques, arabesques, automatons, skeletons, hand, saraband*), enforce the distorted impression which he wishes to convey:

> Sometimes a clockwork puppet pressed
> A phantom lover to her breast,
> Sometimes they seemed to try to sing.

In contrast to the early part of the poem the close has an air of fresh naturalness, the mood of some Elizabethan lyric:

> And down the long and silent street,
> The dawn, with silver-sandalled feet,
> Crept like a frightened girl.

It is true that the poem still retains memories from the works of others, but Wilde possesses an independence and consistency of mood that constructs the poem into a single poetic image. *The Sphinx* is a more elaborate poem. Wilde, adapting an incident from J. K. Huysmans's novel, *A Rebours*, imagines that while he is sitting in his room he sees in the corner 'a beautiful and shining Sphinx'. The poem resolves itself into a recollection of all the scenes that the Sphinx in its agelessness has known, and closes with the poet repelled by this object of intricate evil:

> Why are you tarrying? Get hence! I weary of your sullen ways,
> I weary of your steadfast gaze, your somnolent magnificence.

The metre of the poem has often been commended, and the subtle internal rhymes praised, but the metre is merely the *In Memoriam* stanza, written on the page as two long lines instead of four short ones. Wilde had used this metre in his earlier years in poems of self-exploration into which Tennyson's influence directly intruded. Now he employs it with an entirely contrasting effect in the poem which shows most fully the influence of Baudelaire upon his work. The structure of the poem allows him to display his talent for verbal mosaic; as he addresses the Sphinx and recalls the incidents of its history the verbal pageantry passes by. The poem derives from Baudelaire both in spirit and detail, though Wilde also knew Heine's lines, 'O schöne Sphinx'. Baudelaire in *Les Chats* had compared cats to the Sphinx:

> Ils prennent en songeant les nobles attitudes
> Des grands sphinx allongés au fond des solitudes.

Wilde reverses this process and compares his sphinx to 'a curious cat'. Similarly, Wilde's conclusion in which he condemns the Sphinx as a symbol of all that leads to evil is suggested in Baudelaire's lines on *Le Chat*:

> Et, des pieds jusques à la tête
> Un air subtil, un dangereux parfum,
> Nagent autour de son corps brun.

These obligations could be multiplied, but they do not rob the poem of its individuality, found in the theme itself and in the intricate exploration of its bizarre possibilities.

The other poems between 1881 and 1895 are but a few casual pieces. In the sonnet *On the Sale by Auction of Keats' Love Letters*, Wilde uses the sonnet in Miltonic manner for vigorous and sincere protest, while certain of the other pieces, such as *Pan* (*Double Villanelle*) and *Canzonet*, show an attraction to French forms. He was busy in this decade doing other things, and little of the talent and wit which he so abundantly displayed comes through in his poetry. His only other verse is contained in two plays: the fragment, which Sturge Moore completed, *A Florentine Tragedy*, and the play, partly in verse, *The Duchess of Padua*. Both pieces belong to the history of his development as a dramatist, and the verse in them cannot affect one's estimate of him as a poet.

On 25 May 1895 he was sentenced at the Old Bailey to two years' imprisonment with hard labour. On 19 May 1897 he was released, and crossed over to France. There, at Berneval, he completed a poem dealing with his prison life, which was published in 1898 as *The Ballad of Reading Gaol* by C.33. Wilde was only preserving a pseudo-anonymity by this use of his prison number, and in a third edition, also in 1898, the poem was signed by the author. His letters on prison reform and *De Profundis* show that two years in the cells had a deep influence upon him. To be snatched from a life of lavish extravagance and intricate indulgence to bare prison routine was bound to affect one who was ever conscious of his environment. Previously he had created his own atmosphere, elaborate and artificial: 'Oh! that I could live up to my blue china.' Now his atmosphere was created for him, and he responded by producing a poem which matched it. To some extent the *Ballad* is a *cri de cœur*, but mingled with this open sincerity lies a subtle readjustment to his setting of one who remained until the end a consummate actor. While Wilde was in prison a trooper in the Royal Horse Guards was executed for the murder of his wife. Wilde was profoundly moved, and the first draft of *The Ballad of Reading Gaol* was written to explore with stark realism the emotions aroused by this gruesome incident. Allied to this source in experience there was, as always in Wilde, a strong literary influence, and here he relied on a poem from A. E. Housman's *A Shropshire Lad*:

> On moonlit heath and lonesome bank
> The sheep beside me graze;
> And yon the gallows used to clank
> Fast by the four cross ways.

Further, Wilde adapted phrase, mood, and rhythm from *The Ancient Mariner*, though Coleridge's fantasy militated against the grim directness which the narrative demanded. Some of his stanzas are in close imitation of Coleridge:

> Dear Christ! the very prison walls
> Suddenly seemed to reel,

> And the sky above my head became
> Like a casque of scorching steel;
> And, though I was a soul in pain,
> My pain I could not feel.

Thus, with these literary influences, Wilde gradually imposed sophisticated episodes on the simple narrative structure with which the poem had originated. Similarly, there intrude into the elemental harshness of the poem memories of Wilde's pre-prison days. He employs a recollection of Coleridge's pageant of Life-in-Death, and decorates it with exotic rhymes, borrowed from his earlier work:

> About, about in ghostly rout
> They trod a saraband
> And the damned grotesques made arabesques,
> Like the wind upon the sand!
>
> With the pirouettes of marionettes,
> They tripped on pointed tread.

The *Ballad* will remain, in England at least, Wilde's most popular poem. It possesses a human appeal which will compensate in some eyes for its poetic defects. But Wilde, as he returned to those rhymes *saraband, grotesques, arabesques*, was making an unconscious estimate of his own work; there in those few, artificial, Baudelairean poems the thin flame of poetry had grown bright for a time with him.

The materials for any biographical note on Ernest Dowson (1867-1900) are still incomplete, though more is known after Mark Longaker's volume.[5] When he was young his family lived out of England and his early education was casual, though he acquired an intimate knowledge of French and Latin. He emerged as an interesting figure when he went up to Queen's College, Oxford, where he spent but a period of five terms and left without taking a degree. He came from Oxford to London in 1887. Thirteen years were left to him. Intermittently he worked with his father in his business and he chose no regular occupation and had no fixed income; he wandered from England to France and found in Paris some attraction that London lacked. He lived recklessly, careless of where he slept, or how he lived, and utterly improvident of his frail strength. With no settled income he existed precariously, translating a number of works from French, and doing journalism, unwillingly, when it came his way. He would seem to have brought into London the Bohemian life through which Verlaine lived and suffered, where everything about a poet is shabby except his poetry, which is exquisite. It was probably this cult of the French *quartier* that led him, and a number of young poets of this period, with Lionel Johnson and W. B. Yeats among them, to form *The Rhymers' Club*. Arthur Symons has described the gatherings, 'in an upper room of the "Cheshire Cheese", where long clay pipes lay in slim heaps on the wooden tables, between tankards of ale; and young poets, then very young, recited their own verses to one another with a desperate and ineffectual attempt to get into key with the Latin quarter'.[6] Mark Longaker describes the effect on him of his father's declining fortunes and of his mother's suicide, and of his love for Adelaide Foltinowicz, the daughter of a Polish Soho restaurant-keeper. She did not marry him, but remained the most consistent of his attachments. Some have thought her the inspiration of the 'Cynara' lyric, but for this there is very little evidence, and Horace and Propertius seem a more possible source. His conversion to Catholicism left its mark on his poetry, especially in lyrics such as 'Extreme Unction' and 'Nuns of the Perpetual Adoration'. He is alleged to have told Frank Harris, 'I am for the old faith. I've become a Catholic, as every artist must'.

Whatever may be written of Dowson's uncontrolled life, it must be admitted that he achieved a considerable amount of work. Most of it was in prose; apart from his translations, he wrote two novels in collaboration with Arthur Moore, *A Comedy of Masks* (1893) and *Adrian Rome* (1899), and a volume of shorter pieces, *Dilemmas* (1895). His verse, when it was collected by Arthur Symons in 1905, made only one slender volume.

He had published poems in periodicals, such as *Temple Bar*, the *Century Guild Hobby Horse*, and in *The Rhymers' Club's* books (1892 and 1894), before his *Verses* appeared in 1896. Many of his later poems were published in Arthur Symons's journal, the *Savoy* (1896), and a further pamphlet of verse, *Decorations*, followed in 1899. In 1897 he had issued *The Pierrot of the Minute, A Dramatic Phantasy, in One Act*.

Ernest Dowson is the poet symbolic of the eighteen-nineties; he is in verse what Beardsley was in pictorial art. His work is the logical conclusion of the aestheticism of Rossetti and Swinburne, and of the influence of the doctrine of *l'art pour l'art* of the later French romanticists. He removed from his poetry everything except his own narrow circle of sensations, and these, with the sickening sense of sin that lay behind them, he tortured himself to express with exquisite perfection. Even his sense of sin, except in a few places, seemed an artistic rather than a moral value, some self-mutilation necessary to make complete the presentation of his sensations. It was as if Dowson were fulfilling in his poetry the precepts of Walter Pater and recording moments of sensation to the utter exclusion of all moral and philosophical comment. Wilde, the bulk of whose verse belongs to the eighties, never achieved this with equal force, and despite his wide personal influence on the period he seldom approached Dowson's quality as a poet. Many of Dowson's companions in that decade shared his purposes temporarily, and then turned to achieve other things; so Arthur Symons, who developed in the twentieth century as a prose writer and a critic, and W. B. Yeats, who left the London of the nineties to found a new Irish national poetry. Even Lionel Johnson was governed by other loyalties, in which his classicism and his Irish attachments had a part. But Dowson in his brief life gathered into his own distress, and his own darkly beautiful lyrics, all that this final movement in English romanticism had to express.

His poetry arose from two well-defined literary origins, from the French decadents, Verlaine and Rimbaud more particularly, and from the cool, clear movement of Horatian verse. Already in the seventies a group of poets, using the examples of Théodore de Banville, had employed French forms in English verse, and Wilde in the early nineties had derived from Baudelaire his most successful lyrical themes. Dowson penetrated more deeply than any of these into the purposes of French poetry after Baudelaire. He exorcized from his verse all philosophical or social preoccupations, all narrative, with its suggestion of normal employments. The sensations which he analysed he regarded only for their potential poetic value. To this he allied an attraction for the motives which occur in Latin lyrical poetry, the brevity of life and the fading of things that once were beautiful:

> *Vitae summa brevis spem nos vetat inchoare longam*
> They are not long, the weeping and the laughter,
>   Love and desire and hate:
> I think they have no portion in us after
>   We pass the gate.

To the verse of Horace and Propertius he owed suggestions for some of his most imaginative poems, including *Non sum qualis eram bonae sub regno Cynarae*. The name of his mistress he derived from Horace,[7] but the situation in the poem arises from memories of Propertius's *Cynthia*, and some would think from his relations with Adelaide Foltinowicz.

His literary attachments led him naturally to emphasize style. His admiration for Flaubert had induced in him a self-torturing desire for *le mot juste*. Further, he possessed a love of words for their very shapes and appearance on the page, apart from their values of sound and association. This fastidiousness he may have gained from the French *symbolistes*, especially from Rimbaud. Arthur Symons records that Dowson once confessed 'that his ideal of a line of verse was the line of Poe':

> The viol, the violet and the vine,

and 'that the letter "v" was the most beautiful of the letters, and could not be brought into verse too often'. So Dowson opens his own poem, *A Coronal*:

> Violets and leaves of vine.

This sense for words and his attraction for the easily intelligible movement of Latin lyric verse preserved a simplicity in his vocabulary, clear and unalloyed. Guided by his classical reading, he was equally unafraid of the traditional words and phrases of poetry: 'roses', 'vines', 'passions', 'red mouths'; he gathered up these well-worn symbols and gave them the benison of his verse.

He possessed, further, an unusual prosodic skill, not only in the traditional forms, but in modifications and inventions. So the 'Cynara' poem added a new melody to English poetry:

>   Last night, ah, yesternight, betwixt her lips and mine
>   There fell thy shadow, Cynara! thy breath was shed
>   Upon my soul between the kisses and the wine;
>   And I was desolate and sick of an old passion,
>   Yea, I was desolate and bowed my head:
>   I have been faithful to thee, Cynara! in my fashion.

The basic line is the alexandrine, a line which Dowson particularly admired. He contrived to vary the stress and caesura, so that all the weariness which the line draws to itself in English is removed, and there is substituted a moving lyrical quality. Dowson's stanza cannot easily be imitated; the ear adjusting the licences that bring such variations has to be nicely attuned.

Prosodic success and the daring of the theme have given *Cynara* a pre-eminent place in Dowson's work, but many of the other lyrics have an equal mastery of form and theme. *Nuns of the Perpetual Adoration* is Dowson's most profound treatment of his central poetic motive. He knew that the 'world is wild and passionate' and that 'the roses of the world would fade', and he turned with sad admiration to view those whose asceticism allowed them to stand aside and made their nights and days 'Into a long, returning rosary':

>   Calm, sad, secure; behind high convent walls,
>   These watch the sacred lamp, these watch and pray:
>   And it is one with them when evening falls,
>   And one with them the cold return of day.

He employed here the quatrain verse which Dryden and Gray

had used, and infused it with new variety. He returned to the same theme in the *Carthusians*, though here he attempted the difficult task of using the alexandrine in a quatrain with alternate rhymes. He gathered again into this poem the conception that he was driven to seek a life of sensation, but that wherever he went the shadow of sin haunted him even to desolation:

> We fling up flowers and laugh, we laugh across the wine;
> With wine we dull our souls and careful strains of art;
> Our cups are polished skulls round which the roses twine:
> None dares to look at Death who leers and lurks apart.

Not all his poems have the poignancy and originality of his best work. He was in danger at times of imitating Swinburne's more facile rhythms, while an occasional triviality of theme marred some of his lyrics. He had excluded so much from poetry that his range of theme had to be narrow, but he possessed variety, as can be seen in contrasting the macabre *To One in Bedlam*, and the gentle elegy of *The Dead Child*; while his strength as a craftsman appeared in his confident control of the alexandrine in the epigram which opens:

> Because I am idolatrous and have besought.

Dowson's one essay in verse drama is the episode of *The Pierrot of the Minute*, which was published with effective decorations by Beardsley. The dialogue is conducted in the heroic couplet with lyrical interludes. It tells of Pierrot's love for the moon-maiden, and how she caressed him, and then, when he wearied, allowed him to sleep. Yet she left her charm upon him:

> Go forth and seek in each fair face in vain,
> To find the image of thy love again.
> All maids are kind to thee, yet never one
> Shall hold thy truant heart till day be done.

It is the dramatic expansion of the mood found in many of the lyrics, and owed a number of suggestions to Verlaine.

Dowson's poetry when it first appeared met with much harsh criticism: he was described as a disciple of Arthur Symons and a mere versifier in the Swinburnian manner. Verses which justify such stricture exist in his work, but there emerge also some few lyrics in which the dark, narrow beauty of the nineties gains its most adequate expression. Beardsley decorated his work and his pictorial scenes add emphasis to the poems, so that despite its narrow compass Dowson leaves an impression on the sense which is deep and permanent.

Lionel Pigot Johnson[8] (1867-1902) was an associate of the poets who created the 'nineties' poetry; with Dowson he was a member of *The Rhymers' Club*, and his early verses appeared in their *Books*; with Wilde he felt the influence of Pater, and with Yeats he shared in the Irish literary revival. His poetry, however, and the dominant enthusiasms of his mind remain apart from contemporary contacts; the influences which affect him are as wide and as old as Christendom.

He was born at Broadstairs of a military family; his father was a soldier and his grandfather was General Sir Henry Johnson. He was educated at Winchester and at New College, Oxford. Some of his Winchester letters have been printed and show an unusual range of thought and allusion, emerging from a mind that is curious, sensitive and earnest. Along with passages of religious discussion can be found paragraphs marked by the aestheticism of the close of the century: 'I do not love sensuality: I do not hate it; I do not love purity: I do not hate it; I regard both as artistic aspects of life.' Such a passage may have influenced his life, but his poetry is far removed from the schools with which such thought is associated. Johnson's capacities as a critic were already apparent at Winchester, while his Winchester Prize poem, the blank-verse piece, *Sir Walter Raleigh in The Tower*, was published in 1885. At Oxford he achieved scholastic success, and established himself as a prose writer. In 1890, burdened with Oxford debts, he came to London to make a living in literature. He turned to prose, ever the more lucrative medium, and apart from journalism and reviews, which included in 1891 an early and acute article on Robert Bridges, he published *The Art of Thomas Hardy* (1894), a critical study of much insight. A selection of his critical essays was issued in 1911 as *Post Liminium*, and a further collection, in 1921, as *Reviews and Critical Papers*. In the best of his prose work he combined the sympathetic approach of Pater with that regard for principles and for sanity which marked his attachments to Samuel Johnson.

In 1891 he entered the Roman Catholic Church. Love of tradition, present in his poetry and in his prose style, had drawn him, since his Winchester days, towards the Church whose history went back to the earliest days of Christianity. His poetry was published in two volumes, *Poems* (1895) and *Ireland with other Poems* (1897); a collection of the poems appeared in 1915. His Irish interests had shown themselves in an edition of James Clarence Mangan's prose writings, and in contacts with the Irish Literary Association. He claimed Irish nationality, but apart from his grandfather's military operations in Ireland, his contacts appear to have been of his own invention. He had had an 'arid home life, a lonely school life'; in London he found himself in the easy company of writers, who regarded moral conventions as a hindrance, and who drank almost as a literary discipline. Enough is known to see that Johnson, despite the restraint of his work and his mental asceticism, accepted these licences: 'I do not love sensuality: I do not hate it.' Running counter to all the best qualities of his prose and verse, he possessed inclinations towards indulgence. The final tragedy occurred in September 1902: he fell in Fleet Street, and died a few days later without recovering consciousness. A sense of pathos clings around Lionel Johnson's life, strengthened by the elegiac vein of his poetry and by his own consciousness of fate's irony. The lines from Walt Whitman which preface his Winchester Prize poem seem to symbolize his life to the end:

> I do not know what you are for, (I do not know what I am
>   for myself, nor what anything is for),
> But I will search carefully for it even in being foiled,
> In defeat, poverty, imprisonment – for they too are great.
> Did we think victory great?

> So it is – but now it seems to me, when it cannot be helped,
>   that defeat is great,
> And that death and dismay are great.

Johnson's most enduring work is contained in his first volume, *Poems* (1895). He was already freeing himself from the temptations of contemporary patterns into a grave yet superb verse, classical in its effects and in its husbanding of resources. So in *By the Statue of King Charles at Charing Cross*,

> Comely and calm, he rides
> Hard by his own Whitehall:
> Only the night wind glides:
> No crowds, nor rebels, brawl.
> Gone, too, his Court: and yet,
> The stars his courtiers are:
> Stars in their stations set;
> And every wandering star.

This verse has the unerring rightness which A. E. Housman also commanded and the power of drawing illimitable suggestion from the short lines of a brief lyric. A universal experience stands revealed, fresh in the glamour of a new recognition of its truth. The same restraint, combined with security of effect, is found in *Mystic and Cavalier*, where he explored a more subjective mood:

> Go from me: I am one of those, who fall.
> What! hath no cold wind swept your heart at all,
> In my sad company? Before the end,
>   Go from me, dear my friend!

The same volume had such admirable though less well-known pieces as *A Burden of Easter Vigil, In England, The Roman Stage, The Dark Angel* and *Lines to a Lady Upon her Third Birthday*. Johnson, already in this first volume, showed an enthusiasm for Celtic themes, strengthened by his walking tours in Cornwall and Wales; in his sonnet on *Wales* he speaks of the 'Voices of Celtic singers and of Celtic Saints'. A number of political and personal associations led him to transfer the centre of this Celtic attachment to Ireland, and this was confirmed by his visit there in 1891, and by his adoption of Catholicism in the same year. Already in the volume of 1895 Irish interests are found in such poems as *Parnell, Celtic Speech, Ways of War*. Into *Ireland* (1897), his second volume, the Irish element entered more liberally. Some of the poems in this volume are early pieces, such as *Julian at Eleusis*, a blank-verse dramatic monologue on Julian the Apostate. The title-poem itself is an elaborate ode in regular stanzas incorporating the story of Ireland's woe. His creative impulses, apparent in the earlier volume, seem somehow cramped by this increased preoccupation with Ireland and Catholicism. At times, however, he recovered that eloquent brevity of epithet which marked his most secure work. This strength can be seen in the magnificent conclusion to *Cromwell*, which opens as a satire in the ode form:

> Nay, peace for ever more!
> O martyred souls! He comes,
> Your conquered conqueror:
> No tramplings now, nor drums,
> Are his, who wrought your martyrdoms.
>
> Tragic, triumphant form,
> He comes to your dim ways,
> Comes upon wings of storm:
> Greet him, with pardoning praise,
> With marvelling awe, with equal gaze!

These enthusiasms were genuine, but as with Swinburne's attachment for Italy they were not poetically fortunate: Ireland gained predominance over his mind without yielding adequate experience to his poetry. At the same time he eradicated from the second volume the few traces present in his work of the love poetry of the school of Wilde and Dowson. In 1895 it had entered into such poems as *A Dream of Youth* and *The Precept of Silence*:

> I know you: solitary griefs,
> Desolate passions, aching hours!
> I know you: tremulous beliefs,
> Agonized hopes, and ashen flowers!

Johnson, in his most distinctive verse, is a literary poet whose work, like that of Gray, cannot be appreciated without a conscious interest in style and a knowledge of preceding traditions. He frequently writes, as did poets in the eighteenth century, a poetical commentary in verse, as in *Oxford Nights* or in *Winchester*:

> here came Keats,
> Chaunting of autumnal sweets;
> Through this city of old haunts,
> Murmuring immortal chaunts;
> As when Pope, art's earlier king,
> Here, a child, did nought but sing.

Nature, words, mood, experience are for him a heritage shared with other poets and remembered through his memory of them, and so in *Laleham* he writes:

> Go past the cottage flowers, and see,
> Where Arnold held it good to be.

His allegiance was to classicism and to tradition; the poets that influenced him, apart from Latin and Greek writers, were Milton and Gray and Arnold, and less directly the eighteenth-century couplet writers. He was never crudely derivative; his vocabulary had an economy which could never have been gained in imitating Milton or Gray. Yet his impersonal approach, his calm themes, the elimination of personal and perfervid elements showed the ultimate origin of his attachment. So in the last decade of the nineteenth century Johnson revived in *Winchester* the music of *L'Allegro*:

> To the fairest!
> Then to thee
> Consecreate and bounden be,
> Winchester! this verse of mine;

and when, as in *Plato in London*, he allowed a personal reflection to intrude it was with the same calm gravity as Arnold had employed in *Dover Beach*, though without Arnold's persistent questioning,

> Lean from the window to the air:
> Hear London's voice upon the night!
> Thou hast bold converse with things rare:
> Look now upon another sight!
> The calm stars, in their living skies:
>   And then, these surging cries,
>   This restless glare!

Arnold's influence extended further upon his thought than that of any other poet; in *In Falmouth Harbour*, and in poems of elegiac mood, he expressed that world-weariness which had been Arnold's central poetic mood.

The diction of his best poetry remains, distinct from these derivatives and removed from his own decade. He established a poetical rhetoric, economical of phrase, simple in vocabulary, but compelling by the justness with which its elements have been collected. It can be seen most successfully in *By the Statue of King Charles at Charing Cross*, where the six-syllable lines are so compact that they have the strength of a longer-lined stanza. Similarly he refined his poetic vocabulary until his lyrics have that same elimination of the unnecessary which is found in Jonson and Marvell; so in *Trentals* he wrote a lyric where the effect is gained by brief unerring rightness of phrase:

> Gray, without, the autumn air:
> But pale candles here prepare,
> Pale as wasted golden hair.
> Let the quire with mourning descant
> Cry: *In pace requiescant!*
> For they loved the things of God.
> Now, where solemn feet have trod,
> Sleep they well: and wait the end,
> Lover by lover, friend by friend.

Johnson's poetical independence can best be seen in viewing his work amid that of his contemporaries. The infectious melodies of Swinburne rarely intruded into his verse; the Pre-Raphaelites were seldom re-echoed; the coloured effects of romanticism were laid aside. The French influences which affected Wilde and Dowson were not dominant, though he wrote an alexandrine sonnet on *Our Lady of France*, and dedicated it to Dowson, and in the 1897 volume he had a number of sonnets in alexandrines. He was adventurous within his own methods; six-line stanzas, octosyllabics, blank verse, the ode, macaronics, and stanzaic and irregular forms are all found. His calm, clean verse retained its freshness after much of contemporary ornateness had been dulled. He might have done more, and there lay the element of pathos in his life, but some of his lyrics have an unquestioned perfection, a certainty of intention and achievement.

The major writers whose production fell into the decade 1890-1900 have been considered above; many who then practised verse, such as W. B. Yeats, made their main contribution in the twentieth century, and a detailed estimate of their work has been excluded from this volume. Here an attempt is made to outline briefly some of the varied activities of this *fin de siècle* to which criticism has given an unusual glamour,[9] as if believing that it bore some symbolical relationship to the whole of the preceding century. The eighteen-nineties certainly remain one of the most compact movements of modern times, but poetry had only a limited share in its significance. Max Beerbohm spoke truthfully when he jested that he belonged 'to the Beardsley period', for the final impression from this decade rested not in the new poetry or in the new journalism, but in the pictorial art of this genius who died when he was 26. Aubrey Beardsley (1872-1898), working under the influence of Japanese art, drew the human form in a way that possessed indefinable suggestions of furtiveness and sin. Nature and homely human occupations were banished from a world of elegant artifice, maliciously conveyed; the life of Pope's *The Rape of the Lock* etched out satirically with Hogarthian severity. 'He never walked', wrote Arthur Symons of Beardsley, 'and I never saw him look at the sea'; he withdrew to places where he could watch cynical or passion-wasted faces made ashen in a gleam of dead white. Beardsley once wrote of Pope's satire on Sporus: 'The very sound of words scarifies before the sense strikes.' So it is with Beardsley's drawings: however varied the legend which they individually convey, they assault the imagination persistently with their elegant brutalities. The most lasting impression left of the eighteen-nineties is in the drawings in the *Yellow Book* and the *Savoy* and in the illustrations to *Salomé*.

Beardsley's drawings served further to draw general public attention upon art and the work of the artist in England. Whistler had commenced that good work in 1878 with his lawsuit against Ruskin, for describing him as 'a coxcomb' who asked 'two hundred guineas for flinging a pot of paint in the public face'. Whistler had continued the same defiance of the compact majority with his lecture *Ten o'Clock* (1888): 'Art and Joy go together, with bold openness and high head, and ready hand – fearing naught, and dreading no exposure.' Beardsley, sometimes half-jestingly, challenged the public with this independence of the artist, and the resulting conflict was one of the most important results of the decade. A public occupied with commerce, and the rapid construction of unlovely things, was forced to recognize the presence of artists, antagonistic to all that standardized civilization and the dull habitual round of modern life which it represents. *The Times* expressed the anger of many minds when it described Beardsley's work as 'a combination of English rowdyism and French lubricity'. This onslaught on the public taste was not an attempt to convert anyone; rather, the artist thus revenged himself on a society that was rapidly making life impossible for him. The artist knew that he was in a minority; so Whistler had dedicated *The Gentle Art of Making Enemies* (1890), 'To the rare Few who early in Life have rid themselves of the Friendship of the many'. Beardsley aroused antagonism by his work alone; Wilde exploited his own personality, and this not without vulgarity, to bring upon himself the scorn and anger of the multitude. Wilde's trial in 1895 remains a symbolical event in that decade; it was society complacently asserting that it had been right all the time about the meretriciousness of art and its purveyors.

It is difficult to relate the poetry of this decade to this larger movement which extended far outside poetry into the complexities of morality and taste. The clearest element lay in the adhesion of certain writers to French models, to Baudelaire and Verlaine in particular, from whom they gained a desire to break with conventional values, to seek themes from pleasures which the virtuous forbade, and to inflict agonies upon themselves to achieve perfection of form. Ernest Dowson, whose work has already been considered, is as symbolical a figure as Beardsley was in pictorial art. Swinburne had already been subject to similar influences, but he had other and wider contacts than the poets of the nineties would allow, enthusiasm for medieval legend, for Elizabethan drama, apart from tense if theatrical political partisanship. For Dowson, and the other poets of his tradition, all must be excluded except the record of a few deeply moving moments of passion or sadness, or emotional exaltation or distress. These must be conveyed for their own sake only with exquisite brevity. They had encountered this conception not only in the study of French models but in the critical work of Walter Pater, and their adherence to these self-imposed limitations separated them from earlier English romanticism and from Pre-Raphaelite verse. Pater in his essays on the Pre-Raphaelites, and above all in his *Conclusion* to *Studies in the Renaissance*, had given a double suggestion which was never long absent in the verse of this group. First there accompanied life an inevitable mortality, the 'undefinable taint of death' was upon all things; and secondly, out of life may be seized some few moments of deep passion or high intellectual endeavour. It is true that the nineties poets emphasized the passion rather than the intellect, and there was some justification for the bias in Pater: 'While all melts under our feet, we may well grasp at any exquisite passion, or any contribution to knowledge that seems by a lifted horizon to set the spirit free for a moment, or any stirring of the senses, strange dyes, strange colours, and curious odours, or work of the artist's hands, or the face of one's friend. Not to discriminate every moment some passionate attitude in those about us, and in the very brilliancy of their gifts some tragic dividing of forces on their ways, is, on this short day of frost and sun, to sleep before evening.'

Apart from Ernest Dowson the most consistent follower of the movement was Arthur Symons[10] (1865-1945). As a critical writer of distinction, and working under Pater's influence, he had explored in *The Symbolist Movement in Literature* (1899), a study later to influence T. S. Eliot, the French writers whom his contemporaries in the nineties had so much admired. He became the biographer of both Beardsley (1898) and Dowson (1905). His own early verse included *Days and Nights* (1889); *Silhouettes* (1892); *London Nights* (1894); *Amoris Victima* (1897); *Images of Good and Evil* (1902). Nine volumes of *The Collected Works* were published in 1924, but the series was not continued. Of his personality more is known since the publication of Roger Lhombreaud's sympathetic biography in 1963. Though he lived to old age he suffered a period of almost complete mental breakdown. What he endured can be seen by comparing an early portrait with that painted by Augustus John in 1917. He recovered, partially at least, by 1910, and wrote *Confessions*, some time before 1917. These were published in a limited edition in New York, and many of them appeared in Desmond McCarthy's *Life and Letters* of March 1930. Though he came back thus to writing, his mind remained in the past. He had been brought up in a family of rigorous Methodist background, and at first a strong moral influence appeared in his criticism, as when he wrote that there were passages in *Venus and Adonis* which 'we cannot excuse: we can but regret them'. The break came in his life when he lost his faith and sought emancipation and independence. Though this change was not violent, it must have had a profound influence on him. His education was irregular, but he made himself an accomplished linguist and a scholar of distinction. Lhombreaud notes that much of his early life was spent either in small towns or the country, and that as a result 'he fell passionately in love with the great city and the London crowds'. One of the sustaining influences of his difficult years was a friendship with Havelock Ellis, whom he had first met when Ellis was editor of the *Mermaid Series*. John Betjeman, who saw him a few years before his death, wrote a poem in the autograph book of the Manager of the Café Royal which gives a brilliant image of him as an old man:

> I saw him in the Café Royal
> Very old and very grand.

It is as a critic that he will probably be best remembered. In verse he never had Dowson's unfaltering perfection, where the image burns clearly and steadily. He represented effectively themes which were unusual in English poetry. He introduced all the nineties paraphernalia of music-hall, ballet, warm elegant interiors, and furtive amorous shabbiness, with never a glimpse of a tree or natural light of sun; and all the puppets, pierrettes, borrowed loves, and ballet-girls like those in Beardsley's drawings move in and out of his poems. It would be unfair to Symons's achievement to suggest that all his verse was of that type; nature returned later, and there are the tragedies; but his most pungent verse remained in those lyrics of the nineties. Apart from his original poems, he made in the same years a number of verse translations, and those from French poetry, Gautier, Mallarmé, Verlaine, show a sensitiveness beyond that which is found sometimes in his original work.

No poet follows as closely as do Dowson and Symons in this central nineties tradition. John Davidson, as has been noted above, though a few of his lyrics conform to the tradition, soon abandoned it in a lonely and strenuous effort to define his own faith. Herbert Trench (1865-1921), a poet whose work has never gained adequate recognition, did not begin until 1901 with *Deirdre Wedded*, and one has to wait until 1907 for *New Poems* and the excellent allegory of *Apollo and the Seaman*. Trench's work lies outside the century chronologically, and his contacts with philosophy and mysticism remove him from the nineties tradition. Lionel Johnson, who shared with Dowson a never-appeased desire for perfect form, had sympathies and loyalties far different from those of the nineties poets. Similarly W. B.

Yeats, though he began as an associate of Dowson in *The Rhymers' Club*, arose, as has been noted, out of the world of the nineties to go to Ireland and attempt to build a poetic and dramatic literature for that nation. Thus also, Laurence Binyon, very little of whose work appeared in the old century, had far wider contacts with earlier traditions, both Pre-Raphaelite and classical, than the formula of the nineties would allow. Norman Gale, who began a long career in poetry with *A Country Muse* (1892), though his work issued from John Lane, the publishers of the *Yellow Book*, had a gentle bucolic talent, which is the denial of the Beardsley mode. Richard le Gallienne, a figure popular among his contemporaries, may be better remembered as a chronicler of this decade than as a poet; his *Retrospective Reviews* (1896) have some interesting judgements on contemporary poets, and these have been supplemented by later chronicles. The quality of nineties verse can be discovered much more distinctly in the work of John Gray, *Silverpoints* (1893) and *Spiritual Poems* (1869). The second volume contains mainly translations of religious verse, but *Silverpoints* has the authentic nineties quality in its short lyrics and translations; in both he seemed to be a Dowson whose technical education was not yet complete. Theodore Wratislaw, in *Love's Memorial* (1892) and *Caprices* (1893), showed influences derived from Baudelaire and Arthur Symons; while Richard Middleton represented a link between the nineties and the poetry of the twentieth century. Yet when the verse produced in the decade 1890-1900 has been passed under review, it is surprising how little of it belongs to this Beardsley tradition. Even Wilde wrote frequently in other manners, and his actual production in the nineties is limited to a few poems. Beardsley himself, had he continued to exercise the discipline of words, might have become Dowson's most proper companion in poetry. His verse collected in *Under the Hill* (1904) consists of three poems – which seem the verbal counterpart of his drawings. The actual production of this *fin de siècle* school was small, though its influence on contemporary taste and the development of poetry in the twentieth century was considerable.

The poetical significance of the poetry produced in the nineties can, however, in no way be confined to the Beardsley school. It is full of fresh works in other traditions, and among the poets who stand apart while sharing some of the motives is A. E. Housman, many of whose lyrics were written in 1895, the year of Wilde's trial.

Rudyard Kipling

Rudyard Kipling[1] (1865-1936) was a poet, a short-story writer, and, less successfully, a novelist. Few writers succeed with equal originality in verse and prose, but this Kipling did in his short stories and ballads; both seem the product of a genius that is altogether his own. The degree of his success was phenomenal, for from the late nineties until 1910 he was, probably, the most widely read English author. From the period of the First World War a number of influences entered to affect his reputation, and his vigorous notion of patriotism and his genuine acceptance of imperialism were in disrepute. Still the record of republication shows how large and constant was the circle of his readers, and among critics Somerset Maugham has spoken well of his prose and T. S. Eliot of his verse.[1] His verse is best studied in the *Definitive Edition* (1940) and the extent of his activity as a poet is shown by the fact that this volume contains over eight hundred pages. The only drawback to this edition is the puzzling placing of many of the poems outside their chronological order. The *Definitive Edition* includes many poems that do not appear in the separate volumes: for Kipling placed poems in his books of short stories and there appear other pieces not previously collected.

Kipling is a figure different from anyone else, different indeed from the legend, and oddly unaccountable. When he was born in 1865 his father, John Lockwood Kipling, to whom he was deeply attached, was Professor of Architectural Sculpture at

Bombay. He was a man of great intelligence and an author himself in *Man and Beast in India*. Kipling's mother, Alice Macdonald, came of a remarkable family. She was one of five daughters of a Wesleyan minister: one of them married Sir Edward Burne-Jones, another Sir Edward Poynter, and a third Alfred Baldwin, who was the father of the Prime Minister, Lord Baldwin of Bewdley. It was Burne-Jones and the Pre-Raphaelite influence that had the most vivid effect on Kipling and he had recollections of meeting William Morris when he was a child.

Kipling's earliest memories were of Bombay; the 'gaily dressed Parsees wading out to worship the sun', and the 'menacing darkness of tropical eventide'. Here he first saw the vision of the India which is so brilliantly described in *Kim*, the vision of a child. When at the age of 3 he accompanied his parents on a visit to England his impression was of 'a dark land and a darker room full of cold, in one wall of which a white woman made a naked fire'. He cried out in dread, for he had not seen such a thing before. England was always to some extent an alien country against which in later years he protected himself with the fantasy of the Sussex mythology. When he was 5 he returned to England with his sister and, away from the warm and compact devotion of his family, he was placed in Southsea from his sixth to his eleventh year. It may well be that these were the most important years of his life, that here he came to understand cruelty and violence and to realize that the only weapon against these was stoicism. Because of the absence of affection he came to treasure the family circle whether in the form of parents or a wife. As a very small boy he had known all the warmth of a close and united family and the variegated colour of the Indian scene: then all this suddenly had been removed.

As a lonely boy of 12 Kipling entered the United Services College, a school about which he was later to speak in an admiring way as the 'school before its time', but the scarifying portraits and anecdotes which he presents in *Stalky & Co.*, particularly in the character of Beetle, give his own revelation of these years. In 1882 he returned to India, to Lahore, where his father was Curator of the Museum, and the years of isolation and misery were over. But something had happened deeply within his personality, some wound from which he was never to recover. England had led him to insecurity, frustration, and fear. Now he was back again with his family in the Indian scenes of his early childhood. In Lahore he became for five years assistant editor of the *Civil and Military Gazette*, and then for two years he was on the staff of the *Pioneer* at Allahabad. For seven years he worked with a desperate fierceness, and found with what facility he could write short stories, verses, and essays. The contrast of a hated and imprisoned life in school to the emancipation to full manhood in Lahore encouraged his genius to expand. On his return to India 'the Hindu child who had lain dormant in England came to life'. But he was never to be like other people: his way of life and his experience were to be so different, and the nature of his imagination was to keep him as a man apart. In 1889, at the age of 24, he left India for the last time. He was already known as a writer; within a few years he was famous, and within a decade, still very young, he was the most widely read author in the English-speaking world.

Kipling's success left him a man of independent resources, and he must have been baffled by the suddenness with which fame had come. Yet his life continued to be strange and unpredictable; much of it is so odd and inconsequent that it lacks reality, and, as already noted, India, with which he was so closely linked in the popular imagination, filled only a few years of his adult life. There followed a strange and inconsequent period, his friendship with the New Englander, Wolcott Balestier, with whom he collaborated to write *The Naulahka, a Novel of East and West* (1892); his voyages to Australia and New Zealand, his sudden return on Wolcott's death and his marriage to Carrie, Wolcott's sister, who cherished and dominated him for the rest of his life; his happy years in Vermont, marred by a tempestuous quarrel with his brother-in-law Beatty. Then came more wanderings with long though intermittent residence in South Africa, where Cecil Rhodes had given him a house, and finally to 'Bateman's' in

Sussex, and to the 'mythological' England that protected him from realities.

In the cool-weather season of 1886-1887 Kipling, only just 21, wrote the poems and short stories which were first to make him famous. A selection of the stories were to appear later as *Plain Tales from the Hills* (1888). The verses, topical and satirical of the social life of the English in India, appeared first as *Departmental Ditties* (1886), an Indian edition by Thacker Spink & Co. He had no illusions about the value of most of these pieces, which were first condescendingly reviewed in England. They were mainly clever reflections on the social life and vanities of the English in India, particularly at Simla. Many of them were written for English newspapers in India and they possess what Eliot describes as 'the precocious knowingness about the more superficial level of human weakness that is both effective and irritating in some of his early stories of India'. But already the ballad manner, and the Biblical directness were coming through as in 'The Story of Uriah' or 'The Grave of the Hundred Dead'. The theme of the galley ship haunted his imagination and he used it in 'The Galley-Slave' to express his farewell to India. It was to recur in his writings, and in one of the most brilliant of his short stories, 'The Finest Story in the World', he employs it in a passage of rhythmical prose as imaginative as anything he ever wrote: 'It was the kind (of ship) rowed with oars, and the sea spurts through the oar-holes and the men row sitting up to their knees in water.'

London first became aware of Kipling with a poem in the December number of *Macmillan's Magazine* for 1899:

> Oh, East is East, and West is West, and never
> the twain shall meet,
> Till Earth and Sky stand presently at God's great
> Judgment Seat.

1899 was the year of his great success with over eighty short stories, but it was Henley in the *Scots Observer* who confirmed his reputation as a poet. He continued publishing poems in periodicals. On 22 February 1890 'Danny Deever' appeared and the effect on the literary world was electric. 'Tommy' appeared on 1 March; 'Fuzzy-Wuzzy' on 15 March; 'Loot' on 29 March; 'The Widow at Windsor' on 26 April; 'Gunga Din' on 7 June; and 'Mandalay', most admired of all, on 22 June. A genius was acclaimed and Kipling was famous. Wilde might describe him as a 'man of talent who drops his aspirates' and there might be those later who would accept this view, but for the moment all was praise, as if the audience had been stunned by this new voice. He withheld the poems from volume publication until 1892, when they appeared as *Barrack-Room Ballads*: the book was reprinted three times in that year and fifty times in the next thirty years, becoming the most popular book of verse in the world for more than a generation[2]. The poems showed a much-deepened vision, though the volume has often been misunderstood. The soldier of the Queen is the major theme, the often despised 'Tommy Atkins':

> I have tried for to explain
> Both your pleasure and your pain,
> And, Thomas, here's my best respects to you!

'Danny Deever', with which the volume opens, is a ballad of authenticity, compassion, and high imagination ('The Regiment's in 'ollow square . . . they're hangin' him to-day'); Kipling is desirous of making the public sympathize with and understand the ordinary private soldier. So 'Loot' was no commendation of 'the thing to make the boys git up an' shoot', but an attempt to see it all from the fighting private's point of view. There was not present here the imperialism for which he was later condemned. Rather it was an appreciation of those who have toiled in strange ways and are neglected. The introductory poem illustrates the general theme:

> Beyond the path of the outmost sun through utter
>   darkness hurled –
> Farther than ever comet flared or vagrant star-dust
>   swirled –
> Live such as fought and sailed and ruled and loved and made
>   our world.

Achievement was the main theme, though national pride has its place, particularly in one of the more ambitious poems in the volume 'The English Flag' ('And what should they know of England who only England know?'). Here was his emotional definition of his isolation from the England that had tormented him in his childhood and his home-living countrymen who had no conception of what he regarded as the destiny of the Empire. There was a recognition of vast responsibilities which those contemptuously described as 'the poor little street-bred people' are not likely to understand.

In his early days in India Kipling had turned out his topical newspaper verses because he needed the cash. Now his prose commanded such handsome prices that he could turn to verse only when the mood pleased him. *The Seven Seas* appeared in 1896 after he had finished the second of his *Jungle Books* ('that ends up Mowgli and there is not going to be any more of him'). The final volume of poems was *The Five Nations* (1903), which contained among other pieces the South African poems. Though it had very large sales, it did not reach the same enormous circulation as the earlier volumes: 1903 was not the best of years for poems on the South African War. Already in 1901 *Kim* had appeared, possibly the greatest of his prose works and one of his most popular, which showed India through the eyes of a child. *The Five Nations*, which contains many of his best poems, appeared in 1903, to be followed by *The Years Between* (1919) and supplemented with the pieces that appear in the *Definitive Edition*.

If genius is ability of the highest order whose origins cannot be related to previous experience or intellectual study, then Kipling had this unpredictable quality in a high degree. Where, to take a single instance, did he acquire the literary counterpart of the language of a cockney and a private soldier? How did he come to write ballads, often composed to actual tunes, subtle in their literary composition, however deceptively easy at first sight, which were read in barrack-rooms, and sung in privates' messes, as well as being appreciated, until politics confounded the issue, in literary circles.

What is often forgotten when his legend is rehearsed is that he spent so few years in India and all before he was 24, and that he had, as *Kim* shows, such a genuine love for the country and its people. It is often assumed that the theme of 'The White Man's Burden' came out of his contact with India, but this is not so. It was in South Africa that he first fully felt the call of imperialism and it was Cecil Rhodes who gave definition to this consciousness. He developed a special relationship with *The Times* under the editorship of Moberly Bell and used it as a special platform for his poetical messages to the nation. 'The Native-Born' was the first to appear in 1895, an appeal from those born overseas for a little understanding from the home-born Englishmen. The special quality of these *Times* poems was indicated by the fact that Kipling took no payment for them, and during the next forty years some twenty of them were given to *The Times*, including 'Our Lady of the Snows', 'Recessional', and 'The White Man's Burden'. This last, sometimes falsely identified with Kipling's Indian period, was written in 1899 and addressed to the American people during the Spanish American War, when Kipling pleaded that the United States had a civilizing function to perform in the Philippine Islands.

Charles Carrington in his biography gives a well-reasoned account of what in general Kipling meant by 'The White Man's Burden'. He wrote, Carrington suggests, 'in contemporary colloquial language, the language of the streets. In the eighteen-nineties the phrase "a white man" did not only mean a man with an unpigmented skin, it had a secondary symbolic meaning: a man with the moral standards of the civilized world.' He notes the cockney private's comment in 'Gunga Din':

> An' for all 'is dirty 'ide
> 'E was white, clear white, inside.

Carrington further comments that 'no one will assert that Rhodes and Kipling and Theodore Roosevelt believed in the political equality of all men, regardless of their social status, as it is asserted today; they would have contemptuously rejected any such notion. It is equally unjust to suppose that they believed in the absolute superiority of certain racial types. They lived in a world in which the British and the Americans were immeasurably the most progressive of nations; in which their standards of conduct prevailed wherever civilization spread; in which they were in fact spreading those standards over the world.'

Kipling's verse is far more subtle than at first it seems. One might think that it derived from the happy intuition of some untutored poet, and Eliot admits that he at first underestimated Kipling's skill as something simple until he came to the *Sestina of the Tramp Royal*, 1896. Influences there must have been, something from the Pre-Raphaelite influences of his childhood and from Swinburne. Browning's monologues taught him something of the dramatic monologue in poetry, though his dramatic ballads are less complicated than Browning's poems. But all this is little compared with the originality of his genius: as his life is not like that of other men, neither is his poetry. He fits into no tradition of nineteenth-century verse. Eliot, obviously puzzled by Kipling's verse, has said some of the wisest things about him. He comments that while some poets have to be defended from obscurity, Kipling must be protected 'against the charge of excessive lucidity'. In his analysis of Kipling's verse Eliot confesses that the ordinary instruments of criticism do not seem to work, nor does he find introspection into his own processes of any assistance: 'part of the fascination of this subject is the exploration of a mind so different from one's own'. Eliot then adds a most revealing passage on Kipling's verse: 'An immense gift for using words, an amazing curiosity and power of observation with his mind and with all his senses, the mask of the entertainer, and beyond that a queer gift of second sight, of transmitting messages from elsewhere, a gift so disconcerting when we are made aware of it that thenceforth we are never sure when it is *not* present: all this makes Kipling a writer impossible wholly to understand and quite impossible to belittle.'

Alfred Edward Housman

A. E. Housman[1] (1859-1936) holds an individual place in the later years of the century and in the beginning of the twentieth century. He was a classical scholar of the rarest distinction, to rank with Scaliger and Bentley, a critic and a lyrical poet of individual quality. Further, as a personality, he made a profound impression on those who knew him best. As a poet some critics have assailed him, yet his verse at its best has undeniable excellence, and he has remained widely known not only to readers of poetry but to those who have heard his lyrics sung to musical accompaniment. He was born in Fockbury, Worcestershire, and he and his brothers went to Bromsgrove School. His childhood spent in the country was happy until his mother's death when he was 12, and some have thought that this was one of the most important events in his life. Poetry and the countryside mingled in his childhood, as in the life of his brother, Laurence Housman. At St John's College, Oxford, his distinction in 1879 in Classical Moderations led to the possibility that he might become a university classical scholar of accepted reputation, but two years later he failed in 'Greats'. His disappointment with Oxford was profound. It is alleged that Jowett, the great Master of Balliol, uttered a false quantity in his lectures and that Housman never returned. George L. Watson in *A. E. Housman, A Divided Life,* in a cogently argued but unproven thesis, suggests that his passionate and lifelong friendship for a fellow undergraduate at St John's, M. J. Jackson, evidently inspired some of his most deeply felt poems, and the emotional disturbance of that friendship accounted not only for the poetry but for his academic failure.

As a result of his failure at Oxford he had to accept in 1882 a position in the Patent Office, but publications on classical themes drew the attention of members of University College, London, and in 1892 he was nominated as Professor of Latin. For the next nineteen years he worked at University College, London, in Gower Street. These were the happiest and most creative years of his complex life. He came among a distinguished group of colleagues: R. W. Chambers, W. P. Ker, F. W. Oliver, Karl Pearson, J. A. Platt, Sir William Ramsay, E. H. Starling. Without exception they found him friendly, even on occasions affable, though with much of the malicious and sardonic wit common, especially at that period, in academic circles. In 1911 he left London for a Professorship of Latin and a Fellowship at Trinity College, Cambridge, for 'an asylum in all senses of the term', but his main creative period was in his years in Gower Street. Throughout all this time, whether in London or in Cambridge, his main energies were absorbed by classical scholarship of an unrelenting severity. This is what separates him from other English poets, with the partial exception of Gray. Classical scholarship dominated his mind in an obsessive manner. His first paper on Manilius, the difficult astronomer poet of the age of Tiberius, appeared in 1899, and later, between 1903 and 1930, that adventurous publisher Grant Richards, who cared little for Manilius but a great deal for Housman personally and for his poetry, issued an edition by Housman of Manilius's *Astronomica*. There have been few readers for the text, but many have been amazed by the merciless treatment in the preface of all editorial rivals. Housman published other editions of classical works, *Juvenal* (1906) and *Lucan* (1926). O. L. Richmond comments that scholars have been astonished by the quantity of his published work: 'a list of his publications had one hundred and eighteen items on Latin subjects, over forty on Greek and five on

English'.[2] It could be argued that he avoided as an editor authors where his great sensibility would be engaged, yet a fellow scholar, Otto Skutsch, has spoken of the distinctive quality of his work: 'Almost every word that Housman wrote, however coolly controlled by the brain, vibrates with the peculiar passion which the passion of truth aroused in him.'[3] The reason why Housman chose Manilius was that he was himself an expert in classical astronomy and astrology. A. N. Marlow has indicated to me that 'there was no question of his avoiding the poets who engaged his great sensibility, and in any case an emotional reaction could not be sustained indefinitely in the labour of a critical edition of any poet however great'. A. N. Marlow, further, writes to me: 'Housman was drawn to Manilius by the special problems involved, and this is true of all his work. He had no fear of the great poets, but the problems raised by Aeschylus, for example, are insoluble, and whereas Virgil offers very few problems of textual criticism, Lucan and Juvenal abound in them.' 'Nor', he adds, 'do I find much evidence of shyness or embarrassment about his poetry. The refusal to take money for it (later relaxed) was through a deep-seated loathing of money and all the evils it brings (he expressed this feeling to Percy Withers) and was part of a deliberate pose, as was his attitude to the publication of his own prose. He was a Professor of Latin and all else was to be put firmly into a subordinate place.'

It was during the years of his Professorship at University College, London, that there appeared in 1896 the slim volume of lyrics *A Shropshire Lad*, which, despite reminiscences of Stevenson and Kipling, seemed detached from contemporary moods in poetry. Housman had to pay for the publication of *A Shropshire Lad* after more than one rejection, so the view that he did not want to see his poems published is untenable. Even *Last Poems* (1922) was suggested first by Housman to Grant Richards, and not by the publisher to the poet: many of these had been written in the nineties, in the period of *A Shropshire Lad*. A prefatory note warned the reader that he must expect no more: 'I can no longer expect to be revisited by the continuous excitement under which in the early months of 1895 I wrote the greater part of my other book, nor could I well sustain it if it came.' In 1936 his brother Laurence Housman made a further selection of his unpublished work as *More Poems*, 'published by his permission, not by his wish': it is significant that nearly all these poems belong to the 1895 period. The most convenient edition is *Collected Poems*, edited by John Carter, 1939, of which a fourteenth revised impression had been called for by 1953. All his prose and his verse fragments Housman ordered to be destroyed. Unfortunately Laurence Housman sold them to the Library of Congress and the verse fragments were used by T. B. Haber in *The Manuscript Poems of A. E. Housman* (1955). This has led to severe criticism by John Carter in *The Times Literary Supplement* in October 1953 and in *The Book Collector* (1955).

In 1933 Housman delivered the Leslie Stephen lecture in Cambridge on *The Name and Nature of Poetry*. This and the Inaugural Lecture which he delivered at University College, London, in 1892, are among the most important documents in the assessment of his personality. In the Cambridge lecture he had in his audience critics of literature, many of them at that time highly theoretical, even a little desiccated, and an element of mischief often intrudes into his discourse. He knew precisely what his intention was when he quoted from Coleridge's *Anima Poetae* that only a poet could be a critic of poetry and then, for good measure, added Coleridge's conclusion 'Supposing he is not only a poet, but is a bad poet! What then?' With a deliberate reference to the audience he confronted, he emphasized the importance of versification and, in a somewhat cryptic manner, added that 'a few pages of Coventry Patmore and a few pages of Frederic Myers contain all, as far as I know, or all of value, which has been written on such matters'.

As a poet he remained a romantic in an age which was aggressively following other ways. He did not much like his contemporaries, either as critics or poets, and he detested their pretentiousness. With what delight he must have answered in *The Times Literary Supplement* of 20 December 1927 T. S. Eliot's disparaging comment on what was the meaning of Shelley's lines:

>Keen as are the arrows
>Of that silver sphere
>Whose intense lamp narrows
>In the white dawn clear
>Until we hardly see, we feel that it is there.

'Although this ode', Housman wrote, 'is not one of Shelley's best poems and enjoys more fame than it deserves, it is good enough to be worth interpreting. Quintilian says that you will never understand the poets unless you study astronomy: and as this subject is not now much studied in girls' schools, it was only to be expected that Mr Moore's *Egeria* should darken with misinformation the ignorance of Mr Eliot. In this stanza . . . the silver sphere is the Morning Star, the planet Venus; and Shelley is giving a true description of her disappearance and using an apt comparison. The moon, when her intense lamp narrows in the white dawn clear, is not a sphere, but a sickle: when she is a sphere at sunrise she is near the western horizon, visible in broad daylight and disappearing only when she sets; so that nothing could be less like the vanishing of a skylark.'

The most significant element in the Cambridge lecture was the disparagement of the eighteenth century, and here again the attack on some of his contemporaries was mixed with his more serious thought: 'The period', he said, 'lying between Samson Agonistes in 1671 and the Lyrical Ballads in 1798, and including as an integral part and indeed as its most potent influence the mature work of Dryden.' In that passage Housman could not have forgotten the praise of Dryden by Eliot and some of his contemporaries. There follows a far more profound passage. It admits the excellence of eighteenth-century verse, but adds that 'Man had ceased to live from the depths of his nature; he occupied himself for choice with thoughts which do not range beyond the sphere of the understanding; he lighted the candles and drew down the blind to shut out that patroness of poets, the moon. The writing of poetry proceeded, and much of the poetry written was excellent literature; but excellent literature which is also poetry is not therefore excellent poetry, and the poetry of the eighteenth century was most satisfactory when it did not try to be poetical.'

All Housman's poems were short lyrics, frequently in the ballad stanza, or in verse patterns with, superficially at least, a simple appearance. The vocabulary never distressed the reader with abstruseness, often, though delusively, it seemed to have the simplicity of conversation. The themes had equal clarity; they were dramatic incidents and narratives, quickly and allusively conveyed. The compelling quality of these short, stabbing lyrics was immediately apparent, though the rare and even intricate artistry supporting them had been cunningly concealed, for Housman's art was as studied as that of Gray, though its final result was gained with greater economy. Working from the basis of a common vocabulary, he had highly individualized his use of words. He could seize upon an ordinary word and so divert its meaning that it became full of new suggestion, as with the single word 'sprinkle' in the lines:

> He stood, and heard the steeple
> Sprinkle the quarters on the morning town.

Similarly from Latin literature he derived a verbal economy with a frequent and enlightening use of an English rendering of a Latin phrase. So in the most momentous of his lyrics, *Epitaph on an Army of Mercenaries*, he introduces a natural English equivalent for *summa rerum* in the concluding lines:

> What God abandoned, these defended,
> And saved the sum of things for pay.

Nor is he without a subtle relationship to earlier English poets, and often, in unexpected places, one lights upon the devious roads by which he travelled Shropshire county. Even the ballad of Richard Corbet, the seventeenth-century Bishop of Norwich, seems to have been encountered before he came to write the final poem of *Fancy's Knell*. The pattern and even the vocabulary of the following stanza of Corbet's lyric seem to have entered into Housman's poem:

> At Morning and at Evening both
> You Merry were and Glad;
> So little care of Sleep and Sloath
> These pretty Ladies had.
> When Tom came home from Labour
> Or Cisse to milking rose;
> Then merrily, merrily went their Tabor
> And nimbly went their Toes.

In fact, the literary influences were very considerable and from widely different sources. Housman gave the chief influences of which he was conscious as 'Shakespeare's songs, the Scottish border ballads, and Heine'. There were memories in movement and vocabulary of Shakespeare's lyrics and in particular the beautiful song from *Cymbeline* powerfully affected him:

> Fear no more the heat o' th' sun,
> Nor the furious winter's rages,
> Thou thy worldly task hast done,
> Home art gone and ta'en thy wages.
> Golden lads and girls all must,
> As chimney sweepers, come to dust.

He recalls the lines in

> Rest you so from trouble sore,
> Fear the heat o' the sun no more,
> Nor the snowing winter wild,
> Nor you labour not with child.[4]

and in the following poem he writes:

> Dust's your wages, son of sorrow,
> But men may come to worse than dust.

Few poems can have affected him more deeply. For in *Cymbeline* he found the word 'lads' that occurs in so many of the lyrics and 'wages' which he used so effectively in the *Epitaph on an Army of*

Mercenaries. Often the recall is less obvious, and frequently the mood of the original is altered. So Ariel's song at the end of *The Tempest*:

> Merrily, merrily shall I live now
> Under the blossom that hangs on the bough

yields to the more sombre:

> Loveliest of trees, the cherry now
> Is hung with bloom along the bough,
> And stands about the woodland ride
> Wearing white for Eastertide.[5]

The Scottish border ballads were a more direct influence. Housman was attracted by their dramatic themes, and by the terseness of their vocabulary and metre. He used the quatrain of the ballads in the majority of his poems, delighting in the mainly trochaic rhythm which he was able to employ. How deep was his admiration for the old 'fifteener', which broken up into 'eight' and 'seven' was the basis of the quatrain, can be seen from his praise in *The Name and Nature of Poetry* of Dr Watts's lines:

> Soft and easy is thy cradle;
> Coarse and hard thy Saviour lay,
> When his birthplace was a stable
> And his softest bed was hay.

'That simple verse', he wrote, 'bad rhyme and all, is poetry beyond Pope.'

Kipling's influence can be found both in his rhythms and vocabulary and, though this has been questioned, in his interest in soldiers, while his reading of Victorian street ballads confirmed his preoccupation with hangings and violent deaths. While there were these strong modern influences, Housman was naturally affected by the lyrics of the Greek Anthology and by the Latin lyrics which he knew so well.

Everywhere in his poems, and again in *The Name and Nature of Poetry*, one comes on the influence of the Authorized Version of the Bible and of Coverdale's translation of the Psalms: most of the latter he must have known by heart. Even when he is not captured by some direct recollection, his mind seems to employ naturally a Biblical language and imagery. So he writes: 'That Pope was a poet is true; but it is one of those truths which are beloved of liars, because they serve so well the cause of falsehood. That Pope was not a poet is false; but a righteous man, standing in awe of the last judgment and the lake which burneth with fire and brimstone, might well prefer to say it.' He must have studied very closely the Scriptures of a God in whom he professed not to believe, and whose injustice he hated.

It was not unnatural that among a younger generation there should be strong and at times virulent criticism of Housman's verse. While, in the early years, *A Shropshire Lad* was slow to gain popularity, it ultimately attained that rare position of being read by those who normally did not read poetry. This acclaim was widened when some of the lyrics were put to music by Vaughan Williams, George Butterworth, Arnold Bax, Ivor Gurney, John Ireland, and others.[2]

The attack on his romantic, Pre-Raphaelite quality, was led by Cyril Connolly in 1936,[6] within a month of Housman's death, suggesting 'a triteness of technique, equalled only by the banality of the thought'. The extreme of such comment was earlier to be found in Ezra Pound's contribution in the *Criterion* for January 1934. Housman himself had been separate and away from the groups which attempted to control critical opinion in the thirties. Housman's supporters overcrowded the *New Statesman* in the week after Connolly's article appeared. L. P. Wilkinson from Cambridge spoke of Connolly's 'eccentric note' and John Sparrow from Oxford wrote of the article as a 'brilliant piece of journalistic opportunism'. There were more balanced comments than Connolly's, which were still adverse; these refrained from uncritical eulogy, drawing attention to the features in Housman's verse which were strange and unpredictable.

The strangest thing is that a mind so discriminating should be, in some ways, so uncritical of even the work that he sanctioned for publication. At his best he creates 'a poetic region of his own where none approach', as O. L. Richmond comments, 'and it needs comparison with the giants to make quite clear that his poetic gift, so nearly perfect in its kind, so sure of a measure of immortality, is yet a less gift than his matchless contribution to scholarship'.[2] Yet, at the same time, O. L. Richmond emphasizes the range of his work as a scholar compared with his output as a poet. 'Accuracy', Richmond suggests, 'had been a passion with him.' In poetry his 'sense of beauty has been so coldly restrained that it is not always even there, except in the outward form'. '*More Poems*', he adds, 'showed up most unkindly the narrowness of the vein of inspiration.'[2] There are also the sudden lapses in his work, the sudden failure in the quality of the verse, the morbid preoccupations with graves, dead soldiers, and hangings ('lads are in love with the grave'), the immeasurable distance between what is best and what is most banal.

Housman disdained the subjective moods of many of his contemporaries in the nineties and explored brief, often tragic, moments of experience in the dramatic and narrative methods of the ballad. Yet he is at one with Dowson in rejecting all dross from his verse and with Pater in conveying that quickened urgency to experience which the sense of the brevity and mortality of life conveys:

> From far, from eve and morning
> And yon twelve-winded sky,
> The stuff of life to knit me
> Blew hither: here am I
>
> Now – for a breath I tarry
> Nor yet disperse apart –
> Take my hand quick and tell me,
> What have you in your heart?

He gave to the best of his lyrics the largeness and amplitude of great imaginative work; as in the *Epitaph* already mentioned, where eight lines gather up a theme of epic dimensions and reveal it in its fullness. The same quality enters frequently, the subtle and awe-inspiring suggestion of the whole vaulted sky outlined as a mute and terrifying witness to the human scene. The problem remains whether there was any autobiographical element in the poems. Laurence Housman notes that the poet told a French inquirer that 'the Shropshire Lad is an imaginary character, with something of my character and view of life. Very little in the book is autobiographical.'[7]

Let it be admitted that as a man and a poet he is most puzzling. It is difficult to dismiss altogether that some deep emotional disturbance affected the whole of his life both as a scholar and a poet. His failure at Oxford was probably at the centre of crisis. But something must have caused the Oxford crisis. O. L. Richmond wrote: 'I am driven to suppose that something more acute than self-consciousness left a sting embedded in his experience. One might guess that, though he was made for love, none would ever love him, because of his physical disabilities, caused by precocious intellectual strain.'[2] Grant Richards, his friend and publisher, and his sister, Mrs Symons, strongly opposed this diagnosis. One cannot ignore the friendship with Moses Jackson. It is unnecessary to postulate an active homosexual relationship, but there is evidence that his friendship for Jackson was deep and intimate, and that he was aware of the further and for him forbidden ways in which it could easily develop. It comes through in lines published posthumously:

> Because I liked you better
> Than suits a man to say,
> It irked you, and I promised
> To throw the thought away.

John Sparrow deals with the whole matter sympathetically,[8] though without a precise conclusion, possibly because the evidence for such does not exist. His criticism of Watson's style and classical knowledge in *A. E. Housman, A Divided Life* is severe, but this does not affect Watson's main argument that Housman's horror at discovering that his friendship for Moses Jackson might slip into active homosexuality led to his failure at Oxford and to the tragic themes of the poems. Sparrow argues that Housman with his independent and atheistical mind would not be so moved:

> The laws of God, the laws of man,
> He may keep who will and can;
> Not I: let God and man decree
> Laws for themselves and not for me.

Sparrow further suggests that Watson misinterprets the Jackson influence partly because he does not understand how the study of the classics was the dominant element in Housman's life. Sparrow admits that Jackson was a dominant influence and that the main inspiration of his 'love' poems was the frustration of his feelings for Jackson and his knowledge that they must always remain frustrated. There was none of the 'horror' postulated by Watson.

My own summary, and again I am helped by A. N. Marlow's suggestion, is that there was an unresolved tension in Housman's life and that this arose from his feeling for Moses Jackson. On his own statement this feeling was so strong that it dominated his life. He had a bitterness within because he had turned away from half of life. His Cyrenaicism proved at times insufficient and his atheism was restless, as is shown by the profound influence of the Scriptures on his prose. I add, as a personal suggestion, that the influence of Wilde's trial in 1895, and the cruel sentence that followed, may have been profound. It was at this date that something stirred him into composition, as at no other period in his life, and there are reflections of the Wilde theme in his verses:

> Oh who is that young sinner with the handcuffs on his wrists?
> And what has he been after that they groan and shake their fists?
> And wherefore is he wearing such a conscience-stricken air?
> Oh they've taken him to prison for the colour of his hair.

A most revealing comment of an entirely different order came from his sister, Mrs E. W. Symons, in the introduction to Grant Richards's *Housman, 1897-1936*. She suggests that it is unwise to seek the bitterness in Housman's poetry from his failure at Oxford or his own emotional life. She believes that the failure of the ideals which he had set himself in youth contributed to the condition. In his lecture at University College, London, in 1892, he was still able to say, 'Our business here is not to live, but to live happily . . . our true occupation is to manufacture from the raw material of life the fabric of happiness.' He quoted Dante speaking through the mouth of Ulysses: 'Ye were not formed to live like brutes, but to follow virtue and knowledge.' He added that 'the pursuit of knowledge, like the pursuit of righteousness, is part of man's duty to himself'; 'for knowledge resembles virtue in this, and differs in this from other possessions, that it is not merely a means of procuring good, but is good in itself simply: it is not a coin which we pay down to purchase happiness, but it has happiness indissolubly bound up with it'. Housman was later to condemn this lecture as 'rhetorical and not wholly sincere'. Mrs Symons suggests that he made this comment because he knew that the pursuit of knowledge and virtue had not brought him happiness:

> He, standing hushed, a pace or two apart,
> Among the bluebells of the listless plain,
> Thinks, and remembers how he cleansed his heart
> And washed his hands in innocence in vain.

NOTES

Introduction

[1] Estimates of the nineteenth century as a whole can be found in *A Survey (1830-1880)*, O. Elton (1920); *Die englische Literatur des 19 und 20 Jahrhunderts*, Bernhard Fehr (Potsdam, 1931). *The Literature of the Victorian Era*, Hugh Walker (1910), is an earlier attempt, as is G. Saintsbury's brief study *A History of Nineteenth Century Literature (1780-1896)* (1896, etc.). For the minor poets of the century *The Poets and the Poetry of the Century*, ed. A. H. Miles (1893, etc.), is still a useful guide. For the transition from the nineteenth century to the twentieth see *Modern English Writers (1890-1914)*, Harold Williams (revised ed., 1925).

[2] Essay prefixed to the selections from Keats in Ward's *English Poets*, vol. IV (1880).

[3] The *Nineteenth Century* (January 1888).

[4] See *Ruskin (and others) on Byron*, R. W. Chambers, English Association Pamphlet (November 1925); *Byron in England*, S. C. Chew (1924).

[5] Preface to *Poetry of Byron* (1881).

[6] In criticism as apart from creation, Byron does gain appreciation later in the century. See Chambers loc. cit. in 4.

[7] *Letter to John Murray*, etc. (7 February 1821).

[8] *Table Talk* for 12 September 1831.

[9] *London and Westminster Review* (August 1838).

[10] *Coleridge on Logic and Learning*, Alice D. Snyder (1929); *Coleridge as Philosopher*, J. H. Muirhead (1930).

[11] *The Romantic Revolt*, C. E. Vaughan (1907).

[12] I heard this phrase used of Arnold by W. P. Ker. I am not aware that it occurs in his published work.

[13] For an interesting and unusual view of Clough, see Humbert Wolfe in *The Eighteen-Sixties* (1932).

NOTES TO INTRODUCTION

[14] Preface to *Poems* (1853).
[15] Lascelles Abercrombie has a study in *The Eighteen-Sixties* (1932).
[16] For details see *Memoir of W. E. Aytoun*, Theodore Martin (1867).
[17] *Letters of Edward Fitzgerald* (1907), I, 348.

Chapter 1 · Dante Gabriel Rossetti

[1] The main authority is W. M. Rossetti, though he states frankly that he is not prepared to reveal the whole truth about his brother; *Dante Gabriel Rossetti as Designer and Writer* (1889); *D. G. Rossetti, his Family Letters, with a Memoir*, 2 vols. (1895); *Pre-Raphaelite Diaries and Letters* (1900); *Rossetti Papers (1862-1870)* (1903); and valuable information in the preface and notes to *The Works of D. G. Rossetti* (1911). The literature on Morris is so closely related to the literature on Rossetti that they should be studied together. Also the references under Christina Rossetti and W. M. Rossetti and such volumes as *Memorials of Edward Burne-Jones*, 2 vols. (1904). W. M. Rossetti's daughter, Helen Rossetti Angeli, added new information with her *Dante Gabriel Rossetti, His Friends and Enemies* (1949). The fullest account is *A Victorian Romantic, Dante Gabriel Rossetti*, by Oswald Doughty (1949; revised edition with additional information, 1960), which has a useful select bibliography of manuscript and printed material. Rossetti Angeli and Doughty give the most revealing record of Rossetti's personal life. To these may be added *Letters to Janey* (1964, *The Journal of the William Morris Society*, vol. 1, No 4), R. C. H. Briggs: this gives an account of the letters from Morris and Rossetti to Jane Morris deposited in the British Museum by Dr Robert Steele, literary executor of Jane Morris's second daughter, May; (the letters from William Morris to Jane (Add. MS. 45, 338) have been available for study since 1946, but the letters from Rossetti were released only in January 1964); *Letters to Fanny Cornforth*, edited by Paull Franklin Baum (Baltimore, The Johns Hopkins Press, 1940); *The Rossetti Macmillan Letters* (1963), ed. L. M. Packer. A comprehensive edition of *Letters of Dante Gabriel Rossetti* is being prepared by J. R. Wahl and Oswald Doughty for early publication in the Clarendon Press. On Rossetti's work, one of the earliest volumes still has value, *Dante Gabriel Rossetti: an Illustrated Memorial of his Life and Art* (1899),

NOTES TO CHAPTER ONE

H. C. Marillier. William Sharp's life (1882) is an 'undertaker's' biography, but it has some interesting critical judgements; Sir Thomas Hall Caine wrote his *Recollections of Rossetti* in 1882 and 1928; A. C. Benson (1904) combined biography and criticism in his life; a later and more effective study is *Rossetti* (1928), Evelyn Waugh; R. L. Mégroz in *D. G. Rossetti* (1928) has a full critical estimate. To these may be added *The Rossetti Family (1824-1854)* (1932), Ross D. Waller; E. R. Vincent, *Gabriele Rossetti in England* (1936); and the illuminating but fictional *The Wife of Rossetti*, by Violet Hunt (1932). D. G. Rossetti's letters, in addition to those mentioned above, can be found in *Letters of D. G. Rossetti to W. Allingham (1854-1876)*, ed. G. B. Hill (1897), and *The Letters of D. G. Rossetti to F. S. Ellis*, ed. Oswald Doughty (1928); and Janet Troxell (ed.) *The Three Rossettis, Unpublished Letters to and from Dante Gabriel, Christina, and William* (1939). The best general essays are still Walter Pater's essay in *Appreciations* (1889) and A. C. Swinburne's *The Poems of Dante Gabriel Rossetti* in *Essays and Studies* (1875); single aspects of Rossetti's personality and work have been studied by H. T. Dunn, *Recollections* (1904): Dunn is unreliable, but he knew Rossetti and was one of his assistants. L. A. Willoughby in *D. G. Rossetti and German Literature* (1912) makes a full correlation of Rossetti's German reading and his poetical achievement. Other suggestive studies are: *Un Italien d'Angleterre*, Henri Dupré (1921); *Pre-Raphaelite and Other Poets*, Lafcadio Hearn (1923); *The Blessed Damozel: The unpublished manuscripts, texts, and collation*: with an introduction by Paull Franklin Baum (1937); and *Thanks Before Going*, John Masefield (1946). Much information on the poems can be gained from vols. 4, 8, 9, and 10 of *The Catalogue of the Ashley Library*, T. J. Wise.

On Pre-Raphaelitism, apart from the above volumes, the most useful works are *Autobiographical Notes*, W. B. Scott (ed. W. Minto), 2 vols. (1892); *Memorials of Edward Burne-Jones* (1904); *Ruskin, Rossetti; Pre-Raphaelitism*, edited W. M. Rossetti (1899); *Rossetti*, Ford Madox Hueffer (1902). Max Beerbohm's cartoons *Rossetti and his Circle* (1922) are most revealing. A discriminating account of the movement in its literary aspects will be found in *The Victorian Romantics (1850-1870)*, T. Earle Welby (1929); *The Pre-Raphaelite Tragedy*, by William Gaunt (1942).

[2] See *Gabriele Rossetti*, a versified autobiography, translated and supplemented by W. M. Rossetti (1901); and refs. in 1 above.

NOTES TO CHAPTER ONE

³ *Ruskin, Rossetti and Pre-Raphaelitism*, W. M. Rossetti (1899).
⁴ *Memoir* (1895), vol. I, p. 135.
⁵ *Century Guild Hobby Horse* (1887).
⁶ R. D. Waller, *Modern Language Review* (April 1931).
⁷ *Die älteste Fassung von D. G. Rossetti's Ballade Sister Helen*, Max Foerster (Leipzig, 1929).
⁸ *The House of Life*, P. F. Baum (Cambridge, Mass., 1928).
⁹ W. Sharp, *Rossetti* (1882), maintains that this poem arose from Meredith's *In the Woods*.
¹⁰ See Willoughby, loc. cit. in 1, p. 27.
¹¹ Such at least is the evidence of Dunn, loc. cit. in 1.

Chapter 2 · *Algernon Charles Swinburne*

¹ There are a number of biographical and critical studies. The best place to begin is with Cecil Y. Lang's *The Swinburne Letters* (Yale University Press, 6 vols., 1959-1962). Apart from the *Letters*, this edition contains Edmund Gosse's previously unpublished life, to which frequent reference is made. There are a number of critical works. The standard volume is still *Swinburne*, E. Gosse (1917), revised for the *Bonchurch Edition*, where it appears as vol. 19. He wrote at a time when caution was necessary and, anyway, he was naturally cautious; the volume can now be supplemented by his manuscript life, to which reference is made above. Apart from Gosse there is *La Jeunesse de Swinburne (1837-1867)*, by G. Lafourcade, 2 vols. (1928), and his *A Literary Biography* (1932). Many of the Swinburne manuscripts and related material were in the possession of T. J. Wise, who issued *A Bibliography of A. C. Swinburne*, vol. I (1919) and vol. II (1920), *A Swinburne Library* (1925), and the bibliography in *The Bonchurch Edition* (1925-1927). See also T. J. Wise's *The Catalogue of the Ashley Library*, vols. VI and VII. Swinburne's works in verse and prose, with a number of letters, were issued in *The Bonchurch Edition*, E. Gosse and T. J. Wise, 20 vols. (1926-1927). The Swinburne manuscripts passed to the British Museum from the collection of T. J. Wise. For the less happy side of Wise's devotion to the Swinburne manuscripts see J. Carter and G. Pollard, *The Firm of Charles Ottley, Landon and Co.* (1948). Aspects of Swinburne's biography and work have been studied by John Drinkwater (1913); Mary C. J. Leith, *The Boyhood of A. C.*

Swinburne (1917); W. B. D. Henderson, *Swinburne and Landor* (1918); T. Earle Welby, *A Study of Swinburne* (1926); S. C. Chew (1929); F. Delattre, *Charles Baudelaire et le jeune Swinburne* (1930); W. R. Rutland, *Swinburne, A Nineteenth Century Hellene* (1931); C. K. Hyder, *Swinburne's Literary Career and Fame* (Duke University Press, 1933); Randolph Hughes, *Swinburne, A Centenary Survey* (1937), and *Unpublished Swinburne etc* (1948); Humphrey Hare, *Swinburne a biographical approach* (1949); *Swinburne*, H. J. C. Grierson (1955). In 1950 *The Golden Cockerel Press* published Randolph Hughes's edition of Swinburne's *Pasiphae*. C. K. Hyder has a chapter on Swinburne in *The Victorian Poets, A Guide to Research*, ed. F. E. Faverty (Cam. Mass., 1956). Lafourcade is the fullest account of Swinburne's earlier work, but interesting estimates are found in Paul de Reul's *L'Œuvre de Swinburne* (1922) and in Harold Nicolson's *Swinburne* (1926) and *Swinburne and Baudelaire* (1930). On Swinburne's relationship with women there is a valuable article in Cecil Y. Lang's *Swinburne's Lost Love* (P.M.L.A., March 1959, vol. 74, No 1), material from which has been used in the text of the chapter.

[2] See above.
[3] Quoted in Lang.
[4] Quoted in Gosse, *Swinburne*.
[5] Quoted from Lang.
[6] The details can be found in Lafourcade, *La Jeunesse de Swinburne*, vol. I, 178.
[7] Meredith portrayed Swinburne as Tracy Runningbrook in *Sandra Belloni*.
[8] *Bonchurch Edition*, vol. I.
[9] *Joyeuse Garde* (a Tristram fragment), *Lancelot*, and the *Rudel* poems (a possible Browning influence).
[10] *Ballads of the English Border*, W. A. MacInnes (1925).
[11] *Dedicatory Epistle*.
[12] The sources of the Mary Stuart plays have been admirably worked out by E. F. James in an unpublished thesis of the University of Bristol, and I am indebted to him for permission to quote his findings.
[13] See Lafourcade, *La Jeunesse*, vol. II, p. 384, and the same author in *La Revue Anglo-Américaine* (December 1925).
[14] For the prosody of the poem see Lafourcade, vol. II, p. 408.
[15] Floris Delattre, loc. cit. in 1 (1930); G. Turquet-Milnes, *The Influence of Baudelaire in France and England* (1913).

16 See Lafourcade for a detailed account of the chronology of this volume, studied with the aid of Swinburne's manuscripts.
17 An interesting account of this volume is to be found in Harold Nicolson's *Swinburne*, and from this I have borrowed suggestions.
18 *The Eve of Revolution*.
19 Swinburne quoted by Gosse, *Swinburne*, p. 177.

Chapter 3 · Christina Georgina Rossetti

1 Lona Mosk Packer's *Christina Rossetti* (1963) is essential even if one does not fully accept her theory of Christina's relation to William Bell Scott. Her 'Selective Bibliography' is by far the fullest yet to be issued. She notes as Manuscript Sources the Angeli Collection; the Rossetti papers, now on loan to the Bodleian Library; the British Museum Collection; T. J. Wise's *The Ashley Library, A Catalogue of Printed Books, Manuscripts and Autographed Letters*, the original material now mainly in the British Museum. Lona Packer also lists a number of other manuscript sources. Among bibliographical sources, apart from T. J. Wise, there is Howard M. Jones, 'The Pre-Raphaelites' in *The Victorian Poets*, ed. F. E. Faverty (Cam., Mass., 1956), and Austin Wright, *Bibliographies of Studies in Victorian Literature for the Ten Years, 1945-1954* (Urbana, Ill., 1956). The main biographical source is still W. M. Rossetti: *The Rossetti Papers (1862–1870)* (1903) have a number of letters; these can be supplemented by *The Family Letters of C. G. Rossetti*, ed. W. M. Rossetti (1908), which has a brief biographical notice. The early biographies are disappointing. H. T. M. Bell's study, *C. G. Rossetti* (1898), is criticism with meagre biography. Elizabeth L. Cary, *The Rossettis* (1907), deals only incidentally with Christina Rossetti. Ellen A. Proctor's modest *Brief Memoir* (1895) has details of Christina's early reading not mentioned elsewhere. The *Poetical Works* (1904) have a memoir by W. M. Rossetti. The centenary year brought two new volumes: Mary F. Sandar, *The Life of C. Rossetti* (1930), and Dorothy M. Stuart, *Christina Rossetti* (1930), a discriminating study. For a study of the verse see also *C. Rossetti and her Poetry*, Edith Birkhead (1931), and *C. Rossetti*, Fredegond Shove (1931). The article by Richard Garnett in the *Dictionary of National Biography* is vaguely hostile; he overemphasizes the melancholy and morbidity of the poems. Watts-Dunton has a

NOTES TO CHAPTER THREE

notice in the *Athenæum* (5 January 1895). See also Alice Meynell, preface to *Poems, C. G. Rossetti* (1910), and the note on the biographies of D. G. Rossetti. For *Goblin Market* see B. I. Evans, *Modern Language Review* (April 1933).
2 *Family Letters*, p. 103.
3 ibid., p. 31.
4 These included: No 1, *Dreamland, An End*; No 2, *A Pause of Thought, Six Roses for the Flush of Youth, A Testimony*; No 3, *Repining*.
5 *Family Letters*, p. 31.
6 See A. Proctor's *Brief Memoir* (1895).
7 *D. G. Rossetti*, vol. I, p. 44, W. M. Rossetti (1895).
8 *Life*, Mackenzie Bell.
9 *Family Letters*, facing p. 36.
10 *Macmillan's Magazine* (1863), p. 68.

Chapter 4 · William Morris

1 The standard life is by J. W. Mackail, *The Life of William Morris*, 2 vols. (1899); critical and biographical material is also to be found in *The Collected Works*, ed. by May Morris (1910-1915), and in her two volumes *William Morris, Artist, Writer, Socialist* (1936). See also *Memorials of Edward Burne-Jones*, 2 vols. (1904). The literature on Rossetti is so closely related to the literature on Morris that they should be studied together. Mackail paid but limited attention to Morris's political activities, and this is adjusted in E. P. Thompson's *William Morris, Romantic to Revolutionary* (1955): Thompson has also additional biographical material; see also R. D. Macleod's *Morris Without Mackail* (1954), showing Morris 'as seen by his contemporaries'. Philip Henderson's edition of *The Letters of William Morris to his family and friends* (1950) is valuable, particularly for some of Morris's autobiographical descriptions, and his *William Morris* (1952); for the Rossetti and Morris letters to Jane Morris see *The Journal of the William Morris Society* (1964, vol. 1, No 4), R. C. H. Briggs. Other works on Morris are mainly critical and derive their biographical sources from Mackail; *Wm. Morris*, Alfred Noyes (1908), attempts a criticism of Mackail; *The First Morris*, Dixon Scott, in *Primitiae* (1912), is a spirited study of *The Defence of Guenevere*. *Wm. Morris*, John Drinkwater (1912), is an interesting but somewhat personal

appreciation of the poems. *Four Poets, A Study of Clough, Arnold, Rossetti, Morris* (1913), A. Stopford Brooke. *Wm. Morris*, A. Clutton Brock (1914), is an able survey of all aspects of Morris's work and influence. See also *The Books of W. Morris*, etc. (1897), H. B. Forman; *W. Morris*, etc. (1897), A. Vallance; *W. Morris and the Early Days of the Socialist Movement* (1921), J. B. Glasier; *William Morris and his Poetry* (1925), B. I. Evans; *William Morris* (1926), Holbrook Jackson; *Mittelalter und Antike bei William Morris* (Berlin and Leipzig, 1928), Elisabet C. Küster; *William Morris* (1934), Paul Bloomfield; *William Morris* (1934), Montague Weekley; *Portrait of W. Morris* (1947), Esther Meynell; *William Morris: Selected Writings and Designs* (1962), ed. with an introduction by Asa Briggs, with an illustrated supplement by Graeme Shankland.

² *The Collected Works*, ed. May Morris, vol. viii.
³ *The Record of an Adventurous Life*, H. M. Hyndman (1911).
⁴ Swinburne, *Essays and Studies* (1875).
⁵ See *Primitiae* (loc. cit. in 1).
⁶ *Letters*, ed. Hake and Compton-Rickett (1918).
⁷ 'Top' is Morris's nickname.   ⁸ *Art and the Beauty of the Earth.*

Chapter 5 · Minor Pre-Raphaelite Poets

¹ The main biographical source is *Autobiographical Notes*, edited W. Minto, 2 vols. (1892); this is supplemented by additional information in the *Dictionary of National Biography*; there are frequent references to Scott in the memoirs of D. G. Rossetti by W. M. Rossetti (see p. 443); a new and major source of biographical information is L. M. Packer's *Christina Rossetti* (1963); see also the chapter on Christina Rossetti.

² A copy of this volume was the first work ever tooled by Cobden-Sanderson, a beautiful volume in gold-tooled morocco, now in the British Museum.

³ *W. Allingham, A Diary* (1907), ed. H. Allingham and D. Radford; *Letters to W. Allingham* (1911), ed. H. Allingham and E. Baumer Williams; *Letters from W. Allingham to E. B. Browning* (1914). A. H. Miles's *The Poets and Poetry of the Century* (1892) has an essay on him by W. B. Yeats; there is biographical material in Allingham's prose work, e.g. *Rambles in England and Ireland*, Patricius Walter

(pseud. for W.A.) (1873). See also *William Allingham und seine Dichtung*, Hans Kropf (Bern, 1928), which deals with Allingham and Ireland; and A. P. Graves in *Transactions of the Royal Society of Literature*, 2nd series, vol. XXXII, part III. *A Bibliography of William Allingham* (1945), P. S. O'Hegarty.

4 Quoted in the *Dictionary of National Biography*.

5 See *Memories*, Amy Woolner (1917), largely a collection of letters between Woolner and his numerous correspondents.

6 The *Dictionary of National Biography*.

7 Apart from Dr Richard Garnett's discreet notice in the *Dictionary of National Biography*, and a brief life by Louise Chandler Moulton (1894), there is no biographical material.

8 In the preface, A. W. Newport Deacon refers to 'the mass of unpublished manuscript found amongst his literary remains'.

9 *The Life of John Payne*, Thomas Wright (1919).

10 Written before *The Masque of Shadows*.

11 A biographical sketch by Louise Chandler Moulton in *A Last Harvest* (1891), and by the same author in *Collected Poems* (1892); *P. B. Marston*, C. C. Osborne (1926).

12 Other volumes were issued in the United States.

13 *William Sharp*, Elizabeth A. Sharp (1910, enlarged 1912).

Chapter 6 · Coventry Patmore and Allied Poets

1 For the study of the Catholic elements in poetry, see *The Catholic Spirit in Modern English Literature*, G. N. Shuster (1922), and C. Alexander, *The Catholic Literary Revival* (1935). On Coventry Patmore a valuable study is J. C. Reid, *The Mind and Art of Coventry Patmore* (1957): to this I am indebted in a number of places; it has a select bibliography with a useful list of Patmore's contributions to periodicals. There are Patmore manuscripts at Princeton University Library and at Boston College Library. Further on Patmore see Dr Richard Garnett's notice in the *Dictionary of National Biography*; *Memoirs and Correspondence of Coventry Patmore*, 2 vols. (1900), Basil Champneys, which is the official life; *Coventry Patmore* (1905), Edmund Gosse; *The Idea of Coventry Patmore* (1921), Osbert Burdett; *Patmore – A Study in Poetry* (1933), Frederick Page, a sympathetic study of Patmore's verse; *Portrait of My Family* (1935) and *The Life and Times of Coventry Pat-*

more (1949), by Derek Patmore; *Patmore's Theory and Hopkins's Practice* (1949), Margaret R. Stobie. There is an early study of *The Angel* in *Essays* (1858), George Brimley, and also in Alice Meynell's preface to *The Angel* (1905). There are a number of essays: *The Moderns* (1916), John Freeman; *Splendid Failures* (1932), Shane Leslie; *In Defence of Shelley* (1936) and *The Great Victorians*, vol. II (1938), by Herbert Read; *Further Letters of Gerard Manley Hopkins, including his correspondence with Patmore* (1938); *Œuvres Complètes*, vol. III (1951), Valéry Larbaud; *La Crisi Dell'Eroe Nel Romanzo Vittoriano* (1952), Mario Praz.

² *Poems* (1844) is published by Edward Moxon, and *Tamerton Church-Tower and other Poems* (1853) by William Pickering. *The Angel in the House, The Betrothal*, was published by John W. Parker in 1854; this was followed by *The Angel in the House*, book II; *The Espousals* (John W. Parker) in 1856. In 1858 the same publisher issued both books revised, in one volume. In 1860 *Faithful for Ever* (Parker) was published, and in the same year *The Angel in the House* (books I and II). Parker is the name of the publisher on the title-page and Macmillan on the cover. In 1863 there is a reissue of the Parker volume of 1860, to which a Macmillan title-page, dated 1863, has been inserted. Also in 1863 (presumably taken over by Macmillan) there is an edition of *The Angel in the House, Faithful for Ever*, and *The Victories of Love*; some of the earlier poems are also added. In 1866 Macmillans issued a one-volume edition, all the parts of the *Angel*, with a shorter selection from the earlier poems. In 1878 G. Bell took over *The Angel* (parts I and II) and issued a new one-volume edition, and a further edition of 1885 (books I and II); in 1878 G. Bell issued *The Victories of Love*, which is a rearrangement of the poems in *Faithful for Ever* and *The Victories of Love*.

In 1878 *Amelia*, with a number of the early poems, was published, and a long prefatory study of English metrical law. Already in 1868 Patmore had printed privately a collection of nine odes. In 1877 a collection of thirty-one odes was published under the title *The Unknown Eros*, and this was expanded by further editions in 1878 and 1890. *Amelia* and *L'Allegro*, the two new poems of the 1878 volume, were published in *The Unknown Eros* (1890), though kept apart from the other poems. Both *The Angel* and *The Unknown Eros* have been frequently reprinted.

³ Burdett (loc. cit. in 1) finds a compactness in this poem which I fail to discover.

⁴ For this reference I am indebted to Professor R. M. Hewitt.

⁵ In his essay on Francis Thompson, Patmore seems to suggest 1867 as the date when he began to write odes. *Fortnightly Review* (London, January 1894).

⁶ *Whate'er thou dost* and *No praise to me* were extracted from *The Unknown Eros* in 1890 and published separately; *Go up, thou Baldpate* was excluded altogether.

⁷ In the Francis Thompson essay (loc. cit. in 5).

⁸ There are some parallels between the prosodic theories of Patmore and G. M. Hopkins, but no collaboration.

⁹ *The Times Literary Supplement* (12 May 1932).

¹⁰ In the *Dictionary of National Biography*.

¹¹ Champneys (loc. cit. in 1), vol. I, p. 175.

¹² *Francis Thompson* (1907), Wilfrid S. Blunt; *Le Poète Francis Thompson* (1909), F. Delattre; *Francis Thompson* (Marburg, 1912), George Ashton Beacock, is an excellent study; *Francis Thompson* (1913), J. K. Rooker; *Francis Thompson* (revised edition, 1926), E. Meynell; *Francis Thompson* (1927), R. L. Mégroz; *Francis Thompson and his Poetry* (1927), T. H. Wright; *Francis Thompson et les poètes catholiques d'Angleterre* (1932), A. de la Gorce; *Francis Thompson* (1935), F. Olivero; *Francis Thompson* (1936), F. C. Owlett; *An Account of the Books and Manuscripts of Francis Thompson* (1937), Terence L. Connolly; *Francis Thompson and Wilfrid Meynell* (1952), Viola Meynell; *Francis Thompson*, etc. (2nd edition, 1955), Vincent J. MacNabb.

¹³ loc. cit. in 5.

¹⁴ The *Contemporary Review* (London, February 1894).

¹⁵ *Manus Animam Pinxit*.

¹⁶ *To a Poet Breaking Silence*.

¹⁷ Francis Thompson's debt to other poets and his neologisms have been fully studied by G. A. Beacock (see loc. cit. in 12). This thesis is now difficult to obtain, and I am indebted to Wilfrid Meynell, who kindly sent me Everard Meynell's copy.

¹⁸ The *Athenæum* (3 February 1894).

¹⁹ *Francis Thompson*, E. Meynell (1926).

²⁰ *Alice Meynell*, Viola Meynell (1929); *Mrs Meynell and her Literary Generation*, Anne K. Tuell (1925). *An Autobiography* (1922), by Mrs Meynell's sister, Lady Butler, though in itself an interesting volume, contains little information on Mrs Alice Meynell.

NOTES TO CHAPTER SIX

21 *Poems, E. B. Browning*, ed. Alice Meynell (1903).
22 *Poems, C. G. Rossetti*, ed. Alice Meynell (1910).
23 To Professor A. A. Cock, quoted in the life by Viola Meynell (loc. cit. in 20).

Chapter 7 · George Meredith

1 *George Meredith: Some Characteristics* (1890), R. Le Gallienne, with a Bibliography by J. Lane; *Bibliography of the Writings in Prose and Verse of George Meredith* (1907), A. J. K. Esdaile, and the same author's *A Chronological List of George Meredith's Publications (1849-1911)* (1914); *A Bibliography of the Writings in Prose and Verse of George Meredith* (1922), M. B. Forman, and the author's supplement to this work *Meredithiana* (1924); *The Poetry and Philosophy of George Meredith* (1906, expanded in later editions), G. M. Trevelyan, a standard work, also the same author's notes to *Poetical Works* (1912) and to *Selected Poems* (1955). *The Letters of George Meredith*, 2 vols. (1912), were edited by his son William Maxse Meredith; there have been a number of smaller collections of letters: to Edward Clodd and Clement K. Shorter (1913); to Richard Henry Horne (1919); to Swinburne and Watts-Dunton (1922); to Alice Meynell (1923); to 'various correspondents' (1924). There was a standard edition of *The Works* (1922-1924). Most of the critical essays fall within a decade of this publication, for of late Meredith has been the most gravely neglected author of the whole period. There are studies by H. Lynch (1891); W. C. Brownell (1902); W. C. Jerrold (1902); May S. Henderson, afterwards Gretton (1907 and 1926); R. H. P. Curle (1908); M. B. Forman (1909); J. A. Hammerton (1909); C. Photiades (1910); J. W. Beach (1911); Archibald Henderson (1911); Laura Torretta (1915); J. H. E. Crees (1918 and 1921); *Memories of Meredith* (1919), Lady Butler; Stewart M. Ellis (1919); R. Galland (1923); Lucien Wolff (1924); W. Chislett (1925); Gladys R. Milnes (1925); J. B. Priestley (1926); R. E. Sencourt (1929); Robert Peel (1931); Mona E. Mackay (1937); H. Littmana (1938); Guy B. Petter (1939); Siegfried L. Sassoon (1948 and 1959); Jack Lindsay (1956). See also *Mythology and the Romantic Tradition in English Literature* (1937), D. Bush, and an edition of *Modern Love* with the revised text of 1892 and an introduction by C. Day Lewis (1948).

NOTES TO CHAPTER SEVEN

² See *Der Einfluss Goethes auf George Meredith*, M. Krusemeyer; *Englische Studien*, LIX (1925); *Wilhelm Meister and his English Kinsmen*, Susanne Howe (1930).

³ Four of these are reprinted by R. Galland, *Meredith et l'Allemagne, Revue de Littérature Comparée*, III (1923), p. 463.

⁴ *The Woods of Westermain.*
⁵ *Earth and Man.*
⁶ *Hard Weather.*
⁷ *Whimper of Sympathy.*
⁸ *The Question of Whither.*
⁹ *A Faith on Trial.*
¹⁰ *Hymn to Colour.*
¹¹ *Earth's Secret.*
¹² *The Empty Purse.*
¹³ *Ode to the Comic Spirit.*
¹⁴ loc. cit. in 13.
¹⁵ *The Woods of Westermain.*
¹⁶ *Phantasy.*
¹⁷ loc. cit. in 15.
¹⁸ loc. cit. in 1.

Chapter 8 · Thomas Hardy

¹ For Hardy's bibliography see *A Bibliography of the Works of Thomas Hardy (1865-1915)* (1916), A. P. Webb; *Thomas Hardy, A Bibliographical Study* (1954), R. L. Purdy. Biographical material is still limited. The official account is by Florence, Hardy's second wife and widow; *The Early Life* (1928) and *The Later Years* (1930) were gathered together in one volume as *The Life of Thomas Hardy, 1840-1928* (1962): it is clear that this was largely composed by Hardy himself 'from notes, letters, diaries, and biographical memoranda'. Mrs Hardy states that for a long time Hardy 'would not care to have his life written at all', and this official volume is a record of outward happenings without intimacies. *Thomas Hardy, A Critical Biography* (1954), Evelyn Hardy, contains some new material. The most important development biographically has been the reinstatement of the influence of the first Mrs Hardy on Hardy's verse, see 7 below and *'Dearest Emmie', Thomas Hardy's Letters to his First Wife*, C. J. Webber (1963). There are numerous critical studies, most of which deal with Hardy as a novelist; *The Art of Thomas Hardy* (1894), Lionel Johnson, has, in the 1923 edition, a chapter on the poetry by J. E. Barton and a bibliography by John Lane; in *Thomas Hardy* (1912) Lascelles Abercrombie deals fully with the poetry up to that date; there are other studies by H. H. Child (1916); H. C. Duffin (1921); J. W. Black

NOTES TO CHAPTER EIGHT

(1922); *Thomas Hardy's Universe* (1924) and *The Life of T. Hardy* (1925), E. Brennecke; *Thomas Hardy and his Philosophy* (1928), Patrick Braybrooke; *Thomas Hardy* (1928), S. C. Chew; *Thomas Hardy* (1929), H. M. Tomlinson; *Thomas Hardy* (1941), Edmund Blunden; *The Pattern of Hardy's Poetry* (1961), Samuel Hynes; *Hardy* (1963), G. Wing. Aspects of Hardy's work are considered also in *Thomas Hardy's Wessex* (revised ed., 1925), Harman Lee; *The Landscape of Thomas Hardy* (1928), Donald Maxwell; *Thomas Hardy* (1931), A. S. MacDowall.

2 *The Pattern of Hardy's Poetry*, Samuel Hynes (1961).

3 See Arthur Symons, loc. cit. in 1; also *Thomas Hardy* (1954), Evelyn Hardy.

4 loc. cit. in 3.

5 See *Le couple humain dans l'œuvre de Thomas Hardy*, P. d'Exideuil (1928).

6 *Tryphena and Thomas Hardy*, Lois Deacon, 1962.

7 *Some Recollections of Emma Hardy, Together with Some Relevant Poems by Thomas Hardy*, notes by Evelyn Hardy and Robert Gittings, 1961.

8 loc. cit. in 1.

9 See the letter to H. H. Child, quoted, *The Later Years* (loc. cit. 1), p. 235.

Chapter 9 · James Thomson

1 *James Thomson*, H. S. Salt (1889); *James Thomson*, B. Dobell (1910); *James Thomson: sein Leben und seine Werke*, J. Weissel; *Weiner Beiträge zur englischen Philologie*, bd. 24 (1906). A critical estimate is provided by Edmund Blunden as an introduction to *The City of Dreadful Night*, etc. (1932). *James Thomson, A Critical Study*, Imogene B. Walker (1950, Cornell University Press). Some biographical matter is to be found in *Charles Bradlaugh*, 2 vols., Hypatia Bradlaugh Bonner (1895). In his lifetime and in the first decade of the twentieth century Thomson attracted a good deal of critical comment, particularly in periodicals.

2 *Satires and Profanities* (1884).

3 *Essays and Phantasies* (1881); *Biographical and Critical Essays* (1896).

4 The Tale of Zobeide in *The Three Calendars*. Thomson notes the source (*Collected Works*, II, p. 443).   5 *Collected Works*, II, p. 442.

Chapter 10 · *Robert Bridges and his Associates*

1 *Poems* (1909), with a memoir by Robert Bridges. *Last Poems* (1905), preface by Mary Coleridge. *A Poet Hidden* (1962), James Sambrook.

2 *Gathered Leaves* (1910), edited with a memoir by Edith Sichel and with extracts from the *Letters and Diaries, Mary Coleridge*; Robert Bridges in *Cornhill* (May 1907); *Poems* (1907), with a preface by Sir Henry Newbolt.

3 A number of references to Robert Bridges are continued in the notes to the chapter on Hopkins, see page 457. Biographical notes are prefixed to *Notes on the Testament of Beauty* (1931), Nowell C. Smith, and I am indebted to him for permission to quote from these; in the *Pelican Record* (Oxford, June 1930) there is a brief article by Oliver Elton; *Robert Bridges* (1914), F. E. Brett Young, is a critical study, as is T. M. Kelshall (1924); in *Pascal the Writer* (*Bulletin of the John Rylands Library*, vol. XV, No 2, 1931) Samuel Alexander compares Pascal and Bridges; in *Poetry, Its Music and Meaning* (1933) Lascelles Abercrombie has an account of the metre of *The Testament of Beauty*; *Oxford Lectures on Poetry* (1934), E. de Sélincourt; *Robert Bridges* (1944), E. H. Thompson. Much valuable information on Bridges's mind and his critical development is to be found in his own prose essays, and especially in the critical memoirs, *D. M. Dolben* (1911); *G. M. Hopkins's Poems* (1918); *Henry Bradley* (1928); see also the collected memoirs in one volume, *Three Friends* (1932). For the bibliography of Bridges see *Bibliographies of Modern Authors*, No 1 (1921); see also for critical studies, *Quarterly Review* (July 1913); *Fortnightly Review* (July 1928); on *The Testament of Beauty* there is an important article in the *Hibbert Journal* (April 1930), by E. de Sélincourt, and another study appears in *Poetry and the Criticism of Life*, H. W. Garrod (1931).

4 *Dolben* (loc. cit. in 3).

5 *Collected Essays*, IV (1927, etc.), p. 158; the spelling has been normalized.

6 *Collected Essays*, I (1927, etc.), p. 5.

⁷ *Henry Bradley* (loc. cit. in 1 above).
⁸ *Collected Essays*, III (1927, etc.).
⁹ A much enlarged edition appeared in 1921.
¹⁰ *Monthly Review* (London, July 1903); *New Quarterly* (London, January 1909).
¹¹ See *Poetical Works* (Oxford, 1912), p. 410.
¹² This was prefaced with an essay on Virgilian hexameters.
¹³ *Milton's Prosody* (Oxford, 1921).
¹⁴ See references in 1; I am indebted in my account to Professor de Sélincourt's admirable article.   ¹⁵ *Poor Poll*, 1921.

Chapter 11 · Gerard Manley Hopkins

¹ *Poets and Poetry of the Nineteenth Century*, A. H. Miles (1893); *Lyra Sacra*, ed. H. C. Beeching (1895); *The Spirit of Man*, ed. by Robert Bridges (1915).

² A number of critical studies followed Bridges's edition of 1918: J. Middleton Murry in *Aspects of Literature* (1920); 'Father Gerard Hopkins', by Frederick Page, *Dublin Review* (1920); I. A. Richards in *The Dial* (September 1926); Laura Riding and Robert Graves in *A Survey of Modernist Poetry* (1926). In 1930, after the publication of the second edition, the critical interest was massive: *Gerard Manley Hopkins* (1930), G. H. Lahey, S.J.; *Seven Types of Ambiguity* (1930), William Empson, in which chap. VII has a consideration of Hopkins, especially on 'The Windhover'; *Form in Modern Poetry* (1932), Herbert Read; *New Bearings in English Poetry* (1932), F. R. Leavis; *The Poetry of G. M. Hopkins* (1933), Elsie E. Phare; *A Hope for Poetry* (1934), Cecil Day Lewis (Day Lewis, as a poet, was much under Hopkins's influence); *Aspects of Modern Poetry* (1934), Edith Sitwell; *New Verse, No. 14*, a 'Hopkins Number' (1935); 'The Wreck of the Deutschland', W. H. Gardner, in *Essays and Studies* (1935); *The Mind and Poetry of G. M. Hopkins, S.J.* (1935), Bernard Kelly; *Gerard Manley Hopkins, A Study of Poetic Idiosyncrasy in Relation to Poetic Tradition*, 2 vols., vol. I, 1944, revised 1948, and vol. II, 1949, W. H. Gardner; *A Bibliographical Study of Hopkins Criticism 1918-1949* (1950), Maurice A. Charney; *Poems and Prose of Gerard Manley Hopkins* (1953), W. H. Gardner; *Gerard Manley Hopkins* (1955), G. E. H. Grigson.

NOTES TO CHAPTER ELEVEN

³ *The Letters of Gerard Manley Hopkins to Robert Bridges*, edited by C. C. Abbott (1935); *The Letters of G.M.H. and R. W. Dixon*, edited by C. C. Abbott (1935); *The Note-books and Papers of G. M. H.*, edited by Humphrey House (1937); *Further Letters of G.M.H. including his Correspondence with Coventry Patmore*, edited by C. C. Abbott (1938; second edition enlarged, 1956); *The Notebooks and Papers of G. M. Hopkins*, 2 vols. (1959): vol. I, *The Journals and Papers*, ed. by Humphrey House, completed by Graham Storey; vol. II, *The Sermons and Devotional Writings*, ed. by Christopher Devlin.
⁴ *Robert Bridges and Gerard Hopkins, 1863-1889, A Literary Friendship* (1960).
⁵ See *In Defence of Shelley and other Essays* (1936).
⁶ *Robert Bridges* (1944).
⁷ This poem appeared in *Once a Week* (14 February 1863), and was thus Hopkins's first published work. The version appearing in *Poems* shows much revision.
⁸ *Poems* (1918), ed. Robert Bridges.
⁹ *G. M. Hopkins*, W. H. Gardner, vol. I, p. 9 (1948).
¹⁰ *G. M. Hopkins*, vol. I, chap. II (1948).
¹¹ *The Common Pursuit* (1952).
¹² Bridges, as in 9 above.
¹³ Bridges, as in 9 above.
¹⁴ *Poems*, edition of 1930.
¹⁵ As in 14 above.
¹⁶ Gardner, vol. II, p. 263.
¹⁷ Letters of G. M. H. to R. Bridges, ed. C. C. Abbott.
¹⁸ *The Poetry of G. M. Hopkins* (1933).

Chapter 12 · Lighter Verse, Comic and Nonsense Verse

¹ *Miscellanies* (London, 1796); see also *Letters on Literature* (1889), Andrew Lang.
² For a further account of the use of these French forms in English, see *The Ballade*, H. L. Cohen (New York, 1915), and *Lyric Forms from France*, H. L. Cohen (New York, 1922); also *Ballads and Rondeaus*, etc., ed. (1887) Gleeson White.
³ *Latter-Day Lyrics* (1878), W. D. Adams.

NOTES TO CHAPTER TWELVE

⁴ *Austin Dobson. Some notes by Alban Dobson. With chapters by Sir Edmund Gosse and George Saintsbury* (1928); *Austin Dobson. An Anthology* (1924), Alban Dobson.

⁵ *A Bibliography of Austin Dobson* (First Edition Club, 1925), Alban Dobson.

⁶ See Stephen Gwynn in the *Dictionary of National Biography*.

⁷ *The Library of Edmund Gosse* (1924), E. H. M. Cox; *The Life and Letters of Sir Edmund Gosse* (1931), Sir Evan E. Charteris; *The Correspondence of André Gide and Edmund Gosse, 1904-1928* (1960); *Sir E. Gosse's Correspondence with Scandinavian Writers* (1960), ed. Elias Bredsdorff.

⁸ loc. cit. in 7.

⁹ It was Andrew Lang's desire that no official biography should be published; there is an excellent notice in the *Dictionary of National Biography*, by G. S. Gordon, and this can be supplemented by the same author's *Andrew Lang Lecture* (1927): a number of studies have appeared; *Lang, Lockhart and Biography* (1934), H. J. C. Grierson; *Andrew Lang's Work for Homer* (1929), A. Shewan; *Andrew Lang as Historian* (1930), J. Omerod; *Andrew Lang and the Border* (1933), J. Buchan; *Andrew Lang's Poetry* (1937), A. B. Webster; *The Poetry of Andrew Lang* (1943), James Omerod; *Andrew Lang and St Andrews. A Centenary Anthology* (1944), ed. J. B. Salmond; *Andrew Lang* (1946), R. L. Green; *Andrew Lang the Poet* (1948), G. G. A. Murray; *Concerning Andrew Lang, Being the Andrew Lang Lectures delivered before the University of St Andrews, 1927-1937* (1949); see also the critical symposium on Lang's work in the *Quarterly Review* (April 1913), and the article in the same review by George Saintsbury (October 1923).

¹⁰ Mrs Andrew Lang has some comments in her introduction on the ethics of preserving fugitive verse. But who is to decide what is fugitive verse?

¹¹ 'In Ercildoune' in *Ban and Arrière Ban* (1894).

¹² *Edward Lear* (1938 and 1950), Angus Davidson; *The Field of Nonsense* (1952), Elizabeth Sewell; see also *The Letters of Edward Lear to Chichester Fortescue*, etc. (1907), ed. by Lady Strachey; *Further Letters* (1911), ed. by Lady Strachey.

¹³ With E. V. Lucas's account in the *Dictionary of National Biography* see *The Life and Letters of Lewis Carroll*, Stuart Dodgson Collingwood (London, 1898); *The Collected Verse of Lewis Carroll*, etc.,

with an introd. by J. F. McDermot (New York, 1924); there are also studies by I. Bowman (1899), Belle Moses (1910); and *A Handbook of the Writings of Rev. C. L. Dodgson*, S. H. Williams and F. Madan (1931); for a list of the works see *A Bibliography of the Writings of Lewis Carroll (C. L. Dodgson, M.A.)*, S. H. Williams (1924); *The Life of Lewis Carroll* (1932), Langford Reed; *Lewis Carroll* (1932), Walter de la Mare; *Lewis Carroll* (1947), Florence B. Lennon; *The Story of Lewis Carroll* (1949), R. L. Green; *The Field of Nonsense* (a study of the works of Lewis Carroll) (1952), Elizabeth Sewell; *The White Knight* (1952), A. L. Taylor; *The Diaries of Lewis Carroll*, 2 vols. (1954), ed. R. L. Green; *Lewis Carroll* (1954), Derek Hudson; *Lewis Carroll Mathematician* (1956), Warren Weaver; *Lewis Carroll* (1960), R. L. Green; *The Lewis Carroll Handbook* (1962), S. H. Williams and F. Madan.

14 Most of the studies deal with the operas. There are biographies; *Sir W. S. Gilbert* (Boston, 1913), Isaac Goldberg; *W. S. Gilbert* (1923), Sidney Dark and Rowland Grey; *The World of Gilbert and Sullivan* (1950), W. A. C. Darlington; *Gilbert and Sullivan* (1950), Hesketh Pearson; *Gilbert and Sullivan* (1951), A. Jacobs; *Gilbert, his life and strife* (1957), Hesketh Pearson.

15 *Cornhill* (December 1863).

16 *The Literary Remains of Charles Stuart Calverley* (1885), with a memoir by W. J. Sendall; *Calverley and some Cambridge Wits* (1929), R. B. Ince.

17 See Calverley's prose papers on translation in loc. cit. in 16.

Chapter 13 · Minor Poets: I

1 *George Macdonald and his wife*, Greville M. Macdonald (1925); *George Macdonald*, Joseph Johnson (1906), a somewhat enthusiastic critical study; *George Macdonald, An Anthology*, C. S. Lewis (1946); a bibliography was published by J. M. Bulloch (1925).

2 *A Note on Dante Rossetti* in *A Look Round Literature* (1886).

3 Lives and studies of R. W. Buchanan have been issued by Archibald Stodart-Walker (1901), Henry Murray (1901), Harriet Jay (1903), and by Arthur Symons in *Studies in Prose and Verse* (1904).

4 Monckton Milnes's preface to *The Luggie* (1862); *David Gray and other Essays*, Robert Buchanan (1868).

NOTES TO CHAPTER THIRTEEN

⁵ There is a biographical sketch of Gerald Massey attached to the edition of his poems edited by S. Smiles (1861).
⁶ *Studies in Poetry and Criticism* (1905).
⁷ *The Life-History of Alexander Anderson,* David Cuthbertson (1929); a biographical sketch by Alexander Brown is attached to *Later Poems* (1909).
⁸ *Joseph Skipsey,* R. Spence Watson (1909).

Chapter 14 · Minor Poets and Poetry: II

¹ *Sir William Watson* (1956), Cecil Woolf, with a check-list of first editions.
² *Martin Tupper* (1930), John Drinkwater; *Martin F. Tupper and the Victorian Middle Class Ballad* (1941), Ralf Buchanan; *Martin Tupper: his rise and fall* (1949), Derek Hudson.
³ *E. Arnold as poetizer and paganizer* (1884), W. C. Wilkinson.
⁴ The *Observer* (5 June 1932); see also Sir Denison Ross's introduction to *The Light of Asia* (1926).
⁵ Biography by Sir H. M. Durand (1913).
⁶ See *Lady Blake's Love Letters* ('the theme from which Owen Meredith took his . . . poem of Lucile') (1884), P. MacCarty; *The Birth of Rowland* (an exchange of letters between Lord Lytton and his wife in 1856) (1956); see preface by Lady Betty Balfour to *Selected Poems* (1896).
⁷ For biography see *J. B. L. Warren,* Hugh Walker (1903). See Edmund Gosse, *Critical Kit-Kats* (1896) for impressions of De Tabley's verse; and Robert Bridges, *Collected Essays* (1927).
⁸ An interesting and favourable estimate will be found in *Michael Field,* Mary C. Sturgeon (1922); T. Sturge Moore has a note *A Selection from the Poems* (1923); *Works and Days* (1933), edited from the journal of Michael Field by T. and D. C. Sturge Moore.
⁹ For biography there is a discriminating notice by Prof. H. B. Charlton in the *Dictionary of National Biography.* The critical studies are coloured by the high esteem in which Phillips was held at the beginning of the century, *Dramatists of To-Day,* E. E. Hale (1906); *Two Poets,* etc., R. A. Streatfield (1901).
¹⁰ See *The Autiobiography* (*1835-1910*), 2 vols. (1911).
¹¹ *Ionicus* (1923), by Reginald, Viscount Esher; a volume based on

about one-fourth of the letters written by Cory to Viscount Esher; *William Cory* (1950), Faith Compton Mackenzie.

12 There is a note by Robert Buchanan in *Poems, a selection* (1892); a biographical essay by P. Addlesham with *Selected Poems* (1897), and a note by J. A. Symonds in *The Collected Poems* (1902).

13 *John Addington Symonds* (1964), Phyllis Grosskurth, is the fullest biography based on material from an autobiography which cannot be fully published until 1976; it discloses the strange complexity of Symonds's homosexual life. See also *Letters and Papers of J. A. Symonds*, H. E. Brown (1923); the same author has an earlier study in 1903; Van W. Brooks (1914) has a psychological interpretation of Symonds.

14 For biography see *My Diaries (1888-1914)* (1919-20); *Wilfrid Scawen Blunt* (1961), Earl of Lytton; *Three Victorian Travellers* (1964), T. J. Assad.

15 See autobiographical material in *Collected Poems* (1921).

16 *Aubrey de Vere: Victorian Observer* (1953), Mary P. Reilly; Wilfrid P. Ward, *A Memoir* (1904); critical estimates are found in *Quarterly Review* (April 1896 and April 1902); an excellent anthology of English verse by Irish poets is contained in *A Treasury of Irish Verse*, S. A. Brooke and T. W. Rolleston (1900).

17 C. Dickens wrote an introduction to *Legends and Lyrics* (1866); see also Ferdinand Janku, *A. A. Procter, ihr Leben und ihre Werke* (Vienna, 1912).

18 *Recollections*, Jean Ingelow (1901); *An Appreciation of Jean Ingelow* (1935), E. A. Stedman.

19 *Poetical Works*, edited by Arthur Symons, with a memoir by R. Garnett (1900).

Chapter 15 · *William Ernest Henley and Robert Louis Stevenson*

1 There is an appreciative, brief memoir, *W. E. Henley*, L. C. Cornford (1913); biographically, *W. E. Henley*, Kennedy Williamson (1930), adds little to the information in the excellent notice in the *Dictionary of National Biography*; a fuller account is to be found in *W. E. Henley*, 'John Connell' (1949): the author had available the letters of Henley to Charles Whibley.

NOTES TO CHAPTER FIFTEEN

² *Poems* (1898), *Advertisement*.

³ A large literature has grown around Stevenson and his 'legend'. The official biography is *The Life of R. L. Stevenson* (2 vols.), Sir Graham Balfour (1901, etc). This accepts the 'official' view of Stevenson's personality, as does *The Letters of R. L. Stevenson* (4 vols.), ed. Sidney Colvin (1911). A more dependable portrait is to be found, *R. L. Stevenson*, J. A. Steuart (1924), and particularly in *The True Stevenson*, G. S. Hellman (1925); to this must be added Hellman's editions of the unpublished poems, see 4 below. Some additional letters have been published: *Henry James and R. L. Stevenson* (1948) and *Letters to Charles Baxter* (1956). There have been numerous studies, listed here in chronological order; the title, unless quoted is *Robert Louis Stevenson*: L. C. Cornford (1899); G. K. Chesterton (1902); J. A. Hammerton (1907); *R. L. Stevenson, An Appreciation* (1920), H. H. Harper; *R. L. Stevenson, his work and personality*, essays ed. by A. St. J. Adcock (1924); *An Intimate Portrait of R.L.S.*, Lloyd Osbourne (1924); *La Vie de R. L. Stevenson*, J. M. Carré (Paris, 1929); *R. L. Stevenson* (1947) and *Stevenson and the Art of Fiction*, D. Daiches (1951); John Bowman (1949); Henry Cowell (1950); *The Strange Case of R. L. Stevenson*, Malcolm Elwin (1950); G. B. Stern (1952); *Portrait of a Rebel*, Richard Aldington, 1957.

⁴ The sources of the new poems, and the poems themselves, were edited for *The Bibliophile Society* (Boston) by George S. Hellman (1916 and 1921). A reprint from this collection was issued in England as *New Poems* (1918).

Chapter 16 · John Davidson

¹ There is a brief notice in the *Dictionary of National Biography*. See also *John Davidson, a Study of the Relation of his Ideas to his Poetry*, H. Fineman (Philadelphia, 1916); *John Davidson und sein geistiges Werden unter dem Einfluss Nietzsches*, Gertrud von Petzold (Leipzig, 1928); there are also two essays on J. Davidson in *Collected Prose*, J. E. Flecker. *John Davidson, a selection of his poems*, preface by T. S. Eliot, edited by Maurice Lindsay, with an essay by 'Hugh McDiarmid', 1961; *John Davidson*, by J. Benjamin Townsend (Yale University Press; additional biographical material, 1961).

² Maurice Lindsay as above.

NOTES TO CHAPTER SIXTEEN

³ Epilogue to *Mammon and his Message*.
⁴ *The Triumph of Mammon*.
⁵ Epilogue to *Mammon and his Message*.
⁶ *Mammon and his Message*.
⁷ *Testament of an Empire Builder*.
⁸ I frequently employ Davidson's own words from his summary, in his preface to this play.

Chapter 17 · Oscar Wilde, Ernest Dowson, Lionel Johnson and the Poetry of the Eighteen Nineties

¹ There is a large biographical literature; much of it concerns Wilde's life and the trials. Of the biographies the most satisfactory is *Life of Oscar Wilde*, Hesketh Pearson (1954); *The Trials of Oscar Wilde* was edited with an introduction (1948) by H. Montgomery Hyde. For the life in its brilliance and its shabby conclusion the essential volume is *The Letters*, edited (1963) by Rupert Hart-Davies. Among other studies are *Oscar Wilde* (1911), R. H. Sherard; *O. Wilde* (1912), Arthur Ransome; *Oscar Wilde and Myself* (1914), Lord Alfred Douglas; *Oscar Wilde* (1918), Frank Harris; *Oscar Wilde* (1930), Arthur Symons; *Aspects of Wilde* (1936), Vincent O'Sullivan, valuable for Wilde in his last days and for a portrait of Leonard Smithers, the publisher of the nineties poets. Very little of this literature gives attention to Wilde's poetry.

² These pieces, some of which were collected into the volume of 1881, are to be found in the *Month*, the *Illustrated Monitor*, the *Irish Monthly*, *Kottabos*, *Time*.

³ *Walter Pater's Einfluss auf Oscar Wilde*, Bonner Studien zur englischen Philogie, VIII (1913), E. J. Bock; *Studien zu Oscar Wilde's Gedichten* (1918), Dr Bernhard Fehr, *Palaestra*, 100.

⁴ 23 July 1881.

⁵ Memoir by Arthur Symons prefixed to *The Poems of Ernest Dowson* (1905); *Ernest Dowson 1888-1897: reminiscences, unpublished letters, and marginilia*, with a bibliography (1914), V. G. Plarr; *The Poetical Works of E. C. Dowson* (1934), ed. Desmond Flower: this has a valuable critical introduction; *The Dowson Legend* (1939), 'John Gawsworth'; *Ernest Dowson* (1944), J. M. Longaker.

⁶ Memoir, loc. cit. in 5.

⁷ *Carmina,* Lib. IV.i.

⁸ *Selections* (1908) with a prefatory memoir by Clement K. Shorter. *Some Poems of Lionel Johnson* (1912), with an introduction by Louise Imogen Guiney; *Poetical Works* (1915), edited with a preface by Ezra Pound; *The Religious Poems* (1916), with a preface by Wilfrid Meynell; *Some Winchester Letters of Lionel Johnson* (1919). Further letters appeared in *The Criterion* (1925); *The Complete Poems* (1953), ed. by Iain Fletcher.

⁹ *The Renaissance of the Nineties* (1911), W. B. Murdoch; *The Eighteen-Nineties* (1913), Holbrook Jackson; *The Men of the Nineties* (1920), Bernard Muddiman; *Le Mouvement esthétique et décadent en Angleterre (1873-1900)* (Paris, 1931), A. J. Farmer; *The Beardsley Period* (1925), Osbert Burdett; *The Romantic 90's* (1925), Richard le Gallienne.

¹⁰ The standard biography, based on much original material, is *Arthur Symons* (1963), Roger Lhombreaud.

Chapter 18 · *Rudyard Kipling*

¹ There is a considerable literature on Kipling, though, naturally, most of it deals with his achievement in prose and fiction. There are bibliographies: *Bibliography of the Works of R. Kipling, 1881-1921* (1923), E. W. Martindell; *Bibliography of the Works of Rudyard Kipling* (1927; Supplement, 1938), F. V. Livingston; *Rudyard Kipling, a bibliographical catalogue* (1959), J. McG. Stewart; the fullest biography is *Rudyard Kipling, his Life and Works* (1955), Charles Carrington; see also *Schooldays with Rudyard Kipling* (1936), G. C. Beresford, and Kipling's own unrevealing account of his life *Something of Myself* (1937). There are numerous studies of varying importance, quoted here in the order of appearance: *The Lamp and the Lute* (1929), Bonamy Dobrée, and the same author's *Rudyard Kipling* (1951); *Rudyard Kipling* (1936), A. Chevrillon; *Rudyard Kipling* (1940), E. Shanks; *A Choice of Kipling's Verse* (1941), T. S. Eliot's anthology with an admirable and sympathetic introduction, where he rightly asserts that the verse and the prose should be studied together; *The Wound and the Bow* (1941), Edmund Wilson, one of the most penetrating attempts to analyse Kipling's personality; *Rudyard Kipling* (1945), H. C. Brown; *A Choice of Kipling's Prose* (1952), Somerset

Maugham; *La Poétique de Rudyard Kipling* (1958), F. Léaud; *The Art of Rudyard Kipling* (1959), Joyce M. S. Tompkins; *Kipling's Mind and Art* (1964), ed. Andrew Rutherford.

2 Carrington, see 1 above.

Chapter 19 · *Alfred Edward Housman*

1 Among bibliographical studies are *A Bibliography of A. E. Housman* (1941), T. G. Ehrsalm, and *An Annotated Hand-list* (1952), J. W. Carter and John Sparrow: there is *A Concordance to the Poems of A. E. Housman* (1940), C. K. Hyder. The most informative volumes about Housman are *Author Hunting* (1934) and *Housman 1897-1936* (1941), by Grant Richards. He was Housman's publisher and though different in almost all aspects of their personalities a great friendship grew up between them. The most convenient text is *The Collected Poems* (1939), which, in addition to the poems in the two volumes published in Housman's lifetime, includes forty-eight poems published as *More Poems* (1936) and twenty-three additional poems and three translations from the Greek. Many of Housman's manuscripts were acquired by the Library of Congress, and it has been a subject of dispute whether the fragments and unpublished pieces from his notebooks should have been published. They appeared as *The Manuscript Poems of A. E. Housman* (1955), T. B. Haber, and they are incorporated into *Complete Poems* (1959), introduction by Basil Davenport and a history of the text by T. B. Haber. There have been a number of studies of Housman: *A. E. Housman, A Sketch* (1936), A. S. F. Gow: Gow knew Housman well during his years at Cambridge, and the volume includes a list of Housman's writings and indices to his classical papers; *Memories of A. E. Housman* (1936), Katharine E. Symons; *A.E.H.* (1937), a biography with letters and some unpublished poems, and *The Unexpected Years* (1937) are by Housman's brother, Laurence Housman; *A Buried Life* (1940), P. Withers; *A. E. Housman, An Annotated Check-List, Library* (September 1940), and as a volume (London, 1952), John Carter and John Sparrow; *A. E. Housman, W. B. Yeats*, etc. (1955), Richard Aldington; *A. E. Housman* (1955), Ian S. Kilvert; *A Poet's Scholarship, A Study of Housman as a Critic* (1955), A. Norman Marlow; *A. E. Housman, A Divided Life* (1957): George L. Watson elaborates the consequences of Housman's friendship with M. J.

Jackson: the homosexual theme is elaborated and the volume has been much criticized, but it is a serious contribution with much new material; *A. E. Housman: man behind a mask* (1958), Maude M. Hawkins; *A. E. Housman: scholar and poet* (1958), Norman Marlow, a volume on Housman's poetry by a classical scholar and especially valuable for its account of the literary influences and of Housman's reputation. I am much indebted to this volume and to suggestions made to me personally by Norman Marlow; *Catalogue of an exhibition on the centenary of his birth* (1959), J. W. Carter and J. W. Scott; *A. E. Housman* (1960), Otto Skutsch, deals mainly with Housman as a scholar. I am also much indebted to John Sparrow for reading this text and commenting.

2 *Housman 1897-1936*, Grant Richards (1941).
3 *A. E. Housman*, Otto Skutsch (1960).
4 *A Shropshire Lad*, XLIII.
5 *A Shropshire Lad*, II.
6 *New Statesman* (23 May 1936, p. 801).
7 *Last Poems* (1922).
8 *Independent Essays*, John Sparrow (1963).

INDEX

Main entries are indicated by heavier type; separate works are indicated by italics; and single poems, etc, by quotation marks.

Abbot, C. C., on G. M. Hopkins, 458
Abercrombie, Lascelles, on Sir Henry Taylor, 443; on Thomas Hardy, 217, 455; on Robert Bridges, 456
Adams, W. D., *Latter-Day Lyrics*, 459
Adcock, A. St. J., on R. L. Stevenson, 463
Addlesham, P., on Hon. Roden Noel, 462
'A.E.' (George Russell), 350
Aeschylus, 67, 431
Aldington, R., on A. E. Housman, 466; on R. L. Stevenson, 463
Alexander, C., on the Catholic element in nineteenth century poetry, 450
Alexander, Sir George, 338
Alexander, S., on Robert Bridges, 456
'Alleyn, Ellen' (pseud. of Christina Rossetti)
Allingham, Helen, 133
Allingham, William, 26, 28, **132–8**, 350, 449–50
'Æolian Harp', 135
Ashby Manor, 133
Blackberries, 133
By the Way, 133, 135
Day and Night Songs, 133
Day and Night Songs and the Music Master, 133
Diary, 135
'Evening, An', 134
Evil May-Day, 133, 134
'Fairies, The', 134
'Four Ducks on a Pond', 134
Irish Songs and Poems, 133
'Lady Alice', 133
Laurence Bloomfield in Ireland, 133, **135–6**
Music Master, The, 133
Nightingale Valley, 133
'Pilot's Song, The', 133
Poems 133,
Rambles in England and Ireland, 450
Songs, Ballads and Stories, 133
'Therania', 135
Varieties in Prose, 133
'Witch-Bride, The', 134
'Would I knew', 135
Alma-Tadema, Sir Lawrence, 130
Anacreon, 164
Anderson, Alexander, **321–2**, 461
Ballads and Sonnets, 321
'Cuckoo, The', 321
'Cuddle Doon', 322
'In Rome', 322
Later Poems, 321
Songs of Labour, 321
Songs of the Rail, 321
Two Angels, The, 321
Andrews, Emily (Mrs Patmore), 156, 167
Angeli, Helen Rossetti, 443
Anglo-Saxon verse, comparisons with, 81, 122, 277, 284, 285
Anodos (pseud. of Mary Coleridge).
Apollodorus, 67
Apollonius of Rhodes, 67
Apuleius, 119, 257

[468]

INDEX

Aquinas, 167
Arabian Nights, The, 93, 95, 119, 143, 229, 328
Arnold, Sir Edwin, **327-8**, 329, 330, 461
  Feast of Belshazzar, The, 327
  Light of Asia, The, 327, 328
  Light of the World, The, 328
  Poems National and non-Oriental, 328
Arnold, Matthew, ix, 2, 3, 8-10, 12, 17, 55, 84, 159, 167, 228, 229, 235, 265, 273, 332, 333, 346, 359, 393, 397, 398, 412, 413, 443
  'Balder Dead', 9
  'Dover Beach', 9, 412
  'Empedocles on Etna', 9-10
  'Forsaken Merman, The', 10
  'Heine's Grave', 359
  Merope, 9
  New Poems, 12
  'Philomela', 359
  Poems (1853), 9
  'Resignation', 8
  'Rugby Chapel', 265
  'Scholar-Gipsy, The', 10, 397
  'Sohrab and Rustum', 9
  'Strayed Reveller, The', 10, 359
  'Thyrsis', 397
Art and Poetry, 21
Arthurian influences, 12, 54, 85, 113, 225, 379
Assad, T. J., on W. S. Blunt, 462
Athenæum, The, 26, 57, 103, 176
Augustine, St, *Confessions*, 176
Austen, Jane, 165
Austin, Alfred, **340-2**
  Autobiography, 461
  Fortunatus the Pessimist, 340
  Garden that I Love, The, 341
  Interludes, 341
  Poetry of the Period, The, 341
  Randolph, 340
  Sacred and Profane Love, 341
  Tower of Babel, The, 340
Aytoun, W. E., 11, 287
  Firmilian, 11

Bailey, P. J., *Festus*, 11
Baillie, A. W. M., 272
Baldwin, Alfred, 422
Balestier, Beatty, 423
Balestier, Carrie (Mrs R. Kipling), 423
Balestier, Wolcott, 423
Balfour, Lady Betty, on 'Owen Meredith', 461
Balfour, Sir Graham, on R. L. Stevenson, 363, 463
Ballads, influence of, 27, 34, 43, 55, 94, 313-14, 373, 379 et seq., 424, 435-7
Bandello, 143
Banville, Theodore de, 288, 289, 295, 405
Barham, R. H., *The Ingoldsby Legends*, 287
Barnes, William, 207-8, 211, 307
Barton, J. E., on T. Hardy, 455
Baudelaire, C., 14, 51, 72, 86, 140, 145, 394, 396, 398, 399, 400, 402, 405, 416, 419
Baum, P. F., on D. G. Rossetti, 443, 444, 445
Bax, Arnold, 437
Beach, J. W., on G. Meredith, 453
Beacock, G. A., on Francis Thompson, 452
Beardsley, Aubrey, 404, 407, 408, **414-15**, 416, 417, 418, 419, 420
  Under the Hill, 419
Beddoes, T. L., 4, 48
  Death's Jest Book, 48
Beeching, Canon H. C., 253, 457
Beerbohm, Max, 414, on D. G. Rossetti, 444
Bell, H. T. M., on Christina Rossetti, 447
Benson, A. C., on D. G. Rossetti, 444; on W. Johnson Cory, 342, 345
Benson, Sir Frank, 335
Bentham, Jeremy, 4
Bentley, R., 429
Beresford, G. C., on R. Kipling, 465
Betjeman, John, 418
Binyon, Laurence, 336, 419
Birkhead, Edith, on Christina Rossetti, 447
Black, J. W., on T. Hardy, 455
Blackwood's Edinburgh Magazine, 11, 158
Blake, William, 14, 33, 72, 83, 86, 130, 233, 242, 255, 323, 365, 387
  'Evening', 255
Blind, Mathilde, 354
  Ascent of Man, The, 354

INDEX

Blind, Mathilde—*cont'd.*
Birds of Passage, 354
Dramas in Miniature, 354
'Fantasy, A', 354
Heath on Fire, The, 354
'Hunter's Moon, The', 354
Prophecy of St Oran, The, 354
Songs and Sonnets, 354
'Songs of Summer, The', 354
Bloomfield, Paul, on W. Morris, 449
Blunden, Edmund, on James Thomson, 455; on T. Hardy, 455
Blunt, W. Scawen, **347–8**, 462
Diaries, 347
Esther, 347, 348
Francis Thompson, 452
Seven Golden Odes, The, 347, 348
Sonnets and Songs by Proteus, 347, 348
Boccaccio, Giovanni, 139, 143, 157
Bock, E. J., on O. Wilde, 464
Bonner, H. Bradlaugh, 455
Book Collector, The, 432
Borrow, George, 313
Boughton, Rutland, 152
Bowman, I., on 'Lewis Carroll', 460
Bowman, J., on R. L. Stevenson, 463
Boyd, Alice, 25, 88, 129
Boyle, Anne (Mrs W. E. Henley), 357–8
Bradlaugh, Charles, 227, 230
Bradley, Henry, 247
Bradley, Katharine. See 'Field, Michael'
Brantôme, 57, 59
Braybrooke, P., on T. Hardy, 455
Bredsdorff, E., on E. Gosse, 459
Brennecke, E., on T. Hardy, 455
Breviary, The Paris, 304
Bridges, Robert, x, xi, 13, 154–5, 236, 237, 238, 239, 240, 241, **243–67**, 268, 269–70, 271, 272, 273, 274, 275–6, 289, 353, 408, 456–7
Achilles in Scyros, 244, 261, 262
'Cheddar Pinks', 256
Christian Captives, The, 244, 261
Classical prosody, experiments in, 245, 247, 253 et seq.
'Clear and Gentle Stream', 248
Critical essays and comments: on Henry Bradley, 247, 456; on Mary Coleridge, 241; on Lord De Tabley, 461; on Canon Dixon, 238, 239; on D. M. Dolben, 236, 245, 247, 456; on G. M. Hopkins, 268, 274, 275–6; on John Keats, 245–6; on Milton's prosody, 253–4, 255, 256
Demeter, a masque, 244, 258, 259
'Downs, The', 249
Dramas by R. Bridges, 258 et seq.
'Elegy', 248
'Epistles', 255
Eros and Psyche, 244, 257, 259
Feast of Bacchus, The, 244, 260, 261
'Garden in September, The', 251
Growth of Love, The (sonnet sequence), 244, 246, **251–3**
Humdrum and Harum-Scarum, 255
Humours of the Court, The, 244, 261
Ibant Obscuri, 255
'Invitation to the Country', etc., 249
'Joy sweetest lifeborn joy', etc., 250
'Kate's Mother', 256
Later Poems, 253
'London Snow', 245, 250
'Long are the hours the sun is above', 249
Milton's influence on R.B., 248 et seq.
Nero (1885 and 1894), 244, 259–60 262
New Poems (1899), 253
New Verse (1921), 244, 255
'North wind came up yesternight, The', 251
Now in Wintry Delights, 244, 254–5
October, etc., 244, 255
'Ode to Music, Henry Purcell', 253
'On a Dead Child', 250
Palicio, 244, 261
Poems (1873), 243, 244, 248, 289
Poems (various issues from 1876–96), 244
Prometheus the Firegiver, 244, 258–9
'Reply', 249
Return of Ulysses, The, 244, 261–2
Sonnet, Bridges's use of, 251 et seq.
'South Wind, The', 253
Spirit of Man, The, 244, 246, 247
Testament of Beauty, The, 243, 244, 246, 247, 250, 253, 254, 255, 256, **262–7**
'There is a hill', etc., 249

[470]

INDEX

'To a Socialist in London', 255
Yattendon Hymn Book and *Psalter*, 244
Briggs, Asa, on W. Morris, 449
Briggs, R. C. H., on D. G. Rossetti and W. Morris, 443, 448
Brimley, George, on Coventry Patmore, 451
Brontë, Emily, 11–12, 48, 56
Brooke, A. Stopford, on W. Morris, 449
Brooks, Van W., on J. A. Symonds, 462
Brown, A., on A. Anderson, 461
Brown, Ford Madox, 19, 107, 138
Brown, H. C., on R. Kipling, 465
Brown, H. E., on J. A. Symonds, 462
Brown, Oliver Madox, 146
Brown, T. E., 357
Browning, Elizabeth Barrett, 48, 82, 90, 100, 184, 185, 331, 352
  Aurora Leigh, 48, 331
Browning, Oscar, 342
Browning, Robert, ix, x–xi, 3, 4, 5, 6–7, 8, 9, 10, 12, 17, 27, 28, 29, 56, 62, 66, 112, 113, 118, 119, 132, 141, 149, 158, 159, 167, 184, 193, 196, 210, 213, 232, 246, 247, 248, 264–5, 283, 288, 304, 305, 306, 309, 331, 332, 334, 335, 341, 348, 353, 354, 355, 428
  Balaustion's Adventure, 118
  Christmas Eve and Easter Day, 6, 232, 265
  'Guardian Angel, The', 232
  Men and Women, 5
  Pauline, 3, 5
  'Porphyria's Lover', 113
  Ring and the Book, The, 5, 6, 62, 305
  'Saul', 6
Brownwell, W. C., on G. Meredith, 453
Brunelleschi, Filippo, 397
Buchan, J., on A. Lang, 459
Buchanan, R., on Martin Tupper, 461
Buchanan, Robert Williams, 26, 39, **311–16**, 460
  'Antony in Arms', 312–13
  Balder the Beautiful, 314
  'Ballad of Judas Iscariot, The', 315–16
  'Ballad of Mary the Mother, The', 315

Ballad Stories of the Affections, 312, 313
Book of Orm, The, 314
City of Dream, The, 314
David Gray and other Essays, 312, 460
Devil's Case, The, 314
Earthquake, The, 315
Fleshly School of Poetry, The (under pseud. of 'Thomas Maitland'), 26, 39, 311
Idyls and Legends, etc., 312, 313
'Jane Lewson', 313
'Little Milliner, The', 313
London Poems, 312, 313
'Nell', 313
North Coast, etc., 312, 313–14
'Northern Wooing, The', 314
'Outcast, The', 314
'Poet Andrew', 313
Saint Abe and his Seven Wives, 315
'Satyr, The', 312
'Sigurd the Saxon', 314
Undertones, 312
'Vision of the Man Accurst, The', 314
Wandering Jew, The, 314, 315
White Rose and Red, 315
'Willie Baird', 313
Bulloch, J. M., on G. Macdonald, 460
Burden, Jane. See Mrs Wm. Morris.
Burdett, Osbert: on Coventry Patmore, 450; on the Nineties, 465
Bürger, G. A., 27, 34
  'Lenore', 27
Burne-Jones, Lady (Georgie), 116, 422
Burne-Jones, Sir Edward Coley, 22, 48, 56, 105, 106, 237, 322, 422
Burns, Robert, 246, 322, 366, 370
Burton, Sir Richard Francis, 50, 84
Bush, D., on G. Meredith, 453
Butler, Lady Elizabeth, 182–3, 184, 452, 453
Butterworth, G., 437
Byles, Caroline (Mrs C. Patmore), 156
Byron, Lord, 1, 3, 14, 16, 18, 28, 39, 48, 65, 66, 86, 306, 331, 390, 442
  Beppo, 3
  Doge of Venice, The, 65
  Don Juan, 3, 331
  Giaour, The, 28
  Manfred, 11

INDEX

Byron, Lord—*cont'd.*
  Vision of Judgement, The, 3
'Bysshe, Vanolis. See Thomson, James.

Caine, Sir Thomas Hall, on D. G. Rossetti, 116, 444
Cairoli, Signora, 77
Calderon, 261
Calverley, Charles Stuart (born Blayds), **303–5**, 460
  'Auld wife sat at her ivied door, The', etc., 305
  'Cock and Bull story, The', 305
  Fly Leaves, 304
  'Ode to Tobacco', 305
  Theocritus translated into English Verse, 304
  Thomasius's hymn translated by C.S.C., 304
  Translations into English and Latin, 304
  Verses and Translations, 304
Calverley, Walter, 303
Campbell, Mrs Patrick, 380
Carlyle, Thomas, 1, 6, 132, 199, 201, 203, 309
Carr, J. Comyns, 336
Carré, J. M., on R. L. Stevenson, 463
Carrington, C., on R. Kipling, 427–8, 465
'Carroll, Lewis' (pseud. of Charles Lutwidge Dodgson), **299–302**, 459–60
  Alice's Adventures in Wonderland, 300
  Euclid and his Modern Rivals, 300
  Hunting of the Snark, The, 300, 301–2
  'Jabberwocky', 301
  Phantasmagoria, 300
  Rhyme? and Reason?, 300
  Sylvie and Bruno, 300
  Through the Looking Glass, 300
Carter, J.; on W. J. Cory, 342, 343; on A. E. Housman, 432, 466, 467; on A. C. Swinburne, 446
Cary, Elizabeth L., on the Rossettis, 447
Catholic influences on nineteenth-century poetry, 8, 13, 19, 33, 154, 173 et seq., 186, 237, 268 et seq., 395, 403, 411, 450–1
Catullus, 48
Cavalcanti, Guido, 37

Cayley, C. Bagot, 87, 94
Cazalis, Henri, 142
Century Guild Hobby Horse, The, 404, 445
Chambers, R. W., 430; on Byron, etc., 442
Chambers, Robert, 7
Chambers's Journal, 189, 206
Champneys, B., on Coventry Patmore, 450
Chapman, George, 65
Charles d'Orleans, 295
Charlton, H. B., on Stephen Phillips, 461
Charney, M. A., on G. M. Hopkins, 458
Charnock, R. S., 189
Charteris, Sir Evan, on E. Gosse, 459
Chaucer, Geoffrey, 39, 117, 119, 120, 193, 246
Chesterton, G. K., on R. L. Stevenson, 463
Chevrillon, A., on R. Kipling, 465
Chew, S. C., 442; on A. C. Swinburne, 446; on T. Hardy, 455
Child, H. H., on T. Hardy, 455
Chislett, W., on G. Meredith, 453
Chopin, 142
Civil and Military Gazette (India), 423
Clare, John, 4
Clodd, Edward, 453
Clough, Arthur Hugh, 9, 443
Clutton-Brock, Arthur, on William Morris, 449
Cockerell, Sir Sydney, 207
Cohen, H. L., on the ballade, 458
Coleridge, Mary Elizabeth (pseud. 'Anodos'), 155, 238, **240–3**, 456
  Collected Poems, 240
  'Depart from me, I know thee not', 242
  Fancy's Following, 240
  Fancy's Guerdon, 240
  'Imagination', 242
  King with Two Faces, The (prose work), 240
  Letters and Diaries, 240
  'Master and Guest', 241
  'Moment, A', 242
  'Mother to a Baby', 242
  'Other Side of a Mirror, The', 242
  Preface to *Last Poems* of Canon Dixon, 457

[472]

INDEX

'Thee have I sought, divine Humility', 242
'Wilderspin', 241, 242
'Witch, The', 241
Coleridge, Samuel Taylor, xi, 2, 3–4, 5, 6, 14, 17, 44, 76, 92, 97, 129, 157, 162, 178, 180, 181, 182, 211, 240, 241, 301, 401, 402, 432
  'Ancient Mariner, The', 44, 92, 97, 99–100, 157, 178, 301, 401
  'Kubla Khan', 180
Collingwood, S. D., on 'Lewis Carroll' 459–60
Collins, J. Churton, on Gerald Massey, 319
Collinson, James, 87
Colvin, Sir Sidney, on R. L. Stevenson, 363, 463
Commonweal, The, 109
Congreve, W., 303
'Connell, John', on W. S. Henley, 357, 358, 462; on R. L. Stevenson, 358
Connelly, T. L., on F. Thompson, 452
Connolly, Cyril, on A. E. Housman, 437
Contemporary Review, The, 26, 311
Cooper, Edith. See 'Field, Michael'.
Cope's Tobacco Plant, 227
Coppée, François, 142, 380
  Pour la Couronne, 380
Corbet, Richard, Bishop of Norwich, 434–5
Cornford, L. C., on W. E. Henley, 462; on R. L. Stevenson, 463
Cornforth, Frances, 24–25
Cornhill, The, 228, 288, 352
Cornish, F. Warne, on W. Johnson Cory, 343
Cornwall, Barry, 81
Cory, William Johnson, 241, **342–5**, 461–2
  'Eton Boat Song', 343
  Ionica (1858; 1877; 1891), 344
  Lucretilis, 343
  'Mimnermus in Church', 344
  'They told me Heraclitus you were dead', 344
Cowell, Henry, on R. L. Stevenson, 463
Cowper, William, 97, 280, 379
  'Castaway, The', 97, 379
  'Loss of the Royal George, The', 280

Cox, E. H. M., on E. Gosse, 459
Crabbe, George, 135, 161, 162, 166
Crashaw, William, 174, 175, 176, 180, 181
Crees, J. H. E., on G. Meredith, 453
Criterion, 437, 465
Curle, R. H. P., on G. Meredith, 453
Cuthbertson, David, on A. Anderson, 461

Daiches, D., on R. L. Stevenson, 463
Daily Telegraph, 327
Daniel, Samuel, 56
Danish ballads, influence of, 313, 314
Dante, 17, 29, 35–36, 37, 38, 39, 117, 160, 185, 321, 339
  Divina Commedia, 17, 29, 36, 87
  Vita Nuova, 36
Dark, Sidney, on W. S. Gilbert, 460
Darley, George, 4, 191
  'Serenade of a Loyal Martyr', 191
Darlington, W. A. C., on W. S. Gilbert, 460
Darwin, Charles Robert, 7
Davenport, B., on A. E. Housman, 466
Davidson, A., on E. Lear, 459
Davidson, John, xii, 74, 338, **372–89**, 418, 463–4
  Ballad in Blank Verse, etc., 377, 378
  'Ballad of a Nun, A', 377
  'Ballad of an Artist's Wife, A', 378
  'Ballad of Heaven', 377–8
  Ballads and Songs, 375, 377
  Bruce, 373–4
  Fleet Street, etc., 373, 380, 389
  Fleet Street Eclogues, 375, 376
  Fleet Street Eclogues (Second Series), 375, 378
  Godfrida, 381, 384
  'Good Friday', 376–7
  Holiday, 380, 389
  In a Music Hall, 375–6
  Knight of the Maypole, The, 381, 384
  'Lammas', 378
  Last Ballad, The, 375, 379
  Mammon and his Message, 381, 382, **384–5**
  'May-Day', 378
  'New Ballad of Tannhäuser, A', 378–9
  New Ballads, 375, 378
  'Ordeal, The', 379

INDEX

Davidson, John—*cont'd.*
'Piper, Play', 378
Plays, 374, 380
Random Itinerary, A, 375, 379
Romantic Farce, A, 374
'Runnable Stag, A', 389
'St Swithin's Day', 376
Scaramouch in Naxos, 374–5
Self's the Man, 381, 384
Smith, 375
Testament of a Man Forbid, The, 380, 386
Testament of a Prime Minister, The, 380, 387–8
Testament of a Vivisector, The, 380, 381–2, 385
Testament of an Empire-Builder, The, 380, 382, 386–7
Testament of John Davidson, The, 380, 382, 388–9
Testaments by J. Davidson, 377, **380–3**, 384, **385–9**
Theatrocrat, The, 380, 381, 383, 384, 385
Triumph of Mammon, The, 380, 381, **384–5**
Unhistorical Pastoral, An, 374
'Woman and her Son, A', 378
Deacon, A. W. N., on A. W. E. O'Shaughnessy, 450
Deacon, Lois, on T. Hardy, 455
Dee, Dr John, 43
de la Gorce, A., on F. Thompson, 452
de la Mare, W., on 'Lewis Carroll', 460
Delattre, F., on A. C. Swinburne, 446, 447; on F. Thompson, 452
De Quincey, Thomas, 173, 226, 232
De Tabley, Lord. See Warren, J. B. L.
Deverell, Walter, 22
Devlin, C., on G. M. Hopkins, 458
Dickens, Charles, 52; on A. A. Procter, 462
Disraeli, Isaac, 286, 287
Dixon, Richard Watson (Canon), 155, 236, **237–40**, 242, 246, 268, 269, 456
Christ's Company, 238
'Fall of the Leaf, The', 240
'Fallen Rain', 240
'Feathers of the Willow, The', 238–9
Historical Odes, 238, 239
History of the Church of England, The, 238

'I rode my horse to the Hostel Gate', 239
'Joseph of Arimathea', 239
Last Poems, 238
'Legion', 239
Mano, 238
'Mercury to Prometheus', 239
'Mystery of the Body, The', 239
'Nicodemus', 239
'Ode on Conflicting Claims', 239
'Ode: The Spirit Wooed', 240
Odes and Eclogues, 238
St John in Patmos, 238, 239
'St Mary Magdalene', 239
'St Thomas in India', 239
Selected Poems, 238
Songs and Odes, 238
'Story of Eudocia', 238
'Ulysses and Calypso', 239
Dobell, Bertram, 228; on James Thomson, 455
Dobell, Sydney Thompson, 11, 288, 314, 316
Balder, 11
Dobrée, Bonamy, on R. Kipling, 465
Dobson, Alban, on Austin Dobson, 459
Dobson, Henry Austin, 248, **289–92**, 293, 295, 296, 353, 359, 376, 459
At the Sign of the Lyre, 290
'Ballad of Beau Brocade', 292
'Before Sedan', 290
Collected Poems, 290
'Gentleman of the Old School, A', 291
'Gentlewoman of the Old School, A', 291
'Old Sedan Chair, The', 291
Old-World Idylls, 290
'On a Fan', 291
'Prayer of the Swine to Circe, The', 290
Proverbs in Porcelain, 290
Rondeaus of the Great War, 290
'Some Foreign Forms of Verse', 289
'Une Marquis', 290–1
Vignettes in Rhyme and Vers de Société, 290
Dodgson, Charles Lutwidge. See 'Carroll, Lewis'.
Dolben, Digby Mackworth, **236–7**, 243, 245, 247
'From the Cloister', 237
'Home Factus est', 237

[474]

INDEX

Poems ed. with a memoir by R. Bridges, 236
Donne, John, 102, 175, 181, 201, 211, 284
Doughty, Oswald, on D. G. Rossetti, 443, 444
Douglas, Lord Alfred, on O. Wilde, 392, 464
Dowden, Edward, 350, on G. M. Hopkins, 270
Dowson, Ernest, xi, 372, **402–8**, 411, 414, 416, 417, 418, 419, 438, 464
  Adrian Rome, 403
  'Carthusians', 407
  Comedy of Masks, A, 403
  'Coronal, A', 405
  'Cynara'. See 'Non sum qualis eram'.
  'Dead Child, The', 407
  Decorations, 404
  Dilemmas, 403
  'Non sum qualis . . . Cynarae', 403, 405, 406
  'Nuns of the Perpetual Adoration', 406
  Pierrot of the Minute, The, 404, 407
  Propertius, his influence on E. Dowson, 403, 405
  'To one in Bedlam', 407
  Verses, 404
  'Vitae summa brevis', 405
D'Oyly Carte, R., 302
Drayton, Michael, 56
Drinkwater, John, on W. Morris, 449; on A. C. Swinburne, 446; on M. Tupper, 461
Dryden, John, 136, 205, 338, 406, 433
Dublin Review, The, 183
Duffin, H. C., on T. Hardy, 455
Dugdale, Florence. See Mrs F. Hardy.
Dumas, Alexandre, influence on Swinburne, 57
Dunn, H. T., on D. G. Rossetti, 444, 445
Dupré, Giovanni, 253
Dupré, Henri, on D. G. Rossetti, 444
Durand, Sir H. M., on Sir A. Comyns Lyall, 461
Dürer, Albrecht, 234, 235
Düsseldorf, Album, The, 35

Ehrsalm, T. G., on A. E. Housman, 466

Eighteen-Nineties, poetic movements in the, 414–20, 465
Eliot, George, 183, 228, 319
Eliot, T. S., 417, on J. Davidson, 372, 463; on R. Kipling, 358, 421, 424, 428, 465; on A. E. Housman, 432–3
Elizabethan influences, 48, 51, 54–55, 56, 66–67, 221, 246, 251, 252, 253, 335, 338, 373, 374, 399
Elliott, Ebenezer, 4
Ellis, Havelock, 383, 417
Ellis, S. M., on G. Meredith, 453
Elton, Oliver, 442; on R. Bridges, 456
Elwin, Malcolm, on R. L. Stevenson, 463
Emerson, Ralph Waldo, 130, 143
Empson, W., on G. M. Hopkins, 457
Esdaile, A. J. K., on G. Meredith, 453
Esher, Reginald, Viscount, on W. Johnson Cory, 342, 461
Euripides, 67, 75
Examiner, The, 158
Exideuil, P. d', on T. Hardy, 455
Eyrbyggja Saga, 121

Fane, Julian, 74, 332
  Poems, 332
  Tannhäuser (with 'Owen Meredith'), 74, 332
  Translations from Heine, 332
Farmer, A. J., on the Nineties, 465
Farrar, F., 342
Faulkner, Jane. See Jane Simon.
Faverty, F. E., 446, 447
Fehr, Bernhard, 442, on O. Wilde, 464
Ferguson, Sir Samuel, 351
  Congal, 351
  Lays of the Western Gael, 351
'Field, Michael' (pseud. of Bradley, Katharine, and Cooper, Edith), **334–5**, 461
  Attila, my Attila, 335
  Callirrhoë, 334
  Canute the Great, 334
  Cesare Borgia, play on the theme of, 335
  Deirdre, play on the theme of, 335
  Fair Rosamund, 334
  Father's Tragedy, The, 334
  Herod, play on the theme of, 335
  Julia Domna, 335

INDEX

'Field, Michael'—*cont'd*
   Race of Leaves, The, 335
   Stephania, 335
   Tragic Mary, The, 334
   Tristam, play on the theme of, 335
   William Rufus, 334
   World at Auction, The, 335
Fineman, H., on J. Davidson, 463
Fitzgerald, Edward, 12, 74
   Rubáiyát of Omar Khayyám, 12, 74
Flaubert, Gustave, 405
Flecker, J. E., on J. Davidson, 463
Fletcher, I., on L. Johnson, 465
Flower, Desmond, on E. Dowson, 464
Foerster, M., on D. G. Rossetti, 445
Foltinowicz, Adelaide, 403, 405
Forbes-Robertson, J., 380
Ford, George, on A. C. Swinburne, 55
Fora, John, 172
Forman, H. B., on W. Morris, 449
Forman, M. B., 453
Forster, Sir John, 158
Fortnightly Review, The, 51, 228, 270
Fraser's Magazine, 132, 135
Free verse. See Irregular verse forms.
Freeman, John, on C. Patmore, 451
French influences, 13, 15, 27, 140, 141, 202, 208, 288 et seq., 363, 403
   See also French verse forms.
French Revolution, influence of the, 13, 14, 202
French verse forms, 248, 288 et seq., 295 et seq., 376, 400, 404–5, 413–14, 416
   ballade, 288, 289, 291, 295 et seq.
   chant royal, 288
   rondeau, 248, 288, 376
   rondel, 288, 376
   triolet, 248, 288, 289, 292
   vilanelle, 288, 376
Froissart, Lord Berners's trans. of, 111, 112, 113, 114
Froude, James Anthony, influence on Swinburne, 61, 66, 132

Gale, Norman, 419
   Country Muse, The, 419
Galland, R., on G. Meredith, 453
Gallienne, Richard le; 419, on G. Meredith, 453; on the Nineties, 465

Retrospective Reviews, 419
Gardner, W. H., on G. M. Hopkins, 274–5, 276, 280, 282, 457–8
Garibaldi, G., 77
Garnett, Richard: critical work, on Mathilde Blind, 354, 462; on A. W. E. O'Shaughnessy, 450; on C. Patmore, 172, 450; on Christina Rossetti, 447–8; on T. Woolner, 137
   poetical work of, 355
Garrod, H. W., on R. Bridges, 456
Gaunt, William, on the Pre-Raphaelites, 445
Gautier, Théophile, 14, 72, 81, 86, 140, 418
'Gawsworth, John', on E. Dowson, 464
Gay, John, *The Beggar's Opera,* 292
Genlis, Madame de, *Le Palais de la Vérité,* 302
Germ, The, 12, 21, 89, 91, 105, 136, 137, 138, 193
German influences, 27, 188, 201–2, 226, 231, 309, 310
   (See also under Goethe, Heine, etc.)
Gesta Romanorum, 34, 119
Gibbon, E., 335
Gide, André, 390
Gifford, Emma Lavinia. See Mrs E. Hardy.
Gilbert, Sir William Schwenck, **302–3**, 304, 460
   Bab Ballads, The, 302, 303
   'Captain Reece', 303
   Fun, contributions to, 302, 303
   More Bab Ballads, 302
   Operas of Gilbert and Sullivan, 302, 303
   Palace of Truth, The, 302
   Trial by Jury, 302
Giotto, 397
'Giraldus' (pseud. of W. Allingham).
Gittings, R., on T. Hardy, 215, 455
Gladstone, William Ewart, 356
Glasier, J. B., on W. Morris, 449
Goethe, 10, 27, 34, 42, 188, 310, 320, 322, 359
   Faust, 10, 27
Goldberg, Isaac, on W. S. Gilbert, 460
Golden Treasury, The, 137
Goldsmith, Oliver, 135
Gordon, G. S., on A. Lang, 459

INDEX

Gordon, Mary, 49–50
Gosse, Sir Edmund W., 45, 46, 47, 49, 50, 70, 77, 82, 248, 288–9, **292-3**, 295, 359, 376, 459
  Collected Poems, 293
  Critical work, on A. Dobson, 459; on Coventry Patmore, 450; on Lord De Tabley, 461; on A. C. Swinburne, 45–46, 47, 49, 50, 70, 77, 445, 446, 447; on verse forms, 288–9
  Father and Son, 292
  Firdausi in Exile, 293
  In Russet and Silver, 293
  New Poems, 293
  On Viol and Flute, 293
  'Philomel in London', 293
  'Plea for certain exotic forms of verse, A', 288
  'Winter Night's Dream, A', 293
Gow, A. S. F., on A. E. Housman, 466
Graham, James Lorimer, 81
Graves, A. P., on W. Allingham, 450
Graves, Robert, on G. M. Hopkins, 457
Gray, David, 11, 312, 313, 314, **316-18**, 460
  'In the Shadows', 317–18
  Luggie and other Poems, The, 316, 317
  'Sometimes when sunshine', etc., 317
Gray, John, 419
  Silverpoints, 419
  Spiritual Poems, 419
Gray, Thomas, 123, 176, 177, 192, 406, 412, 430, 434
  'Elegy', 176, 177, 306, 345
Greek influences, 15, 48, 49, 67, 69, 70, 72, 118, 123, 246, 257, 258–9 et seq., 296, 297, 333, 359, 396, 397, 412, 430 et seq.
Green, R. L., on A. Lang, 459; on 'Lewis Carroll', 460
Grey, Rowland, on W. S. Gilbert, 460
Grierson, H. J. C., on A. Lang, 459; on A. C. Swinburne, 446
Grigson, G. E. H., on G. M. Hopkins, 458
Grosskurth, Phyllis, on J. A. Symonds, 346, 462
Guiney, L. I., on L. Johnson, 465
Gurney, Ivor, 437
Gwynn, Stephen, 459

Haber, T. B., on A. E. Housman, 432, 466
Hafiz, 143, 319
Hale, E. E., on S. Phillips, 461
Hallam, Arthur Henry, 7
Hammerton, J. A., on G. Meredith, 453; on R. L. Stevenson, 463
Hardy, Evelyn, on T. Hardy, 211–12, 215, 454, 455
Hardy, Mrs (Emma Lavina Gifford), 212, 214–15, 218
Hardy, Mrs (Florence Dugdale), 213, 214, 454
Hardy, Thomas, x, xii, 15, 188, 201, **205-25**, 266, 379, 409, 454–5
  'After a Journey', 216
  'Alarm, The', 220
  'Amabel', 208
  'At Madame Tussaud's', etc., 210
  'Beeny Cliff', 216
  'Bridge of Lodi, The', 221
  'Dance at the Phoenix, The', 221
  Desperate Remedies, 206
  'Duel, The', 212
  'During Wind and Rain', 215
  Dynasts, The, 205, 207, 212, 219, 220, **221-5**
  'England to Germany in 1914', 220
  Famous Tragedy of the Queen of Cornwall, The, 207, **225**
  'Five Students, The', 216
  'Her Immortality', 214
  How I built myself a house (prose essay), 206
  Human Shows, etc., 207
  'I found her out there', 216
  'In a Museum', 218
  'In Eweleaze near Weatherbury', 214
  'In Tenebris', 213
  'Interloper, The', 216
  'In the Days of the Crinoline', 212
  Jude the Obscure, 207, 214
  Late Lyrics and Earlier, etc, 207, 208, 213
  'Leipzig', 221
  'Let me enjoy the earth no less', 217
  'Little Old Table, The', 214
  'Lonely Days', 215
  'Man was drawing near to me, A', 216
  'Marble-Streeted Town, The', 215
  'Meeting with Despair, A', 217–18

INDEX

Hardy, Thomas—*cont'd.*
   Moments of Vision, 207, 210
   'Mother Mourns, The', 218
   'Nature's Questioning', 217
   'Near Lanivet, 1872', 210
   'New Year's Eve', 218
   'Old Furniture', 209
   'One We Knew', 221
   'Peasant's Confession, The', 221
   'Pity of it, The', 220
   'Place', 215
   'Poems of Pilgrimage' (in *Poems of the Past and the Present*), 208
   Poems of the Past and the Present, 207, 208, 212, 219
   'Poems of War and Patriotism' (in *Moments of Vision*), 220
   Poor Man and the Lady, 206
   'Rain on a Grave', 215
   'Rival, The', 216
   Satires of Circumstance, etc, 207, 208
   'She opened the Door', 216
   'Sick Battle-God, The', 219–20
   'Then and Now', 220
   'Thoughts of Ph—a', etc, 214
   Times's Laughingstocks, etc, 207
   'To an Orphan Child', 214
   'Tramp Woman's Tragedy, A', 216
   Trumpet Major, The, 205, 220
   'Under the Waterfall', 216
   'Valenciennes', 221
   Veteris vestigia flammae, 215
   Well-Beloved, The, 207
   Wessex Poems, etc, 207
   'West-of-Wessex Girl, The', 215
   'What of the faith and fire within us?', 220
   Winter Words, etc, 207, 216–17
   'Woman I Met, The', 209
Hare, H., on A. C. Swinburne, 446
Hargreaves, Mrs Reginald, 300
Harper, H. H., on R. L. Stevenson, 463
Harris, Frank, 403; on O. Wilde, 464
Hart-Davies, Rupert, on O. Wilde, 392, 464
Hartmann von Aue, *Der Arme Heinrich*, 27
Hawkins, Maude M., on A. E. Housman, 466
Hazlitt, William, 155
Hearn, Lafcadio, on D. G. Rossetti, 444
Heine, H., 74, 143, 149, 188, 189, 226,
   231, 232, 233, 234, 241, 322, 331, 353, 360, 362, 368, 400, 435
   Buch der Lieder, 362
   Confessions, 234
   'Ich bin die Prinzessin Ilse', 232
   'Nord-See', 362
   'O Schöne Sphinx', 400
   Romancero, 360
Hellman, G. S., on R. L. Stevenson, 363, 369, 463
Henderson, A., on H. Meredith, 453
Henderson, May S. (later Gretton), on G. Meredith, 453
Henderson, P., on W. Morris, 448
Henderson, W. B. D., on A. C. Swinburne, 446
Henley, W. E., 183, 289, 347, **357–63**, 364, 368, 424, 462
   'Ballade of Dead Actors', 360–1
   Book of Verses, A, 358, 359
   'Casualty', 360
   'Clinical', 360
   Collected Works, 358
   For England's Sake, 358, 362
   Hawthorn and Lavender, 358
   'In Hospital', 359, 361
   Irregular verse forms used by W. E. H., 359–61
   'London Voluntaries', 358, 361–2
   Lyra Heroica,, anthology, ed. by W. E. H., 358
   National Observer, The, ed. by W. E. H., 183, 358
   'Of a Toyokuni Colour-Print', 359
   'Operation', 359
   'Or ever the knightly years were gone', 359
   'Out of the night that covers me', 359
   Passing of Victoria, The, 358
   Poems, 358, 363
   'Pro Rege Nostro', 362
   Scots Observer, The, ed. by W. E. H., 358
   Song of Speed, A, 358, 361
   Song of the Sword, The, 358, 361
   Tudor Translations, The (supervised by W. E. H.), 358
   'Villon's Straight Tip', etc, 363
Herbert, George, 177, 274, 284, 329
   'Discipline', 177
Herrick, Robert, 29, 286, 366
Hervilly, Ernest d', 142

INDEX

Hewitt, R. M., on C. Patmore, 452
Hill, G. B., 22; on D. G. Rossetti, 444
Holst, Theodore von, 301
Homer, 42, 124, 262, 294, 297
Hone, William, *Every Day Book*, 94
Hood, Thomas, 287, 320
Hopkins, Gerard Manley, x, xi, 13, 154, 155, 236, 243, 251, 256, 267, **268–85**, 457–8
  'Bugler's First Communion, The', 283
  'Caged Skylark, The', 282
  'Carrion Comfort', 282–3
  'Escorial, The', 273
  'Felix Randal', 282
  'God's Grandeur', 278, 281
  'Harry Ploughman', 284
  Health and Decay in Art, 275
  'Hurrahing in Harvest', 282
  'In the Valley of the Elwy', 282
  'I wake and feel', etc, 284
  'Loss of the Eurydice, The', 269, 280–1
  'Penmaen Pool', 280
  'Pied Beauty', 282
  Poems of G.M.H., 268
  'Preface on Prosody', 277
  'Silver Jubilee, The', 280
  'Sonnet to Henry Purcell', 277, 282
  'Starlight Night, The', 281
  Vision of the Mermaids, A, 268, 269, 273–4
  'Windhover, The', 281–2
  'Winter with the Gulf-Stream', 274
  'Wreck of the Deutschland, The', 269, 270, 273, 274, **275–6, 279–80**, 282
Horace, 403, 404, 405
Horne, R. H., 11, 189, 453
Orion, 11, 130, 189
Houghton, Lord (R. Monckton Milnes), 2, 11, 50, 156, 316, 317, 318, 460
House, Humphrey, on G. M. Hopkins, 273, 458
Household Words, 133, 189, 193, 352
Housman, A. E., 277, 283, 401, 410, 420, **429–41**, 466–7
  Collected Poems, 432
  Critical editions of Juvenal, Lucan, Manilius, 430
  'Epitaph on an Army of Mercenaries', 434, 435–6, 438
  Fancy's Knell', 434–5
  'From far, from eve and morning', 438
  Last Poems, 431
  More Poems, 432, 438
  Name and Nature of Poetry, The (Lecture), 277, 432, 436–7
  Shropshire Lad, A, 401, 431, 437, 439
  University College Inaugural Lecture, 432, 441
Housman, Laurence, 429, 432, 439, 466
Howe, Susanne, on G. Meredith, 454
Hudson, D., on 'Lewis Carroll', 460; on M. Tupper, 461
Hueffer, Ford Madox, on D. G. Rossetti, 444
Hughes, Randolph, on A. C. Swinburne, 51, 446
Hugo, Victor, 51, 52, 59, 81, 82, 85, 140, 181, 295, 331
  'Feuilles d'Automne', 181
  Marie Tudor, 59
Hunt, J. H. Leigh, 2, 132, 158
Hunt, Violet, on D. G. Rossetti, 444
Hunt, William Holman, 19
Huxley, Thomas Henry, 8
Huysmans, J. K., *A Rebours*, 399
Hydge, H. Montgomery, on O. Wilde, 464
Hyder, C. K., on A. E. Housman, 466; on A. C. Swinburne, 446
Hyndman, H. M., on W. Morris, 109, 449
Hynes, S., on T. Hardy, 208, 210, 455

Ibsen, H., 373
Icelandic influences on nineteenth century poetry, 15, 106–7, 119, 120–1, 123–4
Illustrated Monitor, The, 464
Ince, R. B., on C. S. Calverley, 460
Ingelow, Jean, 352, 462
  'Divided', 352
  'High Tide', etc, 352
  Poems (1863), 352
  Poems (1885), 352
  Recollections, 462
  Story of Doom, A, 352
Ingoldsby Legends, The (R. H. Barham's), 287
Ireland, John, 437
Irish Literary Association, 409

INDEX

Irish Literature, the influence of, 133, 134, 135, 136, 350–1, 404, 409, 411
Irish Monthly, The, 464
Irregular Verse Forms, 255, 359
Italian influences and Italian verse forms, 13, 15, 17, 27, 36–37, 38, 72, 77, 91, 100, 185, 246, 249, 251, 346
  canzone, 72, 246, 249
  ottava rima, 231, 331
  terza rima, 114, 238

Jackson, Holbrook, on the Nineties, 465; on W. Morris, 449
Jackson, M. J., 430, 439, 440, 466
Jacobs, A., on W. S. Gilbert, 460
James, E. F., 61, 446
Jamieson, Robert, 313
Janku, F., on A. A. Procter, 462
Japanese Art, the influence of, 359, 414
Jay, Harriett, on R. Buchanan, 460
Jerrold, W. C., on G. Meredith, 453
John, Augustus, 417
Johnson, General Sir Henry, 408
Johnson, Joseph, on G. Macdonald, 460
Johnson, Lionel Pigot, xi, 350, 403, 404, **405–14**, 418, 464, 465
  Art of Thomas Hardy, The, 409
  Bridges, Robert, L.J.'s article on, 408
  'Burden of Easter Vigil, A', 410
  'By the Statue of King Charles', etc, 410, 413
  'Celtic Speech', 411
  'Cromwell', 411
  'Dark Angel, The', 410
  'Dream of Youth, A', 411
  'In England', 410
  'In Falmouth Harbour', 413
  Ireland, etc, 409, 411
  'Julian at Eleusis', 411
  'Laleham', 412
  'Lines to a Lady', etc, 410
  'Mystic and Cavalier', 414
  'Our Lady of France', 414
  'Oxford Nights', 412
  'Parnell', 411
  'Plato in London', 412–13
  Poems, 409, 410
  Post Liminium, 409
  'Precept of Silence, The', 411
  Reviews and Critical Papers, 409

  'Roman Stage, The', 410
  Sir W. Raleigh in the Tower, 408, 409–10
  'Trentals', 413
  'Wales', 410
  'Ways of War', 411
  'Winchester', 412
  Winchester Letters, 465
Johnson, Dr Samuel, 176, 205, 245, 409
Jones, Ebenezer, 11
Jones, Howard M., on C. Rossetti, 447
Jones, Sir William, 348
Jonson, Ben, 366, 413
Jowett, Benjamin, 48, 70, 77, 271, 429
Justice, 108
Juvenal, 430, 431

Keats, John, xi, 1, 2, 5, 11, 14, 27, 34, 44, 50, 55, 72, 76, 86, 111, 119, 123, 129, 162, 191, 193, 231, 245–6, 247, 250, 257, 269, 273, 274, 317, 345, 346, 393, 396, 397, 398
  Endymion, 2, 274
  Hyperion, 2, 55, 123
  'Isabella', 231
  'La Belle Dame sans Merci', 111, 274
  'Ode to Psyche', 257
Keightley, Thomas, *The Fairy Mythology*, 94
Kelly, Bernard, on G. M. Hopkins, 457
Kelmscott Manor House, 106, 107, 116
Kelmscott Press, 110, 111
Kelshall, T. M., on R. Bridges, 456
Ker, W. P., 430, 443
Kilvert, I. S., on A. E. Housman, 466
Kingsley, Charles, 190
King's Quair, The, 43
Kipling, John Lockwood, 421–2, 423
  Man and Beast in India, 422
Kipling, Rudyard, 16, 180, 306, 319, 328, 329, 358, 362, 375, **421–8**, 431, 436, 465
  Barrack Room Ballads, 425
  'Danny Deever', 425
  Definitive Edition, 421 426
  Departmental Ditties, 424
  'English Flag, The', 426
  'Finest Story in the World, The', 424
  Five Nations, The, 426
  'Fuzzy-Wuzzy', 425
  'Galley-Slave, The', 424
  'Grave of the Hundred Dead, The', 424

'Gunga Din', 425
Jungle Books, 426
Kim, 422, 426, 427
'Loot', 425
'Mandalay', 425
'Native Born, The', 427
Naulahka, The (with W. Balestier), 423
'Our Lady of the Snows', 427
Plain Tales from the Hills, 424
'Recessional', 427
'Sestina of the Tramp Royal', 428
Seven Seas, The, 426
'Something of Myself', 465
Stalky & Co., 422
'Story of Uriah, The', 424
'Tommy', 425
'White Man's Burden, The', 427
'Widow at Windsor, The', 425
Years Between, The, 426
Kipling, Mrs R. (Carrie Balestier), 423
Kottabos, 464
Krasinski, Count, 331
Kropf, Hans, on W. Allingham, 450
Krusemeyer, M., on G. Meredith, 453
Küster, E. C., on W. Morris, 449

Lafourcade, Georges, on A. C. Swinburne, 50, 55, 445, 446, 447
Lahey, G. F., on G. M. Hopkins, 457
Lamb, Charles, 67, 155
Landor, Walter Savage, 51, 73, 82, 319, 320
Lane, John, 419, 453; on T. Hardy, 455
Lang, Andrew, 174, 287, 289, **293–8**, 363, 458, 459
  'Almae Matres', 297
  'Ballade of Autumn', 296
  'Ballade of Sleep', 295–6
  'Ballade to Theocritus, in Winter', 296
  Ballads and Lyrics of Old France, 294, 295
  Ballads of Books, 294
  Ban and Arrière Ban, 294
  'El Desdichado', 294–5
  'Fairy Minister, The', 296
  Grass of Parnassus, 294
  Helen of Troy, 294, 296
  'Hesperothen', 295, 296
  'Jn Ithaca', 297

Letters on Literature, 294
'Odyssey, The' (sonnet), 297
Rhymes à la Mode, 294
'Romance', 297
'Sunset on Yarrow, A', 295
xxxii Ballades in Blue China, 294, 295
'Three Portraits of Prince Charles', 297
xxii Ballades in Blue China, 294, 295
'Twilight on Tweed', 295
Lang, Mrs Andrew, ed. of A. Lang by, 294, 296, 459
Lang, Cecil Y., on A. C. Swinburne, x, 45, 47, 49–50, 72, 445, 446
Larbaud, Valéry, on C. Patmore, 451
Latin influences, 48, 110, 206, 260–1, 304, 343, 403, 404, 405, 406, 412, 430 et seq.
Laxdaela Saga, influence of, on W. Morris, 106, 119, 120
Lear, Edward, **298–9**, 459
  Book of Nonsense, A, 298, 299
  Family of the Psittacidae, The, 298
  Knowsley Menagerie, The, 298
  Laughable Lyrics, 298
  Letters, etc, 459
  More Nonsense Songs, etc, 298
  Nonsense Songs, etc, 298
Léaud, F., on R. Kipling, 465
Leavis, F. R., on G. M. Hopkins, 276–7, 457; on T. Hardy, 209
Leconte de Lisle, 140
Lee, Harman, on T. Hardy, 455
Lee-Hamilton, E. J., 331, **348–9**
  Apollo and Marsyas, 348–9
  Fountain of Youth, The, 348
  Gods, Saints and Men, 348
  Imaginary Sonnets, 331, 348, 349
  'Leonardo da Vinci to his Snakes', 349
  New Medusa, The, 348, 349
  Poems and Transcripts, 348
  Sonnets of the Wingless Hours, 348, 349
Leith, Mary C. J., on A. C. Swinburne, 446
Lemprière (Classical Dictionary), 118–19, 374
Lennon, F. B., on 'Lewis Carroll', 460
Leopardi, 226, 232, 234

INDEX

Leslie, Shane, on C. Patmore, 451
Levy, Amy, 353–4
  London Plane Tree, A, 353–4
  Minor Poet, A, 353–4
  'Swing and Sway', 354
  Xantippe, 353, 354
Lewes, G. H., 312
Lewis, C. Day, on G. M. Hopkins, 457; on G. Meredith, 453
Lewis, C. S., 308; on G. Macdonald, 460
Lewis, Matthew Gregory ('Monk' Lewis), 27
  Tales of Terror, 27
  Tales of Wonder, 27
Lhombreaud, Roger, on A. Symons, 417, 465
Liddell, Dean, 300
Lindsay, J., on G. Meredith, 453
Lindsay, M., on J. Davidson, 372, 463
Lister, Joseph (Lord Lister), 357
Littmana, H., on G. Meredith, 453
Livingston, F. V., on R. Kipling, 465
Lloyd, Constance (Mrs O. Wilde), 391
Locker, Frederick, 287–8
  London Lyrics, 287
  Lyra Elegantiarum, 287
London and Westminster Review, The, 442
Longaker, J. M., on E. Dowson, 402, 464
Longfellow, Henry Wadsworth, 300
Lucan, 430, 431
Lucas, E. V., 300; on 'Lewis Carroll', 459
Lucian, *The Dialogues*, 398
Ludlow, J. M., 46
Lyall, Sir Alfred Comyns, 328–9, 461
  Amir's Message, The, 329
  'Old Pindaree, The', 329
  Theology in Extremis, 329
  Verses Written in India, 328
Lynch, H., on G. Meredith, 453
Lytton, E. G. E., Lytton Bulwer Lytton (1st baron), 138, 158
Lytton E. R. Bulwer (1st earl of Lytton). See 'Meredith, Owen'.

Mabinogion, The, 124
McCarthy, Desmond, on A. Symons, 417

MacCarty, P., on 'Owen Meredith', 461
McDermot, J. F., on 'Lewis Carroll', 460
'McDiarmid, Hugh', on J. Davidson, 372, 463
MacDonald, Alice (Mrs J. L. Kipling), 422
MacDonald, George, **308–11**, 460
  Book of Strife, A, 310
  Collected Poems, 308
  Diary of an old Soul, The, 308, 310
  Disciple, The, 308, 310
  'Hidden Life, A', 308, 309
  Luther's *Hymn Book*, translated by G.M., 310
  Phantastes, 308, 310
  Poems, 308, 309
  'Songs of the Days and Nights', 311
  'Waesome Carl, The', 310
  'Within and Without', 308, 309
  'Yerl of Waterydeck, The', 310
MacDonald, Greville M., on George Macdonald, 460
MacDowall, A. S., on T. Hardy, 455
MacInnes, W. A., on A. C. Swinburne, 446
Mackail, J. W., on W. Morris, 116, 448
Mackay, Mona E., on G. Meredith, 453
Mackenzie, Compton, 293
Mackenzie, Faith Compton, on W. Johnson Cory, 342–3, 462
Macleod, Fiona. See Sharp, William.
Macleod, R. D., on W. Morris, 448
Macmillan's Magazine, 97, 424
MacNabb, V. J., on F. Thompson, 452
Madan, F., on 'Lewis Carroll', 460
Magnússon, Erikr, 106
Mahaffy, Professor Sir John Pentland, 391
'Maitland, Thomas'. See Buchanan Robert.
Mallarmé, Stéphane, 418
Malmesbury, William of, *De Gestis Regum Anglorum*, 119
Malory, Sir Thomas, 85, 105, 111, 112
Mandeville's *Voyage and Travel*, 119
Mangan, James Clarence, 350, 409
Manilius, ed. by A. E. Housman, 430, 431
Manning, Cardinal, 156, 177

[482]

INDEX

Marie de France, influence on A. W. E. O'Shaughnessy, 140, 141
Marillier, R. C., on D. G. Rossetti, 444
Marlow, A. N., on A. E. Housman, 431, 440, 466, 467
Marlowe, Christopher, 81
Marston, Cicely, 146
Marston, Eleanor. See O'Shaughnessy, Mrs.
Marston, John Westland, 139, 146
Marston, Philip Bourke, 139, **146-9**, 228, 450
   'All in All', 146, 147
   'Ballad of Monk Julius, The', 148
   Collected Poems, 146
   'In places that have known', 148
   Last Harvest, A, 146, 148
   'New Garden Secrets', 149
   'Old Churchyard of Bonchurch, The', 148
   Song-Tide, 146, 147
   'Speechless, Upon the Marriage of two Deaf and Dumb Persons', 147
   Wind-Voices, 146, 148
Martial, 370
Martin, Sir Theodore, 287; his Memoir of W. E. Aytoun, 443
Martindell, E. W., on R. Kipling, 465
Marvell, Andrew, 413
Masefield, John, on D. G. Rossetti, 444
Massey, Gerald, **318-20**, 461
   Ballad of Babe Christabel, The, 318, 320
   Craigcrook Castle, 318
   'Down in Australia', 319
   'Havelock's March', etc, 318, 319
   My Lyrical Life, 319
   Poems and Chansons, 318
   Robert Burns, 318
   'Sea Kings, The', 319
   'Sir Richard Grenville's Last Fight', 319
   'Song of the Red Republican', 320
   'Tale of Eternity, A', 318, 320
   Voices of Freedom, etc, 318
   War Waits, 318
Mathews, Elkin, 240
Maugham, Somerset, on R. Kipling, 421, 465
Maurice, F. D., 318
Maxwell, Donald, on T. Hardy, 455

Mazzini, Giuseppe, 18, 48, 51, 65, 77, 78, 397
Mégroz, R. L., on D. G. Rossetti, 444; on F. Thompson, 452
Meinhold, 27
   Amber Witch, The, 27
   Sidonia the Sorceress, 27
Mendès, Catulle, 142
Meredith, Arthur Gryffydh, 189
Meredith, George, x, xii, 11, 15, 23, 25, 47, 50, 51, 93, **188-204**, 206, 228, 231, 266, 277, 305, 348, 379, 453-4
   'Alsace-Lorraine', 203
   'Antigone', 193
   Ballads and Poems of Tragic Life, 190
   'Beggar's Soliloquy, The', 196
   'Chillianwallah', 189
   'Daphne', 193
   'Earth and Man', 197-9, 204
   'Empty Purse, The', 197, 199
   Evan Harrington, 1889
   'Faith on Trial, A', 18, 197, 199
   'Flower of the Ruins, The', 191, 192
   'France, An Ode', 202
   'Grandfather Bridgeman', 196
   'Hymn to Colour', 197
   'Juggling Jerry', 196
   'Lark Ascending, The', 197
   Last Poems, 190
   'London by Lamplight', 193
   'Love in the Valley', 190-1, 203
   'Modern Love', **194-6**, 203-4, 253, 348
   Modern Love and other Poems, 189, 194-200
   'Napoléon', 202, 203
   'Ode to the Comic Spirit', 197
   'Ode to the Spirit of Earth in Autumn', 192, 196-7
   Odes in Contribution to the Song of French History, 190, 201
   'Old Chartist, The', 196
   'Olive Branch, The', 193
   'Pastorals', 191-2
   'Phoebus with Admetus', 193, 199
   Poems, 189, 190-3
   Poems and Lyrics of the Joy of Earth, 190
   Poems, The Empty Purse, with Odes, etc, 190

Meredith, George—cont'd.
  Reading of Earth, A, 190
  Reading of Life, A, 190
  'Revolution, The', 202
  Shaving of Shagpat, The, 189
  'Shipwreck of Idomeneus, The', 193
  'Sleeping City, The', 193
  'South-west Wind in the Woodland, The', 191, 192, 197
  'Teaching of the Nude, The', 199
  'Test of Manhood, The', 197, 199
  Translations from Heine, by G.M., 189
  'Two Blackbirds, The', 191
  Vittoria, 189
  'Wild Rose and the Snowdrop, The', 191
  'With the Persuader', 199
  'Woods of Westermain, The', 197, 200–1
Meredith, Mrs George (born Peacock), 189
'Meredith, Owen' (pseud. of the 1st Earl of Lytton), 74, **330–2**, 461; on W. S. Blunt, 462
  Chronicles and Characters, 331
  Clytemnestra, 330
  Fables in Song, 331
  Glenaveril, 331
  Julian Fane, 332
  King Poppy, 331, 332
  Lucille, 330, 331
  Orval, 330
  Tannhäuser (with Julian Fane), 74, 332
  Wanderer, The, 330
Meredith, William Maxse, 453
Merimée, Prosper, influence on A. C. Swinburne, 57
Merry England, 174, 183
Meynell, Mrs Alice, 154, 156–7, 174, 175, 181, **182–7**, 452–3; on C. Patmore, 451; on C. G. Rossetti, 448
  Ceres Runaway, 183
  'Dead Harvest, A', etc, 186
  Father of Women, A, 183
  'I touched the heart that loved me', 185
  Last Poems, The, 183
  Later Poems, 183
  'Meditation', 186
  'My heart shall be thy garden', 185
  Other Poems, 183
  Poems (1893), 183
  Poems (1913), collected ed., 183
  Poems on the War, 183
  Preludes, 183, 185
  'Renouncement', 184, 186
  'Shepherdess, and Other Verses, The, 183, 185
  'Study, A', 185
  'Summer in England, 1914', 186
  Ten Poems, 183
  'We never meet', 185
Meynell, Esther, on W. Morris, 449
Meynell, Everard, on F. Thompson, 173–4, 183, 452
Meynell, Viola, on Mrs Alice Meynell, 183, 452; on F. Thompson, 452
Meynell, Wilfrid, 174, 183, 452; on L. Johnson, 465
Middleton, Richard, 419
Miles, A. H., ed. of The Poets and Poetry of the Century, 442, 449, 457
Mill, John Stuart, 4
Millais, Sir John Everett, 18–19, 115, 133
Milnes, Gladys R., on G. Meredith, 453
Milnes, Monckton R. See Houghton, Lord.
Milton, John, 124, 165, 176, 224, 246, 248, 249, 250, 253–4, 255, 256, 258, 259, 266, 284, 322, 330, 336, 337, 338, 341, 361, 392, 393, 394, 397, 400, 412
  'Comus', 259
  'L'Allegro', 412
  'On the Death of a Fair Infant', 250
  Paradise Lost, 42, 124, 164, 224, 254, 256, 258, 266, 337
  Samson Agonistes, 256
Minto, W., on W. Bell Scott, 444; on the Pre-Raphaelites, 449
Molesworth, Dr, Vicar of Rochdale, 243
Month, The, 464
Monthly Observer, The, 189
Moore, Arthur, 403
Moore, George, 293
Moore, T. Sturge, 400; on 'Field, Michael' (with D. C. Sturge-Moore), 461
Morley, John, Viscount Morley of Blackburn, 71, 206

INDEX

Morris, Sir Lewis, 329–30, 461
  Epic of Hades, 329–30
  'Organ Boy, The', 329
  Songs of the Worlds, 329
  'To an Unknown Poet', 329
  'Vision of Saints, A', 330
Morris, Marshall, Faulkner & Co., 24, 106, 107
Morris, Miss May, on W. Morris, 116, 127, 448
Morris, Mrs William (born Jane Burden), 21, 23, 24, 25, 26, 38, 39, 106, 116
Morris, William, 12, 13, 15, 21, 24, 41, 43, 47, 48, 53–54, 55, 73, 74, 84, 85, 92, **104–27**, 128, 138, 145, 154, 155, 236, 237, 238, 239, 246, 257, 273, 296, 321, 367, 379, 394, 396, 422, 448–9
  Aeneids, The, 110
  Aims of Art, The, 110
  Art and the Beauty of Life, 449
  'Atalanta's Race', 118
  'Bellerophon at Argos', 118
  'Bellerophon in Lycia', 118
  Beowulf, translated by W. Morris, 111
  'Blue Closet, The', 111
  Child Christopher, 110
  'Concerning Geffray Teste Noire', 114
  'Cupid and Psyche', 118, 119
  'Death of Paris, The', 118
  Defence of Guenevere, The (volume), 12, 92, 105, **111–14**
  'Defence of Guenevere, The' (poem), 113
  'Doom of King Acrisius, The', 118
  Dream of John Ball, A, 110
  Earthly Paradise, The, 74, 106, 107, 115, **117–21**, 126, 145, 257
  'Error and Loss', 126
  'Fostering of Aslaug, The', 119
  'Garden by the Sea, A', 126
  'Gilliflower of Gold, The', 111
  'Golden Apples, The', 118
  'Golden Wings', 115
  'Haystack in the Floods, The', 113–14, 115
  'Hill of Venus, The', 74, 119
  Hopes and Fears for Art, 110
  House of the Wolfings, The, 110
  'Iceland First Seen', 126
  Icelandic influences on W. Morris, 106–7, 119, 120–1, 123–4
  'King Arthur's Tomb', 113, 115
  'Lady of the Land, The', 119
  'Land E. of the Sun and W. of the Moon, The', 119
  Lectures on Socialism, 110
  Life and Death of Jason, The, 106, 118, 126
  Love is Enough, 107, 124–6
  'Love of Alcestis, The', 118
  'Lovers of Gudrun, The', 106, 119, 120
  'Man born to be King, The', 119
  'Man who never laughed again, The', 119
  'Near Avalon', 111
  News from Nowhere, 110
  Odyssey, The, translation of, by W. Morris, 110
  'Ogier the Dane', 119
  Poems by the Way, 111, 126
  'Proud King, The', 119
  'Pygmalion and the Image', 118
  'Rapunzel', 111
  'Ring Given to Venus, The', 119
  Signs of Change, 110
  Sigurd the Volsung, 107, 122–4
  'Sir Galahad', 113, 115
  'Sir Peter Harpdon's End', 113, 115, 379
  'Son of Croesus, The', 118
  'Story of Acontius and Cydippe, The', 118
  Story of the Glittering Plain, The, 110
  'Story of Rhodope, The', 118
  Story of the Sundering Flood, The, 110
  'Summer Dawn', 111
  'Tale of Orpheus and Eurydice, The', 118
  Three Northern Love Stories, 106
  'Tune of Seven Towers, The', 111
  ''Twas in Church on Palm Sunday', 54
  'Two Red Roses across the Moon', 112
  Volsunga Saga, translation of, with E. Magnússon, 106, 107, 123–4
  'Watching of the Falcon, The', 119

INDEX

Morris, William—*cont'd.*
  Water of the Wondrous Isles, The, 11
  Well at the World's End, The, 110
  Wood Beyond the World, The, 110
  'Writing on the Image, The', 119
Moses, Belle, on 'Lewis Carroll', 460
Moulton, Louise C., on P. B. Marston, 146, 450; on A. W. E. O'Shaughnessy, 138, 450
Muddiman, Bernard, on the Nineties, 465
Muirhead, J. H., on S. T. Coleridge, 442
Munro, H. A. J., on W. Johnson Cory, 343
Murdoch, W. B., on the Nineties, 465
Murray, G. G. A., on A. Lang, 459
Murray, Henry, on R. Buchanan, 460
Murry, J. Middleton, on G. M. Hopkins, 457
Musset, Alfred de, 289
Myers, F. W. H., **349–50**, 432
  Implicit Promise of Immortality, The, 350
  Passing of Youth, The, 350
  Renewal of Youth, The, 350
  St Paul, 349–50

Naden, Constance, 356
Napoleon Bonaparte, 202, 203, 205, 221, 223; in *The Dynasts,* 205. 221, 223
Napoleon III, 48, 80, 202
National Liberal League, The, 107
National Observer, The, 183, 358
National Reformer, The, 227, 231
Nerval, Gérard de, 294, 298
Nesbit, Mary, 146, 148
Nettleship, J. T., 138
New Statesman, The, 437
Newbolt, Sir Henry, on Mary Coleridge, 240, 456
Newman, Cardinal John Henry, 12, 271, 272
Nibelungenlied, Das, 122
Nichol, John, 48
Nicolson, Sir Harold, on A. C. Swinburne, 446, 447
Nietzsche, F. W., 373, 383
Noel, Hon. Roden, **345-6**
  Beatrice, 345
  Behind the Veil, 345
  'Little Child's Monument, A', 345
  Livingstone in Africa, 345
  Modern Faust, A, 345
  Red Flag, The, 345
  'Water-nymph and the Boy, The', 345
Novalis, 226, 227, 310
Noyes, Alfred, on W. Morris, 448

Observer, 282
Ogier le Danois, 119
O'Hegarty, P. S., on W. Allingham, 450
Oliver, F. W., 430
Olivero, F., on F. Thompson, 452
Omar Khayyám, 143
Omerod, J., on A. Lang, 459
Orwell, George, on G. M. Hopkins, 282
Osborne, C. C., on P. B. Marston, 450
Osbourne, Lloyd, on R. L. Stevenson, 463
Osbourne, Mrs. See 'Stevenson, Mrs R. L.'
O'Shaughnessy, A. W. E., **138–43**, 144, 145, 146, 150
  'Azure Islands', 142
  'Bisclaveret', 140–1
  'Chaitivel', 141
  'Christ will Return', 143
  'Cleopatra', 140
  'Colibri', 143
  'Creation', 139–40
  'Daughter of Herodias, The', 140
  'Disease of the Soul, The', 141
  Epic of Women, An, 138, **139–40**, 141, 142
  'Laustic', 141
  'Lay of Eliduc, The', 141
  'Lay of Two Lovers, The', 141
  'Lay of Yvenec, The', 141
  Lays of France, 139, 141
  'Lover, The', 139
  Music and Moonlight, 139, 141, 142
  'Ode', 142
  'Song of Palms', 142
  Songs of a Worker, 139, 142–3
  'Thoughts in Marble', 142
  Toyland (with Mrs O'Shaughnessy), 139
  'We are the music makers', 142
  'Wife of Hephaestus, The', 140
O'Shaughnessy, Mrs, 139, 146

INDEX

Ossian, 151
O'Sullivan, V., on O. Wilde, 464
Ouida, 150
Ovid, 48, 67, 75
Owlett, F. C., on F. Thompson, 452
Oxford and Cambridge Magazine, The, 105
Oxford Movement, The, xi, 12, 103, 104, 154

Packer, L. M., on C. Rossetti, 87–88, 89, 100, 129, 443, 447; on W. Bell Scott, 129, 449
Page, F., on G. M. Hopkinson, 457; on C. Patmore, 156, 162, 167, 450
Pall Mall Gazette, The, 183
Pater, Walter, 38, 155, 250, 257, 275, 393, 396, 397, 398, 399, 404, 408, 409, 416–17, 438
  Marius the Epicurean, 257
  Rossetti, D. G., W. Pater on, 444
  Studies in the History of the Renaissance, 393, 416
  'Winkelmann', 393
Patmore, Coventry, x, xi, 13, 21, 35, 82, 132, 137, **154–73**, 174, 175, 176, 177, 186, 268, 277, 320, 331, 432, 450–1; on F. Thompson, 452
  Amelia, 157, 168, 170–1
  Angel in the House, The, 137, 156, 157, 158, **160–7**, 169, 171, 172, 182, 320
  'Child's Purchase, The', 170
  'Contract, The', 170
  Courage in Politics and other Essays, 156
  'Dead Language', 168
  'Deliciae Sapientiae de Amore', 170
  'Departure', 168
  'English Metrical Law' (Essay prefacing *Amelia*), 168, 277
  'Eros and Psyche', 171
  'Espousals, The', 162
  'Faithful For Ever', 165
  'Go up thou Baldpate', 452
  'How I managed and improved my Estate', 156
  'Ladies' Praise', 160
  'Lilian', 157, 158, 159
  'Love's Apology', 160
  'No praise to me', 452
  Poems, 155, 157–9
  Principle in Art, 156
  'Prophets who cannot sing', 168
  'Regina Coeli', 171
  Religio Poetae, 156
  'River, The', 157
  Rod, the Root and the Flower, The, 156
  'Saint Valentine's Day', 171
  'Sir Hubert', 157
  'Sonsa Dei', 169–70
  Tamerton Church-Tower, etc, 157, 159–60
  'Tired Memory', 169, 171
  'To the Body', 170
  'Toys', 168
  Unknown Eros, The, 156, 157, **167–72**, 175
  'Victories of Love, The', 164, 165
  'Wedding Sermon, The', 164
  'Whate'er thou dost', 452
  'Woodman's Daughter, The', 157, 158
Patmore, Derek, on C. Patmore, 156, 451
Patmore, Mrs. See 'Andrews, Emily'; 'Byles, Caroline'; 'Robson, Harriet'.
Patmore, Peter, 155, 157
Recollections, 157
Paul, Henry, on W. Johnson Cory, 342
Payne, John, 138, 142, **143–6**, 450
  'Ballad of Shameful Death, The', 145
  Carol and Cadence, 144
  Collected Poems, 144
  Flower o' the Thorn, 144
  Intaglios, 143, 145–6
  Lautrec, 143
  Masque of Shadows, The, 143
  New Poems, 143
  'Rhyme of Redemption, The', 144
  'Sir Floris', 144
  'Sir Winfrith', 144, 145
  Songs of Consolation, 144
  Songs of Life and Death, 143
  Translations by J. Payne, 143
  Vigil and Vision, 144
  Way of the Winepress, The, 144
Peacock, Thomas Love, 189, 312
Pearson, Hesketh, on W. S. Gilbert, 460; on O. Wilde, 464
Pearson, Karl, 430
Peel, Robert, on G. Meredith, 453
Peel, Sir Robert, 2

INDEX

Peele, George, 65
Pen, 183
People's Friend, The, 321
Percy, Thomas, *Reliques of Ancient Poetry*, 34
Perils of Flood and Field, 100
Peter Parley's Annual, 92
Petrarch, influence of, 185, 251
Petter, G. B., on G. Meredith, 453
Petzold, Gertrud von, on J. Davidson, 463
Phare, Elsie E., on G. M. Hopkins, 284, 457
Phillips, Stephen, **335-40**, 461
  Christ in Hades, 336-7
  'Dream, A', 338
  Eremus, 336
  Faust, 336
  Herod, 336, 338-9, 340
  Lyrics and Dramas, 336
  'Marpessa', 337
  Nero, 336, 340
  New Inferno, The, 336
  New Poems, 336
  Orestes, 336
  Panama, 336
  Paolo and Francesca, 336, 339, 340
  Pietro of Siena, 336
  Poems, 335-6, 336, 337
  Primavera, 336
  Sin of David, The, 336, 339-40
  Ulysses, 336, 340
  'Wife, The', 338
Photiades, C., on G. Meredith, 453
Piers Plowman, 277
Pioneer, 423
Plarr, V. G., on E. Dowson, 464
Plato, 164, 262, 263, 398
Platt, J. A., 430
Pliny, 286
Poe, Edgar Allan, 348, 405
Poetry Review, The, 336, 340
Polidori, J. W., 18
Pollard, G., on A. C. Swinburne, 446
Pople Alexander, 5, 16, 48, 53, 135, 245, 322, 338, 414, 436, 437
  Essay on Man, An, 5
  Moral Satires, The, 5
  Rape of the Lock, The, 414
Pound, Ezra, on A. E. Housman, 437; on L. Johnson, 465
Powell, George, 46, 50

Poynter, Sir Edward, 422
Praed, Winthrop Mackworth, 287
Praz, Mario, on C. Patmore, 451
Pre-Raphaelite Brotherhood, The, 20-21, 136, 238
Pre-Raphaelite influences, 13 et seq., 17, 19-20, 21, 48, 54, 56, 72, 92, 128, 131, 132, 135, 136, 138, 143, 144, 147, 148, 150, 177, 236, 238, 239, 241-2, 246, 248, 275, 395, 413, 422, 428, 437
Pre-Raphaelite poets, 21, **128-53**, 154-5, 209, 288, 449-50
Priestley, J. B., on G. Meredith, 453
Prior, Alexander, 313
Prior, Matthew, 286
Procter, Adelaide Anne, 352, 377, 462
  'Legend of Provence, A', 352, 377
  Legends and Lyrics, 352
Proctor, Ellen A., on C. Rossetti, 447, 448
Propertius, 403, 405
Prudhomme, Sully, 142
Purcell, Henry, 257, 277, 282
Purdy, R. L., on T. Hardy, 454
Pusey, Edward Bouverie, 271

Quarterly Review, The, 52
Queensberry, Marquess of, 391, 392
Quintilian, 433

Radford, D., on W. Allingham, 449
Ramsay, Sir William, 430
Rands, W. B., 329, 365
  Lilliput Revels, 365
  Lilliput's Lyrics, 329
  'Polly', 329
Ransome, Arthur, on O. Wilde, 464
Read, Herbert, on G. M. Hopkins, 270; on C. Patmore, 451
Reed, L., on 'Lewis Carroll', 460
Reid, J. C., on C. Patmore, 450
Reilly, Mary P., on A. de Vere, 462
Reul, Paul de, on A. C. Swinburne, 446
Revue Anglo-Américane, La, 446
Rhodes, Cecil, 181, 423, 427
Rhymers' Club, The, 403, 404, 408, 419
Richards, Grant, 380; on A. E. Housman, 430, 431, 439, 440, 466
Richards, I. A., on G. M. Hopkins, 457
Richmond, O. L., on A. E. Housman, 430, 438, 439

[488]

INDEX

Rickett, Compton A., on W. Morris, 449
Riding, Laura, on G. M. Hopkins, 457
Rimbaud, Jean-Arthur, 404, 405
Ritz, Jean-Georges, on G. M. Hopkins, 269
Robson, Harriet (Mrs C. Patmore), 156
Rolleston, T. W., on Irish poetry, 462
Rooker, J. K., on F. Thompson, 452
Roosevelt, Theodore, 427
Ross, Sir Denison, on Sir Edwin Arnold, 327–8; on Sir Lewis Morris, 461
Rossetti, Christina Georgina, xi, 13, 18, 21, 25, 47, **87–103**, 111, 129, 154, 183, 184, 185, 241, 242, 287, 352, 353, 365, 447–8
  'Another Spring', 95
  'Ash Wednesday', 102
  'Autumn', 98
  'Ballad of Boding, A', 99, 102
  'Better Resurrection, A', 96
  'Birthday, A', 95
  'Bitter for Sweet', 95, 96
  Commonplace, 89, 94
  'Convent Threshold, The', 91, 96
  'Cousin Kate', 94
  'Dead City, The', 91, 93
  'Dream Land', 90, 448
  'Echo', 95
  'End, An', 448
  'First Spring Day, The', 95
  'Goblin Market', 89, 90, 91, **92–94**, 95, 96, 97, 99
  Goblin Market and Other Poems, 89, 91, 94, 103, 111
  Goblin Market, Prince's Progress, etc, 89, 99
  'Later Life', 100, **101–2**
  'Life and Death', 98
  'Maude Clare', 94
  'Memory', 98
  'Monna Innominata', **100–1**
  New Poems, 89, 103
  'Noble Sisters', 94
  Pageant, A, 89, 99, 102
  'Pause of Thought, A', 448
  Poetical Works, The, 89, 103
  'Prince's Progress, The', 89, 97
  Prince's Progress and Other Poems, The, 89, **97–98**, 103, 207
  'Repining', 448
  Sing-Song, 89, 93, **99**, 287, 365
  'Sister Maude', 94
  'Six Roses for the Flush of Youth', 448
  'Sleep at Sea', 96–97, 99, 102
  'Song', 95
  'Songs in a Cornfield', 97
  'Spring', 95
  'Testimony, A', 448
  'Three Enemies, The', 96–97, 102
  'Too late, too late', 97
  'Up-hill', 95
  Verses (1847), 89, **91**
  Verses (1893), 89, 102
  'What Would I Give', 98
  'Winter, my Secret', 91
  'Winter Rain', 95
Rossetti, Dante Gabriel, xi, 11, 12, 13, 15, **17–44**, 46, 47, 48, 50, 55, 56, 72, 80, 86, 88, 90, 91, 92, 97, 100, 101, 103, 104, 105, 106, 107, 111, 115, 116, 128, 129, 130, 131, 132, 133, 135, 136, 137, 144, 145, 147, 148, 149, 150, 153, 154, 159, 185, 213, 246, 253, 273, 311, 322, 323, 346, 394, 396, 404, 443–5
  'Annunciation, The', 33
  'Ave', 33
  Ballads ard Sonnets, 22, 26
  'Ballad of Jan Van Hunks, The', 22, 34
  'Blessed Damozel, The', 21, 27, **29–30**, 96, 105, 131
  'Bride's Prelude, The', 26, 33, 34
  'Burden of Nineveh, The', 32, 105
  'Card Dealer, The', 30
  'Cloud Confines', 41
  CollectedWorks of D. G. R., 22
  Dante and his Circle, 22, 26, **35**
  'Dante at Verona', 34
  'David Shand', 34
  Early Italian Poets, The, 22, **35**, 72
  'Eden Bower', 25, 42
  'Hand and Soul', 21
  'Henry the Leper', 27
  'Hill Summit, The', 41
  'House of Life, The', 25, 26, **38–42**, 116, 147, 194
  'Jenny', 28–29
  'King's Tragedy, The', 26, 42–43
  'Last Confession, A', 28
  'Lenore', translated by D. G. R., 27, 37

INDEX

Rossetti, Dante Gabriel—*cont'd.*
  'Love's Nocturn', 30–31
  'Mary's Girlhood', 33
  'Monochord, The', 41
  'My Sister's Sleep', 29
  'Newborn Death', 41
  'Nuptial Sleep', 39
  Poems, 22, 26
  'Portrait, The', 33
  'Rose Mary', 26, 43–44
  'Sir Hugh the Heron', 27
  'Sister Helen', 35
  'Staff and Scrip, The', 34, 105
  'Stratton Water', 42, 43
  'Stream's Secret, The', 25, 41
  'Sun's Shame, The', 41
  'Troy Town', 25, 42
  'Wellington's Funeral', 32
  'White Ship, The', 26, 42–43
Rossetti, Frances, 17, 25, 89
Rossetti, Gabriele, 17
Rossetti, Maria, 18
Rossetti, Mrs D. G. (born Elizabeth Eleanor Siddal), 22–23, 24
Rossetti, William Michael, 18, 19, 20, 22, 38, 87, 88, 89, 100, 103, 190, 443, 444, 445, 447
Ruskin, John, 20–21, 46, 105, 108, 164–5, 250, 273, 415
  Sesame and Lilies, 164–5
Russell, George. See 'A.E.'
Rutherford, Andrew, on R. Kipling, 465
Rutland, W. R., on A. C. Swinburne, 446

Sade, Marquis de, 46
St Augustine, *Confessions*, 176
Saintsbury, George, 47, 442, 459; on A. Lang, 459
Salisbury, Earl of, 340
Salmond, J. B., on A. Lang, 459
Salt, H. S., on W. Johnson Cory, 342, 343; on J. Thomson, 455
Sambrook, James, on Canon Dixon, 456
Sand, George, *Lavinia*, 331
Sandar, Mary F., on C. Rossetti, 447
Sappho, 75
Sassoon, S. L., on G. Meredith, 453
Saturday Review, The, 71, 183
Savoy, The, 383, 404, 415
Scaliger, 429
Schiller, J. F. von, 188, 310

Schopenhauer, A., 219
Schott, J. B., 24–25
Scot's Observer, 358, 424
Scott, Dixon, on W. Morris, 448
Scott, J. W., on A. E. Housman, 466
Scott, Robert, 129
Scott, Sir Walter, 1, 27, 34, 55, 85, 129
  Sir Tristrem, 85
Scott, Mrs William Bell (born Letitia Norquoy), 88, 129
Scott, William Bell, 11, 25, 41, 43, 84, 87, 88, 89, 91, 95, 100, 101, **129–32**, 136, 138, 150, 444
  Autobiographical Notes, 129, 130, 444
  Hades or The Transit, 130
  'Kriemhild's Tryst', 131
  'Lady Janet, May Jean', 131
  Poems (1854), 130, 131
  Poems (1875), 130, 131
  Poet's Harvest Home, A, 130, 131
  'Progress of Mind, The', 130
  Year of the World, The, 130, 131
Sélincourt, E. de, on R. Bridges, 456
Sencourt, R. E., on G. Meredith, 453
Sendall, W. J., on C. S. Calverley, 460
Sewell, E., on E. Lear, 459, on 'Lewis Carroll', 460
Shadwell, T., 299
Shakespeare, William, 16, 52, 67, 129, 181, 246, 247, 319, 322, 341, 346, 372, 373, 393, 435, 436
Shankland, G., on W. Morris, 449
Shanks, E., on R. Kipling, 465
Sharp, Elizabeth, on W. Sharp, 450
Sharp, William ('Fiona Macleod'), **149–53**, 450; on D. G. Rossetti, 149, 444, 445
  Browning, R., Life by W. Sharp, 149
  Canterbury Poets, The, ed. by W. Sharp, 149
  'Dreams within Dreams', 152
  Earth's Voices, 149–50
  'From the Hills of Dream', 149
  Heine, life by W. Sharp, 149
  House of Usna, The, 149, 152
  Human Inheritance, The, 149–50
  Immortal Hour, The, 149, 151–2
  'Motherhood', 150
  Ossian, ed. by W. Sharp, 151
  Pharais, 149
  Romantic Ballads and Poems of Phantasy, 149, 151

INDEX

'Son of Allan, The', 151
Sospir di Roma, 149, 151
'Sospitra', 150
'Vision, The', 152–3
'Weird of Michael Scott, The', 151
Shaw, G. B., 109, 116, 303, 383, 388
Shelley, Percy Bysshe, x, 1, 2–3, 5, 13, 14, 33, 45, 66, 76, 78, 79, 119, 125, 130, 174, 175, 181, 192, 227, 246, 258, 345, 396, 433
Alastor, 125, 229
'Epipsychidion', 175
'Hymn to Intellectual Beauty', 246
Prometheus Unbound, 11
Sherard, R. H., on O. Wilde, 464
Shewan, A., on A. Lang, 459
Shorter, C. K., 453; on L. Johnson, 464
Shove, Fredegond, on C. Rossetti, 447
Shuster, G. N., on the Catholic element in poetry, 450
Sichel, Edith, on Mary Coleridge, 456
Siddal, Elizabeth. See 'Rossetti, Mrs D. G.'
Simon, Jane, 49–50
Sims, G. R., on A. C. Swinburne, 46
Sitwell, E., on G. M. Hopkins, 457
Skipsey, Joseph, 322–5, 461
'Bereaved', 323
Book of Lyrics, 323
Book of Miscellaneous Lyrics, A, 323
Carols of the Coal Fields, 323
Collier Lad, The, 323
'Get up! the caller calls', 324
'Hartley Calamity, The', 323
'Mother Wept', 323
Poems, 323
Poems, Songs and Ballads, 323
Songs and Lyrics, 323
'Violet and the Rose, The', 324
Skutsch, O., on A. E. Housman, 431, 467
Smiles, Samuel, on Gerald Massey, 319, 461
Smith, Alexander, *Life Drama, A*, 11
Smith, Nowell C., on R. Bridges, 456
Smithers, Leonard, 464
Snee, Helen, 138, 139
Snyder, Alice D., on S. T. Coleridge, 442
Social Democratic Federation, The, 108, 109

Socialist League, The, 109
Society for Promoting Christian Knowlege, The, 89, 102
Society for the Protection of Ancient Buildings, 107
Sophocles, 333
Southey, Robert, 2, 300
Spanish verse forms, 360
Sparks, Tryphena, 213–14
Sparrow, John, on W. Johnson Cory, 343; on A. E. Housman, 437, 439–40, 466, 467
'Spasmodics, The', 10–11, 130, 314
Spectator, The, 51, 183, 194
Spencer, Herbert, 8
Spenser, Edmund, 246, 248, 249, 269, 361, 376, 394
Starling, E. H., 430
Stedman, E. A., on J. Ingelow, 462
Stendhal (Henri Beyle), 231
Stephen, James Kenneth, **305–6**
Lapsus Calami, 305
'Last Ride Together, The', 306
Quo Musa Tendis, 306
'R.K.', 306
Reflector, The, 305
Stephen, Sir Leslie, 352, 358, 364
Stern, G. B., on R. L. Stevenson, 463
Steuart, J. A., on R. L. Stevenson, 363, 463
Stevenson, Mrs R. L., 364, 365
Stevenson, Robert Louis, 180, 310, 358, **363–371**, 431, 463
'After Reading Antony and Cleopatra', 369
Ballads, 364, 365, 367
'Canoe Speaks, The', 367
Child's Garden of Verses, A, 364, 365–6, 371
Complete Poems, 364
Familiar Epistle, etc, 363
'Feast of Famine, The', 367
'God gave to me a child in part', 370
'Infinite shining heavens, The', 368
Inland Voyage, An, 364
Kidnapped, 365
'Love, What is Love', 370
Letters, ed. Colvin, 363
Moral Emblems, 363
'My bed is like a little boat', 366
New Poems, 463

Stevenson, Robert Louis—*cont'd.*
  Not I, 363
  'Requiem', 367
  'Song of Rahéro, The', 367
  'Song of the Road, A', 367
  Songs of Travel, 364, **368–9**
  Strange Case of Dr Jekyll and Mr Hyde, The, 365
  'System', 366
  'Ticonderoga', 367
  Treasure Island, 365
  Underwoods, 364, 365, **366–7**, 368
  Young Folks, Stevenson's works published in, 365
Stewart, J. McG., on R. Kipling, 465
Stobie, M. R., on G. M. Hopkins and C. Patmore, 451
Stodart-Walker, A., on R. Buchanan, 460
Stone, W. Johnson, 247, 253
Storey, Graham, on G. M. Hopkins, 458
Strachey, Lady, on E. Lear, 459
Strachey, Lytton, on T. Hardy, 208
Streatfield, R. A., on S. Phillips, 461
Stuart, Dorothy M., on C. Rossetti, 447
Stubbs, William, 49
Sturgeon, Mary C., on 'Field, Michael', 461
Sullivan, Sir Arthur Seymour, 302, 303
Swedenborg, E., 160, 167
Swift, Jonathan, 301
Swinburne, Algernon Charles, x, xii, 11, 12, 13, 14, 15, 22, 25, 26, 33, 35, **45–86**, 90, 92, 97, 111; 112, 115, 128, 138, 141, 142, 147, 148, 154, 163, 194, 201, 203, 207, 235, 248, 278, 289, 292–3, 295, 300, 320, 331, 332, 333, 334, 341, 350, 356, 379, 392, 393, 396, 397, 404, 408, 411, 413, 416, 428, 444, 445–7, 453
  'Anactoria', 75
  Astrophel, 52, 84
  'At a Month's End', 81
  'At Eleusis', 73
  Atalanta in Calydon, 49, 51, 53, 57, 58, **67–70**, 71, 73, 75, 207, 333
  'Ave atque Vale', 81
  'Ballad of Death, A', 72
  'Ballad of Dreamland, A', 81
  'Ballad of François Villon, A', 81
  'Ballad of Life, A', 72
  'Before a Crucifix', 79
  'Before Parting', 73
  'Birthday Ode', 82
  'Blessed Among Women', 77
  Bonchurch Edition of the works of A. C. Swinburne, 47, 445
  Bothwell, 51, **60–64**, 80
  'By the North Sea', 82
  Century of Roundels, A, 52, 83
  Channel Passage and Other Poems, A, 52, 84
  Chastelard, 51, 57, **58–60**, 61
  Death of Sir John Franklin, The, 54
  Dickens, Charles, criticism of, by A.C.S., 52
  'Diræ', 80
  'Dolores', 74
  Duke of Gandia, The, 52, 65, 66
  'Epicede', 81
  Erechtheus, 49, 51, 57, **70–71**, 80
  'Eve of Revolution, The', 77
  'Evening on the Broads', 82
  'Faustine', 74–75, 83
  'Forsaken Garden, A', 81
  'Garden of Cymodoce, The', 82
  'Garden of Proserpine, The', 73, 235
  'Genesis', 79
  George Chapman, 51
  'Halt before Rome, The', 77
  Heptalogia, The, 52, 82, 331
  'Hertha', 12, 79
  Hugo, Victor, criticism of, by A.C.S., 52
  'Hymn of Man', 79, 80
  'Hymn to Proserpine', 73
  'In the Bay', 81
  'Inferiae', 81
  'Itylus', 75–76, 86
  Jonson, Ben, criticism of, by A.C.S., 52
  'Joyeuse Garde', 446
  'Kossuth, To', 80
  'Lancelot', 446
  'Last Oracle, The', 80
  'Last Words to a Seventh-rate Poet', 331
  'Laus Veneris', 12, 74, 379
  'Leave Taking, A', 73
  'Leper, The', 73
  Lesbia Brandon, 50, 51

INDEX

'Litany of Nations, The', 77
Locrine, 52, **65–66**
Love's Cross Currents, 50
Marino Faliero, 52, **65–66**
Mary Stuart, 52, **64–65**
Mary Stuart, A. C. Swinburne's dramas on, 58 et seq.
Masque of Queen Bersabe, The, 73
'Mater Dolorosa', 79
'Mater Triumphalis', 79
'May Janet', 73
'Mentana', 77
Midsummer Holiday, A, 52, 83
'Ode on the French Republic', 80
'Ode on the Insurrection in Candia', 76
'Pasiphæ', 446
'Phaedra', 75
Poems and Ballads (First Series), 46, 47, 51, 55, 58, 60, **71–76**, 78 80, 81, 83, 90
Poems and Ballads (Second Series), 51, 55, 80
Poems and Ballads (Third Series), 52, 55, 84
'Prelude', 77–78
Queen Mother, The, 12, 51, 56–57, 92
'Queen Yseult', 53–54, 86
'Quia multum amavit', 77
'Rizpah', 80
Rosamond, 12, 51, 56, 92
Rosamund, Queen of the Lombards, 52, 65, 66
'Rudel', 446
'Sea-Swallows, The', 73
Shakespearian criticism by A.C.S., 52
Sisters, The, 49, 52, 65, **66**
'Song for Landor', 82
'Song in Time of Order, A', 73
'Song in Time of Revolution, A', 73
'Song of Italy, A', 51, 76, 80
Songs before Sunrise, 46, 51, 65, **76–80**, 81, 154
Songs of the Springtides, 52, 82
Songs of Two Nations, 51, 80
Studies in Song, 52, 82
'Super Flumina Babylonis', 77
Tale of Balen, The, 52, 84, 85–86
'Thalassius', 82–83
'Tiresias', 79
Tristram of Lyonesse, 52, 54, 84–85
Triumph of Gloriana, The, 48, 53
'Triumph of Time, The', 49, 73

'Vision of Spring in Winter, A', 81
'Walt Whitman in America, To', 78
'White Czar, The', 80
William Blake, 51, 72
'Year of the Rose, The', 81
Year's Letters, A, 50
Symonds, J. A., 101, **346–7**, 362
Animi Figura, 346
'For one of Gian Bellini's Little Angels', 346
'Le Jeune Homme caressant sa Chimère', 346
Letters and Papers, 462
Many Moods, 346
New and Old, 346
Sonnets of M. Angelo and T. Campanella, 346
Vagabunduli Libellus, 346
Wine, Women and Song, 347
Symonds, Arthur, 354, 372, 403, 404, 405, 407, 414, **417–18**, 419, 465
Amoris Victima, 417
Collected Works, 417
Confessions, 417
Critical work, on Aubrey Beardsley, 417; on Mathilde Blind, 354, 462; on R. W. Buchanan, 460; on Ernest Dowson, 403, 404, 405, 417, 464; on O. Wilde, 464
Days and Nights, 417
Images of Good and Evil, 417
London Nights, 417
Silhouettes, 417
Symbolist Movement in Literature, The, 417
Symons, Mrs E. W. (Katharine), on A. E. Housman, 439, 440–1, 466

Tannhäuser, legend, versions of the, 74, 119
Taylor, A. L., on 'Lewis Carroll', 460
Taylor, Sir Henry, *Philip van Artevelde*, 10
Temple Bar, 404
Tennyson, Lord Alfred, ix, x, xi, xii, 2, 4, 5–6, 7, 8, 9, 10, 11, 12, 14, 17, 34, 76, 84, 85, 105, 112, 119, 132, 135, 137, 138, 156, 157, 158, 159, 161, 163, 167, 172, 185, 191, 193, 194, 201, 207, 208, 209, 248, 265, 276, 287, 288, 300, 319, 321, 326, 327, 328, 329, 330, 331, 332, 333,

INDEX

Tennyson, Lord Alfred—*cont'd.*
  336, 337, 338, 340, 341, 342, 345,
  350, 352, 395, 396, 399, 400
  'Aylmer's Field', 137
  'Balin and Balan', 85
  'Day Dream, The', 161
  'Dora', 157
  Enoch Arden, 137, 207
  'Gardener's Daughter, The', 157
  Idylls, The, 5, 12, 158, 159, 194, 336
  In Memoriam, 5, 7, 265, 276, 395,
    399, 400
  'Lady of Shallott, The', 85
  'Locksley Hall', 158, 191, 321, 330
  'Miller's Daughter, The', 161
  'Œnone', 193
  Poems (1832), 5
  Poems (1842), 5, 12
  'Revenge, The', 319
  'Sir Galahad', 157
  'Ulysses', 193, 332
Tennyson, Mrs, 137, 172
Terence, 260
Thacker Spink & Co., 424
Thackeray, W. M., 287
Theocritus, 273, 376
Thompson, Alice. See Meynell, Mrs
  Alice.
Thompson, Elizabeth. See Lady Elizabeth Butler.
Thompson, E. H., on R. Bridges and
  G. M. Hopkins, 270, 456
Thompson, E. P., on W. Morris,
  448
Thompson, Francis, xi, 154, **173-82**,
  183, 186, 452
  'Anthem of Earth, An', 181
  'Any Saint', 177, 180
  Collected Works, 174, 181
  'Corymbus for Autumn, A', 176-7
  'Daisy', 177, 181
  'Dread of Height, The', 180
  'Ex Ore Infantium', 180
  'Feuilles d'Automne', translated by
    F.T., 181
  'Hound of Heaven, The', 175, 176,
    177, 181
  'Love in Dian's Lap', 175
  'Making of Viola, The', 177
  'Manus Animam Pinxit', 452
  'Miscellaneous Poems', 175, 176
  'Mistress of Vision, The', 179-80

'Narrow Vessel, A', 180
New Poems, 174, 175, 179-81
'Ode to the Setting Sun', 181
'Orient Ode', 181
'Paganism, Old and New', 181
Poems, 174, 175
'Poems on Children', 175, 177
'Shelley', 174, 181
Sister Songs, 174, 177-9, 812
'To a Poet Breaking Silence', 452
'To Monica thought dying', 177
'To the Dead Cardinal of Westminster', 177
Thompson, Thomas James, 182
Thomson, James (pseud. 'Bysshe Vanolis'), xii, 11, 93, **226-35**, 455-6
  City of Dreadful Night and Other Poems, The, 228
  'City of Dreadful Night, The', 226,
    227, 230, 231, **233-5**
  'Doom of a City, The', 229-30, 234
  'In the Room', 233
  'Lady of Sorrow, A', 226
  'Naked Goddess, The', 231
  Poetical Works, 228
  'Recusant, A', 229
  'Story of a Famous Old Jewish Firm,
    The', 227
  'Suggested by Matthew Arnold's
    "Grande Chartreuse" ', 228, 229
  'Sunday at Hampstead', 227, 231
  'Sunday up the River', 227, 231
  'To Our Ladies of Death', 231-2
  'Vane's Story', 231-3
  Vane's Story, Weddah and Om-el-Bonain, etc, 228
  Voice from the Nile, etc, A, 228
  'Weddah and Om-el-Bonain', 231
  'Withered Leaves', 229
Thomson, James (author of *The Seasons*), 317
Thorpe, Benjamin, 119
  Northern Mythology, 119
  Yule-tide Stories, 119
Tieck, J. L., 119
Time, 464
Times, The, 20, 415, 427
Times Literary Supplement, 432
Tomlinson, H. M., on T. Hardy, 455
Tompkins, Joyce M. S., on R. Kipling,
  465
Torretta, Laura, on G. Meredith, 453

[494]

INDEX

Tourneur, Cyril, 81
Townsend, J. Benjamin, on J. Davidson, 372, 463
Tree, Sir Herbert Beerbohm, 336, 338
Trench, Archbishop, *Sacred Latin Poetry*, 304
Trench, Herbert, 418
   'Apollo and the Seaman', 418
   Deirdre Wedded, 418
   New Poems, 418
Trevelyan, G. M., on G. Meredith, 200, 201, 203, 453
Trollope, Anthony, 160
Troxell, Janet, on D. G. Rossetti, 444
Tuell, Anne K., on Mrs Alice Meynell, 452
Tupper, Martin, 327, 461
   Proverbial Philosophy, 327
Turgeniev, Ivan, 135
Turquet-Milnes, G., 447

Vallance, A., on W. Morris, 449
Vaughan, C. E., 443
Vaughan, Henry, 284, 329
Vega, Lope de, 261
Veley, Margaret, 352–3
   Japanese Fan, A, 353
   'Land of Shadows, The', 353
   Marriage of Shadows, A, 352
   'Sunset', 353
   'Town Garden, A', 353
Vere, Sir Aubrey de, 350, 462
   Mary Tudor, 350
Vere, Aubrey Thomas de, **350–2**
   'Composed at Rydal', 351–2
   Foray of Queen Meave, The, 351
   Inisfail, 351
   Legends and Records, etc., 351
   Legends of St Patrick, The, 351
   St Thomas of Canterbury, 351
   Search after Proserpine, The, 351
   Waldenses, The, 351
   Year of Sorrow, A, 351
Verlaine, Paul, 142, 403, 404, 407, 416, 418
Vers libres. See Irregular verse forms
Victoria, Queen, 181
Villon, François, Swinburne's translations of, 80
   Henley's translations of, 363, Payne's translations of, 143

Vincent, E. R., on D. G. Rossetti, 444
Virgil, 255, 431

Wade, Thomas, 4
Wagner, 74, 332
Wahl, J. R., on D. G. Rossetti, 444
Walker, Hugh, 442, on Lord De Tabley, 461
Walker, Imogene B., on James Thomson, 455
Walker, Patricius (pseud. of W. Allingham)
Waller, Ross D., on the Rossetti family, 444, 445
Ward, W. P., on Aubrey de Vere, 462
Warren, John Byrne Leicester (Lord De Tabley), **332–4**, 461
   'Cardinal's Lament, The', 333
   'Garden of Delight, The', 334
   'Heathen to his Idol, A', 334
   'Hymn to Astarte, A', 334
   Orestes, 333
   Philoctetes (drama), 333
   'Philoctetes' (monologue), 332–3
   'Sale at the Farm, The', 333
   'Strange Parable, The', 334
Warton, Joseph, 357
Watson, George L., on A. E. Housman, 429, 439, 440, 466
Watson, R. Spence, on J. Skipsey, 461
Watson, Sir William, 326–7, 461
   Collected Poems, The, 327
   Lachrymae Musarum, 326
Watts, Dr Isaac, 300, 436
Watts-Dunton, Theodore, 46, 51–52, 82, 138, 448, 453
Waugh, Edwin, 307–8
Waugh, Evelyn, on D. G. Rossetti, 444
Weaver, Warren, on 'Lewis Carroll', 460
Webb, A. P., on T. Hardy, 454
Webb, Sidney, 110
Webber, C. J., on T. Hardy, 454
Webster, Mrs Augusta, 354–5
   Auspicious Day, The, 354
   Blanche Lisle, 354
   Book of Rhyme, A, 354
   'Castaway, The', 355
   Disguises, 354
   Dramatic Studies, 354

INDEX

Webster, Mrs Augusta—*cont'd.*
  'English Stornelli', 355
  'Lilian Gray', 354
  Medea, 354
  Portraits, 354
  Prometheus Unbound (translation), 354
  'Snow Waste, The', 355
  Woman Sold, A, 354, 355
  Yu-Pe-Ya's Lute, 354, 355
Webster, A. B., on A. Lang, 459
Weekley, Montague, on W. Morris, 449
Weissel, J., on James Thomson, 455
Welby, T. Earle, on the Pre-Raphaelites, 445; on A. C. Swinburne, 446
Weller, Christina, 182
Weller, Matilda, 226
Wells, Charles, 48
  Joseph and His Brethren, 48
Whibley, C., 462
Whistler, James McNeill, 415
  Gentle Art of Making Enemies, The, 415
  Ten o'Clock, 415
White, Gleeson, 289, 458
Whitman, Walt, 51, 346, 359, 409
Wilde, Oscar, xi, 176, **390–402**, 404, 405, 408, 411, 414, 415, 420, 425, 440, 464
  'Ave Imperatrix', 393, 395
  Ballad of Reading Gaol, The, 392, **401–2**
  'Ballade de Marguerite', 394
  'Burden of Itys, The', 394, 396–7
  'Canzonet', 400
  'Charmides', 393, 394, 398
  De Profundis, 392, 401
  Duchess of Padua, The, 400
  'Eleutheria', 394–5
  Florentine Tragedy, A, 400
  'Garden of Eros, The', 393, 394, 396
  'Harlot's House, The', 399
  'Helas', 392–3
  'Holy Week at Genoa', 395
  'Humanitad', 393, 394, 397
  'Impressions du Théâtre!', 394
  Letters (ed. R. Hart-Davis), 392
  'New Helen, The', 395
  'On Approaching Italy', 395
  'On the Massacre of the Christians in Bulgaria', 393
  'On the Sale of Keats' Love Letters', 390, 400
  'Pan', etc, 400
  'Panthea', 393, 394, 397
  Picture of Dorian Gray, The, 398
  Poems, 391, 392 et seq.
  Ravenna, 391, 392
  'Requiescat', 395
  'Rome Unvisited', 395
  'Rosa Mystica', 394, 395
  Salome, 391, 415
  'San Miniato', 395
  'Sonnets', 393
  Spinx, The, 391, 399
  'To Liberty', 394
Wilde, Sir William, 390
Wilkinson, L. P., on A. E. Housman, 437
Wilkinson, W. C., on E. Arnold, 461
Williams, Charles, on G. M. Hopkins, 268, 278–9
Williams, E. Baumer, on H. Allingham, 449
Williams, Harold, 442
Williams, R. Vaughan, 437
Williams, S. H., on 'Lewis Carroll', 460
Williamson, Kennedy, on W. E. Henley, 462
Willoughby, L. A., on D. G. Rossetti, 444, 445
Wilson, Edmund, on R. Kipling, 465
Wing, G., on T. Hardy, 455
Wise, T. J., on D. G. Rossetti, 444, 447; on A. C. Swinburne, 47, 445–6
Withers, P., on A. E. Housman, 431, 466
Wolfe, Humbert, on A. H. Clough, 443
Wolff, Lucien, on G. Meredith, 453
Woolf, Cecil, on Sir William Watson, 461
Woolner, Amy, on T. Woolner, 450
Woolner, Thomas, 21, **136–8**, 450
  'Children', 137
  My Beautiful Lady, 21, 136, 137–8
  'Nelly Dale', 137
  'Of My Lady in Death', 136
  Poems, 137
  Pygmalion, 137, 138
  Silenus, 137, 138
  Tiresias, 137, 138
Wordsworth, William, 2, 5, 7, 66, 84,

INDEX

133, 157, 158, 159, 162, 163, 177–8, 191, 192, 263, 350, 351, 352, 370, 397
Excursion, The, 66, 352
Lyrical Ballads, 158, 162
'Ode on Intimations of Immortality', 178
Ode to Duty, 192
Prelude, 178
'Ruth', 157
Wratislaw, Theodore, 419
Caprices, 419
Love's Memorial, 419

Wright, Austin, on C. Rossetti, 447
Wright, Thomas, on John Payne, 450
Wright, T. H., on F. Thompson, 452
Wyatt, A. J., 111
Wyndham, George, 347

Yates, Edmund, 300
Yeats, W. B., 133, 151, 153, 350, 403, 404, 408, 414, 419, 440
Yellow Book, The, 415, 419
Young, F. E. Brett, on R. Bridges, 456
Young Folks, R. L. Stevenson's contributions to, 365

PR
591   Evans, Sir Benjamin I.
E8   English poetry in the
1966a   later nineteenth cen-
             tury.

Date	Issued to
APR 16 1981	

PR
591   Evans, Sir Benjamin I.
E8   English poetry in the
1966a   later nineteenth cen-
             tury.

Framingham State College
Framingham, Massachusetts